INTRODUCTION TO AMERICAN HISTORY

SEVENTH EDITION

VOLUME I — TO 1877

INTRODUCTION TO AMERICAN HISTORY

SEVENTH EDITION

VOLUME I — TO 1877

CARL N. DEGLER
STANFORD UNIVERSITY

VINCENT P. DE SANTIS
UNIVERSITY OF NOTRE DAME

CLARENCE L. VER STEEG
NORTHWESTERN UNIVERSITY

BVT
Publishing

Managing Editor: Traci Burton

Manager of Art and Design: Suzanne Morse

Text Layout: Dan Harvey

Cover Design: Suzanne Morse and Jason James

Text and Cover Printing: Quad/Graphics, Dubuque

Photo Editor: Brae Buhnerkemper

Textbook Editor: Brian Farmer

Copyeditor: Joyce Bianchini

Marketing Manager: Robert Rappeport

Printed in the United States of America

ISBN: 978-1-60229-992-4

BRIEF CONTENTS

1 THE CLASH OF CIVILIZATIONS   1

2 FOUNDING THE COLONIES OF
   NORTH AMERICA   31

3 COLONIAL ADMINISTRATION
   AND POLITICS   65

4 PATTERNS OF COLONIAL SOCIAL
   STRUCTURE   89

5 REVOLUTION AND
   INDEPENDENCE, 1763–1783   133

6 THE EMERGENCE OF A
   NATIONAL CULTURE   187

7 ESTABLISHING THE
   REPUBLIC, 1781–1800   225

8 THE JEFFERSONIAN ERA,
   1800–1824   283

9 AMERICAN CULTURE
   COMES OF AGE

10 THE GROWTH OF DEMOCRATIC
   GOVERNMENT, 1824–1844   373

11 WESTWARD EXPANSION AND
   ECONOMIC GROWTH, 1824–1848   417

12 THE NATION AT MID-CENTURY   459

13 THE SECTIONAL CRISIS, 1848–1861   489

14 CIVIL WAR, 1861–1865   543

15 EMANCIPATION AND
   RECONSTRUCTION, 1865–1877   605

CONTENTS

1 THE CLASH OF CIVILIZATIONS ... 1

THOSE WHO CAME FIRST ... 2
The Land Bridge to Alaska ... 2
The Earliest Americans ... 2
Agricultural Revolution ... 3
The Advanced Societies ... 4
The Anasazi ... 5
The Mound-Builders ... 6
The Five Nation Iroquois ... 7
Commonalities ... 8
BACKGROUND TO COLONIZATION ... 10
The Beginnings of European Expansion ... 10
Christopher Columbus ... 12
Columbus' Tainted Image ... 17
The Conquistadores ... 19
The Encomiendas ... 23
Spanish Colonization in the United States ... 23
Factors in English Expansion ... 25
The Lost Colony of Roanoke ... 25

2 FOUNDING THE COLONIES OF NORTH AMERICA ... 31

THE ENGLISH SETTLEMENTS ... 32
Founding Virginia ... 32
Reorganization ... 34
Indentured Servitude ... 34
Pocahontas ... 35
Governing Virginia ... 36
Catholic Maryland ... 37
Proprietary Colonies ... 39
The Coming of Africans ... 39
The Pilgrims in Plymouth ... 40
The "Great Migration" ... 42
Puritan Society ... 43
Puritans and Human Nature ... 44
Hutchinson Heresy ... 45
Puritans and Quaker Persecution ... 46
Puritans and Witches ... 51
Witches of Salem Village ... 54
Puritan Success ... 54
The Spreading Colonies of New England ... 55
Puritans and the Natives ... 56
The Capture of New York ... 57
The Jerseys ... 59

Penn's Experiment ... 59
Quakers ... 60
Quaker Laws ... 60
Pennsylvania Economy and Growth ... 60
Settlement of the Carolinas ... 61
Carolina Economy ... 62
The Division of Carolina ... 62
Georgia ... 63

3 COLONIAL ADMINISTRATION AND POLITICS ... 65

ENGLISH ADMINISTRATION OF THE COLONIES ... 66
Political Structures in the Colonies ... 67
Local Government ... 68
Colonial Politics ... 69
COLONIAL ECONOMY ... 69
New England ... 69
PEOPLE THAT MADE A DIFFERENCE ... 70
The Southern Colonies ... 73
The Middle Colonies ... 74
English Regulatory Acts ... 75
Conflict with the Native Americans ... 77
Bacon's Rebellion ... 79
Pueblo Revolt ... 81
BRITAIN WINS SUPREMACY IN NORTH AMERICA ... 81
New France ... 81
Early Border Conflicts ... 83
King George's War ... 84
Start of the Great War for Empire ... 84
Albany Conference ... 85
Fort Duquesne, 1755 ... 86
William Pitt Increases British Resolve ... 86
The Capture of Quebec ... 87
Proclamation of 1763 ... 87
Ramifications of Seven Years War ... 87

4 PATTERNS OF COLONIAL SOCIAL STRUCTURE ... 89

COLONIAL SOCIAL STRUCTURE ... 90
Influences on Cultural Development ... 90
Influence of English Society ... 90
Influence of the American Environment ... 92

Women in Colonial America   92
The Structure of Colonial Society   94
MINORITIES IN THE COLONIES   95
European Minorities   95
The Rise of Slavery   98
Stono Rebellion   101
The English and the Native Americans   103
PEOPLE THAT MADE A DIFFERENCE   104
Non-English Settlers in the Borderlands   109
End of the Barrier to Expansion   110
THE SEVENTEENTH CENTURY:
AGE OF FAITH   111
Puritanism in England   111
Puritanism in America   112
Puritan Theology   114
Puritan View of the Bible   115
Puritans and Free Thought   116
Changes in the New World   116
The Transplanted Anglicans   117
THE EIGHTEENTH CENTURY MIND   119
The Enlightenment   119
The Growth of Toleration   121
The Rise of Secularism   122
The Great Awakening   123
Lasting Impact, Division, and Dissent   126
The Enlightenment in America   129
Colonial Roots of American Culture   130

5 REVOLUTION AND
   INDEPENDENCE, 1763–1783   133

BACKGROUND OF THE REVOLUTION   134
Character of the Revolution   134
Early Provocations and Crises   135
The Constitutional Issue   137
Constitutional Confrontations   138
Problems of Defense and Western Lands   139
Ramifications of the Seven Years War   142
The Stamp Act   143
Reaction to the Stamp Act   144
The Townshend Duties   147
Liberty Incident   148
Boston Massacre   149
'TIS TIME TO PART   151
The Boston Tea Party and the Coercive Acts   151

Tea Act Crisis   151
The Provincials Act   155
Lexington and Concord   155
Momentum Toward the Declaration   159
The Declaration of Independence   160
The Internal Revolution   162
The Loyalists   163
PROSECUTING THE WAR   166
The Continental Congress   166
Revolutionary Finance   166
Military Strategy   167
Slavery and the Revolution   168
The War in the North   169
European Aid to the Americans   174
New Campaigns in the North   174
The War in the South   175
Battle of Yorktown   176
The War in Retrospect   178
The Peace of Paris, 1783   179
EFFECTS OF THE WAR   182
Unrestricted Trade   182
The Westward Movement   182
Modifications of American Society   183
The Articles of Confederation   184

6 THE EMERGENCE OF A
   NATIONAL CULTURE   187

THE DEVELOPMENT OF
AN AMERICAN CREDO   188
A Time of Optimism and Pride   188
American Nationalism   188
THE FRAMEWORK OF
THE AMERICAN MIND   190
Adapting the Enlightenment   191
The Professionalization of Science   192
"The Best Mechanics in the World"   193
The Arrival of Romanticism   194
Religious Change   195
Frontier Evangelism   196
Freedom and Equality: The Ideal   198
The Social Problem   199
SHAPING AMERICAN SOCIETY   201
Feeding and Clothing the Republic   201
Marriage, Morals, and Family Life   204

Women's Legal Status 206
New Thinking About Women's Rights 208
THE QUEST FOR AMERICAN ARTS 210
A Native Literature 210
Patterns in American Prose 211
Reading for the People 212
Poetry in the New Republic 213
PEOPLE THAT MADE A DIFFERENCE 214
The Theater and Other Entertainments 216
Architecture 219
Musicians and Painters 221
Winning Artistic Independence 223

7 ESTABLISHING THE REPUBLIC, 1781–1800 225

The King's Friends 226
"Our Old Home" 227
"Go to Hell or Halifax" 227
THE SEARCH FOR STABILITY 228
Balancing Federal with Local Authority 228
The State Governments 230
THE CONFEDERATION PERIOD 232
Establishing a Western Policy 234
Relations with Europe 235
The Difficulties of Trade 237
Frenzied Finances 237
Crisis and Rebellion 238
FRAMING A NEW CONSTITUTION 240
The Drift Toward a New Government 240
The Question of Federalism 241
The Philosophy of the Constitution 242
The Convention at Work 244
Referral to the States 248
Federalists and Antifederalists 249
Ratification of the Constitution 251
LAUNCHING THE GOVERNMENT 253
Washington and Federalist Rule 253
Federalist Finance 256
The Whiskey Rebellion 258
DEVELOPING A NATIVE AMERICAN POLICY 259
"Noble Red Man" or "Barbaric Savage?" 260
Assimilation or Removal 261
PEOPLE THAT MADE A DIFFERENCE 262
Clashes on the Frontier 264

THE PERILS OF NEUTRALITY 266
The French Revolution 266
Genet Affair 267
Strained Relations with Britain 268
Jay's Treaty 269
EARLY POLITICAL PARTIES 271
The Emergence of Party Politics 271
The Election of 1796 273
Federalists and Republicans 276
THE TRIAL OF JOHN ADAMS 277
The XYZ Affair 277
The Treaty of 1800 278
The Alien and Sedition Acts 279
The Election of 1800 280

8 THE JEFFERSONIAN ERA, 1800–1824 283

JEFFERSON IN POWER 284
"The Revolution of 1800" 284
Thomas Jefferson 284
Settling the Barbary Corsairs 286
The Purchase of Louisiana 288
The Problems of Political Patronage 290
Jefferson Versus Marshall 291
Marshall and Constitutional Law 292
Opening the West 292
The "Essex Junto" 296
The Election of 1804 298
AMERICA AND THE WOES OF EUROPE 299
Neutrality in a World at War 299
The British at Sea 300
The "Obnoxious Embargo" 301
The Election of 1808 302
The Drift to War 302
The War Hawks 304
"Mr. Madison's War" 304
THE WAR OF 1812 305
War on the Land: First Phase 305
War on the Land: Second Phase 309
War at Sea 309
War on the Land: Final Phase 311
The Hartford Convention 312
A Welcome Peace 313
The Results of the War 314
The War and Canada 314

AMERICA MAKES A NEW START   315
  A Confident Nation   315
  The Aftermath of War   315
  A Protective Tariff   316
  Renewing the Bank of the United States   316
  Building Better Connecting Links   317
AMERICA MOVES WEST   318
  Land Hunger Versus Native American Rights 318
  Resistance to Federal Policy   320
GROWING PAINS   321
  The Election of 1816   321
  The "Era of Good Feelings"   322
  Prosperity and Panic   323
"FIRE BELL IN THE NIGHT"   324
  Sectionalism and Slavery   324
  The Missouri Compromise   325
EVOLVING A FOREIGN POLICY   327
  Catching Up on Old Problems   327
  The Monroe Doctrine   330
  The Triumph of Isolation   331

9 AMERICAN CULTURE COMES OF AGE   333

LAYING THE GROUNDWORK   334
  The Excitement of Progress   334
  Technological Change and
    Economic Development   334
THE ROLE OF REFORMERS   338
  American Women   338
  Fighting Ills, Woes, and Evils   340
PEOPLE THAT MADE A DIFFERENCE   342
  Communitarianism   345
  Progress in Education   347
FAITH AND INTELLECT   348
  Religion and the People   348
  Mormons   350
  The Unitarian Influence   353
  Romanticism Revisited   353
THE GOLDEN AGE OF LITERATURE   354
  Emerson and Transcendentalism   354
  Henry David Thoreau   356
  The Boston Brahmins   357
  Nathaniel Hawthorne   358
  Herman Melville   358
  James Fenimore Cooper   359

  Southern Romanticism   360
  Edgar Allan Poe   361
JOURNALISM AND POPULAR CULTURE   362
  Writing for the People   362
  Magazines and Books for Women   363
  Sports, Humor, and Realism   364
ARTS, SCIENCES, AND POPULAR TASTE   365
  The "Higher Culture"   365
  Popular Music and Drama   366
  Sculpture, Architecture, Painting   367
SLAVERY AND DEMOCRACY   368
  Garrison and Abolition   368
  The Literary Antecedents to Civil War   369
  Alexis de Tocqueville's America   370

10 THE GROWTH OF DEMOCRATIC
    GOVERNMENT, 1824–1844   373

THE ELECTION OF 1824   374
  Four Political Factions   374
  Adams Defeats Jackson   375
THE J. Q. ADAMS INTERLUDE   377
  Adams in the White House   377
  Democratic Republicans, National Republicans 378
  Foreign Relations   380
JACKSON TRIUMPHANT   381
  The Election of 1828   381
  "King Mob"   383
  Andrew Jackson: Man of the People   384
  Reorganization of the Cabinet   386
  Changing Problems, Changing Arguments   387
  Webster's "Second Reply to Hayne"   389
  Two Controversial Vetoes   390
  The Election of 1832   391
"KING ANDREW"   392
  Crisis Over Nullification   392
  The United States Bank   393
  Hard Money and Land   394
  Jackson's Foreign Policy   396
  The Supreme Court   397
JACKSONIAN DEMOCRACY—A LOOK BACK   398
  The Influence of Economic Factors   398
  Characteristics of Jacksonian Democracy   400
  Evaluation of Jackson's Administration   401
DEMOCRATS AND WHIGS   402

The Election of 1836   402
The Panic of 1837   403
The Caroline Affair   404
Tippecanoe and Tyler Too   405
President Without a Party   408
The Webster-Ashburton Treaty   408
Return of the Democrats   410
Features of American Democratic Growth   411
PEOPLE THAT MADE A DIFFERENCE   412

11 WESTWARD EXPANSION AND ECONOMIC GROWTH, 1824–1848   417

THE BACKGROUND OF EXPANSION   418
Manifest Destiny   418
Native American Removal   420
The Pathfinders   423
The Santa Fe Trail   425
The Oregon Trail   426
Western Army Posts   427
CONQUERING THE WEST   428
A National Question   428
The Oregon Dispute   428
Settlement of Texas   431
War for Independence   433
The Republic of Texas   434
Annexation of Texas   435
War with Mexico   437
The Treaty of Guadalupe Hidalgo   440
Gadsden Purchase   441
Eruption of the Slavery Issue   441
Filling Out the West   443
THE ECONOMICS OF EXPANSION   446
The West and the Transportation Revolution   446
The Northeast and the Industrial Revolution   449
The Corporate Revolution   450
The Rise of Industrial Populations   453
The Rise of Labor   455
Growing Sectionalism   457

12 THE NATION AT MID-CENTURY   459

A MODERNIZING UNITED STATES   460
Characteristics of Modernization   460
American Modernization   461

Education and Innovation   462
Technology and Agriculture   463
THE SOCIAL IMPACT   465
Ready-Made Clothing   465
The "Balloon-Frame" House   467
Plumbing, Lighting, and Heating   468
The Icebox   469
The Emergence of the Modern Family   470
MODERNIZATION AND REFORM   470
The Protestant Ethic and Reform   470
Temperance   471
Public Education   474
Higher Education   476
The "Media"   477
Women's Rights   478
The Broadening Antislavery Movement   480
PEOPLE THAT MADE A DIFFERENCE   482
PREJUDICES, POLITICS, AND POLARIZATION   485
The New Immigration   485

13 THE SECTIONAL CRISIS, 1848–1861   489

THE ORIGIN OF SECTIONALISM   490
The Transcontinental Republic   490
The Southern Way of Life   491
Slavery   491
The Northern Way of Life   496
THE BASES OF SECTIONAL ANTAGONISM   496
Economic Causes   497
The Growth of the Slavery Issue   498
The Question of Extending Slavery   500
The Wilmot Proviso   501
The Doctrine of Popular Sovereignty   502
THE COMPROMISE OF 1850   503
Early Secessionist Sentiment   504
The Clay Compromise Proposals   506
The Douglas Strategy   508
The Fugitive Slave Act   508
Resistance Against the Fugitive Slave Law   511
The Election of 1852   512
KANSAS AND NEBRASKA   514
The Douglas Bill   514
"Appeal of the Independent Democrats"   515
The Election of 1854   516

"Bleeding Kansas"   517
"The Crime Against Kansas"   520
The Character of Franklin Pierce   520
ON THE EVE OF WAR   521
The Election of 1856   521
The Dred Scott Decision   523
The Lincoln-Douglas Debates   525
John Brown's Raid   526
The Election of 1860   528
The Democrats   529
The Republican Victory   529
Secession   531
The Failure of Compromise   533
Fort Sumter   534
"CAUSES OF THE CIVIL WAR"   535
PEOPLE THAT MADE A DIFFERENCE   538

14 CIVIL WAR, 1861–1865   543

THE BLUE AND THE GRAY   544
The "American" War   544
The Resources of North and South   545
Southern Strategy   549
Northern Strategy   550
THE WAR IN THE FIELD   554
The Virginia Front   554
The Battle of Bull Run (Manassas)   555
Second Battle of Bull Run   561
Antietam   561
Fredericksburg   563
Chancellorsville   563
Gettysburg   564
The War in the West   566
Confederate Invasion of New Mexico   567
Pea Ridge   568
Forts Henry and Donelson   568
Shiloh   569
Vicksburg   571
Chickamauga and Chattanooga   572
Grant Takes Command   573
Presidential Election and the Peace Movement   575
The Fall of Atlanta   576
Sherman's March   578
Destruction of Hood's Army of Tennessee   579
Sherman's March in the Carolinas   579
Appomattox   580
THE WAR BEHIND THE LINES   581

The Problems of the Confederacy   581
The Importance of Sea Power   582
Prisoners of War   585
Economic Failures of the South   586
Northern Industrialism and
        Republican Ascendancy   587
The Transcontinental Railroad   588
The National Banking System   589
Women and the War   590
The Road to Reunion   593
Emancipation   593
Emancipation Proclamation   594
Lincoln   596
Black Americans and the War   600

15 EMANCIPATION AND
        RECONSTRUCTION, 1865–1877   605

LINCOLN'S PLAN OF RECONSTRUCTION   606
Johnson's Policy of Reconstruction   608
Congressional Radicals   610
Radical Reconstruction   612
The Fall of Radical Reconstruction   617
The Ku Klux Klan   618
Black Sharecroppers   621
Freedmen's Bureau   622
Johnson versus the Radicals   623
The Grant Administration   624
The Hayes-Tilden Election of 1876   627

APPENDIX   631

THE DECLARATION OF INDEPENDENCE   631
THE CONSTITUTION OF THE UNITED
        STATES   634
COPYRIGHT ACKNOWLEDGMENTS;
        PHOTO CREDITS   655

INDEX   661

The opportunity to take a fresh look at the nation's history is always an exciting one. This text represents a solid interpretation of traditional economic and political history, while also including many original insights into social and cultural changes that have influenced and been influenced by economic and political events. Special attention has also been paid to the role of technology. What emerges, in fact, is a vivid picture of the interrelationship of a nation's technology with its culture and its political and economic life. It is hoped that students will gain insights into the ideas and events that inspired this nation's founding and continue to influence its development.

Of special importance are the biographies. The fascinating people profiled range from Phillis Wheatley to W. E. B. DuBois, from Parson Weems to Belva Lockwood, from Dorothea Dix to J. Robert Oppenheimer.

The book that results is an engrossing story of a young nation engaged in what Thomas Paine described as a "bold and sublime experiment" in government. We hope you enjoy the story of the continuing effort to realize the high ideals of this nation's founding.

Cochran, Vincent P. de Santis, Holman Hamilton, William H. Harbaugh, James M. McPherson, Russel B. Nye, and Clarence L. Ver Steeg. These prestigious authors had brought to it many strengths which resulted in a well received and respected textbook for nearly two decades.

We must also extend our appreciation to the many other historians and scholars whose work is reflected in this edition, including Dr. Brian R. Farmer, who provided extensive editing. Special gratitude goes to those teachers and historians who read the manuscript for the previous editions and gave their comments: Frank W. Abbott, University of Houston, Downtown College; Thomas J. Archdeacon, University of Wisconsin at Madison; Morris H. Holman, Eastfield College; Arthur McClure, Central Missouri State University; and Thomas R. Tefft, Citrus College.

Finally, we want to acknowledge the contributions of Dee Andrews of California State University, East Bay, who consulted on early American history, and John Snetsinger of California State Polytechnic University, San Luis Obispo, who consulted about twentieth-century diplomatic history.

The Publisher

SPECIAL ACKNOWLEDGEMENTS

In *Introduction to American History's* earlier iteration the textbook had been a collaboration among Carl N. Degler, Thomas C.

LIST OF MAPS & CHARTS

THE WORLD KNOWN TO EUROPEANS IN 1492   13

VOYAGES OF EXPLORATION   22

MIGRATIONS FROM ENGLAND BEFORE 1640   33

KING PHILIP'S WAR (1675–1676)   79

EARLY SETTLEMENTS IN THE MIDDLE COLONIES   96

GEORGIA AND THE CAROLINAS   99

AFRICAN ORIGINS OF THE SLAVE TRADE   101

EARLY SETTLEMENTS IN THE SOUTH   102

ROUTES TO THE INTERIOR   107

NORTH AMERICA AFTER THE TREATY OF PARIS (1763)   135

MAP OF TERRITORIAL GROWTH 1775   136

PROCLAMATION OF 1763   141

BOSTON AND VICINITY (1775)   153

CENTRAL CAMPAIGNS (1776–1778)   171

NORTHERN CAMPAIGNS (1777)   173

SOUTHERN CAMPAIGNS (1780–1781)   177

NORTH AMERICA IN 1783   180

WESTERN LANDS CEDED BY THE STATES (1782–1802)   233

MAP OF TRANS-ALLEGHENY SETTLEMENTS (1790)   234

MAP OF TERRITORIAL GROWTH (1790)   235

VOTE ON RATIFICATION OF THE CONSTITUTION   252

PINCKNEY'S TREATY (1795)   270

ELECTION OF 1796   274

AMERICAN EXPLORATIONS OF THE FAR WEST   289

TERRITORIAL GROWTH (1810)   296

MAP OF PRESIDENTIAL ELECTION OF 1804   298

MAP OF PRESIDENTIAL ELECTION OF 1808   303

NORTHERN CAMPAIGNS (1812–1814)   306

SOUTHWEST CAMPAIGNS (1813–1815)   310

NEW BOUNDARIES ESTABLISHED BY TREATIES   319

MAP OF PRESIDENTIAL ELECTION OF 1816   322

THE MISSOURI COMPROMISE (1820)   326

POPULATION DENSITY (1820)   329

TERRITORIAL GROWTH (1830)   345

THE PRESIDENTIAL ELECTION OF 1824   376

THE PRESIDENTIAL ELECTION OF 1828   382

THE PRESIDENTIAL ELECTION OF 1832   392

THE PRESIDENTIAL ELECTION OF 1836   402

THE PRESIDENTIAL ELECTION OF 1840   407

WEBSTER-ASHBURTON TREATY AND TREATY OF PARIS BOUNDARIES   409

THE PRESIDENTIAL ELECTION OF 1844   410

IMMIGRATION (1840–1860)   419

SETTLEMENT OF THE MISSISSIPPI VALLEY   424

TRAILS OF THE OLD WEST   427

THE OREGON CONTROVERSY   429

THE TEXAS REVOLUTION   432

MEXICAN WAR CAMPAIGNS   439

PRINCIPAL CANALS AND ROADS   447

MAP OF TERRITORIAL GROWTH (1840)   448

THE RAILROAD NETWORK (1850 AND 1860)   449

MAP OF DISTRIBUTION OF UNITED STATES POPULATION (1840)   456

WHEAT PRODUCTION   465

TERRITORIAL GROWTH (1850)   490

COTTON-GROWING AREAS   492

SLAVERY AND AGRICULTURAL PRODUCTION   495

PRESIDENTIAL ELECTION OF 1848   504

PRESIDENTIAL ELECTION OF 1852   514

THE UNITED STATES IN 1854   516

PRESIDENTIAL ELECTION OF 1856   523

TERRITORIAL GROWTH (1860)   528

PRESIDENTIAL ELECTION OF 1860   530

THE UNITED STATES
ON THE EVE OF THE CIVIL WAR   532

POPULATION DENSITY (1860)   545

FIRST BATTLE OF BULL RUN (1861)   556

PENINSULAR CAMPAIGN (1862)   559

FREDRICKSBURG TO GETTYSBURG (1862–63)   565

WAR IN THE WEST (1862)   566

WAR IN THE EAST (1864)   574

FINAL CAMPAIGNS
OF THE CIVIL WAR (1864–1865)   577

RECONSTRUCTION   613

THE ELECTION OF 1876   628

THE CLASH OF CIVILIZATIONS

THOSE WHO CAME FIRST

The Land Bridge to Alaska
The Earliest Americans
Agricultural Revolution
The Advanced Societies
The Anasazi
The Mound-Builders
The Five Nation Iroquois
Commonalities

BACKGROUND TO COLONIZATION

The Beginnings of European Expansion
Christopher Columbus
Columbus' Tainted Image
The Conquistadores
The Encomiendas
Spanish Colonization in the
  United States
Factors in English Expansion
The Lost Colony of Roanoke

THOSE WHO CAME FIRST

Before the officially documented arrival of Christopher Columbus in 1492, there were approximately four million indigenous people organized into a multiplicity of tribes and speaking hundreds of discrete languages in what would become the United States. Clearly, humans had inhabited the Western Hemisphere thousands of years before Columbus. The exact date of the arrival of the first Americans is in dispute, but historians generally believe that they arrived somewhere between 15,000 and 20,000 years ago. Although prior to the twentieth century, historians believed that the earliest humans had only arrived in North America 3,000–4,000 years ago, a discovery was made in 1908 proved that humans had arrived in North America thousands of years earlier. The artifacts that were found from these early Americans were 19 flint spear points discovered near Folsom, New Mexico, amid the bones of a giant bison, a species that had already been extinct for 10,000 years when the remains were found. One of the spear points was still stuck between the ribs of this extinct giant bison, thus proving that the spear points had not been dropped on the sight at a later date. These "Folsom Points" provided evidence that the first Americans had migrated to the Western Hemisphere at least 10,000 years ago.

THE LAND BRIDGE TO ALASKA

It is believed that these earliest Americans immigrated from Asia during the last ice age when massive continental glaciers covered much of North America. With more water trapped on land in the form of ice (and therefore not in the ocean), the ocean level was low enough to expose a landmass that crossed the Bering Straits from Asia to Alaska. Thousands of migrants then moved south over the millennia occupying a vast region. Using the tools of archaeology, genetics, climatology and dendrochronology—the use of tree rings to date events in the past—scholars have been able to learn a fair amount about these peoples.

THE EARLIEST AMERICANS

The earliest Americans were nomadic hunters that had developed weapon and tool-making techniques. These first Americans apparently specialized in hunting mammoths, long-extinct elephant-like creatures that they killed and processed for food, clothing, and building materials. Most likely, these earliest Americans first migrated to America while following their prey.

The scholars have attempted to make educated guesses where the data are not entirely conclusive. It appears that about 11,000 years ago the early Americans were confronted with a major crisis when a period of global warming evidently caused the extinction of mammoths and other big game animals (mastadons, camels, and ancient species of horses) that they hunted. Thus, as the early Americans spread out over the Western hemisphere, they were forced to adapt to changing environments. The early Americans developed new food sources, including smaller animals, fish, nuts, berries, and insects; and then about 5,000 years ago they began to cultivate corn, squash, and beans. This shift to basic crops is a transformation normally termed as the *agricultural revolution*.

AGRICULTURAL REVOLUTION

In addition to changes in dietary patterns, the agricultural revolution brought other great changes in Native American cultures. Agriculture allowed a food surplus in that many crops, especially grain crops, can be stored and preserved for long period of times. The same could not be said for meat in the era prior to refrigeration. The development of agriculture and a food surplus allowed Native Americans to settle in one place and, therefore, also allowed the development of technology and culture and the accumulation of goods. As long as people hunted and gathered to sustain themselves, they were forced to limit their possessions. Following animal herds required that people travel with as few possessions as possible; hence, there was little room for sculptures or painted pottery that did not directly contribute to the business at hand. Thus, the development of numerous art forms was greatly hindered. Similarly, population growth was limited in nomadic societies, as women could not have more children than they could carry or nurse at one time. After the development of agriculture, however, people were able to have more children because the children would not have to be carried or otherwise assisted while the tribe followed the herds. Technological advancement and advancement in the arts also accompanied the development of agriculture because people had more leisure time and because they no longer had to keep their possessions at a minimum in order to roam more easily with the animal herds.

Gradually, the Native Americans developed a variety of substantial civilizations, whose cultures and living standards varied greatly. For example, the Karankawa tribes of the Gulf coast of Texas had a formidable reputation for cannibalism and bestiality. In the words of one Spanish traveler in the sixteenth century, "They are cruel, inhuman, and ferocious. When one nation makes war with another, the one that conquers puts all the old men and old women to the knife and carries off the little children for food to eat on the way." In contrast to the Karankawas, near the mouth of the Rio Grande were the Coahuiltecans, who lived primarily by digging and grubbing. The Coahuiltecan diet consisted of spiders, ant eggs, lizards, rattlesnakes, worms, insects, agave bulbs, sotol, lechuguilla, maguey, rotting wood, and deer dung. The Coahuiltecans roasted mesquite beans and ate them with sides of dirt. They also ate products from what was known as the "second harvest," seeds and similar items picked from human feces. They also ate prickly pear cactus and chewed another cactus, peyote, which produced a hallucinogenic effect. When the Coahuiltecans caught fish, they roasted them whole and then set them in the sun for several days to collect flies and maggots before eating the bug-enriched food. Because food was obviously scarce for the Coahuiltecans, they also practiced infanticide because they did not have enough food to go around.

THE ADVANCED SOCIETIES

In contrast to the Coahuiltecans, other Native Americans built technologically advanced and elaborate societies. For example, in Peru, the Incas assembled approximately six million people into an empire with irrigated farmland, paved roads, and a complex political system. In Southern Mexico and the Yucatan, the Mayas assembled a civilization that utilized a written language, an advanced system of mathematics, an accurate calendar, and an advanced agricultural system, while building impressive pyramids that stand to this day. Similarly, the Aztecs of central Mexico constructed an elaborate political society complete with educational and medical systems that rivaled those of Europe in the sixteenth century. The Aztec capital, Tenochtitlan, had a population of over 250,000 and impressive temples equal in size to the Great Pyramid of Egypt. In comparison, Seville, Spain, the port from which the Spanish sailed, had a population of approximately 50,000 at the time. The Aztec religion, however, required human sacrifice on a massive scale as evidenced by the 100,000 sculls the Spanish found at one location in 1519. The Aztecs also shocked the Spanish by bringing them a meal soaked in human blood when they mistook the Spanish for bloodthirsty "gods" from their own religious folklore that foretold of the coming of white men.

No civilization of Native Americans in the territory of the present day United States constructed a society as advanced and elaborate as those of the Mayas, Aztecs, and Incas; however, there were numerous Native American societies prior to Columbus that are worthy of note. We can look more closely at a few of these groups about whom the most is known.

The Aztecs constructed an elaborate political society in central Mexico.

THE ANASAZI

When the Europeans arrived in the Southwest in the fifteenth century, the Navajos called the people who had earlier inhabited the region before them the Anasazi, meaning "ancient ones" in Navajo; and that is the name that is commonly employed for a society whose members built so well that some of their structures have survived for 1,000 years. This has been accomplished while the Anasazi wrung a living from their harsh environment. Ancestors of the modern Pueblo Indians, the Anasazi lived in what we now know as the Four Corners region where the states of Arizona, New Mexico, Utah, and Colorado come together. They learned how to grow their crops of corn, beans, and squash in this arid region in such a way as to take advantage of virtually every precious drop of rainfall. They even built irrigation devices to improve their chances of watering the crops adequately. Moreover, archeologists have discovered parrot feathers among their remains, items that could only have originated some 1500 miles to the south in MesoAmerica. We know, therefore, that the Anasazi traded with those who were a long way away. Furthermore, there is compelling evidence that the Anasazi knew how to keep track of key dates, such as the solstices, because various ruins contain spirals pierced by a dagger of sunlight at noon on the day in question. Finally, some 400 miles of roads in one of the most important Anasazi regions, Chaco Canyon in New Mexico, attest to a complex web of interconnectedness within the region itself. The Anasazi

The Anasazi, who lived in the southwestern U.S., built structures into cliffs and hillsides.

road system connected Chaco Canyon by road to more than 70 outlying villages. Several of the Anasazi roads were almost 100 miles long.

Their buildings, however, that have captivated succeeding generations since the first Euro-Americans discovered those structures in the late nineteenth century. Some were built into hillsides, hence the term "cliff-dweller" that has been used to characterize the Anasazi. Others were freestanding and built on a scale that suggests a people with a sophisticated social structure. The largest complex is called Pueblo Bonito, and it is located in Chaco Culture National Historical Park. With at least 650 rooms and stretching up to four stories, Pueblo Bonito poses many mysteries: Was it an apartment complex? A ceremonial center? A storehouse for supplies? What is certain is that the people who built it included master architects and skilled masons.

Beginning around 300 B.C., the Anasazi culture would flourish for more than a millennium; but then, for reasons that are still not known with certainty, around A.D. 1150 the Anasazi abandoned their carefully constructed dwellings and moved on. Generations of archeologists have wrestled with explanations that include environmental stress, conflict, and soil exhaustion.

THE MOUND-BUILDERS

In contrast to the Anasazi, the people who lived in the Mississippi watershed enjoyed an environment that was lush with abundant water and a temperate climate. What the two groups had in common, however, were their ambitious building projects that developed around the same time, A.D. 900–1100. At the largest

Mound-builder settlement, Cahokia located in Illinois just across the Mississippi from St. Louis, there were more than 100 earthen mounds used for ceremonial purposes. The principal one, Monks Mound, is the largest prehistoric earthen construction in the Western Hemisphere, rising 100 feet with a base covering over 14 acres. It is believed that these Native Americans were sun worshipers, and the purpose of the mounds was to elevate elites nearer to the divine power of the sun. Sun calendars have been unearthed at this site, too, as well as many other evidences of a complex social organization led by powerful chiefs. In one mound a man, presumably the chief, was buried with the bodies of more than 60 people who were evidently executed at the time of the chief's burial. Several bodies, presumably either servants or enemies, were buried with their hands cut off. Also in the mound are the bodies of fifty young women, presumably wives, who evidently had been strangled. The entire Cahokia site encompasses almost 20 acres, and it is estimated that it was once home to 20,000 people, easily the largest settlement in North America prior to Columbus.

Also known as the "Mississippians," these people had a well-developed agricultural system, once again based on corn, beans, and squash. They were able to supplement this diet with animal protein, thanks to abundant hunting and fishing, and consequently had a good enough food supply that they could construct actual cities, with houses built around plazas. They, too, engaged in extensive trade; and they, too, abandoned their sites—circa A.D. 1500—for reasons that are not fully known. The contributing factors may have been some combination of war, disease, and depletion of natural resources.

THE FIVE NATION IROQUOIS

When we discuss the Iroquois, we are talking about a group that came into intense contact with Europeans; and hence, the Iroquois entered the historical record. Member tribes of the Iroquois included the Seneca, Cayuga, Oneida, Onondaga, and Mohawk people. They lived in large villages in the woodlands of what is now New York and Ontario, Canada. Their success in the cultivation of corn and other crops allowed them to build permanent settlements of bark-covered longhouses, some of which were up to 100 feet in length and housed as many as ten families. Women were the primary agriculturalists, while male jobs centered on hunting and on frequent warfare. Iroquoian societies were also matrilineal with property of all sorts—not limited to

Male Iroquois chiefs, such as the one shown here, were chosen by the women of the tribe.

but including land, children, and inheritance—belonging to women. Women were considered the heads of households and family clans, and they selected the male chiefs that governed tribes. Jesuit priests who lived among them in New France were much struck by their culture, including the close attention they paid to dreams and their child-rearing practices that seemed overly permissive to Europeans.

It was the Iroquois' breakthrough in political organization for which they are best known. One hundred or so years before the Europeans arrived, that is in the fifteenth century, there was apparently a substantial enough population increase among the Iroquois that they began to put pressure on the hunting grounds of neighboring tribes such as the Algonquian. Not surprisingly, this led to even more frequent warfare. Scholars believe that it was this increased warfare that led the Five Nations to form a confederacy for mutual defense. In the early sixteenth century a prophet by the name of Deganawida appeared among them. He and his chief disciple, Hiawatha, preached the benefits of unity and peace, and persuaded the Five Nations to form a Great League of Peace and Power, which remained powerful well into the eighteenth century on the eve of the American Revolution.

COMMONALITIES

With all of the variability among them, there were certain elements in common among the native peoples. In the first place, one can say with certainty that none had gender roles at all like those among the

Europeans, whose gender roles were profoundly p[...]
some tribes, such as the Iroquois, the sexual divisio[...]
vored relatively greater equality between men and women than anything known to the Old World.

Another commonality lay in their religious beliefs: despite all of
the differences among the tribes, they had in common a way of
looking at the world and its origins that is called "animistic". For the
native peoples, the distinction made by Europeans between "natural" and "supernatural" was non-existent. The native world was
filled with spirits. Rivers, the sun, the moon, forests, the ocean,

great rocks—all had spirits
that one must take care not
to disturb. Moreover, unlike
the Judaeo-Christian tradition, in which creation was
an all-male undertaking,
most tribes had cosmolo-
gies in which there were
Great Mother figures, as well
as Great Fathers.

The natives also had their
own creation myths and their
own "fall of man" myths. For
instance, the Cherokees believed that the land was created by a busy water bug
that built the continent a grain
of sand at a time by diving to
the bottom of the ocean and
bringing earth to the surface.
After trillions of trips, the continents were built. As for the
mountains and valleys, a
giant bird swooped down
and scraped the earth with its
wings, carving out valleys
and depositing the earth into
hills and mountains in the
process. The Cherokees also
explained their fall from
grace as the result of a
Cherokee who distracted

Common among the different native groups of
the Americas was their belief in animism and
spirits, as depicted in this Aztec idol sculpture.

God. According to the Cherokees, God kept all the animals in a cave and allowed the Cherokees to eat them as needed until a Cherokee boy distracted God's attention from his guard duty, allowing all the animals to escape. The Cherokee had, therefore, been forced to chase the escaped game ever since.

Finally, another commonality lay, tragically, in their vulnerability to European pathogens. There were no hogs or cattle in the Western Hemisphere prior to the arrival of the Europeans, and it is from these animals that the diseases smallpox and influenza are believed to have originated. The Europeans had resistance to these diseases from centuries of contact with hogs and cattle while the indigenous peoples of the Western Hemisphere had none. The conquerors brought these animals and the accompanying diseases to which Native Americans had never before been exposed, and the native peoples succumbed in ghastly numbers. Demographers estimate that typically there was only about one tenth of the original native population left after a generation or so of contact with Europeans. Warfare played a role in this decimation, but its role was secondary to that of disease.

BACKGROUND TO COLONIZATION

THE BEGINNINGS OF EUROPEAN EXPANSION

America had been discovered as early as A.D. 1000, when the Vikings dominated northern Europe and the northern Atlantic. Erik the Red led a group of Norsemen from Iceland to Greenland, geographically a North American island, in 982 A.D. There Erik came into contact with indigenous people of North America and established a permanent settlement. In 1001 ad, Erik's son, Leif Erikson, made a voyage from Greenland to North America and landed perhaps at Labrador or Newfoundland. Leif made three more voyages, the last in 1014 when he began a colony he named "Viinland" on the north coast of Newfoundland at a place now called L'Anse aux Meadows. The indigenous peoples of Newfoundland resisted the Norse incursion vigorously. In one engagement, just as the Norse were about to be wiped out in battle, Freydis, the illegitimate daughter of Erik the Red and the first woman known to North American history, saved the Norse by bearing her breasts, slapping them with a sword, and screaming ferociously. At these sights and sounds, the indigenous attackers turned and fled.

Unfortunately, the Norse colonists quarreled among themselves and ended up destroying their own colony. The Norse abandoned Viinland after their brief settlement in 1014, but continued to visit North America for another 100 years. A twelfth century Norse coin recovered from an Native American site in Maine proves that the Norse had continuing contact in North America at least until the early twelfth century.

In spite of this relatively long period of contact between the Norse and North America, their adventures did not stimulate European expansion into the New World. Obviously, a significant change had taken place in Western Europe by the time of Columbus' voyage in 1492, not only making overseas expansion possible but also instilling an adventurous spirit among Europeans so that they were eager to explore new lands and new opportunities.

Essentially, it was a change from medieval agrarianism and the feudal mind to economic developments characteristic of early modern Europe and the inquiring mind. In the Middle Ages, western Europe had been dominated by the feudal and manorial system in which each family's place in society—ranging from the peasantry to the nobility—was determined by the relationship of the male head of the household to the land. The inhabitants of the manor consumed the commodities produced. The rise of early modern capitalism, however, brought a revival of trade, the rise of the city, the emergence of a merchant class, production for an outside market, and the growth of banking. As a result people were no longer dependent exclusively upon their relationship to the land. Business transactions brought an accumulation of money, and money could be employed to finance new enterprises.

The mind of Europe also was awakened. The Crusades, beginning in the eleventh century, introduced Western Europe to the ways of the Near East and to such exotic commodities as spices and silks. Italian merchants—most notably, Marco Polo—journeyed all the way to China and Japan. The fear of the unknown and of new experiences that gripped many people in the Middle Ages began to change with the Renaissance of the fifteenth century, giving way to the spirit of innovators, whose minds were stimulated by a curiosity about the unknown and a wish to exploit the riches of the East. The Renaissance fostered a more expansive outlook and encouraged more creative thinking. The time period also witnessed greater centralization of political authority under a group of leaders whom historians call the New Monarchs. The New Monarchs gained power over the local nobles who had dominated in the feudal system and extracted taxation on the national scale that could be used to fund expansion. As a result, the nation-state system emerged in Europe.

Portugal was the first nation bordering the Atlantic to engage in wide-scale exploration, especially along the western coast of Africa.

This primacy was not accidental. Portugal was the first of the Atlantic nations to be unified, giving its leaders an opportunity to look outward rather than to be preoccupied with internal disorder. Portugal of the fifteenth century enjoyed internal peace and reasonably efficient government at a time when most of Europe was beset by war and internal upheaval. Portugal's location at the intersection of the Mediterranean and Atlantic also made the Portuguese look outward to the maritime possibilities. The Portuguese were aware that Arab caravans crossed the Sahara to bring back gold, slaves, and ivory from sub-Saharan Africa. Arab traders also spoke of how the Mandingo King Musa of Mali controlled more gold than anyone in Europe. The Portuguese believed that an Atlantic voyage to points on the West African coast south of the Sahara could tap into Africa's riches and undercut the Arab traders.

Among the most forward-looking of the Portuguese leaders was Prince Henry the Navigator (1394–1460), who established a center for the study of cartography and astronomy and for the improvement of ships and seamanship. The Portuguese studied the Arab ships, borrowing from the Arab designs and improving upon them. The Portuguese increased the ratio of length to width from a standard 2:1 ratio to 3:1, borrowed the lateen (triangular) sail from the Arabs, and created a new kind of ship called the Caravel, of which the Nina used on Columbus' first voyage was one. The Portuguese also learned how to mount heavy cannon on their ships, made full use of the compass, and borrowed the astrolabe—a device that permitted calculation of latitude from looking at the stars—from the Arabs. Prince Henry sponsored some fifteen voyages along the African coast and launched Portugal's era of expansion. Portugal was eventually rewarded when Bartholomew Diaz rounded Africa's southernmost Cape of Good Hope in 1488 and when Vasco da Gama reached India by way of the Cape of Good Hope in 1498.

The significance of national unity was underscored when Columbus' voyage in 1492 coincided with the expulsion of the Moors from Spain by the capture of Granada. For the first time in centuries, the entire Iberian Peninsula was united under Christian rulers. Columbus' voyage, sailing west to reach the fabulous riches of the East, marked the great historical divide which eventually made the Atlantic rather than the Mediterranean the principal artery of trade and communication.

CHRISTOPHER COLUMBUS

Christopher Columbus was born to a master weaver in 1451 and raised in Genoa, Italy. Columbus began his life on the sea at age 14

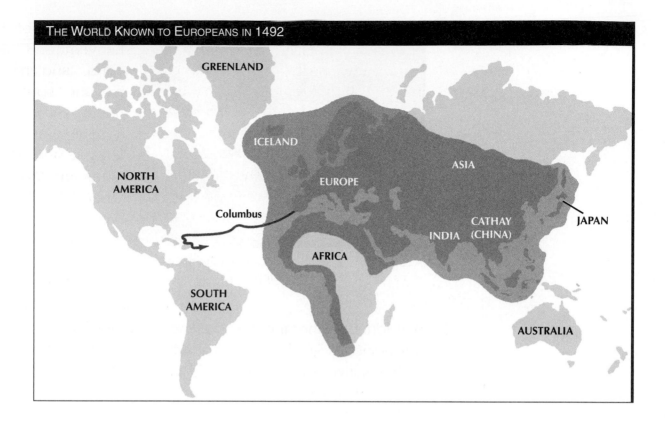

THE WORLD KNOWN TO EUROPEANS IN 1492

and by 1476 journeyed to Lisbon where he would do most of his sailing as a young man in the service of Portugal. Columbus married Felipa Moniz, whose father had been raised in the household of Prince Henry the Navigator. Through Felipa's family, Columbus gained access to a wealth of explorers' maps and papers providing information on navigation of the currents and winds of the Atlantic. Through his seafaring experience, Columbus became intrigued with the possibility of reaching Asia by sailing west. Columbus did not discover that the earth was round. Most fifteenth century mariners understood that fact. The Greek scholar, Ptolemy, had postulated that the earth was round six centuries before Christ; however, Columbus thought that the world was much smaller than it was and expected to find Asia approximately 2,500 miles West of the Canary Islands. His calculations were only off by about 8,000 miles. Since Columbus was unable to find anyone in Portugal that would finance his expedition, he turned to Spain where Queen Isabella agreed to finance his voyage. Isabella outfitted Columbus with his three small ships—the Nina, the Pinta, and the Santa Maria—and ninety men, including the Pinzon brothers who would do his navigation for him. Columbus was a religious man and believed his voyage to be part of a Divine mission. In the words of Columbus, "God made me the

A replica of the Santa Maria, one of the three ships that sailed with Christopher Columbus to the New World

messenger of the new heaven and the new earth, and he showed me the spot where to find it."

Only 33 days after leaving the Canary Islands and after a voyage where he experienced calm seas, Columbus landed on an island in the Bahamas that he named San Salvador on October 12, 1492. Columbus found neither the gold nor the black pepper he had hoped to bring back to Spain, so he instead brought back with him to Spain seven Native Americans, whom he misnamed as "Indians." In his diary Columbus described the natives as friendly but "naked as their mothers bore them." Columbus also reported that the natives had no knowledge of metals because when he showed them swords, "they took them by the edge and through ignorance cut themselves." The natives called themselves "Tainos," which meant "good" or "noble" in their language; and they engaged in agriculture, growing cassava, sweet potatoes, corn, cotton, and tobacco. The natives also fished and traveled from island to island in canoes. Columbus did notice, however, small pieces of gold in the noses of some of the natives, and he sought to find the source of the gold and bring it back to Spain.

Upon Columbus' return to Spain, the Spanish awarded him the title "Admiral of the Ocean Sea"; and the seven Tainos were all baptized as Christians. In 1493, Columbus returned to the Caribbean with 17 ships and a thousand men and began a colony on Hispanola. Upon his return, Columbus found that the Tainos had killed all 39 men he had left on the island. The Tainos had retaliated because Columbus' men kidnapped Taino women and forced them into personal harems.

Finding neither gold nor spices, Columbus forced the natives to bring him either cotton or gold to ship back to Spain so as to make his voyage profitable. Columbus imposed a quota for natives of 25 pounds of cotton or a hawk's bell full of gold. Those that did not comply were severely punished by having a hand, nose, or ear cut off. When those efforts also failed to produce the desired profits, Columbus began selling the natives into slavery.

In 1494, Spain and Portugal almost went to war over who would control the riches of the newly found territories. Spain insisted on complete control over the lands discovered by Columbus while Portugal wanted its share of the new discoveries but, more importantly, to ex-

The landing of Columbus on San Salvador in the Bahamas on October 12, 1492

clude Spain from the coast of Africa which had been explored extensively by Portugal. Pope Alexander VI negotiated a settlement of the dispute that became the Treaty of Tordesillas. The treaty divided the new territory (which all parties still believed to be Asia) by a line of longitude located 270 leagues west of the Azores. Any land west of the line belonged to Spain and those lands east of the line belonged to Portugal. Unknown to all parties at the time, much of undiscovered Brazil lay east of the line.

With the bulk of the new land secured for Spain by the Pope, Columbus made a third voyage in 1498 where he reached the coast of South America. He still believed that he was in Asia, however, and died in 1506 not realizing that he had discovered an entirely different continent. In 1500, Amerigo Vespucci published an account of his voyages across the Atlantic that was sufficient to convince European mapmakers that Columbus had indeed discovered unknown continents rather than Asia. It is, therefore, from Amerigo Vespucci that America got its name. In 1519–1522, Ferdinand Magellan, a Portuguese mariner in the service of Spain, led a voyage around the globe (though Magellan himself was killed in a skirmish with natives in the Philippines), thus putting to rest forever the question of whether or not the earth is round and whether Asia could be reached from Europe by sailing West.

The efforts of Portugal and Spain to find new routes to the East were prompted in large part by their desire to challenge the commercial monopoly of the Italian cities. These cities, because of their geographical position, dominated trade with the East by way of the Mediterranean. By sailing around the world in 1519–1522 and showing a substantial profit despite the loss of all but one ship, the commander, and most of the men, the expedition of Ferdinand Magellan proved that the Mediterranean could be bypassed and the Italian monopoly broken.

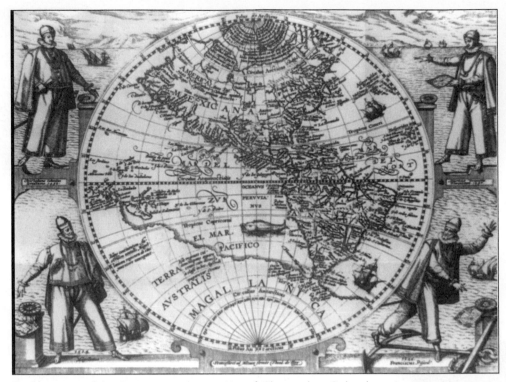

Replica map of the Americas with portraits of Christopher Columbus, Amerigo Vespucci, Ferdinand Magellan, and Francisco Pizarro.

Spain followed up the voyage of Columbus by establishing an American empire, thereby setting an example that the other nations of western Europe attempted to imitate. The Spaniards constructed a tightly knit, closely supervised colonial system whose object was to make its American colonies a source of wealth for the mother country and to prevent any encroachment by other nations. All of the Spanish conquests, including those of Columbus, were cloaked under the guise of Christianity. Wherever Columbus went, he planted a cross, and made (as he said) the "declarations that are required" to claim the land for Spain and Christianity. Spanish explorers that came after Columbus would be required to read to natives a document known as the Requerimiento (requirement) that informed the natives of the truth of Christianity and the necessity to swear immediate allegiance to the Pope and the Spanish crown. The natives were informed that they would be the slaves of the Spanish and those who rejected these blessings of Christianity deserved to die. The actual text of the document read thusly:

> I certify to you that, with the help of God, we shall powerfully enter into your country and shall make war against you in all ways and manners that we can, and shall subject you to the yoke and obedi-

ence of the Church of Their Highnesses. We shall take you and your wives and your children, and shall make slaves of them, and as such shall sell and dispose of them as Their Highnesses may command. And we shall take your goods, and shall do you all the mischief and damage that we can, as to vassals who do not obey and refuse to receive their Lord and resist and contradict him.

Generally, the Requerimiento was read to the bewildered natives in Spanish (which most natives could not understand) after the natives had already been put in chains.

COLUMBUS' TAINTED IMAGE

Though Columbus has been enshrined as an American hero and "Columbus Day" is a national holiday in the U.S., the true history of Columbus is more mixed; and his savagery was such that he has been denounced in many places in Latin America in a manner similar to the Soviet denunciation of Stalin in the 1950s. The denunciation of Columbus is not without warrant. Long before the Requerimiento, Columbus had begun kidnapping and enslaving the Native Americans, even on his very first voyage. On one occasion during Columbus' first voyage, he sent a raiding party ashore to capture some women to keep males he had already captured company because, as he wrote in his journal, his past experience in African slave trading taught him that "the Indian men would behave better in Spain with women of their own country than without them."

On Columbus' second voyage he embarked on a much larger slave roundup and gathered 1600 natives on the Island of Hispanola, 550 of whom he took back to Spain. The Italian nobleman Michele de Cuneo described the involuntary nature of the round-up when he wrote, "Among them were many women who had infants at the breast. They, in order the better to escape us ... left their infants anywhere on the ground and started to flee like desperate people." Of the 550 slaves Columbus took back to Spain, 200 died en route, and many of the others died shortly after reaching Spain. Of the event Columbus wrote, "in the name of the Holy Trinity, we can send from here all the slaves and brazil-wood which could be sold." Columbus even viewed the Native American death rate optimistically, writing, "Although they die now, they will not always die. The Negroes and Canary Islanders died at first." And die they did. Spanish historian Peter Martyr described the situation in 1516 thusly, "Packed in below deck, with hatchways closed to prevent their escape, so many slaves died on the trip that a ship without compass, chart, or guide, but only following the trail of dead Native Americans who had been thrown from the ships could find his way from the Bahamas to Hispanola." This, however, was only the beginning of a campaign of rape, murder, and genocide perpetrated by Columbus and the Spanish on Hispanola.

Upon Columbus' arrival in Hispanola in 1493, he demanded quotas of food, gold, cotton, and sex from the natives. To ensure cooperation, Columbus ordered the cutting off of an ear or a nose of those that did not comply. Concerning the sex demands, Columbus was most explicit. Columbus' friend, Michele de Cuneo reported that he was personally given a beautiful Carib woman by Columbus during Columbus' second voyage. De Cueno states, however, that "I conceived desire to take pleasure. I wanted to put my desire into execution but she did not want it and treated me with her finger nails in such a manner that I wished I had never begun. But seeing that, I took a rope and thrashed her well, for which she raised such unheard of screams that you would not have believed your ears. Finally, we came to an agreement."

In 1500, Columbus wrote to a friend and gleefully proclaimed, "A hundred castellanoes are as easily obtained for a woman as for a farm, and it is very general and there are plenty of dealers who go about looking for girls; those from nine to ten are now in demand."

In 1495, the natives attempted a rebellion, but Columbus brutally put down the rebellion. According to Columbus' son Ferdinand, "The soldiers mowed down dozens with point blank volleys, loosed the dogs to rip open limbs and bellies, chased fleeing Native Americans into the bush to skewer them on sword and pike, and with God's aid soon gained a complete victory." The Spanish reports of their own deliberate cruelty are legion. In the words of one observer, "For a lark they tore babes from their mother's breast by their feet and dashed their heads against the rocks. The bodies of other infants they spitted ... together. After losing in battle, many natives chose suicide rather than live in slavery for the Spanish." As Pedro de Cordoba wrote in 1517, "Occasionally a hundred have committed mass suicide. The women, exhausted by labor, have shunned conception and childbirth. ... Many, when pregnant, have taken something to abort and aborted. Others after delivery have killed their children with their own hands, so as not to leave them in such oppressive slavery."

The Spanish annihilation of the natives on Hispanola was thorough and complete. At one point, the Spanish even hunted the natives for sport and fed the natives to their dogs. Historians estimate the population of Hispanola to be as high as 8 million people upon Columbus' arrival. By 1496, Columbus' brother Bartholomew estimated the population of adults at 1.1 million. By 1516, the native population was only 12,000 and by 1555, there were no Native Americans remaining. Elsewhere in the Caribbean, what natives still survived were all enslaved by the Spanish by 1525. Although the vast majority in this great holocaust surely died from European diseases such as influenza, the brutal Spanish policies of slavery and subordination clearly share blame. What's more, the pattern of genocide perpetrated by the Spanish was carried out on other Caribbean Islands as well, including the Bahamas where Columbus first landed. By 1516, Spanish historian Peter Martyr reports that the Bahamas were "deserted." Similar patterns were repeated on Puerto Rico and Cuba.

THE CONQUISTADORES

Very early in the sixteenth century, the Spanish ceased to view the New World as an obstacle to the prospects of wealth in Asia and began to look at the New World as a place that could provide riches for Spain in and of itself. In 1519, the Spanish under Hernan Cortes began an exploration of Mexico with the purpose of finding and conquering a great kingdom that other Native Americans had informed them about in the Caribbean. Aided by an Native American woman named Malinali, whom Cortes received from a native chief in the Yucatan, Cortes eventually found the capital of the Aztec (called Aztecs by the Spanish, but the people referred to themselves as Mexicans) empire at Tenochtitlan (located at present-day Mexico City). The Aztec leader Montezuma mistook the Spaniards for the coming of the Aztec god Quetzalcoatl, whose arrival had been prophesied in the Aztec religion. Malinali had previously informed Cortes about the legend of Quetzalcoatl and encouraged Cortes to don some native ceremonial regalia indicating to the Aztecs that he was indeed the prophesied Quetzalcoatl. Hoping to please the God, Montezuma sent Cortes not only a large quantity of food soaked in human blood, but also a large golden disk the size of a cartwheel, proof of the Aztec's wealth. Montezuma welcomed the Spanish into Tenochtitlan and presented Cortes and his men with gifts. Cortes,

An Aztec calendar carved from stone

however, quickly took Montezuma hostage and held him under house arrest. Cortes then ruled from the background, attempting to use Montezuma as a puppet until the Aztecs revolted on June 30, 1520. Cortes and his men were forced to flee from Tenochtitlan to Tlaxcala, approximately 100 miles away where they made an alliance with the Aztec's enemies, the Tlaxcalans. Cortes and his men had also left behind the deadly smallpox virus, producing an epidemic so horrible in Tenochtitlan that the Aztecs lacked the manpower to bury all the bodies.

In the spring of 1521, Cortes, his men, and tens of thousands of Tlaxcalan allies laid siege to the city. Cortes destroyed the Aztec's food and water supplies, burned the magnificent Aztec public buildings, marketplaces, parks, gardens, and aviaries with thousands of wondrous birds. The city that the Spanish had just months earlier described as the most beautiful city on earth quickly became a place of rubble, dust, flame, and death. Because the city was built on canals, burning was not always the most efficient means of destruction; so the Spanish crushed houses and other buildings and piled the debris into the canals. Cortes wrote that his intention was to kill everyone in Tenochtitlan and that there were so many bodies in the streets that the Spanish were forced to walk upon them. Lastly, the Spanish burned the books of Aztec religion and learning and fed the Aztec priests to the Spanish dogs.

The Spanish conquerors fanned out from Tenochtitlan, searching for more gold and plunder, so that over the next 100 years, 95 percent of the indigenous populations of Mexico and South America would perish. It is estimated that Spanish troops under Pedro de Alvarado alone were responsible for as many as five million deaths in Southern Mexico and Central America between 1525 and 1540. In South America, the Spanish under Francisco Pizarro in 1532 repeated the pattern established by Columbus, Cortes, and Alvarado when they conquered the Incan empire of nine million people with only 200 men. Pizarro and his men captured the Incan Emperor Atahualpa and held him for ransom. The Incas responded with a pile of gold and silver equal to 50 years worth of precious metal production in Europe in the sixteenth century. After receiving the ransom, the Spanish then executed Atahualpa anyway. Over the next 100 years, 95 percent of the Incan population would perish.

In place of the Native American population, the Spanish immigrated to the New World in large numbers. In 1574, long before the English had established a successful colony in the New World, the Spanish population in Mexico City alone exceeded 15,000; throughout the New World it exceeded 160,000. By 1650, over 450,000

Spaniards had immigrated to the New World. More than 200 Spanish cities and towns had been founded, and Mexico City boasted a university. Most of the immigrants were single males seeking economic opportunity. The principal agency used by Spain to transplant the culture of the Old World to the New was the Catholic Church, the only church in existence in the Western world at the time the Spanish colonial system was founded. The Church established missions throughout the New

The Incan city of Machu Picchu, rediscovered in 1911, may have been used for religious purposes.

World, many of which are in Florida and the Southwestern United States.

The Spanish colonial policy, unlike that followed later by the English, considered native peoples as subjects of the sovereign and American resources as wealth to be plundered. The result was a fusion of cultures, still characteristic of Latin America today, and the shipment of 200 tons of gold and 16,000 tons of silver back to Spain between 1500 and 1650. The influx of metals into Spain, however, had the negative effect of producing inflation since gold and silver were used for the currency and the money supply, therefore, greatly expanded—faster than the growth of tangible goods.

The Spanish colonial system extended into territory that has since become part of the United States. As early as 1512 Ponce de Leon had launched an expedition from the West Indies to explore the coast of Florida, returning on a second voyage some seven years later. In 1528 Panfilo de Narvaez led a disastrous expedition of about 600 men, equipped with horses, livestock, and other supplies, which landed on the Gulf Coast of Florida. After exploring the region extending westward to Alabama and encountering illness, starvation, and hostile Native Americans, the survivors of the expedition were forced to kill their horses and build barges of horse hide in an attempt to follow the coastline to Mexico. The barges foundered, and the Spanish were forced ashore on the Texas coast. The Spanish then attempted

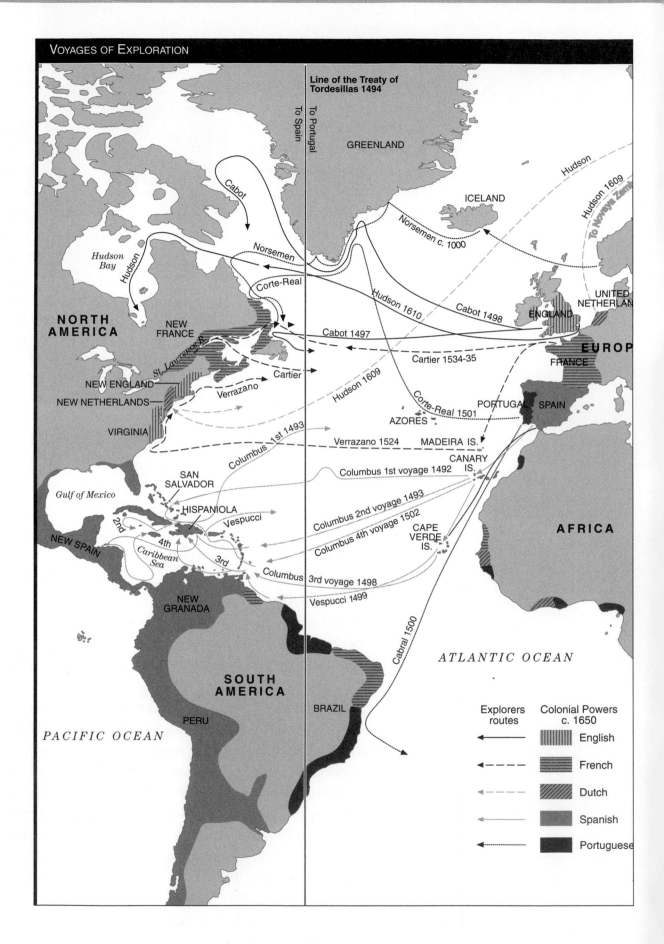

VOYAGES OF EXPLORATION

to trek overland to Spanish settlements in Mexico. Only four members of the group led by Cabeza de Vaca, reached Mexico City some eight years later, after suffering almost unbelievable hardship, including enslavement by native tribes in Texas. In 1539, Hernando de Soto and 600 men landed in Florida, and de Soto and his men explored the southeastern United States all the way to Texas. De Soto himself died in 1542 and was buried in the Mississippi River before his men turned back without finding another city of gold like Tenochtitlan. Similarly, Francisco Vasquez de Coronado left northern Mexico in 1540 and headed north into New Mexico, Texas, and Kansas in search of the legendary "seven cities of gold." Coronado did find a small Zuni Pueblo, but nothing resembling a "city of gold." That same year (1542), Juan Rodriguez Cabrillo led an expedition along the coast of California all the way to Oregon, but he too failed to find another Tenochtitlan. Cabrillo himself died on the Island of Catalina.

THE ENCOMIENDAS

The Spanish Empire in the New World was primarily the effort of private entrepreneurs with little direct support from the Spanish government. For individuals that desired to launch expeditions into the New World, it was required that they first get licenses from the Spanish government. Those who obtained licenses (encomiendas) were essentially rewarded with possession of conquered native villages. Those encomenderos (those with encomiendas) were given the authority to demand labor from the natives in return for their legal protection and religious guidance.

SPANISH COLONIZATION IN THE UNITED STATES

In 1565 Menendez de Aviles founded St. Augustine, the earliest continuous settlement within the present limits of the United States. The Spanish expansion into what are today Texas, the American southwest, and California was sufficiently powerful to leave an enduring imprint. Spanish soldiers and Franciscan priests established a chain of garrisons and mission stations throughout the territory. Santa Fe, New Mexico, was founded in 1610 and San Antonio, Texas, in 1718. In the eighteenth century more than twenty missions were organized in California, including San Diego, San Francisco, and Santa Barbara.

By the end of the sixteenth century, the Spanish Empire was the largest in the history of the world including most of South America, Central America, Mexico, the Caribbean, Florida, and the Southwestern United States. The Spanish, however, had imposed a small ruling class that existed to serve the Spanish crown and had not established anything resembling European society in the New World. The fact that the Spanish largely came as single men (men outnumbered women ten to one) meant that the Spanish men in America typically took Native American wives and thus fused the bloodlines and the cultures. Eventually, what emerged in Latin America became known as the "fifth great race" (the Latin Americans). The majority of people in Latin America by the eighteenth century were mestizos or persons of mixed Spanish and Native American ethnicity. More men of the Spanish ruling class brought their European wives with them than did commoners; consequently, Latin America, in general, became dominated by an ethnically European elite, ruling over the mestizo masses. The Spanish also brought eleven million African slaves to Latin America, further diversifying the ethnic mix. Brazil and the Caribbean were the destination for most of the African slaves, and the population of Haiti remains at over 90 percent African origin in the twenty-first century. In some of the more remote regions of Latin America, such as the Amazon Basin and some areas high in the Andes, the Spanish mixed very little with the indigenous populations so that the Native American populations remained much larger than those in North America and have remained so through the present.

The Spanish also imported new crops to the Western Hemisphere, including sugar and bananas and new livestock including cattle, pigs, sheep, goats, cats, chickens, and, perhaps most importantly, horses. With no natural enemies, the population of new animals grew rapidly in the new land. The Native Americans quickly learned to cultivate the new crops and domesticate the new animals, thus furthering the spread of the flora and fauna, but also changing forever the Native American cultures. By the mid-19th century, for instance, the great plains Indians of North America were known for their expertise in horsemanship. The exchange was not all one way, however. The Spanish also brought the new crops, corn and tobacco, back with them to Europe along with their Native American slaves and epidemics of syphilis. This transatlantic exchange of people and goods became known as the Columbian exchange.

As the sixteenth century came to a close, the Spanish Empire was beginning its decline and the Spanish were facing new challenges from the French, Dutch, and English in Europe, on the open seas, and in the New World. The sixteenth century, however, belonged to the Spanish who had not only discovered the New World but, also, exploited it for their own benefit. The Spanish had subdued the people of the New World and instituted the Columbian exchange, thus providing a model for those who would come later. The lesson that the Spanish example taught the rest of Europe was that there were riches in the New World and that they were there for the taking. As other European powers rose to challenge Spanish dominance, they would launch their own expeditions purposed to do just that; however, the English colonial attempts of the seventeenth and eighteenth centuries in North America would take a much different course.

FACTORS IN ENGLISH EXPANSION

Although John Cabot, representing the English crown, explored the eastern coast of North America within a decade of Columbus' voyage, (1497) successful English settlement was delayed for a century. Cabot landed on the North American coast, perhaps at Newfoundland or Labrador, but did not journey further than the range of a crossbow from the shore line. The English would not attempt to establish a settlement in North America until 1583 when Henry Gilbert led an expedition to Newfoundland. Gilbert did land on the coast of Newfoundland, but he proceeded along that coast in search of a good place for a military outpost until he became caught in a storm and was lost at sea.

THE LOST COLONY OF ROANOKE

Undeterred by Gilbert's failure, in 1585 Sir Walter Raleigh dispatched a group under the command of Richard Grenville to an island called Roanoke off the coast of North Carolina. The English experienced problems with the natives almost immediately as the English accused the natives of

Sir Walter Raleigh, shown with his wife, dispatched a group of English settlers to the island of Roanoke, off the coast of North Carolina, in 1585.

Sir Francis Drake arrived in Roanoke in 1586.

theft of a silver cup. In retaliation, the English destroyed a native village, leading to enmity with the natives. When Sir Francis Drake arrived on Roanoke in the spring of 1586, the colonists boarded his ship and abandoned the colony. The next year (1587), Raleigh dispatched another expedition of 91 men, 17 women, and nine children that he hoped would begin a successful plantation. Shortly after arrival, one of the women gave birth to a daughter, Virginia Dare, the first person born in North America to English parents. Dare's grandfather, John White, returned to England a few weeks after her birth to recruit more settlers and bring more supplies. When he returned to Roanoke in 1590, he found the island deserted and no clues to the fate of the settlers other than the inscription "Croatoan" carved on a post.

Theories abound as to what happened to the settlers. Some argue that they were all killed in a war with the Native Americans. Others argue that they were adopted by the natives and then taken off the island. Perhaps segments of both theories are correct, but no conclusive evidence has ever been found to prove either. In any case, it would be twenty years before another English group would attempt to establish a colony in North America.

Other factors, however, would lead to further English colonial attempts in North America. The economic, religious, and political factors affecting the English colonies were entirely different from those that had influenced the Spanish colonies. Two outstanding economic changes were in trade and agriculture. Whereas no trading companies flourished in 1500, over 200 English trading companies operated aggressively by 1600, including the Muscovy Company (1553), the Levant Company (1592), and the famous East India Company (1600). In 1500 German and Italian merchants dominated English trade. By 1600 this domination had been eliminated and a strong group of English merchants had emerged. In 1500 most of the raw wool raised in England was shipped to Flanders to be made into cloth. By 1600 an English textile industry in England absorbed much of the wool produced in England.

These economic changes had a direct effect upon the development of the English colonies. The first three successful English colonies in America—Plymouth, Virginia, and Massachusetts Bay—were planted by cooperatively owned joint-stock companies, precursors of modern corporations, in which a number of investors pooled their capital. Many of those engaged in the American enterprises had gained their experience in trading companies elsewhere, and they continued to participate in trading enterprises throughout the world. As Charles M. Andrews, a prominent historian of the colonial period, has written: "English America would hardly have been settled at this time had not the period of occupation coincided with the era of capitalism in the first flush of its power."

The experience in trade influenced mercantilist thought in England. Mercantilism embodied a set of economic ideas held throughout western Europe from 1500 to 1800, though the precise measures taken differed from country to country. The mercantilist advocated that the economic affairs of the nation should be regulated to encourage the development of a strong state. A number of propositions were customarily included in this policy. A nation could become stronger by exporting more than it imported, resulting in a "favorable balance of trade." National self-sufficiency should be encouraged by subsidy of domestic manufactures. A nation's wealth was to be measured by the amount of precious metals it could obtain (thus the emphasis on the accumulation of bullion). Labor should be regulated for the wellbeing and benefit of the state. And colonies should be established to provide the nation with raw materials that it was unable to produce.

Although this does not exhaust the list of propositions supported by mercantilist thinkers, it does show that trade was considered one of the most important measures of a nation's wealth and that colonies were valued because they contributed to that wealth. In England the mercantile emphasis between 1500 and 1600 was upon internal regulation. After 1600 the emphasis was on external regulation, particularly the commercial relationship of England to its colonies. The phenomenal increase in English mercantile activity not only provided an agency—the joint-stock company—to create colonies but also provided a national purpose for doing so.

A second significant economic change took place in agriculture. Between 1500 and 1600 an enclosure movement gained strength in Britain. Essentially, "enclosure" meant that smaller landholdings in certain areas of England were incorporated into larger holdings, forcing some people off the land. The result was a dislocation of population that caused many political thinkers to conclude that England was overpopulated and that therefore almost anyone should be permitted to go to the New World to reduce "overpopulation." Spain, by contrast, had restricted immigration to selected individuals favored by the crown.

In the sixteenth century the Protestant Reformation swept through Europe and profoundly affected the religious and political development of England, which in turn placed an enduring stamp upon its colonies in America. In 1500 England (and the Continent) was within the fold of the Catholic Church. By 1600 not only had England broken away and established the national Anglican Church, but the religious rupture had also encouraged the rise of religious splinter groups.

The story of this religious rupture in England is too involved for extended treatment in this text. What is particularly important is that in the process of waging his contest with the Roman Catholic Church, King Henry VIII enlisted the aid of Parliament. Parliament passed a series of enactments creating a national church, culminating in the Act of Supremacy (1534), which made Henry, instead of the pope, the ecclesiastical sovereign of England. Eventually, by means of parliamentary acts, lands in England belonging to the Roman Catholic Church were taken over by the king, greatly enhancing his wealth.

The ramifications of these actions invaded almost every sphere of English life, but two had most effect on the colonies: (1) The king, by utilizing the support of Parliament, demonstrated that in practice the authority of the crown was limited, a concept carried to the English colonies in America and a concept in direct contrast to Spanish doctrine, which held the power of the sovereign to be without restriction; and (2) the break with the Catholic Church opened the way for a wide diversity of religious groups.

King Henry VIII, with the help of Parliament, broke from the Roman Catholic Church in 1534 and was made the ecclesiastical sovereign of England.

Some people, believing that separation from the Catholic Church should never have taken place, remained Roman Catholics. Others felt that Henry VIII and, later, Elizabeth I had not gone far enough. The Puritans, an impassioned and vocal minority, believed that the Reformation in England had stopped short of its goal, that ritual should be further simplified, and that the authority of crown-appointed bishops should be lessened. However, they resolved to stay within the Church of England and attempt to achieve their goals—that is, "purify" the church—without a division. The Separatists, a small minority, believed that each congregation should become its own judge of religious orthodoxy. They were no more willing to give allegiance to the crown than they had been to give it to the pope.

This religious factionalism was transferred to the American colonies. Of the first four settlements, Virginia was Anglican, Plymouth was Separatist, Massachusetts Bay was Puritan, and Maryland was Catholic.

Early in the seventeenth century, a number of English "dissenters"—men and women who were dissatisfied with political, economic, or religious conditions in England—were ready to migrate to the New World; English trading companies provided an agency for settlement.

FOUNDING THE COLONIES OF NORTH AMERICA

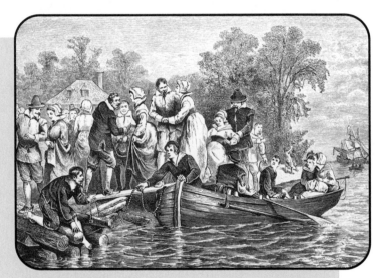

THE ENGLISH SETTLEMENTS

Founding Virginia
Reorganization
Indentured Servitude
Pocahontas
Governing Virginia
Catholic Maryland
Proprietary Colonies
The Coming of Africans
The Pilgrims in Plymouth
The "Great Migration"
Puritan Society
Puritans and Human Nature
Hutchinson Heresy
Puritans and Quaker Persecution
Puritans and Witches
Witches of Salem Village
Puritan Success
The Spreading Colonies of New England
Puritans and the Natives
The Capture of New York

The Jerseys
Penn's Experiment
Quakers
Quaker Laws
Pennsylvania Economy and Growth
Settlement of the Carolinas
Carolina Economy
The Division of Carolina
Georgia

THE ENGLISH SETTLEMENTS

One hundred fifteen years after Columbus' discovery of America, the English had not established a single permanent foothold in the Western Hemisphere. As late as 1600, although they had made several voyages and two attempts at settlement, they had not one colony to show for their efforts. By 1700, however, some 20 colonies, with 350,000 inhabitants, stretched all the way from Newfoundland on the North Atlantic to the island of Barbados in the southern Caribbean. Heavy losses originally deterred growth, but promoters and settlers learned to adjust to the new environment. Thus by the end of the 1600s their settlements had taken root, attained prosperity, and entered upon a stage of steady growth. The English dream of expansion overseas had become a reality, and Britain looked with pride upon its American empire.

FOUNDING VIRGINIA

The first permanent English colony in America was Virginia. In the year 1606 King James I granted a group of London merchants the privilege of establishing colonies in "the part of America commonly called Virginia." Securing a charter, this Virginia Company of London raised sufficient funds by the sale of shares to outfit three ships, the Godspeed, the Discovery, and the Susan Constant, with 144 men and sent them to Virginia, where on May 24, 1607, the 104 men and boys that survived the voyage established a settlement, Jamestown, on a peninsula extending from the banks of the James River. Unfortunately, the colonists did not choose their site wisely. The peninsula was low and swampy in addition to being hot and humid in the summer, resulting in an abundance of mosquitoes that caused malaria outbreaks among the colonists. The site was chosen, however, because it appeared to be a good place to build a defensible fort, and the colonists wanted to avoid the Native American attacks that were believed to have destroyed the colony at Roanoke.

The early Jamestown settlers had no experience in colonization. Many of them had come for adventure rather than from any desire to become permanent residents in the wilderness. They knew nothing of subsistence farming and displayed little ingenuity. Approximately a third of the original colonists were "gentlemen" who were, in the words of John Smith, "averse to work." Another third of the colonists were criminals who had been given a second chance in the New World. They, too, according to Smith, were averse to work. Although the

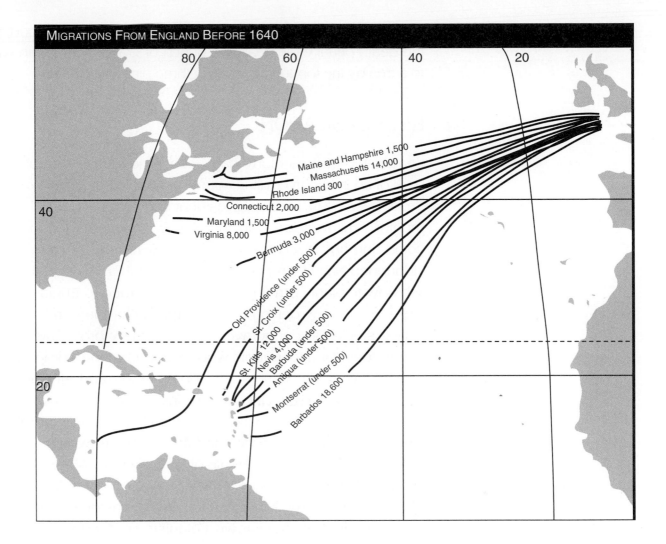

MIGRATIONS FROM ENGLAND BEFORE 1640

80 60 40 20

40

Maine and Hampshire 1,500
Massachusetts 14,000
Rhode Island 300
Connecticut 2,000
Maryland 1,500
Virginia 8,000
Bermuda 3,000
Old Providence (under 500)
St. Croix (under 500)
St. Kitts 12,000
Nevis 4,000
Barbuda (under 500)
Antigua (under 500)
Montserrat (under 500)
Barbados 18,600

40

20

James River teemed with fish, they nearly perished for want of food. Instead of fishing and engaging in agricultural pursuits, the colonists spent their time on fruitless hunts for gold. Of the 104 that had landed in Jamestown in May, only 38 survived until a ship full of supplies arrived in January; even that many might not have survived if it were not for the Native Americans offering to barter food for English goods in the fall of 1607. Of the first 5,000 people who migrated to Virginia, fewer than 1,000 survived. The winter of 1609–1610 was particularly harsh and became known as the "starving time." John Smith had alienated the Native Americans by raiding their food supplies, so the natives retaliated by killing off the livestock in the woods and keeping the colonists barricaded within their settlement. The English lived by eating dogs, cats, rats, snakes, toadstools, horsehides, and even cannibalizing the bodies of the dead. One man reportedly sat and watched his wife die and then quickly chopped up her body and salted down the pieces. The man was executed for eating what Smith referred to as "powdered wife." The English imposed draconian laws for stealing food, including the death penalty for stealing a bunch of grapes. One man was nailed to a tree by the tongue for stealing three pints of oatmeal.

REORGANIZATION

Leadership of the colony had been divided between several members of an ineffective ruling council. In the fall of 1608, however, John Smith became the council president and imposed his will on the community. Smith traded with the Native Americans for food when he could and organized raids to steal their food at other times. He also kidnapped Native Americans and forced them to explain to the English how to plant corn. In 1609, Smith returned to England after suffering a severe powder burn. The Virginia Company raised money by selling stock and encouraged immigrants by providing free passage to the New World for people who would serve the Company for seven years. Smith's successors, Sir Thomas Dale and Sir Thomas Gates, imposed harsh discipline, organizing settlers into work gangs and sentencing offenders to flogging, hanging, or being broken on the wheel. Eventually, Dale decided that colonists would work harder if he permitted private ownership of land. Still, life in Virginia was harsh, and mortality rates remained high. Over 9,000 people immigrated between 1610 and 1622, but the population was only 2,000 by 1622.

Gradually, the Jamestown colonists devised ways of making a livelihood. John Rolfe developed the skill of growing tobacco profitably and planted the first tobacco crop in 1612. Rolfe's contribution ensured Virginia's prosperity, for tobacco was a commodity much in demand in Europe very soon after its introduction from the New World. The first commercial shipment of tobacco reached England in 1617. In 1620, the colony with fewer than a thousand residents sent 60,000 pounds of tobacco across the waters. By 1700, there were approximately 100,000 colonists in Chesapeake Bay, and they exported 35 million pounds of tobacco. The Virginia colony was finally an economic success, but one built on smoke. Even King James I's denunciation of tobacco as "loathsome to the eye, hateful to the nose, harmful to the brain, and dangerous to the lungs" failed to slow the expansion of tobacco exports.

INDENTURED SERVITUDE

Tobacco is a labor-intensive crop and successful cultivation required Virginia planters to find a reliable supply of low-cost labor. To fill this need, Virginia tobacco growers turned to indentured servants, who willingly sold themselves into a form of temporary slavery for a set number of years (normally four years) in exchange for passage to the New World. Eighty percent of seventeenth century immigrants to the Chesapeake colonies came as indentured servants. Approximately 75 percent were single males under the age of 25.

Life for indentured servants in the seventeenth century Chesapeake colonies was harsh. Approximately half of the indentured servants died before fulfilling their indenture contract and securing their freedom. The harsh working conditions of the tobacco plantations along with tropical diseases decimated the indentured workforce. Masters often cared only if their servants survived the years of their contracts and thus worked them from "can" (can see or sunrise) to can't (can't see or sundown). Indentured servants could also be sold for the remainders of their contracts and, therefore, had no control over whom they might work for. Masters were even known to gamble away indentured servants in card games. Women could also be sold into indenture, often enduring sexual abuse from masters. To make matters worse, women had time added to their indenture contracts (two years) for pregnancy and childbirth. Time was also added for both men and women if they attempted to run away or committed crimes, such as stealing food or livestock. Women could be released from indenture through marriage if prospective grooms had the resources with which to purchase their indenture contracts; hence, many indentured women actively sought husbands. Both women and men received compensation at the end of their indenture contracts in the form of one suit of clothing and one barrel of corn.

POCAHONTAS

The daughter of the Native American chief Powhatan, Pocahontas, became famous both for saving the life of John Smith and for marrying the English tobacco planter John Rolfe and thus securing a temporary peace between the English and the Native Americans. Shortly after arriving in Jamestown in December 1607, John Smith wrote that he was "feasted by the Indians according to their best, barbarous manner" and then taken and held down upon a rock where a Native American with a large rock threatened to "beat out his braines." Right before the Native American was to crush his skull, Pocahontas, whom Smith described as a "well featured, but wanton young girl," probably 11 years old, placed her own head on the rock next to Smith's so as to save him from certain death. Smith wrote that Pocahontas "hazarded the

Pocahontas saving the life of Captain John Smith

beating out of her own braines" to save his. Instead of a story of romance, however, historians generally interpret the story as part of a staged ceremony that signified Powhatan's power over the life and death of Smith. Instead of a love story, it was most likely a ceremony of subordination. The English eventually captured Pocahontas in a raid on Powhatan's camp in 1613. When Powhatan refused English ransom demands, Pocahontas remained with the English, converted to Christianity and married the English tobacco planter, John Rolfe. After giving birth to a son, Thomas Rolfe, Pocahontas accompanied Rolfe back to England in 1616 and became known as a gracious woman in English society. Unfortunately, Pocahontas died of European diseases in 1617 probably at the age of 21.

GOVERNING VIRGINIA

In governing the colony, the Virginia Company at first adopted a policy of having severe laws administered by a strong-armed governor. After this failed, it made the momentous decision to let the settlers share in their own government. When Governor George Yeardley arrived in Virginia in 1619, he carried instructions to call annually an assembly to consist of two members, or burgesses, from the various local units in the colony. These burgesses were to be elected by residents on a basis of almost complete male suffrage. This assembly, which met in the church at Jamestown in the summer of 1619, was the first representative law-making body in English America and as such was the forerunner of representative government in the United States. Even when the Virginia Company at last succumbed to bankruptcy in 1624 and lost its charter, with the result that Virginia became a royal colony, the company's greatest contribution was preserved intact: The Virginia House of Burgesses continued to meet. It was ironical that this transfer took place under King James I, for it meant that the very monarch who was the most severe enemy of Parliament in England was also, unwittingly, the one who permitted representative government in America to become a regular part of the system of colonial government under the crown.

CATHOLIC MARYLAND

While Virginia was gradually gaining vitality, a neighboring colony developed on its northern flank. In 1632 Sir George Calvert, First Lord Baltimore, received from Charles I a charter for the tract of land extending from the fortieth degree of north latitude to the south bank of the Potomac River. Calvert, a Roman Catholic, intended to make Maryland a refuge for oppressed Catholics. He died before he could settle his grant, but his son Cecilius became lord proprietor and sent his brother Leonard to take possession of Maryland. The first group of Catholic settlers landed on March 25, 1634.

A "proprietary colony" such as the Calverts obtained was a return to a feudal and baronial system which in the seventeenth century was becoming outmoded. The manorial system of land tenure, which made the inhabitants of Maryland tenants of the Calverts instead of landowners, was the source of much unrest and would never have lasted at all had the Calverts not made tenancy similar to ownership. Calvert planned an aristocratic society ruled from the top, but those who immigrated to Maryland created their own democratic structures and often ignored rule from above.

From the outset, in order to attract settlers and make the colony pay, the Calverts encouraged Protestants, as well as Catholics, to go to Maryland. Though most of the manorial families were Catholic, Catholics never constituted a majority of the population. Catholics and Anglicans held separate worship, and Lord Baltimore would not allow the Jesuits in the colony to place any restrictions upon Protestants. In 1649 he sponsored the famous Maryland Toleration Act, which guaranteed freedom of worship to all Christians. This was not yet full liberty of conscience because there was a death penalty for non-Christians; but the act marked an advance in the direction of full religious freedom. Calvert attracted settlers with low cost land, however, with the result that the majority of Maryland's population was Protestant, rather than Catholic, in the seventeenth century. Economically, Maryland resembled Virginia in the seventeenth century with its economy based on tobacco agriculture, but Maryland became more open both religiously and politically. Maryland granted citizenship rights to women and Native Americans. A black man, Matthias de Souza, became the first African American to vote in North America in 1647, and Margaret Brent became the first woman to exercise the franchise in the same election.

Religious tolerance would end in 1689, however, when the Anglicans in Maryland accused the Calverts of refusing to bow to the new Protestant King in England, William of Orange. In reality, the Calverts had simply not yet received word of the new king. Anglicans deposed the Calverts, but they also declared the end of Catholic worship, closing and later destroying the Catholic Churches. Catholics would not be able to worship in public again in Maryland until the American Revolution. The Anglicans were also harsh to the Puritans, whom they viewed as traitors for failing to aid in the revolt against the Calverts. As a result, Puritans were arrested and jailed for treason. The Anglicans then made the Anglican Church the official State Church of the colony.

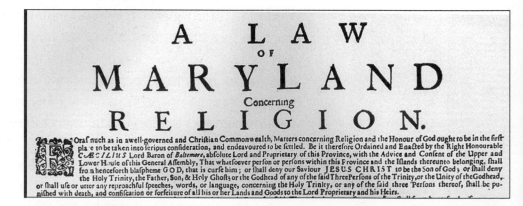

In 1649 Lord Baltimore sponsored the Maryland Toleration Act to guarantee freedom of worship to Christians.

PROPRIETARY COLONIES

Except for Maryland, the original colonies were established by joint-stock companies, but after 1660 almost all the newly founded colonies were proprietaries. Joint-stock companies, as a whole, did not make a profit, and business enterprisers became less interested in investing in colonial establishments. After 1660 King Charles II began to grant large segments of American land to those who had supported the Stuart claim to the throne during the period of Puritan control in England (1642–1660). Proprietors had been unsuccessful in the late sixteenth century because they could neither command sufficient capital nor sustain a colonizing effort over an extended period of time; but with the successful founding of Virginia, Maryland, Plymouth, and Massachusetts Bay, the risk of founding proprietary colonies was greatly reduced. As a result, the territory of the Carolinas was given to a number of proprietors in 1663, and Pennsylvania was founded as a proprietary colony in 1682. New Jersey began as a proprietorship but eventually was made a crown or royal colony, one where affairs were directed by crown officials. New York also began as a proprietary colony under the Duke of York after its capture from the Dutch. It became a crown colony when York ascended the throne as King James II.

THE COMING OF AFRICANS

The first Africans came to Virginia in 1619 as part of what would become a vast and very profitable Atlantic trade in human flesh, a trade that had begun about 100 years earlier with the slaves sent to the West Indies. The records do not reveal whether the Africans brought to Virginia in 1619 came as servants or slaves, but it is known that by 1650 Virginia had both black freemen and black slaves. African immigration grew slowly during the seventeenth century. In 1680 Africans, mostly slaves, comprised only four percent of the total population, widely scattered throughout the eastern seaboard.

Late in the seventeenth century the pace of importation of African slaves quickened. Most were brought to the Southern colonies of Maryland, Virginia, North Carolina, South Carolina, and eventually Georgia. By the beginning of the American Revolution blacks comprised 20 percent of the population, and the number of blacks—400,000—was equal to the total population of New England. Given the size of this single ethnic group, it is hardly surprising that the unwilling immigrants from Africa had an enduring impact on life in what was to become the United States of America. In the next chapter we will learn more about the treatment and the culture of these African immigrants.

THE PILGRIMS IN PLYMOUTH

Colonists who arrived off Cape Cod at Plymouth Rock in the *Mayflower* in December of 1620 made the first permanent settlement in New England. They had been granted permission to settle farther south, but their ship had been blown off course. The core of the group of about 100 settlers was a small, devoted band of Separatists, part of a larger number of religious dissenters who had left England for Holland in 1608. The Separatists viewed the Anglican Church as corrupt and beyond correction; thus, proper service to God required that they separate themselves from the Anglican Church and establish their own separate society. The Separatists first moved to rural England but, finding it impossible to escape Anglican decadence in England, moved to Maryland in 1608. The Separatists would find constructing a pure society of uncorrupted Christians in the Netherlands to be futile as well. In the words of Separatist leader

Mayflower Pilgrims arriving at Plymouth, Massachusetts, in 1620

William Bradford, "many of their children, by the great licentiousness of youth in Holland, and the manifold temptations of the place, were drawn away by evil examples." Unsuccessful in the Netherlands, the Separatists obtained permission to settle in the New World in the lands granted to the Virginia Company. In August 1620, 102 Pilgrims boarded the Mayflower to emigrate to the New World. The expedition, which put out from Plymouth, England, was financed by a joint-stock company in which the Separatists, their fellow passengers, and outside investors participated.

The story of these Separatists, who now called themselves Pilgrims, has become a part of the American legend: the hardships of the first winter, the friendship of the Native Americans Samoset and Squanto, who taught the settlers to plant corn, and the first harvest and thanksgiving festival.

During their 11-week voyage, the Pilgrims were blown off course and ended up far north of the Virginia Company's lands. Realizing that they had no legal authority to settle at Plymouth, the Pilgrims drew up the Mayflower Compact the day they arrived as a document that would provide a claim to legitimacy and provide security and order. In the document, the Pilgrims agreed to "covenant and combine ourselves together into a civil Body Politick, for our better Ordering and Preservation." The signatories also agreed to enact and obey just laws. William Bradford was quickly elected Governor.

Unfortunately, the Pilgrims got off to a difficult beginning in the New World. William Bradford's wife jumped overboard and committed suicide by drowning in Plymouth Harbor before ever setting foot in North America. Arriving in November, the weather was harsh and food was scarce. As a result, half the Pilgrims died that first winter and they were only able to build seven houses. More might have died of starvation had the Pilgrims not stolen Native American corn while the Native Americans were away from their houses toiling in the fields. Bradford credited God with sending the Native Americans away so that the Pilgrims could steal the Native Americans' food. The Pilgrims at first attempted a communal lifestyle with no private property, but Bradford explains that this early attempt at communism was abandoned in 1623 because it apparently sapped the work ethic.

Squanto arrived in the Pilgrim's camp in March of 1621 with the simple greeting, "Welcome Englishmen." Obviously, this meant that Squanto had had previous experience with Englishmen, but Bradford interpreted Squanto as a "special instrument sent from God for the Pilgrims' good." Historians believe that Squanto had been sold into slavery in Virginia in 1614 and had been transported to Spain, France, and then England where he convinced the Newfoundland

Company that he could be a useful guide and trade broker. Consequently, the English Newfoundland Company evidently returned Squanto to North America.

Bradford writes that Squanto taught the Pilgrims the Native American way of planting corn, directing that the Pilgrims place four fish in each corn mound and that the corn mounds be 1.5 feet apart. Unfortunately, historians doubt that the Pilgrims could have followed such a method since it would have meant using 27,844 fish per acre or 2,784,400 fish per 100 acres. Furthermore, there is no evidence of any other Native Americans in North America were using fish for fertilizer in the manner and quantity prescribed by Squanto. Instead, there is evidence that fish waste was used for fertilizer in coastal Spain and France in the seventeenth century. It is therefore suggested that Squanto, in actuality, gained the fish-for-fertilizer idea during his time as a slave in Europe. Squanto also often kept portions of goods traded between the English and Native Americans for his own personal profit. Historians believe that he coerced Native Americans into trading with the English by telling them that the English kept the plague in the ground and they would release it on the Native Americans if the Native Americans refused to trade. Instead of an instrument from God, it appears that Squanto was primarily a salesman and an opportunist.

THE "GREAT MIGRATION"

Although the character and heroism of the Pilgrims bequeathed a poetic heritage to the American people, the larger colony of Massachusetts Bay contributed more to New England's civilization. The main body of Puritan settlers, under the leadership of John Winthrop, arrived in the summer of 1630 in the *Arbella*. This was one of four ships that carried the first wave of the "Great Migration" that between 1630 and 1640 brought some 20,000 people into Massachusetts. The Pilgrims of Plymouth would be, essentially, overwhelmed and absorbed by the larger Puritan society. The Puritans, like the Pilgrims before them, were a splinter group from the Anglican Church who viewed the Anglican Church as corrupt. In contrast to the Pilgrims, who viewed the Anglican Church as beyond reform, the Puritans sought to reform or "purify" the Anglican Church from within.

The Winthrop group managed to obtain a royal charter for the Massachusetts Bay Company. Unlike other colonial enterprises, this company vested control not in a board of governors in England but in the members of the company who themselves were emigrating. They came bringing their charter with them and were self-governing, subject only to the English crown. Voting privileges were granted to those who were members of the Congregational Puritan Church of the colony, and during the early years of settlement a close relationship between church and state was the key to authority and lifestyle. In all cases, however, the civil magistrates, not the clergy, held preeminence.

Massachusetts Bay Company Governor John Winthrop

Similar to other seventeenth century colonies, however, the Puritans of Massachusetts Bay suffered hardships upon their arrival in the New World. Over 200 Puritans died the first year, including Winthrop's son and 11 of his servants. A group of over 100 decided that immigration to the New World had been a mistake and boarded boats back to England. In spite of these problems, however, Puritans would continue to emigrate from England due to persecution of Puritans, at the time, by the Anglican King Charles I, who charged Anglican Bishop William Land with "harrying them (the Puritans) out of the land."

During the 10 years after the landing of the *Arbella*, Massachusetts Bay became the most populous English colony in the New World. From towns established at Boston, Cambridge, Dorchester, Salem, and elsewhere, groups from time to time broke away and moved into fresh territory. In the summer of 1636, for example, the Reverend Thomas Hooker, with about 100 of his followers, set out on foot from Cambridge and settled a new township at Hartford, in what became Connecticut. Other towns proliferated in similar fashion.

PURITAN SOCIETY

From the very beginning, Puritan society was very Democratic in form for Puritan men and the Puritan society stressed religion, work, family, and education. Leaders in the Puritan community were university trained ministers, and Harvard University was begun in 1636 as a theological seminary for Puritans. In 1647, all towns with 50 families were ordered to establish elementary schools and towns of

100 families were required to establish secondary schools, making the Puritan colonies of New England the most educated of the American colonies. The Puritans also established the first printing press in the New World.

The Puritans began democratic self-government almost immediately. Male church members elected a governor and colonial legislature as well as local selectmen that handled most political matters. Annually, all townspeople would meet at a town meeting to decide local political matters (a practice that continues through the present). Puritans had a multiplicity of municipal offices including surveyors of deer, town criers, measurers, and purchasers of grain. Ten percent of all adult males held some sort of municipal office.

Each Puritan town was founded by a grant from the Massachusetts Colony General Court in Boston. Settlement grants were given only to groups of Puritans that signed a compact signifying the unity of their purpose. "We shall live by all means, labor to keep off from us such as are contrary minded, and receive only such unto us as may be probably of one heart with us." After receiving a charter from Boston, Puritan communities had local autonomy.

PURITANS AND HUMAN NATURE

Puritans espoused the negative view of human nature, believing that humans are naturally bad and untrustworthy. Consequently, single men and women were prevented from living alone because it was expected that people would sin if left to their own devices. In the words of Thomas Hooker, "Every natural man and woman is born as full of sin as a toad is of poison." In order to compensate for the depravity of human nature, Puritans believed that coercion was necessary to ensure proper behavior; civil and religious transgressions, therefore, were severely punished. Puritans also believed that people were naturally slothful, but work was Godly; and, therefore, work was stressed as the primary method of serving God. To ensure that Puritans served God faithfully through work, the Puritans meted out punishment for slothfulness. Puritans purged themselves of all luxuries to focus on God's work. Physical beauty and aesthetics were disparaged. In 1634, the General Court forbade garments with any lace, silver or gold thread, all cutworks, embroidered or needlework caps, bands and rails, all gold and silver girdles, hatbands, belts, ruffs, and beaver hats, and all clothing whereby the nakedness of the arm may be discovered. The Court also forbade long hair, neither Christmas nor Easter were celebrated, and religious wedding ceremonies were outlawed. A magistrate married couples in a civil ceremony.

Laws were also passed ensuring that one was not entertained. Prohibited entertainment included sledding, swimming, music, and dancing. According to Puritan leader Increase Mather, "Mixt or Promiscuous Dancing of Men and Women could not be tolerated since the unchaste Touches and Gesticulations used by Dancers have a palpable tendency to that which is evil." Also prohibited were cards, dice, shuffleboard, and other games of chance. To make sure that Puritans did not waste time entertaining themselves, the Court specifically forbade enjoyment when one might be better employed, enjoyment on the Sabbath, Sunday walks, and visits to the harbor. In 1670, John Lewis and Sarah Chapman were convicted of "engaging in things tending much to the dishonor of God, the reproach of religion, and the prophanation of the holy Sabbath." Lewis and Chapman, specifically, were "sitting together on the Lord's Day, under an apple tree in Goodman Chapman's orchard." Perhaps the most notorious case of all, however, was the case of Thomas Granger, who was executed in 1642 for having sex with a mare, two cows, five calves, two goats, five sheep, and a turkey. William Bradford reports that all of the animals were also put to death according to the instructions of Leviticus 20:15, their carcasses were thrown in a pit, and all persons were ordered to make no use of them.

HUTCHINSON HERESY

In 1636, the Puritan Community of Boston became divided between the male clergy and the theological teachings of Anne Hutchinson. Hutchinson considered herself a devout Puritan, but she challenged the Puritan view of women as subservient. In I Timothy 2:10–11, the writer states that women should be submissive to men, silent in Church, and not teach men. Hutchinson essentially violated all three, teaching her own version of the gospel, and built up a major following at her home after church services. Hutchinson had no official church training or standing, but she gained a wide respect from converts within the community through her teachings. Hutchinson stated that the "Holy Spirit was absent in the Preaching of some Ministers," thus challenging the spirituality and legitimacy of the Puritan leadership.

Hutchinson was, therefore, placed on trial by male clergy and judges in 1637, convicted of sedition and contempt, and banished as a "woman not fit for our society, cast out and delivered to Satan to become a heathen and a leper." Hutchinson was also convicted

Statue of Ann Hutchinson outside the State House in Boston

of the heresy of prophecy and "erroneous" claim that God revealed his will directly to a believer instead of exclusively through the Bible. On the stand in her trial, Hutchinson claimed, "the Lord hath let me see which was the clear ministry and which was wrong by the Voice of God's own Spirit into my Soul." In claiming that God had spoken to her directly, Hutchinson committed heresy before the Puritans' very eyes. In all, Hutchinson was convicted of preaching 82 heresies and banished from the Massachusetts colony, only to help found a colony of dissenters in Rhode Island. In establishing Rhode Island, however, the Puritan dissidents did not prove to be any more open-minded. The Rhode Island Constitution of 1644 persecuted Catholics and Quakers for "Belching out fire from Hell."

PURITANS AND QUAKER PERSECUTION

In furtherance of their goal of unity, the Puritans persecuted Quakers for blasphemy when members of the competing sect began arriving in Massachusetts in the 1650s. The General Court ordered that any Quaker literature found in the colony should be publicly burned; and the first Quakers that arrived in Boston (a pair of housewives) were arrested before they had even disembarked from their ship.

The Puritan interpretation of "contrary minded" was essentially broadened to include those that not only thought differently but also acted or looked differently. For instance, Puritans identified the Quakers among them as "persons who wore hats in the presence of magistrates" (a violation of Puritan customs) and used outdated terms such as "thee" and "thou" in conversation. In fact, the first two Quakers arrested in the Massachusetts Bay Colony in the seventeenth century were actually identified, arrested, and committed to jail after one of them was heard using the word "thee" in conversation.

In this instance, the two Quaker women were jailed, stripped naked and body-searched for marks of the devil, the Puritan belief being that the Devil's children (witches) had a mark on their body where the Devil had physically touched them when he made them his own. The windows of the jail were boarded so that the women could not infect the rest of the community with their heresies. The women were deported to Barbados, in spite of the fact that there was no Puritan law per se against Quakerism at the time. The Quaker books that were in the possession of the women were then burned in a ceremony in the public marketplace.

Puritans did nothing, however, without finding justification for what they were doing in the Bible; hence, in order to charge the Quakers with blasphemy, the Puritans searched the Bible for a Biblical basis on which the charge could rest. The failure of Quakers to "put off their hats" in the presence of the magistrates was a practice that was particularly galling to the Puritans. The Quakers had their own Biblical reason for refusing to do so in that they believed that all were equal in the eyes of God, and the custom of tipping the hat violated God's natural equality. Puritans, however, searched the scriptures until they found what they interpreted as a command from God against the practice within the Ten Commandments themselves. Specifically, the Puritans ruled that failure to "put off the hat" violated the commandment to "Honor thy mother and father." The following conversation between a Puritan magistrate and Quaker Edward Wharton illustrates this point.

Wharton: "Friends, what is the cause and wherefore have I been fetched from my habitation, where I was following my honest calling, and here laid up as an evil-doer?"

Magistrate: "Your hair is too long and you are disobedient to that commandment which saith, 'Honor thy mother and father.'"

Wharton: "Wherein?"

Magistrate: "In that you will not put off your hat before the magistrates."

The Quakers were also condemned for a number of other practices foreign to the Puritans that most Protestant Christians in later generations would view as within Biblically imposed limits on Christian behavior. In particular, the Quakers were known to sometimes gather together in private for religious services rather than appear as a group at the "Lord's Barn." In doing so, the Quakers' religious separateness was interpreted as blasphemy. Consequently, in October 1656, the Puritans passed a law against "that cursed sect of heretics lately risen up in the world," providing fines for ship captains who brought Quakers to Massachusetts and larger fines for Puritans who sheltered Quakers. Finally, it was decreed:

> "what person or persons soever shall revile the office or persons of magistrates or ministers, as is usual with the Quakers, such persons shall be severely whipped or pay the sum of five pounds."

The Quakers reacted to the persecution by choosing martyrdom, and Quaker efforts to infiltrate the Puritan community actually increased, rather than decreased, as a result. The Puritans, not learning from their heavy-handed mistake that had only created a religious "cause" for Quakers, reacted the next year by passing the following harsher law, including the extremes of corporal punishment and amputations, against Quakerism:

> "And it is further ordered, that if any Quaker or Quakers shall presume, after they have once suffered what the law requireth, to come into this jurisdiction, every such male Quaker shall for the first offense have one of his ears cut off, and be kept at work in the house of correction till he can be sent away at his own charge, and for the second offense shall have his other ear cut off, and kept in the house of correction, as aforesaid; and every woman Quaker that hath suffered the law here and shall presume to come into this jurisdiction shall be severely whipped, and kept at the house of correction at work till she be sent away at their own charge, and so for her coming again she shall be alike used as aforesaid; and for every Quaker, he or she, that shall a third time herein again offend, they shall have their tongues bored through with a hot iron, and kept at the house of correction, close to work, till they be sent away at their own charge."

Three persons lost an ear for violating the law, but there were numerous beatings, imprisonment, and other tortures. One man was beaten with 117 blows from a corded whip and left for dead. A witness to the event stated,

> "his flesh was beaten black and as into jelly, and under his arms the bruised flesh and blood hung down, clotted as it were into bags; and it was so beaten into one mass, that the signs of one particular blow could not be seen."

In October 1658, the General Court passed another new law that required that anyone guilty of Quaker disorders would be banished from the territory "upon pain of death." In other words, Quakers were not only to be banished, but if Quakers failed to honor the conditions of their banishment, they would be executed. The law was quickly implemented, with the result that in May 1659, the General Court banished six persons from Salem, Massachusetts for Quakerism; and two young Quaker children were promptly sold into slavery in order to satisfy claims against their parents.

Additional banishments of Quakers followed in the summer of 1659, with the result that several Quakers, prepared to die as martyrs, defied the law by returning to Boston in protest during a meeting of the General Court. A group of Puritans from Salem who sympathized with the Quakers came to the Court with them, one person bringing linen "wherein to wrap the dead bodies of those who were to suffer." The General Court proceeded to arrest all of the protesters, over 20 people in total, and incarcerated them in the Boston jail. The Court then selected three persons from those incarcerated, William Robinson, Marmaduke Stevenson, and Mary Dyer (who formerly had been a follower of Anne Hutchinson), and sentenced them to death. The two men were

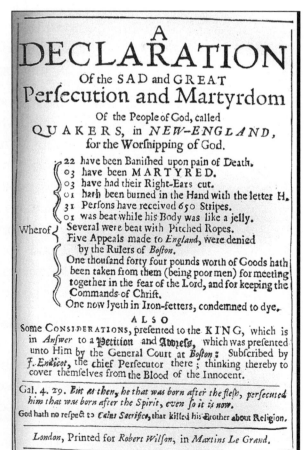

The Puritans passed a number of laws resulting in the persecution of Quakers

hanged, but Mary Dyer was given a reprieve and taken down from the scaffold at the execution due to unrest among the Puritan audience attending the public execution. Dyer would continue to defy the Puritan Courts, however, and was hanged for her defiance the next year in 1660.

In the months following the executions, local constables conducted a purge of their community, complete with household raids, confiscations of property, and public floggings. The executions and increased persecution, however, had the opposite effect than that intended by the Puritan magistrates. Instead of being cowed by the Puritans' display of savagery, the Quakers "came together in the moving and power of the Lord, to look your bloody laws in the face, and to accompany those who should suffer by them." In other words, the Quakers rebelled in demonstrative, open defiance of the laws and offered themselves as martyrs, forcing the Puritans to either relent or play the role of mass slaughterers.

Noteworthy of the Quaker demonstrations which the Puritans found impossible to ignore was that of John Burton, who accused the Puritan Court of being "robbers and destroyers of the widows and the fatherless" and argued that the "Puritan worship was not the worship of God," in front of the magistrates in the Puritan Court itself. Other Quakers engaged in equally bold and bizarre types of "impossible-to-ignore" behavior. For example, Thomas Hutchinson, governor of Massachusetts at the time before the American Revolution, later wrote:

> "At Boston one George Wilson, and at Cambridge one Elizabeth Horton, went crying through the streets that the Lord was coming with fire and sword to plead with them. Thomas Newhouse went into the meeting house at Boston with a couple of glass bottles and broke them before the congregation, and threatened, 'Thus will the Lord break you in pieces.' Another time M. Brewster came in with her face smeared and black as coal. ... One Faubord, of Grindleton, carried his enthusiasm still higher and was sacrificing his son in imitation of Abraham, but the neighbors hearing the lad cry, broke open the house and happily prevented it."

Two Quaker women performed the outrageous act of parading naked in public as a protest of their unjust treatment by the Puritans. The demonstrations, of course, were merely further proof to the Puritans of Quaker wickedness, and the naked-parading women were punished. The sentences from the Essex County Court were as follows:

> "The wife of Robert Wilson, for her barbarous and inhuman going naked through the town, is sentenced to be tied at a cart's tail with her body naked downward to her waist, and

whipped from Mr. Gidney's gate till she come to her own house, not exceeding thirty stripes."

Similarly, Quaker woman Lydia Wardell was ordered by the Court to be "severely whipped and to pay costs to the Marshall of Hampton upon her presentment for going naked into Newbury meeting house."

Each of the Puritans' escalating stern actions, however, only caused the Quakers to be even more defiant, with the results that the number of Quakers awaiting execution overflowed the jails and the waiting list for Quaker trials grew to an unmanageable length that overwhelmed the Puritan Courts. It soon became clear that either the Puritans would have to develop new tactics in order to deter the Quakers or they would have to engage in a bloodbath of unprecedented proportions, even for the Puritans. In late 1661, however, the insanity was laid to rest when the Massachusetts General Court received a letter from King Charles II prohibiting the use of either corporal or capital punishment in cases involving Quakers.

PURITANS AND WITCHES

The Puritan rationale concerning witch trials and executions had its origin in Exodus 22:18, which states, "Thou shalt not allow a witch to live," obviously meaning to the Puritans that there were such things as witches and that it was the duty of God's children not only to seek them out, but to kill them when they were found. The Bible, however, does not contain a complete and concise discussion of how to identify and apprehend witches, so the Puritans were forced to rely on traditions that had developed over the prior centuries. In Medieval Europe prior to the Protestant Reformation, the Catholic Church had shaped many of the Puritans' ideas concerning witches. The Puritans were merely the beneficiaries of ideas developed and handed down over the centuries. The official pre-Enlightenment Catholic Church position on witches was spelled out in detail in the *Malleus Maleficarum* of 1484, written by Heinrich Kramer and James Sprenger; and the ideas contained therein remained ideas concerning witches that were prevalent in society among Protestants and Catholics alike in the seventeenth century English colonies.

Kramer and Sprenger in the *Malleus Maleficarum* explained for the Catholic Church the concept of witches, their power, and how the authorities should deal with them. The Catholic Church approved the *Malleus Maleficarum* as valid in 1487, and its prescriptions and procedures became the official policies of the Inquisition in the late fifteenth and sixteenth centuries. In this truly incredible work, Kramer and Sprenger argue such absurdities as that "devils" can "truly and actually remove men's members" as well as "work some prestidigitatory illusion so that the male organ appears to be entirely removed and separate from the body." Furthermore, Kramer and Sprenger explain that witches are able to:

> "collect male organs in great numbers, as many as twenty or thirty members together, and put them in a bird's nest, or shut them up in a box, where they move themselves like living members, and eat oats and corn, as has been seen by many and is a matter of common report?"

Kramer and Sprenger also provide the story of a "certain man," who explained,

> "when he had lost his member, he approached a known witch to ask her to restore it to him. She told the afflicted man to climb a certain tree, and that he might take which he liked out of a nest in which there were several members. And when he tried to take a big one, the witch said: You must not take that one; adding, because it belonged to a parish priest."

A courtroom scene of the Salem Witch Trials

Kramer and Sprenger also explain how men can be turned into "werewolves," both voluntarily and involuntarily, and how one such "werewolf" was condemned by the court of Dole, Lyons, in 1573 and burned alive. Other nonsensical creatures explained by Kramer and Sprenger include Fauns, Trolls, and Incubus devils (with penises of ice) and Succubus devils, both of which are known to have sex with humans.

In an atmosphere of such scientific ignorance and superstition, almost anything supernatural becomes possible in the minds of the believers. In the cases of witches, the Puritan court accepted without question the idea that Satan could take the "shape" of persons and use that shape to terrorize innocent Christians (as had been argued by Kramer and Sprenger two centuries before). The Puritans also contended that the Devil could not assume the "shape" of an innocent person; thus, if someone testified that they were visited by a "specter" that came to them in the "shape" of a particular person, it was a foregone conclusion that the person whose shape the Devil assumed was, therefore, guilty of "signing the Devil's book" that had allowed him to thus use that person's "shape."

During an early hearing in the Salem witch proceedings, a young girl had been named as one whose "shape" had terrorized the other young girls in Salem Village. When the Puritan authorities inquired of the girl "How comes your appearance to hurt these (girls)?" the girl replied, "How do I know, he that appeared in the shape of Samuel, a glorified saint, may appear in anyone's shape," a reference by the girl to I Samuel 28: 7–17, where the Witch at Endor conjures the shape of the prophet Samuel at the behest of Israel's King Saul. By any sound rule of logic, the girl had just proven through the very Bible itself that if the Devil can take the "shape" of humans, then he must be able to take the shape of innocent humans since he took the shape of Samuel, whom Puritans all knew to be prophet and an "innocent" man of God. The Puritans, however, were not persuaded by the testimony and continued to condemn persons to death based on "spectral evidence."

As if this were not enough, the Puritans also altered the rules of evidence in witch trials. Puritans normally followed the rule that two eyewitnesses were necessary for conviction in capital cases. In witch trials, however, they abandoned this standard and ruled that any two witnesses, even if they were not necessarily eyewitnesses to the events in question and even if they were testifying about different events at different times, would be sufficient to gain convictions in witch proceedings. Regardless of how they stacked their cards, however, the Puritans' efforts to squelch heresy and witchcraft would inevitably end in failure due to the massive immigration and accompanying religious diversity that would eventually render the narrow Puritan experience untenable.

WITCHES OF SALEM VILLAGE

In Salem Village, the most famous witch trials were preceded by a series of sermons by Samuel Parris in 1692 on demons, the devil, and witchcraft. Following Parris' sermons, nine-year-old Betty Parris and her 11-year-old cousin Abigail Williams baked "witchcakes" with the aid of Tituba, the Jamaican slave of Betty's father Samuel. The cakes were made with cornmeal and human urine and eaten by the two young girls. Afterward, the two girls are reported to have been seized with fits, making wild gestures and speeches. The strange behavior then spread to other young girls in the village. The Village elders interrogated the young girls, who confessed that Tituba and two other old women had bewitched them. Tituba admitted to having practiced witchcraft in the Caribbean prior to coming to Salem (evidently not understanding that the Puritans would punish such a practice through execution). With her confession to witchcraft, fear gripped the town, and other persons came forward with similar tales of bewitching.

Foremost among the accusers was the family of Thomas Putnam, who had been recently left out of his father's will and whose family was suffering from economic hardship. Thomas Putnam accused 12 persons of witchcraft, his daughter Ann accused 21, brother Edward accused 13, and another Putnam cousin accused 16. Any personal misfortunes, bad harvests, illnesses, or even bad dreams in Salem Village were blamed on witches. One woman was accused of witchcraft for stroking a cat and causing a nearby batch of milk to sour. The trials lasted through the summer of 1693, and 19 witches were eventually hanged on Witches Hill. One man, 81-year old Giles Corey, was crushed under heavy rocks. The insanity finally ended when officials from Harvard declared that henceforth no one could be convicted upon spectral evidence. That being the case, the remaining suspects were released and the ordeal was over, but not before more people were executed for witchcraft than in any other single incident in American history.

PURITAN SUCCESS

Puritans had astounding success in terms of survival as compared to the Chesapeake colonies. Ordinary settlers came as family units with men and women being almost equal in numbers. Very few were indentured servants. Puritan's economy was a mix of agriculture, fishing, timber, and fur trade. Puritans farmed in open fields, shared by all, and grazed livestock in open meadows. Firewood was cut from communal woodlands. Life expectancy was 60 years by 1700, exceeding the life expectancy in England, and 90 percent survived childhood to marry (only 50 percent survived childhood in the United States in 1900). The Puritan population doubled every 27 years to reach 100,000 in population by 1700. Furthermore, most of the population increase is accounted for by natural increase since only 25,000 immigrated to New England in the seventeenth century. Large scale Puritan immigration ended after 1642 due to an English Civil War that ended their persecution. In contrast to the Puritans' success, 75,000 immigrants to Chesapeake in the seventeenth century yielded a population of 70,000 by 1700. By 1680, the average Massachusetts household had a kitchen, parlor, and sleeping loft instead of just one room, and Puritan living standards were equal to those in England.

THE SPREADING COLONIES OF NEW ENGLAND

Occasionally colonists left Massachusetts Bay because they had offended the ruling authorities or because they were discontented with a thoroughgoing Puritan commonwealth that punished nonconformists severely and tried to impose its religious tenets upon all comers. Freedom of conscience or religion was not a virtue of Massachusetts Bay. Roger Williams, pastor of the church at Salem, was banished from the colony in 1635 because he had complained publicly that interference of the clergy in politics threatened the freedom of individual congregations, and because he questioned the right of the settlers to take land from the Native Americans. Williams fled in the dead of winter to the Narragansett Indians, and in January 1636 he arranged to purchase land from the Native Americans for a little settlement that he called Providence. Before long, other fugitives from the persecution of the Puritan clergy in Massachusetts Bay found their way to Williams' colony, including a group led by the religious rebel, Anne Hutchinson.

The Providence settlers made a compact which guaranteed liberty of conscience to all, regardless of faith and which provided for the separation of church and state. Other groups came to the area and settled at Portsmouth, Newport, and Warwick, and in 1644 Parliament granted Williams a charter that united the various groups in what is now Rhode Island into one civil government. A royal charter in 1663 once more reiterated the liberties established earlier. This charter remained the basis of Rhode Island's laws until 1842. Rhode Island was far ahead of its time in its legal provisions. As early as 1647, for example, it outlawed trials for witchcraft and imprisonment for debt.

Massachusetts Bay emigrants settled a colony at New Haven under conservative Puritan leadership. As in Massachusetts, only church members were permitted to vote, a policy that in effect gave the church political control over the affairs of the colony. Since the Scriptures made no mention of jury trials, New Haven—in contrast to other New England colonies—forbade such trials and left the dispensation of justice in the hands of the magistrates.

In 1662 Connecticut received a royal charter that confirmed the rights of self-government and provided for the Fundamental Orders, a platform of government extending the franchise to nonchurch members. New Haven, to its distress, was absorbed into Connecticut, and its citizens thereby gained the guarantees of Connecticut's charter.

Other Massachusetts Bay residents moved into New Hampshire and Maine, where settlers had already settled small fishing villages. Massachusetts laid claim to both regions, but after many disputes New Hampshire in 1679 gained a royal charter and freed itself from the domination of Massachusetts. Maine was not separated until 1820.

PURITANS AND THE NATIVES

Natives in Massachusetts Bay were estimated to number around 125,000 in population in 1600; but English fishermen brought smallpox to the area, and an epidemic wiped out over half the population by 1610, 20 years prior to arrival of the Puritans. In 1633, three years after the Puritans' arrival, a second smallpox epidemic hit the natives and again wiped out over half the population. The Puritans believed the epidemic was proof that God had given them the Native American land, just like God had given Canaan to the Israelites by allowing the Israelites to kill all of the inhabitants of the land of Canaan. In this case, God had wiped out the indigenous inhabitants himself through pestilence. After the plagues, the remaining Native Americans welcomed the Puritans because the Puritans now had surplus land and lacked the manpower to tend all the land they had cleared. Untended land in New England will very quickly return to forest. The natives also needed trade with the Puritans, who had many things the Native Americans could use, including steel blades, axes, guns, and steel kettles for boiling water and cooking food. The remaining Massachusetts Bay Indians also recognized the value of English protection from tribal enemies to the north and thus hoped that the Puritans could be an aid to their own security.

Puritans sought to Christianize the Native Americans and succeeded in converting over 1,000 natives by 1640. The Puritan Charter claimed that the Puritans' "Principal end is to convert the natives to Christianity." Some natives resisted Christianization, leading to a war in 1637 that was won by the Puritans. In typical Puritan fashion, William Bradford credits God for giving the Puritans the victory over the Native Americans in the Pequot War, recounting how the Puritans massacred 400 Native Americans in a raid on the natives' village, with most of the Native Americans dying in a fire set by the Puritans that burned the Native Americans out of their homes. In the words of Bradford:

> "It was a fearful sight to see them thus frying in the fire and the streams of blood quenching the same, and horrible was the stink and scent thereof; but the victory seemed a sweet sacrifice, and they gave the praise thereof to God, who had wrought so wonderfully for them, thus to enclose their enemies in their hands and give them so speedy a victory over so proud and insulting an enemy."

At the close of the war, all the Native Americans in eastern Massachusetts were essentially under Puritan control; but, in order to aid in the conversion of the Native Americans and avoid security threats from the Native Americans in the future, it was decreed that all Puritan men were to be trained in the use of firearms.

THE CAPTURE OF NEW YORK

While in search of a "Northwest Passage" to Asia in 1608, Henry Hudson, an Englishman in the employ of the Dutch East India Company, sailed the Hudson River as far as the present town of Albany. In 1623, after the monopoly of a private Dutch company in the area had run out, the Dutch West India Company was formed to develop trade in the region along the river that Hudson had discovered. In 1626, Dutch West India Company director Peter Minuit purchased Manhattan Island from the Native Americans for trade goods equal to a dozen beaver pelts. A settlement was begun on Manhattan known as "New Amsterdam," which became the trading center for the new Dutch colony that was named New Netherlands.

Despite incompetent governors, quarreling inhabitants, and frequent wars with the Native Americans, the colony made progress; and New Amsterdam (New York City) became an important shipping point for furs and farm products. By the 1660s, with a population of 2,500, it was second only to Boston as a trading port. The colony as a whole had about 8,000 settlers, some of them English.

Since the citizens of Holland were largely content, the new company had trouble finding colonists, so the early settlers included French Protestant refugees and non-Dutch emigrants from Holland. From the earliest times, New Netherlands (later New York) was a polyglot region. The Dutch tried to attract settlers by granting "patroonships—allotments of 18 miles of land along the Hudson River—to wealthy stockholders who would bring 50 families to the colony. Only one patroonship succeeded; and the settlers that were attracted were diverse peoples from Sweden, Holland, France, and Germany. The Dutch sent a minister of the Dutch Reformed Church to oversee religion in the new colony, and the minister wrote back and complained that the colonists were unreceptive. In his words, "Several groups of Jews have recently arrived, adding to the religious mixture of Papists, Mennonites, and Lutherans among the Dutch, and many Puritans and many other atheists who conceal themselves under the name of Christians." Due to the diversity, the Dutch West India Company imposed religious freedom on the Colony in 1664, declaring, "the consciences of men should be free and unshackled."

The English had never admitted the right of the Dutch to the territory they had occupied. In 1664 Charles II named his brother James, Duke of York, proprietor over lands occupied by the Dutch in the New World. York sent out an expedition to take over New Netherlands with the English claiming that this was not an act of war but merely an action to regain from the Dutch West India Company territory that was rightfully English. With an English fleet in the harbor of New Amsterdam, the Dutch governor, Peter Stuyvesant, surrendered on September 9, 1664. The town and territory were both rechristened New York in honor of the royal proprietor. The English lost the colony back to the Dutch in a second war in 1673, and then recaptured the colony permanently in 1675. The Duke of York continued the religious freedom that had begun under the Dutch, and New York never had a state-church blend such as Massachusetts. New York City grew quickly due to its harbor location and access to the interior via the Hudson and Oneida Rivers.

The Dutch occupation of the Hudson Valley had benefited the English far more than the new overlords cared to admit. Had the Dutch not been in possession in the first half of the seventeenth century, when English settlements on the Atlantic seaboard were too sparse and weak to prevent the French from moving down the Hudson from Canada, England's traditional enemy, France, might have divided the thin line of English colonies along the coast.

THE JERSEYS

Soon after the Duke of York took over New Netherlands in 1664, he granted the land between the Hudson and the Delaware to John Lord Berkeley and Sir George Carteret, royalists who had defended the island of Jersey against the Parliamentarians during the Puritan Revolution in England. Berkeley sold his proprietary right to two Quakers, and in 1676 the province was divided into East Jersey (belonging to Carteret) and West Jersey (which became a Quaker colony). The later division of the two portions of New Jersey among many heirs of the proprietors bequeathed a land problem so complex that it vexes holders of real estate in that state to the present day.

PENN'S EXPERIMENT

In 1681 King Charles II granted to William Penn, a Quaker, a charter to the land between New Jersey and Maryland, naming him and his heirs forever owners of the soil of Pennsylvania, as the domain was called. Penn set about establishing a colony that would serve as a refuge for persecuted Christians from all lands. He drew up his celebrated first Frame of Government and made various concessions and laws to govern the colony, which already had a conglomerate group of English, Dutch, Swedish, and Finnish settlers scattered here and there. After his own arrival in Pennsylvania, he provided for the calling of a popular assembly on December 4, 1682, which passed the "Great Law," guaranteeing, among other things, the rights of all Christians to liberty of conscience. Penn's colony is generally considered the most democratic and free of any colony in the New World to that point. Legislative power was vested in a directly elected assembly and suffrage was granted to all free males, not just Church members. In addition, trial by jury was guaranteed to all citizens.

Penn determined to keep peace with the Native Americans and was careful to purchase the land that his settlers occupied. The tradition of a single "Great Treaty" signed under an ancient elm at Kensington is probably a myth, but Penn held many powwows with the Native Americans and negotiated treaties of peace and amity after purchasing needed land. To the credit of Penn and the Quakers, these agreements with the Native Americans were, for the most part, conscientiously kept. Penn's colony became the only colony where land from the Native Americans was purchased, rather than taken. In the words of Voltaire, "This was the only league between the Indians and Christians that was never sworn to and never broken."

QUAKERS

Like Puritans and Pilgrims, Quakers were a literalist Protestant sect that regarded the Anglican Church as corrupt and renounced its formalities and rituals. Based on their reading of Hebrews, Chapters 4–8, Quakers rejected all church officials and institutions, instead claiming that every individual could claim salvation on an individual basis. Quakers were persecuted in England after the 1650s since they challenged the legitimacy of the existing church (and therefore the political hierarchy since Anglican Clergy sat in the upper house of Parliament).

Quakers were despised by English nobles for their failure to observe customary deference (for instance, the tipping of one's hat to noblemen). The Quakers refused such deference because they believed that all men were equal before God; consequently, no one should be tipping one's hat in deference to anyone else based on birthright. Quakers also refused to pay church taxes that went to the Anglican Church and refused to sign witness oaths on the Bible (Jesus said "swear not"). Quakers also refused violence, including military service, taking Jesus' admonition to "turn the other cheek" literally. All of these beliefs and practices set them at odds with the Anglican Church and the political authority in England.

QUAKER LAWS

Though persecuted by others both in England and in the New World, the Quakers, like Anglicans and Puritans, also used civil government to enforce religious morality. One of Pennsylvania's first laws provided severe punishment for "all offenses against God, such as lying, profane talking, drunkenness, drinking of healths, obscene words, all prizes, stage plays, cards, dice, May games, gamesters, masques, revels, bull-baiting, cock-fighting, bear baiting, and the like, which excite the people to rudeness, cruelty, looseness, and irreligion."

PENNSYLVANIA ECONOMY AND GROWTH

Pennsylvania's growth from the first was phenomenal. Penn's success was largely due to his own skill as a promoter, for he wrote enticing tracts and on preaching journeys described the opportunities offered by his colony. Mennonites from Switzerland and Germany—especially Pietists from the Rhineland, which had so often been overrun by invading armies—soon were coming to Pennsylvania in large numbers. Dutch sectarians, French Huguenots, Presbyterian Scots from Ulster, Baptists from Wales, and distressed English Quakers also came. Somewhat after the Mennonites, Lutheran emigrants from Germany swarmed into Pennsylvania's backcountry, where they cleared the forests and developed fertile farms. From the beginning Pennsylvania was prosperous. Pennsylvania avoided the starvation periods that beset the other colonies due to its fertile ground and a longer growing season than in the northeast and, also, a lack of tropical diseases that plagued the South. Philadelphia became a major international port due to its excellent harbor on the Delaware River and was larger than New York City by 1700.

SETTLEMENT OF THE CAROLINAS

Among the later colonies to be settled was Carolina, which also began as a proprietorship. In 1660, the Monarchy was restored to the throne in England; and King Charles II rewarded those who helped him regain the throne, including a Barbadian Planter named John Colleton and seven other men, with a Charter to establish a colony south of Chesapeake and North of Spanish Florida. The proprietors drew up an instrument of government called the Fundamental Constitutions (probably the handiwork of the English political philosopher John Locke). This document provided for a hierarchy of colonial nobility and set up a platform of government with a curious mixture of feudal and liberal elements. Eventually it had to be abandoned in favor of a more workable plan of government. For the short term, however, Colleton and the small group of nobles officially monopolized political power in the new colony, but they also followed the Chesapeake example of settlement by enticing immigration through the promise of 150 acres of free land and free religion. In 1670, the first settlement was founded just across from present day Charleston.

Most of the early settlers were Englishmen from the English Caribbean colony of Barbados. Carolina was the only seventeenth century English colony to be settled principally by colonists from other colonies rather than from England. The colonists were a diverse mix of Swiss, Scotts, Irish, French, English, and African slaves (who made up one-fourth of the first settlers). Religious diversity prevented any group from creating a Church/State relationship. The new settlers generally ignored the political rule of the nobles and opted instead for local self-rule.

CAROLINA ECONOMY

The leaders of Carolina sought to exploit the Native Americans in Carolina for deerskin trade. In the words of Colleton, "All of Carolina is one continuous deer park." Settlers, however, found greater profit in the trade of Native Americans as slaves for sale in New England or the West Indies. Local planters would arm and reward one tribe for helping them bring in enemy tribes; then the planters would capture and sell the tribe that helped them and sell them into slavery as well. By 1700, the native population of Carolina was essentially wiped out. The end of the native population caused the British to begin the importation of African slaves to South Carolina since white Europeans refused to work in the swamps of the Carolina rice and indigo plantations. In 1680, South Carolina was 80 percent white. In 1720, South Carolina was 70 percent black. Like Virginia and Maryland, the climate of South Carolina was conducive to malaria and high mortality rates. John Colleton described it thusly, "Carolina is in the Spring Paradise, the Summer Hell, and in the Autumn, a Hospital."

THE DIVISION OF CAROLINA

The division of Carolina into two distinct colonies came about gradually. English settlers were already occupying land around Albermarle Sound when the proprietors received their charter, and Albermarle continued to attract a scattering of settlers. It was geographically remote from the other settlement on the Ashley and Cooper rivers to the south. As the two separate sections gained population, they set up separate legislative assemblies, approved by the proprietors. In 1710 the proprietors appointed a governor of North Carolina, "independent of the governor of Carolina," thus recognizing the separation of North from South Carolina. In 1721 South Carolina was declared a royal province, and eight years later North Carolina also became a crown colony. North and South Carolina also had different economies and different demographics. North Carolina's economy was a mix of livestock, tobacco, and naval stores. Naval stores provided lumber, rope, and pine tar for sailing ships. Those that worked in the pine tar industry gained the name "tar heels." In terms of population, while South Carolina was 70 percent African slaves by 1700, North Carolina remained 80 percent white.

GEORGIA

For two decades 20 trustees in England administered Georgia, founded in 1733. Georgia was established to serve many purposes: as an extension of the southern provincial frontier; as a buffer or a first line of defense between the Spanish colony of Florida and the English settlements; as a planned Utopia where the trustees hoped to establish a model society; as a refuge for persecuted Protestants from Europe; as a new opportunity for men who had been released from debtor's prisons in England; as an Enlightenment project to make productive use of England's "deserving poor" and as a model "colony" that would produce commodities that England wanted, notably silk and citrus fruits.

In its inception, Georgia was governed strictly by its Board of Noble Trustees and had no popularly elected assembly. The Trustees brought in silkworms from China and grapes from France for their planned economy of silk and wine. Alcohol was prohibited in Georgia so as to dissuade the laziness of poor people and "second chance" criminals. Slavery was prohibited for the same reasons.

The "model colony," however, envisioned by the Board of Trustees, never materialized, due to multiple problems. The wine business failed in Georgia due to grape-eating bugs and birds. The silk business also failed because it turned out that silkworms needed the trees from China and Georgia birds feasted on the imported silkworms. As a consequence, the population of Georgia was only 2,800 in 1750; hence, Parliament passed the legalization of slavery and alcohol in Georgia. Georgia then developed into a rice and indigo plantation economy based on slave labor like that in South Carolina.

COLONIAL ADMINISTRATION AND POLITICS

ENGLISH ADMINISTRATION OF THE COLONIES

Political Structures in the Colonies
Local Government
Colonial Politics

COLONIAL ECONOMY

New England
The Southern Colonies
The Middle Colonies
English Regulatory Acts
Conflict with the Native Americans
Bacon's Rebellion
Pueblo Revolt

BRITAIN WINS SUPREMACY IN NORTH AMERICA

New France
Early Border Conflicts
King George's War
Start of the Great War for Empire
Albany Conference

Fort Duquesne, 1755
William Pitt Increases British Resolve
The Capture of Quebec
Proclamation of 1763
Ramifications of Seven Years War

ENGLISH ADMINISTRATION OF THE COLONIES

In London, administrative agencies to govern the colonies were slow in evolving. Originally, the Lord Commissioners for Plantations, a committee of the King's Privy Council, directly supervised the colonies. Variations of this committee operated until 1675, when the Lords of Trade was created—an agency whose vigorous actions set a new standard in colonial policy. It opposed the disposition on the part of the crown to issue proprietary grants and advocated revoking them, thus bringing such colonies under direct royal control.

The most important effort of the Lords of Trade was made in 1686, when it established the Dominion of New England. The charter of Massachusetts Bay had been annulled in 1684, and the Dominion represented an attempt to centralize the authority of the crown by creating a super-colony, including Massachusetts, New Hampshire, Connecticut, Rhode Island, New York, and New Jersey. It was expected that eventually Pennsylvania would also be incorporated within the framework of the Dominion. The crown, acting upon the recommendation of the Lords of Trade, appointed Edmond Andros as governor. He was to reside in Boston while his deputy was to reside in New York. No provision was made for an assembly although there was to be a council of advisers. Andros, unfortunately, was of limited mind and petty spirit. He was scarcely the man to carry out such a dramatic, far-reaching colonial experiment. Resentment among the colonies included within the Dominion was intense, not only because their original charters had been arbitrarily set aside and the arbitrary Andros appointed, but because they lacked a representative assembly.

England's Glorious Revolution of 1688 deposed the despotic James II and firmly championed Parliament—and thus representative government—in England. This twist of fate provided an opportunity for the colonials to overthrow the Dominion. Acting on the premise that Governor Andros now represented a discarded royal regime, the colonials imprisoned him as a signal of their allegiance to the new government in England set up under William and Mary. Each colony that had been included within the Dominion hastily returned to its previous path of colonial self-government. Thus the Glorious Revolution marked the end of an experiment to consolidate the colonies within a larger framework and administer them more directly by home authorities.

In many respects, the experiment of the Dominion of New England was a turning point in colonial political affairs. At this time the colonials were not yet strong enough to defeat the royal will. If the experiment had been a success, individual self-government within the colonies would have been eliminated and the entire course of American history might have been changed. With the fall of the Dominion, the individual colonies received a new lease on life, and they used it to gain strength politically and economically.

In 1696 the Lords of Trade were replaced by the Board of Trade, an administrative agency that survived into the period of the American Revolution. During the eighteenth century Parliament was overwhelmed with its own problems—namely, the internal political transition to parliamentary supremacy in England and the turmoil of foreign policy—and could not spare the time to formulate new policies for the empire. As a result, the general policies formulated very early in the century were followed throughout the period despite changing circumstances. An instruction issued to a governor in 1750 was little changed from instructions given in 1700. The American provinces were changing, but British imperial policy remained, for the most part, unchanged.

POLITICAL STRUCTURES IN THE COLONIES

English colonies in America experienced a vigorous political life, in contrast to the colonies of other western European countries. The concept of self-government was transferred to the English colonies almost from the outset in most settlements, but the political structure generally took more definitive shape early in the eighteenth century.

The political structures that evolved in royal, proprietary, and charter colonies were remarkably similar. Each colony had a governor who executed colonial laws, served as commander in chief of the militia, presided over the colony's highest court of appeals, and enforced relevant British enactments. In a proprietary colony like Pennsylvania the governor looked after the interests of the proprietor, most notably in the disposition of land, but he was also expected to enforce the imperial policies laid down by the home authorities. Usually the crown appointed the governor although in proprietary colonies the proprietor held this prerogative and in Rhode Island and Connecticut the governor was elected by the legislature.

Most colonies had a council whose members served as advisers to the governor. This council comprised the upper house of the legislature and sat as the highest court of appeal in the colony.

Generally the crown, upon the recommendation of the governor, appointed council members, but exceptions were made. Members of the council were customarily the more affluent colonials, who had powerful friends in England. In a number of colonies the council, although acting in self-interest, was the spokesman for the people against the prerogative of the governor. The council wished to control office patronage, the distribution of lands, and the like.

The freemen elected a colonial assembly, which served as the lower house of the legislature. By the eighteenth century every colony had instituted property requirements as a requisite for freemanship, but recent research has demonstrated that these requirements did not seriously restrict the number of eligible voters. Property requirements for office holding, however, were frequently much higher than the requirements for suffrage, so that a member of the assembly had to be a person of some means. "Professional politicians" who had no other means of livelihood were rare in the provinces.

During the eighteenth century the assemblies of every colony gained power. Among the specific powers obtained by most assemblies were the rights to initiate legislation, to judge the qualifications of their own members, and to elect their speakers. The assemblies were somewhat less successful in determining when elections should be held and in extending their membership.

Whereas the basic constitutional position of the home authorities was that the power of the assemblies and the grant of self-government itself were merely an extension of "the royal grace and favor,"—to be offered, modified, or even eliminated as the crown determined—the constitutional position held by the assemblies was that their power and authority was derived from the consent of the governed. The assemblies conceived of themselves as replicas of the British House of Commons, and they attempted to imitate it in waging their contest for power against the prerogative of the governor, representing the crown or the proprietor.

LOCAL GOVERNMENT

The structure of English local government at the time the colonies were founded was transplanted, for the most part, to the New World. Among the more important officials were the county sheriffs and the justices of the peace. Other positions that were important in England, such as lord lieutenant, did not flourish in the New World. Local government in the United States today descends directly from the colonial period.

Local disputes over land titles and other matters were settled by the county courts. The justices of the peace in cooperation with the sheriff enforced colonial legislation, and the sheriff collected taxes. In practice, therefore, local government served as a major link between the people and the colonial government.

COLONIAL POLITICS

In every colony, at some time or another, domestic disputes developed which were fought out in the political arena. The issues of land, currency, proportionate representation, defense, and the Native American trade were among those that arose most frequently. In a colony such as Virginia, where tobacco was the principal staple, tobacco inspection acts aroused lively political disputes. (See "Alexander Spotswood: Colonial Governor.") Seldom did political parties develop. Generally, a coalition of forces, drawn in most cases from various parts of a province, united to support or defeat a particular measure. Once the issue was decided, the coalition disintegrated.

A political split between the eastern and western parts of the province was characteristic of Pennsylvania, which was growing at a swifter pace than most of its sister colonies. By contrast, the major political division in New York was between influential families whose wealth was based on land and influential families whose wealth was based on commerce. These political issues and the conflicts they aroused were evidence not of internal disorder but of political maturity—of vigorous, healthy self-government in action.

COLONIAL ECONOMY

NEW ENGLAND

The rise of capitalism throughout western Europe, which coincided with the founding of the English colonies, determined that the American provincial economy would be capitalistic in orientation with an emphasis on trade, production for market, and eventual regional specialization. Each colony's economy at the outset was rather primitive—merely an appendage of the economy of the mother country—but shortly after the mid-eighteenth century an indigenous, well-developed capitalism emerged.

The economic development of New England was strongly influenced by the systems of land distribution and of trade. In the seventeenth century land was granted by the legislature to groups—usually

PEOPLE THAT MADE A DIFFERENCE

Alexander Spotswood: Colonial Governor

When His Majesty's Ship Deptford dropped anchor off Hampton Roads, Virginia, on June 20, 1710, in preparation for its assignment to escort the tobacco fleet to England, it carried more than its usual complement of men and supplies. Aboard was Alexander Spotswood, with his commission as lieutenant governor of the colony of Virginia. Perhaps no royal governor better exemplified the political relationship that existed between the crown and the British colonies on the North American continent.

The Spotswoods had been royal and Anglican for five generations, and they had waged wars for the crown and church. Alexander's great-grandfather, Archbishop of St. Andrews and historian of Scotland, had assisted Archbishop Laud in introducing the Book of Common Prayer into Scotland, a defiant act in a Presbyterian stronghold. Alexander's grandfather, Secretary for Scotland, had been executed in 1646 for his opposition to the politics of the Presbyterian Party and his loyalty to King Charles I.

Alexander was born in 1676 in Tangier where his father was serving as physician to the English garrison. Following his family's rugged tradition, he became an ensign in the regiment of the Earl of Bath at the age of 17, serving first in Flanders. Later, by then a lieutenant colonel, he was wounded at the Battle of Blenheim and captured by the enemy. No less a person than the Earl of Marlborough negotiated for his release.

Although his contemporaries and historians of early America refer to him as Governor, he was in fact the deputy of George Hamilton, the Earl of Orkney. The common practice of the time was to award a lucrative office in the colonies in return for a fee or favor to the crown. No work was required, and the pay was excellent. The governor invariably appointed a lieutenant who actually conducted the official duties in the colony. The governor and lieutenant governor shared the salary and other perquisites of office.

Alexander Spotswood assumed his responsibilities at a difficult time. In the absence of a governor, Edmund Jennings, President of the Colonial council, had governed Virginia by law during the previous four years. Although the king had appointed the council members, they had assumed executive power and used it to further their personal interests. Thus the Colonial Council had granted land, defended the colony, appointed subordinate officials, collected taxes, and—with the cooperation of the House of Burgesses—decided on the priority of expenditures.

Spotswood's early years can be read as a continuous attempt to regain and reinforce the authority of the royal governor. Measured against this standard, he failed; however, the contest for authority fore-

church congregations that in turn distributed the land among their members. The result was the encouragement of the famous New England township system, whose principal aim was to maintain an effective social-religious community. After provision for the church, sometimes a school, and a village green had been made, each family was customarily granted a town lot. Plots of land outside the town shadowed the growing tension between Britain and all of its colonies that would finally surface in the War for Independence.

Among Governor Spotswood's earliest concerns was the lucrative Native American trade. He believed that this trade should be strictly controlled for the British welfare, which (pleasantly enough) closely coincided with his own personal fortunes. To this end, he succeeded in persuading the Burgesses and the council to adopt an "Act for the Better Regulation of the Indian Trade." To participate in the Native American trade, a colonist or anyone else now needed to purchase a share in the Virginia Indian Company at a cost of 50 pounds—comparable to a year's salary for an experienced minister. To Spotswood's dismay, both the colonials and the London merchants raised strenuous objections, and the Indian Act was soon repealed.

Spotswood tackled another, even thornier, issue when he got a Tobacco Inspection Act passed. The idea had merit. Inferior tobacco was being shipped to England and passed off as tobacco of the highest grade. Because no standard existed, buyers had become wary; and the market for Virginia tobacco had sagged. How better to set things right, argued the governor, than to establish tobacco inspection points in Virginia and prohibit the export of all inferior grades?

Spotswood had a hidden motive, however. He wished to appoint tobacco inspectors who supported his political objectives and thus, through patronage, to build a governor's party in Virginia.

To everyone's surprise, the small planters rebelled. The added expense of transporting their tobacco to places of inspection was burdensome. Moreover, they did not want to have the governor's favorites deciding whether their tobacco was fit for the London or Amsterdam market. In the next elections the rebellious voters turned almost all of those who had accepted appointments as inspectors out of office.

Angered and frustrated, Spotswood summoned the House of Burgesses and read a scathing attack on its members and their motives. Their laws were "Giddy Resolves," their quality as persons was "illiterate Vulgar," and their behavior was "drunken conventions."

Thereafter, the disputes over the Native American trade and tobacco inspection invaded all the political issues and affected basic social and economic policy in the colony, including the distribution of land. The strife ended only when Spotswood began to take on the self-interest of a Virginia planter and made peace with the Colonial Council and the House of Burgesses.

Spotswood was an able organizer and administrator. By 1722, when he was replaced as lieutenant governor, he had become a major landholder in the colony, an explorer of its western territories, and founder of the Spotswood Iron Works. After six years in England, he returned to Virginia where he spent his later leisurely years as a flourishing patrician planter. At his passing on June 7, 1740, he was mourned by Virginians who had pitted their political strength against him while he represented the authority of the crown.

were then distributed among members of the group, with common land retained for grazing purposes and a specified number of acres reserved for latecomers.

Distributing the land in this fashion meant that all members of the group would be in close proximity to the church, the heart of the Puritan community. It also meant that sending youngsters to school would raise no serious problems and that towns would become the basis for representative government with town meetings providing the political structure to resolve local issues.

In the eighteenth century the New England land system changed. Because it was no longer so important to create concentrated social-religious communities, church groups seldom made settlement along western frontier lands. Instead, people of influence and means began to buy large blocks of land for speculative purposes, selling off smaller parcels to individual farmers or prospective farmers.

Even in the older towns conditions changed. Original settlers or descendants of original settlers moved out, often selling their land to newcomers. Absentee ownership of town lots and township lands was common. Whereas in the seventeenth century town proprietors were nearly always residents of the town, this was less often the case in eighteenth-century communities.

Although farming was the predominant occupation in New England up to 1640, trade gained increasing importance thereafter. From 1640 to 1660 the English were preoccupied with civil war and political upheaval at home, and colonials began to replace the English merchants as the trading enterprisers. It was at this time that the developing resources of New England fisheries helped open up trade between the Puritans of New England and Puritans who had settled in the West Indies.

New England merchants gradually gained a position of economic and political primacy. By the end of the seventeenth century they had already begun to replace the Puritan magistrates as the source of economic and political power. By the 1760s they constituted the single strongest voice in New England.

It is important to remember that merchants were not alone in their dependence on trade for prosperity. The artisans who repaired canvas and built vessels and the farmers who exported meat products—in fact, the entire population in one way or another—were partly dependent upon prosperous commercial relations. Meat, fish, and lumber—the principal articles of export—found their major market in the West Indies. New England was also dependent on its role as a carrier of exports from other provinces and of imports from England.

For labor, New Englanders depended largely on members of their own families, though they sometimes hired local servants and imported indentured servants. New England, in contrast to some of the other regions, was attractive to skilled workers because they could find a ready market for their talent in an area dominated by a town system. Each town needed a carpenter and a blacksmith, for example. Slavery, though never as important to the northern economy as it was further south, was fully legal in each of the New England colonies.

THE SOUTHERN COLONIES

Three significant factors affected the economic development of the Southern colonies: the distribution of land, the evolution of the plantation system, and the tremendous production of staples for market. In the seventeenth-century Chesapeake colonies (Virginia and Maryland) land was distributed directly to individuals, in contrast to the practice in early New England. Moreover, the colonials scattered up and down the rivers of the Chesapeake area instead of settling in groups. Each planter tried to have his own landing where an ocean-going vessel could readily load the tobacco he produced and unload the goods he had ordered from England. This method of settlement made the county the basis of local government, discouraged the establishment of a school system because of the distances involved, and markedly influenced the transplantation of the Anglican Church.

Skilled workers, such as blacksmiths, found ready markets in New England towns.

In the seventeenth century the average landholding was relatively small since labor to cultivate extensive landholdings was lacking. The headright system, whereby a planter could obtain 50 acres of land for each dependent or servant brought to the colonies, allowed the first accumulations of land to occur. It was not until the eighteenth century, however, when American colonists obtained control of the machinery to distribute land, that large grants become fairly common.

Although slaves were imported into the Chesapeake colonies and into South Carolina in the seventeenth century, the principal labor force was composed of indentured servants, including convicts and paupers who were sentenced to labor in America. Over 1,500 indentures were imported annually into Virginia alone in the 1670s and the 1680s.

In the following years the plantation system became larger, the black slave became a relatively less expensive source of labor, and the Middle colonies—New York, the Jerseys, Pennsylvania, and Delaware—expanded to compete for indentured servants. At the same time the supply of English indentures decreased because the demand for labor in England increased. As a result, the institution of slavery became fastened upon the eighteenth-century Southern colonies. A planter elite, whose power was based on black slaves, now dominated a society that had been made up largely of yeomen.

Tobacco continued as the main staple in the Chesapeake colonies, but rice became prominent in South Carolina; and the indigo introduced by Elizabeth Pinckney became an important crop. Naval stores became a major export of North Carolina. Deer hides were the important goods obtained through trade with the Native Americans.

In the seventeenth century no merchant group developed in these colonies because planters sold directly to English merchants. In the eighteenth century an important merchant group developed in strategically located Charleston, South Carolina, trade center for a vast hinterland. No major tensions developed between merchants and planters in the South, however, because the prosperity of one was directly related to the wellbeing of the other. In fact, the same individual might belong to both groups since many merchants bought land and planters sometimes became merchants.

THE MIDDLE COLONIES

During the eighteenth century English migration decreased because demand for laborers and opportunities for advancement greatly increased at home as Britain expanded its trade and manufactures. However, a tremendous influx of non-English peoples—Germans,

Scotch-Irish, Irish, Swiss, and French Huguenots—into the Middle colonies resulted in expansion of that region at a rate exceeding that of New England or the Southern colonies.

The reasons for the migration of non-English peoples were fundamentally economic, although religious intolerance and fear of destructive wars at home sometimes played a part. Opportunities for the Scotch-Irish in Ireland were limited, whereas opportunities in the New World appeared much more attractive. German Pietists came to Pennsylvania in large numbers because that colony offered an attractive land policy as well as religious toleration.

Land policies in Pennsylvania, the Jerseys, and New York varied greatly. In New York land was granted to royal favorites, who established extensive manors. An ordinary settler was often forced to accept a leasehold and become a renter instead of obtaining a clear title to the land. The distribution of lands in Pennsylvania was much more favorable. Small grants could be obtained by outright purchase. In fact, Scotch-Irish settlers on the frontier of Pennsylvania frequently assumed title to the land by right of settlement and refused to pay the proprietors.

New York and Philadelphia developed into major ports in the eighteenth century with Philadelphia becoming the second largest city within the British Empire. Both cities developed a strong mercantile class and attracted skilled artisans—cabinetmakers, silversmiths, gunsmiths, and the like. Both exported grain. Grain was the principal commodity of the Middle colonies, which became the "breadbasket" of colonial America.

Pennsylvania's rapid growth and early economic maturity reflected the astonishing general growth of the colonies. The handful of English settlers had become 250,000 strong by 1700. By 1760 the colonies provided a good livelihood for a population of approximately 2,000,000—almost half the population of England. No wonder, then, that trade quadrupled, that banking and currency became important issues, that tradesmen and merchants carried on sophisticated economic practices, that a stable society was formed, and finally, that the American economic system was sufficiently developed to sustain the shock of political separation from the mother country and to finance a war for independence. All the ingredients of a well-developed commercial capitalism were present.

ENGLISH REGULATORY ACTS

As the economy of the American provinces matured, imperial regulations were enlarged to prevent foreign commercial competition and the competition of colonial manufactures with those of the mother country. Although restrictions were placed on the tobacco trade as early as the 1620s, a series of enactments passed from 1651 to 1700 laid the actual framework for the English imperial system.

The Navigation Act of 1651 was designed primarily to reduce competition from foreign shipping. It provided that non-European goods brought to England or its possessions could be transported only in English (including colonial) ships and that goods from the Continent could be brought into England or its possessions only in vessels belonging to the country that had produced the goods. A second Navigation Act (often called the Enumeration Act), passed in 1660, closed the loophole that had permitted colonials to import directly from Europe. It provided that all goods, regardless of origin, could be imported into or exported from any English colony only in English ships. "Enumerated" goods—including sugar, cotton, indigo, dye goods, and tobacco—of colonial origin were to be shipped only to England or its colonies; they could not be exported directly to other European countries.

The Enumeration Act was particularly hard on Virginia and Maryland, for it meant that colonial tobacco—which the English market could not absorb—had to be shipped to England and then exported from there back to Continental markets. These additional exportation costs—including handling charges, storage charges, and the costs of frequent loss of tobacco stored in English warehouses—were extremely high. Historians have suggested that the enumeration of tobacco produced an economic depression in Virginia and Maryland in the late seventeenth century and was responsible for the later concentration of land ownership, since only the large-scale producer could meet the disadvantages of the market.

In 1663 a third Navigation Act—the Staple Act—required that most commodities (excluding salt, servants, and wine) imported into the colonies from Europe had to be shipped from England in English-built ships. The colonists, however, found a loophole. Often ships stopped at several colonial ports before returning to Europe. Colonial merchants would load enumerated goods at one port supposedly designated for a later colonial port; actually the goods would remain on the ship and go directly to Europe.

To close this loophole, a fourth Navigation Act was passed in 1673. It provided that whenever the vessel carried enumerated commodities, a plantation duty—that is, a bond—had to be paid before a ship could clear a colonial port. A final enactment in 1696 provided for the creation of vice-admiralty courts in America to place the enforcement of the navigation laws in the hands of men appointed directly by the crown. Research indicates that the burden of the Navigation Acts was greater at the end of the seventeenth century than at any other time during the colonial period and that the acts were seldom evaded. Evasion was to come later with the Molasses Act of 1733.

Whereas in the seventeenth century the English regulations were directed principally at commerce, in the eighteenth century—with the maturing of the American economy—the regulations were directed principally at manufactures. The Woolen Act of 1699, which forbade colonial export of wool products, had little impact upon the American colonies because their exportation of textiles was limited anyway; but the Hat Act of 1732—which prohibited exportation of hats from one colony to another and severely restricted the colonial hat industry—adversely affected New York and New England, which had been usurping a vital European market. The act eliminated this colonial enterprise and greatly benefitted London hatters, who had exerted pressure in Parliament to pass the bill.

The Molasses Act of 1733 placed a heavy duty upon sugar, rum, molasses, and other commodities imported into the colonies from the non-British West Indies. This enactment seriously hampered the trade of the American colonies. They had been importing these commodities—molasses in particular—in quantity from Spanish and French colonies at a price cheaper than could be obtained in the British West Indies. Because the act seriously encroached upon this customary channel of trade, the Molasses Act was evaded by extensive smuggling.

The Iron Act of 1750 encouraged the colonial production of pig and bar iron for use by the English iron and steel industry but prohibited the building of slitting mills, forges, and other iron-finishing equipment in the colonies. Certain colonies, notably Pennsylvania, defied the prohibition; and when war broke out between France and England in 1752, the home authorities were unable to enforce the act with vigor. After 1763, of course, the continual crises between the mother country and the colonies prevented effective enforcement.

CONFLICT WITH THE NATIVE AMERICANS

Throughout the seventeenth century, there was conflict with the Native Americans, who saw themselves being dispossessed of their land and their way of life. In 1622, for example, the Powhatans under Opechancanough nearly succeeded in wiping out the new settlement of Jamestown in Virginia. After the English murdered a

Powhatan war captain and religious leader, Nemattanew, Opechan-canough and the Powhatan's waged a war on the white population of Virginia that led to the death of a fourth of the English population. By the time the Native Americans were finally subdued, the Virginia Colony was bankrupt.

After Opechancanough's revolt, the English adopted a policy of "perpetual enmity" toward the natives in Virginia and only viewed them as obstacles to English progress that must be eradicated. John Smith was given orders from England to "root out the Indians from being any longer a people." John Smith wrote that many believed that the orders would be good for the plantation because "now we have just cause to destroy them by all means possible." In 1623, the English invited the Native Americans to a feast in celebration of peace and then served the Native Americans poison wine, leading to the death of approximately 200 Native Americans.

The following decade, in 1636–7 the Puritans fought a bitter war of annihilation against the Pequots. The next big war in New England occurred in 1675–76. Known as King Philip's War, it entailed fierce fighting along the frontier. In 1671, the Plymouth colonists had forced Native American leader Metacomet (referred to as King Philip by the colonists) to surrender the Native Americans' stock of guns and accept a Treaty of Submission acknowledging English rule. In 1675, a Native American informant was murdered, and the Puritans retaliated by executing three Native Americans that were accused in the murder. The executions sparked a war of retaliation led by Metacomet as the Native American tribes banded together and launched an offensive against their white oppressors, who now had superior numbers and greater technology.

At first, the Native Americans scored resounding victories. In all, the Native Americans under King Philip attacked 52 of the 90 Puritan towns and completely destroyed 13. In reaction, in 1676 New England passed the first military draft law in American history. By the spring of 1676, the Native American offensive had been thwarted, and the colonists had nearly exterminated the Narragansetts, Wampanoags, and Nipmucks. King Philip was killed in battle, and his head was put on public display in Plymouth for 25 years. The conflict left so strong a legacy that one scholar, Mary Beth Norton, has argued that it was a contributing factor in the hysteria about witches that erupted in Salem in 1692. The estimated cost of the war was greater than all the personal property held in New England. For 40 years, the fear of evoking another Native American war prevented the New England colonists from extending their boundaries any further into Native American territory.

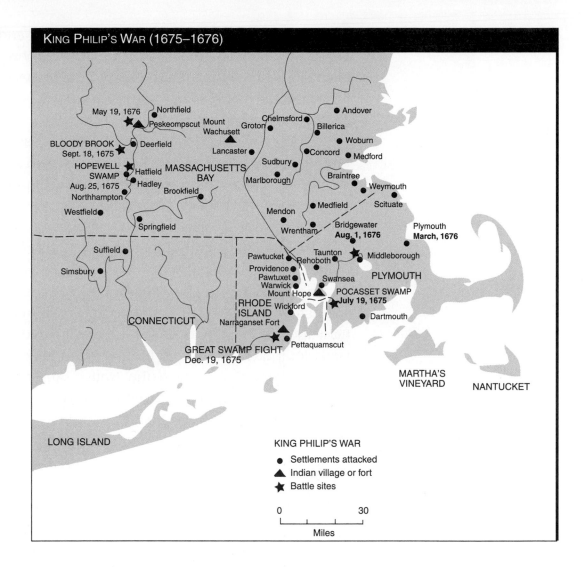

KING PHILIP'S WAR (1675–1676)

KING PHILIP'S WAR
● Settlements attacked
▲ Indian village or fort
★ Battle sites

0   30
Miles

BACON'S REBELLION

Precipitated by the belief of a faction of settlers that they were not receiving enough protection against the Native Americans, a serious rebellion in Virginia, Bacon's Rebellion, was fought among white men. Led by a wealthy planter named Nathaniel Bacon, 500 former indentured servants took up arms against the constituted authorities in 1676. Violence had erupted periodically in the 1660s and early 1670s between whites and Native Americans, and then overflowed in the summer of 1675 when a group of frontiersmen attacked and killed a small group of Susquehannock Indians. In retaliation, the Native Americans attacked and killed 36 Virginians during the winter of 1675. In turn, the frontiersmen retaliated under the leadership of 25-year-old Nathaniel Bacon with a series of attacks on the Native Americans.

Bacon was a cousin of Governor Berkeley and demanded that Berkeley appoint him to lead an army against the Native Americans.

Berkeley refused, pronounced Bacon a rebel, and threatened to punish him for treason. Berkeley then called for new elections of the Virginia House of Burgesses, hoping to purge Bacon's supporters from the legislature. To Berkeley's surprise, Bacon's supporters swept the election, and Bacon himself was elected to the House of Burgesses.

In June 1676, the Virginia House of Burgesses passed a series of laws known as Bacon's Laws. The laws gave landowners a voice in setting tax levies, forbade officeholders from demanding bribes for carrying out their duties, placed limits on the holding of multiple offices, and required officials to be residents of Virginia for three years. The House also declared that all free men could vote (property requirements were abolished).

Bacon followed his legislative success by marching into Jamestown with 500 armed men and demanding a commission to fight the Native Americans. Faced with overwhelming firepower, Berkeley pardoned Bacon for any wrongdoing, and authorized his military campaign against the Native Americans. Bacon and his army then departed to go fight Native Americans, but the Elite Planters complained to Governor Berkeley that Bacon was more dangerous than the Native Americans and urged him to reconsider. Berkeley complied by again charging Bacon with treason and sending 300 militiamen into the Virginia wilderness to apprehend Bacon. When Bacon learned that he had again been branded a traitor, he declared war against Berkeley and the other Grandees and headed into the wilderness to recruit more soldiers. Bacon then waged war against both the Native Americans and Berkeley's forces for three months. Berkeley's militia retaliated by plundering the homes of Bacon's supporters. Both Berkeley and Bacon recruited slaves and indentured servants by promising freedom to them if they joined their cause. Hence, most of Bacon's rebels were discontented indentured servants who desired freedom and Native American land.

In September of 1676, Bacon marched on Jamestown, defeated Berkeley's militia, burned the State House, and forced the Governor to flee. Berkeley then sent word of the crisis to England; and the King responded by sending 1,100 troops, though it took three months to get a message to England and receive the troops back from the King as a reply. Before the troops could arrive, Bacon died of either swamp fever or dysentery in October 1676; and most of his followers disbanded. Berkeley then rounded up 23 known Bacon followers and hanged them without a trial.

The King launched an investigation of the entire affair, which resulted in the removal of Governor Berkeley. The new governor installed by the King subsequently nullified Bacon's laws and imposed an export tax on tobacco.

In the end, Bacon's rebellion secured the Native American land for the white settlers and, through the expansion into Native American land, quelled the divisive land tension between whites. A slow down in immigration to Chesapeake during the 1680s and 1690s due to an improving economy in England also reduced land pressures and tension.

PUEBLO REVOLT

Finally, though we have been focusing on the English colonies, it should be mentioned that in 1680 the Pueblo Indians (descendants of the Anasazi) staged a revolt that succeeded in driving the Spanish out of colonial New Mexico for 13 years. Led by the shaman Pope, villagers from some two dozen pueblos repudiated Christianity and even massacred several hundred Spaniards, driving the remaining 2,000 south along the Rio Grande. The Pueblos were conquered again in the 1690s. In the eighteenth century, the English/Native American conflict took place within a context of European struggle for empire that will be discussed in the next chapter.

BRITAIN WINS SUPREMACY IN NORTH AMERICA

NEW FRANCE

France had originally laid claims to America because of the voyages of Giovanni da Verrazano in 1523 and of Jacques Cartier in 1534, but not until 1608 was the permanent settlement of Quebec established by Samuel de Champlain. New France, as the French settlements on the North American continent were called, was slow to grow, being virtually all male. Trading in furs was the most lucrative enterprise, and it flourished in a wilderness setting. Settlers in farms and villages intruded upon the wilderness and its inhabitants.

In the 1660s the French became more determined in expanding their hold on North America. As a consequence, families were encouraged to settle in New France. They were provided with land, livestock, seed, and tools. Women were sent to become wives of unmarried men. Those who elected to remain unmarried were required to pay special taxes and were excluded from some of the subsidies provided to married settlers. In five years the population in New France doubled.

The French, much like the Spanish, encouraged exploration of the interior, sending Jesuit priests along with specially selected explorers.

Father Jacques Marquette and Louis Jolliet exploring the Mississippi River

In 1673 Father Jacques Marquette, whose personal goal was to establish missions among the Illinois Native Americans, was ordered by his superior in Quebec to accompany Louis Jolliet, picked by the governor of New France, to explore the "Great River," the Mississippi. Accompanied by five trappers, Marquette and Jolliet followed the Wisconsin River down to the Mississippi River, which awed them with its grandeur. No less a surprise downstream was the roar of the Missouri River emptying into the Mississippi.

Marquette kept a lively journal describing the buffalo, the Native Americans along the route, the heat—it was mid-July—and their experiences and encounters along the route. After feasting on dog meat and other delicacies with the Native Americans on the Arkansas River, the explorers decided to return to Canada, in part because of their fear of capture by the Spanish should they proceed to the mouth of the Mississippi.

Robert de La Salle launched a less successful expedition in 1683, although he did reach the mouth of the Mississippi. Both explorations not only gave New France a strong claim to the interior of the territory of mid-America but also encouraged the French to fortify the Mississippi and Ohio rivers, laying the background for an inevitable clash of interests between the British and French colonies on the North American continent.

EARLY BORDER CONFLICTS

The shifting balance of power in eighteenth-century Europe, brought about in part by the emergence of France and Britain as the major nations of the Western world, produced a ceaseless contest for position in both the Old World and the New. To the English colonials, the strength of New France was a particular danger. French fur traders in the wilderness were capable of stirring up the Native Americans to hostility against English traders and settlers who began to penetrate the transmontane region; and French control over the interior threatened to curb the westward expansion of the English colonies in America. The French had a problem, however, in that the French population in North America in 1690 was only 12,000, as compared to 200,000 English; and the French were scattered from Quebec to New Orleans.

The growth of both French and English ambitions in the New World led to protracted wars between the English and the French in the New World. Between 1689 and 1713, the French and the British were at war for 19 of 24 years with King William's War (1689–1697) and Queen Anne's War (1702–1713). In King William's War, the French attacked New England, proving to the colonists that British military protection was necessary for their security. The War of the Spanish Succession (1702–1713), or Queen Anne's War as it is known in America, saw a conflict of the colonists with both Spanish and French forces.

The Colonists were again heavily involved in the English war effort in Massachusetts. Twenty percent of able-bodied men in Massachusetts participated in the war, and the death rate for colonial soldiers was 25 percent. The war debts incurred by the colony of Massachusetts, (50,000 British pounds), exceeded the colony's GDP. The war left numerous widows and orphans in Massachusetts and a war ravaged economy. The New England economy would not rebound for a generation. Nevertheless, the war ended with a British victory; and in the Peace of Utrecht that officially ended the War in 1713, the British gained Newfoundland and Nova Scotia along with the Hudson Bay Territory (Ontario) from the French. The British takeover of these areas eventually led to an out-migration in the years of 1755–1762 of French inhabitants who did not desire to be ruled by the British. Flotillas of refugees left French Acadia (Nova Scotia) for New Orleans that was still possessed by France. The locals misunderstood the Acadians when they arrived in New Orleans due to differences in dialect, and the "Acadians" became known as "Cajuns."

KING GEORGE'S WAR

In 1739 Great Britain attacked Spain in a conflict that soon merged into the War of the Austrian Succession, or King George's War (1740–1748). Believing that the time was ripe to neutralize French power in Canada, the governor of Massachusetts organized a force of militia. On June 17, 1745, the Americans, in one of the most audacious—and lucky—episodes in the colonial wars, captured Louisbourg, a fort on Cape Breton Island. In 1748, however, the British returned the fortress to the French in exchange for Madras in India.

START OF THE GREAT WAR FOR EMPIRE

The French now showed a greater determination than ever to hold Canada and the Ohio and Mississippi valleys. In furtherance of their goals, they erected blockhouses to fortify the Ohio and Allegheny River valleys against the British. In the meantime, planters from Virginia and Maryland had organized the Ohio Company to exploit virgin lands as far west as the present site of Louisville, Kentucky. To prevent these western lands from falling into possession of the French, the governor of Virginia in 1753 sent George Washington, a young surveyor, into the Ohio Valley to remonstrate with the French commander. George Washington delivered a letter from the Royal Governor of Virginia, Robert Dinwiddie, to a French outpost near Lake Erie, warning the French that they were intruding on Virginia land. Washington returned with a scornful reply from the French; and, in addition, Washington gathered military intelligence about the French positions.

In May 1754, Dinwiddie sent Washington and 160 armed men into the Ohio territory to oust the French intruders. Mingo Indians, helping Washington, killed and scalped 14 Frenchmen including their commander—a massacre unintended by Washington. Washington knew there would be a French retaliation and quickly assembled a fort called Fort Necessity, built in just one week in an indefensible position. Washington received 200 reinforcements; but his Native American allies abandoned the Colonists and instead helped the French, who attacked the Fort in July of 1754. A third of Washington's men were killed or wounded in the battle, and Washington was forced to surrender. The French then sent Washington back to the Virginia governor with the message that the French would not depart from the disputed territory. Thus began the conflict that was to develop into the French and Indian War and explode in Europe as the Seven Years War (1756–1763), allying England and Prussia against France, Austria, and Spain. In 1754, both England and France dispatched 3,000 new troops into the New World and charged them with securing their colonial territory.

ALBANY CONFERENCE

With the danger of an Native American war threatening the whole frontier, the colonies were particularly concerned with counterbalancing the Native American allies of the French. To conciliate the powerful Iroquois, who had given invaluable support to the English in the past, the British government called a conference in Albany of commissioners from seven Northern and Middle colonies. This "Albany Congress" was more important for its political proposals than for its few accomplishments in dealing with the disaffected Iroquois. Because the delegates realized that a closer union of the colonies was needed to provide better collective defense and control of Native American affairs, they listened attentively to the "Plan of Union" put forward by one of Pennsylvania's leading citizens, Benjamin Franklin. Franklin's proposals would have brought all of the colonies under "one general government" with an executive and legislature, but with each colony retaining its separate existence and government. Ben Franklin's plan for a union of the colonies could not be agreed upon by the seven colonies. Although all agreed a union for defense was needed, none could agree on the actual form. Thus, no colony gave the plan serious consideration, and the British government disregarded it altogether. The Iroquois left the conference with 30 wagonloads of gifts, but never committed to help the English.

Benjamin Franklin

FORT DUQUESNE, 1755

Instead of helping the English, the Iroquois initially helped the French because it was the French with whom they engaged in more trade. To protect the colonies, the British government sent two regiments of regulars and a British fleet, but the French and Native Americans repeatedly routed the British Army under General James Braddock. In an attempt to dislodge the French from Fort Duquesne, a strategic position that controlled the upper Ohio valley, a detachment of regulars and colonial militia under British General Edward Braddock marched toward the fort, but it was ambushed and routed by French and Native American forces. Almost half of the 2,000 British were killed, including Braddock. Washington narrowly escaped and survived having two horses shot out from underneath him. With the loss of Braddock, young Washington was given the responsibility of protecting more than 300 miles of the Virginia frontier against incursions of Native Americans and French marauders. The year 1755 was a period of almost unrelieved misfortune for the British; and for the next two or three years the war raged intermittently and disastrously along the whole frontier, with the French under Marquis de Montcalm winning a succession of victories in the north.

WILLIAM PITT INCREASES BRITISH RESOLVE

By 1757, the British had not accomplished their objectives; and French Canada, with only 70,000 inhabitants, was winning the war against the British colonies that had a population nearly 20 times larger. In 1757, William Pitt, who was determined to break the French resistance in the New World, became the English Prime Minister. William Pitt, who had become British Secretary of State for War in 1757, realized that part of the trouble in America lay in the incompetence of Britain's officers. To remedy this, he ordered to America fresh troops under a new command. He also won more wholehearted cooperation from the American provincials by promising that Britain would reimburse the individual colonies for their war expenditures.

Pitt dispatched 23,000 new British army troops to North America in 1757 and 1758 along with a 14,000-man naval force. Pitt altered British strategy to one of cutting off French trade with the Native Americans. Pitt correctly surmised that if Iroquois' trade were disrupted the Iroquois would change sides. The overwhelming force of the British army was successful in defeating the French in several major battles in 1758, resulting in British control of the St. Lawrence River. With British control of the St. Lawrence, the Iroquois were effectively cut off from French trade goods, thus convincing them to aid the English. With the Native Americans on their side, the British took Fort Duquesne from the French in 1758. In 1759, the Iroquois helped the English defeat the French at Fort Niagara and Fort Ticonderoga.

THE CAPTURE OF QUEBEC

The victory that finally decided the issue in Canada came on September 13, 1759, when General Wolfe led a successful attack on Quebec, which had been under siege since late June. The capture of Quebec sealed the fate of France in North America. Elsewhere—in Europe and India—British arms were also victorious, and France could do nothing but capitulate. In 1762 France ceded Louisiana to Spain in recompense for aid in the war and a year later, by the Treaty of Paris, ceded to Great Britain all of Canada except the tiny islands of St. Pierre and Miquelon. Paradoxically, the very magnitude of the British victory paved the way for the disintegration of the British Empire in America.

PROCLAMATION OF 1763

In order to have good relations with the Native American tribes, the English issued the Proclamation of 1763, in which England ceded all land west of the Appalachians to the Native Americans; and whites living West of the Appalachians were ordered to withdraw. The Proclamation of 1763 failed miserably. Neither England nor the colonies had the resources necessary for its enforcement, and whites west of the Appalachians refused to pull up and move east.

RAMIFICATIONS OF SEVEN YEARS WAR

The ramifications of the Seven Years War were immense. Although the French would later temporarily gain the land between the Mississippi River and the Rocky Mountains from Spain, they would quickly sell the territory to the United States in 1803. The French were never again to be a colonial force in North America.

The long and costly war also had major economic ramifications. The war left England and the colonies with massive debt, and the booming wartime colonial economy was followed by an economic recession. There were huge human casualties in the colonies (especially in New England), resulting in a sex imbalance in New England (women outnumbered men) and a widows and orphans problem.

In addition, the war had major political ramifications as the colonial legislatures gained power at the expense of colonial governors. During The Seven Years War, governors were forced to make numerous concessions to the legislatures in efforts to gain legislative support for the British war effort. The war also left the colonies replete with a generation of seasoned military veterans, who would be less averse to taking up arms later when they believed their livelihood was threatened. Additionally, the colonies gained a sense of national identity through working together in the war against the French. Finally, France was no longer a security threat to the colonies; and, therefore, the colonists no longer viewed English military protection in the colonies as necessary. When the British Crown would insist that the colonists do their part to support the British military, the colonists would resist.

CHAPTER *4*

PATTERNS OF COLONIAL SOCIAL STRUCTURE

COLONIAL SOCIAL STRUCTURE

Influences on Cultural Development
Influence of English Society
Influence of the American
  Environment
Women in Colonial America
The Structure of Colonial Society

MINORITIES IN THE COLONIES

European Minorities
The Rise of Slavery
Stono Rebellion
The English and the Native Americans
Non-English Settlers in
  the Borderlands
End of the Barrier to Expansion

THE SEVENTEENTH CENTURY:
AGE OF FAITH

Puritanism in England
Puritanism in America
Puritan Theology
Puritan View of the Bible
Puritans and Free Thought
Changes in the New World
The Transplanted Anglicans

THE EIGHTEENTH CENTURY MIND

The Enlightenment
The Growth of Toleration
The Rise of Secularism
The Great Awakening
Lasting Impact, Division, and Dissent
The Enlightenment in America
Colonial Roots of American Culture

COLONIAL SOCIAL STRUCTURE

INFLUENCES ON CULTURAL DEVELOPMENT

In intellectual and social life, as in political and economic life, the first English settlers in America shared the attitudes, ambitions, and habits of thought of their peers in the home country. During the colonial period, however, these characteristics were modified. In part this was because of the changing intellectual life in England, which affected the colonies in a variety of ways. In part it was because the men and women born and educated in America knew first-hand only the ways of their colonial neighbors. They experienced English culture and English intellectual currents second-hand.

Furthermore, the immigration of non-English peoples brought added diversity and dimension to the social and intellectual scene. An evaluation of the degree of distinctiveness of American culture depends on the relative weight placed upon these elements—English, American, and non-English. Because individual historians have placed different emphasis upon these factors, their judgments have differed. All agree, however, that conditions in the New World influenced social and intellectual development.

INFLUENCE OF ENGLISH SOCIETY

In Elizabethan England, the social rank of a family was determined strictly by the status of the male head of the household. The top level of this patriarchal and paternalistic society consisted of noble families, whose position depended upon extensive landholdings and the favors that accrued to a privileged segment of society. The nobility was not quite a closed circle. Younger sons who did not inherit a substantial estate or title generally sought their fortunes through the life of the gentry, through commercial connections, or through such professions as the army and the church. It was possible for a highly successful entrepreneur to penetrate the nobility, though full-fledged acceptance was often delayed for several generations.

Below the nobility ranked the gentry, the country gentlemen. The life of the gentry centered on the land. The country gentleman knew his tenants and their problems, and he experienced at first hand the uncertainties, as well as the blessings, of farming. The gentry served as the backbone of governing authority, in part because the sovereign encouraged their participation as a shield against ambitious nobles. The gentry formed the largest group in Parliament, and they held those local offices that were mainly responsible for enforcing the statutes of the state. Marriage alliances between gentry and families engaged in trade were fairly frequent; and gentry families often contributed younger sons to trade, to adventure, to the military, to the church, and sometimes to the universities.

Below the gentry ranked the yeomen, who could be leaseholders or owners of small estates. A yeoman was the dirt farmer of Elizabethan days, a man attached to the soil, who lived a simple life and farmed with frugality. The laborers and servant classes of Elizabethan England ranked below the yeomen. A laborer might be an apprentice who in time would enter a trade and make a good living, or he might be a man who worked for daily wages and whose chances of rising to a better social and economic position were remote. In the same fashion, to be a servant could mean to serve with a gentry family in the expectation that by means of a good marriage or hard work an elevation of status could be secured; or it could involve the meanest kind of position, from which no escalation of status seemed possible.

The English social structure was not transplanted intact to America. Members of the English aristocracy did not come to America. They were relatively content and well off at home, so they had no incentive to migrate to a primitive New World wilderness. Occasionally, younger sons of noble families came to America to try their fortune, but even this element was rare.

For the other end of the social structure—day laborers and servants—migration to the New World was restricted because of the transportation costs. Often gentry transported their servants. Laborers, too, sometimes migrated by taking advantage of the system of *indentured servitude,* in which they bound themselves to a master for service in the colonies for a specified length of time, usually three to five years, in exchange for their passage. This system became widespread after the mid-seventeenth century.

The first settlers, then, were drawn principally from the yeomanry and the gentry, the latter bringing servants with them. At the outset, these class divisions, and their patriarchal framework, were scrupulously maintained. In early Massachusetts, to cite an illustration, a laborer's wife who appeared at church wearing a frock or hat of a quality that, in the eyes of the elders, exceeded the social station of laborer was severely admonished.

INFLUENCE OF THE AMERICAN ENVIRONMENT

Modifications in this structure during the colonial period gave rise to a social structure indigenous to English America. The gradual growth of a system of indentured servitude enabled people without money to emigrate to America, where they eventually became yeoman farmers or free laborers. Men who arrived as hired servants or as yeomen sometimes acquired substantial estates through industry or good fortune. Ships' captains who brought immigrants to certain colonies claimed headrights—an allotment of 50 acres of land for each person transported—and these grants formed the nucleus around which some landed estates were formed. Labor was so scarce that a skilled workman not only could make a good living but also could become an employer. Men of modest means who engaged in trade built up strong mercantile firms, and wealth brought an elevation of social status and, often, political power.

Among the most important determinants of social position in America was the possession of land; and its very abundance—as the Native Americans lost ground—helped encourage a more mobile society. Nowhere was this more clearly demonstrated than in the Chesapeake colonies. In the first century of settlement the vast majority of the settlers in Virginia and Maryland were yeomen or indentured servants who were able to rise to the status of yeomen after completing their term of servitude. During various crises of the seventeenth century, especially during the Puritan ascendancy in England of the 1640s and 1650s and immediately after the restoration of the Stuart monarchy in 1660, members of gentry families or, more rarely, younger sons of noble families migrated to Virginia. But they acted as no more than leaven to the loaf. The Virginia gentry class that gradually emerged was made up primarily of those who had risen to this status in America. It was not a gentry group transplanted to America.

WOMEN IN COLONIAL AMERICA

The practice of bringing families to the New World set the English colonies apart from those of other nations. Women were in great demand, not only as companions or to satisfy sexual appetites, but as partners in the enterprise of settlement. John Winthrop of Massachusetts, who preceded his wife to New England, wrote her most lovingly of the life and excitement they would share in America. Some became influential. The religious views of Anne

Governor John Winthrop

Hutchinson of Massachusetts led to her being ousted from the colony but attracted a following that found refuge with her near Providence—Native Americans eventually killed her and her family. Anne Bradstreet is now recognized as the most sensitive poet in colonial America. Most women, like most men, worked day in and day out in the fields and the household, making a living, raising a family, and looking forward to better times. Whether as slaves, indentured servants, or housewives their labor made an essential contribution to the success of the colonial economy.

Women in colonial America did not have the vote and could not, in most cases, hold property. Their opportunities were severely restricted. None became lawyers or ministers. Some practiced a trade, such as blacksmithing or printing, but almost none made a name in business. Yet their influence was keenly felt, and without them there could have been no society to win its freedom and found a nation. Some Scholars have suggested that the extreme Protestant devotion to the Bible may have offered women a strong incentive to literacy;

and this may, in turn, have laid the ground work for the reforming role women, white and black, would play in the new nation.

THE STRUCTURE OF COLONIAL SOCIETY

The structure that evolved in colonial society differed from that of English society in three important respects. First, the process of transplantation sheared off the top level of English society—the nobility. Second, the composition of American classes was not the result of direct transplants from England. Third, the parts of society were present in somewhat different proportions.

In America there were more slaves who were condemned to perpetual servitude and who had little if any mobility; but there were fewer servants because the opportunities to acquire land and other forms of wealth were so abundant. American society ranged, therefore, from the colonial elite—the important merchants in Massachusetts and Rhode Island, the planters along the Chesapeake and in the Carolinas, and the large landholders in New York and Pennsylvania—to the small farmers and skilled workers, to the unskilled workers and servants, and finally, at the base, to the slaves.

The special contours of American society also reflected a modification of male professional opportunities. An upper class Englishman could advance professionally through the church, the military, or the law. In America, the church in New England offered an avenue for advancement for a time, but by the eighteenth century a man looking for advancement generally sought out land and commerce, not the church. Moreover, American men, accustomed to their special militia forces, could not advance professionally through the naval or military service. In America, a man who had already

John Dickinson

achieved status as a merchant or landholder was placed in command of a colonial expedition.

Not until the 1730s and 1740s did the practice of law gain sufficient status to become an avenue for advancement. In earlier periods, merchants and landholders frequently served as their own lawyers. Only as colonial society became more sophisticated did the practice of law become a profession. A number of colonials, some that were already in a substantial social position—James Otis and John Adams in New England, John Dickinson in the Middle Colonies, and Patrick Henry and Charles Pinckney in the Southern colonies—improved their status by becoming expert in the practice of law. The seed of American society was English, but the American environment dramatically affected its growth. Its evolution, as a result, was distinctive, not a replica.

MINORITIES IN THE COLONIES

In the eighteenth century, the population of the colonies included large groups of non-English: Irish, Germans, Scots, and French. These minorities gave a flavor to American society that endures to the present time.

Two groups of Americans, however—the Native Americans and the immigrant Africans—were excluded from the colonial social structure. True, black Americans were very much a part of the economic structure, and trade with the Native Americans had great economic significance for the colonists. In both cases, however, the relationship between the races was marked by a cultural clash rather than cultural fusion; also, in both cases, white culture had enough power to establish its dominance.

EUROPEAN MINORITIES

The reasons for the inflow of non-English Europeans were numerous, but a change of policy in England was a critical factor. By the eighteenth century England was less enthusiastic about exporting its population to America. As its agriculture became increasingly commercial, as trade expanded a hundredfold, and as manufacturing began to take root, its people were needed at home. As the supply of labor from the mother country was reduced, the Middle and Southern Colonies, especially, brought indentured servants from northern and western Europe.

Francis Daniel Pastorious, a man of exceptional intellect, led the first German settlers into Pennsylvania in 1683, founding Germantown north of Philadelphia; but the principal migration of Germans did not begin until after 1710. From that date until 1770, a wave of 225,000 German immigrants came to the New World—almost half of which migrated to Pennsylvania. Statistically, about 80 percent settled in the Middle Colonies of Pennsylvania, New York, and New Jersey, and about 20 percent settled in the Southern Colonies from Maryland to Georgia. Less than one percent settled in New England.

The settlement of newcomers from France, Scotland, and Ireland tended to conform to the pattern of the German migration. In fact, the migration of Scotch-Irish from northern Ireland to Pennsylvania became so heavy that James Logan of Pennsylvania observed: "It looks as if Ireland is to send all its inhabitants hither. ... The common fact is that if they thus continue to come they will make themselves proprietors of the Province."

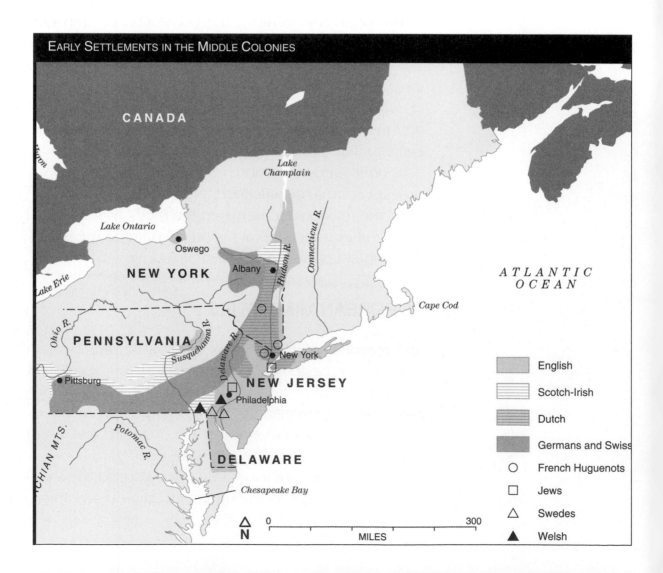

The consequences of non-English migration were numerous. The population of provincial America grew; demographic patterns changed, and new cultural patterns and influences, such as German Pietism, were introduced. In those colonies where immigration was greatest—such as Pennsylvania, where Quakers constituted the elite and the Germans and the Scotch-Irish were regarded as the lower classes—the social structure was affected. New sources of labor became available at a time when colonial economic expansion demanded them. The colonies became more cosmopolitan with a broader interaction of cultures.

The non-English influence was primarily cultural, not political. English political customs and institutions, modified by American colonial conditions, continued to be practiced without challenge because most of the newcomers had never before experienced self-government. Non-English cultural life in the broadest sense—the classical music of the Moravians, the new languages, Scottish Presbyterianism, the special methods of breeding high grade cattle brought by the Scottish Highlanders—enriched provincial America.

The population growth provided by the new immigrants occurred mainly in the country rather than in the cities. In fact, this was one of the few periods in American history in which the urban proportion of the population declined rather than increased. Yet the five major colonial cities—Boston, Newport, New York, Philadelphia, and Charleston—tripled their populations between 1690 and 1742. More significantly, a great number of smaller urban communities developed—port towns in Massachusetts and inland towns such as Albany.

In each case the importance of the urban areas exceeded a strict population count because, as centers of distribution for goods and commodities, they became more influential economically, politically, socially, and culturally. By 1776 Philadelphia, ranking second among the cities within the British Empire, had become an important cultural center with its scientific societies,

Benjamin Franklin

its university, its public library, its newspaper, and its first citizen, Benjamin Franklin— amateur scientist, inventor, and noted publisher of *Poor Richard's Almanac*.

THE RISE OF SLAVERY

By far the largest group of immigrants to come to the English colonies in North America during the eighteenth century was the blacks from Africa and the West Indies. It was a forced migration. The first blacks were brought to Virginia in 1619; and evidence indicates that until the middle of the seventeenth century they were both slaves and servants, as has been noted. The numbers involved were relatively insignificant. Less than four percent of the population of Virginia in 1670 was composed of slaves, with similar percentages in New York and Rhode Island.

In the 1690s slavery suddenly boomed. The proportion of slaves in the population of Virginia rose to 25 percent in 1720 and to 41 percent in 1750. Slavery became the labor base upon which the large-scale plantation system in Virginia, Maryland, and North and South Carolina was founded.

Two considerations in particular account for the abrupt change. First, neither intellectual nor moral restraint existed. Blacks were considered property rather than people. Liberty as understood in the seventeenth and eighteenth centuries protected property and, as a consequence, protected slavery. No important social institution within Virginia or, indeed, in the Western World condemned slavery in 1700.

Second, Virginia, Maryland, and South Carolina were desperately in need of workers. In the seventeenth century, indentured servants had been the primary labor force in Virginia and Maryland; and indentures in modest numbers were introduced into New England where family labor predominated. Beginning in the late seventeenth century, however, and accelerating in the eighteenth century, indentured servants were increasingly attracted to the Middle Colonies. As a result, the Southern Colonies were correspondingly desperate for labor as large landholdings became more numerous.

The chief reason for the increase of black slave importation in the Southern Colonies, then, was economic. Although twice as expensive as an indentured servant at the outset, a slave provided permanent service; and in every colony the laws made slaves in perpetuity of the offspring of female slaves. Soon slaves outstripped land as an investment. In a broadside written by Thomas Nairne of South Carolina in 1704 informing prospective colonists of the relative costs of establishing a plantation, the cost of two slaves, even for a modest plantation of 200 acres, constituted one half of all costs, including tools, land, a house, livestock, and a year's provisions. The land cost only £6 compared with £80 for the two slaves.

The human cargo arrived in colonial America from Africa under particularly cruel conditions. Having purchased captured Africans from African middlemen, the traders loaded them onto ships for the infamous "Middle Passage". Two competing goals were in play for the

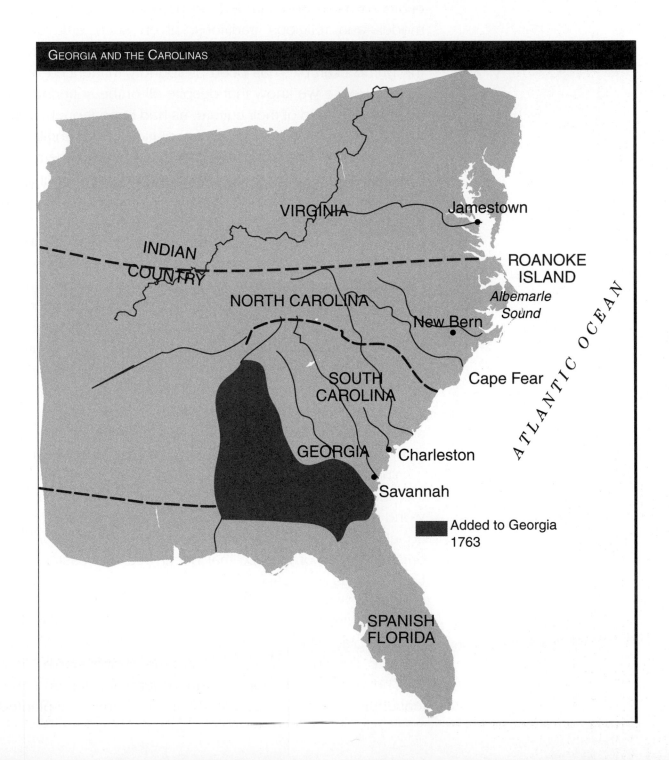

GEORGIA AND THE CAROLINAS

traders. On the one hand, it was in their economic interest to deliver their goods alive and in good enough health to be sold into slavery. On the other, they wanted to cram as many people in as they could, once again to maximize their profits. Typically, the captives made the long voyage to America below decks and in shackles.

Once put on shore and sold, the captives found themselves the property of people speaking an unfamiliar language and with unfamiliar customs and laws. Scholars debate the extent to which slaves were able to reconstitute their own culture, family life—which was centered more on extended kin networks than was the European model—and religious traditions, given such unfavorable circumstances. What is clear is that much of American culture, jazz being the prime example, has been profoundly influenced by the African legacy. Hence we know that despite all of the suffering, the Africans were not stripped of their culture, as had been thought formerly.

By 1775, 20 percent of the population of the English colonies in North America was composed of blacks, most of them slaves. More than 400,000 lived in the colonies of Maryland, Virginia, North Carolina, South Carolina, and Georgia—a number almost equal to the total population of New England.

Although it has often been asserted that the British Royal African Company brought most of the slaves to America, free traders were the principal conveyors of blacks. New Englanders, infrequently the Dutch, and later Southern merchants or planters imported slaves from the Caribbean as well as from Africa. Most of the colonies tried to end by law the increasing importation of slaves, but the British Board of Trade rejected each act adopted by the individual colonial legislatures. Because of the profitability of the slave trade, Britain considered it to be the basis for its entire trading structure. Indeed, a charge excised from the Declaration of Independence that condemned the crown for imposing slaves upon the colonies, had a basis in fact.

That the slaves came to the English colonies with no skills and that the culture of Africa was vastly inferior to that of the Western World are myths that feed a racial bias. Most slaves came with skills equal to those of an ordinary laboring Englishman. For example, the original source of the rice that became a successful crop in South Carolina was Madagascar, where Africans had been cultivating it for centuries. When Eliza Pinckney of South Carolina was unsuccessful in making the commercial dye indigo with a white overseer, she imported a black slave whose knowledge, together with her own perseverance, culminated in an important marketable staple.

The agricultural tools of the African farmer and the English leaseholder did not vary greatly. In time, the transplanted African

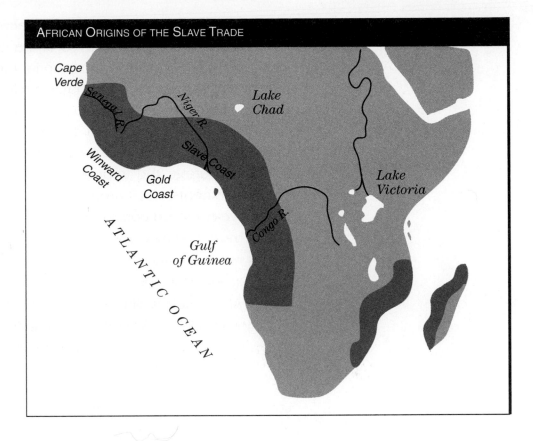

became the skilled worker in the Southern colonies—the cook, cooper, cobbler, and blacksmith. It was not unusual for a planter to put in a request for a slave from a special region of Africa because of the particular skills of its inhabitants.

STONO REBELLION

The devastating social consequences of slavery pervaded every aspect of colonial life. Conflict between blacks and whites led to the enactment of elaborate codes for the conduct of slaves. Open rebellions by slaves were rare, but such a rebellion occurred at Stono, South Carolina, in 1739. On a Sunday morning before dawn, a group of some 20 slaves attacked a country store and killed the store's two shopkeepers while confiscating the store's guns and ammunition. The slave rebels placed the severed heads of their victims on the store's front steps and then headed toward Spanish Florida, attacking Southern plantations along the way and enticing other slaves to join their rebellion. The slave rebels burned and plundered over a half-dozen plantations and killed over 20 white men, women, and children. A force of whites was quickly assembled to put down the revolt; and the rebels were killed and their heads placed atop mileposts along the road as reminders to other slaves of the consequences of rebellion. The fate of the rebels illustrated the fact that slaves had no chance of overturning slavery and that rebellion would lead to certain death for the rebels. The Stono Rebellion stunned the white population, however, and fear of future revolts prompted defensive measures. Laws were passed to restrict the importation of slaves and to encourage the importation of white indentured servants. White settlements were promoted on the frontier as protection for older slave-centered communities.

The most common form of slave resistance, however, was not outright rebellion; and there were no successful slave revolts in the United States. More often slaves resisted their masters covertly by working slowly, faking illnesses, breaking tools, and carrying out their instructions poorly. The covert resistance should not be overstated, however, because masters obviously were able to get sufficient work

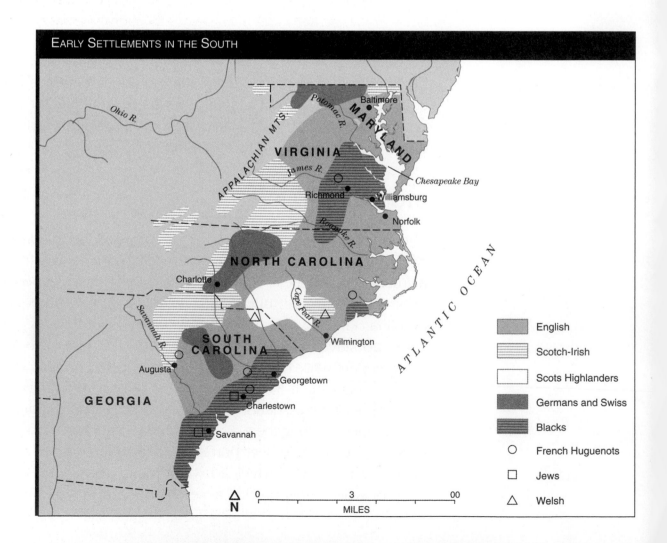

EARLY SETTLEMENTS IN THE SOUTH

from their slaves or the slave system would have been scrapped for a wage labor system.

The most enduring effect of slavery was to set Africans outside the existing social strata and, with minor exceptions, to condemn them to perpetual bondage and lowest status in a caste system. The black was deprived of rights often described as peculiar virtues of the American system—the chance to improve one's position through hard work and the opportunity to provide a better life for one's children. Slavery alienated all but a few Africans from the American tradition. (See "Phillis Wheatley: Black Poet.")

The eighteenth century, therefore, witnessed a strange spectacle: a developing consciousness with respect to a definition of political liberty, consummated by the American Revolution, at the same time that slavery was being imposed on a vast number of human beings—the Africans who came to the colonies under compulsion.

THE ENGLISH AND THE NATIVE AMERICANS

The relationship between the English in North America and the Native Americans was different from that between indigenous peoples and any other European group. A small number of Spanish conquistadors under Hernando Cortez, for example, were able to dominate Mexico by conquering the Aztecs, who held lesser tribes in subordination; but the English in North America faced a different situation that produced a decidedly different result. Powerful tribes blocked the westward expansion of the English settlers: (1) in the triangular area between Lakes Ontario, Erie, and Huron, the Hurons; (2) along the spine of the Appalachians, the Iroquois in New York and Pennsylvania, the Susquehannas in Pennsylvania and Virginia, and the Cherokees in the Carolinas; (3) in the Mississippi Valley below the Ohio River, the Chickasaws and, farther south, the Choctaws. There were many other tribes interspersed throughout; however, no single nation had achieved ascendancy. Defeat for one tribe did not mean defeat for all.

Since the most powerful groups of Native Americans in English America did not dwell along the Atlantic seacoast, the first white settlers from England frequently faced tribes that were friendly or, if warlike, easily defeated. If the Native Americans had joined forces to drive the English from North America at any time during the first half century of colonization, they could have succeeded. Lack of will—of unity of purpose—not an absence of power, explains their failure to do so.

From the beginning, the English treated Native Americans as members of separate nations or separate tribes, never as subjects

PEOPLE THAT MADE A DIFFERENCE

Phillis Wheatley: Black Poet

Phillis Wheatley

There are few enslaved Africans brought to the British colonies in North America whose lives are as well documented as that of Phillis Wheatley. Part of the explanation lies in the Wheatley family history. More importantly, Phillis Wheatley herself left a living, written record in her verses.

In both respects, her life was very different from those of the great majority of Africans brought to America. Yet her story represents the importance of the forced migration from Africa, not only because the numbers of people involved exceeded the migration of peoples from Western Europe in the colonial eighteenth century, but also because of the many talents brought to America by Africans. Unlike many other blacks, Phillis Wheatley was encouraged to develop her talents and was accepted into white society.

Phillis Wheatley was first seen in America as a delicate little girl, about eight years old, aboard a slave ship from Senegal that reached Boston in 1761. Susannah Wheatley, wife of tailor John Wheatley, wished to have a special personal servant. John purchased the young slave, brought her home, and named her Phillis.

At the time Phillis entered the Wheatley household, it included, in addition to the husband and wife, a son, Nathaniel, and a daughter, Mary. Three other children had died in their early years.

Susannah Wheatley and her daughter Mary, who was 18, observed that Phillis absorbed her lessons quickly. As a result, they began to instruct her, giving preference to biblical teachings. Within about 16 months Phillis could read difficult passages in the Bible with ease. Encouraged, Mary taught Phillis a smattering of astronomy, ancient and modern geography, ancient history, and even a few of the Latin classics. Homer became Phillis's favorite author, and soon she began to write verse. In the household, she was increasingly considered a daughter rather than a slave, and it became a familiar treat among the Wheatley friends to have Phillis recite the poetry of others or verses of her own. Her first poem, entitled "A Poem, by Phillis, a Negro Girl, in Boston, On Death of the Reverend George Whitefield," appeared in print in 1770.

In 1771, Mary Wheatley married the pastor of the Second Church in Boston, the Reverend John Lathrop. In that same year, Phillis became a member of the congregation of the Old South Meeting house, a significant departure for that faith. Because Phillis's health appeared to fail, the Wheatley family physician recommended sea air. Nathaniel was about to leave for England on business, and so it was decided that Phillis would sail under protection of her foster brother. She was made a freed person before she left in May 1773.

The Countess of Huntingdon, for whom Whitefield had served as chaplain, welcomed Phillis in England. She attracted wide attention, not only because of her writing talent but also because of her unusual gift of conversation. Brook Watson, the Lord Mayor of London, was sufficiently impressed to present Phillis with a 1720 Glasgow edition of Paradise Lost.

Phillis was urged to stay in London, but word reached her that Susannah Wheatley was seriously ill and longed for her return. Turning aside all entreaties to remain in London, Phillis left for Boston. However, before departing she arranged to have her collection of poems published under the title Poems on Various Subjects, Religious and Moral.

Little but despair greeted her return to Boston. Susannah Wheatley died in March 1774, and four years later Susannah's husband John died, followed soon after by Mary Wheatley Lathrop. Nathaniel, the only remaining member of the family, was living abroad.

In April 1778 Phillis became the wife of John Peters. In her letters she wrote of him as an agreeable man, but she quickly discovered that he lacked qualities to which she had become accustomed in the Wheatley household—among them diligence and industry. Pursued by poverty, deeply affected by the war that cut her off from friends in England, Phillis finally earned her living by doing daily chores in a lodging house. She died December 1784, preceded in death by two of her three children.

Phillis Wheatley was a tragic figure, a victim of slavery who was rescued by a loving and talented family, a victim of a war that turned minds to politics rather than to poetry; yet her verses live on. First editions of her poems appeared in 1793. Since then, her verses and her life have been the subject of continuous study.

Her piety and upbringing in the Wheatley family are revealed in these lines from "On the Death of the Reverend Mr. George Whitefield."

> Thou, moon, hast seen, and all the stars of light,
> How he was wrestled with his God by night.
> He prayed that grace in ev'ry heart might dwell;
> He longed to see America excel;
> He charged its youth that ev'ry grace divine
> Should with full luster in their conduct shine.

Somewhat surprisingly, Phillis's references to slavery are limited. When it surfaces, as in her dedicatory verses to the Earl of Dartmouth, she links it to a larger context of freedom, a commentary on her extraordinary perception, well in advance of her time and place, and a fitting epitaph.

> Should you, my lord, while you peruse my song,
> Wonder from whence my love of Freedom sprung,

continued

PEOPLE THAT MADE A DIFFERENCE *continued*

Phillis Wheatley: Black Poet

Whence flow these wishes for the common good,
By feeling hearts alone best understood,
I, young in life, by seeming cruel fate
Was snatched from Afric's fancied happy seat:
What pangs excruciating must molest,
What sorrows labor in my parent's breast!
Steeled was that soul, and by no misery moved,
That from a father seized his babe beloved:
Such, such my case. And can I then but pray
Others may never feel tyrannic sway?

of the crown. Warfare and negotiation involved two nations: England and the particular tribe or nation in question. In contrast to the fusion of cultures that took place under the Spanish colonial system, the white and Native American cultures remained separate in English America.

In need of labor, English settlers sometimes tried to make slaves of the Native Americans captured in skirmishes. That did not work. The captives could too easily slip off and return to their own people. In some colonies—South Carolina, for instance—captured Native Americans were shipped off to the West Indies as slaves around 1700.

Efforts were also made to convert Native Americans to English ways. Schools were established for them in several colonies; but once the Native Americans returned to their own people, they took up their traditional ways and customs.

On occasion, the practice of treating a Native American people as a foreign power had gratifying results for the English. When Iroquois and Cherokee leaders were brought to London to sign treaties of friendship, the crown made these occasions festive and special. Both Native American nations remained invaluable allies of England for a century.

In the colonial period powerful nations of Native Americans blocked English access to the interior of the continent. These Native Americans controlled the interior trade by their defensive position along the Appalachian range and were strengthened by their ability to play off the European rivals, France and England, against each other. They held the balance of power in America for a century (1660–1760). Not until the French had been eliminated as a major participant in colonizing the continent were the English finally able to penetrate the Appalachian barrier in any great numbers.

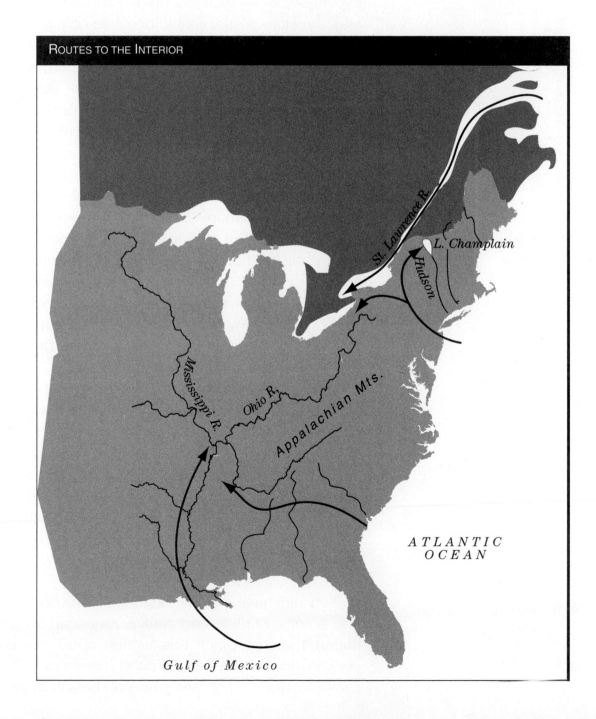

ROUTES TO THE INTERIOR

Ironically, by forcing the American provincials to stay principally in the coastal areas, the Native Americans may have contributed to their own destruction. Prevented from moving westward, the colonists established a mature, vigorous, developed society from which to launch an assault to conquer the inland wilderness. If the English had been able to penetrate deeply into the interior of America soon after settlement, the strength provided by cohesive, highly developed colonies would not have been achieved.

Also, if deep penetration had been possible, the tie with England would unquestionably have been much less influential. The political experience of the settlements would have been less sophisticated and, therefore, less valuable because only relatively stable communities could provide such experience. In contributing to the creation of a vigorous, structured provincial society, the formidable Native American barrier thus contributed to the development of political, economic, and intellectual institutions. These institutions, in turn, became so deep-rooted that the sweeping westward movement of the nineteenth century failed to alter them in any fundamental way.

Trade represented one of the most important contacts between the settlers and the Native Americans and accounted for the founding of many of the first modest provincial fortunes. In South Carolina, for example, the early road to riches was gained not by raising rice but by trading in deerskins, one of the most valuable exports from the Carolinas until well into the eighteenth century. In Pennsylvania James Logan's emergence as the first citizen of that colony was made possible through what he called the "stinking" fur trade. In New York the trade brought a fortune and a title to Sir William Johnson.

During the eighteenth century the locus of the fur trade shifted. By 1730 New England's share was limited, if not negligible. The Middle Colonies, the area of greatest expansion, had become the center of the trade with New York and Pennsylvania well in the lead. In the South, Virginia had controlled the principal trade with the Cherokees and the Chickasaws in the late seventeenth century, but early in the eighteenth century South Carolina developed into a serious rival. Then Georgia moved into contention. By the mid-eighteenth century, New York and Georgia were perhaps the two colonies most deeply engaged in the trade with the natives.

Scholars have recently begun to focus on a more informal trade, one among English and Native American women. The historian Laurel Thatcher Ulrich has written about "exchange relations" in needlework and basketry among members of the two groups, for example, using an Native American basket in the collections of the

Rhode Island Historical Society as the point of departure for exploring the nature and meaning of such relations in the colonial period.

NON-ENGLISH SETTLERS IN THE BORDERLANDS

While the English settlers were being held in check, Spanish and French colonists were settling in territory that would eventually become part of the United States. From the sixteenth to the early nineteenth century, the Spanish advanced into Florida, Texas, the American Southwest, and along the Pacific coastline of California. The French established their first settlement in Quebec, Canada, in 1608 and in the seventeenth and eighteenth centuries posted settlements of explorers and soldiers from New Orleans to the western Great Lakes and from the headwaters of the Ohio River, near present-day Pittsburgh, to its outlet into the Mississippi.

The Spanish and French coupled exploration and conquest with missionary stations. Many of the Spanish missions in the American Southwest and California, originally housing a garrison of soldiers, a parcel of priests, and a community of Native Americans, remain to be visited today. Those established by France proved to be somewhat less durable.

The objective of the Spanish defense of its borderlands was to extend the empire and, at the same time, "to Christianize, civilize, and purify" the native inhabitants—the Native Americans. To achieve these goals the Spanish established a chain of *presidios*, or army outposts, from Florida to California. These were linked to and often coupled with mission stations. A *presidio* consisted of some 60 or more soldiers, often living in a modest hut surrounded by a mud palisade. They were accompanied by their families, Native American servants, Native American warriors, and hangers-on of various types of frontier adventurers.

The missions, somewhat in contrast, tried to organize Native American society. On the whole the priests, largely Franciscans, did not find settled Native American communities and so set out to establish them. They gathered the Native Americans into mission stations typically made up of a *plaza*, or square, dominated by the church and surrounded by official buildings, granaries, blacksmith shops, tanneries, and stables, as well as living quarters for the Native Americans and the missionaries.

The object was to impose Spanish "civilization" upon this created Native American community. Native Americans learned to speak the Spanish language, to cultivate crops, to raise livestock, to raise and ride horses. They also learned carpentry, European style. They became winemakers and candle-makers, and, of course, they were held to daily sessions of work and prayer.

A traveler to the missions in California described how everyone, Native Americans and missionaries alike, awakened at first light. They attended prayers and mass, after which *atole*, a type of barley ground up and boiled, was served for breakfast. Then everyone was sent out to work. Men tilled the soil; women cared for the household and the children. A bell summoned the workers for the noonday meal of a stew made of wheat, corn, peas, and beans. The inhabitants of the mission station worked for several hours in the afternoon, after which everyone, once again, attended religious services.

Hunting and fishing were allowed, and the Native Americans raised livestock. At the same time, they retained some of their lifestyle. Their shelters, clothing, and games remained the same. Intermarriage between the Spanish and Native Americans was encouraged, and, in some mission stations, polygamy was permitted.

Out of this came the mixed Spanish-Native American customs: the rodeo and cattle roundup, the stylized concept of the cowboy with chaps, lasso, and lariat, riding a bronco. Out of it also came the fierce Apache warrior on horseback, defending the tribe against further colonial encroachment. Much more subtle as an outgrowth of the Spanish colonization of the borderlands was the hybridization of people and customs in the region, that has endured. Among some of the peoples in the Southwest, such as the Navajos, the Hopis, and the Pueblos, there has been extraordinary cultural survival over the centuries, with tribal groups in some instances holding on to their religious beliefs in tandem with their Catholic practices.

The French did not impose themselves in the same way on their mission-garrison stations. Trading played a larger role. The French did not attempt to keep whole Native American populations under their control, but they wooed and won the friendship of many tribes who stood against English encroachment. They also fortified the basins of the Mississippi and Ohio Rivers, as well as the region surrounding the Great Lakes.

END OF THE BARRIER TO EXPANSION

In the wars that erupted during the eighteenth century between England and France, Native Americans played a key role. Each side tried to win allies among them, and for almost a century there was a standoff; but in the Great War for Empire, 1754–1763, the English defeated the French and caused them to abandon North America. In the process the Native Americans who had previously been able to take advantage of the rivalry between England and France to suit their own interests abruptly lost their strategic position. It was not by chance that the English settlements, which for 150 years had failed to penetrate more than 200 miles into the interior of North America, suddenly were able to surge thousands of miles in a few decades after 1800 to reach the Pacific Ocean.

THE SEVENTEENTH CENTURY: AGE OF FAITH

In America's intellectual and religious life, as in its social structure the American environment modified English ideas and practices transplanted to the New World.

The late sixteenth and early seventeenth centuries in England were an Age of Faith, and the characteristics of this age were indelibly stamped upon the English colonies in America. The Protestant Reformation in Europe had unleashed a flood of ideas concerning the role of the church, qualifications for church membership, and the individual's relationship to God—particularly the degree of a person's freedom of will. Were individuals elected by God and thus saved from eternal damnation? Or could each person win salvation through individual faith and the exercise of free will? The English of the early seventeenth century were endlessly concerned with points of doctrine like these.

PURITANISM IN ENGLAND

When Henry VIII broke with the Roman Catholic Church and established the Church of England, specific church practice and doctrine were little altered; but within the Anglican Church, opposition groups, who became known as Puritans, gradually emerged. All Puritans agreed that to become a member of God's elect, an individual must undergo a "conversion experience," in which a spiritual rebirth was sensed. Most agreed that certain rituals within the church service should be changed. Puritans disagreed, however, on the question of church government.

One group, the Presbyterian Puritans, followed the precepts of John Calvin. They believed in a close church-state relationship in which policies would be established by the ruling hierarchy and, once adopted, would be enforced among the individual congregations. In addition, the Presbyterian Puritans believed that the church

John Calvin

should include the non-elect as well as the elect, since mortals were not capable of knowing with certainty whom God had elected for salvation.

Comprising a second group of Puritans were the Non-Conforming Congregationalists. They believed, first of all, that a church should be composed only of the elect and that such men and women could be identified. In their view the invisible church (God's elect) and the visible church (the church in daily operation) were one. The Non-Conforming Congregational Puritans held that individual congregations should rule themselves and that the individual congregation, not by a superior church hierarchy, should enforce church doctrine and practice. Both these groups of Puritans—the Presbyterians and the Congregationalists—were willing to remain within the Church of England and to carry out their reforms, their "religious revolution," within the structure of the established church.

Closely related to the Puritans—although less influential—were the Non-Conforming Congregational Separatists. As their name indicates, these people held many of the same views as the Non-Conforming Congregational Puritans. But the Separatists believed that reforming the Church of England was an impossible task, so they wished to separate from it. In the eyes of the king their views were particularly dangerous, because by following their religious inclinations they were in effect repudiating the king as head of the church.

PURITANISM IN AMERICA

In New England, a small, uninfluential group of Non-Conforming Separatists founded Plymouth, while Non-Conforming Congregational Puritans founded Massachusetts Bay and spread throughout New England. Puritanism was to have a dramatic career in England where the Presbyterian Puritans, at least for a time, gained control; but in

America Puritan ideas were transformed into a distinct social organization only in New England.

The Puritans there conceived of themselves as a covenanted people. In essence, the "covenant theology" held that God had made a contract with humans setting down the terms of salvation. God had pledged Himself to abide by these terms. This covenant in no way changed the doctrine that God elected the saints, but it explained why certain people were elected and others were not. Individuals knew that they were numbered among the elect by experiencing God's grace and reflecting this *regeneration*—spiritual rebirth—before their peers.

Because the terms of the covenant were to be found in the Bible, the Bible was the source of the rules of conduct and was constantly searched for meaning and interpretation. Because of the covenant, each law, each act, each policy demanded literal Biblical support. Believing in the vigorous use of reason, the Puritans supported the idea of a highly trained clergy and a literate laity. They firmly opposed all religious enthusiasms or any evidence of self-revelation (the doctrine that God revealed Himself directly to an individual). For this reason, both the Puritans and the Anglicans abhorred the Quakers. The notion of an "inner light"—which the Quakers claimed involved a mystical force and a direct communication between God and the individual—was offensive to the New England Puritans. They demonstrated their abhorrence when they hanged several Quakers who refused to leave Massachusetts Bay.

The New Englander Puritans turned to congregationalism as a form of church government. They attempted informally, however, to establish close ties among the individual congregations by means of synods, or assemblies of delegates, for discussion and decision on ecclesiastical affairs. Theoretically, each congregation could select its own course of action, but in practice a consensus of the Puritan leaders usually determined the course.

It would be a mistake to think that the Puritan clergy were all-powerful; indeed, civil authority enforced conformity to Puritan beliefs. Lay leaders like John Winthrop, not the leading ministers, were primarily responsible for the banishment of colonials who protested against the Puritan doctrines.

The premises of New England Puritanism affected every sphere of life—political, economic, cultural, social, and intellectual. For example, land was distributed to church congregations so that a social-religious community could be created and sustained. Settlements by towns enabled the Puritans to center their lives and activities around the church, and designated practice could easily be enforced. With the Puritans in political control, and thus able to determine those groups who were to receive land grants, the objective of creating a Bible Commonwealth could be achieved.

Because the Puritans firmly believed in a rational religion, they soon began to think about establishing a center of higher learning to continue the tradition of a learned ministry untainted by divergent strains of theology. The upshot was the founding of Harvard College in 1636. Town settlements made schools practical. In 1642 an act was passed which required every town of 50 or more householders to establish an "elementary school" to teach the fundamentals of reading and writing. Both boys and girls attended. An enactment of 1647 required each community of 100 householders or more to provide a "grammar school," a school to prepare students for college by means of vigorous instruction in the Greek and Latin classics.

New England Puritans expressed themselves in prose and poetry. Sometimes their tone was harsh, but it was always unmistakably clear. Sermons were cultivated as a literary form and were published by the press founded in Massachusetts Bay in 1639. This press became the voice of Puritanism in America. Its productivity was fabulous. Its output exceeded that of the presses of Cambridge and Oxford in England.

PURITAN THEOLOGY

Puritanism is representative of a religious and political movement to return society to a "better, vanished time," in this case, the time of the Christian Church in the days of the Acts of the Apostles. The Puritans viewed the first century as an uncorrupted golden age of Christianity that had become corrupted over the centuries, first by the Catholic Church and then the Anglican Church, complete with defiling and unnecessary traditions, rules, and decorations. Human history, in the Puritan view, was a history of religious (and, therefore, human) decline and increasing human depravity.

The Puritans were heavily influenced by John Calvin and believed Calvin's doctrine of predestination, which holds that before the creation of the world, God exercised his divine grace and chose a few human beings to receive eternal life. Only God, however, could know who the elect are, and nothing could change God's choice; however, if one were among the elect, one would be expected to act like it and the saintly behavior would be visible to all.

An obvious problem with the Puritan predestination doctrine, however, is that if one is predestined to eternal bliss, and nothing could change God's mind, why worry about sin? In another apparent contradiction with Calvin's predestination doctrine, the Puritans stressed the conversion of "those who could not find God's truth in their hearts." If the decision was predestined by God before the beginning of the world and has nothing to do with humans, why evangelize?

The Puritans rarely saw the contradictions in their religious logic. Even when they were forced to do so, they continued to believe that their position was sound because it came from God; and the Puritans were confident that they knew the truth from God in its entirety. Consequently, their logic was necessarily infallible—regardless of any problems that seemed to be obvious contradictions on the surface. Puritan logic was not a method of discovery or of learning the truths in science and nature. Instead, Puritan logic was a rhetorical means of communicating the logic received from God to others. Since the Puritans already knew the truth by the Divine Revelation of the Bible, there was little need for inductive reasoning.

Nevertheless, the Puritans viewed the salvation of themselves as well as the salvation of others within the Congregation as the concern of everyone in the Puritan community, and each Puritan was responsible for helping others achieve their spiritual goals. To further this purpose, the Puritans engaged in "Holy Watching," or moral surveillance of each other to ensure that they did not sin. Puritan houses were built in close proximity so that Puritans could hear their neighbors and know what they were doing. Curtains on the windows were forbidden so that one could see inside of the house of one's neighbor and ensure that no one inside was engaging in sin. The physical layout of the towns was such that houses faced inward toward their neighbors so as to allow Puritans to keep better watch on one another and guard against ungodly behavior.

PURITAN VIEW OF THE BIBLE

The Puritans viewed the Bible as a complete guide to societal organization. "God's laws," as outlined in their Holy Book, also should be civil laws. In the Puritan mindset, everything that occurred in their world was somehow analogous to some event in the Bible and, therefore, a reproduction of divine will. The fact that the Bible was "complete" meant that anything that could not be justified by a passage from somewhere in the Bible was forbidden. In the minds of the Puritans, they spoke when the Bible spoke and were silent when the Bible was silent. The Puritans were extremely legalistic in their approach to the Bible and paid great attention to Biblical details, so much so that they were often open to the criticism that they were paying more attention to the Biblical "trees" than to the forest. In the words of historian Kai Erikson,

> "The Scriptures not only supplied rules for the broader issues of church polity but for the tiniest details of everyday life as well, and many Puritans were fully capable of demanding that a clergyman remove some emblem from his vestments unless he could justify the extravagance by producing a warrant for it from the pages of the Bible."

PURITANS AND FREE THOUGHT

Like the seventeenth century Anglicans and the Catholics whom they disparaged with unrestrained zeal, the Puritans refused to tolerate those that thought differently than themselves in religious matters. Such heretics were, therefore, vigorously persecuted. The Puritans not only believed in the literal interpretation of the inerrant Bible but, also, believed that the teachings of the Bible were moral absolutes that transcended time and place. Furthermore, they believed that they had possessed the correct interpretation of the Bible to the exclusion of all other groups with whom they disagreed. As a consequence, if anyone offered a persuasive argument that shook the Puritans' certainty, or if someone developed a clever line of reasoning that could confuse the Puritan or cause him to question his beliefs, the Puritans suspected that Satan must somehow be involved. In order to prevent such confusion, settlement grants in the Puritan colony were granted only to groups of Puritans that signed a compact signifying the unity of their purpose. The compact stated that,

> "we shall live by all means, labor to keep off from us such as are contrary minded, and receive only such unto us as may be probably of one heart with us."

CHANGES IN THE NEW WORLD

During the seventeenth century, Puritanism in America was gradually modified by New World conditions. Modifications were made in theology, in church practice, and in everyday life. The changes were many, but for purposes of this text a single example—the adoption of the Half-Way Covenant in 1662—will suffice.

The church, you will recall, was presumably made up exclusively of the elect, the covenanted people. Children of the elect, however, sometimes failed to evidence "conversion" and, thereby to demonstrate the election that would qualify them for full membership within the church. As the body of church members became smaller in proportion to the total population, the clergy feared that the influence of the church in the community at large would be seriously undermined. By the terms of the Half-Way Covenant, therefore, the children of the elect who had not entered full membership in the church were nevertheless permitted to have their children baptized. Baptism enabled the children to participate in some, though not all, of the sacraments of the church. This opening wedge made an association with the church possible without proof of "election." It was gradually widened until a number of prominent ministers advocated opening the church to those who tried to live according to the precepts of the church even though they could not demonstrate election.

The New World environment affected other areas of Puritan intellectual life as well. The intellectual vigor of Harvard College declined. Its intellectual direction became, at least to old-line Puritans, "radical," which meant that it diverged from early Puritan precepts and intellectual rigor. The enforcement of the school acts lagged, and few intellectuals of late seventeenth-century New England could match the intellectual creativity of the first-line Puritans.

Making the terms of church membership easier was important outside intellectual and spiritual life as well. During most of the seventeenth century only male church members could vote in the colony-wide elections of Massachusetts Bay. A substantial majority of the population, therefore, failed to qualify for the franchise. Thus, broadened church membership had direct political effects. In 1691 a new charter made property ownership the basis for franchise and the Puritans lost outright control of Massachusetts. The Congregational Church as a social-religious institution, however, was a powerful influence in New England well into the nineteenth century.

THE TRANSPLANTED ANGLICANS

In the Age of Faith the Anglican Church was transplanted to Virginia, beginning with the first English colony at Jamestown. Jamestown's charter declared that the Anglican Church would be the official state religion of the colony and that bringing Christianity to the natives was the true purpose of the colony. John Smith, however, debunked this façade by stating, "it was absurd to cloak under the guise of religion the true intentions of profit." Smith added that what quickened the heart of most Chesapeake folk was a "close horse race, a bloody cock-fight, or a fine tobacco crop." The religion of Jamestown was officially Anglican, but the passion of the people was most certainly tobacco, which was not only the primary source of income but also smoked constantly by virtually all inhabitants. Still, most of the colonists of Jamestown were nominally Anglican, and attendance at Sunday services and conformity to Anglican doctrines were required of all Virginia colonists. The Anglicans officially did not allow religious dissent. Thus Baptists, Presbyterians, Catholics, Quakers, and other "heretics" were persecuted, whipped, fined, imprisoned, and forced to financially support the Anglican Church through a Church tax. Anglican Church Courts punished fornicators, blasphemers, and served notice on those who spent Sundays "goeing a fishing." Fines were imposed for fornication; and in 1662, a law was passed making the fine double if one were caught fornicating with a negro. The Anglican Church would remain the official state religion of Virginia until Thomas Jefferson's Virginia Statute on Religious Liberty separated church and state in Virginia in 1786.

From Virginia, the Anglican religion expanded into the Carolinas and Maryland, and, in the eighteenth century, to the Middle Colonies and New England. In contrast to Puritanism in America, Anglicanism did not center on formal theological inquiries and dogmas. The theological structure of Anglicanism was exclusively the product and concern of the clerical hierarchy within England, and a highly learned Anglican ministry did not migrate to America.

As a result, the influence of the New World environment is measured in terms of its modifications of church practice and church ceremonials rather than modification of doctrine. For example, while the Anglican Church in England was highly centralized and carefully supervised by its hierarchy, in America it became a decentralized church ruled by lay members. The clergy who migrated to America were almost impotent before the lay leaders.

The Anglican parishes in seventeenth-century America were much too large, and this, too, affected church practices. A minister could not readily serve a congregation when its membership was widely scattered. Lay leaders, therefore, began to read the services on the Sabbath, and they soon exercised a role in religious functions that violated the canons of the church.

Because people found it difficult to travel ten or twelve miles to church on horseback or by boat, attendance at services suffered. Moreover, because of the distances, weddings took place on a plantation rather than in church; and the dead were buried on the plantation in an unconsecrated family plot rather than in church ground—again a violation of church ordinances.

The absence of a guiding intellectual premise in the Chesapeake colonies dramatically affected education. The scattered nature of the settlements made community schools impractical. By the time the children arrived at the schoolhouse by horseback or boat, it would be time for them to return home. Consequently, responsibility for education was placed upon the family, not upon the community, and the finances and intellectual values of an individual family determined its response.

Obviously, in a plantation system that made public schools well nigh impossible, the Virginia gentry had a decided advantage over lesser folk. Occasionally, when enough plantations were close to each other, Old Field Schools were founded in which the children were taught by a minister or by the wife of a planter. More often a family or a group of families hired an indentured servant to teach the children. With no way of obtaining an advanced education in the colony, those planters who wished their children to receive a college education sent them to England.

THE EIGHTEENTH CENTURY MIND

THE ENLIGHTENMENT

During the seventeenth century, English intellectual life underwent a transformation triggered by the momentous advance of science and the application of the theoretical framework of science to all phases of human experience. The writings of the father of scientific reasoning, Francis Bacon, marked the beginning of a movement called the Enlightenment. This movement was consummated by the great scientific discoveries of Sir Isaac Newton, whose *Mathematical Principles of Natural Philosophy* (1697) set forth, by precise demonstration, the laws of motion and gravitation. Newton was to the eighteenth century what Einstein was to the twentieth.

The Enlightenment also affected religious thinking. Newton had used reasoning to discover laws in the physical universe. Many reasoned that laws must govern the relationship between the human race and the spiritual universe too. In this view, God was seen as the Prime Mover who had created the universe with a perfectly operating, harmonious system of unchangeable laws—the laws of nature. Once the universe had been created, so the reasoning went, God no

Sir Isaac Newton, 1642–1727

longer took an active part in ruling it; and the natural laws set the requirements for human behavior.

Fortunately, these laws could be discovered; and once they were known, people had only to adjust their lives and their political and educational systems accordingly—in conformity with the requirements set by natural law. The closer to alignment between human activity and the laws of nature, the closer human institutions would be to perfection.

In this view, people were perfectible and progress was inevitable. These ideas about God and the universe were called *deism*. They contrasted sharply with many of the basic tenets of Puritanism. The deists believed that there was a God or supreme being that created the Universe. They viewed him essentially as a "great watchmaker" who sets all of the laws of nature in motion, but does not intervene in human affairs. The deists did not accept Jesus of Nazareth as the "Son of God," instead viewing him as a "cynic sage" endowed with great wisdom. As for the human existence, the deists believed that life is what humans make of it and little, if anything, is left to fate or some Divine plan. Prominent deists included Ben Franklin, who described himself as a "thorough deist" in his autobiography, Thomas Paine, Ethan Allen, and perhaps Thomas Jefferson, though he stated, "I never told anyone my own religion."

In spite of the influence of deism on some prominent Americans, it should be emphasized that the ideas of the Enlightenment affected only a small minority of the English and far fewer colonials. Most people went about their daily lives unaware of intellectual trends. Enlightenment ideas did not gain strong advocates in America until the mid-eighteenth century, and even then their influence was sharply restricted. Whereas in England Enlightenment ideas permeated literature as well as political thought, in America they found expression chiefly in political thought. The Declaration of Independence appeals to the "laws of nature and nature's God."

The Enlightenment constituted only one current in the mainstream of intellectual life in eighteenth-century America. Whereas the English Age of Faith had dominated seventeenth-century colonial America, the widespread immigration of non-English groups brought a diversity of cultures. By the eighteenth century the colonies reflected what was to become a characteristic of the American mind—a wide diversity of intellectual streams.

THE GROWTH OF TOLERATION

Thomas Paine

The Toleration Act adopted by Parliament in 1689 gave sufferance to all Protestant sects in England. In America the background for toleration had been laid as early as 1636, when Roger Williams founded Rhode Island.

In a sense, Williams backed into the principle of religious toleration. He had found the Puritans of Massachusetts Bay imperfect in their religious fervor, and he consequently vowed to pray only with those he knew to be regenerate, spiritually reborn. Because he was unsure of other folk, he finally was forced to pray only with his wife. From this restricted, impractical position, Williams took the long step to religious toleration on the premise that since he could not determine precisely which persons were regenerate, he had no alternative but to extend toleration to everyone with religious convictions. Williams' ultimate attitude of toleration was well in advance of the mainstream both in England and in America.

The Maryland Toleration Act of 1649 lent impetus to the growth of toleration, though it arose not from broad humanitarian principles but from immediate circumstances. Protestants were heavily populating Maryland, established originally as a Catholic refuge. Not only had the Catholics become a minority but, because of the Puritan domination in England, they were seriously threatened by persecution. The Toleration Act, advocated by Lord Baltimore, was intended to protect the Catholic minority and to forestall action against Baltimore's proprietorship.

Toleration flourished in the eighteenth century, in part because of seventeenth-century precedents but, more important, because the realities of the eighteenth century made intolerance an anachronism. The migration of dissenter sects from Germany; the emergence of an inter-colonial Presbyterian church increasingly fortified by newly arrived Scots and Scotch-Irish; the spread of Anglicanism throughout the colonies; the migrations from Pennsylvania south to Georgia; the settlements of Jews in Rhode Island, Georgia, and other colonies; the application of the English Toleration Act in America—these developments made toleration a necessity. The diversity of religious faiths made any other course impossible.

Toleration for provincial America did not mean disruption of church-state establishments. Householders of all faiths were taxed, for example, to maintain the Anglican Church in Virginia and the Congregational Church in Massachusetts, although in each colony people could practice other faiths without undue molestation. The separation of church and state did not become a question of principle until during and after the American Revolution, when it was apparent that no single church was sufficiently strong to be elevated to the status of a national church.

THE RISE OF SECULARISM

Greater toleration, in turn, provided a climate in which *secularis*—a concern with worldly rather than religious matters—could grow. The people who migrated to America in the eighteenth century were primarily seeking opportunity, not religious toleration. If toleration had been their principal desire, the German Pietists could easily have migrated to Rhode Island—and at an earlier date. Choice Pennsylvania land, in combination with religious toleration, proved to be a superior attraction, however. Moreover the new generations of Americans who were native-born turned with avidity to enrichment and advancement. They were less concerned than their seventeenth-century forebears with the saving of souls.

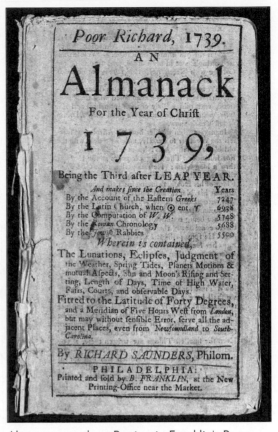

Almanacs, such as Benjamin Franklin's Poor Richard's Almanac, were best sellers in the eighteenth century.

Perhaps the best index of the rise of secularism is the production of the provincial press. In the eighteenth century, newspapers flourished. The first was published in Boston in 1704, and by the 1750s almost every colony had one newspaper and a number had several. In contrast to Michael Wigglesworth's *Day of Doom* of the seventeenth century, almanacs became the best sellers of the eighteenth century. *Poor Richard's Almanac*, which Benjamin Franklin edited in Philadelphia from 1732 to 1758, sold 10,000 copies a year and became the most popular reading matter in the colonies—except for the Bible.

The emergence of secularism can also be detected in the appearance of touring companies of English actors. Williamsburg had a theater in 1716. In the 1770s satirical patriotic plays by Mercy Otis Warren were published, as were the verses of Phillis Wheatley, who had been brought from Africa as a slave.

THE GREAT AWAKENING

The growth of toleration and the emergence of secularism should not obscure a third significant and persistent theme of eighteenth-century intellectual and social life. It was the Great Awakening, an evangelical religious movement—a series of revivals preached by stirring evangelists—that swept through colonial America and caused great excitement.

There are numerous reasons that the colonies experienced a religious "Awakening" in the eighteenth century, but one of them is certainly the changing demographics of the time. The sex imbalance between men and women in the Southern Colonies that had been so severe in the seventeenth century had largely disappeared by the mid-eighteenth century. Thus, the southern colonies, like those in the north, became societies based on the family unit rather than the young single male laborer and adventurer. The family-based society introduced numerous different social dynamics, but one of those was an increase in religiosity. Secondly, rural America at the time was an extremely "unchurched" society due to a shortage of trained clergymen from England and the difficulty of attending church from rural areas in the horse-drawn era. Most historians estimate church membership in the colonies at approximately 10 percent in the mid-eighteenth century. In Virginia in 1761, for instance, there were only 60 clergymen for a colony with a population of 350,000. Furthermore, churches were small, averaging only about 70 members. That being the case, it appears that less than two percent of Virginians in 1761 were attending church with any regularity. Thus, the colony was "primed" for a religious revival.

To compound matters, many of the colonial clergymen that made it to America were simply the worse that England had to offer. Drunkenness, brawling, and womanizing were unfortunately all too common among colonial clergymen. The clergymen were also trained in theological seminaries in England and often unable to connect with the common uneducated people of the American colonies.

The Great Awakening began in the Middle Colonies, and there were three main reasons that it was there that it had its beginnings. German migration, much of which went to the Middle Colonies, carried with it the Pietist movement from Europe. The rapid expansion characteristic of the Middle Colonies tended to overtax traditional religious institutions and thus to encourage the creation of new organizations and new forms for religious expression. Finally, a church-state relationship did not exist to thwart an evangelical movement.

In the 1730s the Great Awakening extended into New England where its fire-and-brimstone preachers drew large revivalist crowds in cities and towns. In the 1740s and 1750s the movement reached into the Southern colonies, carried along in part by the migration of the Scotch-Irish and Germans southward along the eastern edge of the Appalachians.

Among the noted preachers associated with the Great Awakening was Jonathan Edwards of the Northampton Church in Massachusetts. Often called the greatest theologian America has produced, Edwards used Enlightenment reasoning to construct a theological contradiction to Enlightenment ideas. Beginning in the 1720s, many New England ministers were influenced by a theology basing salvation on human moral effort as well as divine grace. Edwards opposed this tendency and reasserted the absolute justice of God's power to elect or to condemn as He chose, defending with exceptional skill the basic Calvinistic position that God was omnipotent and that, before God, humans were impotent.

Another gifted evangelist who lit the fires of religious revival in America was George Whitefield, a gifted Anglican who arrived and toured the American seaboard in 1739. Whitefield spoke to huge crowds, including a farewell sermon to 25,000 in Boston in 1740. Whitefield also successfully connected his religious message with the politics of his age, attacking wealthy merchants who were hated by the common people as "gripping and merciless usurers who heaped up vast estates" at the expense of the common people.

Two years later, evangelist James Davenport would take the political thesis even further. Upon his arrival in Boston, Davenport found every church closed to him; consequently, Davenport took his message to the street and probably reached more people with his message than he might have reached in the churches themselves.

Simultaneously, William Robinson began preaching tent revivals in the rural south. Robinson and other preachers (including Davenport) so stirred up the rural masses that the Virginia governor banned all traveling preachers in 1750. This only caused the circuit riders to have even greater resolve, and the "persecution" helped prove to the masses that the preachers were genuinely men of God sent to do the Lord's work.

Successful preachers stressed the conversion experience and often eschewed theological arguments in favor of playing on emotions. New Light tent revivals became replete with speaking in tongues, barking, jerking, uncontrollable dancing, falling, and slithering on the ground like snakes. In some instances, people crawled on the ground on all fours and dragged their tongues on the ground in displays of humility. Tent revivals could last for a weekend or an entire week and became immense social gatherings in the rural areas. Some revivals were also replete with drunkenness, and some argue that as many souls were conceived as were saved among those in attendance. Successful Enlightenment preachers in the Southern Colonies also tended to be uneducated ministers who were able to speak to the common people in their own language. Given that preaching in the Awakening South was not reserved only for those with theological training, but was open to anyone who felt the spirit, the number of preachers quickly and exponentially multiplied.

LASTING IMPACT, DIVISION, AND DISSENT

The Great Awakening caused divisions within existing church organizations. Church members attracted to the evangelical group were called "new lights," and they attempted to wrest control of the church from the conservative members who held power, the "old lights." The Awakening fervor also was responsible for the founding of four colleges by separate religious denominations: Dartmouth (Congregationalist), Princeton (Presbyterian), Brown (Baptist), and Rutgers (Dutch Reformed). The premise in each case was that the existing institutions of higher learning—Yale, for instance, which had been founded in 1701—were unsuitable for training acceptable "new light" ministers. The Awakening also altered the face of American religion so that the Methodists, who were only three percent of Americans in the mid-eighteenth century, were the largest denomination in America in the mid-nineteenth century. Baptists and Presbyterians also experienced exponential growth.

The Awakening, because it was an inter-colonial movement, strengthened inter-colonial ties. Many historians have advanced the idea that, by emphasizing the individual and his or her relationship to God, the Awakening aroused a democratic spirit that influenced the revolutionary generation. This generalization cannot be proved or disproved, but it seems fair to suggest that in reviewing traditional institutions—which in this case happened to be ecclesiastical institutions—the Awakening encouraged a climate of freedom. It also offered women the choice of whether to stay with an Old Light congregation or affiliate with the New Lights, no mean thing in a period when women lacked a political voice and married women were unable to control property, except under unusual circumstances.

As immigration increased in the early eighteenth century, and with it increasing religious diversity, the more established Puritans and Anglicans both opposed the new religious diversity and sectarianism as heresy, violations of God's will and contrary to Apostle Paul's (I Corinthians 14:40) admonition, "Let all things be done decently and in order." Puritans and Anglicans viewed the new sects as not only erroneous and heretical, but also exceedingly unruly and therefore unpleasing to God. In the words of Isaac Stiles, a Puritan clergyman, members of other religious sects were:

> "subversive of peace, discipline, and government, lay open the sluices, and make a gap to let in a flood of confusion and disorder, and very awfully portend the ruin of these churches. If sectarianism increased, Connecticut would soon be an habitation of dragons and a court for owls."

Anglicans, like the Puritans, tended to believe that their Church was the only one among English-speaking Protestant Churches founded on the principle of Apostolic succession; therefore, the Anglican church was the only one that was valid. To the Anglicans, ministers in other sects were not truly ordained, and other sects were a perversion of sound church doctrine, organization, and discipline that undermined civil society. For example, Lieutenant Governor Colden of New York essentially blamed land riots in the 1760s on trouble caused by "religious dissenters from the diverse sects."

Similarly, Anglican minister Jonathan Boucher described the sectarians as those referenced by Apostle Paul as "persons having itching ears and unstable in all their ways," who are "easily tossed about with every wind of doctrine." Boucher declared, "those who are not for the (Anglican) Church are against it," and viewed the dissenting sects as representative of revolts not only against the Church, but also against the state and society. Boucher argued for rigid enforcement of regulations and laws against dissenting sects and warned of the ultimate destruction of society if the sects were allowed to go unpunished.

Anglicans and Puritans, however, were also disdainful of each other, as well as the upstart sects. Anglicans were particularly appalled by the democratic leanings within the Puritan community that they viewed as an affront to the hierarchical structure of the Anglican Church. In the words of Anglican rector of Stratford in 1760, Samuel Johnson,

> "All the disadvantages it (Puritan Connecticut) labors under are owing to its wretched constitution, being little more than a mere democracy, and most of them upon a level, and each man thinking himself an able divine and politician; hence the prevalence of rigid enthusiasms and conceited notions and practices in religion, and republican and mobbish principles and practices, next door to anarchy, in polity."

Samuel Johnson

Johnson's sentiments were most certainly the dominant views of the Anglican Church hierarchy throughout the early colonial period; however, by the time of the American Revolution and the subsequent writing of the American Constitution, the Anglicans had come to recognize that suppression of dissent, no matter how distasteful, was no longer possible. Nevertheless, during the reign of King James II, the governors of all royal provinces had instructions,

> "to permit a liberty of conscience to all persons except Papists, so they be contented with a quiet and peaceable enjoyment of the same, not giving offense or scandal to the government."

Eventually, the diversity of the population produced from massive immigration would mean that laws punishing heretics and dissenters would be overturned and eliminated on a state-by-state basis between the end of the Seven Years War and the Jacksonian Era. Thomas Jefferson's famous Virginia Statute on Religious Liberty of 1786 declaring, "no one shall be compelled to contribute to any opinion with which he disagrees" became a model for other states to follow and its ideas gradually supplanted official intolerance as the norm.

The Anglican Church, in particular, had a special proclivity to oppose the movement toward freedom of conscience in the colonial period given that it was the established Church, not only in a number of the colonies, but in the mother country as well. Thus, for political reasons, specifically the motivation to retain their preferred positions both in England and in the colonies, as well as reasons theological and ideological, the Anglicans could be expected to resist religious tolerance. The resistance was futile in the long run, however, as the Awakening proved that religious diversity was unavoidable and that complete unity of religious thought was impossible. Furthermore, the Awakening enlarged the idea that ordinary persons could challenge the religious and political authorities, thus helping to lay the groundwork for the American Revolution that would arise on the tail of the Awakening.

THE ENLIGHTENMENT IN AMERICA

The greatest influence of the Enlightenment in America was the encouragement it gave to scientific inquiry. Cotton Mather, the most prominent New England clergyman in the late seventeenth and early eighteenth centuries, was attracted to scientific investigation. He was an advocate of smallpox inoculations when others greeted this medical advance with uncertainty or fear. William Byrd II of Virginia, along with other colonials, belonged to England's Royal Society and frequently sent observations of New World phenomena to his friends in England.

The contribution of most colonials was to that aspect of science called "natural history." Almost every botanical specimen collected in America constituted a contribution to knowledge because it added to the storehouse of scientific information. Carolus Linnaeus of Sweden, the foremost botanist in Europe, called John Bartram, who collected specimens throughout the provinces and cultivated rare species in his garden at Philadelphia, the finest contemporary "natural botanist". A celebrated work was Mark Catesby's extraordinary Natural History of Carolina.

Only Benjamin Franklin contributed to theoretical science, although many of his provincial contemporaries pursued allied investigations with vigor and persistence. Fortunately for Franklin, he entered a field of physics in which relatively little work had been done, and thus he was not handicapped by his lack of background, particularly his limited knowledge of mathematics. His identification of lightning as electricity (though it was his son William, not Ben, who dangerously flew the kite in the lightning storm) and his observations concerning the flow of electricity and the equalization that took place between highly charged particles and those less highly charged were contributions that won him a reputation throughout Europe.

Endowed with an active and inventive mind, as well as quick wit, Franklin famously invented bifocals, the lightning rod (which greatly reduced the incidents of barn fires in America), and the Franklin Stove, an invention that proved to be a much more energy-efficient way of burning wood than a brick fireplace.

Franklin is also representative of the fact that although science became increasingly important in the colleges, those outside the institutions of learning pursued it most fervently. As proper eighteenth-century generalists, they were interested in politics, science, writing, and other broad-gauged, stimulating activities. As the impact of science in colonial America makes clear, the Enlightenment, unlike Puritanism, was peculiarly the possession of the educated and social elite.

Yet in important ways Enlightenment ideas affected the whole people. For one thing, provincial America, because it represented a new, formative society, appeared in the eyes of some European and American observers to be the laboratory of the Enlightenment. American society, free from the incrustations of the centuries, could presumably adjust to the unchangeable laws of nature more readily than could that of Europe. Indeed, American intellectuals were confident that a perfect society was already being created.

In political thought and practice, too, provincial Americans regardless of status or location embraced many Enlightenment ideas. The right of citizens to challenge a governmental system when it stood athwart the laws of nature, and to replace such a government with one that conformed to nature's laws, were two assumptions of the Enlightenment that deeply penetrated the American mind.

COLONIAL ROOTS OF AMERICAN CULTURE

Colonial America made no great progress in the arts, nor could such manifestations of cultural life be expected of a people whose principal energies were devoted to creating a new civilization. Philadelphia stood as a cosmopolitan city, however, second in population only to London within the British Empire. The American cities in the aggregate, as well as the American countryside, provided a stimulating atmosphere that nourished people of intelligence, indeed of genius, whose contributions would endure beyond those of most of their cultivated counterparts in England.

The standard criteria for evaluating the level of intellectual life, therefore, do not apply to provincial America. What were important were its zest for learning, its new modes of society, its mobility, its ability to prosper and to set examples that in time would be imitated. The promise of the American "minds" fashioned from the experience of the seventeenth and eighteenth centuries formed

In addition to founding the first public library and first volunteer firefighting company, Benjamin Franklin founded two colleges, including Franklin and Marshall College shown here.

the foundation upon which American nationhood and an American culture were to be built.

Here Benjamin Franklin, born in New England but enjoying his prime in Philadelphia, can be seen as representing the best of colonial American culture A man of the Enlightenment, interested in all of the new ideas, he also devoted himself to bettering his adopted city and played a role in founding the first public library there, the first volunteer firefighting company, and two colleges, the University of Pennsylvania and Franklin and Marshall College. An early advocate of colonial unity, he would play a role second only to that of George Washington in the success of the American Revolution. To that epoch we now turn.

REVOLUTION AND INDEPENDENCE, 1763–1783

BACKGROUND OF THE REVOLUTION

Character of the Revolution
Early Provocations and Crises
The Constitutional Issue
Constitutional Confrontations
Problems of Defense and
  Western Lands
Ramifications of the Seven Years War
The Stamp Act
Reaction to the Stamp Act
The Townshend Duties
Liberty Incident
Boston Massacre

'TIS TIME TO PART

The Boston Tea Party and
  the Coercive Acts
Tea Act Crisis
The Provincials Act
Lexington and Concord
Momentum Toward the Declaration
The Declaration of Independence
The Internal Revolution
The Loyalists

PROSECUTING THE WAR

The Continental Congress
Revolutionary Finance
Military Strategy
Slavery and the Revolution
The War in the North
European Aid to the Americans
New Campaigns in the North
The War in the South

Battle of Yorktown
The War in Retrospect
The Peace of Paris, 1783
EFFECTS OF THE WAR

Unrestricted Trade
The Westward Movement
Modifications of American Society
The Articles of Confederation

BACKGROUND OF THE REVOLUTION

CHARACTER OF THE REVOLUTION

The American Revolution was the first revolution of modern times, and even more remarkably, it was founded on the principles of self-government and the protection of individual liberty. In this context, it became a beacon to light the way for peoples the world over.

The American Revolution was, in fact, many-sided. It was a War for Independence in which the colonies fought to be separated from the strongest nation in the world, Great Britain. It was a civil war in which Englishmen fought Englishmen and, occasionally, colonials fought colonials. It was part of a world war. It involved a struggle for power within each colony. In addition it was a nationalist movement in which the colonies, after separating from Britain, formed a lasting union—an important decision that Americans today take for granted but that was not necessarily predestined. Although the purpose of the Revolution was not to establish democracy any more than it was to establish a union, one of the results of the struggle within certain states was to give the average white male American a greater voice in government.

Finally, it should be remembered that the first revolt by colonials against the homeland in modern times—the American colonies against Britain—occurred under the most enlightened and least burdensome imperial system of contemporary Europe. The whites that lived in the English colonies enjoyed far more privileges in every sphere of life than did their counterparts in the French and Spanish colonies.

Why were the least restricted colonials the first to revolt? The American colonials had enjoyed what they thought of as their liberties for a century or more, and they had no intention of seeing these liberties restricted, even if, comparatively, they were better off than colonials elsewhere. Although the Revolution was not inevitable, any action to limit existing privileges automatically produced friction. How deep the friction was to become depended upon the course of events and the response to these events by American colonials and by the authorities in Britain.

EARLY PROVOCATIONS AND CRISES

The crises within the empire from 1763 to 1776 were provoked by a series of specific enactments, but to review the prelude to revolution in such narrow terms is to misconstrue the essential issues that were in dispute. An adjustment in the relationship between Britain and its

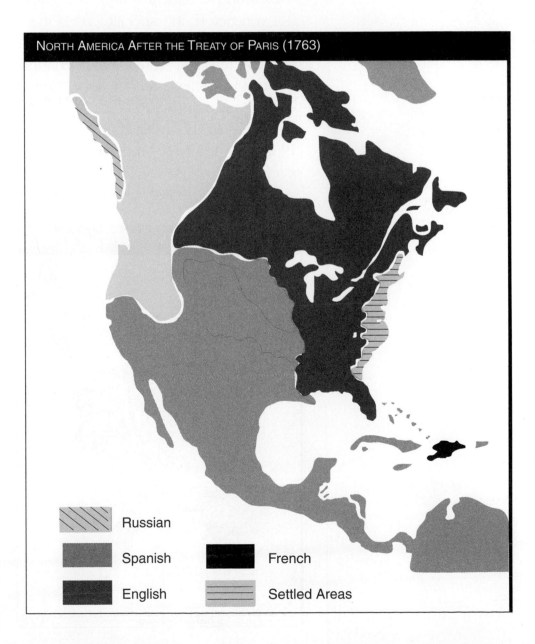

NORTH AMERICA AFTER THE TREATY OF PARIS (1763)

Russian

Spanish

English

French

Settled Areas

colonies was made inevitable by several sweeping changes that had been occurring during the eighteenth century.

The colonial and commercial systems of Britain had been established in the seventeenth century, based on the mercantilist theory—already several centuries old. That theory had seen colonies as important, primarily, for the wealth that could be extracted from them. During the course of the eighteenth century, colonies began to be important primarily for the role they played in British commerce. Moreover, when the system was inaugurated, England possessed only a few colonies. After the Peace of 1763, Britain had more than 30 colonies, each with its individual characteristics, scattered throughout the world. Did the policies initiated in the 1660s suit conditions in the colonies in the 1760s? Should the same system apply to India and Massachusetts?

Even before the specific crises that occurred between 1763 and 1776, the British-colonial relationships required adjustment to meet the new realities. Three major changes were clearly evident. The American colonies had matured. The political transition in England by which Parliament had steadily gained power at the expense of the crown required a redefinition of relationships within the empire. The colonies in the New World had become a critical factor in the European balance of power.

By 1760 the British colonies in America were no longer infants dependent solely upon the protection of the mother country. From limited self-government to mature self-government, from inexperience to experience with authority, from a primitive to a complex, well-developed indigenous economy—this had been the course of the American colonies. Any imperial system that failed to recognize these realities was doomed. As it existed, the imperial system had become, in some of its parts, an anachronism. The American provinces had become an insatiable mar-

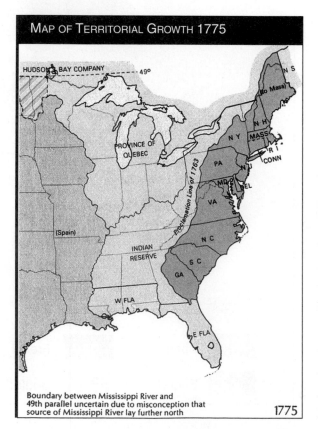

MAP OF TERRITORIAL GROWTH 1775

HUDSON'S BAY COMPANY — 49°

N S
(to Mass)
N H
PROVINCE OF QUEBEC
N Y
MASS
R I
CONN
PA
N J
MD
DEL
VA
Proclamation Line of 1763
(Spain)
INDIAN RESERVE
N C
S C
GA
W FLA
E FLA

Boundary between Mississippi River and 49th parallel uncertain due to misconception that source of Mississippi River lay further north

1775

ket for British goods, but the British system failed to adjust to this fact. The American colonies required a more enlightened money and banking policy, but the British tried to continue outworn theories. The American colonies produced statesmen, and even geniuses, but most American talent was unacknowledged.

The political transition in England required a rethinking of the constitutional structure of the empire. The colonies had been established under the auspices of royal charters. They had been administered through the king, the executive authority. As Parliament assumed greater authority, fundamental questions arose. Did Parliament have unlimited legislative supremacy over the colonies? Did Parliament gain the executive power previously exercised by the crown? The home authorities said yes; American colonials said no. Moreover, the Industrial Revolution of the eighteenth century in England introduced new problems with regard to mercantile theories—notably the importance of colonies as markets—that were never resolved.

During the eighteenth century the Spanish, French, and British colonies in the New World had become increasingly critical factors in the European balance of power. Beginning particularly with the Peace of Utrecht in 1713, the European powers attempted to establish equilibrium in that balance. It was clearly tipped in England's favor by the Peace of Paris in 1763, when Britain acquired New France in North America as well as French possessions elsewhere in the world.

These British acquisitions created uneasiness and uncertainty throughout Western Europe, and France began to explore avenues to redress the balance of power. Soon after 1763 the French recognized the possibility of doing so—not by recapturing its lost colonies or by capturing British colonies but by encouraging a separation between Britain and its colonies in America. This reasoning was responsible for French intervention in 1778 on behalf of the Americans.

Any one of these major changes in the eighteenth century—the maturation of the colonies, the political and economic transition in Britain, and the diplomatic evolution—was destined to produce problems in the relationship between England and the colonies. Together, they helped to produce a revolution.

THE CONSTITUTIONAL ISSUE

As mentioned previously, the British and the American colonials had differing concepts of the constitutional structure of the empire. The British assumed that the self-government practiced by the separate colonies was a favor granted by the mother country—a favor that could be enlarged, curtailed, or even eliminated. The ultimate authority rested in Britain. The colonies possessed no power except that granted by the home authorities. The colonials, on the other hand, held that self-government rested upon the consent of the governed (the colonial electorate), not upon royal grace and favor. The Americans believed they possessed rights (at first called the Rights of Englishmen and later called American Rights) that Britain could in no way curtail. Each colonial assembly viewed itself as struggling against a royal governor (and thus against the king), much like the House of Commons, in its struggle to gain power at the king's expense. During the Seven Years War, the colonial assemblies gained power in juxtaposition with the colonial governors as a result of their roles in extracting taxation from the colonists. Governors were unable to collect the necessary taxes without assistance from the colonial assemblies. The assemblies provided that assistance, but they extracted concessions of power from the governors in return for their role in revenue extraction.

The increase in the power of Parliament, along with the rising power of the colonial assemblies, posed an additional question: What were the limits to the legislative power of Parliament over the colonies? Conflict on this point was inevitable, and it became a critical issue in the revolutionary crisis that developed.

CONSTITUTIONAL CONFRONTATIONS

During the French and Indian War several British policies annoyed the American provincials. In 1759 the Privy Council instructed the governor of Virginia to refuse to sign any bill that failed to include a "suspending clause"—that is, a clause preventing the act from becoming effective until it had been approved by the home authorities. In 1761 general writs of assistance empowered officers of the British customs service to break into and search homes and stores for smuggled goods. This provoked strong opposition from the provincials, who claimed that the writs were contrary to law and to the natural rights of men. In that same year the Privy Council prohibited the issuance in New York and New Jersey of judicial commissions with unlimited tenure, specifying that such commissions must always be subject to revocation by the king, even though in England judges no longer held their posts at the king's pleasure. In 1764 the Currency Act extended to all colonies the restrictions on the issuance of paper money that previously had applied only to Massachusetts. All colonists would now have to pay British merchants in gold or silver, thus severely diminishing colonial buying power in an economy that was already in recession following the Seven Years War.

PROBLEMS OF DEFENSE AND WESTERN LANDS

The Peace of Paris of 1763 eliminated the French threat to English expansion on the North American continent and made available to English colonials opportunities in the West (West of the Appalachians, primarily the Ohio Valley) that had been denied them for a quarter of a century. However, the Peace of Paris raised problems with regard to the administration and distribution of this land. It also raised the issue of how to raise the necessary revenue to pay the cost of administering the empire. Most importantly, the Peace of Paris, by eliminating the French threat, made the American provincials bolder in stating their views since they no longer viewed themselves as in need of English protection against the French; and, once they had adopted a position, more tenacious in clinging to it.

Among the principal problems faced by the British was the settlement of the territory west of the Alleghenies. The issue was complicated by the revolt in 1763 of the western Native Americans under the leadership of Pontiac, chief of the Ottawa tribe. Farms and villages along the entire colonial frontier from Canada to Virginia were laid waste. The uprising was put down largely by British troops, but the problem of future defense assumed great importance. This incident, together with a previous policy of appointing a commander in chief for America, produced a major decision on the part of the British: to quarter 10,000 British regulars on the American mainland and in the West Indies.

However well intentioned, this action met with stern provincial opposition. Americans who had faced the French competition at close quarters for a century could not understand why British troops were needed now that the French menace had been eliminated. Ill will between the British redcoats and the colonials increased the tension, especially in New York (after 1765) and in Boston (after 1768) where the troops were stationed. Moreover, the colonials were not accustomed to the accepted British practice of expecting the people who were being "defended" to quarter the troops. The Quartering Act of 1765, which required New York colonials to house the soldiers and to make supplies available, was bitterly resented. The British did not actually intend for the colonists to quarter the British army in private homes. Instead, the British intended for the colonists to fund and build barracks for the British troops, and the threat of quartering the soldiers in private homes was to serve as a motivation for the colonists to build housing for the troops. Instead, the Quartering Act provided colonial revolutionaries with a symbol of British oppression.

The solution to the problem of western lands beyond the Appalachians was equally irritating. If the colonies in immediate proximity

Native American war art

to the western lands—like Pennsylvania, New York, Virginia, and the Carolinas—were permitted to extend their boundaries westward, colonies without a hinterland—Connecticut, Rhode Island, New Jersey, and Maryland, to name the most obvious—would be placed at a disadvantage. Should new colonies, therefore, be formed in the territory beyond the Appalachians?

The solution formulated by the British government was the Royal Proclamation Line of 1763, which established a line along the crest of the Alleghenies west of which colonials could not take up land. This policy of delay seemed sensible in London, but the colonials were impatient to take advantage of the new territory. Virginians had fought in the French and Indian War specifically to open this area to settlement. Not only were frontiersmen eager to exploit these opportunities, but also land companies in Pennsylvania, Virginia, and New England, whose membership included affluent colonials and Englishmen wished to act. For these men the Proclamation Line was a disappointment—an unexpected barrier to enterprise and opportunity.

The Proclamation Line, intended originally as a temporary measure to gain time for a permanent policy, was not revoked before the Revolution. Meanwhile, the Quebec Act of 1774 further annoyed the provincials by annexing the western lands north of the Ohio River to the Province of Quebec. The former French colony, viewed by the colonials as the enemy, was to be rewarded while the faithful

PROCLAMATION OF 1763

- - - - Proclamation line of 1763

colonists who had fought to free that territory from French control were denied the fruits of their sacrifices.

The problems of western lands and defense did not bring on the Revolution, but they caused a lingering grievance. When added to the other irritations of British rule, they decreased the probability of compromise and increased the chances of hostility.

RAMIFICATIONS OF THE SEVEN YEARS WAR

The Seven Years War not only effectively redrew the map of North America and eliminated France as a major colonial power in North America, it also had immense and lasting political and economic impact on the British colonies of North America. The war had produced an economic boom in the colonies as American merchants were awarded British military contracts to outfit the British military with ships, arms, uniforms, shoes, and food. When some 30,000 British troops departed from North America, however, an economic recession and unemployment followed as the war orders ceased.

During the war, colonial governments licensed American privateers (legally commissioned pirates) to attack and seize French shipping, often at great profits to the privateers. For example, John MacPherson in 1758 seized 18 French ships in privateering and purchased an estate near Philadelphia for £14,000. With the close of the war, this lucrative but dangerous business would cease. All colonists who served in the war, however, had not been so fortunate. For example, the 1764 census of Boston counted 3,612 adult females and only 2,941 adult males. War deaths created the sex imbalance, but the deaths also created poverty in New England due to a severe widow and orphan problem.

Finally, the Seven Years War left England with massive financial obligations. The British now controlled French Canada with its anti-English population, and forward placement of troops would be required to keep the newly acquired territory under control. Britain's new Prime Minister, George Grenville, also viewed the American colonies as unruly and believed that the stationing of troops in the American colonies was also necessary to keep the colonists in line. The forward placement of troops would be costly; England was already saddled with 145 million pounds in debt from the war. In order to service the debt and finance the forward placement of troops, Lord Grenville would propose new taxation both in England and the colonies. Without the threat of the French, the colonists would view the forward placement of troops, as well as the new taxation as unnecessary; and the contentment among the colonists with being British subjects, which appears to be widespread as late as 1762, would come to an abrupt end.

THE STAMP ACT

Prime Minister George Grenville was neither an imaginative nor a clever man, but he was a determined one. Coming into office just at the close of the French and Indian War and feeling, as most of his countrymen did, that the American colonists would be the greatest beneficiaries of the vast territory bordering the Ohio and Mississippi rivers that had been won from the French, he was determined that the colonists should pay at least part of the costs of defending and pacifying this territory. Currently no revenue was coming from the colonists to aid in imperial defense. Smugglers were evading duties imposed by the Molasses Act of 1733. In fact, the American customs service was costing more to operate than it was collecting in fees.

Thus, in 1764 Grenville led Parliament to adopt the Revenue Act or Sugar Act, an act intended to produce revenue—a purpose clearly stated in its preface—by enforcing the payment of customs duties on sugar, wine, coffee, silk, and other goods. The act declared that a number of colonial commodities could only be imported from England and required tighter control over ships' cargo. American shippers would have to post bonds guaranteeing observance of the Revenue Act before loading their cargoes. The act also strengthened the admiralty courts where the violators of British customs laws were prosecuted. Although the act reduced the duty on molasses bought from non-British sources from six pence to four pence per gallon, which on the surface was an attractive reduction, provincials actually had been smuggling in molasses for no more than a pence and a half per gallon as a bribe to customs officials. Now Grenville intended to enforce the trade laws by stricter administrative procedures. The crux of the issue, however, was the British intention to tax the colonists for purposes of revenue. Before this, duties had been imposed merely as a means of regulating the trade of the empire. The New York legislature protested that any tax by Parliament solely for the purpose of raising revenue, rather than to control trade, violated the rights of overseas English subjects who were taxed without representation in Parliament.

The issue of taxation, raised by the Sugar Act, was brought to a crisis in the Stamp Act of 1765, which provoked spontaneous opposition throughout the colonies. Grenville announced his intention to extend to

America stamp duties that he had already imposed in England. Grenville gave the colonies one year to propose an alternative way to raise the same amount of revenue. Instead of coming up with a plan, the colonists spent the next year denouncing the idea of the Stamp Act, and the year elapsed with the colonists offering no revenue-raising plan of their own. In November 1765, The Stamp Act went into effect, placing a stamp fee on all legal documents, deeds and diplomas, custom papers, and newspapers, liquor licenses, playing cards, and dice. It directly affected every articulate element in the community—including lawyers, merchants, preachers, and printers. Moreover, the act raised not only the question of who had the right to tax but also the more significant questions: Who had what power? Could Parliament legislate for the colonials in all matters? Was Parliament's authority without limit or were there bounds beyond which it could not reach—bounds based upon certain rights inherent in all Englishmen?

REACTION TO THE STAMP ACT

The conflict was contested on two levels, that of action and that of constitutional debate, and the massive American reaction to the Stamp Act shocked the British government. In every colony the men appointed as Stamp Act collectors were forced to resign, sometimes under the threat of force. Newspapers defied the act by printing skull and crossbones in the corner where the stamp belonged. Sons of Liberty were organized in key colonies to enforce the colonially imposed prohibition on the use of stamps.

Occasionally mob spirit carried opposition to extremes, as it did in Massachusetts when a band of provincials rioted in what is known as the Stamp Act Riot. On August 14, 1765, Bostonians hanged an effigy of Boston Stamp Distributor Andrew Oliver from a tree on the south end of town. That evening, a crowd of several thousand people paraded the effigy through town and held a mock trial before beheading and burning the effigy. The crowd then destroyed the new stamp

Newspapers defied the Stamp Act by printing a skull and crossbones in place of the stamp.

distribution office at the wharf. Stamp Distributor Oliver resigned the next day out of fear for his life; and twelve days later another angry mob ransacked the home of the lieutenant governor, Thomas Hutchinson, whom the Bostonians mistakenly believed to be in support of the Stamp Act. A reward of £300 was offered for the arrest and conviction of the riot organizers, but not a single person came forward with a lead. The courts and the ports, which could not operate legally without using the stamps, continued after a momentary lull to carry out their regular functions in defiance of the act.

Boston's riots sparked similar actions by other Sons of Liberty in almost 50 towns throughout the colonies, and stamp distributors resigned throughout the colonies. Each colonial legislature met to decide on a course of action, the most famous incident occurring in the Virginia House of Burgesses, where Patrick Henry introduced resolutions declaring that the "General Assembly of this Colony have the only and *sole exclusive* Right and Power to lay Taxes and Impositions upon the Inhabitants of This Colony." Any other course, said Henry, would tend "to destroy British as well as American Freedom." One of Henry's resolutions, which did not pass because the Virginia House of Burgesses feared it might be treasonous, declared it "illegal, unconstitutional, and unjust" for anybody outside of Virginia to tax Virginians. Henry also resolved that Virginians did not have to obey any externally imposed tax and labeled anyone who denied Virginia's exclusive right to tax as "an enemy of the colony." Though Henry's radical resolutions did not pass, they were widely circulated throughout the colonies creating a furor. Massachusetts's governor Francis Bernard termed the Virginia resolves as "an alarm bell for the disaffected."

At the invitation of Massachusetts, nine colonies sent delegates to New York in October 1765 to form the Stamp Act Congress, in which a set of resolutions was adopted denying the authority of Parliament to tax the colonials. A boycott of British goods—the use of economic coercion to achieve political ends—was introduced on the theory that the colonial market was so necessary to Britain that it would abandon the act to regain the market. It should be noted that scholars of women's history have argued that the use of the boycott following the Stamp Act began to bring women into the political process since consumer choices about what to buy have typically been part of women's domain. Moreover, in many instances, women were required to produce the goods no longer being purchased.

On the second level, that of defining constitutional theory, the respective arguments of the colonials and the authorities in England developed differently. Colonials argued that they could not be free without being secure in their property and that they could not be secure in their property if, without their consent, others could take it away by taxes. This argument revealed the close tie between property and liberty in the minds of the eighteenth-century Anglo-Americans.

The British responded by saying that the Americans were not being taxed without their consent because they were "virtually," if not directly, represented in Parliament. They argued that many areas in Britain—notably Manchester and other substantial communities—were not directly represented in Parliament; yet no one denied that an act of Parliament had authority over those communities. The same concept of "virtual representation," asserted the British leaders, applied to the colonies.

The colonies vigorously opposed this interpretation of representation. Most of the colonial legislatures echoed Maryland's argument "that it cannot, with any Truth or Propriety, be said, That the Freemen of this Province of Maryland are Represented in the British Parliament." Daniel Dulany, a Maryland attorney, in his *Considerations on the Propriety of Imposing Taxes in the British Colonies*, argued that even those people in Britain who did not have the right to vote were allied in interest with their contemporaries.

"But who," he asked, "are the Representatives of the Colonies?" Who could speak for them?

> The Right of Exemption from all Taxes without their consent, the Colonies claim as *British* Subjects. They derive this Right from the Common Law, which their Charters have declared and confirmed. ... A Right to impose an internal Tax on the Colonies, without their Consent *for the single Purpose of Revenue,* is denied; a Right to regulate their Trade without their Consent is admitted.

In brief, the colonists argued that Parliament had power, but not unlimited power. It could *legislate* and thus impose external duties to regulate trade, but it could not *levy a tax* for revenue. In time, as the revolutionary crisis deepened, the colonial position was modified to deny Parliament's authority to legislate for or tax the colonists for any purpose whatsoever.

George Mason of Virginia, who implicitly denied the indefinite subordination of the colonies, expressed a view much closer to the eventual stand taken by the colonists. "We rarely see anything from your [the English] side of the water free from the authoritative style of a master to a school boy: 'We have with infinite difficulty and fatigue got you excused this one time; pray be a good boy for the future, do what your papa and mama bid you.'" He warned the British "such another experiment as the stamp-act would produce a general revolt in America."

Parliament backed down—not on the principle at issue, but on the act itself. The Stamp Act was repealed in 1766. At the same time, however, the Declaratory Act was passed, stating that Parliament possessed the authority to make laws binding the American colonists. "in all cases whatsoever." The Americans mistakenly believed not only that their arguments were persuasive but also that the economic pressure brought on by the boycott of English goods had been effective. The boycott, in fact, only delayed British reaction; but the Americans, unaware of its failure, were to employ the boycott as a standard weapon against the British at each time of crisis.

THE TOWNSHEND DUTIES

The next major crisis arose in 1767. Misinformed by Benjamin Franklin, who in February 1766 had told the House of Commons that the provincials objected only to internal taxes, not to taxes on trade, the British Parliament in 1767 enacted the Townshend Duties on glass, lead, paper, paints, and tea. These import or "external" taxes were designed to exploit the distinction between internal taxes and external duties that Parliament mistakenly supposed the Americans were making. At the same time, Parliament reorganized the customs service by appointing a Board of Customs Commissioners to be located at Boston. The Townshend Act also designated that customs officials were to be paid directly from the duties collected (an incentive for customs officials to be diligent collectors).

The Massachusetts House of Representatives responded to the Townshend Acts by sending a circular letter written by Sam Adams, denouncing the Townshend duties to all the other colonies. Adams declared that the payment of customs officials from duties collected was unconstitutional. Parliament quickly demanded that Massa-

Sam Adams

chusetts rescind the circular; and when the Massachusetts Legislature refused, Parliament declared the legislature to be dissolved.

LIBERTY INCIDENT

Tension mounted in Boston in the summer of 1768 when customs officials seized the *Liberty*, a ship owned by John Hancock, for evading customs duties. An angry mob of Bostonians reacted by attacking the customs officials, who fled to the safety of a British warship in Boston Harbor.

In response, the British sent two regiments of troops to Boston, in part at least because of the urging of Customs Commissioners. By the time all the British troops were in place, there were 4,000 British soldiers in Boston, which only had a population of 16,000. Such numbers were perhaps a formula for disorder without any other accompanying political stimulants.

Though the Townshend Duties failed to awaken the spontaneous reaction of the Stamp Act, they tested once again the colonial versus British theory of the empire and posed anew the question: What were the limits to the power of Parliament? Again the American colonists resorted to a boycott although no inter-colonial congress was called. John Dickinson, in his *Letters from a Farmer in Pennsylvania*, reaffirmed the position of the colonials that duties, even "external" duties, could not be levied primarily to obtain revenue, though measures enacted to regulate trade were admitted as a proper prerogative of Parliament. Dickinson's essays were not revolutionary in tone or in spirit. Neither, however, did they back away from the fundamental position taken by the colonists—that they alone could levy a tax upon themselves.

As for the British, the Board of Customs Commissioners that came to enforce the Navigation Acts, the Sugar Act of 1764, and the Town-

John Hancock

shend Duties carried out its responsibility in such a perfidious way that the commissioners were properly accused of customs racketeering. The real significance of the Board, however, was the breadth of opposition it aroused. Not merely those colonists most vulnerable to its activity—particularly New England merchants—were disposed to stand against the British, but a consensus of opposition pervaded all the colonies, many of which experienced no serious problem with customs officials. This consensus was made possible because of the more profound issue: Where did the regulatory power of Parliament end and that of the colonials begin?

The Townshend Duties disappointed their advocates, for they did not produce the revenue expected due to colonial boycotts that caused imports of British goods to decline as much as 40 percent. In 1770, therefore, the British repealed the Townshend Duties (except the duty on tea, which was retained as a symbol of Parliament's right to tax). The Americans relaxed their opposition and reopened their ports to British goods, though they condemned tea drinking as unpatriotic.

BOSTON MASSACRE

Violence erupted, however, in February 1770 as colonists surrounded the house of Ebeneezer Richardson, a low-level British customs official. Richardson fired his gun into the crowd in an attempt to get them to disperse and accidentally killed a 17-year-old boy. Though the boy's death was an accident, some view it as the first death of the American Revolution. Violence would be greater the next month on March 5, 1770, when by coincidence the same day the Townshend Duties were repealed, the "Boston Massacre" took place. A small group of townspeople, described by the Boston lawyer John Adams as a "motley rabble of saucy boys, negroes, and mulattoes, Irish teagues and outlandish Jack Tars," shouted catcalls and insults and hurled snowballs and rocks at British troops on duty. The crowd referred to the British soldiers as "lobsterbacks" due to their red coats and referred to a British soldier as a "damned rascally scoundrel lobster son of a bitch." A scuffle erupted, and the redcoats opened fire, killing five persons and wounding six more. Among the slain was Crispus Attucks, an escaped slave who, according to one witness, had led the charge against the redcoats.

Acting governor Thomas Hutchinson ordered the removal of British regiments in Boston to an island in the harbor so as to prevent further bloodshed. Hutchinson then jailed the eight British soldiers until they could stand trial. John Adams and Josiah Quincy

The March 5, 1770, massacre between British soldiers and the citizens of Boston.

defended the British soldiers in court. Adams defended the British soldiers so as to show that even unpopular suspects in America could receive a fair trial. All but two of the British soldiers were acquitted; and the remaining two were convicted of manslaughter, but given the "benefit of clergy" and branded on their thumbs as punishment.

Following the trial, a form of informal truce developed between the colonists and the British. Imports of British goods again increased, and the American boycotts essentially collapsed. The colonists continued to boycott tea since the British had symbolically retained the small Townshend duty on tea; but it appeared at the end of 1771 that revolt might be averted after all.

'TIS TIME TO PART

THE BOSTON TEA PARTY AND THE COERCIVE ACTS

Beginning in 1772, the informal truce collapsed and new unrest erupted. In June 1772, a British patrol boat, the Gaspee, ran aground in Narragansett Bay south of Providence. The Gaspee's commander, Lieutenant Dudingston, was detested by the colonists for what they viewed as overzealous prosecution of smugglers and illegally seizing ships' cargo. Colonists, therefore, seized the opportunity for revenge and burned the Gaspee to the water level as it sat helpless in Narragansett Bay. To make matters worse, the colonists arrested Lieutenant Dudingston and convicted him of illegally seizing what he believed was smuggled rum and sugar. The British attempted to try the colonial culprits for the arson, but no witnesses to the events could be found.

Shortly thereafter, Governor Thomas Hutchinson announced that the British Crown, rather than the local legislature, would now pay the governor and colonial judges. The colonists viewed the action as an attempt by the British to bias the courts and government against them. In reaction, a Committee of Correspondence was established in Massachusetts at the urging of Sam Adams, John Adams' radical cousin. By the end of 1772, 80 Massachusetts towns had such committees and all but three of the other colonies followed the Massachusetts pattern and by the end of 1773 formed such committees in order to keep one another informed of possible British action.

TEA ACT CRISIS

In 1773 and 1774, with the Boston Tea party and the passage of the Coercive Acts, the conflict between Great Britain and its colonies entered a new and conclusive phase. In the early 1770s, colonists had been drinking moderate amounts of English tea (from India) and paying moderate duties on the tea without major objections; but they were also smuggling large quantities of Dutch tea, thus cutting into the tea sales of Britain's East India Company and also cutting into the British government revenues gained by taxes on tea. With the Tea Act of May 1773 the British government permitted the British East India Company, which had built up an excess stock of tea in England (an estimated 17 million pounds in English warehouses), to market— "dump" would perhaps be a better term—it in America. The East India Company's overstock had been caused partially by colonial boycotts and partially by competition from Dutch tea smuggled into the colonies. Normally, the East India Company sold its tea to British wholesalers who in turn sold to American wholesalers who then distributed the tea to local colonial merchants for sale to the public. By eliminating English middlemen and British import taxes, the Tea Act would allow the colonists to purchase less expensive tea and the East India Company could undersell smuggled Dutch tea. The British government would get modest revenue from the small Townshend duty that remained on tea and the East India Company would be saved from bankruptcy. The company was also authorized to employ its own agents in this transaction, rather than go through public auction to the independent wholesalers and thus cut out the middlemen, in effect, to seize monopolistic control of the American market.

With this act the British reawakened the latent hostility of the American colonists. Some Americans objected to what they viewed as a British attempt to control American trade. Colonial merchants denounced the "monopoly" given to the East India Company and predicted that other monopolies would follow and colonial middlemen of all types would be eliminated. Others viewed the Tea Act as a British plot to induce Americans into buying more duties tea. Many colonists believed that the real goal of the act was to increase British revenue, which in turn would be used to pay royal governors and judges. The Tea Act was, therefore, viewed by many as an insidious example of Parliament's claim to the power to tax and legislate for the colonies "in all cases whatsoever," a principle that many colonists rejected. When Americans drank the tea, they would also be "swallowing" the British right to tax Americans and control their trade.

Before any of the East India Company's tea arrived in Boston, the Sons of Liberty had already pressured British tea agents to resign and vowed that the "obnoxious" tea would be stopped at the water's edge. When the ships carrying the tea arrived, they were met with unbroken opposition. In some ports, the ships were forced to return to England without unloading; in other cases the tea was placed in a warehouse to prevent its distribution. In Boston, 5,000 persons gathered at the Old South Church on December 16, 1773. The colonists resolved that the Governor, Thomas Hutchinson, clear the ships for a return to England, but the Governor refused. At nightfall, a band of 100 to 150 colonists, haphazardly disguised as Native Americans, dumped the 342 chests of tea valued at 11,000 pounds (approximately one million dollars in 2008) into the harbor.

The reaction in England was prompt and decisive: The prevailing mood in Parliament was that punitive legislation must be passed

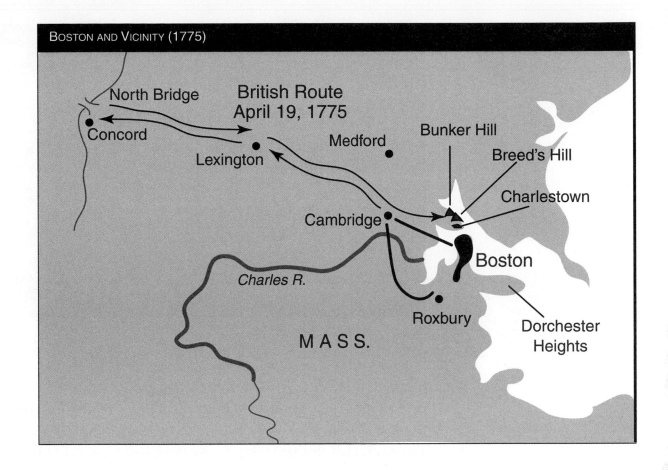

BOSTON AND VICINITY (1775)

to teach those property-destroying Massachusetts provincials a lesson. Even members of Parliament previously well disposed to the Americans endorsed this position. In quick succession, three Coercive or Acts (denounced as "Intolerable Acts by the colonists) were passed: the Boston Port Act (March 31, 1774), which closed that port to commerce until the colonists paid for all of the destroyed tea; the Massachusetts Government Act (May 30, 1774), which altered the manner of choosing the Governor's Council from election by the lower house to appointment by the governor, authorized the governor to prohibit all but annual town meetings, installed General Thomas Gage as governor of Massachusetts, and—more significantly—indicated to the Americans that parliamentary power knew no limits; and finally, the Administration of Justice Act (May 30, 1774), which removed certain cases involving crown officials from the jurisdiction of Massachusetts courts. British officials were declared immune from local court trials for acts committed while suppressing civil disturbances in the colonies.

The other colonies immediately rallied to the support of Massachusetts in opposing these "Intolerable Acts"—much to the surprise

Boston Tea Party, December 16, 1773

of the British authorities, who had expected the support rather than the condemnation of the colonies outside Massachusetts. After all, had not property been destroyed? No action on the part of the Americans revealed the basic issue so clearly. Essentially, the issue was not customs racketeering, or the presence of redcoats, or the problem of western lands, or even taxes. The issue was: Who had what power?

The Coercive Acts set in motion a series of actions and counteractions that led directly to separation. If there was any one point at which the Revolution seemed to become inevitable it was in 1774, with the passage of the Coercive Acts and the colonial response to those acts. The colonists asked themselves, What would Parliament do next? Change the administration of justice in Virginia? Eliminate self-government in New York? Close the port of Philadelphia? Once the supremacy of Parliament in all areas was conceded, self-government would live merely on sufferance.

The colonials at this stage were not calling for independence. Such a step was too frightening. The Americans had lived within the British Empire for more than a century. It was the most enlightened government of its time, where liberty was a word that meant something. Separating from Britain in the 1770s was somewhat similar to abruptly changing today the form of government under which we have lived since 1789. It was not a step to be taken, as the revolutionary fathers later declared in the Declaration of Independence, for light and transient causes.

THE PROVINCIALS ACT

Events proceeded once again on two levels—that of action and that of theory. The First Continental Congress was called to meet in Philadelphia in September 1774. A number of important decisions made early in the deliberations set the tone of the meeting. Carpenters Hall, instead of the legislative chambers of Pennsylvania, was selected as the meeting hall—a victory for Sam Adams of Massachusetts and those who wished to take firm action against Britain. A more important show of strength came when resolutions proposing a union of colonies were offered, resolutions regarded as conciliatory. They were tabled by a close vote; and the Suffolk Resolves were adopted, asserting that the colonies should make no concessions until Britain first repealed the Coercive Acts. The burden of conciliation was thus upon the home authorities.

In addition, the First Continental Congress adopted a series of resolutions embodying its position and sent them off to the king. The colonists claimed that they were not represented in Parliament and claimed that each colonial government had the exclusive right to legislate and tax for its own people. The colonists acquiesced to British trade regulations so long as the regulations were not covert forms of raising revenue. At the same time a Continental Association was established to cut off trade with the British. Although Congress avowed its "allegiance to his majesty" and its "affection for our fellow subjects" in Great Britain, the stand it took placed Britain on notice.

LEXINGTON AND CONCORD

When the First Continental Congress adjourned, its members agreed to meet again in the spring of 1775 if no action was forthcoming from Britain. Conditions failed to improve; in fact, they became worse. In Massachusetts "minutemen" were training to guard against possible actions by British redcoats stationed in Boston.

The raising of the first flag at Independence Hall in Philadelphia

Guns, powder, and other military stores were being collected at Concord. On April 14, 1775, British military governor General Thomas Gage received his orders to arrest the "aiders and abettors of the rebellion."

On April 18, 1775, Gage sent out from Boston about 700 British regulars to destroy the stores at Concord. Paul Revere and William Dawes mounted their horses and rode out to warn the minutemen of the British advance. When the British reached Lexington, they were met by minutemen. The British demanded that the colonists lay down their weapons and disperse, but someone—no one knows who—fired; and in the next two minutes more of both Americans and British fired their weapons. By the time the firing stopped, the Americans dispersed, but eight Americans were killed and 10 were wounded. The first shots of the Revolution, termed by the Americans as the "shots heard round the world," had been fired. The British then continued their march toward Concord, some 15 miles west of Lexington while colonists gathered to defend Concord. When the British arrived at Concord, they were unable to find the bulk of the American ammunition because the Americans had quickly removed most of it; but the British burned what little they did find. The British were engaged by the minutemen at Concord's Old North Bridge, where two Americans and three British soldiers were killed. The British retreated to Boston; but the colonists, hiding in the trees, attacked them along the way.

The battle at Lexington, Massachusetts

General George Washington and the Continental Army

Before their day was spent, the British had suffered nearly 300 casualties and had escaped total destruction only because reinforcements came from Boston. Dogging the regulars all the way, the minutemen encamped on the land approaches to Boston and began a siege. The colonial effort had not come without a cost, however, as 95 Americans were killed by the time the British reached Boston and the American Revolution had begun.

When the Second Continental Congress met in May 1775, the thin line between peace and war was in danger of vanishing. Congress appointed a Virginian, George Washington, commander in chief of the provincial forces surrounding Boston. His nomination by John Adams, a Massachusetts man, revealed the determined effort of the Americans to present a united front. Congress also authorized the outfitting of a navy under the command of Commodore Esek Hopkins of Rhode Island. In order to finance the war effort, Congress authorized a paper currency issue of $2 million. Congress tried to win Canada to its cause but failed.

Meanwhile, on May 10, New England forces led by Benedict Arnold and Ethan Allen captured Fort Ticonderoga on Lake Champlain. Subsequently, they moved northward to seize points along the Canadian border. In June, colonists seized Breed's Hill and Bunker Hill in Boston with the intention of shelling the British positions on the peninsula of Boston. The colonists set up defenses on Breed's Hill, and General William Howe and 2,500 British troops assaulted the hill on June 17, 1775 to drive them off. In what the colonists referred to as the battle of Bunker Hill (though it was actually fought on Breed's Hill), the colonists twice turned the British back before the British were able to take the hill when the colonists ran out of ammunition. It was for this reason that the famous order, "don't fire until you see the whites of their eyes" was issued, as the colonists, short on ammunition, needed to make sure that every shot counted. The battle lasted only two hours, but the British suffered 1,000 casualties and the Americans 400. Though the British accomplished their objective, the battle proved to the colonists that they were capable of taking on the British army. In the words of British General Henry Clinton, "It was a dear bought victory; another such would have ruined us." The heavy casualties on both sides also reduced any chance for a negotiated settlement, and the spilling of so much blood only caused each side to become more determined to force the other to submit militarily. General Howe perhaps erred in failing to pursue the Americans as they fled Bunker Hill. If Howe had pushed westward after the battle, many military historians suggest that he might have decisively defeated the Continental Army. Instead, Howe held his army in Boston and abandoned the town without a fight nine months later.

In July of 1775 Congress adopted the "Declaration of the Causes and Necessity of taking up Arms," in essence, a declaration of war, in an attempt to assure fellow Britons that dissolution of the union was not intended, but that neither would Americans back away from their convictions. "Our cause is just. Our union is perfect. Our internal resources are great, and, if necessary, foreign assistance is undoubtedly attainable." The "Declaration" stated that the British government had left the American people with only two alternatives: "unconditional submission to the tyranny of irritated ministers or resistance by force." Congress simultaneously pursued war and peace, however, as they also drafted and sent to the king an "Olive Branch Petition" that humbly begged the king to remove obstacles to reconciliation. Congress also moved to secure the neutrality of the Native American tribes, erected a post office, and approved plans for a military hospital.

In August 1775 the king declared that his subjects were in rebellion, effectively rejecting the Olive Branch Petition, and began to recruit foreign mercenaries and prepare the British regulars. Twenty thousand British troops were sent to the colonies to quell the rebellion. Parliament also passed the "Prohibitory Act," which closed the colonies to all overseas trade and made no concessions to American demands. The British enforced the Prohibitory Act with a naval blockade of colonial ports.

During the remainder of 1775 the Americans under Benedict Arnold and Richard Montgomery attempted the conquest of Canada, chiefly in order to deprive Britain of a base of attack before British reinforcements could arrive. After capturing Montreal, Montgomery pushed northeastward to Quebec while Arnold pushed north to Quebec from the territory of Maine. Arnold's contingent was decimated by smallpox and freezing rain, and more colonists died in the campaign from disease than from battle with the British. Nevertheless, Arnold and the colonists heroically reached Quebec and jointly attacked the British with Montgomery; but the American attack was repulsed, and the Americans were forced to withdraw.

MOMENTUM TOWARD THE DECLARATION

Beginning in January 1776 the movement for independence gained ground. On January 1, 1776, the British gave the Americans a military shove by shelling Norfolk, Virginia. Thomas Paine published his *Common Sense*, asserting "tis time to part." To this point, few Americans had questioned the legitimacy of the king. In this pamphlet, however, Paine condemned the monarchy as a form of government in bold language, stating that "nature disapproves it; otherwise she would not so frequently turn it to ridicule by giving mankind an ass for a lion." Paine not only denounced the monarchy in general, but also King George in particular, referring to him as a "Royal Brute" and the "hardened sullen-tempered Pharaoh of England." To replace the monarchy, Paine advocated republican government based on the consent of the people. Appreciatively read by thousands upon thousands, *Common Sense* helped to crystallize opinion. The denunciation of the king as an "ass" helped to break down the traditional British deference that most Americans still had for the monarchy. The British also gave the independence movement a boost when news that the British were using Hessian mercenaries reached the colonies. The use of mercenaries, who had a reputation for rape and pillage, was considered ungentlemanly and an improper thing for the British to do in a dispute with their American brothers. By late spring a number of colonies instructed their delegates to the Continental Congress to advocate independence.

On June 7, 1776, Richard Henry Lee of Virginia, once again reflecting the unity of the colonials regardless of region, introduced a resolution calling for independence. Thomas Jefferson was appointed chair of a committee to draft the document that was presented to Congress on June 28. Congress debated the document on July 1. Though many delegates were apprehensive, it was adopted on July 2 by a unanimous vote with twelve colonies voting for independence and New York abstaining so that the vote could be unanimous. On July 4, 1776, the document went to the printer and became public knowledge.

THE DECLARATION OF INDEPENDENCE

Action and theory were moving together. In 1774 James Wilson, later a Supreme Court justice, had published Considerations on the Authority of Parliament, which posed a series of questions: "And have those, whom we have hitherto been accustomed to consider as our fellow-subjects, an absolute and unlimited power over us? Have they a natural right to make laws, by which we may be deprived of our properties, of our liberties, of our lives? By what title do they claim to be our masters? ... Do those, who embark freemen in Great Britain, disembark slaves in America?" Wilson answered by affirming, without qualification, that Parliament had no authority over the colonies. Their dependence upon Britain was exclusively through the crown. The colonies were "different members of the British Empire ..., independent of each other, but connected together under the same sovereign."

Wilson's assumption underlay the philosophy of the Declaration of Independence. The colonists directed the entire document against the king. Nowhere is Parliament mentioned.

The Continental Congress could have separated from Britain by means of a simple declarative resolution. An elaborate document to explain the reason for revolution was unnecessary. That such a document was written is in itself an insight into the nature of the Revolution, for it did not feature tattered flags, starved and desperate people, or lawlessness. Its leadership included some of the most substantial and prominent individuals in America. Because of their influential position and their regard for law, they and their associates felt a deep need to explain to a "candid world" why they took such a drastic step.

Five delegates of the Continental Congress, among them John Adams and Benjamin Franklin, were assigned the task of writing the Declaration, but the draft was composed primarily by Thomas Jefferson of Virginia. The members of the committee made modest changes, and the document was then debated in Congress where more changes were made.

The philosophy upon which the Declaration was based was that which underlay treatises written by John Locke on the occasion of the English Glorious Revolution of 1688. The similarity in ideas and even in phraseology is striking. The Declaration appealed to the highest authority within the intellectual structure of the eighteenth century, "the Laws of Nature and Nature's God." It asserted that all men are created equal, that each person is endowed with certain rights that cannot be set aside, that included among these rights are "life, liberty, and the pursuit of happiness."

What this felicitous phrase meant was to be defined more carefully later in state and national constitutions. But the Declaration reaffirmed what Americans in their experience had long practiced: that governments, based upon the consent of the governed, are established to secure these rights; and if governments become destructive to these rights, they should be abolished. The king, the symbol of the British government, had failed to honor his obligation to protect rights and instead had become destructive to them; thus, the king's government should be abolished.

The Declaration included a list of specific charges that add up to a devastating indictment, too often treated by historians as an excuse or a rationalization for an act already taken. The list of grievances was meant to show that the Declaration was not based on transient causes, but rather upon a long pattern of abuse. With the acceptance of the Declaration by the Continental Congress, the British view that the rights of the colonies depended on the sufferance of the royal grace and favor was forever demolished. Ben Franklin added some gallows humor that reflected the grave nature of the situation by stating

The Declaration of Independence

to John Hancock, "we must all hang together, or surely we will all hang separately" when signing the Declaration of Independence.

With the Declaration, the character of the conflict changed too. Whereas the colonials had been secretly soliciting aid from France since 1775, the Continental Congress, representing an independent people, now established ministries throughout Europe to obtain recognition and help for the independent colonies, soon to become the United States. Washington, who had been leading a militia force to obtain recognition of the rights of colonials, now headed an army fighting for American independence. Thirteen colonies became thirteen states with the problem of working out appropriate constitutions.

Facing the experience of union, the Americans also had to work out an acceptable constitutional structure for the national government. With the Declaration, the Continental Congress was no longer an extralegal body of rebels but the symbol of a sovereign nation.

THE INTERNAL REVOLUTION

Emphasis has been placed on the principal issue—what were the limits of the power of Parliament? But historians have investigated a second question: Within each colony, who was to possess authority? Their point of view has ranged widely on this question. Some have insisted that the issue of who was going to rule at home was preemi-

The signing the Declaration of Independence

nent, that the break with Britain was brought about by radical dissenters within each colony who were so anxious to overthrow the power structure in their colony that they worked for revolution to accomplish this purpose. Other historians contend that those who held power in the late colonial period were willing to fight to maintain it. This argument is fueled by the undisputed fact that in many colonies, the number of people living in poverty was on the increase in the years before the Revolution.

The present consensus among historians is perhaps best expressed as follows: Conflicts within individual colonies contributed to the coming of the Revolution because some people hoped to correct grievances under a new regime. However, this internal struggle for control was not the decisive or preeminent force. The principal issue was the conflict over the constitutional framework of the empire. Even without an internal struggle, the Revolution would have occurred. The internal grievances were related, however, to later developments in the revolutionary and post-revolutionary periods as Americans set about to resolve their own problems. Between the explosive potential for human freedom contained in the words of the Declaration and the heady release of democratic fervor in the early days of the new nation, those developments would be transformative.

THE LOYALISTS

The Declaration of Independence was a divisive rather than a unifying document, and it had an impact upon every colony, county, and town and almost every family. With its adoption, people had a decision to make: Would they remain loyal to Britain and its government? Or would they join those who advocated independence and be called rebels?

Regardless of their political views or associations, the present generation of Americans claims the American Revolution as their rightful heritage and, consequently, regards this decision as a foregone conclusion. The literal "patriots" of 1776 were those who upheld the existing British government: The word *patriotism* derives from *patrios*, meaning "established by forefathers."

In discussing the division between those who supported separation from Britain and those who opposed it, historians have customarily used rather gross figures, holding that one third of the revolutionary generation remained loyal to Britain, one third remained uncommitted, and one third supported independence. Closer examination reveals that the percentage varied substantially among colonies as well as among localities within colonies.

The best recent figures indicate that 20 percent, about 500,000, of the white population became Loyalists. As many as 100,000 persons altogether left the colonies for Canada, England, the West Indies, and other places of exile. Historian Robert R. Palmer has calculated that 24 persons per thousand of the population left the colonies compared with five persons per thousand of the population of France during the French Revolution, a startling fact that raises the issue of Loyalists to a new level of importance.

These divisions were reflected among families and friends. Gouverneur Morris of New York took up the cause of independence. His mother and many other members of his family remained loyal to Britain. Benjamin Franklin's son William, who was governor of New Jersey, became a Loyalist, causing Franklin to write that his son caused him more personal grief by this act than he had experienced in a lifetime. Close friends and trading associates Thomas Willing and Robert Morris of Philadelphia took opposite sides: Willing remained a supporter of the crown, while Morris became a principal leader of the Revolution.

Some of the most distinguished and honored leaders in these and other provinces left. Daniel Dulaney of Maryland, who wrote so convincingly about the evils of the Stamp Act, could not bring himself to accept independence. Neither could Joseph Galloway, Speaker of the House in Pennsylvania. Chief Justice William Smith of New York finally decided to migrate to Canada after refusing to take a loyalty oath to the revolutionary government in New York.

To list these names tends to imply that only the upper social strata became Loyalists, but the total of 500,000—a full 20 percent of the population—demonstrates that people from every social class became Loyalists. Slaves left plantations to follow the British in the hope of gaining freedom, but servants and artisans also sought the protection of the British government and army.

During the course of the War for Indepen-

Spirit of '76 fife and drum

dence, it is estimated that as many as 30,000 Loyalists served in the British army. In 1780 alone as many as 8,000 Loyalists served in the British forces. Washington's forces at that time numbered no more than 9,000.

What is more difficult to ascertain is the number of Loyalists who remained in the colonies, trying not to offend the supporters of the Revolution but assisting the British troops when they came. The colonies of Georgia, New York, and South Carolina were the staunchest Loyalist strongholds, followed by New Jersey and Massachusetts. Indeed, the British planned military campaigns in these provinces in the expectation that Loyalists would flock to their standard. The decision to concentrate on New York in 1776 and again in 1777 was based, at least in part, on this assumption. The decision in 1779–1780 to redirect the military effort to Georgia and South Carolina was also prompted by the expectation of winning support throughout the countryside.

Gouverneur Robert Morris

Loyalists who did not wish to speak out had good reason to retain a low profile. To leave was to abandon their homes and land, for few Loyalists were able to convert their possessions into cash. Revolutionary governments confiscated Loyalists' property to be resold to the highest bidders. For this and many other reasons, few Loyalists, with the critical exception of those who migrated to Canada, left an imprint upon their adopted homelands.

Those that left for England were probably the ones who became most disenchanted. The nation and the government they had held in such high esteem seemed unrecognizable at close range. The rampant corruption, the flagrant bidding for position and favor, even the lifestyle of eighteenth-century England seemed alien to provincial leaders. Persons accustomed to leadership in the colonies became, for the most part, inconsequential in England. One dedicated Loyalist, Henry Van Schaack, longed to return to America and eventually did so.

On the whole, the Loyalists, because they chose the losing side, became lost among their contemporaries and, in many respects, to history.

PROSECUTING THE WAR

THE CONTINENTAL CONGRESS

To make independence a reality, the war had to be won. Though the Continental Congress had neither a specific grant of authority nor a fixed constitutional basis until 1781, it resolved financial, military, diplomatic, and constitutional questions during this critical period. Occasionally, action lagged and arguments centered upon trivialities, but the Continental Congress should be remembered for its major achievements rather than for its minor failures. It unified the American war effort and fashioned an instrument of national government without violating individual liberty and without producing dissension so divisive as to splinter the Revolution. Most of America's greatest leaders served at one time or another in the Congress, gaining their first political experience at the national rather than at the colony-state level.

REVOLUTIONARY FINANCE

One of the early problems facing Congress was how to finance the war. Four major methods were used: Loan Office Certificates, the equivalent of present-day government bonds; requisitions, that is, requests for money and later supplies from individual states; foreign loans, which were *insignificant* until 1781; and paper currency.

Congress made the first issues of paper money before the Declaration of Independence. This avenue of revenue was one that had been used by many colonies during the colonial period. At first the paper money circulated at its face value; but as more money was issued, its value declined (although intermittently the value of the currency increased when successful military operations revived hopes for a quick victory). States contributed to the decline in the value of the currency by issuing paper currency of their own. By the spring of 1781 the value had declined so precipitously that paper currency cost more to print than it was worth once it was printed. Up to that point, however, paper money paid for no less than 75 percent of the cost of the war. At one point, inflation reached 12,000 percent. What this means is that the Americans essentially paid for the Revolution through the depletion of their own savings caused by price inflation from the currency issues. The currency issues, in turn, were necessary because the colonists refused to tax themselves sufficiently to pay for the war.

After 1781 foreign loans became especially important, because these loans provided capital for the establishment of a national bank, the Bank of North America. From it the government borrowed money in excess of the bank's capitalization. After 1781, Morris Notes—a form of paper currency backed by the word of Robert Morris, the Superintendent of Finance—helped to restore the public credit. At the conclusion of the war the national government as well as the various states had incurred a substantial debt that was to figure in the movement to write the federal Constitution of 1787.

MILITARY STRATEGY

The British did not take advantage of their most promising military strategy until 1782, when, too late, they managed to blockade all the American ports. An intensive blockade, if it had been coordinated with swift, devastating land campaigns to lay waste the resources of the Americans, might have brought success, for the British, in order to win, had to demand unconditional surrender. The Americans, to be successful, needed an army in the field as a symbol of resistance. Any negotiations automatically recognized the United States as an independent nation because under international law a sovereign power does not negotiate with rebels.

The first military operations of the British were concentrated in the Middle states with an eye to dividing the United States physically, crippling its unity, and exploiting the possibility of support from American Loyalists, which was much stronger in New York than in Massachusetts. Control of New York, with its excellent harbor and river connections to the interior, was also viewed as crucial to the strangulation of American trade. The British believed that control of the Hudson River system would allow them to isolate New England, which they viewed as the center of the rebellion. British armies could then descend on New England from Canada while simultaneously pushing northward from New York and while strangling New England trade with the blockade. The British believed that once New England was subdued, Loyalists in the middle colonies would force New York, Pennsylvania, and New Jersey to fall in line. When the New York strategy failed to sufficiently divide the colonists and end the war, the British emphasis shifted to the Southern theater of operations beginning in 1780 with the intention of exploiting Loyalist sentiments in the South so as to subdue troublesome rebels in Virginia.

SLAVERY AND THE REVOLUTION

The policy on enlisting blacks in the Continental forces changed throughout the course of the war. At the beginning of the fighting the Continental Army and most state militias accepted black enlistments, both slaves and freemen. Prince Estabrook, a black, fought at Lexington, for example, and Peter Salem fought at Lexington, Concord, and Bunker Hill. One Rhode Island regiment included 125 blacks, of whom 30 of which were freemen.

Early attitudes changed. The Council of War convened by General Washington in Massachusetts in October 1775 decided not to accept further enlistment of blacks because other troops, especially those from the South, refused to accept them as equals. Free blacks protested to Washington, and in December 1775 he ordered the reopening of enlistments to free blacks. Meanwhile, he requested the Continental Congress to review the issue. In January 1776 Congress ruled that free blacks, that had already served could reenlist; but other blacks, whether slave or free, were excluded. State militias followed the pattern set by the Continental Army.

The British attitude fluctuated as much as that of the American provincials. The British recognized that recruiting slaves would cripple the planter colonies, so they promised freedom in exchange for service. They offered indentured servants the same promise. When planters found their slaves leaving to answer the British call, they became alarmed and angry. In Virginia slave patrols were doubled to catch runaways. Each planter in the Southern colonies tended to keep a sharper eye on the men and women in bondage.

Toward the end of 1776 and early in 1777, Continental policy changed once again. Blacks were recruited for the Continental and state navies. The state of Maryland enlisted blacks in its militia, and even the Virginia militia was willing to accept blacks. By 1779 the Continental Congress recommended that South Carolina and Georgia raise a military force of 5,000 black soldiers. Owners of slaves who enlisted were to be compensated, and the slaves in return would receive freedom and $50 in cash. The two states rejected the recommendation, but enlistment of blacks did grow in the North. In 1781 Baron Von Closen found that one fourth of the encampment of soldiers at White Plains was composed of blacks.

A few faltering steps were taken toward emancipation during the war years. In 1780 Pennsylvania provided for the gradual abolition of slavery. In 1784 Connecticut and Rhode Island followed Pennsylvania's lead, and soon thereafter New York and New Jersey followed suit. In 1783 the Supreme Court of Massachusetts ruled that the phrase "men are created free and equal" meant what it said, thereby freeing slaves in that state. In contrast, a proposal in the Maryland legislature to free slaves lost by a vote of 32 to 22. Significantly, no grand plan of emancipation was adopted anywhere in the new nation.

The reason was largely the attitude of the whites toward the blacks. Jefferson, in a public statement called *The Summary View*, acknowledged that slaves should be freed, but he also declared that blacks were inferior human beings. He could never bring himself to free his own slaves, even though Washington eventually did. The fear of living with blacks as equals, the loss of property, and the social consequences paralyzed the movement to free the slaves. So the possibility faded, to be taken up again by a later generation that resolved the issue on the battlefield.

THE WAR IN THE NORTH

In March 1776 Washington forced the British under General Sir William Howe to abandon Boston by capturing Dorchester Heights, from which they could shell British positions from the high ground. Howe loaded his troops on transports and sailed to Nova Scotia to prepare for an attack on New York. He took with him more than 1,000 Loyalists who preferred residence in Canada to independence from Great Britain, thus demonstrating the divisiveness among the American colonists even in the revolutionary hotbed of Boston.

In an effort to prevent Howe's taking New York, Washington moved south and occupied Brooklyn Heights on Long Island. There on August 27, 1776, Howe with an army of 33,000 attacked and defeated Washington, who withdrew to Manhattan Island under the cover of night and fog after suffering some 1,500 casualties. Washington then attempted to hold his ground against the British by occupying Forts Washington and Lee on either side of the Hudson River. In November, Howe attacked the forts, forcing Washington to retreat across New Jersey into Pennsylvania. Howe pursued Washington across New Jersey and at one point was only one hour behind the fleeing Continental Army; but Howe rested his

George Washington on his horse

men for a day and allowed Washington to escape. The Continental Congress, however, meeting in Philadelphia, fled to Baltimore as the British army approached. Military historians tend to argue that Howe failed to press his advantage while he had Washington on the run and contend that had Howe attacked Washington's army at Philadelphia, he would have taken the city and crushed the Continental Army. Instead, Howe decided to winter his Hessian troops in quarters along the Delaware River and delay his advance until spring, confident that the colonists would be unable to mount an attack. Instead, on December 25, 1776, in a freezing rainstorm Washington moved his army across the Delaware River in the dead of night and attacked the unsuspecting Hessians early in the morning, taking 900 prisoners. Washington read to the troops a selection from a Thomas Paine pamphlet entitled "American Crisis" the famous words, "These are the times that try men's souls ... The summer soldier and the sunshine patriot will, in this crisis shrink from the service of their country, but he that stands it now deserves ... love and thanks." A week later on January 3, Washington continued his surprise attacks with an assault on Princeton before moving his army to winter quarters at Morristown. The colonial victories in New Jersey were important less for their strategic significance than for their boost to morale. The victories convinced many Americans that they should continue the fight though the strategic prize, New York City, would be occupied by British troops for the duration of the Revolution.

In 1777 Howe bestirred himself sufficiently to send an army by sea against Philadelphia. Washington proceeded overland south of Philadelphia and met units of Howe's army at Brandywine Creek on September 11, 1777, suffering defeat after being badly outmaneuvered. Howe entered Philadelphia with ease, but British units were severely tested when Washington launched an unexpected counter-attack at Germantown on October 4. Just when it appeared that the American army would prevail, Washington's troops suddenly retreated in confusion. Though the American army was defeated, its offensive spirit aided the cause of independence at home and in France. Washington then withdrew his army to Valley Forge, Pennsylvania, where a combination of freezing weather, bad food, a shortage of blankets and shoes, and disease cost 2,500 American lives. Washington complained to congress that nearly 3,000 of his men were "unfit for duty" because they are bare foot and otherwise naked. Food and clothing were available elsewhere in the different states, but states were reluctant to send their own supplies of blankets, shoes, and food for use outside of their home states. To make matters worse, the American supply lines were fraught with corruption. Teamsters who hauled barrels of salt pork drained out the brine to lighten their load, thus allowing the meat to rot in transit. Blankets

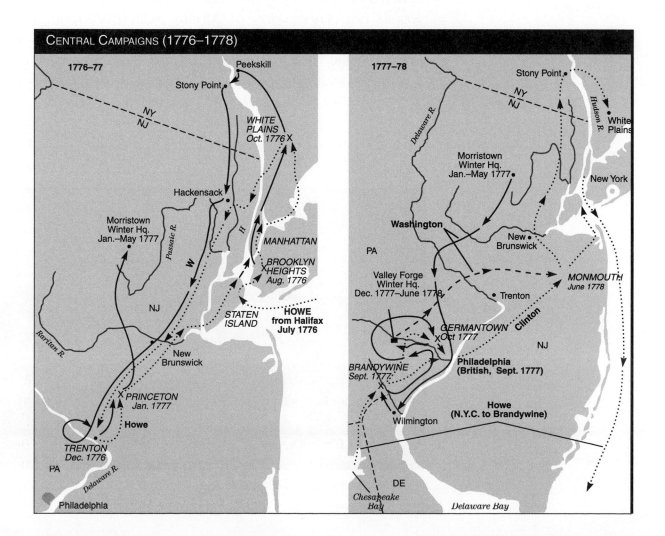

CENTRAL CAMPAIGNS (1776–1778)

were delivered that were only a fourth of the normal size, and gunpowder often turned out to be defective.

In the meantime the British had planned a three-pronged attack to capture the Hudson Valley and thus isolate New England from the colonies to the south. From Canada, General Sir John Burgoyne was to push southward down Lake Champlain and the upper Hudson with the expectation of joining Howe moving up the Hudson from New York City. Burgoyne would then join Howe in an attack on Philadelphia and the occupation of other rebel territory to the south. But Howe had received conflicting orders and decided that the immediate capture of Philadelphia was more urgent than cooperating with Burgoyne, thus delaying his scheduled rendezvous with Burgoyne's army descending from the north.

Burgoyne had also expected to converge with a third British force under Barry St. Leger (mostly Loyalists and Native Americans) moving eastward from Lake Ontario along the Mohawk Valley, but this force was beaten back by American troops at the Battle of Oriskany. The Americans suffered heavy losses with 500 of the 800 Americans killed, but the British forces were forced to retreat and would not rendezvous at Albany with Burgoyne. Nevertheless, throughout the summer of 1777 Burgoyne pressed southward toward Albany. Burgoyne captured Fort Ticonderoga in July after 3,000 American defenders, low on food and supplies, fled when

Washington crossing the Delaware

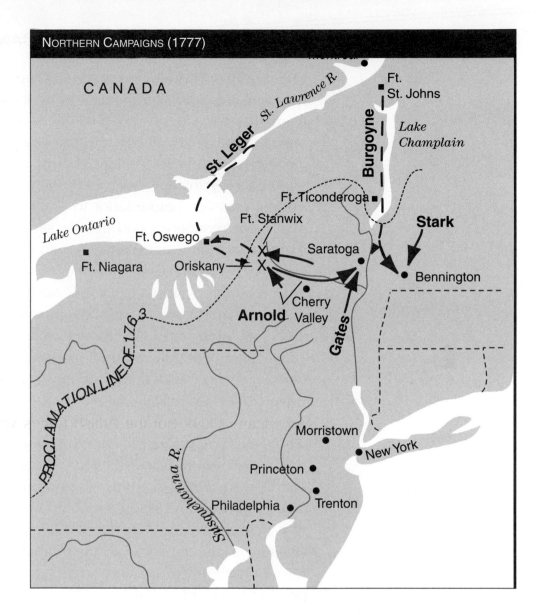

NORTHERN CAMPAIGNS (1777)

they saw the coming British army. Burgoyne was slowed in his march because some 1,000 laundresses, cooks, and musicians, as well as 400 Native American warriors and scouts, accompanied his troops. Burgoyne required 400 horses to pull his heavy artillery and also carried 30 trunks of personal belongings including his wardrobe and fine wines. At last, failing to receive aid from either Howe or the force from Lake Ontario, he suffered complete defeat to American forces under Horatio Gates and Benedict Arnold in two battles fought near Saratoga. On October 17, 1777, with food supplies running out, Burgoyne surrendered his entire army of 5,800 men to American General Horatio Gates. Thus ended the British hope of isolating New England by occupying the Hudson Valley.

EUROPEAN AID TO THE AMERICANS

The victory over Burgoyne at Saratoga and the Battle of Germantown had significant political results. They indicated to European politicians that the Americans could win independence and that British power could be crippled by the loss. France, of course, was anxious for revenge upon its ancient enemy, and the efforts of American diplomats in Paris now began to bear fruit. Benjamin Franklin proved a most effective ambassador to France. Wearing a fur cap as the symbol of republican and frontier simplicity, he soon became the toast of Paris and made friends with those politicians best able to help the American cause. Recent research in French archives has revealed how very skilled a diplomat he was.

On February 6, 1778, he consummated a Treaty of Alliance and a Treaty of Amity and Commerce with France. France recognized American independence, thus granting America status as an independent nation under international law. France promised to the United States full military support until England recognized U.S. independence; and both France and the United States agreed that neither would sign a separate peace with England. Finally, the United States was to be militarily allied with France indefinitely. France immediately supplied limited funds to aid the American cause and in 1780 dispatched troops and ships. French ports were now opened to such war vessels as the Americans had, and privateers could attack British vessels and stand a better chance of getting away to a safe haven. The French navy provided sea power that the colonies had previously lacked.

Eager to gain the access to American markets that Great Britain had long prevented, Holland also provided aid, largely in the form of loans underwritten by the French. Thus European aid, prompted by self-interest, contributed to the American victory. Since Spain was at the time closely allied to France, America expected aid from Spain also, but these hopes were never fulfilled.

NEW CAMPAIGNS IN THE NORTH

General William Howe, notorious for his dilatoriness, was relieved in 1778 by Sir Henry Clinton, who evacuated Philadelphia and returned to New York for a new campaign in the North. Washington, without the power to inflict defeat, could only hang on the flanks of the British army. He established a base at White Plains, New York and saw to it that West Point on the Hudson was fortified. The arrival off New York ot a French naval force under Count d'Estaing did little to help the American cause, for d'Estaing showed little audacity and soon sailed away to the West Indies. Only from the western frontier was the news encouraging. George Rogers Clark, leading a group of frontiersmen, helped to hold the West against the British.

THE WAR IN THE SOUTH

In 1778, the British adopted a new strategy designed to take advantage of Loyalist sentiments in the South and play on the destabilizing factor of the presence of thousands of slaves who could be freed by a British victory. The British hoped to reestablish British rule in the southern colonies one by one, beginning with lightly defended Georgia, and then moving north up the southern colonial coast. The British captured Savannah in December 1778, and subsequently installed a Loyalist government. Fourteen hundred Georgia militiamen then signed an oath of allegiance to the king and agreed to fight for the British against American rebels. In April and May 1780, the British laid siege to Charleston where 3,300 Americans were forced to surrender after five weeks of fighting. As in Georgia, pardons were offered to Carolinians who swore loyalty oaths to the king and then proved their loyalty by taking up arms for the British. When the Continental Army under Horatio Gates attempted a counterattack at Camden, South Carolina in August, American militiamen dropped their weapons and ran when they saw the approaching British cavalry. By the second day of the battle when the Americans tried to regroup, only 700 of the 3,000 American troops showed up, the rest were killed, captured, or deserted.

The British victories in the South were aided by information the British gained from America's most famous traitor, Benedict Arnold. Arnold had been a hero at Saratoga but had been denied the command of the Southern army that was given to Horatio Gates, whom both Arnold and many military historians viewed as Arnold's inferior on the battlefield. Instead Arnold was given command of a fort at West Point, a post he did not want. This combined with a romantic relationship with a pro-British lover evidently pushed Arnold to espionage. Arnold's treason was discovered when a man was caught carrying plans of West Point's defense from Benedict Arnold to British General Henry Clinton.

In South Carolina, Washington replaced Horatio Gates after the defeat at Camden with General Nathanael Greene, who divided his army into small guerrilla bands and launched a series of hit and run

Benedict Arnold

attacks on the British. Some 6,000 men engaged in 26 battles with the British and Loyalists, and the guerrilla war spread into Georgia and North Carolina. Both patriots and Loyalists committed murders and atrocities and ravaged their opponents' property, and the southern backcountry slipped into near anarchy. In the worst of these fratricidal skirmishes, on October 7, 1780, patriots massacred 1,400 Loyalists at King's Mountain in western South Carolina. In January, 1781, the patriots followed with a brilliant victory of Daniel Morgan and his farmer-cavalrymen at the Battle of Cowpens, South Carolina, where local militia units backed by the Continental Army defeated the British Army.

These successes turned the tide in the Carolinas. Through the winter, spring, and summer of 1781, General Nathanael Greene, commander of the American army in the South, skillfully threw militia, cavalry, and guerrilla forces against the British armies. By autumn those British who had not moved north to Virginia with Cornwallis were pocketed in a small area about Charleston, South Carolina.

BATTLE OF YORKTOWN

Meanwhile, in 1780 the French dispatched an army of 5,500 men under an able soldier, the Count de Rochambeau, to aid Washington. These troops encamped at Newport, while Rochambeau and Washington waited to see what success collaborative effort would bring. The Count de Grasse, a brilliant French naval commander with a well-equipped squadron, had arrived in the West Indies.

After an exchange of correspondence, de Grasse decided that his squadron could attack more successfully in the Chesapeake than in the harbor of New York, so a decision was made for a coordinated land and sea attack in Virginia, where Cornwallis' army, supplemented by troops under the turncoat Benedict Arnold, was being engaged by forces led by French general Lafayette. Washington and Rochambeau began to move their armies southward, a maneuver that the British believed was a feint to catch them off guard in New York, where they expected the main attack to take place.

With de Grasse controlling the Chesapeake Bay area and with a French and American force of 15,000 men surrounding Cornwallis' camp on the York peninsula, Cornwallis was doomed. He surrendered on October 19, 1781. As his men marched out to lay down their arms, a band played "The World Turned Upside Down." When the news of Yorktown reached Britain, the king's ministers agreed that peace must be made with the rebellious colonies. Though the nation of Great Britain still had resources with which to continue the fight, the war had been too costly both in terms of economic damage and in human casualties. The British people lacked the will to continue the unpopular fight.

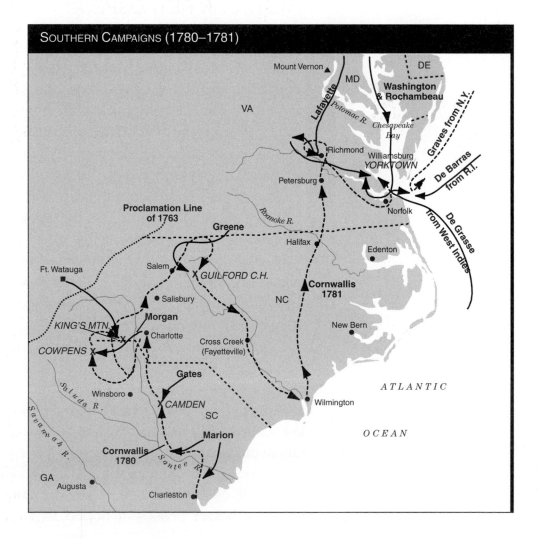

Cornwallis surrendering at Yorktown

THE WAR IN RETROSPECT

The war had been a strange and at times hopeless one for the Americans. But Washington had emerged as a persistent, determined leader. He may have lacked brilliance as a military tactician, but he had the courage, integrity, and character essential to successful command. Despite the demoralization of his forces by lack of supplies, by desertions, and occasionally by mutinies, he held on until the Americans, with French help, achieved victory.

British incompetence played a part in the eventual outcome of the war. Without the assistance that British commanders—Howe and Clinton, particularly—unwittingly gave the patriots, the end might have been different. It was the good fortune of America that Great Britain had been engaged in a world war, and that some of its best troops and more competent commanders were in India, Africa, the West Indies, and elsewhere.

Although a few young Frenchmen like Lafayette came to America to fight for the patriots out of sheer idealism, the alliance of the Bourbon powers, France and Spain, against Great Britain was not motivated by love of liberty or of the republican principles so nobly stated in the Declaration of Independence. By a trick of fate, these very principles of liberty would exercise an enormous influence in France within a few years and would overturn the French monarchy. But in the conflict between the colonies and Great Britain, France was merely playing the game of power politics. It hoped to wreak revenge on an ancient enemy and perhaps to regain some of the American territory it had lost.

Spain also had an interest in territory west of the British possessions in North America. To weaken Great Britain's strength in the New World would provide possible opportunities for later aggrandizement there for both France and Spain. A weak and struggling republic without money and friends would be easy to dominate and perhaps to devour.

France had promised its satellite, Spain, that it

French general Gilbert du Motier, Marquis de Lafayette

would help wrest Gibraltar from the British, but had attacked Gibraltar in vain. Now France proposed to appease Spain with territory west of the Appalachians. In the peace negotiations, which had begun even before Yorktown, the disposition of western territories was a critical consideration.

THE PEACE OF PARIS, 1783

To negotiate a peace with England, Congress appointed five commissioners: Benjamin Franklin, envoy in France; John Jay, American agent in Spain; John Adams, envoy in Holland; Henry Laurens; and Thomas Jefferson. Only the first three, assembled at Paris, took an active part in the discussions. At the outset, Jay was suspicious of the motives of the Count de Vergennes, the French foreign minister, and of the British agent, Richard Oswald. Oswald had come with instructions to treat with the commissioners as if they represented rebellious colonies. Jay insisted that Oswald go back and obtain new instructions to treat with the representatives of the "Thirteen United States," which would be tantamount to recognizing at the outset the independence of the new republic. This Oswald did.

Although the commissioners had received from Congress full power to negotiate the best treaty possible, Congress had specifically instructed them to take no steps that France would not approve. Since Jay was convinced that France was determined to sacrifice American interests to satisfy Spain, he persuaded Adams and Franklin to deal secretly with England and to make a preliminary treaty that promised favorable terms.

The news leaked out and Vergennes was incensed, but Franklin, a great favorite of the French, managed to placate him by admitting that their action was merely an "indiscretion." Nevertheless, the preliminary treaty had established the pattern for the final treaty, which was signed on September 3, 1783.

Great Britain, partly to sow dissension between the Bourbon allies and partly to win the friendship of the late colonies and keep them from becoming satellites of France, offered such favorable

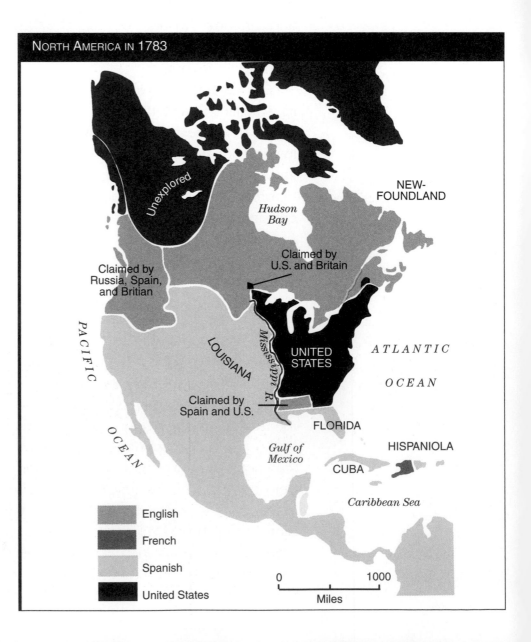

NORTH AMERICA IN 1783

terms that Vergennes in anger declared that the English were ready to "buy peace rather than make it." Instead of letting Spain have the trans-Appalachian region, Great Britain agreed that the Mississippi should be the western boundary of the United States. Although Franklin had tried to obtain all of Canada "to insure peace," it was agreed that the Great Lakes should determine the northern border. In the end, Great Britain gave the Floridas back to Spain, and the treaty set the southern border of the United States at 31° north latitude. The provisions of the treaty seemed clear, but in some areas the boundary lines were not stated precisely. In Maine (at that time still part of Massachusetts) the border remained in dispute for years.

The treaty also provided that American citizens were to enjoy the same fishing rights in Canadian waters as British subjects. The two countries agreed that the Mississippi River would be forever open to navigation by both American and British shipping. The British demanded restitution of Loyalist property confiscated during the war, but all Congress could do was to recommend that this be done. The treaty also stipulated that the United States would not impede the payment of debts to the British, but Congress had no means by which to force any American debtors to pay their British creditors. Since Congress also had no authority over the states, it was agreed that suits might be brought by British subjects in the state courts for the recovery of debts. Congress ratified the Treaty of Paris the next year on January 14, 1784.

Washington resigning his commission after the war

EFFECTS OF THE WAR

UNRESTRICTED TRADE

Wars traditionally result in social and financial upheavals, and the American Revolution was no exception. Within the 20 years of controversy and war, old and settled traditions were altered, and the patterns of a new society emerged.

No longer were the American colonies the source of raw materials supplied exclusively to Great Britain. Dutch, French, Spanish, and Portuguese ships could slip into American ports and load tobacco, wheat, corn, meat, rice, and other products needed in Europe. Despite the war—even as a result of it—some American merchants made more money than ever before, and some European commodities, received in exchange for produce, were more abundant during the war than previously.

War profiteers made a few fortunes, but, more importantly, a network of colonial merchants experienced the challenges and problems of unrestricted trade on an international scale. Patriotism did not keep some dealers from making 200 or 300 percent profit on clothing and supplies needed by the Continental soldiers. New industries, particularly war industries, developed. Iron foundries multiplied. Gunsmiths flourished, and factories for the manufacture of muskets, gunpowder, and cannon were built, particularly in New England and in Pennsylvania. Since the usual trade in English woolens and other fabrics was cut off, cloth making was encouraged.

THE WESTWARD MOVEMENT

With the elimination of the prohibition against movement into the trans-Appalachian region that the British had tried to enforce after 1763, fresh migrations began. Frontiersmen were soon filtering into valleys and clearings beyond the mountains. In 1776 Virginia had organized into a county a portion of what later became the state of Kentucky. Before the Revolution, frontiersmen from Virginia had settled on the Watauga River in what became Tennessee. After the Revolution, uprooted citizens and restless souls all along the frontier began a trek west that would continue until one day the American continent as far west as the Pacific would be occupied. Land companies were organized, and within a few years speculation in western lands became an obsession. Thus in many ways, one could see the native peoples as "losers" in the Revolution, alongside the British: in the course of twenty years of imperial struggle—and then the War for Independence itself—Native Americans first lost their French allies and then the British as a restraint on American expansionism.

MODIFICATIONS OF AMERICAN SOCIETY

Socially, the Revolution brought changes too. The most immediate result was the elimination of royal governors, other British officials, and the cliques of socially elite that gathered about them. Even in colonies that had had no royal officials, those who were subservient to the mother country were swept out and new leaders took their places. State legislatures gained power at the expense of governors as state governors were forced to rely on legislatures to raise the needed revenue during the war. States wrote constitutions with State Bills of Rights under the premise that part of the reason the British had abused the rights of the colonists was that the British Constitution is unwritten, and there is no stated British Bill of Rights. The revolution also brought about the end of privilege based on birth and its replacement with meritocracy, representative government, and equality under law.

There was also a movement to separate Church and State since the Anglican Church received its share of the blame for British abuses. Prior to the revolution, nine of the 13 colonies had supported religion with taxation. Six of those nine colonies had actually supported multiple religions. By 1833, all states had disestablished religion from the state.

The revolution also brought a movement against slavery. Slavery conflicted with the "All men are created equal" ideal of the Declaration of Independence and the Enlightenment. Additionally, some 5,000 blacks served in the United States military during the revolution. As a consequence, Pennsylvania abolished slavery in 1780 during the revolution. Other northern states followed Pennsylvania's lead so that all northern states had abolished slavery by 1804. The Massachusetts Supreme Court even declared slavery unconstitutional in Massachusetts, and owners of slaves were forced to emancipate their slaves against their will in 1783. Even in the South there was some movement against slavery. In Virginia, slave owners voluntarily freed some 10,000 slaves. All states except Georgia and North Carolina lifted laws prohibiting slave owners from freeing their own slaves.

Along with the movement against slavery, there was a movement for greater rights for women due to the aforementioned Enlightenment thinking and the fact that women were often left in charge of farms and businesses while the men went off to war. In some cases, such as in the celebrated case of Molly Pitcher, women actually fought in the armed forces with the men. Female landowners were allowed to vote in New Jersey until 1807. Divorce laws in northern states were loosened to allow women to escape abusive relationships even if adultery were not an issue. Some schools altered education to be less gender-specific and allowed women to take the same courses as men rather than limit them to a curriculum of cooking, cleaning, sewing, and general "wifery."

Yet as important as these changes were, the United States nowhere experienced the kind of social revolution that swept France a few years later. The structure of American society was modified rather than radically altered. In Virginia, for example, the influence of the tidewater aristocrats diminished somewhat, and back country politicians of the type represented by Patrick Henry gained power. The families that had produced leaders before the Revolution, however, still continued to supply many of the leaders in the new nation.

One reason the new republic moved with relative ease from the status of a colony to that of a self-governing nation was the tradition of local responsibility established in all of the colonies early in the development of the British settlements. This inheritance from the British tradition of local self-government ensured a reservoir of leadership from which individuals could be drawn for any level of responsibility required.

Though lacking a French-style social revolution, it must still be said, in summation, that within a generation or so after the Treaty of Paris, American society had undergone extraordinarily rapid change. As the noted historian Joyce Appleby has argued in a recent book, all sorts of Americans reinvented themselves in the first decades of the new nation, started small businesses, created new products, established organizations, and, in general, found themselves ready to take chances.

In some cases, women such as Molly Pitcher, shown here, fought in the armed forces alongside the men.

THE ARTICLES OF CONFEDERATION

Soon after the Declaration of Independence, a committee was appointed to draw up Articles of Confederation to bind the thirteen states together into a union. It took more than a year to draft the Articles, and they then had to be submitted to the states for ratification. This took until the spring of 1781.

In the meantime—during almost the entire war—the rebel colonies operated under the authority of the extralegal Continental Congress.

Among the most important contributions of the Articles were their preservation of the union and their definition of powers to be granted to the central government as opposed to the state governments. The operation of the Articles, together with the formation and operation of state governments, is more properly the subject of Chapter 6 on the postwar period.

The delay in ratifying the Articles of Confederation was due chiefly to a conflict of economic interests. Massachusetts, Connecticut, New York, Virginia, Georgia, and the Carolinas—under the terms of colonial charters, royal grants, Native American treaties, or proprietary claims—asserted ownership of tremendous grants of lands in the West. To be able to retain these western lands would be a great economic boon since the sale of the back regions would provide the state governments with a steady income and make it unnecessary for them to tax their citizens at all.

Naturally the advantage that would come to states with western land claims was resented by the states with fixed boundaries. They protested that the War for Independence was being fought for the benefit of all and that every state should share in the rewards to be found in western territory. Thus these landless states were reluctant to sign the Articles of Confederation until the westward limits of the existing states were set and until Congress, the central government, was given authority to grant lands and to create new states beyond these limits.

The debate was not motivated entirely by the question of the equality of the states. Land speculators had formed companies in Maryland and Pennsylvania, for example, and had made purchases from the Native Americans in the Ohio valley. Now they wished governmental validation of their titles. How could they secure clear title to land claimed by Virginia and New York when such states were inclined not to recognize the Native American purchases made by out-of-state residents?

Eventually, after considerable political maneuvering and propagandizing, both sides gave in. Between 1777 and 1781 the land companies vacated their claims to western territory purchased from the Native Americans, and upon recommendation of a congressional committee in 1780, the landed states, led by Virginia, New York, and Connecticut, gave up claim to most of the trans-Appalachian country, thus making the western lands the territory of the nation. In February

1781 the last of the landless states, Maryland, ratified the Articles, and on March 1 the Confederation was formally proclaimed. The problem of western lands was now placed squarely before the new central government.

When the war was over, many thoughtful citizens throughout the country feared that the loose provisions of the Articles of Confederation would not permit the evolution of a nation strong enough to survive. For example, in foreign policy much would depend upon the power of a centralized authority. Furthermore, a central authority was required to establish the financial stability of the nation and to deal with problems of credit, the issuance of money, and the maintenance of national defense. These problems and their solution would form an important chapter in constitution making.

A final word should be said about the American Revolution not only as a symbol in the history of the United States, but as a guiding light for generations of people the world over. As the first anti-imperialist, anti-monarchial revolution of modern times, the American Revolution inspired imitators in Europe and Latin America in the nineteenth century and in Africa and Asia in the twentieth. The principles of revolution—government by consent of the governed, and inviolate rights that no government can invade—spoke to the hearts and minds of people in other nations. The fact was, and is, that the American Revolution is not exportable. Other people and other nations are the products of their own particular circumstances and experience; but the language, idealism, and ideas these have taken on a life of their own.

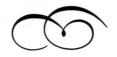

CHAPTER *6*

THE EMERGENCE OF A NATIONAL CULTURE

THE DEVELOPMENT OF AN AMERICAN CREDO

A Time of Optimism and Pride
American Nationalism

THE FRAMEWORK OF THE AMERICAN MIND

Adapting the Enlightenment
The Professionalization of Science
"The Best Mechanics in the World"
The Arrival of Romanticism
Religious Change
Frontier Evangelism
Freedom and Equality: The Ideal
The Social Problem

SHAPING AMERICAN SOCIETY

Feeding and Clothing the Republic
Marriage, Morals, and Family Life
Women's Legal Status
New Thinking About Women's Rights

THE QUEST FOR AMERICAN ARTS

A Native Literature
Patterns in American Prose
Reading for the People
Poetry in the New Republic
The Theater and Other Entertainments
Architecture
Musicians and Painters
Winning Artistic Independence

THE DEVELOPMENT OF AN AMERICAN CREDO

A TIME OF OPTIMISM AND PRIDE

We begin with the cultural context for the founding and development of the new nation. In fact, the period between 1783 and 1824 was a time of extraordinary political, economic, and social revolution. This was the age that saw the close of the American Revolution, the ratification of the Constitution, and the development of the two-party system of government. It was the age of George Washington and Thomas Jefferson, of the Louisiana Purchase and the Lewis and Clark expedition, of the War of 1812 and the growth of textile and iron industries, of Henry Clay and John C. Calhoun, of the Missouri Compromise and the Monroe Doctrine. In Europe it was the age of the French Revolution and the rise and fall of Napoleon, of the Romantic Movement, and of the Industrial Revolution.

In launching a new system of government, Americans looked ahead with a strong sense of hope and experiment. They were optimistic about the future, for they had no significant record of failure to disillusion them. They were impatient of "established" institutions or traditions, for they were just establishing some of their own and had disestablished a good many British ones. Though the society did not grant the Declaration's "unalienable rights" to free blacks, slaves, and Native Americans, or full political and social equality to women or to all classes, nonetheless—thoughtful Americans believed—it afforded more freedom to its citizens than any other society.

This pride in what they had accomplished, joined to their anti-British feelings, made Americans aggressively self-confident. Triumphant in their newly won independence, they became less aware of their social, cultural, and religious indebtedness to Great Britain. Having rejected all the prejudices, superstitions, and errors of the Old World, so Americans felt, they were ready to outdistance it in every sector.

AMERICAN NATIONALISM

Several events favored the growth of American nationalism. For one thing, many democratic and humanitarian tendencies were accentuated or set in motion. During the Revolution and the early national period large Loyalist estates were confiscated and divided. Small businesses and manufacturing were stimulated. Church establishments were attacked. Slavery, imprisonment for debt, and humiliating punishments were regarded with growing disfavor. The idea of universal education at state expense was voiced. Americans were far from being of one mind about these matters, but they did believe that they could, by honest effort and the fortunate circumstances of their society, forge ahead in ways that the nations of the Old World could not. The Americans were a "new" people, as Crèvecoeur put it. They were ready to teach the rest of the world and were no longer content to be taught.

Indeed, Americans considered the United States to be superior to England and Europe in every way. It was, they hoped, the model of a new kind of New World. "Americans are fanatically proud of their own wild country," remarked an English traveler during the period, "and love to disparage the rest of the world." It was America's mission to lead other nations to revolution against the forces of ignorance and oppression or, as Joel Barlow wrote, "to excite emulation throughout the kingdoms of the earth, and meliorate the conditions of the human race." It was America's responsibility to extend the concepts of liberty, equality, and justice over all the earth. This responsibility, James Wilson would say at the Constitutional Convention, was "the great design of Providence in regard to this globe."

In order to accomplish this mission, Americans felt compelled to cultivate their Americanness, emphasize their differences with Europe, and develop their own culture in terms of their own national purpose. "Every engine should be employed to render the people of the country national," wrote Noah Webster, "to call their attachment home to their own country." If the United States was to succeed as an experiment in self-government, the people who governed themselves must have deep faith in it. The patriotic impulse was considered essential to the creation of a national character.

As a consequence, there was a trend in fashion toward American "homespun" clothing even if the American threads were inferior to their British counterparts. American Churches, including, but not limited to the Anglicans and the Catholics, broke with their British hierarchies. The Anglican Church, in particular, even underwent a name change to become the American Episcopal Church. Education was altered to include American history, complete with the American heroes of the Revolution including the General Washington, Jefferson's Declaration, and the word exploits of Patrick Henry, Thomas Paine, John and Sam Adams and the Sons of Liberty, and many, many more. American language education was also altered with the introduction of Noah Webster's *Speller* that included American spellings and pronunciations of words that by 1783 had become, in many

Noah Webster helped alter American language education with the introduction of a book that gave American spellings and pronunciations of words.

cases, somewhat different than those in England. The forging of a truly American identity separate from England and separate from the identities of the 13 individual colonies had begun.

THE FRAMEWORK OF THE AMERICAN MIND

Two great intellectual movements embodied in the Age of Reason and the Age of Romanticism provided the structure of ideas within which Americans achieved their independence. The United States itself, almost purely a creation of the eighteenth century, emerged at a time when the Western world was shifting from one system of thought to another, the two involving quite different views of human nature, the world, and the deity.

ADAPTING THE ENLIGHTENMENT

The American colonies were children of the Age of Reason, or the "Enlightenment." (See Chapter 2 for an earlier discussion.) John Locke, an English philosopher, probably wrote a charter for the Carolinas. Rousseau and Montesquieu were friends of Franklin. Sir Isaac Newton and Cotton Mather were contemporaries. Voltaire was still living when the Continental Congress signed the Declaration of Independence. It was the Enlightenment, not the Puritanism of New England, which provided the first *national* pattern of American thought.

The Age of Reason rested upon three principles: the possibility of human perfectibility, the inevitability of *progress*, and the effectiveness of *reason*. It emphasized the scientific method over the theological, reason over faith, skepticism over tradition and authoritarianism. The thinkers of the Enlightenment believed that humans could subject themselves, their society, the past, and the universe itself to rational analysis. In this way they could discover general laws that would supply them with precise, definitive explanations of human and natural activity. With this knowledge, they could so direct their energies and construct their institutions that their progress would be swift and sure. The Americans who chose the path of revolution, and who, after its successful conclusion, accepted the challenge of making a new nation on new principles, reflected these attitudes.

There was an American Enlightenment, but it was late, eclectic, and singularly American. Eighteenth-century America was not merely an extension or a reflection of contemporary Britain or Europe. First of all, there was a culture lag in the transmission of patterns of thinking from one side of the Atlantic to the other. The Founding Fathers worked with ideas 50 to 100 years old by European standards, developed on another continent for different purposes—and mixed them with latter borrowings and adaptations. The Romanticists—Goethe, Wordsworth, Coleridge, Schiller, and Kant—were writing at nearly the same time that Americans were still quoting the leaders of the Age of Reason—Newton, Locke, and Montesquieu.

Second, Americans chose from British and European thought only those ideas they needed or those in which they had special interest. They adopted Locke's justification of a century-old English revolution as vindication of their own, for example, and used French "radicalism," aimed at Gallic kings, to overthrow a tyranny that really did not exist. The Americans thus bent the Enlightenment to American uses.

THE PROFESSIONALIZATION OF SCIENCE

The intellectual impact of the Enlightenment manifested itself most clearly in the advancement of American science in the late eighteenth century. The colonies had been settled in the scientific age of Galileo and Newton. American intellectuals were never far from the center of the great scientific revolution that marked the European Enlightenment, and, like other educated people of their times, lived by contemporary scientific attitudes. They believed that all problems would respond to scientific investigation. Deriving their view from Newtonian science, they saw the universe as mechanistic, governed by constant natural laws that were discoverable by human reason. They believed that all knowledge was fundamentally scientific and that the inductive method of thinking was quite possibly the only trustworthy method of arriving at truth. From science, the leaders of American thought believed they might find solutions to the problems of human society.

The Revolution suspended practically all scientific activity. But immediately after it, as Dr. Amos Eaton, himself a scientist, wrote, "A thirst for natural science seemed to pervade the United States like the progress of an epidemic." The nation was especially fortunate in receiving a number of brilliant immigrants and refugees during and after the war. Thomas Cooper, geologist and economist, came from England, as did Joseph Priestley, one of the world's greatest chemists; Pierre du Pont de Nemours, a noted chemist, arrived from France. Meanwhile, the United States possessed a number of highly competent scientists among its native-born. President Jefferson was a scientist of repute himself, and the Lewis and Clark expedition that he sent west-

A statue of Lewis and Clark, whose "Corps of Discovery" expedition was one of the most significant scientific projects in American history

ward in 1804 was one of the most significant scientific projects in American history.

Though long neglected by the colleges and universities, the study of science began to appear in the curriculum, usually as astronomy, chemistry, or physics. Indeed, science itself was becoming a profession rather than a hobby for interested amateurs. The tremendous growth in the amount of scientific knowledge, and the equally great impact of that knowledge on contemporary life, meant that there was no longer a place for the "natural philosopher" who took all scientific knowledge as his province. The day of the academic jack-of-all-trades like Dr. Samuel Latham Mitchill of Columbia, who ranged through chemistry, medicine, mathematics, botany, zoology, and poetry, was nearly over.

American scientists readily admitted that they had made no major contributions to scientific theory and that Europe and England still dominated the various fields. Yet their achievements were not negligible, especially in identifying and classifying the flora and fauna of their continent and in exploring the extent of its resources. Americans were confident that their own great scientific contributions would inevitably come.

"THE BEST MECHANICS IN THE WORLD"

While America had produced few scientists of worldwide repute (always excepting Franklin), Americans were quick to apply scientific knowledge to practical ends. Born in the midst of the Industrial Revolution, the United States knew no other than a technological environment. The steam engine, the iron industry, the chemical revolution, and the discovery of electricity, for example, all preceded Yorktown. Americans embraced technology with great enthusiasm. Machinery, Salmon P. Chase would write, "is an almost infinite power. It is in modern times by far the most efficient cause of human improvement, producing almost unmingled benefit, to an amount and extent of which we have as yet but a very faint conception."

Technology was particularly important to a new nation that needed to catch up with the rest of the industrialized world. One of Congress' first acts in 1790, after the Constitution had been ratified and gone into effect, would be to pass a patent law, and the first patent went to a process for making potassium carbonate, essential to the glassmaking industry. By 1830 the United States Patent Office was issuing annually four times as many patents as were being issued in England. Foreign visitors often commented on "Yankee ingenuity." Americans, a French observer wrote, "are the best mechanics in the world ..., engineers from birth." The country had ample power, unparalleled natural resources, and a chronic shortage of labor. A stream of new processes and new machines supplied the missing element needed for an efficient, productive society.

When the country needed something done, somebody quickly invented or adapted a machine, tool, or technique to do it. Examples are too numerous to list, but the iron I-beam, the copying lathe, the breech loading rifle, the iron plow, the electromagnet, the milling machine, the miner's lamp, the compound steam engine, Portland cement, the screw propeller, the stone-crusher, the high-speed steam printing press, insulated wire, wire nails, the spinning mule, the ice refrigerator, canned food, the railroad T-rail—to name a few—were all in use before 1830. These, and many other technologies like them, had immediate economic value and powerful influence on the way Americans lived and worked.

The New England textile industry is a case in point. The area had plenty of water power, good transportation, and a labor shortage. Before 1800 cloth was made almost wholly by hand. After 1820 it was made almost wholly by machinery. Cheap factory-made cloth of good quality had effects in the home, in society, in the domestic market, and in world trade. This example could be duplicated in a hundred other cases.

THE ARRIVAL OF ROMANTICISM

The rise of Romanticism disturbed the orderly patterns of the Age of Reason. During the latter years of the eighteenth century, philosophers and critics in America and Europe became increasingly uncomfortable within the framework of thought erected earlier by Newton, Locke, and Pope. They were no longer content with a rationalism and classicism that, it seemed to them, had hardened into traditionalism. Thinkers on both sides of the Atlantic began to question seriously some of the attitudes of the Enlightenment and to alter their conceptions of nature, human nature, and society.

Many of these "Romantic" ideas were not new, nor were they ever assimilated into a unified system. But the climate of opinion that characterized the intellectual activity in both America and Europe from the closing decades of the eighteenth century to the middle of the nineteenth was coherent and consistent enough to warrant calling the period the Age of Romanticism.

The Romantic view of society rested on three general concepts. First, it rested on the idea of *organism*—of wholes, or units, with their own internal laws of governance and development. A society had a life of its own, a "national spirit," a "national destiny." Second, it rested on the idea of *dynamism*, of motion and growth. Institutions and beliefs were assumed to be fluid, changing, and capable of improvement and adaptation. The age had a dislike of finality. Third, it rested on the idea of *diversity*—the value of differences in opinions, cultures, tastes, societies, and characters—as opposed to the value of uniformity of the Enlightenment.

To the Age of Reason, conformity meant rationalism. Diversity meant irrationality, and therefore error. To the Age of Romanticism, consensus seemed less important than individual judgments. It was "natural" and "right" for things and people and ideas and societies not to be all alike.

Those who fought the Revolution and set the Republic on its way were largely products of the Age of Reason and derived their intellectual inspiration from it. The next generation of leaders was shaped less by the Enlightenment than by Romanticism. What Americans thought about their country, their arts, and the organization of their political and social relationships, as well as about themselves and the natural world around them, was powerfully influenced in the early 1800s by this new set of ideas.

RELIGIOUS CHANGE

At the time of the Revolution there were approximately 3,000 churches in the United States. The majority of these were Calvinist and belonged to the Presbyterians and Congregationalists, whose differences lay less in creed than in matters of church government. The Anglican Church was seriously divided by the Revolution, supplying, on the one hand, the largest number of Loyalists of any church and, on the other hand, the majority of the signers of the Declaration of Independence.

The Methodists, a Protestant group founded by John Wesley whose first missionaries had arrived only in 1769, were growing rapidly, as were the Baptists; and both groups would explode in growth after the Revolution. Lutheran and Reformed church membership lay chiefly in German- and Dutch-settled areas. The small Catholic population was concentrated primarily in Maryland. In 1782 there were still fewer than 25 priests in America. The first American bishop, Father John Carroll, was appointed in 1789.

Ministers of the postwar years generally believed American Protestantism to be in a "low and declining state." The Presbyterian Assembly of 1798 noted "a general dereliction of religious principles and practice among our citizens." Congregations were often restive with authority and impatient of the old doctrines. In 1800 even the powerful Congregational and Presbyterian churches could count less than 10 percent of the people of New England and the Middle Atlantic states as church members. All the major Protestant sects were split by argument and dissension. None of the older Calvinist groups, in fact, had been able to make the necessary adjustments to the great new surge of scientific information, and none had kept direct touch with the secular, optimistic, republican spirit of the time.

Nor was this all. The churches faced a threat in the form of a religious philosophical movement transported from England and Europe in the latter decades of the eighteenth century under the name of *deism*. (See Chapter 2 for an earlier discussion.) Rooted in the Enlightenment's faith in reason and science and closely in tune with the secular, rationalistic temper of the period, deism had a strong appeal to intellectual and political leaders such as Franklin, Jefferson, Paine, and the poets Joel Barlow, and Philip Freneau. Cutting away the intricacies of Calvinistic doctrine, the deists proclaimed God's benevolence but, also, His detachment from the running of the Universe. They also believed in human rationality, goodness, free will, and in nature's order, harmony, and understandability. If people would but live by these beliefs, said Ethan Allen of Vermont, "they would ... rid themselves of blindness and superstition, gain more exalted ideas of God, and make better members of society."

Against the deists the orthodox theologians put up a sturdy defense, but against the inroads of another "heresy," *Unitarianism*, they had less success. Partly imported from England and partly the legacy of the Old Lights of Great Awakening fame, Unitarianism was so named because it rejected the idea of the Trinity and emphasized the human personality, rather than the divinity, of Jesus. "Liberal" Unitarian doctrines, which assumed that most persons possessed the ability to discern religious truth, interested more and more orthodox Calvinist parishioners and ministers after 1790.

Harvard College, the traditional fortress of New England Calvinism, surrendered to the "liberals" in 1805. The "Conference of Liberal Ministers," called in 1820 to furnish leadership for those dissatisfied with Calvinistic orthodoxy, six years later became the American Unitarian Association. This association was a separate group of 125 churches, among them 20 of the oldest Calvinist churches in New England.

FRONTIER EVANGELISM

At the same time, there were indications, as early as the 1790s, that the religious fervor that had been embodied in the Great Awakening might once again provide a revitalizing force in American churches. The Methodists and Baptists, especially, produced a number of evangelist preachers, though revivalism was never really popular in Presbyterian and Congregational circles. On the frontier, in particular, the evangelists' simple, direct, and emotionally satisfying version of Christian faith was well suited to the needs of a pioneer community. There the new institution of the camp meeting took on great importance, and by 1800 traveling preachers had spread revivalism through western Pennsylvania, Kentucky, Ohio, and Tennessee. Famous exhorters such as James McGready and Barton Stone, preaching a vivid religion of hellfire, rigid morality, and salvation, attracted huge crowds.

At the great Cane Ridge camp meeting of 1801 in Kentucky, between 10,000 and 20,000 people heard 40 evangelists preach over a six-day period. Such meetings spread across the country—Methodist Bishop Francis Asbury counted 400 of them in 1811, chiefly in the South and West—and continued through the 1850s.

While frontier evangelism sometimes encouraged emotional excess, it helped bring stability and order to new communities, increased church membership, and gave churches great influence in social and political affairs, especially valuable given that the Revolution had disrupted traditional patterns of authority and destroyed earlier institutions. Calvinism itself was powerfully affected by the impact of this "second Great Awakening," which, in addition to exerting a strong democratizing force on religion, emphasized individual responsibility, morality, and social action. The new Romanticism, by reason of its insistence on the individual, the validity of human emotions, and the ability of the individual to make things better, also contributed significantly to the impetus of revivalism. From the religious enthusiasm generated by this "Awakening," churches became involved in reform causes such as temperance, so

Methodist Bishop Francis Asbury

cial welfare, prison reform, and eventually the abolition of slavery. The historian of religion Mark Noll has characterized the evangelical developments of this era as "democratized Christianity."

FREEDOM AND EQUALITY: THE IDEAL

Thomas Jefferson put into the Declaration the phrase "all men are created equal," using the word *men* in the eighteenth-century sense of "any human being." Those who signed the Declaration apparently agreed that this was part of that body of "self-evident" truth enumerated in the document and supported by natural law. Equality and liberty, the Declaration implied, were coexistent. *Liberty* was the more easily defined; *equality* was more difficult, yet the need for defining its meaning was imperative.

Neither Puritans nor Virginians came to the colonies looking for equality. The company settlers were in search of more wealth, while the Puritans brought with them the elements of an aristocratic theology. Both carried to the new country many of the distinctions of the British social system.

Calvinism also pointed in another direction: It rejected much of the church hierarchy, believed in the priesthood of all believers, and introduced elective methods into portions of church policy. Later, philosophers of the Enlightenment included the principle of equality within their listings of "natural rights," and John Locke and Jean Jacques Rousseau added wider dimensions to the term's meaning.

More important, however, the idea of equality had a strong practical basis in the American colonial experience. The wilderness stripped away the distinctions of civilization and tended to put white men on an equal footing. Native Americans, disease, starvation, and other hazards of frontier life killed an earl's or a tinker's child with equal disregard. The lack of fixed organization in a new society made it possible for Americans to be both free and equal in an actual, visible sense. Social mobility allowed them to change their status, within limits, rather rapidly. The rough equality forced on American society by the frontier was the most compelling fact about it.

Colonial and republican society, like England's, was built on stratifications that no one questioned. Everyone recognized, a Virginian wrote in 1760, that there were "differences of capacity, disposition, and virtue" among people, which divided them into classes. Yet these strata were broader and more vague than England's. Colonial society possessed the whole range of criteria for class distinctions, including wealth and property, dress, manners, speech, and education, but these carried less weight than they did abroad. There was not so much doffing of caps, bowing or curtseying, and pulling of forelocks; British General Carleton complained that it was hard to uphold "the dignity of the throne and peerage" in American society. Few foreign travelers failed to remark on the fluidity of American classes, much of it the result of broad economic opportunities offered by an expanding society.

THE SOCIAL PROBLEM

After 1783, when Americans faced the necessity of implementing the terms of the Declaration, almost every leader gave attention to the problem of equality and of how to make it an integral part of the new nation's life. Jefferson's "glittering generality," as John Adams called it, had provided an inspirational rallying cry for revolution but had not provided a practical definition for constructing a government in a disjointed postwar society. Some, like Fisher Ames, believed the doctrine "a pernicious tool of demagogues"; others, like Thomas Paine, thought it "one of the greatest of all truths" in political theory.

Franklin, while remarking that "Time, Chance, and Industry" created social and economic distinctions, believed that everyone was equal in "the personal securities of life and liberty." Jefferson and John Adams discussed the matter in their old age, concluding, in Jefferson's phrase, that there was a "natural aristocracy" of "virtue and talents," but that there was also an equality of rights belonging to all. (Or, as Nathaniel Ames said succinctly in his popular *Almanac*, "Men are by nature equal, but differ greatly in the sequel.")

Generally, the leaders of the postwar generation agreed that the new nation needed a government in which the better and more able governed, and also one in which the rights of all were equally protected and maintained. On this basis the nation began to build its society, with the implications of the term *equality* still to be explored more fully by future generations.

Thoughtful Americans were well aware that it was inconsistent to have slavery in a society based on "natural rights" and to wage a revolution to free people who held others in bondage. There was no dearth of opposition to slavery. Between 1776 and 1804 seven states passed legislation for emancipating slaves. Jefferson included an antislavery clause in his instructions to the Virginia delegates to the Continental Congress and tried unsuccessfully to place an antislavery provision in the Virginia constitution of 1776. Revolutionary leaders Charles Carroll and William Pinkney also unsuccessfully sponsored an antislavery bill in the Maryland legislature in

George Washington at his Mount Vernon home. Although the leaders of the postwar generation generally agreed in the equally protected rights of all, slavery remained legal in several states for many years.

1789. While slavery was a matter of legal condition, it was also a matter of race, which made a great difference when emancipation legislation and the black slave's future status in an overwhelmingly white society were discussed.

Theories of race were not well developed until the eighteenth century, when continuing contact with Native Americans and blacks forced Europeans to speculate about the different kinds of human beings, their origins, and their qualities. Eighteenth-century scientists, who arranged all life forms in systems, considered the different races as varieties of one human *species*. That species, created by God to occupy a particular place in the design of nature, existed within fixed, unchangeable limits. The varieties of races were the result of geography, climate, and other factors, which produced differences within the species but did not alter its boundaries. Beginning with the Biblical account of the creation of Adam, scientists postulated that at one time all humans had been alike but that different environments had changed them into members of related races, differing in color, size, hair, and other characteristics. Though color was not a wholly satisfactory criterion for identifying these varieties of human beings, it provided the most visible and logical basis for classifying them.

There were also those—claiming Biblical support—that believed the different races were the result not of environmental influence but of a second creation; and later there were still others who believed that each race had originated in one of a series of separate creations. Whatever the theory, it was generally agreed that there were five biologically identifiable groups of humans: Caucasian or white; Mongolian or yellow; Malayan or brown; "American" or red; and Ethiopian or black. Whether or not these races were equal in abilities—or, if not, possessed the potential to be made so—became a question of major importance to the Enlightenment.

Some philosophers believed that since all people, whatever their color, were created as members of the same species, they had the same potentialities and, through education, favorable environment, and other means, could reach equality. Among the American writers who belonged to this school, one of the most influential was Professor (later President) Samuel Stanhope Smith of Princeton. Others disagreed, arguing that the races were separate and not necessarily equal. Thomas Jefferson, in *Notes on Virginia* (1786), took the view that certain races, particularly the red and the black, probably did not possess the proper potential for progressive change and that while their status might be improved, it was doubtful they could attain actual equality. He later modified his ideas, expressing the hope that blacks would someday be "on an equal footing with the other colors of the human family."

As the debate over race continued into the nineteenth century, Jefferson's hope seemed increasingly less likely of realization. Philosophers and scientists on both sides of the Atlantic tended to assume that each race had inherent and quite separate traits. They were not equal, nor could they be made so. Most authorities ranked them in descending order as white, yellow, brown, red, and black, on the basis of pseudoscientific evidence subject to much debate. This theory of racial abilities dominated American thinking about race over the next half century. It both shaped and was used to justify the national policy toward Native Americans and blacks.

SHAPING AMERICAN SOCIETY

FEEDING AND CLOTHING THE REPUBLIC

From the earliest settlement, soil and sea provided Americans with abundance. Nowhere else in the world did people have food in such quantity and variety as in the United States. A visitor to New York City in 1796 counted 63 kinds of fish, 14 kinds of shellfish, 52 kinds of meat and fowl, and 27 kinds of vegetables for sale. Contemporary accounts show that American appetites were impressively large: Count Volney, who was almost hospitalized during a tour of the United States by a breakfast of fish, steak, ham, sausage, salt beef, hot breads, and cider, wrote that Americans seemed to pass "the whole day ... in heaping indigestions upon one another."

Such abundance was unavailable, however, to the less affluent. Habit and ignorance of nutrition, as well as economic deprivation in many instances, made the average American meal ill balanced and monotonous. Frontier diet leaned heavily on game, mush, molasses, beans, peas, and "hawg and hominy." The city laborer's diet was not much different, except that it had less game and fewer vegetables. Its staples were bread and meat—usually salt pork, pickled beef, salt fish, and sausage. For most slaves the diet was even worse, though on occasion a slave mother could smuggle food to her family from the "big house."

Meat was salted or smoked because preservation was a problem. A freshly killed chicken lasted only about 18 hours in a city market. Neither country nor city people, unless they could afford it, consumed much fresh milk, vegetables, or fruit. Scurvy and rickets were common in the lower walks of life.

A great change in diet came after 1820, when new methods of refrigeration and canning partially solved the ancient problem of food preservation. Commercial canning began in 1819, and the substitution of tin containers for glass in the 1830s made the process better and cheaper. Icehouses for storage had been common since the seventeenth century, and efficient home iceboxes came on the market as early as 1803. By 1840, according to the New York *Mirror*, an icebox was as much a necessity as a kitchen table.

American men in the post-Revolutionary years dressed much the same as the British of similar social and economic situation. Though a few older men still wore wigs in 1800, most men wore long hair tied in a queue. Madison was the last President to wear a queue, and by the 1820s the style was gone; James Monroe wore his hair shorter, parted in the middle, and combed in shaggy waves in the reigning style. Beards did not appear until the 1830s and then mostly on radical-bohemian types. They did not gain respectability until the Civil War (Lincoln was the first bearded President) and then flourished in luxuriance until the 1890s.

A well-to-do city man's attire in the 1790s might include a beaver hat, blue cutaway coat with high collar and broad lapels, striped waistcoat, white linen scarf, light-colored doeskin breeches buttoning below the knee, and high soft boots with turned-down tops. Gone were the gaudy colors, gold embroidery, and decorative ruffles of the 1770s. Colors were muted, the emphasis on quality cloth, skilled tailoring, and understated elegance.

By 1810 the full-length pantaloon had replaced knee breeches, and by the 1820s men wore tight-waisted, high-collared, wide-shouldered coats with rolled lapels, contrasting vests, shirts with wide collars, and colored cravats. The city laborer or artisan wore buckskin or ticking (heavy cotton) breeches, a thick shirt of linen (or deerskin or "linsey woolsey," a linen-wool mixture), a coat of "duroy" (coarse woolen cloth) and heavy boots. He probably also had a suit of broadcloth or dark corduroy for church, weddings, christenings, and burials. Fustian, a cotton-flax combination, was used widely in the South for both men's and women's ordinary clothes. Jeans, a wool-cotton mixture, was common in the North.

Improved spinning and looming machinery and the rise of the textile industry changed male clothing habits. A plentiful supply of cheap cloth and the appearance of factory-made, ready-to-wear clothing made class distinctions in style, cut, and fabric less obvious. Without close inspection, foreign travelers observed, it was often difficult on a Sunday to distinguish a mechanic from a clerk or even a banker.

As men's fashions followed London, so women's fashions followed Paris—if the woman belonged to a family that could afford to indulge this predilection. In the postwar period the tremendous hair arrangements dictated for women during the preceding years (some had to be mounted on wire forms) gave way to shoulder-length curled hair, secured by ribbons and combs and sometimes lightly powdered. Rouge and "pearl powder" were common cosmetics. By 1800 hair was shorter, pomaded into tight curls. By 1812 it was longer again, curled into loose tendrils and decorated with leaves, flowers, jewels, and the like.

The trend in fashion at that time was toward sheer, clinging materials, the basic dress a straight narrow tube (almost always white) with drawn-in high waist, puffed sleeves, and a single petticoat or pink tights underneath. Over the next decade there evolved the "Empire" style, patterned after that of Napoleonic Paris, with long narrow sleeves, plunging necklines, and sweepingly draped skirts, done in rich damasks, brocades, silks, and fine light wools or cottons. Fashions shifted dramatically in the 1820s toward bright colors, low waistlines, ankle-length skirts, wide sleeves, large collars, and ballet slippers or low shoes. In the 1830s came stays, stomach boards,

Dolley Madison

French pantelettes, leg-of-mutton sleeves, and full skirts that were soon to give way to hoopskirts.

All this, of course, was high style. A visitor to the White House reported that, like most American women, Dolley Madison at home wore "a plain stuff dress protected by a large apron with a linen kerchief pinned about the neck." The usual costume for housework was a no-nonsense, long-sleeved wool or cotton dress buttoned up to the neck, with lightweight knee-length linen or flannel underdrawers for protection against the chill of unheated houses.

MARRIAGE, MORALS, AND FAMILY LIFE

"Marriages in America," wrote Franklin in 1782, "are more general, and more generally early, than in Europe." With agriculture pushing westward and industry expanding in the cities, young couples did not need to wait for capital to marry—as in Europe they often had to do. And in the newer settlements young women, considerably outnumbered by the men, were in much demand as wives and had much greater freedom of choice.

American marriages tended to be not only early but unusually productive. Families of six to eight surviving children were common. South Carolina authorities recorded one woman with 34 living children. In America, in contrast to Europe, the delicate business of marriage agreements was either neglected or left to the principals. The "arranged" marriage never found wide acceptance in the United States, and much of Europe's nuptial apparatus—the dowry or *dot*, the contract, banns, and the like—had disappeared by the turn of the century. Young men and women could, of course, recognize the advantages of a good match, but observers agreed that American partners paid less attention to economic benefits.

Attitudes toward divorce differed from those current in Britain and Europe. Divorce seemed more frequent (except in Catholic and strict Anglican circles) and somewhat easier to obtain, especially for men. Laws varied from state to state, but cruelty and desertion, as well as adultery (and nearly 20 other reasons), were recognized as grounds for divorce earlier in America than in Europe. In sparsely settled areas, where courts met infrequently, couples sometimes simply separated without legal formalities. Similarly, couples might live together for months or longer until a circuit-riding parson arrived.

The frontier also accepted so-called left-handed marriages in which militia captains, unlicensed ministers, or even the bride's father performed the ceremony. As churches and organized government caught up with settlement, of course, there was less casualness.

Foreign travelers often noted that the American family lacked the unity and patriarchal structure of the European. Although it formed a strong social unit, with clear educative, religious, economic, and protective responsibilities, it was noticeably less tightly knit than its British and Continental counterpart. Factories sprang up in the cities and young people soon became a vital component of the labor market; and on the farms of the West the same was true. Though shamefully exploited, mill girls could earn enough to be independent, while boys could find work at 11 or 12. Family wealth, social caste, and parental influence—matters of importance in European society—counted for less in a fluid society where sons and daughters, by hard work and a bit of luck, could outdo their parents. In America a young man might easily own more land than his father. A young woman might as easily marry, leave home, and set up her own household, better than her mother's. Meanwhile, with the spread of public schooling the family need no longer serve as the sole medium of education and culture. In sum, material conditions in the new nation combined with the ethos of the American Revolution produced a more democratic family on this side of the Atlantic.

Travelers were particularly amazed at the lack of strict parental control in the United States and at the responsibilities parents placed on children. One British visitor wrote that even at 13 "female children rejoice in the appellation of 'Misses' and begin to enjoy all the privileges of self-management." Boys, it seemed to Europeans, were on their own much earlier than abroad. Some thought this the result of lax discipline in an unformed society, while others attributed it to the American feeling of equality. More probably, the fact was that in the new society where population was scattered and opportunities great, children necessarily took on greater responsibilities. In a frontier setting, boys and girls had to make their own way as soon as they could and grew up quickly because they had to.

There was one component of the population, the slaves, whose family life was uniquely vulnerable. Because slaves were property in the eyes of the law, they could not enter into contracts—including marriage. Men and women formed partnerships, but the law did not recognize these relationships, and family members could readily be sold away from one another if a master found this to be in his economic interest. Scholars debate about the extent to which slaves could protect the integrity of their family life under such brutal conditions.

American moral attitudes were much the same as those of contemporary England, but the powerful Calvinistic tradition (and more rigid Anglicanism) in the United States probably produced a stricter code of morals in small town and rural areas. French émigré Moreau St. Mèry found Philadelphia's morals no looser than Europe's, though he was continually surprised at American frankness about sex. The European custom of keeping mistresses, though uncommon in the United States, was not unknown in sophisticated circles. One traveler noted "young and pretty street walkers" in Philadelphia, saw a bevy of attractive "sailors' girls" in Baltimore, and found an entire section of New York, called "Holy Ground," set aside for prostitution.

Travelers rarely failed to comment on the freedom granted to American youth. A study of Massachusetts church records later indicated that of 200 couples married over a 14-year span, 66 admitted to premarital relations. The practice of "bundling," or sharing the same bed, was a result of frontier housing conditions. Its innocence no doubt varied with the participants. But travelers also agreed that there was probably less extramarital activity in America than in Europe. St. Mèry believed that although American girls enjoyed "unlimited liberty before marriage," an American wife "lived only for her husband, to devote herself without surcease to the care of her household and her home."

WOMEN'S LEGAL STATUS

The legal status of women during the later eighteenth century remained much as it had been in colonial days. Many of the earlier laws were carried into the law books of the new states without substantial change. Unmarried women were considered the wards of relatives, married women their husband's chattels. Although they varied from state to state, a wife's rights to property were closely limited. She could not make a will, sign a contract, or witness a deed without her husband's permission because most states upheld the old English common law doctrine of "coverture," whereby a married woman's legal identity was "covered" by her husband's. For a woman to get a divorce, no matter what the provocation, was so difficult in most states as to be next to impossible.

Almost all professions and trades were closed to women, and of course they could neither vote nor hold office—a handicap they shared with some males. In the eyes of the law, as Blackstone tersely put it in summarizing the essence of coverture, "The husband and wife are one, and that one is the husband."

Not only the law but the church supported this view. According to both Catholic and Protestant clergy, woman's subordinate place in society was established by those intellectual and physical limitations placed upon her at her creation, as the Bible said, and forever fixed by her weaknesses as a daughter of Eve.

Nonetheless, the American woman held a higher status in this new and flexible society than it might appear. In the city or country, woman's work—spinning; weaving; sewing; making shoes, soap, candles, clothing; and much else—was absolutely necessary to the maintenance of the home and the functioning of society. Nor were such mundane tasks the extent of her obligations. The development of the child-centered family, which had begun in the Renaissance, powerfully influenced the position of the woman within the home during the eighteenth century. With it came the idea that the family—not society at large—had the crucial task of preparing the young—socially, intellectually, and spiritually—to enter society. This belief placed major responsibility on women as supervisor of home and teacher of children. By the early nineteenth century men were ready to agree that, from this point of view, women's function in society was equal to—possibly superior to—their own. Herein lay the beginnings of a reevaluation of women's place in the world.

Women were not restricted to purely domestic duties. The system of household manufacturing provided opportunities for them to learn a craft and become part of the home labor market. They also helped their husbands in their work, ran the farm or shop when the men served in the militia or went to sea or hunted game, and often took over management of farm or shop when husbands died. Thus Franklin's sister-in-law Ann ran her husband's print shop after his death, and John Singleton Copley's widowed mother kept her late husband's tobacco store.

The growth of the textile industry was particularly influential in opening the way to the employment of women outside the home. Extending them the privilege of working 14 hours a day at a loom

The growth of the textile industry enabled more women to work outside the home.

naturally raised some doubts about their presumed inferiority. Other trades began to accept women workers until, by the early 1830s, Harriet Martineau could list seven kinds of employment dominated by females—teaching, sewing, typesetting, bookbinding, domestic service, textile millwork, and running a boardinghouse.

NEW THINKING ABOUT WOMEN'S RIGHTS

The Revolution itself encouraged new ways of thinking about women's status. The Daughters of Liberty, though not so well publicized as the Sons, aided in the boycott of British goods and the harassment of Loyalists. Not only did the departure of men to serve in the army and the government create vacancies that women had to fill, but the whole drift of the revolutionary argument worked to their benefit. If all human beings were endowed with natural and unalienable rights, why were women not granted them in full? Strong-minded women like Mercy Warren, Margaret Winthrop, and Abigail Adams (not to mention the legendary Molly Pitcher, who joined her husband's artillery crew at the Battle of Monmouth) were likely to ask such questions. Thus Judith Sargent Murray demanded that an American woman be treated as "an intelligent being" with interests beyond "the mechanics of a pudding or the sewing of the seams in a garment." Enlightened men like Franklin, Paine, and Benjamin Rush joined her in asking for a reconsideration of women's rights.

Meanwhile, the winds of feminist ideas abroad blew westward across the water. Americans read Godwin and Condorcet and especially Mary Wollstonecraft's *Vindication of the Rights of Woman* (1792). Women's rights became a topic of discussion in magazines and drawing rooms, especially in Philadelphia, the new nation's largest city. *Alcuin* , a tract written in 1798 by the Philadelphia-born Charles Brockden Brown, was intended to serve as the American version of *Vindication;* and several of Brown's novels, notably *Ormond*, explored issues raised by the debate about women's rights. Judith Sargent Murray could thus confidently predict in 1798 the advent of "a new era in female history."

This was not soon forthcoming, however. Both in England and in the United States, distrust of "radical theories" after the French Revolution led once-enthusiastic reformers to revise their concepts of female rights and return to earlier, more conservative views of woman's place in society. Part of the reaction derived from a revised concept of "motherhood" and of woman's "place in the home". In contrast to the Puritan and neo-Puritan emphasis on the father as chief agent in childrearing, the eighteenth century gradually shifted responsibility for family life to the mother. By 1800 the mother was considered uniquely qualified, by biological and spiritual design, for raising and educating the next generation. This idea of woman's role in American life, with its stress on domesticity, was in a sense an elevation of woman's status. It also served to rationalize a change in attitude toward her rights. If mothers played such a crucial social and moral role in determining the nation's future, their political and legal emancipation seemed really of secondary importance. Their right to rule the home seemed of greater importance than their right to vote or hold property.

Since it was assumed that most would become wives and mothers, the position of the unmarried woman was not of great social concern. Those who did not marry often served as caretakers in a relative's household (as "maiden aunts") or followed careers in teaching or in one of the limited number of semi-skilled professions open to them.

The key to legal (and social) equality, most women's rights advocates believed, lay in the right of self-development through education. The struggle for equal education was hard, for women faced the old tradition of female inferiority, summarized in Rousseau's dictum that woman's "whole education ought to be relative to man." Although men like Jefferson and Burr believed in educating their daughters in something more than the polite and domestic arts, most Americans considered women's minds to be incapable of contending with subjects like law, philosophy, science, or theology.

Here the argument from domesticity proved useful, however. A mother must be well educated herself in order to educate her children to be the citizens of a republic, with all of the responsibility that implied. Moreover, if she was to be in charge of maintaining a virtuous home, a key institution in the new nation, she obviously must be educated in such a way as to enable her do so effectively. The historian Linda Kerber has coined the term "republican motherhood" to characterize this way of thinking.

The thrust for female education gained momentum swiftly during the early decades of the century. Emma Hart Willard, herself an accomplished mathematician, first cracked the wall (with the help of Governor DeWitt Clinton and others) by establishing in 1821 at Troy, New York, the first endowed school for women that was equal to those for men—Troy Female Seminary. A few others appeared during the 20s and 30s—notably Mt. Holyoke Seminary, opened at South Hadley, Massachusetts, in 1837 by Mary Lyon—but it was left to the next generation to give the women's rights movement measurable momentum.

THE QUEST FOR AMERICAN ARTS

A NATIVE LITERATURE

Having gained political independence, Americans sought their own culture as a way to express—in literature, drama, and the other arts—the fundamentals of their civilization. Critics, editors, and authors agreed on the need for native, original art. As Noah Webster wrote, "America must be as independent in *literature* as she is in politics." But it was easier to demand art than to produce it.

The first step toward artistic independence was to declare America's freedom from English and European domination. The second was to define the circumstances and standards by which the new nation could produce its own distinguished literature. The author must have something American to write about and a defined, recognizable, native manner of writing it. True, Timothy Dwight admitted, the United States lacked "ancient castles, ruined abbeys, and fine pictures." On the other hand, the American artist possessed a number of things that neither British nor other European artists possessed.

The American artist had the Native American, the frontier, and a brief but eminently usable past. After 1790 every author of note made at least one attempt to use the American frontier or American history in a major work. In addition, American artists possessed ample material for studies of manners—what dramatist James Nelson Baker called "the events, customs, opinions, and characters of American life."

PATTERNS IN AMERICAN PROSE

The distinguishing development in literature during the period from 1783 to 1830 was the growing popularity of the novel, the poem, the essay, and the drama. This growth was accompanied by a decline of such once-popular forms of writing as the sermon, the journal, and the travel narrative. It reflected in part the higher level of appreciation and sophistication of American society and in part a greater effort by American writers to enter into the mainstream of contemporary literary fashions.

The essay, modeled chiefly after the work of the great British essayists, attracted a number of talented Americans, among them Washington Irving, who became famous with the appearance of *The Sketch Book* (1819–1820). Although most critics did not consider the novel an art form worthy of serious effort, the popular demand for fiction increased rapidly. Magazines printed novels by the score, and libraries stocked greater numbers of them each year.

The most popular ones, such as William Hill Brown's *Power of Sympathy* (1789) and Susannah Rowson's

Washington Irving

Charlotte Temple (1791), copied the novels of the English author Samuel Richardson. The Gothic novel of suspense and terror found a gifted American practitioner in Philadelphia's Charles Brockden Brown, whose *Wieland* (1798) and *Ormond* (1799) were uneven in quality but indicative of genuine talent.

Most popular of all, however, was the historical romance, patterned on the works of Sir Walter Scott, whose novels enjoyed a tremendous vogue in early nineteenth-century America. Dozens of American novelists imitated him, but none successfully fitted the Scott formula to the American scene until James Fenimore Cooper wrote *The Spy* (1821), *The Pioneers* (1823), *The Last of the Mohicans* (1826), and 30 other novels. When Cooper's buckskin-clad hero Natty Bumppo walked into American fiction and leaned on his long rifle, the American novel came of age.

Meanwhile, another American, the afore-mentioned Washington Irving, had included several pieces of short fiction in his *Sketch Book*. Two of these, "Rip Van Winkle" and "The Legend of Sleepy Hollow," provided a pattern for a new literary form, the short story, and their central characters quickly became a part of the American cultural heritage. Irving's popularity, combined with Cooper's, furnished a decisive answer to English critic Sydney Smith's sneer in 1820, "Who reads an American book?"

READING FOR THE PEOPLE

With a near doubling of population between 1790 and 1830, there was a large new mass audience for books. People were unusually literate because of the spread of popular education, and they had a taste for books of every kind. At the close of the Revolution, Boston counted 50 bookstores, New York and Philadelphia 30 or more each. Peddlers and "book agents" hawked books, along with pots, ribbons, and liniments, up to the edge of the frontier. Subscription and rental libraries, developed in the mid-eighteenth century, swiftly multiplied. In 1825 the libraries of the five largest American cities had 20 times more books to *lend* than the entire country *owned* in Washington's day.

With this growing audience in mind, publishers, booksellers, and writers soon worked out better marketing and publication methods. New machinery for papermaking, typesetting, and printing increased production a hundredfold. The steam-powered cylinder press, perfected by the 1830s, turned out thousands of impressions an hour.

Improved mail services and the expanding network of roads meant cheap, quick distribution of reading matter.

This great new market naturally demanded a supply. Fiction was a particularly lucrative field for writers and publishers. "Sentimental" novels, in which characters had to distinguish between "false" and "true" love and surmount heartrending domestic disaster, flooded the market. Written by and for women—some quite skillfully—these novels were the "true confessions" of the day. Often the protagonist was an orphaned girl, that had to learn how to grow into a skilled and virtuous housewife and mother. With this theme, the novels reinforced the cultural authority of woman as household manager and mother and at the same time carried implicit messages of female pride and independence.

Women produced the bulk of American fiction written in the postwar decades and provided by far the largest market for it. Of the approximately 200 American novels published between 1790 and 1820, two-thirds were by female authors. While they tended to feature highly emotional and melodramatic plots, with names such as *The Coquette, The Beggar Girl,* or *Virtue Rewarded,* they nevertheless showed that women's concerns and values were legitimate literary subjects and emphasized the importance of women in the society of the new Republic.

Equally popular were tales of mystery, terror, and crime, such as *Adventures in a Castle* and *The Asylum,* patterned on the British Gothic novel. So, too, were stories of Native Americans, war, and adventure, like *The Prisoners of Niagara, The Champions of Freedom,* and *The Mysterious Chief.* Nearly as much fiction as fact, Parson Mason Weems' biographies of Francis Marion, Benjamin Franklin, and George Washington (including the hatchet-and-cherry-tree story) left indelible impressions on the American mind. (See *"Parson Weems: The Hero Maker".*)

POETRY IN THE NEW REPUBLIC

Poetry found hard going in the period after the Revolutionary War. There were plenty of young people interested in writing verse but the way of the poet was difficult in a world torn by two wars with England, a near-war with France, bitter political rivalries at home, and a whole new political system a-building. Some talented writers, like Joel Barlow, tried their hands at "epics" and retreated to politics; John Trumbull, one of the cleverest, went into law. Timothy Dwight, whose poetic aims were high but whose gifts were of doubtful quality, turned to theology and education.

PEOPLE THAT MADE A DIFFERENCE

Parson Weems: The Hero Maker

Parson Mason Locke Weems occupies a unique place in American history. He gained immortality with one book and one anecdote. The book was The Life of George Washington, with Curious Anecdotes Equally Honourable to Himself and Exemplary to His Young Countrymen, published in 1800. The story was, of course, about young George, his hatchet, and his father's cherry tree. These seem scant reason to warrant fame, but with them Weems created the first authentic, enduring American hero.

Mason Weems was born in Maryland in 1759. Little is known of his childhood and youth. He may have served in the Royal Navy and he may have studied medicine in Scotland. He appeared in England, however, after the Revolution, and with the help of John Adams was ordained a minister in the Church of England in 1784. He returned to take up a church in Maryland and, as was not uncommon for preachers in poor parishes, took another job. He signed up as a book agent and traveled on horseback through the country settlements peddling broadsides, recipes, pamphlets, books, and prints. He did well, married Frances Ewell, a local girl, in 1795, and moved to Virginia.

Here his growing family required more income than his pulpit provided, so he hired on as agent for Matthew Carey of Philadelphia, one of the most aggressive publishers in the East. Weems proved as good at selling as he was at preaching and combined the two until he found he was spending more time taking orders than saving souls. Since he was also an accomplished fiddler, he was much in demand at weddings, dances, and holiday celebrations, and he was well known and well liked in the backcountry settlements from Georgia to Pennsylvania.

Weems was a superb salesman, and wherever he found a crowd he stopped to tout Carey's list of 76 titles and 56 maps and prints. In fact, Weems set a kind of record by selling over 3,000 copies of Carey's Family Bible at the then-astronomical price of $30.00 each. He sensed, though, that the market was ready for something different from anything on Carey's lists. His countrymen were religious and patriotic and liked a good story; they needed a history, and they needed heroes. So Weems suggested to Carey that a series of books about famous Americans "of Courage and Ability" would provide exactly what the public warranted. Washington was the obvious first choice, and when the ex-President died suddenly in late 1799 Weems put out a short biography (dedicated to Martha Washington) within a few months. Three editions, each expanded over the previous one, were sold out within the year.

Weems was, after all, a "parson", whose purpose in life was to "uplift his fellowman" and put his country on the path to righteousness. He believed that Washington's "unparreleled [sic] rise and elevation was due to his virtues," and that he was therefore the best possible model for Americans to emulate. Washington's virtues, he wrote Carey, were "his Veneration of the Diety [sic], his Patriotism, his Industry, his Temperance and Sobriety, his Justice, etc.," all of which (and more) he illustrated by "anecdotes apropos Interesting and Entertaining."

Since Weems conceived of his book as a kind of sermon, he could see no harm in embellishing his anecdotes a bit, or, for that matter, making up ones he needed. Any legend of rumor, if it would add to the story, was therefore fair game. As a dedicated Jeffersonian, Weems was also anxious to show Washington not as a lofty aristocrat, but rather as a heroic, statesmanlike man of the people. The book sold hugely, entranced his readers, and created a legendary Washington who still endures.

Parson Weems, of course, wrote not history but fiction, and he wrote it well. Washington was a skillful mixture of adventure, patriotism, morality, and hero worship that struck, the public exactly right. The cherry-tree incident did not appear until the fifth edition in 1806, and other unverifiable anecdotes appeared from time to time—the Native American who fired at Washington 17 times at the Battle of the Monongahela and mysteriously missed every time; the Quaker observer who saw him praying alone in the woods at Valley Forge; his mother's dream of how little George put out the fire that threatened their home, just as he later saved the nation from the consuming blaze of war and dissension.

There were other stories of Washington's youthful wisdom and strength of character—of how as a boy he refused to allow his classmates to fight and instead adjudicated their quarrels with even justice; of how he showed his precocious military talent by organizing his school friends in mock battles. The man who emerged from the book was precisely the larger-than-life figure the public wanted—strong, pious, just, virtuous, and everything else an American hero should be—a "patriot Hero, a Christian statesman, great in goodness and good in greatness."

Weems, unfortunately, sold the rights to his book to Carey for $1000 in 1808, but the book had a life of its own. It went on and on, through at least 90 editions, and was still on sale for a dime in an abridged edition as late as 1930. William McGuffey picked up the cherry tree story and others for his famous series of school Readers (1836–1857), thus introducing Weems to uncounted millions of youthful readers. Nobody really knows, to this day, how many copies of the Parson's Washington have been sold.

Loss of the Washington did not discourage Weems. He went on to write similar exemplary—and touched-up—lives of Francis Marion (1809), Benjamin Franklin (1815), and William Penn (1822), all successful. He still wanted to make the United States the world's most moral, Christian nation, and he believed that the right kind of reading would help his countrymen accomplish it. Therefore he began a series of books under the general title of God's Revenges, directed against dueling, adultery, gambling, murder, and drunkenness. They warned effectively against those and other sins and were also whacking good melodramas, the soap operas of their times. Who would not be interested, for example, in how handsome, elegant James O'Neale seduced pretty, trusting Matilda L'Estrange, whose brother then pursued the miscreant and shot him twice in the head—all illustrated with seven lurid engravings?

All in all, before he died in South Carolina on May 23, 1825 (leaving 10 children), Parson Weems had authored 25 pamphlets and books in addition to the Washington. As one of Weems' friends remarked of his writings, they were "most admirable in their effect except that you know not what to believe." His readers probably sold over a million copies, which made him clearly one of the best-selling authors of his day.

Later biographers de-fictionalized Washington and made him gradually into the Virginia planter-aristocrat, professional soldier, and indispensable statesman that he no doubt really was. Yet he remains to Americans, in an equally real sense, the boy who could not tell a lie and who grew up to be Father of His Country—as Parson Weems said he was.

This was not the case with Philip Freneau, the first authentic poetic voice to be heard in the new nation. His poems, dealing with nature, beauty, the past, and personal experience, show genuine poetic gifts. The delicacy and skill of his lyric verse were unmatched by any American poet of his day.

These early poets, however, belonged to the formal English tradition. Colonial Americans had imported the British broadside, a sheet of paper with ballad verses written on one side and sold for a penny by street hawkers. These remained popular after the turn of the century. Really a form of versified journalism, they dealt with crimes, battles, deaths of the famous, holidays, natural disasters, and anything else of public interest.

The Revolution and the War of 1812 elicited hundreds of such poems, many anonymous, printed either as broadsides or in magazines, with titles like "A Patriot's Prayer," "A Song for the Redcoats," and "Hale in the Bush." Similarly, funeral poetry, written to commemorate the passing of famous and ordinary alike, constantly appeared in newspapers.

THE THEATER AND OTHER ENTERTAINMENTS

Immediately after the Revolution, people flocked back to the theaters, which had been closed by the Continental Congress in 1774, along with "horse racing, gambling, cockfighting ... and other expensive diversions." Companies catering to elite and relatively affluent audiences presented British, Continental, and some American plays.

American dramatists tended to follow foreign models, using American materials. Royall Tyler's *The Contrast* (1787), patterned on Sheridan's comedy of manners, contrasted true-blue American Colonel Manly with Billy Dimple, an Anglicized fop, much to the latter's disadvantage. James Nelson Barker's *The Indian Princess*, or *La Belle Sauvage* (1808), focused on the Native American-white conflict, a persistent theme. John Howard Payne's *Clan* (1823), introduced the song, "Home, Sweet Home."

The growth of audiences stimulated a wave of theater building in the cities between 1790 and 1840—big theaters, seating as many as 4,000. Where theaters did not exist, companies played in tents, taverns, ballrooms, barns, and anywhere else that an audience could find seats. As audiences increased, prices decreased. Whereas a New York theater box cost $2 in 1800, most city theaters by 1820 had a 75¢ top price, with tickets for the gallery as low as 12-1/2¢. Shakespeare, Goldsmith, and Sheridan, well acted and presented, were successful at the

After the Revolution, the growth of theater audiences stimulated a wave of theater building.

box office, but theatrical emphasis clearly began to shift to mass entertainment. Farces like *The Double-Bedded Room*, melodramas like *Metamora: The Last of the Wampanoags*, and roaring comedies like *The Lion of the West* gave the popular theater audience what it wanted.

"Spectacles" or "pageants," presented either as separate exhibitions or as portions of plays, were as popular as plays. *The Battle of Bunker Hill*, staged at Boston in 1793, reproduced the entire engagement, complete with troops, cannon, gunfire, burning houses, fireworks, and parade. *The Young Carolinian* (1818) included a full-scale battle between the United States Navy and the Barbary pirates. *The Last Days of Pompeii*, presented in Philadelphia in 1830, had 22 spectacular scenes, the last one the eruption of Vesuvius. An evening at the theater in 1820 might also include between-the-acts skits, afterpieces, comic routines, and parodies with names like *Hamlet and Egglet* and *Much Ado About Pocahontas*.

Another popular theatrical form featured the panorama or diorama. A panorama was a painting on the inner walls of a rotunda. To view it, the spectator stood in the middle and slowly turned full circle. A dio-

George Washington leading troops at the battle of Trenton

rama was a continuous strip of painted canvas about 12 feet wide, cranked from one roller to another across a stage to make a moving picture. Music, a lecture, and program notes often accompanied both. Panoramic views of cities—Paris, Rome, London, Jerusalem—were particularly popular. One could take *A Trip to Niagara*, or view *The Battle of Trenton*, or have *A Tour of the Pyramids* for a dollar or less. Probably the largest panorama displayed was the one shown in 1831 of the Battle of Waterloo, Napoleon at St. Helena, and Napoleon's funeral procession, all covering a total of 20,000 square feet.

Animal shows, equestrian shows, jugglers, acrobats, puppeteers, and other itinerant entertainers traveled the countryside in America as they did in England. In 1815 Hachaliah Bailey of Somers, New York, took to the road with a few animals and an elephant named Old Bet. Within a few years more and larger shows followed, some with clowns.

Quite logically, these shows teamed up with traveling acrobatic groups and horse shows to become "circuses", as we use the word.

Where roads did not go, circuses went by boat, down the Ohio and the Mississippi in the 1820s, as far west as Detroit by 1830. The more prosperous shows began to use canvas walls, and later tents, to accommodate larger audiences.

The first circus to travel under "the big top" was probably the Turner show in 1826. A few years later tents were standard for all but the smallest shows. Copying the stage "spectaculars", circuses introduced costumed parades and pageants. Well aware of the popularity of the city "dime museums", they also added "side shows".

ARCHITECTURE

The Enlightenment, as befitting an Age of Reason, preferred spare, clean, harmonious designs derived from Greek and Roman building to the intricate and ornamental baroque and medieval styles inherited from the seventeenth century. There were very few professional architects in the United States at the time of independence, and most existing public buildings were copied from designs imported from Britain. The typical colonial style was, therefore, a modification of Georgian, made popular in England by Inigo Jones and the Adam brothers.

After the Revolution there was an immediate demand for buildings to serve the new state and federal governments, and a corresponding need for professional architects. The current vogue for things Greek and Roman, as well as the prevailing English style, created two distinct architectural traditions—a modified Georgian style, exemplified in Philadelphia's State House, or Independence Hall, and a Romanized style characteristic of the Middle and Southern colonies, best illustrated by Jefferson's Virginia State Capitol at Richmond.

The two greatest practitioners of these architectural styles were Charles Bulfinch of Boston and Thomas Jefferson of Virginia. Deeply impressed by the British style, Bulfinch developed an American version of it, called the Boston or "Federal" style. It emphasized simplicity and balance, with cleanly symmetrical brickwork, graceful doorways separating equal numbers of sash windows, white trim, and classical cupolas. He rebuilt Faneuil Hall in Boston, designed capitols for Boston, Hartford, and Augusta, built a number of churches, and served for a time as architect in charge of the national Capitol in Washington. His influence may still be seen in the small towns of Ohio, Michigan, and Illinois, or wherever the next generation of New Englanders migrated.

Jefferson believed that the United States needed to develop an architectural tradition of its own, free of British influence and worthy of a young, great nation. Perceiving an analogy between the grandeur of the classic past and the future of the Republic, he drew on his study of Roman remains in Europe, and of French and Italian adaptations of the Classical style, to create an American tradition well illustrated by his plans for the University of Virginia. His home at Monticello, on which he worked for 40 years, was his crowning achievement and is one of the gems of American architecture.

After Jefferson, Benjamin Latrobe, whose source was Greek, not Roman, and who further modified the Classical tradition with his followers helped initiate what soon became the Greek Revival era in American architecture. The Federal, Classical, and Greek Revival styles, though they added grace, beauty, and charm to the American scene, still could not yet be called wholly American architecture.

The laborer, farmer, and frontier settler, of course, could not afford a Monticello or a Boston townhouse. The early colonists quickly replaced the medieval gables, thatched roofs, and exposed timbers of the English cottage with shingles and clapboards, better suited to American weather. The result was the graceful, func-

Thomas Jefferson's home at Monticello was his crowning achievement.

tional (and usually unpainted) Cape Cod cottage, translated into brick in the Middle colonies and built with variations throughout the country. In the South the "shotgun" cabins, introduced by Scandinavian settlers, were still built on the frontier; but in the growing settlements people preferred the plank-built, four-square cottage or two-story house.

MUSICIANS AND PAINTERS

The eighteenth-century colonists loved music as ardently as their English contemporaries. French and German immigrants, too, brought their musical tastes to America, and after 1800 such cities as New York, Philadelphia, Boston, and Charleston supported good orchestras, musical societies, studios, and academies. However, American composers and musicians, such as William Billings or James Hewitt, could hardly hope to match their powerful European contemporaries or to compete with the talented, trained immigrants who came to America from the finest European orchestras and schools.

As for popular music, eighteenth-century colonists imported large numbers of songbooks from England. "Singing meetings" were common diversions, and "singing schools" trained not only church choirs but secular choruses, some of professional skill. After the Revolution publishers put together "songsters" or "musical miscellanies" by the hundreds, including such songs as "The Blue Bell of Scotland," "Drink to Me Only with Thine Eyes," "Yankee Doodle," "Auld Lang Syne," and many others that became enduring favorites. These collections (such as the 1808 *Missouri Songster*, which Lincoln remembered using as a boy) proliferated after the 1790s and served as the main source of American popular music over the next century.

Samuel Miller, in his *Retrospect of the Eighteenth Century* (1803), admitted apologetically that American art had as yet produced no great painters, though he could point with pride to Benjamin West, John Singleton Copley, Charles Willson Peale, Gilbert Stuart, and John Trumbull. These painters, all born into the pre-Revolutionary generation and rooted in an English and European tradition, looked to Paris, Rome, and especially London for instruction and inspiration.

Leaving America, West became court painter to England's King George III and successor to Sir Joshua Reynolds as President of the British Royal Academy. A painter in the so-called grand style, he specialized in huge canvases of such famous events as *The Death of General Wolfe*. Copley, one of West's students, left also and became one of the best portrait painters in London. Peale not only painted well but founded the first museum in the United States

West's painting *The Death of General Wolfe*

(1786), organized the first public art exhibition in the country (1794), and in 1805 helped establish the Pennsylvania Academy of Fine Arts. He was friends with—as well as the portrayer of—many members of the founding generation, corresponding with Jefferson, for example, about their mutual interest in invention.

Gilbert Stuart, another pupil of West's, dominated American portrait art for nearly 30 years, producing the amazing total of 1,150 portraits. His realistic, luminous style and his feeling for the person behind the painting made him the best portrait painter of the period. His *Washington*, which appears on a well-known postage stamp, is an example of Stuart at his best. Trumbull, strongly affected by West's manner, became head of the American Academy of Arts in 1817 and exerted considerable influence on American taste and critical standards for many years.

Since the Romantic Age was intensely interested in the individual, the most popular form of painting was the portrait. The market for official portraits of businessmen, judges, legislators, militia officers, and the like was excellent, and the market for family portraits of ordinary folk was even better. From polished professionals to self-taught "limners," painters traveled the land taking commissions, while the better known maintained thriving studios in the cities. There were so many that Gilbert Stuart grumbled in his old age "you kick your feet against a dog kennel, and out will start a portrait painter." For those who could not afford the best, some would "paint in" customers' faces on prepainted figures. For even less, a silhouette cutter provided cheaper immortality.

There were limited opportunities for women to receive art training until after 1800, when female seminaries and art academies introduced studio instruction and a few male painters took female pupils. Nevertheless, there were a few notable women painters in this field traditionally dominated by men—Ellen and Rolinda Sharples, who came from England to do portraits; Jane Stuart, Gilbert's daughter; Sara Goodrich, the miniaturist. There were also Angelica Kaufmann Peale and her cousins Sarah Miriam and Anna Claypoole of the "painting Peale" family.

Sarah Peale and her sister, in fact, were both elected to the prestigious Pennsylvania Academy. Sarah, who had her own studio in Boston for 20 years and in St. Louis for 30, was recognized as one of the more successful portrait painters of her time. She was the first professional woman painter in the United States, supporting herself entirely on her commissions.

In areas free of male competition, however, there developed a strong female aesthetic sense and a tradition of craftsmanship displayed in quilting rugs, lace, furniture decoration, homemade water colors, folk painting, and the like. Female academies and private teachers taught needlework, the best of which required great skill and years of training in technique and design. Though the sampler was the most common form of self-expression, the highest technical and artistic performance was the needlework picture of silk embroidery, based on paintings or original sketches, which could take a year or so to complete. Only in recent years have art historians begun to take such early women's art seriously, and much work remains to be done.

WINNING ARTISTIC INDEPENDENCE

During the period from 1787 to 1830 all the arts in the United States were in large part derivative and imitative—dependent upon Britain and Europe for standards and inspirations. Literature showed much more of an American disposition than painting, architecture more than music. Artistic production on the whole was becoming increasingly nationalistic in spirit, though artists and writers still lacked confidence in their own tastes and ideas. They were fearful about not conforming to traditional, time-tested artistic norms.

What the United States wanted was a Golden Age of its own, built out of American materials and ideas but couched in artistic terms and derived from traditional esthetic theories. Real artistic independence was yet to come. At the popular level, however, there was already a sturdy, quite American tradition that would flourish and grow more independent in the half-century ahead.

The story of American culture will be resumed in Chapter 9. In the following two chapters we shall be concerned with the political, diplomatic, and military events of the period under consideration—the period that witnessed the establishment of the Republic and the developments of the Jeffersonian Era. It was, as we mentioned earlier, a period of precedents, a time in which the new government was seeking to establish its identity and to begin functioning as a viable political system.

ESTABLISHING THE REPUBLIC, 1781–1800

The King's Friends
"Our Old Home"
"Go to Hell or Halifax"

THE SEARCH FOR STABILITY

Balancing Federal with Local Authority
The State Governments

THE CONFEDERATION PERIOD

Establishing a Western Policy
Relations with Europe
The Difficulties of Trade
Frenzied Finances
Crisis and Rebellion

FRAMING A NEW CONSTITUTION

The Drift Toward a New Government
The Question of Federalism
The Philosophy of the Constitution
The Convention at Work
Referral to the States
Federalists and Antifederalists
Ratification of the Constitution

LAUNCHING THE GOVERNMENT

Washington and Federalist Rule
Federalist Finance
The Whiskey Rebellion

DEVELOPING A NATIVE AMERICAN POLICY

"Noble Red Man" or "Barbaric Savage?"

Assimilation or Removal
Clashes on the Frontier
THE PERILS OF NEUTRALITY
The French Revolution
Genet Affair
Strained Relations with Britain
Jay's Treaty
EARLY POLITICAL PARTIES

The Emergence of Party Politics
The Election of 1796
Federalists and Republicans
THE TRIAL OF JOHN ADAMS
The XYZ Affair
The Treaty of 1800
The Alien and Sedition Acts
The Election of 1800

The first two decades of American life after the Revolution were the years in which the work of independence was completed, the Republic shaped, the national character determined, the federal system established, and a foreign policy developed. Fortunately for the nation born during this period, it was blessed with a generation of extraordinary leaders. These men met the challenges forthrightly and left a legacy of dedicated and creative work that still fascinates their countrymen and women.

THE KING'S FRIENDS

As soon the Revolutionary War ended, the new government faced a number of problems, not the least of which was what to do about those who had remained loyal to George III. The Treaty of Paris of 1783 contained two clauses concerning the American Loyalists. One recommended that they be restored their "estates, rights, and properties"; the other, that refugees be allowed to return for a year, without persecution or prosecution, to settle their affairs. The States, however, did not always follow these recommendations. The bitter war that "set Nabor against Nabor" had left fierce antagonisms. Loyalists who had served with the British—there were 21 Loyalist regiments in the British army—faced beatings, tar and feathers, and possibly hanging. Most Loyalists who fled did not return.

There were two waves of Loyalist migration—one in the early years of the war, the other near its close. Refugees in the first wave went chiefly north to Canada. Of those in the second wave of "late Loyalists" in 1781–1784, some were probably motivated as much by the promise of cheap land as by loyalty to the King.

Estimates are hard to substantiate, but about 60,000 Loyalists left the United States. Of those, 40,000 went to Canada, 10,000 to England, and most of the rest (including over 1,000 free blacks and slaves) to the West Indies and Africa.

"OUR OLD HOME"

The Loyalists who went to England, chiefly to London and Bristol, were first lionized and then neglected. Governor Hutchinson of Massachusetts, who on arrival was offered a baronetcy (which he could not afford) and an honorary Oxford degree, wrote two years later, "We Americans are plenty here, and cheap. Few if any of us are much consulted or inquired after."

Some liked London, of course; but others found that they did not like the British and that the British, with their prejudice against colonials, did not particularly like them. Britain's tightly woven, hierarchical society had few openings for them in the usual vocations—church, military, law, politics—and not many had the capital or connections needed for business.

Then, too, the Loyalists were not British, but British-American, and England was not home. "I would rather die in a little country farmhouse in New England," said Hutchinson, "than in the best nobleman's seat in Old England." Nevertheless, a parliamentary commission, appointed in 1783 to deal with Loyalist war claims, eventually paid out three million pounds to about two thirds of the claimants.

"GO TO HELL OR HALIFAX"

Loyalists who went to Canada did much better. The British promised half-pay to ex-officers as well as land, lumber, seeds, stock, tools, and clothing, and kept most of their promises. The larger number went to Nova Scotia—to the great port city of Halifax or to the fertile St. John valley. Others went to the St. Lawrence area. Since the Maritime Provinces of Canada were a geographical and economic extension of New England, and central Upper Canada—north of the St. Lawrence River—was a similar extension of New York State, the Loyalists easily fitted into Canadian society. In fact, the British in 1784 created the Province of New Brunswick to separate them from the more conservative society of Nova Scotia.

The arrival of the Loyalists had significant impact on subsequent Canadian history. It placed thriving English-speaking settlements where none had been before, thus reinforcing Canada's British tendencies at a crucial point in its development. Without them Upper Canada might have gravitated toward New York State, the Maritimes toward New England, and present-day Canada might not exist. Refugees from one North American nation, in a sense, became the founders of another. "By Heaven," wrote Loyalist Edward Winslow from New Brunswick, "we will be the envy of the American States. I am in the midst of as cheerful a society as any in the world." In contrast, one Loyalist wife wrote, as she saw the last ships depart for Massachusetts, "Such a feeling of loneliness came over me that though I had not shed a tear through the entire war, I took my baby in my lap and sat down on the moss and wept."

THE SEARCH FOR STABILITY

BALANCING FEDERAL WITH LOCAL AUTHORITY

Of prime importance in the political life of the United States throughout its history has been the problem of federalism—the division of power between the states and the federal government—or, more simply, the issue of local control or "states' rights" versus national power or central authority. The origins of this problem are to be found in the British imperial system of the mid-eighteenth century. At the center of this system had stood Great Britain, whose government had directed foreign affairs and intercolonial relations with the view of keeping the machinery and policies of the empire working in harmony. At the extremities of this system had been the colonies themselves, each of which had attained the right to govern its internal affairs.

In practice, however, the dividing line between imperial and local affairs was variously interpreted, and out of the conflict of interpretations arose the American Revolution. With the Declaration of Independence, the American colonies rejected the government in London altogether and, under the pressures of war, united sufficiently to set up a central authority of their own making—the Confederation.

When Richard Henry Lee on June 7, 1776, offered a resolution to the Continental Congress declaring American independence, he also proposed, "a plan of confederation be prepared and transmitted to the respective colonies for their consideration and approbation." A little over a month later, on July 12, a committee headed by John Dickinson of Pennsylvania presented such a plan to the Continental Congress. On November 15, 1777, after more than a year of debate, the Articles of Confederation were approved and sent to the states for ratification, a process that took four years. During almost the entire war, therefore, as we have seen, the country operated under the authority of the Continental Congress without a formal central government.

Because the loyalty of individual Americans was strongly attached to their states, it was readily agreed that the states should hold the sovereign powers of government. The Articles were designed to create an assembly of equal states, each of which retained its "sovereignty, freedom, and independence, and every Power, Jurisdiction, and right." The Articles of Confederation therefore created a loose confederation of states with a New Congress almost exactly like the wartime Continental Congress then in existence, in which each state—regardless of size, population, or wealth—had an equal vote. The Articles delegated to Congress the power to declare war, make peace, conclude treaties, raise and maintain armies, maintain a navy, establish a postal system, regulate Native American affairs, borrow money, issue bills of credit, and regulate the value of the coinage of the United States and the several states. However, nine of the 13 states had to give their consent before any legislation of importance could be enacted, and enforcement of the decisions of Congress depended upon the cooperation of all the states. Ultimately, all power

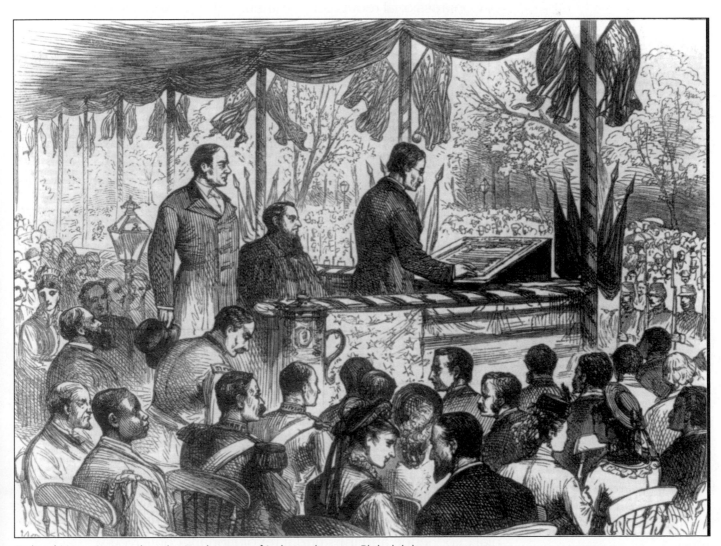

Richard Henry Lee reading the Declaration of Independence at Philadelphia

therefore rested in the states rather than in the national government. For example, Congress could make treaties but could not force the states to live up to their stipulations. It could authorize an army but could not fill its ranks without the cooperation of each state. It could borrow money but had to depend on requisitions from the states to repay its debts. Nor did the Articles provide standing agencies of enforcement. Congress could pass laws, but there was no formal executive or judicial branch to execute and adjudicate them. The day-to-day operations of government were handled rather precariously by officials or committees appointed by Congress.

Because of their recent quarrels with Parliament over questions of taxation and commercial regulation, the states also withheld two key powers from their new central government: the power to levy taxes (Congress could merely request contributions from the state legislatures) and the power to regulate commerce. This proved to be problematic during the Revolution as states actually fulfilled only 10 percent of Congressional requisitions. Without these powers the Confederation government could not depend upon a regular and adequate supply of revenue to sustain its own functions, nor could it attempt to foster a national economy, a factor essential to the political unity of America.

The central government, therefore, was what the Articles called it—nothing more than "a firm league of friendship." Sharing a common cause of facing common danger, its members could work together with some measure of effectiveness. Any suspicion that Congress would infringe upon their own right of independent action, however, would throw the states on their guard.

THE STATE GOVERNMENTS

The Declaration of Independence in 1776 had made necessary the creation of two kinds of government: central and local. While only tentative motions were made toward centralization, the people were quick to make the transition from colonial government to state government. Actually the process was one of revision and adaptation, since each of the former colonies already possessed a government with its own methods of operation. Indeed, two states (Connecticut and Rhode Island) continued to operate under their colonial charters by simply deleting all references to the British crown. Ten other states completed new constitutions within a year after the Declaration of Independence, and the last (Massachusetts) by 1780. The state constitutions, though varying in detail, reflected both the colonial experience and the current revolutionary controversy.

The Federal Hall in New York as it looked in 1789

The framers of these constitutions placed the center of political authority in the legislative branch where it would be especially responsive to popular and local control. As a Massachusetts town meeting bluntly resolved in 1778, "The oftener power Returns to the hands of the people, the Better … Where can the power be lodged so Safe as in the Hands of the people?" Members of the legislature, if they wished to be reelected, had to keep in mind the feelings of their people "back home." Legislators were held constantly accountable by being restricted to brief terms: in 10 states the lower house, which originated tax legislation, was newly elected every year; in Connecticut and Rhode Island it was every six months; in South Carolina, every two years.

Framers of the constitutions, remembering their recent troubles with royal governors and magistrates, restricted the powers of governors and justices almost to the vanishing point. The average governor, contemporary jokesters claimed, had just about enough authority to collect his salary. In Pennsylvania, the position of the governor was abolished and replaced with a council of 12.

The imbalance of power among the branches of government often severely hampered the states' abilities to meet and solve the political and economic problems that faced them during and after the war. Yet whatever their shortcomings, these constitutions were the first attempts to translate the generalities of the Declaration into usable instruments of government. They were constructed on the premise, novel to the eighteenth century, that a government should be formed under a *written* document, thus recognizing the first time in modern political life the difference between fundamental and statute law. The introduction of such precisely formed instruments of governmental law, on such a grand scale, was a major contribution to the science of government.

The state constitutions reaffirmed the powerful colonial tradition of individual freedom in their bills of rights, which guaranteed each citizen freedom of religion, speech, and assembly, trial by jury, the right of habeas corpus, and other natural and civil rights. In general, they extended the voting franchise to the majority of white male citizens. In all states, a man had to own some property to vote. In many, he had to own a more substantial amount to hold office. Since property formed the basis for voting qualifications, and since the states quickly enlarged opportunities to own land, most white males could probably meet the requirements. New Jersey even gave the vote to women, only to withdraw it in 1807. Over the years, gradual abolition of property qualifications further widened the suffrage so that all property requirements were eliminated on a state-by-state basis by 1852.

The popular fear of governmental power tended to render the state governments politically and financially impotent. Afraid to antagonize the voters, who could quickly run them out of office, legislators had difficulty, for example, in passing effective measures of taxation. Even when they did so, revenue men were hard put in forcing collections from the people.

THE CONFEDERATION PERIOD

Such was the political framework within which the new nation entered the "critical period," 1783–1789, from the close of the Revolutionary War to the inauguration of the federal government under the Constitution. The term "critical period" was first introduced by historian John Fiske in 1889, and still possesses some utility. On the one hand, historians have come to believe that the years of the Confederation were more creative and constructive than once was supposed. During these years a peace was won on terms highly favorable to the

United States. An orderly policy for western territorial expansion was established. A postwar recession was overcome and replaced by economic prosperity. The population increased. The Constitution was born. On the other hand, except in regard to western lands, the achievements of the period were due largely to the efforts of particular individuals and groups and to some of the more foresighted state governments. The central government was much too dependent on the conflicting whims of the several states to be consistently effective.

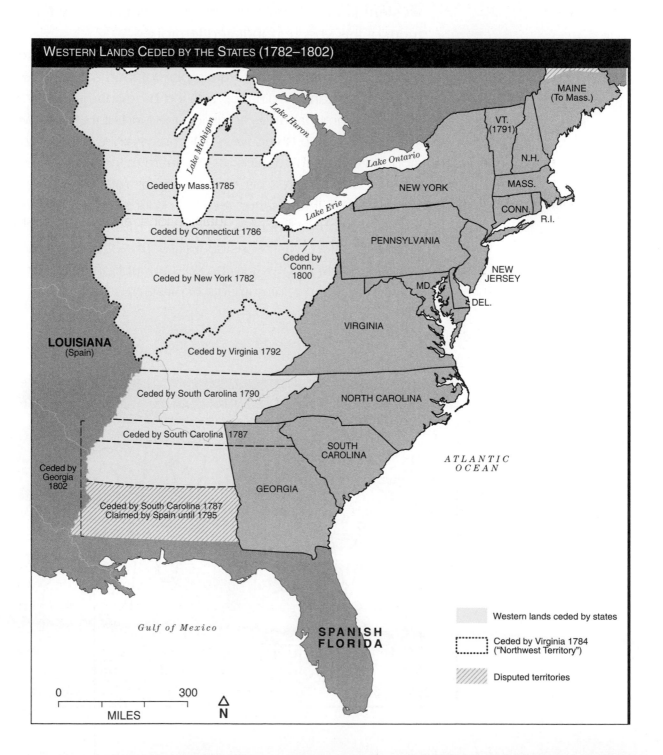

WESTERN LANDS CEDED BY THE STATES (1782–1802)

MAINE (To Mass.)

VT. (1791)

N.H.

MASS.

CONN.

R.I.

Lake Michigan

Lake Huron

Lake Ontario

Lake Erie

Ceded by Mass. 1785

NEW YORK

Ceded by Connecticut 1786

PENNSYLVANIA

Ceded by Conn. 1800

Ceded by New York 1782

NEW JERSEY

MD.

DEL.

VIRGINIA

LOUISIANA (Spain)

Ceded by Virginia 1792

Ceded by South Carolina 1790

NORTH CAROLINA

Ceded by South Carolina 1787

SOUTH CAROLINA

ATLANTIC OCEAN

Ceded by Georgia 1802

GEORGIA

Ceded by South Carolina 1787 Claimed by Spain until 1795

Gulf of Mexico

SPANISH FLORIDA

Western lands ceded by states

Ceded by Virginia 1784 ("Northwest Territory")

Disputed territories

0   300
MILES

N

ESTABLISHING A WESTERN POLICY

The solution to the western land problem (see Chapter 3), which had kept the last state, Maryland, from ratifying the Articles until 1781, was of paramount importance to the new government. It represented a first step toward nationalization and made certain that the nation, as it moved west, would gradually evolve as a unit rather than as 13 colonies with a set of permanent dependent territories. It also meant that since Congress now controlled all the western lands, it could determine a central policy for the development of this vast unpopulated territory.

During and after the Revolution a stream poured west, creating an urgent need for a systematic plan of land sale and territorial government. A Land Ordinance passed by Congress in 1785 provided for a government survey to divide the land of the Northwest Territory (north of the Ohio River, west of Pennsylvania, and east of the Mississippi River) into townships of 36 square miles. Each township was to be split into 36 sections of one square mile (640 acres) each and every section into quarter sections. Four sections in every township were reserved as bounties for soldiers of the Continental Army, and another section was set aside for the use of public schools. The remainder of the land was to be sold at public auction for at least one dollar an acre, in minimum lots of 640 acres.

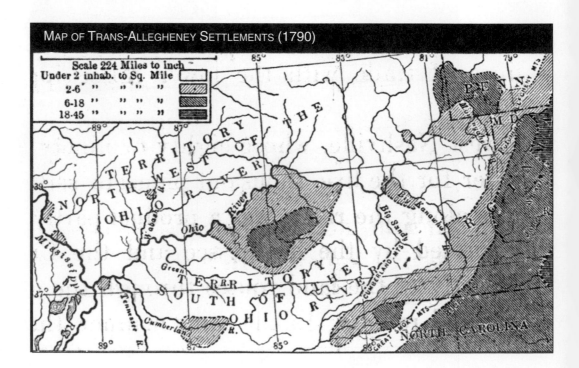

MAP OF TRANS-ALLEGHENY SETTLEMENTS (1790)

The Ordinance of 1785 proved advantageous to wealthy land speculators, who bought up whole townships and resold them at handsome profits. Sensing even greater returns, a group of speculators (including some congressmen and government officials) pressed for further legislation to provide a form of government for the Northwest. The result was the Northwest Ordinance of 1787, based largely on a similar ordinance drafted by Jefferson in 1784 but never put into effect.

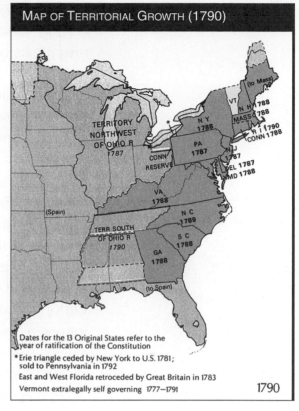

MAP OF TERRITORIAL GROWTH (1790)

Dates for the 13 Original States refer to the year of ratification of the Constitution

*Erie triangle ceded by New York to U.S. 1781; sold to Pennsylvania in 1792

East and West Florida retroceded by Great Britain in 1783

Vermont extralegally self governing 1777–1791

1790

Though it favored the wealthy land speculator over the indigent farmer, the Northwest Ordinance did provide a model for translating the unsettled Northwest, by orderly political procedures, from frontier to statehood. It provided that Congress should appoint from among the landholders of the region a governor, a secretary, and three judges. When the territory reached a population of 5,000 free adult males, a bicameral legislature was to be established. When there were 60,000 free inhabitants (the population of the smallest state at the time), the voters might adopt a constitution, elect their own officers, and enter the Union on equal terms with the original 13 states. From three to five states were to be formed from the territory. Slavery was forbidden in the area, and freedom of worship and trial by jury were guaranteed.

So successfully did the Northwest Ordinance accomplish its political aims that it set the pattern for the absorption of the entire West (as well as Alaska and Hawaii) into the Union. Settlers flooded into the Northwest Territory as soon as the ordinance went into effect. The great drive westward had begun, not to cease for another 100 years.

RELATIONS WITH EUROPE

Perhaps the most serious problems facing Congress under the Articles arose from its lack of a unified, coherent foreign policy and its lack of authority to evolve one. The core of diplomatic power lay equally among the states, each of which possessed the right to arrange its own foreign affairs, with the national government virtually helpless to operate independently.

The United States was in a most delicate position in regard to England, France, and Spain. There was no reason to suppose that Britain intended to allow America to remain independent without interference if Britain's interests dictated otherwise. The United States, for its part, desperately needed agreements with Europe and especially with England, its largest market.

It was also involved in a border dispute with Spain over Florida, and when the Spanish, who controlled the lower Mississippi and New Orleans, closed them to American trade in 1784, the nation was in trouble. If Congress could not open the Mississippi to trade, a number of Western leaders favored either taking New Orleans by force or joining a British protectorate that might help them to do so. Washington felt that the West in 1784 was so near to secession that "the touch of a feather" might divide it from the country.

The Spanish, who needed American trade, seemed willing to negotiate, and in 1785 the Spanish minister Diego de Gardoqui discussed terms with Secretary of Foreign Affairs John Jay. Both diplomats were bound by specific instructions that led to a stalemate, but in 1786 Jay agreed to a commercial treaty. This treaty would have allowed the United States to trade with Spain but not with its colonies—if the Americans would "forbear" navigation of the Mississippi River though not the *right* to use it.

Such a roar of protest went up from the West that Jay let the negotiations lapse. The Spanish helped matters in 1788 by opening the river under restrictions with which the West could live, though not happily, until the Pinckney Treaty of 1795 settled the issue. These negotiations with

Secretary of Foreign Affairs John Jay

Spain not only pointed up the impotence of the Articles in foreign affairs but also left behind in the West a lingering suspicion of the East.

THE DIFFICULTIES OF TRADE

When the colonies left the imperial system, thus giving up their favored economic position, American merchants and shippers found themselves in cutthroat competition with the British, Dutch, and French for world markets. John Adams tried unsuccessfully for three years to make some kind of trade agreement with England, but as Lord Sheffield commented, putting his finger squarely on the commercial weaknesses of the Articles of Confederation, "America cannot retaliate. It will not be an easy matter to bring the Americans to act as a nation. They are not to be feared by such as us."

Sheffield proved to be correct, for when Congress asked the states in 1784 for exclusive authority to regulate foreign trade over a 15-year period, the states immediately refused. Under the Articles of Confederation, Congress was powerless to do more than protest.

Domestic commerce as well as foreign trade suffered from interstate rivalries. The states used their power to levy tariffs against each other, creating barriers that seriously hampered domestic commerce and caused further dissatisfaction with the central government. At the same time, American industry was struggling to survive. The war and blockade had stimulated American manufacturing by cutting off imports from Britain and the Continent. Some of the states, in fact, had offered premiums and subsidies for the production of manufactured goods. With the return of peace much of the artificial stimulation that had encouraged American industry was withdrawn, and the inevitable postwar slump set in. Capital was short, the currency disordered, transportation deficient, and investments risky.

FRENZIED FINANCES

The Articles of Confederation gave the national government no power to tax. If the states refused to pay their levies in full or on time, Congress simply was forced to accumulate ever-larger foreign and domestic debts. The states responded erratically to Congress' requests for revenue, so that while Congress occasionally had money, it never had enough at the right time. Although Congress repudiated most of its war debts by simply canceling out millions of dollars in the currency issued under the Continental Congress, the country in 1785 still owed about $35 million in domestic debts and had a growing foreign debt. The fledgling government owed money to its soldiers that had fought the revolution, but could not pay them. Congress had sold war bonds in an effort to finance the revolution; but those bonds were now coming due, and Congress had no means with which to pay them. As the government defaulted on its obligations, bondholders sold their bonds to speculators for as little as 10 cents on the dollar. The states, meanwhile, had war debts of their own, which they increased after the war by taking on the amounts of the congressional debt that were owed to their citizens.

In addition to the problem of these debts, both national and state governments lacked a uniform, stable, sound currency. There was no trustworthy federal currency, and the states were loaded with badly inflated wartime paper money. Both the states and the central government issued over $200 million in paper currency during the Revolution with the predictable result that inflation reached 12,000 percent at one point in the 1780s. The inflation had the effect of essentially rendering the savings of Americans as worthless. The postwar slump which hit the country in 1783, sinking to its lowest point in mid-1786, affected the farmer and the small debtor most of all. In states where they controlled the legislatures, the solution seemed easy: Seven state legislatures simply approved the issue of paper money in larger quantities. In addition, to help distressed farmers, these states passed "stay laws" to prevent creditors from foreclosing mortgages.

CRISIS AND REBELLION

At the depth of the depression in 1786 there was a severe hard-money shortage. Farmers, especially, were in difficulty. The problems were most acute in Massachusetts where the debt situation led to a decree by the state government that all debt must be repaid at face value. Thus, new taxes were levied to pay the state's debts. The citizens of Massachusetts, however, lacked the resources with which to pay the new taxes. Twenty-nine Massachusetts towns declared their inability to meet their obligations. Tax collector Peter Wood, of Marlborough, Massachusetts, reported that "there was not ... the money in possession or at command among the people" to meet their obligations. Protest meetings in several states won some concessions from the legislatures, but in Massachusetts, a Hampshire County convention of 50 towns met and passed resolutions condemning the state legislature, lawyers, court fees, and the taxation. The Massachusetts county courts became the targets of the citizens' wrath when they issued writs of foreclosure on farmers that had been demanded by creditors and the state taxing authorities. When mobs of unruly men closed the courts at Northhampton, Worcester, and Springfield, thus preventing farm foreclosures and prosecutions for debt, Governor James Bowdoin sent militia to scatter them.

In reply to Bowdoin, Daniel Shays, a veteran of the Revolution and Bunker Hill, began organized resistance to the Massachusetts' government. Shays issued a set of demands, including a demand for new paper money issues, tax relief, a moratorium on debts, and the abolition of imprisonment for debt. Shays organized a band of some 1,200 farmers in the winter of 1786 for an attack on the Springfield Arsenal, from which he hoped to get arms. The governor sent a force of militia of some 3,000 men (paid for by contributions from Boston businessmen) to protect the arsenal, and Shays' poorly mounted attack by outnumbered farmers in February 1787 failed miserably. Four of Shays' men were shot and killed by the Massachusetts militia and 20 were wounded, sending Shays' rebels into retreat. Shays fled toward Canada, though he was arrested and imprisoned; and over 1,000 of his followers were also arrested and jailed. Samuel Adams, who only a decade earlier had led a revolt against the taxation policies of the British government, denounced Shays and the rebels for treason. Two of the rebels were executed, and 16 more were sentenced to death but later granted reprieves. Four thousand more gained leniency by confessing their misconduct and swearing a loyalty oath to the state. The Massachusetts legislature passed a Disqualification Act that prohibited the rebels from voting, holding public office, serving on juries, working as schoolmasters, or operating taverns for a period of up to three years.

Shays' Rebellion had swift effects in Massachusetts. Governor Bowdoin was defeated in the next election by John Hancock, and the legislature prudently decided to grant the farmers some measure of relief. Debtor laws in Massachusetts were reformed, and Shays and his followers were released. The effect on the country at large was equally swift, and much greater. The rebellion shook the confidence of elites in the ability of the confederation to maintain order. As Abigail Adams wrote Thomas Jefferson, when "ignorant, restless desperadoes, without conscience or principles" could persuade "a deluded multitude to follow their standards …" who could be safe, anywhere in the land? "There are combustibles," wrote Washington, "in every state which a spark might set fire to."

FRAMING A NEW CONSTITUTION

THE DRIFT TOWARD A NEW GOVERNMENT

Even the most earnest states' rights advocates were willing to admit the existence of imperfections in the Articles of Confederation, and proposals for conventions to discuss amending them had already appeared in the New York legislature in 1782 and in Massachusetts in 1785. In 1786, under the cloud of Shays' Rebellion, Congress agreed that the Articles needed revision, though as James Monroe told Jefferson, "Some gentlemen have inveterate prejudices against all attempts to increase the powers of Congress, others see the necessity but fear the consequences."

James Madison called for a meeting of delegates at Annapolis Maryland in 1786 to discuss needed changes in the Articles of Confederation and hopefully reach agreement on a uniform tariff. The lack of a uniform tariff had seriously hindered American trade and rendered the confederation impotent in its efforts to retaliate against high British tariffs on American goods. New York, with its busy harbor, opposed high tariffs, preferring more open trade policies in an attempt to boost trade in the port of New York. No agreement was reached in the convention of 1786, and only five states even participated; but it provided the opportunity for Alexander Hamilton of New York to seize the initiative. When Virginia invited representatives from the states to meet at Annapolis in 1786 for a discussion of problems of interstate commerce, Hamilton called upon the states to appoint delegates to a meeting to be held in May 1787 at Philadelphia, to discuss ways "to render the Constitution of the Federal Government adequate to the exigencies of the Union." Since at almost the same time Daniel Shays' men, pursued by Boston militia, were providing an example of the kind of "exigency" Hamilton referred to, his call found receptive audiences in the states. Congress adopted his suggestion and authorized a convention "for the sole and express purpose of revising the Articles of Confederation

Alexander Hamilton

and reporting to Congress and the several legislatures such alterations and provisions therein."

While there were those who believed that the Articles could be amended and reworked into an effective and efficient government, a number of determined political leaders—among them Alexander Hamilton, James Madison, John Jay, and Henry Knox—were convinced that the country's interests demanded a much stronger central government. They believed in executive and judicial control rather than legislative and did not fully trust the decentralized, mass-dominated state governments. There was a general belief among the mercantile and financial classes that, as Madison wrote, the United States needed the kind of government that would "support a due supremacy of the national authority, and leave in force the local authorities so far as they can be subordinately useful."

THE QUESTION OF FEDERALISM

The meetings at Philadelphia began on May 25, 1787. Conspicuously absent were many of the popular leaders of the pre-revolutionary era. These men like Samuel Adams and Patrick Henry, became known as "antifederalists" due to their opposition to a federal form of government that would place more power in the central government at the expense of the states. These men had become involved in the Revolution when it still comprised a scattering of colonial protests and then state revolts, rather loosely guided by the Continental Congress. Deeply devoted to winning independence for their own states, most of them continued to believe that the states should be governed without the interference of a strong central government. Some anti-federalists, like George Clinton of New York, had a vital stake in local state politics, which the enlargement of the powers of a continental government might endanger. Others saw the need to strengthen the Confederation but insisted that the supremacy of the states should not be basically altered. Others feared a strong executive due to what they viewed as abuses of executive power under the English monarch. All of the antifederalists were passionately convinced that a republican system could survive only on the local level, under their watchful eyes. A republic on a continental scale was beyond their imagination.

The 55 delegates who made their appearance in the Philadelphia State House held generally broader views. George Washington (chosen presiding officer of the convention) and Benjamin Franklin were distinguished representatives of an older generation, long experienced in guiding the military and diplomatic affairs of the colonies as a whole. Though Washington, in particular, contributed little to the proceedings at the convention, his presence gave the convention legitimacy in the eyes of the public. Most of the delegates, however, were in their thirties or forties. Their careers had only begun when the Revolution broke out and their public reputations had been achieved as a result of their identification with the continental war effort. With the coming of peace, these "nationalists" had been disquieted by the ease with which the states slid back into their old provincial ways. In vainly advocating revenue and commercial powers for the Confederation Congress, Robert Morris, James Wilson, Gouverneur Morris, James Madison, Alexander Hamilton, Charles Pinckney, and others began to see the futility of trying to govern a large country with 13 states following diverse policies. These men who favored placing more power in the national government became known as "federalists."

These federalists distrusted unchecked power in government as much as their opponents did and favored retaining state autonomy as much as possible. However, they believed that under the current system power *was* being exercised in one quarter without effective restraints. Jefferson branded it the "legislative tyranny" of the states. There was no way to appeal the decisions of the state legislators. The state executive and judicial branches, and even the central Confederation, were powerless to overrule the legislative branch. In addition, nations abroad were beginning to look with contempt upon the disunited states, and there were even dangerous signs of territorial encroachments—by Britain in the Northwest and by Spain in the South and Southwest. The English had not withdrawn all of their troops from American soil in the Ohio Valley. The British remained on American soil in an effort to exploit trade with Native American tribes in the Ohio Valley but, also, to induce the Americans to pay their British debts. Spain controlled the mouth of the Mississippi River and, therefore, could cut off trade to the American interior by closing the Mississippi at their discretion to American trade. The United States had no standing army and was too weak militarily to do anything about either the Spanish or British situation. National survival, and prestige, the federalists insisted, demanded that a stronger central government be created.

THE PHILOSOPHY OF THE CONSTITUTION

The feeling of urgency that permeated the minds of the delegates goes far toward explaining their eagerness to reach compromises on matters in dispute. Whenever the debates became deadlocked, speakers would arise and warn of the consequences should the Convention fail. Said Elbridge Gerry at mid-session: "Something must be done or we shall disappoint not only America, but the whole world. … We must make concessions on both sides." Caleb Strong warned, "It is agreed, on all hands, that Congress is nearly at an end. If no accommodation takes place, the Union itself must soon be dissolved."

Elbridge Gerry

Such warnings climaxed a series of heated arguments during the meetings. There were 569 votes taken at the convention, 60 just to decide on one executive in the form of a president. Of the 55 persons that attended the convention, only 39 signed the document and four voted against it. Of the three New York delegates that attended, only Alexander Hamilton remained at the end as the other two left in disgust. In the end, the document that emerged is best viewed as a political compromise since the founders were not in agreement on many details.

The delegates, generally, believed that the central government must be empowered to act without the mediation of the states and to exercise its will directly upon individual citizens. It must have its own administrative agencies, with the ability to enforce its own laws and treaties, to collect its own revenues, and to regulate commerce and other matters of welfare affecting the states generally.

Second, they believed that power in government, though imperative, must somehow be held in check. Like most enlightened people of the eighteenth century, they recognized that human nature was not perfect. "Men are ambitious, vindictive, and rapacious," said Alexander Hamilton; while his language was strong, his colleagues generally shared his appraisal of human nature. They agreed with the French political philosopher Montesquieu, "men entrusted with power tend to abuse it." The system advocated by Montesquieu to prevent this evil was to distribute the functions of government among three coequal branches of government, each of which would hold a veto or check on the power of the others. John Adams had earlier outlined this doctrine of "separation of powers":

A legislative, an executive, and a judicial power comprehend the whole of what is meant and understood by government. It is by balancing each of these powers against the other two, that the efforts in human nature toward tyranny can alone be checked and restrained, and any degree of freedom preserved in the constitution.

That a three-branch system had failed in the state governments did not shake the delegates' faith in the *principle* of separation of powers. The states had only gone through the motions of creating three branches. In actuality they had not given the executive and judicial branches sufficient checks on the legislatures, which in some states were running riot in control of government.

Finally, most of the delegates were committed to some form of federalism, the political system that would unite the states under an independently operating central government while permitting them to retain some portion of their former power and identity. Few agreed with George Read of Delaware that the states "must be done away." Even Alexander Hamilton, who formally introduced such a scheme, acknowledged that the Convention might "shock the public opinion by proposing such a measure." It was generally agreed that the states must remain. The argument arose over how, in operating terms, power could be properly distributed between the states and the national government.

THE CONVENTION AT WORK

Four days after the Convention opened, Edmund Randolph of Virginia proposed 15 resolutions, drafted by his colleague James Madison. The general intent was clear at once: to proceed beyond mere revision of the Articles of Confederation in favor of forming a new national government. The founders had conflicting goals since they desired to both increase national government power, yet retain state sovereignty. In order to solve this dilemma, Randolph's plan called for a national government sufficient for security, powerful enough to prevent dissension among the states, and strong enough to provide for national development. This "Virginia Plan" proposed a national executive, a national judiciary, and a national legislature consisting of two houses, both representing the states proportionally according to either population or tax contributions, with the lower house popularly elected and the upper house chosen by members of the lower one. Although William Paterson proposed a rival "New Jersey Plan," which in substance would merely have enlarged the taxation and commerce powers of the Confederation Congress, it was never seriously considered.

After four months of debate, amendment, and considerable enlargement, the Virginia Plan became the United States Constitution.

Although the delegates agreed upon the main features of the new government, discord over the details almost broke up the Convention. That a breakup was avoided is attributable in part to the delegates' recognition of the undeniable need for compromise and concession. They were pressed to balance special interest against special interest, the large states against the small, section against section, in order to work out a constitution that the majority could accept. No state could be perfectly satisfied with the result, but each could feel that the half loaf it garnered for its interest was far better than none.

Major opposition to the original Virginia Plan came from the small states. In the existing Congress each of their votes was equal to that of any large state, but under the proposed system of proportional representation in the national legislature they would be consistently outvoted by the larger, more populous states. Delegates from the large states retorted that government should represent people, not geography. "Is (a government) for *men*," asked James Wilson, "or for the imaginary beings called *States*?" The issue came down to the question of how federal the federal government should be. In acknowledging the permanence of the states, were the delegates obligated to go further and introduce the concept of the states into the very structure and representation of the new central government?

The signing of the Constitution

The final answer to this question was yes. In the end, the large states gave in. After the New Jersey Plan was rejected and the principle of a bicameral (two-house) legislature established, the small states, while hesitating to object to proportional representation in the lower house, persisted in claiming the right of equal representation for states in the Senate, or upper house. By threatening to walk out of the Convention, they won. In essence, this "Great Compromise," as it came to be called, was hardly a compromise at all. The major issue concerned representation in the Senate; and when the large states conceded on this point, they received no concession in return. However, the major crisis of the Convention had been resolved.

In the process of accepting this two-house legislature, the delegates acknowledged not only a balance between large and small states but also a balance between the common people and the propertied interests. Many delegates had argued against giving the people a direct voice in government; "The people," said Roger Sherman, "should have as little to do as may be about the government. They want information, and are constantly liable to be misled." Elbridge Gerry pointed to the "evils" that "flow from the excess of democracy." Other delegates agreed, however, with James Madison who stated, "that the great fabric to be raised would be more stable and durable, if it should rest on the solid foundation of the people themselves." Thus the basis of representation in the lower house was set at one representative for every 40,000 persons—each representative to be elected by voters eligible to elect "the most numerous branch of [their] State legislature." On the other hand, the senators of the upper houses—two from each state—were to be chosen by the state legislatures, putting them at a second remove from popular control. As a result, the Senate was expected to represent the more conservative interests, "to consist," as John Dickinson noted, "of the most distinguished characters, distinguished for their rank in life and their weight of property." In sum, the two houses of Congress were to balance the rights of the lower and higher ranks of society, but with the edge given to the higher.

Another issue arose over the manner of choosing the President, the head of the executive branch of the new government. To have the national legislature appoint him, as the original Virginia Plan proposed, might mean, it was argued, that a candidate to that high office would be "a mere creature of the legislature." A second plan, championed by James Wilson, called for popular election of the President, but the delegates had too great a distrust of unchecked democracy to find this plan fully acceptable. Other proposals sought to bring the states into the elective process by having either the state legislatures or the governors combine to elect the nation's chief executive.

The final compromise embodied elements from all these plans. Each state legislature was to appoint a number of presidential "electors" equal to the total number of senators and representatives to which the state was entitled in Congress. The electors would meet in their own states and vote for two presidential candidates, and the candidate receiving the majority of votes from all the states would become President. It should be noted that the method of choosing the

The United States Constitution

electors was left to the decision of the state legislatures. Thus, the legislatures might decide to keep the power of appointment in their own hands, as most of them did, or they could submit the appointment to popular vote, a method that became widespread only much later. In either case, the electoral system was intended to minimize popular influence in the choice of the President.

Few of the delegates, however, believed that the election would end in the Electoral College. It was believed that each state would try to advance a native son, and thus no candidate would receive a majority vote. In that event, the election would be referred to the House of Representatives, where votes would be taken by state delegations with each state having one vote. In effect, this presidential compromise echoed the earlier issue over proportional representation. In the first phase of the election, votes would be drawn on the basis of population. In the second phase, voting would be on the basis of statehood.

The conflict between North and South was not so serious in the Convention as it was later to become, but the differing sectional economies did arouse specific issues of governmental structure and powers. Because the South was an agricultural region dependent on a world market for its staple exports like tobacco and rice, it wanted commercial regulation—tariffs and export duties—eliminated or minimized. Southerners were also committed to slavery, not necessarily through moral conviction of its justice but because of their inescapably large investment in slave labor. Finally, the Southern states, six in number and comparatively less populous than the Northern states, were aware that in Congress the North would outnumber them. They thus felt compelled to secure constitutional guarantees for their sectional interests before launching a new government in which they could be consistently outvoted.

In the North, on the other hand, agricultural products like grain and livestock had for the most part a ready domestic market. Many Northerners were more interested in having the government promote shipping and foster manufacturing by means of protective tariffs. Many also roundly condemned slavery and demanded an end to the "nefarious" slave trade. Their attitude, however, was not entirely without self-interest. The Convention had already agreed that direct taxes were to be assessed on the basis of population. The North was quite willing to have slaves counted as part of the population in apportioning such taxes, thus upping the South's assessments; but Northerners objected to counting slaves in apportioning representation in the House of Representatives, a plan that would enlarge the Southern delegations.

The Convention resolved these differences by negotiating compromises. In regard to commerce, the South won a ban on export taxes and a provision requiring a two-thirds vote in the Senate for ratification of treaties. In return, the North secured a provision that a simple congressional majority was sufficient to pass all other acts of commercial regulation. The slave trade would not be prohibited before the year 1808, but a tax of 10 dollars might be imposed on each slave imported. The so-called three-fifths compromise specified that five slaves would equal three free men for purposes of both taxation and representation.

The influence of the states in the framework of the new constitution was greater than some nationalists would have liked. One of the most important factors shaping the delegates' decisions was their practical recognition that they had to offer a constitution that the people would approve, and popular loyalty to the respective states was too strong to be ignored.

REFERRAL TO THE STATES

By the close of the summer the Constitution was slowly taking shape, and on September 17, 1787, 12 state delegations voted approval of the final draft. Edmund Randolph and George Mason of Virginia, along with Elbridge Gerry of Massachusetts, refused to sign it, feeling that it went too far toward consolidation and lacked a bill of rights. (Randolph, however, later decided to support it.) The remaining 39 delegates affixed their signatures and sent the document to Congress with two recommendations: that it be submitted to state ratifying conventions especially called for the purpose, rather than directly to the voters; and that it be declared officially operative when nine (not 13) states accepted it, since there was real doubt that any document so evolved could ever get unanimous approval. Some of the delegates feared that they had far exceeded their instructions to *revise* the Articles, for the document they sent to Congress certainly represented much more than revision.

Edmund Randolph

FEDERALISTS AND ANTIFEDERALISTS

The new Constitution met with great favor and equally great opposition in the states. Its strongest supporters, who adopted the name "Federalists," were drawn from the ranks of bankers, lawyers, businessmen, merchants, planters, and men of property in the urban areas. Hamilton and Jay favored it in New York. Madison, Randolph, and John Marshall argued for it in Virginia. The fact that Washington and Franklin, the two most honored Americans, supported it was much in its favor. Opposition to its ratification came from the small farmers, laborers, and the debtor, agrarian classes. However, it is misleading, however convenient, to arrange the argument over ratification on lines of economic interest alone. Obviously there were businessmen and merchants who voted for the document because they felt it would mean expanded markets, better regulation of commerce, greater credit stability, and less control of trade by the states. Just as obviously there were farmers and debtors who voted against it for equally self-interested economic reasons.

The lines of demarcation between rich and poor, or mercantile and agrarian interests, were by no means so clear in the voting as one might expect. Claiming that the nation could obtain progress and prosperity under the Articles if they were revised, the Antifederalists accused the Convention of creating a government that eventually, as George Mason of Virginia thought, might "produce either a monarchy or a corrupt aristocracy." There was "apprehension," Rufus King of New York told Madison, "The liberties of the people are in danger." In Massachusetts, the pioneering female historian Mercy Otis Warren, who belonged to an elite family, opposed the Constitution on these grounds.

Happily for the fate of the Constitution, the Federalists, who might more accurately have been called "Nationalists," possessed a group of leaders of great drive and organizing skill. It was not easy to out-argue or outmaneuver men such as Hamilton, Jay, Madison, James Wilson, or Henry Knox. Furthermore, they had the initiative and kept it, giving their opposition little time to temporize or organize. The Federalists immediately began an energetic campaign for ratification in their own states. In New York, where opposition was strong, the Constitution was brilliantly defended in a series of 85 newspaper articles written by Hamilton, Madison, and Jay. The essays later were collected in a single volume called *The Federalist.*

The Antifederalists had only a few such talented leaders. George Clinton, Patrick Henry, Elbridge Gerry, Luther Martin, and James Warren were able men, but none, for example, was capable of producing the brilliant *Federalist* papers or of handling the New York campaign as Hamilton did. The Antifederalists tried to fight the battle piecemeal, without a positive program, and showed a curious reluctance to match the aggressive, shrewd campaigning of the Federalists.

It has sometimes been fashionable among historians, particularly in the early twentieth century, to consider the struggle over ratification as a contest between "conservatives" and "liberals". If the Declaration of Independence represented "radical" or revolutionary thought, the Constitution, it was assumed, represented a conservative counterrevolution that undid some of the Revolution's work. On reexamination, however, it becomes less clear which side deserves which label. It was the Federalists, after all, who proposed the bold, decisive change to carry out to completion the powerful nationalism engendered by the revolutionary effort. This was a daring step—to create from a bundle of disparate states a single, unified nation bound together by common consent and national pride. The Antifederalists, fearful of any power not under their direct restraint, preferred the status quo. To them, apparently, the great experiment in federalism suggested by the Constitution seemed too new, too dangerous.

They could not conceive of a nationalized government that did not threaten republican principles.

RATIFICATION OF THE CONSTITUTION

The ratification of the document proceeded smoothly in most of the smaller states, which were generally satisfied with the compromises set up to protect them. By January 1788 five states (Delaware, New Jersey, Georgia, Connecticut, and Pennsylvania) had accepted it, with strong opposition recorded only in Pennsylvania. The Massachusetts state convention ratified the Constitution by a vote of 187 to 168 after a long dispute, and then only after attaching a strong recommendation for a bill of rights. Maryland and South Carolina ratified, while New Hampshire, the ninth state, took two conventions (the second by a margin of nine votes) to accept it in June 1788. Legally the Constitution could now go into effect, yet most people understood that without New York and Virginia it could not function successfully.

In Virginia, the Federalists won a narrow victory, 89 to 79, on June 25. Like Massachusetts, Virginia attached proposals for 20 changes and a recommendation for a specific bill of rights. In New York, Hamilton and the Federalists pulled the document through on July 26 by the breathtakingly small margin of 30 to 27. North Carolina refused to ratify the Constitution until a bill of rights was actually attached to it and finally approved it in late 1789. Rhode Island held out until 1790.

The debates over the ratification indicated that the chief issue was the Constitution's lack of a bill of rights, so in 1789 the First Congress proposed 10 amendments (ratified in 1791) to guarantee popular government and individual freedom. Of the 10, the First prohibited Congress from interfering with freedom of speech, press, religion, and assembly. The Fifth placed the citizen under "due process" of law, and the Sixth and Seventh guaranteed trial by jury. The Tenth reserved to the people and to the states all powers not delegated to the federal government, thereby providing a guarantee of decentralized political power. Thus this "bill of rights" wrote into law those "self-evident truths" and "natural rights" on which the Declaration had based its case for independence.

The ideas expressed in the Constitution were themselves implicit in the Articles of Confederation, the Declaration of Independence, and the revolutionary argument. The Constitution merely gave those ideas explicit, final form. The idea that government should protect life, liberty, and property was already accepted. The idea that government

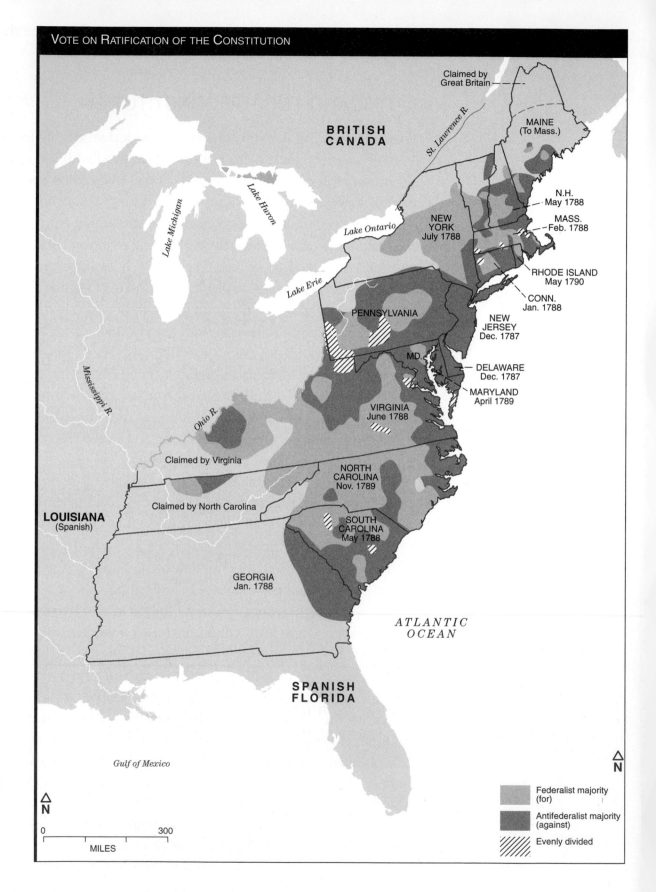

VOTE ON RATIFICATION OF THE CONSTITUTION

Claimed by Great Britain

BRITISH CANADA

MAINE (To Mass.)

St. Lawrence R.

Lake Michigan

Lake Huron

Lake Ontario

N.H. May 1788

NEW YORK July 1788

MASS. Feb. 1788

Lake Erie

RHODE ISLAND May 1790

PENNSYLVANIA

CONN. Jan. 1788

NEW JERSEY Dec. 1787

Ohio R.

MD.

DELAWARE Dec. 1787

MARYLAND April 1789

Mississippi R.

VIRGINIA June 1788

Claimed by Virginia

NORTH CAROLINA Nov. 1789

Claimed by North Carolina

LOUISIANA (Spanish)

SOUTH CAROLINA May 1788

GEORGIA Jan. 1788

ATLANTIC OCEAN

SPANISH FLORIDA

Gulf of Mexico

N

0   300
MILES

N

Federalist majority (for)

Antifederalist majority (against)

Evenly divided

should be powerful enough to perform its functions was already recognized, even in the Articles—though there were sharp differences of
opinion over how powerful that need be.

No one at the Convention, and very few people in the states, argued for retention of the Articles without change. The question was, did the Constitution change the direction of government too much? The difference between the Articles and the Constitution lay almost wholly in the amount and quality of the authority granted to that "more perfect union."

LAUNCHING THE GOVERNMENT

WASHINGTON AND FEDERALIST RULE

After the balloting for President in January 1789, and for Congress under the terms of the new Constitution, the presidential electors met in February to choose George Washington as the first President of the United States. John Adams, who had received the smaller number of electoral ballots, was installed as Vice-President in mid-April. On April 30 Washington, standing on the balcony of the Federal Building at Broad and Wall Streets in New York, was inaugurated as President.

The Presidency for George Washington was the coronation of an American hero who had essentially been "deified" in his own lifetime due to his role as commander of the Continental Army during the American Revolution. Washington was essentially the son of privilege, the heir to a large Virginia plantation who became the wealthiest man in Virginia when he married Martha, the wealthiest woman in Virginia and heir to a large plantation in her own right. Washington was a slave owner who owned some 390 slaves at one time and demanded that they work from "can until can't," meaning can see to can't see, or sunup to sundown. Furthermore, Washington demanded that his slaves "be diligent all the while," and imposed whipping upon slaves for discipline when he felt it was necessary. Washington never freed any of his slaves during his lifetime. He came to the conclusion before his death, however, that he needed to free all of his slaves for economic reasons since he surmised that his expenses would actually be less if he merely hired wage labor

George Washington

rather than taking care of all of the needs of his many slaves through childhood and old age when they were less productive. In his will, Washington decreed that all of the slaves would be free upon Martha's death. This prompted Martha to free all the slaves immediately so as to prevent any slaves from having incentive to secure their freedom through her own untimely death.

As President, Washington desired to make the Presidency a respected position and did so through ceremony. Six horses drew Washington's carriage, and his personal saddle was of leopard skin edged in gold. Twenty-one servants, seven of them slaves, attended his needs at the Presidential Mansion. His preferred title was "His High Mightiness, the President." Washington entertained lavishly at the Presidential Mansion and considered himself a fine dancer, but the Presidential parties ended by 9:30 p.m. so the President could get his needed rest.

Washington was essentially "addicted to appearances" while President. His correspondence with his advisors is often not about what is the proper policy choice, but rather how he, as President, should appear in any given situation. Washington's goal was to appear as a "disinterested and impartial gentleman" who was above the fray. Consequently, Washington left most policy direction to Congress and his advisors because he viewed political bickering as unbecoming of gentlemen. In fact, one time President Washington brought a treaty with Native Americans to the Senate for their advice, and he became so disgusted with their political squabbling that he stated, "I'll be damned if I ever go there again." He never did. Presidents have largely ignored the Senate's "advice" on treaties ever since.

Washington's "disinterested gentleman" approach is reflected in his nonpartisan cabinet where Alexander Hamilton, a top aid to him during the Revolution and a staunch nationalist, was Secretary of Treasury and Thomas Jefferson, a states' rights advocate, was Secretary of State.

Washington was not an intellectual who did not attend college; instead, he viewed colleges as objects of veneration and once stated, "becoming a mere scholar is not desirable for a gentleman." Washington's Vice President, John Adams, would once state of Washington that he was "too unread for his station is beyond dispute." Washington was also a very aloof man and was not considered to be a great writer or speaker. In the words of Jefferson, "His colloquial talents are not above mediocrity. He has neither copiousness of ideas nor fluency of words."

The Washington family by Edward Savage

In spite of his role as commander of the Continental Army, most military historians do not consider Washington to be a great military tactician; however, he most certainly had courage and toughness that won the respect of his men and was endowed with true leadership qualities. Washington felt at home in the heat of battle and, being approximately 6'3" tall, was an imposing figure at a time when the average man was only 5'6" tall. Washington is credited with bringing the fledgling country together as a nation and resisting the temptation to rule it as a monarch. Washington also began the tradition of serving only two Presidential terms (later enshrined in the Constitution with the Twenty-second Amendment in 1951), stepping aside after his second term.

For the first few months of the new administration, Congress and the President moved carefully. Congress quickly created the three executive departments of State, Treasury, and War, and Washington chose Thomas Jefferson, Alexander Hamilton, and Henry Knox to serve as their Secretaries. Congress then passed a tariff on imports and a tonnage duty on foreign vessels, both intended to raise revenue and to protect American trade. The Judiciary Act of 1789 created the office of Attorney General, a Supreme

Court, three circuit courts, and 13 district courts, filling in the outlines of the federal legal system.

FEDERALIST FINANCE

Washington left the most critical problem of his first term to Alexander Hamilton, his confident young Secretary of the Treasury. Hamilton believed, as most Federalists did, that the government should play an active, even decisive role in economic affairs, so that the nation might achieve a self-sufficient, expanding economy, balanced among agriculture, manufacturing, and trade. To this end he proposed, in his *Report on the Public Credit* (1790), *Second Report on the Public Credit* (1791), and *Report on Manufactures* (1791), a firm, unified policy enforced by a strong federal authority.

Hamilton's economic program also had clear political aims. He was convinced that the new government could not last unless the Constitution were strengthened by interpretation and made responsive to changing needs, and unless the forces of wealth and property supported it. Thus he hoped to win business and financial groups to the support of the federal government, and to bind these groups to the national interest. Hamilton fashioned his program from three basic components.

The first laid the foundation for the Hamiltonian system. Under the previous regimes—that is, the Continental and Confederation congresses—the general government had accumulated a foreign debt of about $12 million, owed chiefly to France and Holland, and a domestic debt of about $40 million, owed to American nationals. The separate states owed a total of about $22 million more. Hamilton proposed that the federal government promise full payment of all these debts at par value, thus taking over, or *assuming*, the unpaid debts of the states. Since the federal government did not possess the money to pay this debt, totaling about $74 million, Hamilton recommended *funding* the entire debt. That is, in exchange for their old Continental and Confederation bonds, creditors would be issued new interest-bearing bonds that would be the direct obligation of the new federal government.

No opposition was voiced against payment of the foreign debt in full, but full payment of the domestic debt at face value was another matter. On the open market these old domestic bonds had been selling at far below their original face value. Because the previous central governments had failed to meet interest payments or provide for retirement of the debt, the original owners of the bonds had lost faith in them and had sold them for whatever they could get. The purchasers were usually men of means who were willing to buy cheap on the chance that the government would make good.

Hamilton did succeed in getting Congress to make the old bonds good at face value (many congressmen were themselves bond holders), but in so doing he aroused charges from his opponents that the new government was being operated in the interest of the wealthy. Hamilton's intentions, however, were actually both honorable and farsighted. In his plan, he believed, the middle and upper classes would find a strong motive for sustaining the national government, and their confidence in the solvency and good faith of the government would stimulate business activity. In addition, creditors could use the funded debt, in the form of negotiable bonds, as capital to finance new enterprises.

Vehement opposition to the assumption of the state debts by the federal government was also evoked in the Southern states, which had already paid off most of their debts. Southerners protested the use of national funds to help pay off the obligations of states with large outstanding debts, such as the New England states. Hamilton's assumption program was defeated on its first vote in the House, but he finally won in a bargain with Jefferson. In exchange for an agreement to locate the new national capital on the Potomac across from Virginia, Jefferson's congressional forces agreed to assume the debts of the states.

The second part of Hamilton's program called for the creation of a central bank, somewhat like the Bank of England, which would serve as a depository for federal funds, issue paper money (which the Treasury by law could not do), provide commercial interests with a steady and dependable credit institution, and serve the government with short-term loans. Some leaders in and out of Congress objected to this proposal on two grounds. First four-fifths of the bank's funds were to come from private sources, which might then control the bank's (and the nation's) fiscal policies. More important, the scheme was probably unconstitutional. Jefferson and Madison, among others, argued that since the federal government was not specifically authorized by the Constitution to create a national bank, it would be unconstitutional for Congress to do so.

Hamilton, aware that the bank bill might set an important precedent, argued that Congress was authorized by the Constitution to do what was "necessary and proper" for the national good. If the proposed bank fell within this definition, as he believed it did, the Constitution gave Congress "implied powers" to act in ways not precisely defined in the document. He took the position "that every power vested in a government is in its nature *sovereign* and includes, by *force* of the *term*, a right to employ all the *means* requisite and fairly applicable to the attainment of the *ends* of such power. ..."

Jefferson, to the contrary, argued that the federal government possessed only those powers explicitly granted to it in the Constitution, and that all others, as the Tenth Amendment said, were reserved to the states. The language of the Constitution must be strictly construed. "To take a single step beyond the boundaries thus especially drawn around the powers of Congress," he wrote, "is to take possession of a boundless field of power, no longer susceptible of any definition." Neither the "general welfare" nor the "necessary and proper" clause of the Constitution, he maintained, could be so broadly interpreted. Washington and Congress, however, accepted Hamilton's argument and in 1791 created the Bank of the United States with a charter for 20 years.

THE WHISKEY REBELLION

Third, Hamilton proposed to levy an excise tax on a number of commodities to supply money to the federal Treasury for, he wrote, "... the creation of debt should always be accompanied by the means of its extinguishment." Among the items included in the bill, passed in 1791, was a 25 percent excise tax on whiskey to be paid by farmers when they brought their grain to the distillery. The cost would be then passed on to consumers in the form of higher prices for whiskey. In western Pennsylvania and North Carolina, where conversion into whiskey was an efficient way of getting grain to market while avoiding the high transportation costs of shipping their excess bulk grain over the mountains to the market in the east, Hamilton's excise tax was a tax on the farmer's most valuable cash crop. Farmers viewed the tax as especially oppressive since they already paid half the value of their crop to the distillery to distill their grain; and after the tax was taken out of the farmer's remaining half, less than a third remained. Hamilton exacerbated the farmers' anger by his flippant comment, "Farmers drank too much anyway."

Farmers in Western Pennsylvania gathered in meetings in the summer of 1792, and a convention at Pittsburgh denounced the tax and declared that the people would prevent its collection. Collections fell off in this area in 1792, and irritated Pennsylvania farmers manhandled a few tax collectors in 1793. Some were even tarred and feathered. One tax collector in particular, John Neville, in July 1794 had his house burned to the ground by a crowd estimated at 500; and one man in the crowd was killed and several were wounded as a dozen soldiers inside Neville's house fired into the crowd. In 1794 a sizable force of as many as 7,000 angry whiskey makers vowed to march on Pittsburgh to challenge federal authority at its nearest point.

Memories of Daniel Shays were still fresh in Congress, and President Washington acted quickly. He issued a proclamation ordering the Pennsylvanians to return to their homes, declared western Pennsylvania in a state of rebellion. He mounted his horse and led Hamilton and Henry Lee with a force of 15,000 militiamen, more troops than the average strength of the Continental Army during the American Revolution, to Pennsylvania. The farmers promptly scattered, but Hamilton, determined to teach the unruly frontiersmen a lesson in federal authority, saw to it that a score of the ringleaders were arrested and tried; two were sentenced to death. Washington wisely pardoned them, but neither Hamilton nor Federalism was ever popular in that region again. Hamilton viewed the government's action in the Whiskey Rebellion as a smashing success. Others, however, including Thomas Jefferson and ardent federalist Fisher Ames, opposed the use of federal troops on its own citizens as an abuse of power and viewed the actions of Washington and Hamilton as proof that the national government had been granted too much power under the Constitution.

DEVELOPING A NATIVE AMERICAN POLICY

At the close of the Revolution the issue between Native Americans and white Americans remained as insoluble as ever. It seemed impossible to divert or delay the American drive westward, where the tribes possessed undeveloped lands of great value.

Of the losers in the Revolution, the Native Americans—most had fought with the British—lost the most, as we have previously noted. The Peace Treaty simply left them out. Britain ceded the lands west to the Mississippi to the Americans without mentioning the Native Americans who lived there, while the Americans considered them a conquered people whose lands were subject to confiscation.

"With respect to the Indians," wrote one of the negotiators, "we claim the right of pre-emption; with respect to all other nations, we claim the sovereignty over the territory." Though tribal leaders protested to the British negotiators that they had no right to give away Native American lands, and to the Americans that they had no right to abrogate previous treaties, neither side listened.

"NOBLE RED MAN" OR "BARBARIC SAVAGE?"

Federal and state policy toward the Native Americans was greatly influenced by the white Americans' perception of them. Whites found Native Americans difficult to negotiate with, for few Americans understood much of Native American psychology, politics, or culture. Both Native Americans and whites were heirs of 200 years of constant and vicious warfare. White explorers and settlers, almost from their first contacts with the Native Americans, had developed contrasting images of the "noble red man" on the one hand, and the "barbaric savage" on the other. These images persisted in the minds of later Americans.

Some Americans, particularly the educated minority, viewed the various Native American cultures with respect and sympathized with the Native Americans' plight. These Americans hoped the tribes could be assimilated into American society. Both President Washington and his secretary of war, Henry Knox, who had charge of Native American affairs, believed in assimilation. Knox reaffirmed Native American land claims in a series of reports in early 1789. "Instead of exterminating part of the human race," he wrote, Americans should instead take pride in having "imparted knowledge of cultivation and the arts to the aboriginals of the country. ..."

Delaware Indians hunting buffalo

Others tended to see the Native American as irredeemably—though tragically—savage, incapable ever of learning the ways of civilization. Frontiersmen, too, had vivid recollections of Native American attacks during the French and Indian wars and bitter, still-fresh memories of Loyalist-Native American raids in New York and Pennsylvania during the Revolution. Meanwhile, the possibility of an alliance between the western tribes and the British army, still in Canada, posed a threat to the Ohio-Indiana frontier.

In fact, although the British had promised at the Peace of Paris to give up their posts in the Northwest, they apparently intended to hold them as long as possible. Orders from the Colonial office to the governor-general of Canada, one day before the proclamation of the Treaty in 1784, instructed British commanders to do exactly that. So many Americans were convinced that the only sound policy toward the Native Americans was removal.

ASSIMILATION OR REMOVAL

Relations with the Native Americans developed over two phases in the years before 1812. From the end of the war until the election of Washington in 1789, Congress assumed that all Native American lands belonged to the United States and that all tribes were under government control. Congress appointed commissioners to handle Native American affairs, but most direct dealings with the tribes were carried out by the states.

Land was the issue. Both federal and state policy was to move Native Americans off lands that settlers wanted, but this required more military power and money than either federal or state governments possessed. The removal policy also raised questions among those who saw this as a moral problem as well as a military and political one.

By 1786, both state and federal governments realized that establishing an effective, acceptable Native American policy involved a large set of complex issues. The central problem was how to establish white settlements in Native American country and still treat the Native American with humanity and justice. The lure of open, fertile land, a growing nationalism, and the need for strategic defenses against France, Spain, and British Canada all had to be balanced against the new nation's desire to act in accordance with the principles of its revolution and a Christian conscience.

American leaders therefore reactivated the British colonial policy of recognizing Native American land rights and acquiring the necessary acres by treaties and purchases, meanwhile establishing strict

PEOPLE THAT MADE A DIFFERENCE

Simon Girty: The "White Savage"

The North American Indian wars of the eighteenth century were really not Native American wars at all. They were, rather, wars between white groups—British and French or British and Americans—in which the Native American served as an instrument by which the whites settled the fate of the Native American's homeland. Savage, pitiless wars, they exposed the seamier side of the frontier and created, on occasion, strange patterns of cultural mingling, as the story of Simon Girty will attest.

Simon Girty became notorious as a white colonial man who sided with the Native Americans and then with the British. In fact, more than a few white men and women crossed the cultural line that separated red and white. Within a few years after Virginia's settlement, for example, more than 40 English men had taken Native American wives and several English women had married Native American husbands. Some crossed over simply to escape the rules and responsibilities of their own culture. Others found it the best way to survive on the frontier. Still others found security and status in tribal life. Children who were captured and brought up by Native Americans were particularly susceptible.

Girty was one of these, and 200 years ago almost every American knew his name. His reputation stretched from New England to the Gulf and far into the West. To the white Americans of his era he was the ultimate traitor, the "White Savage of Ohio" who turned against his heritage and his race.

Simon Girty was born in 1741 in Pennsylvania, the son of an Irish immigrant who was killed in 1751 in a fight with an Native American named The Fish. His father's friend John Turner then killed The Fish, married the Widow Girty, and took over her sons, Thomas (the oldest), Simon, James, and George. The entire family, however, was captured in an Native American raid in 1756. After burning Turner at the stake, the Native Americans divided the rest of the family with the exception of Thomas, who escaped. The mother and George went with the Delawares, James with the Shawnees, and Simon with the Senecas, who renamed the boy Katepacoma, taught him their language, and turned him into a skilled woodsman and hunter.

Two years later the Girtys were released and reunited at Fort Pitt. All except Thomas, who entered business, seemed to have been rough, violent young men—three among many such hangers-on around the post who earned a precarious living as scouts and translators. When American independence seemed near, Simon threw in his lot with the British, then changed his mind and found work as an American agent to the Senecas, his old captors. He was soon disciplined for "ill behavior" (probably brawling) and in 1778 changed sides again. This time he went with James and George to Detroit, where they offered their services to British General Henry Hamilton, known as "Hairbuyer" Hamilton because of his reputation for paying bounties on American scalps.

Hamilton sent Simon to Ohio to organize Native American raids against frontier settlements, which he did quite successfully. Ritual torture of captives was a traditional element of the culture of some Eastern Woodland tribes and characteristic of the Shawnee and Mingos that Girty led. (On the other hand, some tribes regarded the white custom of death by hanging as exceptionally cruel and barbaric.) Torture was not restricted to white captives, nor was it considered demeaning to captive or captor. In fact, it was sometimes regarded as an opportunity for a prisoner to demonstrate his personal courage. To the frontier settler and militiaman, however, it understandably represented a barbaric violation of all the codes of war.

Girty, of course, leading Native Americans in battle, did as they did. Soon the Girty legend began to form—stories were told of his cruelty, his pleasure at torture, and his implacable hatred of the Americans. The commandant at Fort Pitt offered $800 in gold for him, to which Simon sent back word that he "expected no quarter and would give none."

In 1782 Girty was part of a British-Native American force that defeated an American militia command near Upper Sandusky, Ohio, under Colonel William Crawford. Girty's Native Americans captured eight prisoners and killed six, saving Crawford and the company doctor for death by torture. Surgeon Knight, who escaped the next night to tell the tale, witnessed Crawford's long and painful death, and the story sped swiftly through the settlements. In August that year, Daniel Boone's militia drove off Girty and 600 Native Americans at Bryant's Station, Kentucky, the last major Native American battle on that bloody ground. Girty's reputation was by that time secure.

After the end of the war in 1783, Simon married a white girl 20 years his junior who had spent four years as a Wyandot captive, and then took up farming (and, according to local stories, heavy drinking) near Amherstburg in Canada. The British, however, soon found they could use him to stir up trouble in Native American country and sent him out once more with war parties into Ohio. But the era of border warfare was drawing to a close. General "Mad Anthony" Wayne's tough frontier army broke the Native American alliance at Fallen Timbers, near Maumee, Ohio, in August 1794, though Girty and his Wyandots escaped.

Girty's life after 1796, when the British finally left the Northwest, was a long anticlimax. In Amherstburg he became a local celebrity, known as a hard-drinking, boastful man given to periodic frightening rages. His wife, tired of beatings, left him in 1798, taking their four children. Girty took no part in the War of 1812, and legend has it that when the British began to evacuate Detroit in 1813 Girty stayed until the last British soldier had left, then jumped his horse from the river bank and swam to Canada (a highly unlikely feat) as a gesture of defiance.

When General Harrison's American army crossed into Canada to occupy Amherstburg, Girty prudently disappeared among the Mohawk villages. He came back to his farm in 1816, old and half-blind but no calmer than before. He died on February 8, 1818, after a drunken spree, and was buried in the iron cold of Canadian winter. When spring came, no one remembered to mark his grave.

There were other renegade white men who played more important roles than he in the Indian wars, but Simon Girty became the frontier's symbol of fear. Tales of tortures clustered about his name. Balladeers chronicled his misdeeds. Soldiers and settlers alike vowed horrible vengeance upon him. Yet in contrast to his reputation, Simon Girty was rather small fry. The British never gave him a responsible military post, nor did they entrust him with any mission that required intelligence or trustworthiness—they used him simply as a guerrilla leader who knew Native Americans and was skilled in forest warfare.

But Americans needed heroes and villains for the Indian wars. For heroes there were Anthony Wayne, Simon Kenton, Daniel Boone, and others. For villains they had such men as Hamilton, Tecumseh, and Girty, the White Savage—the one who most typically personified all that war in the wilderness meant on the frontier. His life, as one chronicler put it, "presents nothing to be imitated. It would be well if the name of this monster could be erased from the annals of history."

In the early twenty-first century, some historians have begun to suggest that the legend of the White Savage, as it has been passed down over the course of American history, has been tinged with more than a little racism, and that Girty looks altogether different when viewed from a Native American perspective.

boundaries to control the advance of white settlers. The Northwest Ordinance of 1787, which had officially opened the West to settlement, stated that Native Americans should be dealt with in "utmost good faith," their "property, rights and liberty" protected, their lands "never to be taken from them without their consent."

This new policy did not fully satisfy the national conscience, however. At best, it was a temporary solution. If land and game disappeared and the tribes were pushed ever farther west by treaty and expansion, the whole race might soon disappear.

Plenty of Americans, particularly on the frontier, did not care. Many others, however, did not want their country, which they believed to be a new and better experiment in enlightened government, held responsible for the destruction of an entire people.

In the view of the Enlightenment, Native Americans were as much part of the human race as were white men. Such differences as existed between them were seen as the results of education and environment. The solution, then, was to "civilize" Native Americans by giving them education, religious training, and the means of making a living, thus bringing them into the mainstream of American society. "In leading them to agriculture, to manufacture, and civilization," said Jefferson, "I trust and believe we are acting for their greatest good."

Westward expansion was thus given a moral basis by being seen as an extension of the advantages of a "higher" social order to a "lower" group. The concept was neither new nor American. It was a common principle in European thought and would continue to be, whether the subjected people were Gauls or Aztecs or Maoris.

CLASHES ON THE FRONTIER

Treaties negotiated with the tribes of the Northwest brought only temporary peace, while in the South the Spanish encouraged the Creeks' harassment of frontier settlements. The Mohawks led by chief Joseph Brant, the Miami led by chief Little Turtle, and the Shawnee led by chief Blue Jacket, led raids against white settlements in Indiana, Ohio, and western Pennsylvania, spreading panic and challenging white control of the Ohio Valley. Meanwhile, the doubling of the American white population to almost four million between the French and Indian War and 1790 created land pressure in the west as thousands of white settlers moved into the Ohio Valley. In such a situation, the Native American resistance was predictable. In response, the Americans took military action.

In 1790 General Josiah Harmar and 1,400 men under orders from Secretary of War Henry Knox marched into western Ohio, burning Native American villages; but his expedition against the Native Americans in the Ohio country was ambushed and scattered by the Miami and Shawnee under Little Turtle and Blue Jacket. Two hundred of Harmar's men were killed, and Harmar was court-martialed for his inept leadership in the humiliating defeat. In 1791 General Arthur St. Clair's larger force of some 2,000 men did no better. St. Clair

Mohawk Chief Joseph Brant

and his men were reduced to about 1,400 through desertion due to the cold Ohio weather that autumn, and Little Turtle with a 1,000 Miami Native Americans ambushed the remaining troops in northwestern Ohio on November 4. Over half of St. Clair's men were killed or wounded, and all but three of the 200 female "camp followers" that accompanied St. Clair's men were also killed. The Native Americans scalped and dismembered the dead and dying and pursued the fleeing survivors out of Ohio. With over 900 dead, St. Clair's defeat was the most costly defeat for the United States in the history of the Indian wars. President Washington denounced St. Clair as "worse than a murderer" and demanded his resignation. In 1793–1794 the tide began to turn as the Tennessee militia temporarily stabilized the Southwestern frontier in a series of small, sharp engagements.

Washington then gave command to General "Mad Anthony" Wayne, who took 4,000 men into northwestern Ohio, where the British had authorized the construction of a fort inside American boundaries. After the signing of the Jay Treaty, the British cut off arms sales to the Native Americans. Without British weapons, the Native Americans, armed with only tomahawks, would be no match for the American forces. Wayne established two military camps, Fort

General "Mad Anthony" Wayne

Greenville and Fort Recovery in western Ohio. Fort Recovery was built on the site of St. Clair's defeat in 1791, and Wayne's men literally had to pick through skeletal remains in order to construct the fort. In the late summer of 1794, Wayne defeated the Native American forces at the Battle of Fallen Timbers, so called because a recent tornado had felled so many trees. The next year the 12 strongest tribes ceded most of the Ohio country to the United States with the Treaty of Greenville—in return for $25,000 worth of shirts, axes, knives, blankets, kettles, mirrors, ribbons, thimbles, and liquor. In subsequent years, the American government continued to supply an annual shipment of liquor to the Native Americans in an attempt to keep them pacified. The unfortunate result was rampant alcoholism among the Ohio tribes. In 1800, Little Turtle proclaimed, "More of us have died since the Treaty of Greenville than we lost by the years of war before, and it is all owing to the introduction of liquor among us. … This liquor that they introduce into our country is more to be feared than the gun and the tomahawk."

THE PERILS OF NEUTRALITY

THE FRENCH REVOLUTION

The outbreak of the French Revolution forced the Washington administration into the first real test of its foreign policy. A good many Americans in 1789 welcomed the news of the French uprisings as the logical outcome of their own revolution. "In no part of the world," wrote John Marshall later, "was the Revolution hailed with more joy than in America." The overthrow of the French monarchy and its replacement with a "Republic" based on the ideals of "liberty, equality, and fraternity" seemed in concert with American Revolutionary ideals. The execution of King Louis XVI and the Reign of Terror that followed, during which France devolved into fratricidal chaos, however, led many to sober second thoughts, while the French declaration of war against England, Holland, and Spain in February 1793 introduced the difficult question of neutrality directly into American foreign policy.

One segment of opinion, holding that Britain was still the United States' major enemy, favored the French cause. Furthermore, technically, the United States was still obligated under the Treaty of Alliance, which had been signed in 1778 during the American Revolution, to defend France when it was attacked. France had aided the United States against Britain during America's time of need; therefore, some argued that the United States must aid France during theirs. Others felt that British trade was so essential to American prosperity that the United States, whatever its sympathies with revolution, could not afford to offend the world's greatest naval and economic power. Still others, observing the chaos of Jacobin Paris, saw France as a threat to the security and order of society everywhere—even to Christianity itself. Up to a third of the population of western France died in the chaos of the French Revolution, and some 20,000 were guillotined as "enemies of the Republic."

In April 1793, when he received news of the outbreak of war between France and Britain, Washington declared a "fair and impartial policy." Although avoiding the word "neutrality"—because Washington believed that since Congress declared war, Congress must also declare neutrality—Washington's proclamation guaranteed the belligerents the "friendly and impartial conduct" of the United States. America, he believed, needed peace—the opportunity to build up its strength—more than anything else. "If this country is preserved in tranquility 20 years longer," he wrote, "it may bid defiance in a just cause to any power whatever. …" His proclamation, which was to influence American foreign policy for the next half-century, derived from his firm conviction that the United States should avoid, at all reasonable costs, the "brawling of Europe." The following year Congress passed a Neutrality Act that made Washington's position the official American policy.

GENET AFFAIR

Nevertheless, many Americans continued to support France both in spirit and in deeds. The supporters of the French Republic noted that the American Republic had been born in blood as well and concluded that the shedding of blood was, therefore, sometimes necessary for the establishment of liberty. In the following words of John Bradford of the Kentucky Gazette:

Instead of reviling the French republicans as monsters, the friends of royalty in this country should rather admire their patience in so long deferring the fate of their perjured monarch, whose blood is ... atonement for the safety of many guilty thousands that are still suffered to remain in the bosom of France.

Citizens' associations formed in support of the French Revolution known as Democratic-Republican societies. In 1793, these associations received a boost with the arrival of Edmund Genet, an envoy dispatched from France to the United States for the purpose of garnering support for the French Republic in its war with England. Instead of meeting with the President or other members of Washington's administration, however, Genet landed in Charleston, South Carolina where pro-French sentiments were much stronger. Upon his arrival in the United States, Genet began commissioning American privateers to seize British shipping, a clear violation of American neutrality. Genet even urged Congress to reject Washington's "friendly and impartial policy" and support Republican France. Washington reacted by demanding that Genet be recalled to France under the premise that his conduct could lead to "war abroad and anarchy at home." Before Genet could return to France, however, the political situation changed in the tumultuous political atmosphere of revolutionary France; and Genet was charged with treason, for which the penalty was death. President Washington granted Genet political asylum under the condition that he withdraw from public life. In doing so Washington began the American tradition of political asylum that has continued through the present.

STRAINED RELATIONS WITH BRITAIN

The British navy was large, the French navy small, and the British blockade of France very effective. When the French, desperate for trade, opened up their West Indian ports to American ships, the British immediately declared that any trade with France was a military act and that ships caught at it were subject to seizure. Not only did British men-of-war confiscate American cargoes, but also, claiming that some American sailors were really deserters from the British navy (as, indeed, a few were), they forcibly "impressed" a number of American seamen into naval service. Still, though American ships were in danger wherever they went in Atlantic waters, wartime trade was so lucrative that many American merchants felt that the profit was worth the risk, and incidents multiplied.

JAY'S TREATY

Hoping to reduce tensions, Congress passed an embargo act in 1794 that forbade British ships to call at American ports and American ships to sail in areas where they might be subject to British seizure. Since this hurt American trade more than it hindered the British navy, the embargo lasted less than two months. However, American protests induced the British to relax some of their rules, and in 1794 Washington requested Chief Justice John Jay to sail for London to discuss a treaty to settle outstanding differences.

Jay's arguments were no doubt good ones, but perhaps more important, French military successes persuaded the British that it was unwise to antagonize the United States unduly. Under the terms of Jay's Treaty (the Treaty of London, signed in 1794) the British agreed to evacuate the frontier posts by 1796; to open the British West Indies to American trade under certain conditions; to admit American ships to East Indian ports on a nondiscriminatory basis; and to refer to a joint commission the payment of pre-Revolutionary War debts and settlement of the northwest boundary dispute.

However, they simply refused to discuss other important points at issue, including impressments and the Native American question; and they made far fewer concessions than Jay had been instructed to get. Washington reluctantly submitted the treaty to the Senate, which ratified it by only one vote. Not only was the Washington administration severely criticized for the settlement, but, also, Jay was burned in effigy in various cities. Alexander Hamilton suffered bombardment of eggs and tomatoes when he attempted to speak in support of the treaty. Americans opposed to the Jay's Treaty began a campaign of graffiti in which they painted on fences the slogan, "Damn John Jay, and Damn everyone who won't Damn John Jay."

Chief Justice John Jay

Not all the news was bad, however. The Jay Treaty allowed the United States to avoid what could have been a disastrous war with England and resume normal trade, thus boosting American well being both in terms of security and economically. Spain, badly mauled by France in the land war, had signed a separate peace in 1795 and, fearing British retaliation for its defection, needed American friendship. In the Pinckney Treaty (the Treaty of San Lorenzo), signed on October 27, 1795, Spain recognized the line of 31° latitude as the United States' southern boundary and granted the United States free navigation of the Mississippi with a three-year right of deposit at New Orleans.

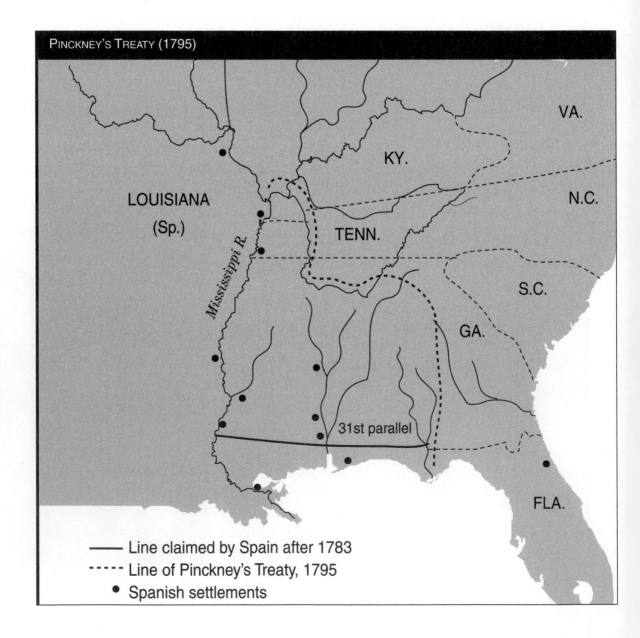

PINCKNEY'S TREATY (1795)

—— Line claimed by Spain after 1783
----- Line of Pinckney's Treaty, 1795
● Spanish settlements

EARLY POLITICAL PARTIES

THE EMERGENCE OF PARTY POLITICS

The dispute over Jay's Treaty revealed a deep division in Washington's administration, as well as growing public opposition to a number of Federalist policies. The French Revolution, the Franco-British War, and subsequent problems in foreign relations created further political differences in Congress. By 1792 opposing factions had begun to coalesce around the two strong men of Washington's cabinet, Hamilton and Jefferson.

Hamilton and Jefferson represented contrasting views of what the American government should be. Both views were implicit in the Declaration and the Constitution, and both still lie beneath the stream of partisan politics. These contrasting views have come to be known as Hamiltonian and state.

Hamilton had no confidence in "the people in the mass." "I have long since learned," he wrote Washington, "to hold public opinion of little value." Most people, he believed, were unreliable, easily swayed by passions, self-interest, and false rhetoric. Since political, social, and economic systems were intertwined, an effective government should be an active force ("a strong government, ably administered," John Jay of New York put it) in promoting the good of the total society. Its control should be vested in those few who had skill and talent—"the rich and wellborn," Hamilton once called them—who would use it best to ensure the forward thrust of the nation.

Jefferson believed deeply in the ability of the majority of people to govern themselves, if properly prepared and allowed to do so. In his view, the individual—in whom he found "substantial and genuine virtue"—was much more important than the state, and the individual's right to pursue liberty and happiness was paramount. People were capable of ruling themselves; thus they needed no strong central government to do it for them. "That government is best," he said, "which governs least." A central government was needed, of course, for foreign policy, defense, commerce, and like matters, but too much control of the individual "begets subservience and venality" and corrupts him. It was ironic that it was Jefferson, the Virginia planter-aristocrat, who did not trust the "rich and wellborn" few and Hamilton, the illegitimate child of a Scottish merchant, who did not trust the "unstable rabble."

Though John Adams had written, "There is nothing I dread as much as the division of the Republic into two great parties, each

John Adams

under its leader," such a split seemed inevitable. This political division, first observable in the arguments over Hamilton's fiscal program, widened noticeably throughout Washington's first administration. The pro-Hamilton, pro-Washington group, using the name adopted by the forces favoring the Constitution during the ratification campaign, called themselves Federalists. The opposition at first called themselves Antifederalists, a somewhat unsatisfactory label but the best that could be devised at the moment.

The Antifederalists opposed the administration's program chiefly because of what they felt was its tendency to concentrate wealth and influence in a relatively small class. Certainly neither Jefferson nor his followers objected to sound currency and credit or to economic stability and prosperity. Rather, they opposed the Hamiltonian methods of obtaining them—the Bank, tariffs, excise taxes (but not the assumption of state debts)—because these measures might serve to create a permanently privileged class whose interests could well become inimical to the opportunities and welfare of the greater number of people.

Through Washington's first term the rivalry between the two factions increased. Despite these internal tensions, however, the Federalists easily reelected Washington for a second term in 1792 against token opposition, with John Adams as his Vice-President.

THE ELECTION OF 1796

James Madison gave the anti-administration forces a better name in 1792, when he spoke of "the Republican party" (not the same thing as the modern Republican Party, but rather the ancestor of the modern Democratic Party). This designation (sometimes "Democratic-Republican") shortly displaced "Antifederalist." Into this loosely organized opposition group, formed about the commanding figure of Thomas Jefferson, came such men as James Monroe and Madison of Virginia, George Clinton and Aaron Burr of New York, Albert Gallatin and Alexander Dallas from Pennsylvania, Willie Jones, the North Carolina back-country leader, and others from the Middle and Southern states. Among the Federalists were Hamilton, Schuyler, and John Jay of New York, Timothy Pickering and John Adams of Massachusetts, Thomas Pinckney of South Carolina, and John Marshall of Virginia, with Washington, of course, at the head of the party.

When Jefferson, convinced that he could no longer work with Hamilton and the administration party, resigned as Secretary of State in 1793, Republican partisan politics began in earnest. Hamilton resigned from the Treasury in 1795, partly because he could not afford to neglect his law and business interests; but he still remained the most powerful Federalist leader since Washington decided not to run again in 1796.

Washington's achievements as President have been overshadowed by his image as "The Father of His Country" and by the dramatic contest during his second term between

Family home of John Adams in Braintree, Massachusetts, as it appeared in 1798

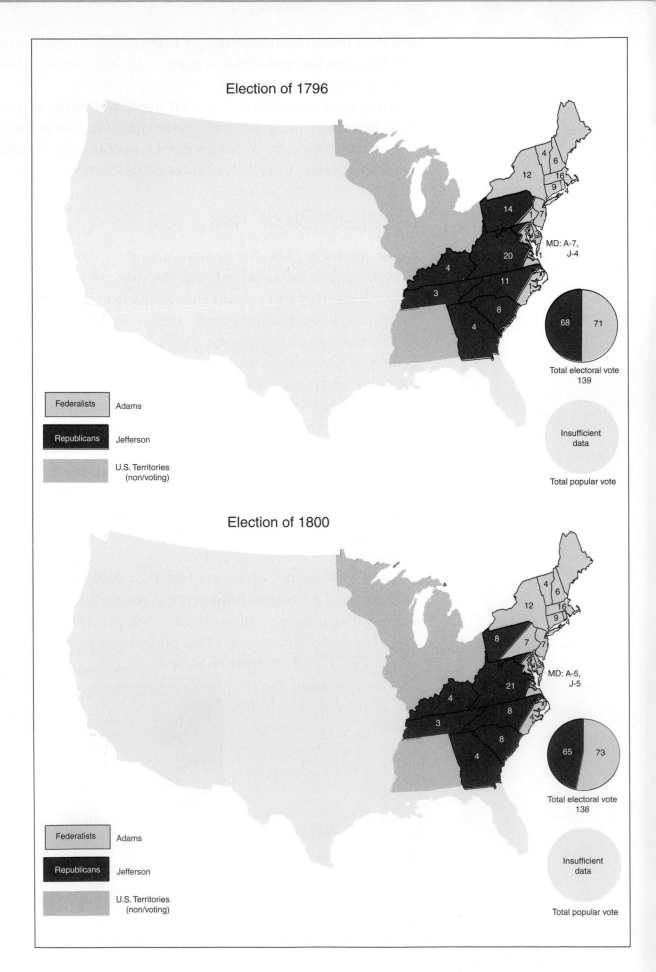

Election of 1796

MD: A-7, J-4

68 | 71

Total electoral vote
139

Insufficient
data

Total popular vote

Federalists — Adams

Republicans — Jefferson

U.S. Territories
(non/voting)

Election of 1800

MD: A-5, J-5

65 | 73

Total electoral vote
138

Insufficient
data

Total popular vote

Federalists — Adams

Republicans — Jefferson

U.S. Territories
(non/voting)

Hamilton and Jefferson. More recently, historians have pointed out Washington's real skill as an administrator and the importance of his contributions to the efficiency of the fledgling government. Since almost every act of his first term set a precedent, Washington did more than anyone else to establish the tone of the presidential office and to establish the whole set of delicate relationships among the executive, the cabinet, the Congress, and the judiciary. Moreover, he imbued the fledgling nation with his immense dignity.

When Washington decided in September 1796 not to seek a third term as President, he submitted to the press a "Farewell Address" which he had written with the aid of Madison and Hamilton. In his valedictory, published in newspapers throughout the nation, Washington explained his reasons for declining to seek a third term. He stressed the necessity of preserving the Union, the "main prop" of individual liberty, and pointed out the obligation of all Americans to obey the Constitution and the established government, "till changed by an explicit and authentic act of the whole People." He warned of the dangers of a party system, particularly one based on a division along geographical lines; urged that the public credit be cherished; and admonished Americans to observe "good faith and justice toward all Nations."

The most enduring passages of the Farewell Address, however, are those in which Washington counseled Americans to steer clear of permanent alliances with the foreign world. Isolationists quoted Washington's admonitions for a foreign policy of neutrality consistently over the succeeding century and a half to justify a long-dominant American policy of avoiding involvement in international politics:

> ... The great rule of conduct for us, in regard to foreign Nations, is, in extending our commercial relations, to have with them as little *Political* connection as possible. ... Europe has a set of primary interests, which to us have none, or a very remote relation.—Hence she must be engaged in frequent controversies, the causes of which are essentially foreign to our concerns.—Hence therefore it must be unwise in us to implicate ourselves, by artificial ties in the ordinary vicissitudes of her politics. ... Taking care always to keep ourselves ... on a respectably defensive posture, we may safely trust to temporary alliances for extraordinary emergencies.

After eight years in office, Washington left behind a government that possessed a reasonably good civil service, a workable committee system, an economic program, a foreign policy, and the seeds of

Aaron Burr, who campaigned with Thomas Jefferson for the Republicans

a body of constitutional theory. He also left behind a party beginning to divide. The election of 1796 gave clear indication of the mounting strength of the Republican opposition. Thomas Jefferson and Aaron Burr campaigned for the Republicans, John Adams and Thomas Pinckney for the Federalists. The margin of Federalist victory was slim: Adams had 71 electoral votes, Jefferson 68. Since Jefferson had more votes than Pinckney, he became Vice-President.

FEDERALISTS AND REPUBLICANS

It is too broad a generalization to say that the Federalists represented the conservative, commercial, nationalistic interests of the Northeast and Middle Atlantic States and the Republicans the more radical, agrarian, debtor, states' rights interests of the South and West, though there is more than a germ of truth in the generalization. In truth, the two parties drew support from all kinds of people in different parts of the country.

The differences in the parties reflected many factors—personalities, religious and educational backgrounds, ideologies, economic interests, political necessities, and the like. It would be more accurate to say that these parties were loose combinations of certain economic, social, and intellectual groupings, held together by a set of common attitudes and interests.

Fundamentally, they reflected two different opinions about the qualities of human nature. Hamiltonians were acutely aware of the "imperfections, weaknesses, and evils of human nature." They believed that if people were fit to govern themselves at all, it must only be under rigid controls imposed upon them by society and government. Jeffersonians, on the other hand, believed that people were by inclination rational and good. If freed from the bonds of ignorance, error, and repression, they might achieve real progress toward an ideal society. Others, of course, took positions between these two extremes.

These contrasting concepts of human fallibility were reflected in contemporary political opinions about the structure and aim of government. The Federalists emphasized the need for political machinery to restrain the majority. They believed in a strong central government and a strong executive, with the active participation of that government in manufacturing, commerce, and finance. They believed that leadership in society belonged to a trained, responsible, and (very likely) wealthy class that could be trusted to protect property as well as human rights.

The Jeffersonian Republicans distrusted centralized authority and a powerful executive, preferring instead a less autonomous, more decentralized government modeled more on confederation than on federalism. They believed in the leadership of what Jefferson called "a natural aristocracy," founded on talent and intelligence rather than on birth, wealth, or station. Most Republicans believed that human nature in the aggregate was naturally trustworthy and that it could be improved through freedom and education—and therefore that wise self-government, under proper conditions, would be possible.

THE TRIAL OF JOHN ADAMS

THE XYZ AFFAIR

John Adams took office at a difficult time, for the Federalist Party that had elected him was showing strain at the seams. Hamilton still dictated a large share of party policy from private life. He did not like Adams and had maneuvered before the election in an attempt to defeat him. Adams was a stubbornly honest man, a keen student of government and law, but blunt, a trifle haughty, sometimes tactless. Indeed, many of his most amiable qualities were reflected in his relationship with his remarkable wife, Abigail, rather than in his conduct as a public figure.

Adams' administration promptly found itself in trouble. Within his party there was a violently anti-French group, including Adams' Secretary of State, Thomas Pickering, who virtually demanded a declaration of war against France. The French minister to the United States, Pierre Adet, had openly tried to influence the 1796 election in favor of Jefferson and the Democratic Republicans. The French, angry at Jay's Treaty and at an American neutrality that appeared to favor Britain, began seizure of American ships at sea carrying British goods. By March 1797, 300 American ships had been seized by

French privateers. France also refused to receive Adams' new minister to France, Charles Cotesworth Pinckney. Adams, who did not want war, sent John Marshall, C. C. Pinckney, and Elbridge Gerry to Paris in 1797 to try to find some way out.

The French foreign minister Talleyrand, dealing with the American commission through three intermediaries called (for purposes of anonymity) X, Y, and Z, demanded not only a loan of $12 million to the French government but also a bribe of $240,000, plus an apology for negative comments that John Adams had made about France. These demands the Americans indignantly refused with Pinckney's retort of "no, not a sixpence." When the news of the "XYZ Affair" leaked out, the ringing slogan "Millions for defense, but not one cent for tribute!" (based on Pinckney's reply) became a rallying point for the anti-French faction in Congress. Adams asked Congress to prepare for war, and the French accelerated the seizure of American ships at sea. The United States Navy was sent to the Caribbean to repel the French navy and, with powder and shot provided by the British, captured over 100 French privateers in what historians refer to as the "Quasi-War" with France since plenty of shots were fired on the open sea but war was not declared.

THE TREATY OF 1800

Capitalizing on the war fever, Congress created a Department of the

Napoleon Bonaparte

Navy, built a number of new ships, armed American merchantmen, and authorized an army of 10,000 men. Though his own party leaders (Hamilton among them) argued that war with France was inevitable, Adams refused to listen, and as it turned out, the French did not want war either. Adams received scathing reviews from Republican newspapers and even endured abuse from members of his own party. After nearly a year of undeclared naval war, the French government suggested that if an American mission were to be sent to Paris it would be respectfully received.

By the time the American commissioners arrived in France in March 1800, the country was in the hands of Napoleon Bonaparte, who quietly agreed to a settlement of differences. The Treaty of 1800 was not popular with the Federalists or Congress, but it was ratified. It avoided a war and also dissolved the French-American alliance forged during the Revolution. "The end of war is peace," said Adams, "and peace was offered me." John Adams got his peace, but probably at the expense of victory in the coming elections for himself and his party.

THE ALIEN AND SEDITION ACTS

The popular outcry against France, and the near-war that carried through 1797–1799, gave the Federalists a good chance, they believed, to cripple their Republican political opponents under cover of protecting internal security. The country was honeycombed, so the Federalist press claimed, with French agents and propagandists who were secretly at work undermining the national will and subverting public opinion. Since most immigrants were inclined to vote Republican, the Federalist Congress capitalized on antiforeign feeling in 1798 by passing a series of Alien Acts which lengthened the naturalization period from five to 14 years, empowered the President to deport undesirable aliens, and authorized him to imprison such aliens as he chose in time of war. Though he signed the bill, Adams did not like the acts and never seriously tried to enforce them.

As the second step in its anti-Republican campaign, Congress passed the Sedition Act, also in 1798. Under this act, a citizen could be fined or imprisoned or both for "writing, printing, uttering, or publishing" false statements or any statements which might bring the President or Congress "into contempt or disrepute." Since this last clause covered almost anything Republicans might say about Federalists, its purpose was quite plainly to muzzle the opposition and its primary targets were newspaper editors that opposed the Adams administration. Under the Sedition Act 25 editors and printers were prosecuted and 12 were convicted—though they were later pardoned and their fines returned by the Jeffersonians.

With the Alien and Sedition laws the Federalists went too far. Republicans opposed the acts on the grounds that they were in violation of the free speech and free press protections of the Bill of Rights. Federalist judges who would not rule against the Federalist Congress or the Adams administration, however, dominated the judiciary branch. Public opinion sided with the Republicans. The legislatures of Kentucky and Virginia (home to Republican leaders Jefferson and

Madison) passed resolutions in 1798 and 1799 (Jefferson drafted Kentucky's; Madison, Virginia's) condemning the laws and asking the states to join in nullifying them as violations of civil rights. Actually none did, but the Kentucky and Virginia resolutions furnished the Jeffersonians with excellent ammunition for the approaching presidential campaign. The Kentucky and Virginia resolutions also put forth the idea that states could nullify federal laws that they found to be unconstitutional. Finally, although the United States had no strong tradition of civil liberties, the Alien and Sedition laws helped to create one by pointing out how easily those rights of free speech and free press, guaranteed by the Bill of Rights, could be violated.

THE ELECTION OF 1800

Washington's death in December 1799 from a throat and upper respiratory infection paired with the detrimental medical treatment of bloodletting, symbolized the passing of the Federalist dynasty. The party that he had led was in dire distress, divided into wrangling factions. The Republicans were in an excellent position to capitalize on a long string of political moves which had alienated large blocs of voters—the handling of the Whiskey Rebellion, Hamilton's tax policies, the Jay Treaty and Jay's negotiations with Spain in 1786, the Alien and Sedition Acts—as well as conflict and resentment within the Federalist party.

As a matter of fact, the Federalists had been unable to maintain a balance between the nationalist business interests that formed the core of their support, and the rapidly growing influence of the middle and lower urban and agrarian classes of the South, the West, and the Middle Atlantic states. After Washington, who had held the party together by the force of his example, no Federalist leader found a way to absorb and control the elements of society that, after 1796, began to look to Jefferson for leadership. The clash of personalities within the Federalist camp, of course, damaged the party further.

John Adams, who through his entire term had to face the internal opposition of the Hamiltonians as well as the Republicans from without, deserves more credit than he is often given. Except for Adams' stubborn desire to keep the peace, the United States might well have entered into a disastrous war with France, and without him the Federalist party under Hamilton's control would probably have killed itself 10 years sooner than it did. Adams' decision to stay out of war, made against the bitter opposition of his own party, was not only an act of courage but also, very likely, his greatest service to the nation.

Although Hamilton circulated a pamphlet violently attacking the President, the party had no other satisfactory candidate for the election of 1800 and decided to nominate Adams again, choosing C. C. Pinckney to run with him. The Republicans picked Jefferson and Burr once more, hoping thus to unite the powerful Virginia and New York wings of the party. The campaign was one of the bitterest in American history. In the end, the Republicans, who won the Middle Atlantic States and the South, emerged with a small edge in total electoral votes.

Under the Constitution, the candidate with the most votes was President and the next Vice-President, but when the Republican electors all voted for Jefferson and Burr, they created a tie. This threw the election into the House of Representatives, still controlled by lame-duck Federalists. The Federalists' hatred of Jefferson was so intense that many of them preferred Burr. At the same time, Burr's own party wanted Jefferson, but Burr refused to step aside. Hamilton, much as he disagreed with Jefferson's principles, considered Burr a political adventurer and deeply distrusted him—as well he might have, given that Burr killed him in a duel a few years later. Hamilton, therefore, threw his influence in Congress behind Jefferson, who was declared President by the House of Representatives on February 17, 1801. Subsequent historians have seen this election as particularly significant because it was the first one in American history in which the party in power lost and then turned that power over to its victorious opponents, peacefully and in legal, democratic fashion.

THE JEFFERSONIAN ERA, 1800–1824

JEFFERSON IN POWER

"The Revolution of 1800"
Thomas Jefferson
Settling the Barbary Corsairs
The Purchase of Louisiana
The Problems of Political Patronage
Jefferson Versus Marshall
Marshall and Constitutional Law
Opening the West
The "Essex Junto"
The Election of 1804

AMERICA AND THE WOES OF EUROPE

Neutrality in a World at War
The British at Sea
The "Obnoxious Embargo"
The Election of 1808
The Drift to War
The War Hawks
"Mr. Madison's War"

THE WAR OF 1812

War on the Land: First Phase
War on the Land: Second Phase

War at Sea
War on the Land: Final Phase
The Hartford Convention

A Welcome Peace
The Results of the War
The War and Canada

AMERICA MAKES A NEW START

A Confident Nation
The Aftermath of War
A Protective Tariff
Renewing the Bank of the United States
Building Better Connecting Links

AMERICA MOVES WEST

Land Hunger Versus Native
  American Rights

Resistance to Federal Policy
GROWING PAINS

The Election of 1816
The "Era of Good Feelings"
Prosperity and Panic
"FIRE BELL IN THE NIGHT"

Sectionalism and Slavery
The Missouri Compromise
EVOLVING A FOREIGN POLICY

Catching Up on Old Problems
The Monroe Doctrine
The Triumph of Isolation

JEFFERSON IN POWER

"THE REVOLUTION OF 1800"

Thomas Jefferson usually referred to his presidential election victory as "the revolution of 1800," though it was hardly a "revolution" in the usual sense. It was, nonetheless, an important election because it shifted national political authority toward the South and West, introducing a new emphasis on decentralized power and state sovereignty. It marked the first successful alliance of agrarian and urban forces, which later President Andrew Jackson consolidated. Since it was also the first really hard-fought American political campaign, it set "faction" and partisanship firmly into the political process. In actual practice, however, Jefferson did surprisingly little to erase what his predecessors had done, and there was much greater continuity from the Federalist decade into his own than there appeared at first glance. Indeed, in his inaugural address Jefferson proclaimed, "We are all Republicans, We are all Federalists."

THOMAS JEFFERSON

Thomas Jefferson, the third President of the United States and first Secretary of State, is viewed by historians as a bit of an enigma and a man of contradictions. Jefferson owned a tobacco plantation but did not smoke. Jefferson drank little alcohol but planted a vineyard and made wine at his Monticello plantation. In a time where the rugged frontiersmen of Virginia tended to be familiar with guns and game, Jefferson did not hunt, ate little meat, and was concerned with protection of the environment. Jefferson was a large plantation owner and a member of Virginia's elite class; but he showed no respect of persons by spending entire days in his housecoat, serving guests himself, and accepting visitors in the order that they arrived rather than in the order of importance. Jefferson was also a slave owner who viewed blacks as inferior and opposed inter-racial "mixing"; yet he also favored the return of blacks to Africa and had sexual relations and children with at least one of his slaves, Sally Hemmings. Jefferson favored a balanced budget for the nation and a small military; yet he was generally known as a spendthrift in his personal life, and for most of his life his personal debts exceeded his ability to pay them. Jefferson believed the nation would be best served if it did not build great cities but, instead, remained a nation of small farmers; yet he built a nail factory on his own plantation where he put slave children to work making nails for profit.

Jefferson is considered one of America's "scholar-Presidents", and few would doubt that he had an active and inquisitive mind. Jefferson wrote over 30,000 personal letters in his lifetime, was very well-read, and after his death his personal library became a major contribution to the beginnings of the Library of Congress. Jefferson is also generally credited with founding the University of

The U.S. Capitol as it looked when first occupied by Congress in 1800

Virginia. Jefferson (primarily) wrote not only the Declaration of Independence, but also in 1786 the Virginia Statute on Religious Liberty that essentially separated Church and State in Virginia. Jefferson's religious views appear to lean toward Deism as evidenced by his letter to his nephew Peter Carr where Jefferson argues that one should "read the Bible as you would Livy or Tacitus." Jefferson also wrote his own gospel where he essentially assembled the sayings of Jesus absent the miraculous deeds depicted in the New Testament

Jefferson is known as an advocate of states' rights and less government, stemming from his negative view of human nature. Jefferson believed that government was a necessary evil- which, by its very nature, limits freedom. In spite of these beliefs, however, Jefferson also expanded the power of the national government with his purchase of Louisiana.

Finally, Thomas Jefferson is credited with forming the first democratic opposition political party, the Democratic Republicans, in opposition to the policies of John Adams and Alexander Hamilton. Jefferson's creation would eventually morph into the Democratic Party as it exists in the twenty-first century.

SETTLING THE BARBARY CORSAIRS

Jefferson's administration had hardly caught its breath before it was plunged into a vortex of swift-moving foreign affairs. The President's first problem involved the depredations of pirates from the Barbary states of North Africa (Tunis, Algiers, Morocco, and Tripoli), who had preyed on Mediterranean commerce for a quarter century, enslaving seamen and levying tribute on shipping. During their administrations, Washington and Adams paid out more than $2 million in ransom and bribes to the Barbary potentates. Jefferson determined to end the affair when the pirates announced an in-

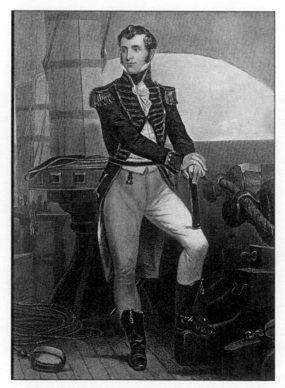

Stephen Decatur

crease in the bounty in the summer of 1781. Jefferson refused to pay the increase, and Tripoli responded by declaring war on the United States and capturing an American ship, the *USS Philadelphia.* In 1803 the United States sent to the Mediterranean four naval squadrons commanded by Stephen Decatur, who reclaimed the *Philadelphia* and in a series of brilliant actions finally forced some of the pirate states to sue for peace. Decatur quickly became an American hero and was famous for his unrestrained patriotism, exemplified by his statement, "My country right or wrong, but may she always be right."

Under a treaty signed in 1805, the United States agreed that it would continue to pay a bounty to the pirates but at the previous, lower price. The United States also agreed to pay a ransom for the return of some captured United States seamen, and the pirates agreed to allow the United States unmolested passage in the Mediterranean. The United States navy remained in the Mediterranean to protect American shipping but was recalled in 1807 by President Jefferson due to conflict with Britain. All of the bounties were not ended until 1815 when Algiers declared war on the United States and resumed disruption of American shipping. The United States navy returned to the Mediterranean and with help from European navies defeated the pirates, thus ending the payment of tributes and piracy.

The USS *Enterprise* capturing the 14-gun Tripolitan corsair *Tripoli*

THE PURCHASE OF LOUISIANA

In 1801 Napoleon Bonaparte recovered the territory of Louisiana, lost by France to Spain in 1763. Jefferson recognized the potential danger to the United States of this sudden shift in ownership of half the American continent from impotent Spain to imperial France. The United States could not afford to have New Orleans, Jefferson wrote, possessed by "our natural and habitual enemy," Napoleon. Jefferson believed in Manifest Destiny and favored the expansion of the United States across the continent. French control of Louisiana was, therefore, counter to Jefferson's long-term goals. Jefferson reacted to the news of French ownership of Louisiana by securing the authorization for 15 gunboats to patrol the Mississippi and the federalization of 80,000 state militiamen for duty along the Mississippi. Jefferson also declared, "The day that France takes possession of New Orleans, we must marry ourselves to the British Navy." Jefferson's actions were in actuality little more than "saber rattling." The French well understood, however, that they could not control the vast territory that was Louisiana; and they may be unable to prevent the United States from taking the territory by force.

In March 1801, Napoleon resumed war against England and could ill-afford to spare troops for the defense of Louisiana in North America. Napoleon had amassed an army for the defense of Louisiana; but his army never made it to the New World because it was iced-in at port in the Netherlands in the winter of 1802–1803. Moreover, Napoleon had tried to conquer Haiti (then called Saint Domingue), which had been lost to France after a rebellion of black slaves led by Touissaint L'Ouverture in 1793. The venture had not been a success, and Napoleon was eager to cut his losses on this side of the Atlantic. In 1802 a slave rebellion cost Napoleon 24,000 French soldiers, most who died from yellow fever. Despite the presence of 50,000 French troops in Saint Dominigue, Napoleon's General Victor Leclerc suggested that 70,000 more troops were needed and that every slave over 12 years of age must be killed. Napoleon, therefore, gave up Saint Dominigue for lost in 1803, proclaiming, "Damn sugar, damn coffee, damn colonies."

The President, therefore, sent James Monroe to Paris to assist the American minister to France, Robert Livingston, and to discuss the possible purchase of New Orleans and East and West Florida (the coastal bend between Baton Rouge and Pensacola). It was either buy now, Jefferson said, or fight for it later. Jefferson privately authorized Monroe to offer as much as $10 million for New Orleans and the Floridas. If France should refuse to negotiate, Monroe was instructed to depart to England and negotiate an alliance with the British (the type of Anglo-American alliance against France that the French greatly feared). Thus, the French emperor decided to sell; and in Paris the French foreign minister Tallyrand asked Livingston if the United States would like to own all of Louisiana rather than just New Orleans. Two days later Monroe arrived in Paris, and Livingston and Monroe agreed that the United States should buy all of Louisiana even though they lacked the explicit authority to commit the United States to such an agreement. In April 1803, the United States offered to purchase the Louisiana Territory and West Florida for $15 million. France accepted the American offer, and the agreement was signed on May 2, 1803. Jefferson, though overjoyed at the bargain, was also embarrassed by the fact that nowhere in the Constitution could he find presidential authority to make it. He finally accepted Madison's view that the purchase could be made under a somewhat elastic interpretation of the treaty-making power, a view he had earlier rejected. Jefferson argued to the Senate, "Strict observance to higher

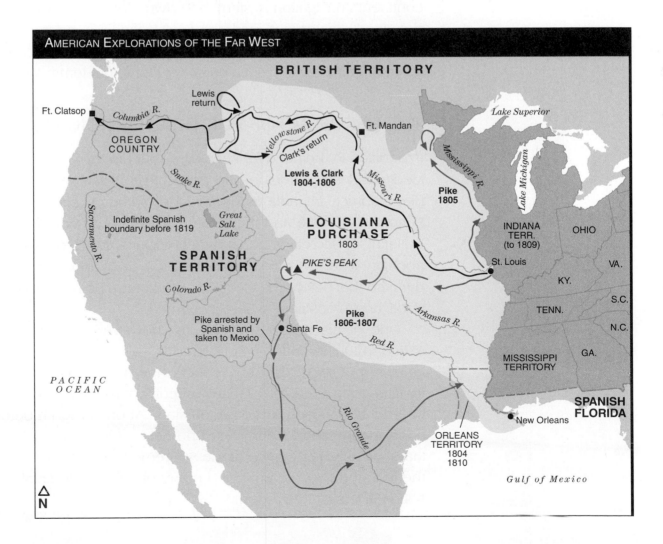

AMERICAN EXPLORATIONS OF THE FAR WEST

law was one of the high duties of a good citizen, but not the highest. The laws of necessity and of self-preservation when a country is in danger are of a higher obligation." The brilliance of the maneuver obscured the constitutional question involved, but the "strict constructionist" doctrine (that the government is limited to powers specifically stated in the Constitution) was never the same again.

The agreement was also problematic in that Spain claimed that under the provisions of an earlier treaty, Louisiana was rightfully Spain's because France had agreed that it could not fall to a third power. Furthermore, it was unclear whether or not the purchase included West Florida. Jefferson had also declared all of the inhabitants of Louisiana to be United States citizens, a power that is not granted to the President by the Constitution. It was also unclear at the time whether or not all of the residents of Louisiana, many of whom were of French heritage, would accept United States citizenship or control.

Whatever its constitutionality, the Louisiana Purchase was one of the most important presidential decisions in American history. At one stroke the United States became a continental power, master of the continent's navigation system, and owner of vast new resources that promised greater (and perhaps final) economic independence from Europe. It also put an end to the likelihood that the West could ever be split from the East and set a precedent for future territorial expansion.

THE PROBLEMS OF POLITICAL PATRONAGE

In addition to the need for keeping a watchful eye on Europe and the Mediterranean, Jefferson had political problems at home. His cabinet, a particularly able group, included James Madison of Virginia as Secretary of State and the brilliant Swiss from Pennsylvania, Albert Gallatin, as Secretary of the Treasury. Quite aware of the utility of patronage, Jefferson quietly replaced Federalist appointments with his own, so that before the close of his first term he had responsible Republicans in positions where it counted.

One of his thorniest problems, however, was that of the so-called "midnight judges" appointed by John Adams under the Judiciary Act of 1801. The act reduced the number of Supreme Court justices to five, created 16 new circuit courts, and added a number of federal marshals and other officials. About a month before Jefferson's inauguration Adams had nominated Secretary of State John Marshall as Chief Justice of the Supreme Court. Then on the eve of the inauguration, Adams filled many of the new judicial posts with solid Federalist Party men.

John Marshall was a stalwart Federalist, but beyond that he was a convinced nationalist who believed that the Constitution was the most sacred of all documents, "framed for ages to come ..., designed to approach immortality as nearly as human institutions can approach it." He did not trust the Jeffersonians, and he entered the Court determined that none should play fast and loose with the Constitution so long as he could prevent it.

JEFFERSON VERSUS MARSHALL

Jefferson was sure that Marshall, that "crafty chief judge," would set as many obstacles as he could in the administration's path, and that the "midnight judges" would undoubtedly follow his lead. In 1802, when Jefferson persuaded Congress to repeal the Judiciary Act of 1801, all of Adams' judges were left without salaries or duties. This, the Federalists claimed, was unconstitutional.

To test the constitutionality of Congress' repeal, William Marbury (one of the "midnight" appointments) asked Secretary of State Madison to give him his commission as justice of the peace of the District of Columbia. This Madison refused to do. Marbury then applied to the Supreme Court for a writ ordering Madison to do so, the famous case of *Marbury v. Madison*. Marshall used the case to promote what Jefferson did not want established—the Supreme Court's right of judicial review of legislation (the power to declare the constitutionality of statutes and actions). The Constitution, wrote Marshall, is "the *supreme* law of the land, superior to any ordinary act of the legislative." "A legislative act contrary to the Constitution is not law," Marshall went on, and "it is the province and duty of the judicial department to say what the law is." In saying so, Marshall had seized for the Court a power that had not been specifically granted to it in the Constitution and thus elevated the judicial branch to coequal status with the legislative branch and the executive.

The Jefferson administration then launched an attack directly on the Federalist-dominated judiciary itself, at one point leading Congress to cut off funding for the Court, effectively closing it for a year. Jefferson and the Democratic Republican Congress began using as its tool the constitutional power of impeachment for "high crimes and misdemeanors" against Federalist judges. The first target was John Pickering of the New Hampshire district court, who was apparently both alcoholic and insane. Pickering was impeached by the House, judged guilty by the Senate, and removed from office. Next, in 1804, the Republicans picked Associate Justice Samuel Chase of the

Supreme Court, a violently partisan Federalist who had presided over several trials of Jeffersonian editors under the Sedition Act of 1798. In 1805, when the Senate decided it could not convict Chase, Jefferson conceded that impeachment was ineffective as a political weapon. Congress gradually created a series of new judgeships and filled them with Republicans, a slower process but one that worked.

MARSHALL AND CONSTITUTIONAL LAW

Jefferson's differences with Marshall were temporarily settled, but Marshall's long tenure as Chief Justice was a most important influence on the rapid growth of the power of the federal government over the next three decades. Marshall served on the Court from 1801 to 1835, participated in more than 1,000 opinions and decisions, and wrote some 500 of them. Whenever opportunity presented itself, as it often did, Marshall strove to affirm two principles: that the Supreme Court possessed the power to nullify state laws that were in conflict with the Constitution, and that the Court alone had the right to interpret the Constitution, especially in regard to such broad grants of authority as might be contained in terms such as "commerce," "general welfare," "necessary and proper," and so on. His opinion did not always become the final version of constitutional issues; but the consistency of his attitudes, carried over a whole generation of legal interpretations, had much to do with the shaping of American constitutional law. Marshall's principles of judicial review and broad construction of the necessary and proper clause of the Constitution, along with the supremacy of the national government in its sphere, remain cornerstones of constitutional law through the present.

OPENING THE WEST

After the Louisiana Purchase there was great anxiety to find out about what the nation had bought, more or less sight unseen. Jefferson, a respected scientist in addition to his many other achievements, had already made plans for the exploration of these newly acquired lands and persuaded Congress to finance an expedition up the Missouri River, across the Rocky Mountains, and if possible on to the Pacific. To lead it Jefferson chose his private secretary, a young Virginian named Meriwether Lewis, and William Clark, brother of George Rogers Clark, the frontier soldier. Congress appropriated $2,500 for an expedition that eventually cost $38,000. The mission itself was political, scientific, and commercial as Lewis and Clark were charged with making note of the landscape, Native Americans with whom the United States could engage in profitable trade, and the plants and animals that could be useful.

In the spring of 1804 Lewis and Clark's party of 48, including several scientists, left St. Louis for the West in one 55-foot keel boat and two pirogues (dugout canoes) and went forth mapping, gathering specimens of plants and animals, collecting data on soil and weather, and observing every pertinent detail of the new country. They journeyed up the Missouri River and wintered in the Dakotas with the Mandan Indians, who welcomed the expedition for their

The Mandan Indians welcomed the Lewis and Clark expedition.

usefulness as a security measure against the Sioux Indians. Sergeant Charles Floyd perished at Council Bluffs from appendicitis, the only death on the expedition.

A French fur trader, Toussaint Charbonneau, and his Shoshone Indian wife, Sacajawea aided Lewis and Clark. Charbonneau and Sacajawea served as language interpreters rather than guides since they did not know the way across the Rocky Mountains to the Pacific. Sacajawea was probably about 15 years old at the time, having been kidnapped in her youth by another Native American tribe, kept as a slave, and then sold as a wife to Charbonneau. Sacajawea's presence with the expedition may have been most helpful in that other tribes viewed the presence of a woman as an indication that Lewis and Clark's group was not a war party. Sacajawea also may have saved the entire expedition when Shoshone warriors aborted what appeared to be a staged attack because they recognized Sacajawea as a family member who had been kidnapped six years prior. Nevertheless, Lewis and Clark were unable to avoid problems with all native tribes along the way. On the return trip one Blackfoot Indian was stabbed while attempting to steal a

Sacajawea may have saved the Lewis and Clark expedition from an attack by Shoshone Indians.

gun, and Lewis shot another for stealing a horse. As a consequence, the expedition traveled 60 miles nonstop over the next three days to escape the pursuing Native Americans.

Lewis and Clark crossed the Rockies and followed the Columbia River to the Pacific, catching their first glimpse of the sea in November 1805. In the Columbia River valley, Lewis and Clark encountered the Clatsop and Chinook Indians, who were very poor tribes that made their existence by spear fishing in the river. The males in these tribes were all blind by age 30, their retinas burned from the sun's reflection on the river. Lewis administered laudanum, an opiate, to the Native Americans. Although Lewis wrote that the Native Americans were not cured, he also stated that they "felt much better." Lewis himself would eventually become addicted to laudanum as a result of the expedition. Once, when Lewis and Peter Cruzatte had gone elk hunting wearing elk-skins, Cruzatte—whose vision was impaired by the fact that he had only one eye—accidentally mistook Lewis for an elk and shot him in the buttocks. Lewis took laudanum for the pain and developed an addiction that would plague him the rest of his life.

By autumn of 1806, the expedition was back in St. Louis. What it brought back was both scientific data and vivid accounts that fed the imagination of fellow Americans, then and since. Lewis and Clark returned with dozens of plant and animal species, including two bear cubs that President Jefferson kept in a pit on the White House lawn. The explorers also made detailed and accurate drawings of other wildlife as well as accurate maps of the Missouri River. Lewis and Clark became national heroes, and Clark was appointed governor of Missouri. Clark died of natural causes in 1838 at the age of 75.

Meriwether Lewis was appointed governor of Louisiana but, addicted to alcohol and drugs, committed suicide in 1809 at age 36. Lewis shot himself in the head and chest; and when servants arrived at his room, they found him cutting himself head to toe with a razor. Lewis stated to his servant, "I am so strong; it is hard to die."

At almost the same time, a party under Lieutenant Zebulon Pike was exploring the upper Mississippi and the mid-Rockies. Pike's expedition was less successful than that of Lewis and Clark because he did not keep accurate records. Nevertheless, Pike's Peak, perhaps the most famous mountain in Colorado, still bears his name. Other explorations followed, and the Louisiana Territory was soon organized on the pattern of the Northwest Ordinance of 1787 (its first state, Louisiana, entered in 1812). The West was no longer a dream but a reality.

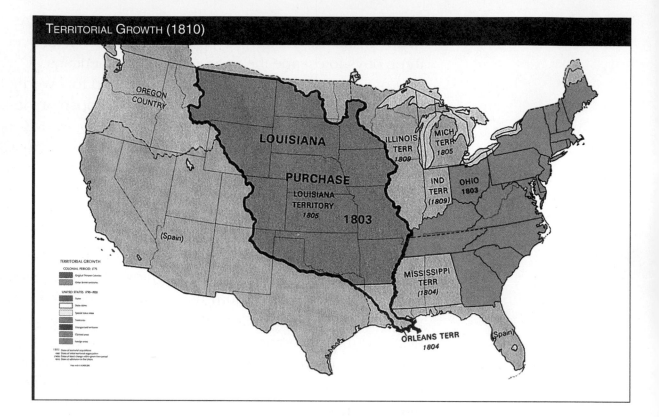

TERRITORIAL GROWTH (1810)

THE "ESSEX JUNTO"

The prospect of more states being carved out of the wide new West greatly disturbed the Federalist Party leaders. Ohio entered the Union in 1803, a soundly Republican state, and the probability that all the new states from the Northwest Territory, plus all those to be developed from the Louisiana Purchase, might lean politically to the Jeffersonians was profoundly worrisome. United only in their common hostility to the President, the Federalists had neither issue nor leader to counter his popularity and had little chance of finding either.

The gloom was especially thick in New England, so much so that a small number of Federalists (nicknamed the "Essex Junto") explored the possibilities of persuading the five New England states, plus New York and New Jersey, to secede from the Union to form a separate Federalist republic—a "Northern Confederacy," said Senator Timothy Pickering of Massachusetts, "exempt from the corrupt and corrupting influence and oppression of the aristocratic democrats of the South."

Alexander Hamilton of New York showed no inclination to join them, so the New Englanders approached Aaron Burr. Since Burr felt it unlikely that he would be nominated for Vice-President again, he consented to run for the governorship of New York, an office from which he might lead a secession movement.

Hamilton disliked Jeffersonians, too, but he considered Burr a dangerous man and campaigned against him. After Burr lost, he challenged Hamilton to a duel—on the basis of certain slurs on Burr's character reported in the press. Hamilton accused Burr of incest with his daughter, while Burr accused Hamilton of adultery with his sister-in-law.

Bust of Aaron Burr

Burr subsequently killed Hamilton in July 1804 with the same gun that had been used to kill Hamilton's son Philip in a similar duel.

Alexander Hamilton died as he had lived, a controversial man who aroused strong feelings. His blunt distrust of "King Mob" and his frank preference for British-style constitutionalism had never endeared him to the public, but the leadership he provided for the country during the crucial postwar years had much to do with its successful transition from a provincial to a federal philosophy. Above all, he had a rare ability to think in large terms about what it would take to create a powerful national economy. Thus Hamilton had made an invaluable contribution when it mattered most.

The duel ruined Burr's reputation and helped to complete the eclipse of the Federalist Party, yet Burr himself was not quite finished. After the Republicans passed him over as their vice-presidential candidate in 1804 in favor of George Clinton of New York, he apparently entered into a scheme to carve a great empire of his own out of the American West, a conspiracy that ended with his trial for treason in 1807. In 1806 Burr and General James Wilkinson, then governor of Louisiana, organized a force of about 80 men at Blennerhassett Island in the Ohio River for the purpose of taking New Orleans militarily from the United States. Wilkinson betrayed Burr to Jefferson, who issued a proclamation warning the nation and calling for Burr's arrest. Burr was brought to Richmond in Jefferson's home state, but Jefferson's nemesis John Marshall tainted the trial. Marshall's charge to the jury was so narrow that Burr's attempt to militarily seize New Orleans from the United States was not defined as treason. Marshall stated to the jury that "organizing a military assemblage … is not a levying of war." Furthermore, Marshall stated that "to advise or procure treason, is not treason itself." Jefferson, however, also tainted the trial by offering a pardon to any Burr associate that would testify against him.

Although Burr was acquitted thanks to Marshall's narrow charges to the jury, everyone drawn into his plan was ruined; and Burr was forced to flee to England to escape further prosecution for Hamilton's death and additional charges of treason in six states. In his old age Burr would eventually return to the United States where he fathered two illegitimate children in his 70's and was divorced by his wife, on the grounds of adultery, at age 80. Meanwhile, the Federalist Party approached the election of 1804 with its brilliant leader dead, its reputation tarnished, and neither candidates nor issues of any public value.

THE ELECTION OF 1804

The election of 1804 was very nearly no contest. The Republican caucus nominated Jefferson for a second time, with George Clinton of New York as his running mate. The Federalists ran the reliable C.

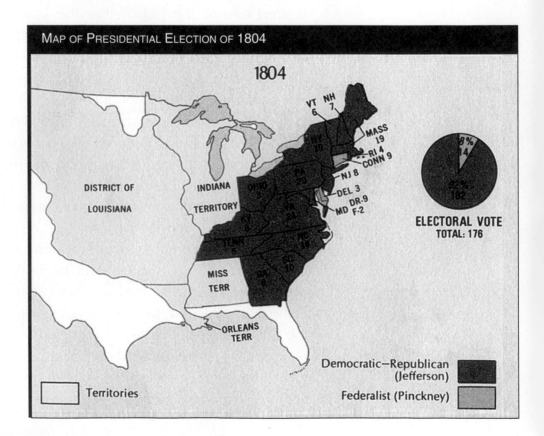

MAP OF PRESIDENTIAL ELECTION OF 1804

C. Pinckney and Rufus King of New York. Jefferson carried every state except Connecticut and Delaware, garnering 162 of the total 176 electoral votes and sweeping in an overwhelmingly Republican Congress with him.

AMERICA AND THE WOES OF EUROPE

NEUTRALITY IN A WORLD AT WAR

Napoleon Bonaparte loomed large in the future of both America and Europe. Jefferson did not like him; but to Jefferson and many other Americans France was still the country of Lafayette, Rochambeau, De Grasse, and the great French philosophers of the Enlightenment. Against Napoleon stood England, whose aim Jefferson believed was "the permanent domination of the ocean and the monopoly of the trade of the world." He did not want war with either, nor did he wish to give aid to either in the war that flamed up between them in 1803.

It would be an oversimplification, of course, to assume that American foreign policy of the period was governed primarily by a like or dislike of France or England. The objectives of Jefferson's foreign policy, like Washington's and Adams', were first, to protect American independence and second, to maintain as much diplomatic flexibility as possible without irrevocable commitment to any nation.

In the European power struggle between England and France that developed after 1790, Jefferson saw great advantages to the United States in playing one against the other without being drawn into the orbit of either. An American friendship with France would form a useful counterbalance against the influence of Britain and Spain, the chief colonial powers in North and South America. A British and Spanish defeat might well mean the end of their American empires.

At the same time Jefferson did not want to tie America's future to the fortunes of Napoleon, who might be an even greater threat to American freedom if he won. The wisest policy therefore, remained in neutrality toward all and trade with anyone—or, as the British wryly put it, America's best hope was "to gain fortune from Europe's misfortune."

America's major gain during the European war stemmed from American misuse of a naval doctrine known as the "doctrine of the broken voyage." Under this doctrine, if merchant ships broke a voyage from French or Spanish islands in the Caribbean by paying duties in an American port, the status of the cargo changed to American. Given that the United States was neutral in the war, the cargo shipped under American flags was not legally subject to seizure by the warring nations. As a result, a "re-export" business boomed in the United States.

In 1806 alone, the United States exported 47 million pounds of coffee, none of which was grown in the United States.

Maintaining neutrality was as difficult for Jefferson as it had been for Washington and Adams before him. The British navy ruled the seas, and Napoleon, after the Battle of Austerlitz in 1805, ruled Europe. The war remained a stalemate while the two countries engaged in a battle of proclamations over wartime naval commerce. Each side set up a blockade of the other's ports, The British argued that the American re-export business was illegal because the United States often rebated 90 percent of the duties paid by a foreign power in its ports. As a consequence, the British argued that the voyages were not "broken" but "continuous" and, therefore, subject to seizure by the British. The British stationed their warships near United States ports, forcing American ships carrying French and Spanish re-exports to Canada for trial in a British admiralty court where the British would confiscate the cargo.

In 1803, the British also angered the Americans by returning to their policy of impressments in an effort to meet the demands for sailors caused by the war against France. The demand for sailors was caused not only by the war but, also, by a high desertion rate (2,500 per year) among British sailors. Many of the deserters found work on American merchant ships. The British, therefore, began stopping American ships and impressing sailors who could not prove American citizenship. The British seized over 10,000 men from American ships between 1803 and 1812, though 3,800 were released after they proved their American citizenship.

To make matters worse, the British did not recognize American naturalized citizens. England claimed that all persons born in England were forever English citizens. Americans exacerbated the situation by forging naturalization papers. In the words of Britain's Lord Vincent, "Every Englishman may be made an American for a dollar."

THE BRITISH AT SEA

From 1806 the British announced the first of a series of "Orders in Council" (orders from the King's privy council) that proclaimed a blockade of Europe. Napoleon retaliated with the Berlin Decree, which declared all British ports closed. The result was that the United States was caught between two warring nations with the United States vessels liable to confiscation by either nation if the vessels obeyed the rules of the other.

Finally, in the summer of 1807, the British *Leopard* stopped the United States navy's *Chesapeake* (a warship, not a merchant vessel), killed or wounded 21 men, and took four sailors (three of whom were

Americans). This was, by any standard, an act of war, and America burst out in a great roar of rage. Had Congress been in session, it almost certainly would have declared war on the spot. Instead Jefferson held his temper, demanded apologies and reparations, and ordered British ships out of American waters to prevent further incidents. Jefferson understood America's naval inferiority at the time and viewed nonmilitary options as preferable. Though the British apologized, they also reaffirmed their right to search American ships and seize deserters. The *Leopard-Chesapeake* affair rankled in American minds for years and had much to do with the drift toward war with Britain in 1812.

THE "OBNOXIOUS EMBARGO"

Neither was sufficiently effective to do much good, however. As the situation between the two nations steadily deteriorated, Jefferson asked Congress for a full-scale embargo—a logical move since Britain needed American trade, especially foodstuffs, in increasing quantities as the war progressed. In late 1807 Congress, therefore, passed the Embargo Act, which forbade American ships to leave the United States for any foreign port or even to engage in the American coastal trade without posting a heavy bond. Jefferson hoped that the Embargo Act of 1807 would do two things: first, that it would discourage the British from seizing American ships and sailors and force them to greater regard for American rights; and, second, that it would encourage the growth of American industry by cutting off British imports.

England suffered shortages, but not enough to matter; France approved of the embargo since it helped at second hand to enforce Napoleon's own blockade of England. American ships rotted at anchor along the Eastern seaboard. Merchants went bankrupt, and farm surpluses piled up. In New York, one traveler wrote, "The streets near the waterside were almost deserted. The grass had begun to grow upon the wharves." American exports dropped 80 percent in 1808, and British exports to the United States dropped 50 percent. The impact of the Embargo Act on the American economy was exacerbated by the fact that the export business was the fastest growing segment of the American economy.

While the shipping interests suffered, however, New England and the Middle Atlantic port states did begin a transition to manufacturing that was soon to change their economic complexion. With foreign competition removed, capital previously invested in overseas trade was available for new factories and mills, which sprang up in profusion along the seaboard. The future economic advantages were difficult to see, however, in the midst of the paralyzing effects of the embargo. American merchants in New England circumvented the act by smuggling goods into Canada and then "re-exporting" the goods to England. Some New Englanders even talked of secession, and New England jurors, sympathetic to the smugglers, often found violators of the Embargo Act not guilty. Jefferson was violently attacked in the taverns and counting houses, and finally Congress repealed the Embargo Act. On March 1, 1809, three days before his successor Madison took office, Jefferson reluctantly signed the bill.

The end of Jefferson's second term came during the bitterest disputes over the embargo; and the President, who had wished for some time to retire to his beloved Monticello, was relieved to accept Washington's two-term precedent and announced his retirement. His eight years in the presidency, begun in such high confidence, ended on a much more equivocal note. Ironically, Jefferson, the believer in decentralized government, found himself under the Embargo wielding more power over American life than any Federalist would have dreamed. Though a "strict constructionist," Jefferson had discovered authority in the Constitution to buy Louisiana; and though a believer in states' rights, he had coerced the New England states into an economic boycott that hurt their commerce badly.

THE ELECTION OF 1808

Jefferson trusted and admired James Madison and easily secured the Republican nomination for him. The Federalists nominated the tireless C. C. Pinckney again, but in spite of the embargo and divided Republican sentiment Madison won by 122 to 47 electoral votes.

James Madison, far from being a mere graceful shadow of Jefferson, was very much his own man. His role in the formation of the Democratic Republican Party was a decisive one, and the political philosophy of the Jeffersonian group owed much to his thinking.

THE DRIFT TO WAR

Madison was an astute practitioner of politics as well as a profound student of it; but when he succeeded Jefferson, he inherited a large bundle of thorny problems. The Non-Intercourse Act, with which Madison replaced the Embargo Act in 1809, allowed American ships to trade with any nations except France and England. The Act also provided that the United States would resume trade with Britain

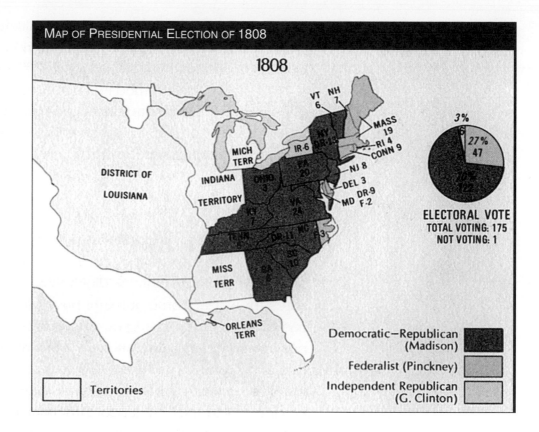

MAP OF PRESIDENTIAL ELECTION OF 1808

1808

ELECTORAL VOTE
TOTAL VOTING: 175
NOT VOTING: 1

Democratic–Republican (Madison)
Federalist (Pinckney)
Independent Republican (G. Clinton)
Territories

or France if either would respect freedom of the seas. The Non-Inter-course Act was ineffective at remedying the economic problems, however, because the vast majority of American trade had been with England and France. Furthermore, the Non-Intercourse Act was unenforceable in that no one could prevent ships from actually sailing to France or England once they had left American ports. When France began confiscating American cargo and seizing and imprisoning American sailors, Congress followed the Non-Intercourse Act with Macon's Bill No. 2 (named after the chairman of the House Foreign Affairs Committee), which relieved American shipping from all restrictions while ordering British and French naval vessels out of American waters. The bill stipulated, however, that if either Britain or France would recognize American rights at sea, the United States would reinstate the Non-Intercourse Act against the other.

Napoleon announced that his government would lift restrictions on United States shipping, thus forcing Madison to invoke the Non-Intercourse Act against England in February 1811. Three months later tensions heightened when an American ship, the *President*, fired on the smaller British ship, *Little Belt*, off the Virginia coast. Nine British sailors were killed and 23 were wounded in the exchange. This failed to influence British policy, but "peaceable coercion" was beginning to hurt England more than the British admitted and more than Madison realized. Parliament was preparing to relax some of its restrictions even as Congress moved toward a declaration of war. In the summer of 1811, the British returned two of the impressed Americans from the Chesapeake (the third had died in prison) and made reparations to the United States for the incident. This simply did not happen soon enough to change the course of events.

THE WAR HAWKS

Jefferson's "peaceful coercion" policy was probably the best that could have been pursued under the circumstances, and except for some exceedingly clumsy diplomacy abroad and mounting pressures for war at home, it might have worked. Much of the pressure came from a group of aggressive young congressmen, the first of the post-revolutionary generation of Western politicians—Henry Clay of Kentucky, John C. Calhoun and Langdon Cheves of western South Carolina, Peter B. Porter of western New York, Felix Grundy of Tennessee, and other so-called "buckskin boys." Intensely nationalist and violently anti-British, this group of "War Hawks," as John Randolph of Roanoke called them, clamored loudly for an attack on Britain via Canada and on the seas.

The regions from which these "War Hawks" came believed they had special reasons to dislike England. The West had fallen on hard times in the years from 1805 to 1809, and it blamed the British navy rather than the Embargo Act. More serious, however, was the charge that the British, from their Canadian posts, were stirring up the Native Americans and arming them for marauding raids across the American frontier. In 1811, there was an Native American uprising in the Ohio Valley led by Chief Tecumseh and his brother "The Prophet." The Native Americans were defeated at the Battle of Tippecanoe by General William Henry Harrison, but the Americans discovered that the weapons used by the Native Americans in the uprising were purchased from the British.

"MR. MADISON'S WAR"

The origins of war are never simple, and the War of 1812, especially, seems to have developed from a bewildering complexity of causes. Historians have advanced a number of explanations as to why the United States, after seven months of somewhat disordered debate in Congress, decided on June 18, 1812, to declare war on Great Britain. The vote was close in the Senate—19 to 13—and not overwhelming in the House—79 to 49.

Nineteenth-century historians tended to agree that the causes of the war were first, to "vindicate the national character" (as the House Foreign Affairs Committee said); and second, to retaliate against British violations of America's maritime rights. The largest vote for war came from the South and West, however, where sea trade was less important. New England, the center of American sea trade, opposed the war. At the news, flags flew at half-mast in New England and there were minor riots in some port cities.

General William Harrison at the battle of Tippecanoe

The Eastern Federalist press dubbed it "Mr. Madison's War," and so it remained. Some, too, regarded it as a stab in Britain's back when that nation stood alone against Napoleon, who in 1812 was on his way to Moscow for what seemed likely to be his last great conquest.

Later historians, noting the rhetoric of the Congressional debates and the distribution of the vote, concluded that the South and West hoped by the war to annex Canada and Florida as room for expansion, an expression of what later became known as America's "manifest destiny" to occupy the continent. Some still favor this expansionist interpretation, but other historians have suggested that fear of Britain's economic dominance—a reassertion of England's old imperial power over her former colony—also played an important role. Whatever the motivations, it was a brief, confused, and, except for a few instances, not very heroic war that, nonetheless, had a crucial role in the national development.

THE WAR OF 1812

WAR ON THE LAND: FIRST PHASE

Many Americans believed that Canada not only ought rightfully to join the United States, but that it wanted to. The Articles of Confederation had provided for Canada's admission to the Union, while the first Congress called itself "Continental" by design. Some Americans believed that the only way to end their problems with the British in North America was to militarily expel them from Canada. Other Americans simply desired land in Canada and believed that Canada would be an easy military conquest. Henry Clay, for instance, argued that taking Canada was "a mere matter of marching." Secretary of War William Eustis wrote in 1812 that "We have only to send officers into the Provinces and the people, already disaffected toward their own government, will rally to our standard."

There was, in fact, a good deal of pro-American sympathy in the Western St. Lawrence region—then called Upper Canada, later Ontario, American Loyalists, however, controlled both the Assembly and the Governor's Executive Council; and as the Anglican Bishop of Upper Canada wrote, they and the British Canadians wanted no part of that "degenerate government ... equally destitute of national honor and virtue," that lay to the south. French Quebec, with vivid memories of Revolutionary anti-Catholic propaganda, feared the loss of its language and its religion under American rule, while neither British nor French merchants in Montreal could see any advantage in a change.

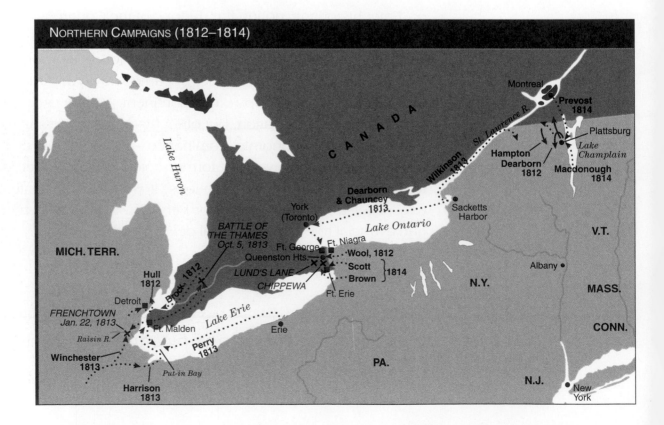

NORTHERN CAMPAIGNS (1812–1814)

In April 1812, Congress imposed a 90-day embargo on all ships in port—an action generally regarded as preparatory to war. That same month in England, disruption of trade and economic recession had spurred enough political unrest that the government announced that it would repeal the Orders in Council if the Americans resumed normal trade and the French rescinded the Berlin Decree. Two months later on June 16, the British announced that they would suspend the Orders in Council on the condition that the United States resume normal trade relations. Congress declared war two days later on June 18, not knowing that England had agreed to suspend the Orders in Council. The Americans were almost as unhappy with the French in 1812 as they were the English, and the call for a War Declaration against France, as well, failed by only two votes.

Upon hearing of the American War Declaration, the British expected Madison to suspend the American War Declaration as soon as he learned of the British suspension of the Orders in Council. Madison did not do so, however, because the British had not agreed to end impressments, which he viewed as an affront to American honor and sovereignty.

The War of 1812 was very unpopular in New England from the outset. New Englanders talked of secession, loaned money to the British, aided British soldiers moving through the country, and traded with Canada and England while the United States was at war. In return, the British allowed New England merchant ships to trade with England.

The United States was totally unprepared for war—its defenses outmoded and its army reduced to about 7,000 badly equipped men, scattered across the frontier and poorly led. Madison called for 100,000 state militiamen, but only 10,000 reported for duty (even though state militia rolls contained 700,000 names). The British situation was no better. Canada had a thousand miles of border, with 6,000 scattered British

James Madison

regulars and a militia pool of perhaps 60,000 to defend it. John C. Calhoun figured that a complete conquest of Canada might take a month. Henry Clay thought one company of Kentucky militia could do it.

American strategy was threefold: first, take Montreal and seal off the St. Lawrence route to the interior; second, invade the Niagara region and secure control of the central St. Lawrence Valley; third, invade western Canada from Detroit, securing the Great Lakes and the Northwest.

None of it worked. The expedition into Quebec failed at Crysler's Farm and at Châteauguay, due chiefly to the stubborn defense of the French-Canadian militia and the fact that some of the American militiamen refused to fight outside of their home states. General William Hull, the American commander at Detroit, crossed into Canada in July of 1812, lost his courage, and quickly returned. British General Isaac Brock, with a smaller force, bluffed Hull (who was later court-martialed and sentenced to death, but pardoned by the President) into surrendering Detroit on August 14, with a fictitious report about the size of the Native American army allied with the British. Hull surrendered, without a shot, to an Native American army half the size of his American force. When Fort Michimilimackinac in upper Michigan and Fort Dearborn in Illinois fell soon after, the British controlled the Northwest. Brock then rushed his army toward Niagara in 1813, where he defeated an American invasion at Queenston Heights in mid-October. The British captured Fort Niagara and burned the town of Buf-

Article of the surrender of Detroit

falo, New York. Brock was killed in the battle, but he had saved western Canada for the British.

The British proclaimed a blockade of the entire United States, and the United States lacked the naval power to do anything about it. At the outset of the war the United States had only 16 seaworthy ships and a fleet of 170 small gunboats that were fit only for harbor or river patrol.

In the middle of these military failures, Madison was nominated for another term. An Eastern antiwar wing of the Republicans, however, nominated De Witt Clinton of New York against him; and the Federalists added their support for Clinton. Madison won, 128 to 89 electoral votes, but, significantly, Clinton carried all of New England and the Middle Atlantic states except Vermont and Pennsylvania. At the same time the Federalists doubled their delegation in Congress.

WAR ON THE LAND: SECOND PHASE

Despite its early disasters, the army kept trying for Canada. In the winter of 1812–1813 American sailors commanded by Captain Oliver Hazard Perry built a small fleet and in September 1813 met and smashed the British lake squadron at the Battle of Lake Erie, near Sandusky, Ohio. Lake Erie was one of the most savage naval actions of the era (Perry's flagship suffered 80 percent casualties). After three hours of fighting, Perry dispatched his message to General William Henry Harrison commanding the forces near Detroit, "We have met the enemy and they are ours." Without control of Lake Erie, the British evacuated Detroit and fell back toward Niagara, but Harrison's swiftly advancing force caught and defeated them at the Battle of the Thames on October 5, 1813.

By reason of the victories of Perry and Harrison, the United States now commanded the Northwestern frontier. London, however, was sending more British regulars, and the Canadian militia was gaining experience. Two American invasions were turned back, Stoney Creek and Beaver Dam, and on July 25, 1814, a bitter battle at Lundy's Lane near Niagara Falls stopped a third attempt. The British then struck back at Buffalo and captured and burned it. Later that year they took Fort Niagara.

WAR AT SEA

The American navy entered the War of 1812 with 16 ships. The British had 97 in American waters alone. The out-numbered Americans, therefore, limited themselves to single-ship actions, in which they did surprisingly well. The *Constitution* ("Old Ironsides"), a 44-gun frigate commanded by Yankee Isaac Hull, defeated the British *Guerriere* on August 19, 1812, in one of the most famous sea fights in history. The big frigate *United States*, commanded by Captain Stephen Decatur, captured the British *Macedonian* a few weeks later, but the American *Chesapeake* lost a bitter fight to the British *Shannon* in 1813.

American privateers contributed most to the success of the war at sea. These swift ships sailed circles around the British, captured or destroyed 1,300 British merchantmen, and even had the impudence to sack British shipping in the English Channel in full sight of the shore. They gave the American public something to crow about now and then, though the overall effect on the outcome of the conflict was negligible. The British naval blockade was quite effective, and by 1813 the majority of American ports were tightly bottled up. British naval captains even forced American cities to pay tribute in order to avoid bombardment.

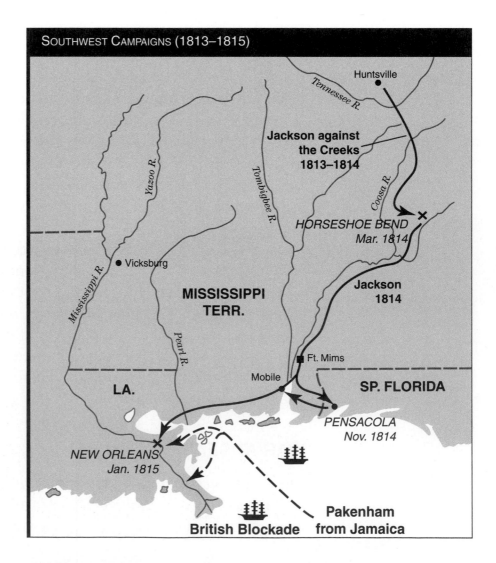

SOUTHWEST CAMPAIGNS (1813–1815)

WAR ON THE LAND: FINAL PHASE

Napoleon abdicated in April 1814 and was exiled to the isle of Elba in the Mediterranean. With Bonaparte gone and the French war finished, England turned its huge army of 14,000 veterans toward American shores. The strategy of the British general staff was to make three coordinated attacks: one from the north, from Canada down Lake Champlain into New York state; a second on the coast, through Chesapeake Bay, aimed at Baltimore, Washington, and Philadelphia; a third up from the south, at New Orleans. The end was in sight, wrote the *London Times*, for this "ill-organized association" of states. Indeed, it looked that way.

The northern campaign began in July 1814. Since Lake Champlain in upstate New York was the vital link in the invasion route, British General Sir George Prevost wanted it cleared of American ships. In September 1814, however, the American lake squadron under Captain Thomas Macdonough decisively defeated the British. Without control of the lake the British drive stalled and eventually dissolved at Plattsburgh, New York, where the British army retreated from an American force it outnumbered 11,000 to 3,300.

The British were more successful at Chesapeake Bay, where in August 1814 General Robert Ross landed a strong force that marched on Washington. The American government fled into Virginia and the British, in retaliation for the American burning of York (Toronto) in 1813, set fire to the White House and the Capitol before moving toward Baltimore. Here they were stopped at Fort

The U.S. Capitol after being burned by the British during the War of 1812

McHenry, where a spirited defense inspired Francis Scott Key to write "The Star-Spangled Banner," putting patriotic words to an old English drinking song. Unable to crack the Baltimore defenses, the British set sail for the West Indies.

The third British offensive, aimed at New Orleans and commanded by General Edward Pakenham, sailed from Jamaica in November 1814 with 7,500 seasoned veterans. To oppose Pakenham, Andrew Jackson took his frontier army on a forced march in December. Though neither Jackson nor Pakenham knew it, American and British representatives were already at work in Belgium on a treaty of peace. Two weeks after the Treaty of Ghent was signed on December 24, 1814, Jackson's Western riflemen almost annihilated Pakenham's army. The British lost 2,000 men (including Pakenham) while Jackson's loss totaled 8 dead and 13 wounded—in a battle that did not really affect the war or the peace.

THE HARTFORD CONVENTION

In 1814, when American prospects seemed darkest, the Federalist Massachusetts legislature called a convention at Hartford, Connecticut, to discuss "public grievances and concerns"—that is, the Republican conduct of the war. The delegates, who came primarily from

The Battle of New Orleans

the Massachusetts, Connecticut, and Rhode Island legislatures, had a great deal to discuss. Some advised amending the Constitution to clip Congress' war-making powers. Others suggested negotiating a separate peace with England.

Curiously enough, the delegates, all Federalists, appealed to the doctrine of states' rights, the same doctrine that the Jeffersonians had used against Federalist centralization during Adams' administration. They argued that since the Republican Congress had violated the Constitution by declaring an unwanted war, those states that did not approve had the right to override congressional action. At the conclusion of the meeting, Massachusetts and Connecticut sent commissioners to Washington to place their protests before Congress. When the commissioners arrived, the war was over; and whatever they had to say was forgotten. The main thing that the Hartford Convention accomplished was to weaken the Federalist Party even further.

A WELCOME PEACE

Early in 1813 Czar Alexander I of Russia had offered to mediate between the United States and England, since he wanted the British free to concentrate their full military force on Napoleon. Madison sent commissioners to Russia, but Lord Castlereagh, the British foreign minister, refused to accept the czar's suggestion. Late that same year, however, Castlereagh notified Secretary of State James Monroe that he was willing to discuss differences between the two nations; and in August 1814 American and British representatives met in Ghent, Belgium.

As the meetings dragged on, it became plain that the British could not successfully invade the United States—or the United States, Canada. The defeat at Plattsburgh convinced the British that the Americans were determined to hold on to their land and continue fighting. Public opposition to the "worthless" war in the Americas, coupled with fears that Napoleon could return to power, pushed the British to genuinely seek a negotiated settlement. Both British and Americans were war weary and wanted to finish it. On December 24, 1814, the commissioners signed a peace treaty. The British had originally demanded American land in the area of the Great Lakes, and the United States had demanded the cession of Canada to the United States Both sides reduced their demands to "*status quo ante bellum,*" or a return to how things were before the war. Based on this principle both sides signed the Treaty of Ghent. Interestingly, it did not mention impressments, blockades, seizures at sea, or any of the major disputes that seemed to have precipitated the war.

THE RESULTS OF THE WAR

The reaction of war-weary Americans to the news of the Treaty of Ghent, which arrived in the United States in February 1815, was swift and spontaneous. Bells rang, parades formed, newspapers broke out in headlines to proclaim the "passage from gloom to glory." Yet "Mr. Madison's War" had accomplished very little in a military or political sense. The treaty realized few if any of the aims for which the war had presumably been fought—most notably, it did not end impressments, which had been Madison's reason for not rescinding the Declaration of War after hearing of British suspension of the Orders in Council.

The most that can be said is that the treaty opened the way for future settlements to be worked out over the next decade with Britain, Spain, and France. The war dislocated business and foreign trade, deranged currency values, and exposed glaring cracks in the national political organization.

To the American people the outcome, ambiguous as it was, marked a turning point in patriotic self-esteem. True, the war might have been avoided by better statesmanship, and it might even have been fought with France on equally reasonable grounds. Yet from the American point of view, the War of 1812 gave notice to the rest of the world that the United States had arrived as a nation. The powers of Europe would tread on American sovereignty only at a price. "Who would not be an American?" crowed *Niles' Register*. "Long live the Republic! All Hail!"

Madison had also used the war to seize both East and West Florida for the United States. Madison had Congress officially annex West Florida in the spring of 1812 and sent troops into West Florida to defend American control of the area. American troops under General James Wilkinson took Mobile from the Spanish in 1813; and Americans under Andrew Jackson took Pensacola from the Spanish in 1814, though the United States returned East Florida to Spain at the conclusion of the war.

THE WAR AND CANADA

The War of 1812 marked the first step in the creation of Canada, which was to emerge a half-century later as a sovereign nation. In the conflict between England and the United States, British and French Canadians were caught in the middle, as they had been in the American Revolution. For England to strike at the United States, the route lay through Canada. For the United States to strike at England, the only vulnerable point was Canada.

To the average Canadians, British or French, the war's causes meant little, however; and they had small stake in it. Canada's problem was simply survival, and it survived. Whatever their differences, French, British, and Loyalists joined in common cause to outlast a long, hard war and preserve their part of the British Empire.

America's attempted invasions intensified already strong anti-American feelings, while Canada's repulse of them was understandably a source of growing national pride. Opposition to the United States and wariness of its motives thus became continuing factors in subsequent Canadian-American relations. The war strengthened Canada's Britishness, and at the same time gave it the beginnings of its own sense of identity.

AMERICA MAKES A NEW START

A CONFIDENT NATION

The War of 1812 marked the end of America's lingering sense of colonial inferiority. It was hardly a "second war of independence," as some called it; but from it there did come a new spirit of national consciousness. Albert Gallatin wrote, "It has renewed and reinstated the national feeling and character which the Revolution had given, and which were daily lessening. The people now have more general objects of attachment. ... They are more Americans; they feel and act more as a nation."

After the Treaty of Ghent the United States turned toward the great hazy West, where half a continent lay virtually empty. America could now concentrate on its domestic problems with less concern for European standards, ideals, and entanglements. Indifference to foreign affairs after 1814 was so great that even Napoleon's escape from Elba, his return to France, and his final defeat at Waterloo in June 1815, excited little attention in the American press. The interest of the United States centered on perfecting and expanding the nation it had constructed out of two wars and a generation of experiment. In other words, its chief task lay in developing modern America.

THE AFTERMATH OF WAR

The most persistent postwar problems were economic. Finances during the war had been handled almost as ineptly as military affairs. Banks had multiplied profusely and without proper control. The country was flooded with depreciating paper money. Prices were at the most inflated level in America's brief history. The shipping industry had been badly hurt by war and blockade. On the other hand, the value of manufacturing had increased tremendously—the total capital investment in American industry in 1816, it was estimated, was somewhat more than $100 million. The West, now producing food-stuffs and raw materials in abundance, balanced on the verge of a tremendous boom. As soon as peace was established, the Republican Congress began to consider a three-point program for economic expansion: a tariff to protect infant American industry; a second Bank of the United States, since the charter of Hamilton's original Bank had expired in 1811; and a system of roads, waterways, and canals to provide internal routes of communication and trade.

A PROTECTIVE TARIFF

The protection of America's infant industries was a matter of first priority. New factories, encouraged by the war, had grown in great numbers, especially in the textile industry where, for the first time, the workforce was comprised of young women. As soon as the wartime blockade ended, British-made products streamed toward the United States; and young industries that had flourished under conditions of embargo and war found it quite another matter to compete in an open peacetime market. Whereas the total value of United States imports in 1813 had been $13 million, by 1816 it had leaped to $147 million while American manufacturers begged for protection.

Congress in 1816 passed a tariff to protect the new factories—the first United States tariff passed not to raise revenue but to encourage and support home industry. The argument over this protective tariff exposed some potentially serious sectional economic conflicts and marked the first appearance of a perennial political issue. Southern producers and New England shippers opposed the tariff; but the growing factory towns of New England supported it, as did some of the younger Southern cotton politicians, who hoped to encourage industrial development in the South. The Middle Atlantic states and the West favored it, and the Southwest divided on the issue.

RENEWING THE BANK OF THE UNITED STATES

In 1816 Congress turned its attention to the National Bank. The charter of the first Bank of the United States had been allowed to expire because the Republicans believed that, as Jefferson originally claimed, banking powers properly belonged to the states and Hamilton's centralized bank was therefore unconstitutional. The new contingent of Western congressmen were much less interested in the bank's constitutionality than in its usefulness. Henry Clay, who had opposed the first bank in 1811 on constitutional grounds, now supported the second bank, he explained, because it was necessary for the national (especially Western) interest to have a stable, uniform currency and sound national credit. Therefore, Congress in 1816 gave the second bank a 20-year charter, on much the same terms as before but with about three and a half times more capital than the first and substantially greater control over state banks.

Henry Clay

BUILDING BETTER CONNECTING LINKS

The British wartime blockade and the westward movement had exposed a critical need for roads, improved waterways, and canals. When coastal shipping was reduced to a trickle by British offshore naval patrols, forcing American goods to move over inland routes, the roads and rivers were soon choked with traffic. The Republican program of improved internal communications was especially popular in the West; but more conservative Easterners, including President Madison, doubted the constitutionality of federal assistance for roads and canals unless an amendment to the Constitution was adopted for the purpose.

Calhoun introduced a "bonus bill" into Congress in 1816, empowering the use of federal funds for internal improvements. It cited the "general welfare" clause of the Constitution as providing authority for such action. The bill was passed, but Madison vetoed it on his last day of office in 1817. Many of the states began digging canals and building roads themselves. President Monroe later agreed that the federal government did have the authority to fund such internal improvements, inaugurating the great canal and turnpike era of the 1820s.

AMERICA MOVES WEST

The Treaty of Ghent released a pent-up flood of migration toward the West. In 1790 a little more than two percent of the population lived west of the Appalachian mountain chain. In 1810 it was 14 percent; in 1820, 23 percent, with the proportion still rising. The stream of migration moved west in two branches following the east-west roads and rivers—one from the South into the Southwest, the other from the northeastern states into the Northwest Territory.

There were a number of reasons for this great westerly movement. One was America's soaring population, which almost doubled in the first two decades of the nineteenth century, from 5.3 million in 1800 to over 9.6 million in 1820. Another was the discharge of war veterans, accompanied by a rush of immigrants from Europe, who moved west to look for new opportunities. Still another was improved transportation. Whereas there had been few good routes to the West, the number of roads and turnpikes now grew, while the Great Lakes-Ohio River waterway provided an excellent route for settlers to move into the Northwest.

The most compelling force behind the westward migration, however, was land—the rich black bottom-lands of the Southwest and the fertile forest and prairie lands of the Northwest. Governor William Henry Harrison of Indiana Territory persuaded Congress in 1800 to reduce the minimum requirement for the sale of land to a half section at two dollars an acre, with four years to pay. In 1804 Congress reduced the minimum to a quarter section, and in 1820 to 80 acres at a base price of $1.25 an acre. This was the great magnet that drew settlers west. Unfortunately, Native Americans sometimes already occupied the land.

LAND HUNGER VERSUS NATIVE AMERICAN RIGHTS

While it was clear from the first that the new American government wanted swift access to the Native Americans' tribal lands, Congress in 1789 had assured the Native Americans that their "land and property shall never be taken from them without their consent." In appropriating funds to pay certain tribes for land claims, Congress had tacitly recognized, as Secretary of War Henry Knox said, the Native Americans' right to ownership as "prior occupants." At the time, however, Washington had remarked that despite the government's good intentions, he doubted that "anything short of a Chi-

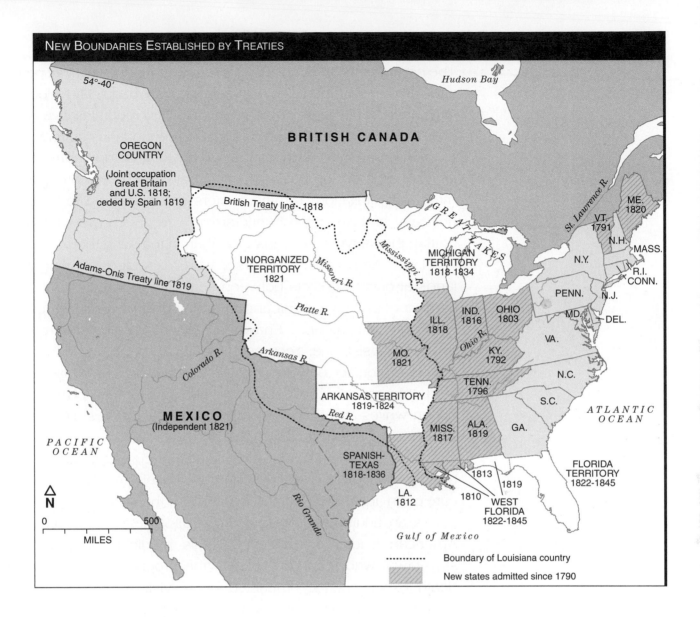

NEW BOUNDARIES ESTABLISHED BY TREATIES

54°-40'

OREGON COUNTRY

(Joint occupation Great Britain and U.S. 1818; ceded by Spain 1819)

British Treaty line 1818

Adams-Onis Treaty line 1819

Hudson Bay

BRITISH CANADA

GREAT LAKES

St. Lawrence R.

ME. 1820

VT. 1791

N.H.

MASS.

N.Y.

R.I.

CONN.

N.J.

PENN.

MD.

DEL.

UNORGANIZED TERRITORY 1821

Missouri R.

Mississippi R.

Platte R.

MICHIGAN TERRITORY 1818-1834

ILL. 1818

IND. 1816

OHIO 1803

Ohio R.

VA.

MO. 1821

KY. 1792

N.C.

Arkansas R.

ARKANSAS TERRITORY 1819-1824

Red R.

TENN. 1796

S.C.

Colorado R.

MEXICO (Independent 1821)

SPANISH-TEXAS 1818-1836

MISS. 1817

ALA. 1819

GA.

ATLANTIC OCEAN

PACIFIC OCEAN

Rio Grande

LA. 1812

1813

1810

WEST FLORIDA 1822-1845

1819

FLORIDA TERRITORY 1822-1845

N

0   500

MILES

Gulf of Mexico

· · · · · · · Boundary of Louisiana country

New states admitted since 1790

nese wall" would ever keep land-hungry settlers out of the Native Americans' lands.

Washington was right. The Native Americans, reported Thomas Forsyth from frontier country in 1818, "complain about the sale of their lands more than anything else." The settler, he wrote, "tells the Indian that that land, with all that is on it, is his," and, treaty or not, "to go away or he will kill him etc."

Such constant clashes between Native American and settler had forced the Native Americans to surrender much of their land. Congress' Native American policy was neither sufficiently definite nor sufficiently aggressive to satisfy impatient settlers, traders, land speculators, or Native Americans.

RESISTANCE TO FEDERAL POLICY

The hope that the two races might live together in "perpetual peace and affectionate attachment," as Jefferson had hoped, quickly faded. Particularly in the South, state governments resisted federal Native American policy. On the frontier few paid attention to boundaries or treaties.

Nor were Native Americans willing to give up more and more land, treaties or not. Each advancing encroachment brought resentment and retaliation. Turning hunters and warriors into farmers was not easy, and American frontiersmen were much more interested in getting the Native Americans' land than in teaching them to farm it.

Native Americans, of course, were expected to relinquish their lands at once. Conflicts between settlers and Native Americans became increasingly violent and frequent, and the emergence of a remarkable leader, the Shawnee Tecumseh, crystallized Native American resistance. Tecumseh was born in Ohio in 1768 during a period of conflict between Native Americans and white men over land. Tecumseh's childhood was marred by repeated violence between whites and Native Americans; and five times, between 1774 and 1782, young Tecumseh experienced raids by American soldiers that destroyed his homes and villages. Tecumseh's father and two brothers were killed in battles, and Tecumseh's mother left him in the care of an aunt at age 10 and left Ohio for the South.

As an adult, Tecumseh rejected all American claims to Native American lands; and along with his medicine-man brother Tenskwatawa, who renamed himself "the Prophet" after having a near death experience accompanied by a "vision" in 1805, Tecumseh sought to unite all Native Americans against white encroachment. The Prophet urged Native Americans to return to traditional ways and preached that white men were the children of the Evil Spirit, destined to be destroyed. Tecumseh and the Prophet organized a village along Tippecanoe Creek (Indiana), which they called Prophetstown, and attracted thousands of followers to their message of spiritual regeneration, unity of the Native Americans, and resistance to the white men. Tecumseh and the Prophet began to organize the tribes of the Northwest into a loose and effective alliance, beginning as early as 1800. Tecumseh traveled throughout the Great Lakes area, encouraging tribes to join a pan-Native American confederacy. In 1811, Tecumseh traveled to the South, visiting tribes in Mississippi and Georgia and encouraging them to join his Native American confederacy and resist white encroachment on their lands.

This alliance was finally broken by General William Henry Harrison, governor of Indiana Territory, at the Battle of Tippecanoe in November 1811, while Tecumseh was absent. Tecumseh then joined the British army in Canada and reappeared with 800 of his Native American warriors in the War of 1812. He was killed at the Battle of the Thames in 1813, and with him died the Native Americans' efforts to organize and resist.

At the close of the war, with the British threat removed from the Northwest and the French from the Southwest, the federal government could at last proceed with its policy of assimilation or removal. After 1815 the political power of those who, like Andrew Jackson, wanted to clear the Native American lands immediately, was too strong to resist. In 1817 the Senate Committee of Public Lands recommended exchanging public lands in the trans-Mississippi region for the Native American lands east of the Mississippi, but only with the consent of the tribes.

Very soon it became clear that the Native American tribes were not willing to consent. The only remedy, John C. Calhoun wrote in 1820, was to place them "gradually under our authority and laws." "Our opinions, and not theirs," he continued, "ought to prevail, in measures intended for their civilization and happiness." In 1825 Calhoun, then Secretary of War, and President Monroe presented Congress with a plan to remove the eastern tribes into the region beyond Missouri and Arkansas—a plan opposed by those who felt such an act a betrayal of the national honor. The opposition was inadequate, however, and by the 1830s the tribes were removed—many to present-day Oklahoma and Kansas. By 1848 twelve new states had been created from what had once been Native American country.

That the postwar policy of peaceful expansion and assimilation did not succeed did not necessarily mean that other solutions to the problem would have been possible. For example, the creation of an Native American state, closed to white settlement, in the rich lands of the Mississippi-Ohio basin—as some proposed—would never have succeeded. Considering the alternatives and the limitations imposed by them, what *should* have been done about the Native American and what *could* have been done were not necessarily the same.

GROWING PAINS

THE ELECTION OF 1816

Madison selected James Monroe of Virginia for his successor in the presidential election of 1816; and although some Republicans favored William H. Crawford of Georgia, the party caucus agreed to

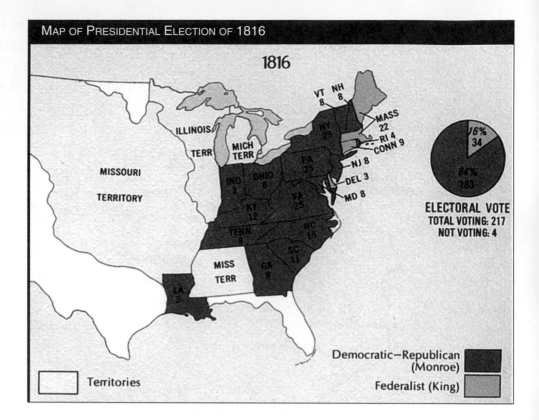

MAP OF PRESIDENTIAL ELECTION OF 1816

choose the third Virginian in succession for the presidency. The Federalists, disheartened by the Hartford Convention, failed to nominate an official candidate, though in some states they supported Rufus King of New York. King received only the votes of Massachusetts, Connecticut, and Delaware, and Monroe won easily by 183 to 34 electoral votes.

A tall, distinguished, quiet man, James Monroe had studied law with Jefferson and was the older statesman's close friend and disciple. He drew his advisers impartially from different sections of the country, choosing John Quincy Adams (son of John and Abigail Adams) of Massachusetts as Secretary of State, William H. Crawford of Georgia as Secretary of the Treasury, John C. Calhoun of South Carolina as Secretary of War, and William Wirt of Maryland as Attorney General. Henry Clay of Kentucky, the Speaker of the House, and others of the Western group dominated Congress, with Daniel Webster of New Hampshire and other New Englanders furnishing the opposition.

THE "ERA OF GOOD FEELINGS"

Because of the virtually unchallenged Republican control of political life until 1824, these years are labeled "The Era of Good Feelings." The

Federalist Party was dead, and it seemed for a time that the two-party system itself was ending. There were no European wars of consequence during the period to involve the United States, nor any crucial issues in foreign affairs. President Monroe possessed a personality that seemed to bring people together. Monroe toured New England, the area that had been fraught with secessionist discontent during the War of 1812, espousing a position of national-

James Monroe

ism to enthusiastic crowds. Like all labels, this one was true only in part: Feelings were "good," but subterranean conflicts were soon to destroy the political peace.

Sectional interests and aspirations were growing and changing. The new Northwest, as it gained stature and stability, demanded greater influence in national policy. The South, tied more and more to cotton, and New England, changing from an agricultural to a manufacturing economy, were both undergoing inner stresses that took outward political form. Specifically, these sectionalized rivalries were shortly to appear in two issues—tariffs and slavery—that terminated the good feelings and produced new bad ones.

PROSPERITY AND PANIC

After 1815, the national economy flourished mightily with the resumption of normal trade that followed the War of 1812. The wartime boom continued, industry grew strong behind its tariff wall, and American ships carried goods and raw materials the world over. Yet much of this prosperity had a hollow ring. Too many small Southern and Western banks had issued far too much paper money in excess of their capital reserves, and in 1818 the second Bank of the United States (which suffered from mismanagement itself) began to close out some of these "wildcat" banks by collecting their notes and demanding payment.

The purpose was fiscally sound—to force stricter control of banking practices—but the effect was disastrous. By early 1819 a number of shaky banks had already collapsed and others were about to follow. In fact, the entire national banking system, which had not been sound for several years, was nearly ready to topple.

In 1819 more and more banks crashed, businesses failed, and a wave of losses and foreclosures swept over the nation, especially through the West. The consequences of the 1819 crisis continued to be felt until 1823. For the part they had played in precipitating the crisis, the second Bank of the United States and the financial interests of the East earned the undying resentment of the West.

"FIRE BELL IN THE NIGHT"

SECTIONALISM AND SLAVERY

As the tariff issue of 1816 had exposed some of the sectional economic tensions beneath the surface of "good feelings," so the panic of 1819 revealed more. The second great issue, the question of the existence and extension of the institution of slavery, was also projected onto the national stage in 1819, coming before Congress that year because of Missouri's impending statehood.

Slavery had been a submerged issue in national politics since Washington's time. In 1793, during his administration, Congress had passed a fugitive slave law and later forbade the further importation of slaves, beginning in 1808, without unduly arousing sentiment in North or South. In fact, there were many in both sections that hoped that the 1808 act might lead to the eventual extinction of the entire system. In the North, where slavery was unprofitable and unnecessary, all the states had legally abolished it by 1804 (as the Ordinance of 1787 already had abolished it from the Northwest Territory). In the South antislavery societies actively campaigned against it. Still, after 1816 there was growing harshness in Northern and Southern discussions of the slavery question.

The most important area of disagreement over slavery concerned its economic relationship to Southern cotton culture. Eli Whitney's invention of the cotton gin (1793), the introduction of new strains of cotton, the expanding postwar textile market at home and abroad, and the opening to production of the rich "Black Belt" lands of the Southwest—all combined to make cotton an extremely profitable cash crop. Cotton was on the way to becoming "King" in the South.

The first cotton gin

Cotton required a large, steady supply of cheap, unskilled labor. Many believed that black slaves filled this need. At the same time, it was found that the delta lands of Louisiana and Mississippi were ideal for sugar cane, while tobacco culture moved from the coastal South into Kentucky and Tennessee. These too needed cheap labor.

In 1800 there were about 894,000 blacks in the United States, almost wholly concentrated in the eastern South. In 1808, when the importation of slaves ceased, the figure stood at over one million; and by 1820 the South's investment in slaves was estimated to be nearly $500 million. It was perfectly clear that slavery and cotton provided the foundation of Southern society and would continue to do so.

THE MISSOURI COMPROMISE

Early in 1819 Missouri, carved out of the territory acquired in the Louisiana Purchase, counted 60,000 persons and applied for entry to the Union as a slave state. No doubt the bill for its admission would have passed without appreciable comment, had not James Tallmadge, Jr., of New York introduced in the House an amendment requiring the gradual abolition of slavery in the new state as a condition of its admission. This amendment immediately exposed the heart of the issue.

As the nation moved west, the tendency had been to maintain a rough balance of power between slave- and free-state blocs in Washington. The North and Northwest, however, had gained a million more persons than the South and Southwest since the 1790 census, thereby proportionately increasing their congressional representation. The slave states were already outvoted in the House; only in the Senate were the sections equally represented, a situation that might not continue for long.

Of the original 13 colonies, seven became free states and six slave. Between 1791 and 1819 four more free states were admitted and five slave. So when Missouri applied for entrance to the Union in 1819, the balance was even, and Tallmadge's amendment involved far more than Missouri's admission alone.

Slavery was already barred from the Northwest Territory but not from those lands acquired through the Louisiana Purchase. Should Missouri and all other states subsequently admitted from the Louisiana Purchase lands be admitted as slave states, the balance of

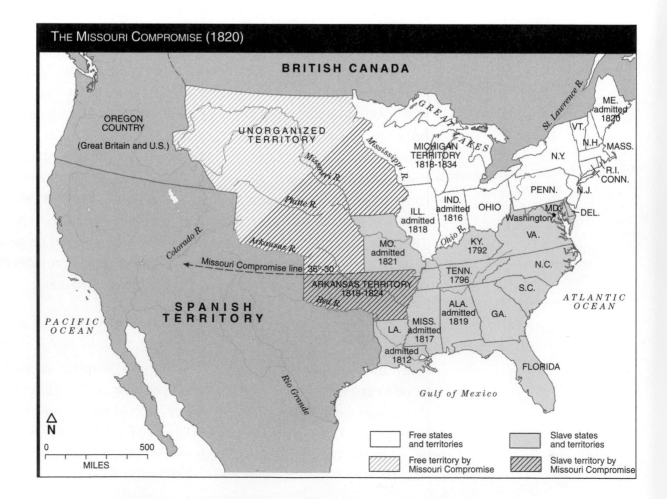

THE MISSOURI COMPROMISE (1820)

federal political power would be tipped toward the South and slavery. If they were to be free states, their entry favored the North and emancipation.

At stake lay political control, present and future, of the Union. "It is political power that the northern folk are in pursuit of," Judge Charles Tait of Alabama wrote to a friend concerning the Missouri question, "and if they succeed, the management of the Gen'l Gov't will pass into their hands with all its power and patronage." At this time, most Northerners were not opposed to slavery on moral grounds; but they believed that the three-fifths Compromise gave southern states disproportionate strength in Congress since they could count three-fifths of their growing slave population for purposes of representation in the United States House of Representatives.

Tallmadge's bill finally passed the House in February, after hot and protracted debate. Congress adjourned, however, until December, and during the interval Maine, long attached to Massachusetts, applied for statehood. Sensing compromise, the Senate originated a bill accepting Maine as a free state and Missouri as slave, thereby preserving the balance. The House accepted it, but added a proviso that slavery be banned forever from the Louisiana Purchase lands above the line of 36° 30′.

The bill was passed and signed in March 1820; but this so-called Missouri Compromise merely delayed the ultimate confrontation of the problem of slavery, and everyone knew it. The "momentous question," wrote Jefferson from Monticello, "like a fire-bell in the night, awakened me and filled me with terror." The debates over Missouri sparked the first protracted public discussion of the contradiction between the ideals expressed in the Declaration of Independence and the institution of slavery—thus foreshadowing the decades of sectional conflict to come. Hence, the reason for the aging Jefferson's alarm.

EVOLVING A FOREIGN POLICY

CATCHING UP ON OLD PROBLEMS

Following the Treaty of Ghent the United States and Britain gradually worked out their differences one by one. In 1815, the United States and England signed a commercial convention that established a reciprocity agreement in trade. Nevertheless, the United States and England still distrusted each other, and each began fortifying its possessions on the Great Lakes. The Rush-Bagot Agreement of 1817 demilitarized the Great Lakes, but both countries retained land fortifications. The United States-Canadian border remained a guarded border until 1871. The Convention of 1818 gave United States nationals fishing rights off the coasts of Labrador and Newfoundland, established the northern boundary of the Louisiana Purchase at the 49th parallel, and left the Oregon country, which both claimed, under joint occupation for 10 years.

America and Spain, too, settled some old disputes. The United States took one section of Florida in 1810 and another in 1813. Secretary of State John Quincy Adams continued negotiations for the rest of the territory, but his diplomacy was disturbed by Florida's Seminole Indians, who kept up raids (with Spanish and British assistance) on the Georgia border. In 1818 General Andrew Jackson raised an army and marched into Florida, claiming that he had received a letter from President Monroe authorizing the invasion. Monroe denied that he had given his approval; and Jackson claimed that he burned the letter, so any evidence that Monroe ordered the invasion was destroyed—if it ever existed. Jackson led 3,000 Americans and 2,000 Native American allies into Florida, captured two Spanish forts, and executed two suspected British agents in what is known as the First Seminole War.

Americans were divided over Jackson's actions. Secretary of War John C. Calhoun called for Jackson's court martial since Jackson had acted without authority from Calhoun's War Department. Congressman Henry Clay introduced a motion of censure in Congress, which failed to pass. Meanwhile, local governments in New York and Philadelphia praised Jackson's actions. Britain viewed Jackson's invasion as a violation of international law and demanded an explanation for the execution of two British citizens. Jackson replied, "The execution of these two unprincipled villains will prove an awful example to the world and convince the government of Great Britain that certain though slow retribution awaits those un-Christian wretches who, by false promises, delude and excite a Native American tribe to all the horrid deeds of savage war." The British were particularly unimpressed with Jackson's explanation, but they decided not to press the issue because they believed Jackson's principle could become useful to them in the future should they experience border problems with the United States in Canada.

John Quincy Adams argued that Jackson's invasion was an act of self-defense against the chaos that Spain had been unable to control and unable to prevent from spilling over into the United States. Adams announced an ultimatum to Spanish minister Luis de Onís in October, 1818: Maintain order in the Floridas or cede them to the United States.

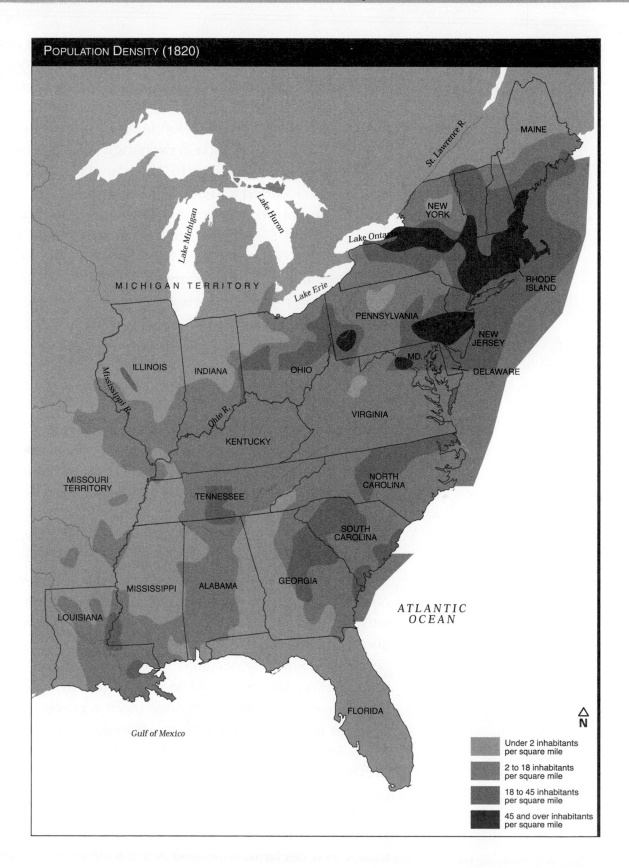

POPULATION DENSITY (1820)

Under 2 inhabitants per square mile

2 to 18 inhabitants per square mile

18 to 45 inhabitants per square mile

45 and over inhabitants per square mile

The Spanish posts captured by Jackson were quickly returned to Spain; but Jackson's action helped precipitate a treaty, signed by Adams and Spanish minister Luis de Onís in February 1819, by which Spain renounced its claims to West Florida and ceded East Florida to the United States. Spain at the time had greater problems than Florida with insurrections erupting all over Latin America and lacked the military resources to force the United States to back away from its ambitions in Florida. That being the case, the Spanish opted to give up Florida in exchange for favorable boundaries in the West and a secure claim to Texas. In the Adams-Onís Treaty the Spanish also agreed to a boundary line stretching across the continent to the Pacific, redefining the Louisiana Purchase line, and dividing the old Southwest from Spanish Mexico. In addition, the Spanish gave up their somewhat vague claims to Oregon in return for a clear title to Texas, where the United States relinquished any claims. The United States also assumed $5 million worth of claims by United States citizens against Spain.

THE MONROE DOCTRINE

Reduced to a third-rate power and racked by internal dissension, Spain was losing its empire in Central and South America. Beginning in 1807, its colonies revolted one after another until, by 1821, nearly all had declared themselves independent republics. By 1830, all of Latin America except Cuba and Puerto Rico had gained independence. Sympathetic to such revolutions and alert to opportunities for new markets, the United States waited until its treaty with Spain was accepted and then recognized these republics early in 1822.

Spain, of course, continued to consider the new Latin American nations simply as Spanish colonies in rebellion. In Europe, meanwhile, Austria, Prussia, Russia, and France had formed an alliance and "congress system" for the purpose of crushing popular revolutions wherever they occurred. The United States feared that the alliance would decide to send an army to restore Spain's lost colonies, making royal Catholic Spain once more a power in the New World. Nor was the alliance the only threat to the Americas. Russia had already established trading posts in California, and in 1821 Czar Alexander's edict claimed part of the Oregon country for Alaska and barred foreign ships from a large area of the northwest Pacific.

The British, who had no desire to see Spain regain its empire or Russia expand its colonial holdings, offered to join with the United States in a declaration against any interference in the Americas on the part of the alliance, but Secretary of State John Quincy Adams convinced President Monroe and the cabinet that the United States should handle the problem alone. For one thing, Adams did not want his country, he said, to "come in as a cockboat in the wake of the

British man-of-war." Furthermore, Adams and others recognized the potential value of the new Latin American republics as markets. And lastly, no one wanted to write off the possibility of American expansion southward if one or more of the new republics asked to be annexed to the United States.

President Monroe in his annual message to Congress on December 2, 1823, therefore stated the official attitude of the United States on the issue. The Monroe Doctrine, as it came to be called, rested on two main principles—noncolonization and nonintervention.

Concerning the first, Monroe stated that any portions of the Americas were "henceforth not to be considered as subjects for future colonization by any European power." In regard to the second, he drew a sharp line of political demarcation between Europe and America. "The political system of the allied powers is essentially different ... from that of America," he said. "We should consider any attempt to extend their system to any portion of this hemisphere as dangerous to our peace and safety." At the same time, Monroe promised that the United States would not attempt to interfere with the internal affairs of European nations or with any of their existing colonies in the New World, such as Cuba.

These ideas had been implicit in all American foreign policy since Washington's Farewell Address, but Monroe's message restated in precise terms the classic American principles of hemispheric separation and avoidance of foreign entanglements that had motivated the diplomacy of his predecessors. His enunciation of American domination over half the globe seemed "arrogant" and "haughty" to European statesmen, and the Latin American republics were not particularly pleased with such doubtful protection. Both knew, whether Monroe or the American public cared to admit it, that it was the British navy and not the Monroe Doctrine that barred European expansion into the Americas.

THE TRIUMPH OF ISOLATION

The Monroe Doctrine simply articulated what Americans had believed since the beginnings of their foreign policy—that there were two worlds, old and new, contrasted and separate. The Old World of England and Europe seemed to Americans regressive, corrupted, and plagued by wars and ancient hatreds. The New World was thought to be democratic, free, progressive, and hopeful. The objective of the United States, reflecting these attitudes, was to keep these worlds apart, lest the "taint" of the old besmirch the "fresh future" of the new.

The first generation of American statesmen, from Washington to Monroe, unanimously insisted that the United States should, whenever possible, avoid entanglements in Old World politics or problems. At the same time it was perfectly clear to them that the United States could not exist without European trade and that, since the major European powers still held territorial possessions in the New World, it would be extremely difficult to avoid some sort of implication in their almost continuous wars. The foreign policy of every president from Washington to John Quincy Adams was shaped by this constant tension between the dream of isolation and the reality of involvement. In 1815, however, American isolation was aided by the Congress of Vienna that, combined with the defeat of Napoleon, ushered in a period of great power peace in Europe and aided the United States in its quest to avoid European squabbles.

Still, there were certain accepted positions on foreign affairs that the United States throughout the period believed it must maintain—freedom of the seas, freedom of trade, neutrality in European disputes, national integrity, and, above all others, the promotion of the cause of liberty throughout the world. In practice, American diplomats found it hard to work out solutions within this somewhat rigid framework. Did maintenance of freedom of the seas, for example, justify involvement in a European war? Would American assistance to other nations' revolutions justify entanglement in European affairs, even for the best of motives? Should American policy, when it coincided with that of a European power, be pursued jointly? Ought the United States to assume responsibility for internal affairs of democracy in other American republics?

In attempting to answer these and similar questions, the makers of American foreign policy during the early years of the Republic followed rather closely the principles laid down by Washington and the first generation. Fortunately for them, Europe was so preoccupied with its own power conflicts that American diplomacy had time to temporize and room to make a few mistakes. Still, every statement about foreign affairs in the early decades of the nineteenth century derived from the American assumption that the United States was detached from Europe and must remain so, always free to pursue its special ends.

AMERICAN CULTURE COMES OF AGE

LAYING THE GROUNDWORK

The Excitement of Progress
Technological Change and Economic
   Development

THE ROLE OF REFORMERS

American Women
Fighting Ills, Woes, and Evils
Communitarianism
Progress in Education

FAITH AND INTELLECT

Religion and the People
Mormons
The Unitarian Influence
Romanticism Revisited

THE GOLDEN AGE OF LITERATURE

Emerson and Transcendentalism
Henry David Thoreau
The Boston Brahmins
Nathaniel Hawthorne
Herman Melville
James Fenimore Cooper
Southern Romanticism
Edgar Allan Poe

**JOURNALISM AND
   POPULAR CULTURE**

Writing for the People
Magazines and Books for Women
Sports, Humor, and Realism

**ARTS, SCIENCES, AND
   POPULAR TASTE**

The "Higher Culture"
Popular Music and Drama
Sculpture, Architecture, Painting

SLAVERY AND DEMOCRACY

Garrison and Abolition
The Literary Antecedents to Civil War
Alexis de Tocqueville's America

Laying the Groundwork

THE EXCITEMENT OF PROGRESS

In the half-century preceding 1830, the United States had made great progress in establishing itself as a viable nation. The victory at Yorktown, the Constitution, the Bill of Rights, the Louisiana Purchase, the Battle of New Orleans, the Missouri Compromise, and the Monroe Doctrine were landmarks passed within the memory of many citizens living in 1830. The increase in the population, the growth of the national domain, and the development of cities and industries were only a few of the reasons for Americans' sense of gratification

The wonder was that one could see such substantial cultural growth in so short a time. At the close of the Jacksonian Era, only about six decades had elapsed since the eventful months of ratification of the Constitution. Yet distinctive intellectual, artistic, and scientific progress had been made, especially during the most recent 20 years. Authors, artists, and scientists already were giving eloquent and sustained proof of the richness and variety of American life and thought. Ordinary Americans were participating. They and their descendants reaped the benefits.

TECHNOLOGICAL CHANGE AND ECONOMIC DEVELOPMENT

Such heady developments should not obscure the fact that the majority of Americans lived simple lives. In the decades before the Civil War, most of them still were farmers and most farms still were small. Subtly or abruptly, however, what happened to them from dawn to dusk was changing. Since the arrival of Europeans in the New World, the amount of physical labor that had been required to convert unimproved land to cultivated fields had limited agricultural productivity. The agriculturalists of the eastern United States had spent countless hours swinging axes against trees, removing stumps, and digging rocks out of their fields. As Americans opened land further west, rainfall declined, but so did the number of trees; and much of the soil further west was less rocky than that in the East, especially New England. In 1813, Richard B. Chenaworth developed a cast iron plow made in three separate pieces that made possible the replacement of broken parts. The plow was used with success in the East, but the heavy western soils would stick to the cast-iron plow that then proved too brittle to break the ground of the western prairies. In

1837, John Deere patented a steel plow that provided the solution to breaking the western land.

In 1834, Cyrus McCormick patented the mechanical reaper, which greatly reduced the labor involved in harvesting grain. Prior to McCormick's invention, farmers still cut grain by hand, swinging cradles that cut swathes through the grain. The cut grain then was gathered in sheaves and hauled away for threshing. The mechanization of this process through use of McCormick's reaper greatly increased agricultural production. With the coming of the cast-iron plow, the steel plow, and the mechanical reaper, more food and fiber could be produced on the same amount of land. This led many farmers to acquire and cultivate more soil. It also meant that increasing numbers of them, no longer agriculturally essential, would be free to move to cities where—mainly in the Northeast—mills and factories were springing up.

No invention wrought more changes in everyday living than the steam engine. Machines found their way into diverse settings, most importantly the new factories that were located in towns and small cities, thereby transforming once-rural people into urbanized workers with year-around income. Steam-propelled riverboats, with their cheap and smooth transportation, speeded the expansion of river cities like Cincinnati and St. Louis. Railways, from the 1830s and 1840s on, were to have a similar impact on inland communities. One of the most amazing changes, barely beginning in this period, was the coming together of ship and rail traffic, notably at a spot where a small village, Chicago, was incorporated in 1837.

The first steam locomotive (a European invention) built in America was that of Peter Cooper in 1830. By 1850, 9,000 miles of rail had been laid, most of it on the Eastern seaboard. By 1860, 30,000 miles of rail had been laid, more miles of track than that built by the rest of the world combined. Railroads had tremendous spin-offs into the American economy at large. Trains traveling at 20 miles per hour allowed farmers in far-flung locations to get their produce to market before it spoiled. The railroads also allowed a real agricultural specialization as different areas of the country could import agricultural products rather than grow their own. Railroads stimulated movement west and the development of frontier towns as water stops for the trains. Railroads also stimulated the production of iron, steel, coal, and timber to meet the needs of the trains. They also stimulated the telegraph industry as telegraph lines were built alongside railroad tracks so that the railroad men could signal by telegraph from any location whether or not there were problems with tracks or anything else along the way.

The railroads were essentially financed by federal land grants to private railroad corporations. The federal government granted to the railroads up to six square miles of land for every mile of track laid by the railroad corporation. The railroads then sold their land to settlers for profits, thus both financing the railroad operation and spurring settlement of the American West. By 1860, Congress had granted to the railroads 20 million acres of federal land, thus providing great wealth to the railroads that would last for decades.

The railroads also stimulated the American banking system since the building of the railroads required large amounts of capital. The number of state chartered banks in the United States at the close of the War of 1812 was less than 100, but by 1830, there were over 300. Banks stimulated the economy by making loans to railroads, manufacturers, and merchants, thus expanding the money supply and enabling the expansion of America's rail, manufacturing, and commerce.

Concurrently, the ever-increasing use of the cotton gin (invented by Eli Whitney in 1793 for separating the cotton fiber from the seed) combined with the stepped-up demands for cotton to influence the Southerners' way of life. Prior to Whitney's cotton gin, farmers tediously plucked cotton fibers from each cottonseed by hand. Because of the gin, the southern climate, the nature of the land, and the presence of cheap slave labor, the South was in an economic position to supply what expanding American and international markets needed. If there had been no cotton gin, slavery might have been far less profitable. Thus it is clear that the gin was a potent factor, affecting both the status of slavery and the proslavery thinking of many Southerners. By the time of the Civil War, a full 20 percent of the British workforce was employed in the textile industry, most of which was driven by cotton from the American south. In the words of British historian Lord Macaulay, "What Peter the Great did to make Russia dominant, Eli Whitney's invention of the cotton gin has more than equaled in relation to the power and progress of the United States."

Other scientific thought and technological action had similar economic and social impacts. Samuel F. B. Morse, an admirable portrait painter, invented the telegraph and sent his first message in 1844. For the first time in human history, communication over long distances became instantaneous. Charles Goodyear discovered the process known as the vulcanization of rubber, which made rubber much more useful by preventing it from sticking and melting in hot weather. Goodyear's process made possible the manufacture of a wide array of rubber products, most notably the

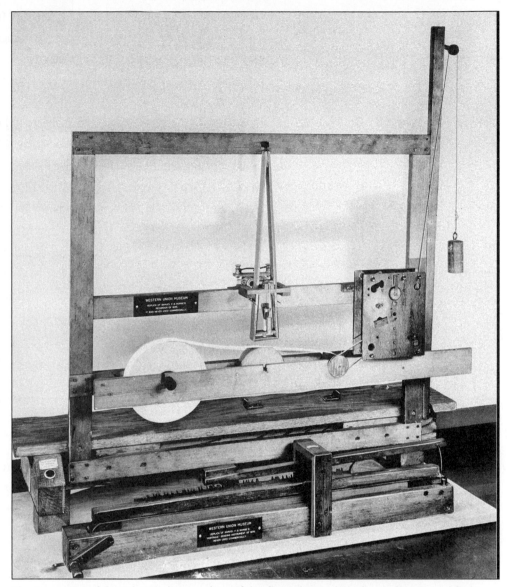

The invention of the telegraph (a replica of the first telegraph is shown here) enabled instantaneous communication over long distances for the first time in human history.

overshoe. From the mind and skill of Samuel Colt came the first practical firearm with a revolving chamber, and Elias Howe is given credit for the first sewing machine. Indeed, the sewing machine reminds us that during this period there were countless other inventions of a more humble nature that changed the nature of housework, such as the first appearance of the cast iron stove for cooking—as opposed to cooking over an open hearth.

During this period, too, medical and dental pioneers in Georgia and New England helped ease the suffering of future millions by applying anesthesia to surgery. In 1842, Crawford Long was the first to administer ether in surgery, thus reducing both pain and the risk of patients going into shock during surgery. William Beaumont, an

American army doctor on the Michigan frontier, was the first student of gastric digestion in a living patient; and Oliver Wendell Holmes, the Massachusetts poet-physician, saved the lives of countless mothers and babies by showing that antiseptics could prevent puerperal ("child-bed") fever.

Because of the technological changes, the growth of industrial production, and improved transportation, more and more goods that had previously been produced at home began to be commercially available—goods such as soap, textiles, and men's clothing. This, in turn, meant that the women who had traditionally produced them could now fill their days with other activities. They had more time to read, for example, and more time for needlework of an aesthetic nature. They also began to be able to join a variety of new organizations, in some cases through their churches and in others, organizations of an explicitly reformist nature.

THE ROLE OF REFORMERS

AMERICAN WOMEN

By twenty-first-century standards white women received very inequitable treatment. Most of them spent their lives at hard, repetitious labor in frontier cabins, isolated farm houses, or urban dwellings, though their work was being somewhat lightened by the new goods. Some left farms and villages to tend machines in such new "mill towns" as Lowell and Lawrence, Massachusetts, where textile mills provided the primary employment in the towns. Newly arrived immigrant girls took menial jobs—often as domestic servants—in Atlantic Seaboard cities and interior communities.

Certain legal restrictions on women carried over from earlier periods into the Jacksonian Era and down toward modern times. Women still could not vote. Wives' property rights were circumscribed at best. Often laws prevented wives from controlling their own inheritances. With rare exceptions, women, no matter how talented or ambitious, found themselves excluded from most professions. Yet in these years, women began to lay the groundwork for considerable progress.

The 1820s, 1830s, and 1840s marked the start of major reforms, many of them spearheaded by women. Fundamental to these efforts were the improved education opportunities being extended to girls in hundreds of private female academies that emerged all over the United States. Beginning in the 1930s, states began to open teacher-training academies known as "normal schools," which were exclusively for female students. Many of the noteworthy reformers—women's rights advocate Elizabeth Cady Stanton being the prime example—had attended one of the new academies.

Oberlin College in Ohio began admitting white women and black men in 1851 and graduated its first women in 1855. No other colleges admitted women until after the Civil War, but several private "female seminaries" were established to provide college-equivalent education to women. Emma Willard, who founded Troy Seminary in New York in 1821, and Mary Lyon, who founded Mount Holyoke in Massachusetts in 1837, were the two most well-known pioneer educators. Mention should also be made of Catherine Beecher, sister of the novelist Harriet Beecher Stowe, who founded the Harford Seminary in Connecticut. Harriet Beecher Stowe, who taught at the Hartford Seminary, argued that women are better teachers than men. In the words of Stowe, "If men have more knowledge, they have less talent at communicating it. Nor have they the patience, the long-suffering, and gentleness necessary to superintend the formation of character."

Women also became involved in the abolitionist movement. Sarah and Angelina Grimké, of a prominent South Carolina family, were among the many who crusaded in the North for the abolition of slavery, thereby challenging the taboo against respectable women speaking in public. The Grimkes were among the first, but they would be followed by many other courageous women, white and black alike. Dorothea Dix was another earnest friend of the unfortunates. (See *Dorothea Lynde Dix: Humanitarian.*) Many women were widely known as writers and editors. It was an augury of the future when Elizabeth Blackwell entered medical school in the 1840s, becoming the first woman to receive an M.D. degree in 1849.

Above all, these years were distinguished by the first appearance of a women's suffrage movement, launched at a gathering in Seneca Falls, New York in 1848. The two women who called the meeting, Elizabeth Cady Stanton and Lucretia Mott, had first met at an anti-slavery convention in London in 1840. There they had been denied the right of full participation on account of their gender. This slight had rankled the women. When they met again in the upstate New York town where Stanton lived with her husband and four children, they decided to call a meeting for a week hence—the first national women's rights convention in the United States—and, thereby, inaugurated what would become a revolution in gender mores. Stanton drew up a document, modeled on the Declaration of Independence, to present to the approximately 300 people who attended the meeting. In this "Declaration

Lucretia Mott

of Sentiments" she announced "All men and *women* are created equal" and cited 18 specific injuries that women suffered at the hands of men (as Jefferson had adduced evidence against George III), including the denial of access to the professions and to higher education. Stanton stated, "The history of mankind is a history of repeated injuries and usurpations on the part of man toward woman, having in direct object the establishment of an absolute tyranny over her." Stanton added that through the doctrine of male supremacy men had "endeavored in every way that could to destroy her confidence in her own powers, to lessen her self-respect, and to make her willing to lead a dependent and abject life." Stanton demanded that women be granted all the rights and privileges that men have as United States citizens, including—most radical of all—the vote, an act which was then seen as belonging entirely to "the male sphere." The great black abolitionist, Frederick Douglass, was in attendance; and he spoke on behalf of woman suffrage, which the delegates voted to support after a lively debate. It would be decades before suffrage was attained, but many of the other items on the list, such as a married woman's right to control her own property, began to be redressed in that era. From 1848 forward, a network of women's rights advocates emerged. Over 20 other women's rights conventions would be assembled before the Civil War, each also calling for the franchise. It was not yet a social movement, and its progress would be interrupted by the Civil War; but it was the beginning of one.

FIGHTING ILLS, WOES, AND EVILS

The zeal of reformers, both men and women, found many targets in the very nation where so many opportunities for improvement and advancement beckoned. The number of people arriving from Europe, particularly from the 1840s on, was larger than America could neatly accommodate. Many immigrants, poor and uneducated, crowded into port cities where they received low wages for working long hours and lived in squalor in what later came to be known as slums.

Attempts to cope with such problems in 1824–1848 proved rudimentary and, on the whole, unsuccessful. Most of the effort to improve the lot of urban workers came from the relatively weak labor unions, which will be analyzed in greater detail in Chapter 11. The unions, however, consisted mainly of skilled artisans. They were interested principally in bettering their own lot, not that of the unskilled newcomers. In general, the chief gain for both groups stemmed from workers' demands for free public schools, which were established in New York in 1832 and in Philadelphia two years later.

Both urban and rural Americans ate too much fat meat, too many fried foods, and too few fruits and vegetables. Reformers like Sylvester Graham, for whom Graham bread and Graham crackers were named, did their best to promote dietary change. Graham, in the 1830s, argued that the keys to better health could be found through proper diet, exercise, and hygiene. Graham also argued, however, that celibacy was essential to proper health and that women should have intercourse only for procreation. A medical doctor, and associate of Grahams, added that women ought not to be educated because the blood needed for the women and procreation would be diverted to the head, thus breeding "puny men." As for men, Graham's associate argued that semen was not to be expelled, but should be saved for reproductive purposes and should not be used for pleasure either in masturbation or in intercourse. Such use of semen, the doctor argued, would lead to "enervation, disease, insanity, and death." Furthermore, the doctor argued that expenditure of sperm would mean a loss of needed energy from the economy and that such a drain of energy from business to sex was wasteful and a contributor to social disorder.

While Graham was preaching clean living and celibacy, the heavy drinking in America, by children and teenagers as well as adults, had been appalling (by modern standards) ever since colonial times. In the words of one historian, "A house could not be raised, a field of wheat cut down, nor could there be a log-rolling, husking, quilting, a wedding, or a funeral, without alcohol." The evil of what we now call *alcoholism* and the reformers' determination to reduce or exterminate it are set forth in Chapter 12. Many men, women, and children "took the pledge" that they would drink no more alcoholic beverages. Then

PEOPLE THAT MADE A DIFFERENCE

Dorothea Lynde Dix: Humanitarian

by James M. McPherson

Dorothea Lynde Dix

The remarkable career of Dorothea Lynda Dix illustrates several important themes in early and mid-nineteenth century America: the upwelling of humanitarian reform; the changing role of women; the development of modern institutions for deviant members of society; the growth of more humane and scientific concepts of "insanity." She is known primarily as a pioneer in the field of mental health. Although her achievements were built on the foundation of earlier reforms, her single-minded dedication to improving conditions for people suffering from mental illness or retardation was the most important agency of progress in this field.

Dorothea Dix was born on April 4, 1802, in the frontier village of Hampden, Maine (then part of Massachusetts). From her Puritan forebears she gained an intense commitment to education, duty, hard work, and self-discipline. But these Protestant Ethic values seem to have skipped her improvident, ne'er-do-well father, from whose chaotic household Dorothea escaped at the age of twelve to live in Boston with her stern but supportive grandmother, the widow of a successful physician and businessman.

At the age of nineteen, Dorothea opened a grammar school for girls in Boston, the type of school then known as a "dame school." For the next twenty years she alternated between teaching and periods of recovery from incipient tuberculosis. Much influenced by the great Unitarian clergyman, William Ellery Channing, Dorothea became a Unitarian and published several undistinguished books of a devotional and poetic nature.

Approaching her fortieth year, Dix seemed headed for a typically genteel but sterile existence as a New England spinster. But an incident in March 1841 changed her life and launched her career as a reformer. Visiting an East Cambridge jail to teach a Sunday school class for women inmates, she found female "lunatics" freezing in filthy, unheated cells. Shocked by such cruelty, she publicized the conditions and won public support for improving them.

From this experience, Dix went on to make an eighteen-month study of jails, almshouses, and other public institutions in Massachusetts. In 1843 she presented to the legislature a hair-raising report of "helpless, forgotten, insane and idiotic men and women" confined "in *cages, closets, cellars, stalls, pens: Chained, naked, beaten with rods*, and lashed into obedience!" Five years later, after traveling 30,000 miles to make similar investigations in more than a dozen states, she presented a petition to Congress: "I have myself seen *more than nine thousand idiots, epileptics, and insane in these United States, destitute of appropriate care and protection* ... bound with galling chains, bowed beneath fetters and heavy iron balls attached to drag chains, lacerated with ropes, scourged with rods, and terrified beneath storms of profane execrations and cruel blows."

In truth, the treatment of the mentally ill was not this bad everywhere. There had been much progress beyond the medieval practice of treating insanity as a form of possession by demons, to be cured or punished by exorcism or scourging. The Quakers, in particular, had in the eighteenth century influenced the establishment of "lunatic asylums" where the mentally ill received humane treatment. About a dozen such asylums existed in the United States at the time Dix began her crusade.

These hospitals reached only a small percentage of the mentally ill. Most persons believed to be insane were either locked up at home by embarrassed relatives or incarcerated as lunatic paupers in jails and poorhouses, where conditions were often as bad as Dix portrayed them.

Dix's tireless, selfless work in state after state, all the more heroic because of personal shyness and chronic ill health, paid off with extraordinary victories. Her first success was the enlargement of the state insane asylum at Worcester, Massachusetts, in 1843. From there she went on to persuade the New Jersey legislature in 1845 to establish the state's first mental hospital, which Dix called "my firstborn child."

During the next thirty years she was directly responsible for the founding of 32 mental hospitals at home and abroad, and indirectly responsible for the establishment of many more. From 1854 to 1856 she visited several European countries and inspired the same kinds of reforms in the care and treatment of the insane there as she had done in the United States. Wherever Dix went, a network of voluntary associations was created to aid her cause and sustain her initiatives after she moved on. By 1880, when she retired from active work, the dozen American mental hospitals of 1840 had increased tenfold to 123.

Dix's observations of jails and penitentiaries led her into the cause of prison reform, a subject on which she produced influential writings. She also sympathized with other reform movements, especially the movements for temperance, women's rights, and education, but she focused her active efforts on the plight of the mentally ill, except during the Civil War when she served as Superintendent of Female Nurses for the Union army.

Single-minded in her ideas of how things should be done and no longer shy about expressing herself, Dix sometimes clashed with army surgeons and intimidated inefficient nurses, who called her "Dragon Dix"; but she also won the commendation of the secretary of war for her services. Dix's wartime activities were part of a broader development in which nursing was evolving from a menial occupation into a genuine profession. This in turn opened up new career opportunities for women.

After the war Dix resumed her work for better institutional treatment of the insane. Although she favored therapeutic rather than merely custodial care, she contributed little directly to the development of psychiatry or to the psychology of mental illness. However, her institutional achievements did create a framework for future advances in psychiatry. In 1881, old and infirm, she retired to live with her "firstborn child," the Trenton State Mental Hospital, where she died on July 18, 1887.

as now, of course, there was cynicism as to how well such pledges would be kept, but vast improvement in drinking habits did occur in the Jacksonian period—far more than with respect to eating.

Reformers similarly progressed substantially in many other areas. One was the struggle to eliminate imprisonment for debt. In addition, headway was made in the movement to end the traditional flogging of wayward sailors. The horrors of war anywhere and everywhere led Elihu Burritt, the learned blacksmith of Connecticut, to champion the cause of pacifism. Thomas H. Gallaudet labored ably on behalf of the deaf. Samuel G. Howe, with equal dedication, educated the deaf and the blind. Horace Mann was an effective crusader for public education in Massachusetts. As a member of the Massachusetts legislature in the 1830s, Mann persuaded the legislature to provide support for the schools in the form of taxation and to establish a state board of education, of which he became the head. Mann argued that private property was actually held in trust for the good of the community and, therefore, "is pledged for the education of all its youth up to such a point as will save them from poverty and vice, and prepare them for the adequate performance of their social and civil duties." Mann's framing of the argument for public education as a means to teach morality, discipline, and order to potential ruffians and revolutionaries converted the middle and upper classes to support the funding of education with tax money. As a consequence, the public schools of the nineteenth century taught not only math, English, and science, but also the Protestant values of industry, punctuality, sobriety, and frugality stressed in *McGuffey's Eclectic Readers* (1836). Millions of American children, therefore, learned to read while also learning of the terrible consequences of sloth, drunkenness, or wastefulness, as taught in McGuffey's parables. Critical thinking, unfortunately, was largely ignored.

That so much humanitarian reform was taking place in mid-nineteenth century owed much to religious changes, to be discussed more fully later in the chapter. In brief, the older emphasis on original sin and human depravity was giving way to a more optimistic set of beliefs in human possibility, doctrines appearing in many sectors of American Protestantism. The theory and practice of democracy, when carried to their logical conclusions, likewise led humanitarians to devote days, years, and even lifetimes to helping unfortunates. Numerous reformers were motivated also by the desire to impose order on the fast-changing society of which they were a part. Finally, we should consider the influence of the Romantic Movement, with its emphasis on the individual's insights, intuitions, and personal responsibilities.

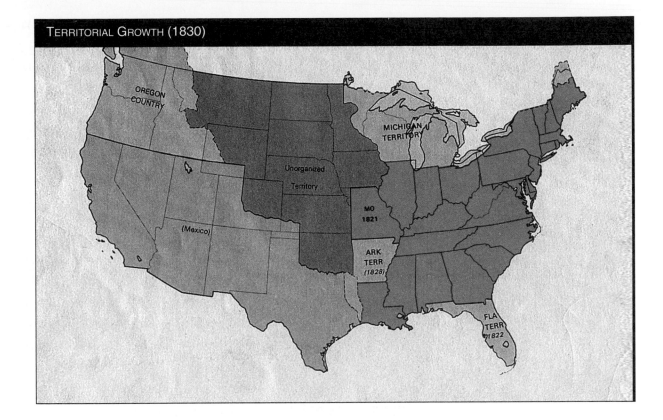

TERRITORIAL GROWTH (1830)

Just as not everyone was politically active, the number of stead-fast participants in some of these reforms was small; but enough Americans believed in human perfectibility to make reform a key characteristic of this period.

COMMUNITARIANISM

For some idealists, devotion to reforms *within* established society could not suffice. A small minority of American men and women looked upon the current social order, in which the majority toiled and suffered so many privations and indignities, as so utterly harsh and materialistic that it should be forsaken in favor of communitarianism. The communitarians' idea was for a limited number of people to live together in a little community, wholly or mainly self-sufficient and more or less apart from the general society surrounding it.

These communities could be either religious or secular. Among the Christian communitarians were the Shakers, who founded settle-ments in New England, New York, Kentucky, and elsewhere, and who believed in separation from the cruel and wicked world, in sim-plicity of language, and in celibacy. Religious communities were sponsored also by the Mormons and by several Adventist sects.

Secular communities resembled the Christian communities in that the purpose was to join people together so as to face collectively the challenge of the frontier or to confront collectively the trends toward industrialization. Among the secular experiments were New Harmony in Indiana, the North American Phalanx in New Jersey, and Fruitlands in Massachusetts. A number of transcendentalists inaugurated a Massachusetts community named Brook Farm, widely known because of its gifted residents.

One of the longest-lived communities was Oneida, founded in upstate New York by the sexual radical John Humphrey Noyes. Deeply religious, Noyes also believed in a system of "complex marriage," which was a rejection of monogamy. Noyes argued that the root of evil was in marriage and in "men's conviction that women are their private property." Noyes also argued that when the will of God is done on earth as it is in heaven, there would be no marriage on earth because Jesus stated that in heaven people do not marry. In order to reproduce this vision of heaven on earth, Noyes advocated complete sharing in family relationships as a step toward what he called "perfect cooperation." That being the case, Noyes and his 51 followers shared everything, both economic and sexual. Child rearing was the responsibility of the entire community, and there was no differentiation of gender roles in work. All private property was relinquished to the community.

In Noyes' complex marriage, every "saved" man was married to every "saved" woman. All who were "saved" were considered to be without sin. Although Noyes preached complete sharing of everything, he also decreed that only certain "spiritually advanced" males were allowed to have sex and father children. Noyes also taught that women could become "spiritually advanced" through sex with "spiritually advanced" males. Noyes considered himself to be "first husband," helping many women to "spiritual advancement." One Oneida community woman, Mary Cragin, appears to have been one of Noyes' favorite partners, and she describes her sexual experiences with Noyes as spiritual experiences as well. In the words of Cragin, "In view of God's goodness to me and of his desire that I should let him fill me with himself, I yield and offer myself, to be penetrated by his spirit, and desire that love and gratitude may inspire my heart so that I shall sympathize with his pleasure in the thing, before my personal pleasure begins, knowing that it will increase my capability for happiness."

Noyes also argued that sex should be a public act that should be performed in public to the pleasure of all, much like music or dancing. Noyes even argued that watching such public sex would give pleasure to "older people who have nothing to do in the matter." In addition to these oddities, to his credit, Noyes also tried a number of expedients to give women more freedom, such as communal nurseries. Oneida lasted from 1848 to 1879, when Noyes fled to Canada to avoid prosecution for adultery. After that, his followers abandoned complex marriage and set up an animal trap, silverware, and kitchenware manufacturing enterprise that survived into the twenty-first century.

The Oneida community was consistent with other religious and secular communitarianism in that it usually shared such features as vegetarianism, prohibition of alcoholic beverages, equitable division of labor (though not necessarily in terms of gender), and community ownership and control of property. Many secular communities had their philosophical bases in the social contract theories of the eighteenth century.

Most secular experiments did not last long, perhaps owing to an absence of explicitly Christian zeal that, in the case of the Mormons and the Shakers, proved a reliable source of community strength. In all, only a few thousand people committed themselves to communitarianism. Those communities, however, have received much attention then and since because they embodied visionary goals of social justice, perhaps inspired by the French theorist Charles Fourier or, in the case of New Harmony, by the ideas of the British thinker, Robert Owen.

PROGRESS IN EDUCATION

Among the most striking reforms of the Jacksonian period were those in the field of education. If some citizens objected to paying for the instruction of other people's children, most of them—at least in the Northeast—endorsed the drive for public schools below the college level. The impetus came from sources as contrasting as Harvard graduates and New York union members. Parents wanted sons and daughters to have the educational exposure they themselves had lacked. More and more children grew familiar with Noah Webster's excellent grammar and speller. As young Americans read and memorized the offerings of William Holmes McGuffey, some of the finest literature of the ages became part of their consciousness.

What we now take for granted as public elementary and high schools did not spread evenly across the face of the land. Primary and secondary education in rural regions was handicapped by the long distances separating farm families, with the resultant problem of assembling students under one roof. As there were more situations of this sort in the South and West than in the Northeast, it was

Southern and Western girls and boys living outside towns and cities who were most frequently deprived of the advantages of public education. Wealthy parents tried to compensate by sending their children to private academies or by hiring tutors for them, but this practice was of no help to any but the well-to-do.

In higher education, prestige continued to be identified with Harvard, Yale, and Princeton. The University of Virginia admitted its first students in 1825. Generally, however, small denominational colleges were more typical, making Latin, Greek, and mathematics available in out-of-the-way places. Such institutions received marginal support from their respective churches.

There were few medical schools, and fewer still in engineering. Most young lawyers got their training in offices of established attorneys. Nevertheless, sons of farm and village families had access to opportunities denied their fathers—even though few state universities thrived. The era also provided a beginning for the higher education of women when coeducation was inaugurated at Ohio's Oberlin College in the 1830s.

FAITH AND INTELLECT

RELIGION AND THE PEOPLE

Religion played an important part in the lives of average Americans. The Baptist and Methodist churches had more members than any others, but the Presbyterian, Congregational, Episcopal, and other denominations also appealed to substantial numbers. Sunday schools constituted a standard medium for indoctrinating the young, and Methodists and Baptists were successful in developing black congregations.

Religious diversity should likewise be stressed. With the influx of Irish and German immigrants by the hundreds of thousands during the 1840s and 1850s, growing numbers of Americans adhered to the Roman Catholic and Lutheran faiths. Supplementing churches with European origins were indigenous ones like the Disciples, Mormons, and various Adventist groups.

Widespread evangelistic endeavors also characterized the era. Especially in the South and West, the example of Bishop Francis Asbury inspired his Methodist successors to "ride the circuit" and present in graphic language the punishments for sin and the rewards of salvation. In the East and then in Ohio and Indiana, Lyman Beecher and his sons preached powerful Calvinistic sermons and attacked such social ills as dueling and alcoholic indulgence.

More popular than any other evangelist in the West and North, Charles Grandison Finney in countless revival meetings emphasized the individual's ability to repent. Salvation, Finney believed, represented only the start of a useful life: The person saved should then save others. Finney's theology, lacking the orthodox Calvinistic tenet of predestination, won converts by the tens of thousands.

Lyman Beecher

No longer were clergymen as apt as in the past to bewail a "low state" of American Protestantism. No longer did religion—as in the 1790s—appear to be removed from the masses in Middle Atlantic and other communities, with church memberships declining and the dissensions and arguments of ministers severely damaging their sects. If—as the French traveler Alexis de Tocqueville thought in the 1830s—religion was the foremost American institution, there were solid reasons for its number one rank. The "Second Great Awakening," which had begun with the turn of the century, continued into the time of de Tocqueville's visit and its spiritual force was felt long after that.

The evangelists of the Second Great Awakening did much of their preaching and exhorting outside the doors of churches, reaching the people at huge camp meetings in the countryside or at medium-sized revivals. A significant part of their ultimate effect was to lead zealous converts into Baptist and other church folds where continuing inspiration, strength, and comfort could be found.

There was also a close relationship between the assailing and reforming of social sins and the Protestant Ethic concept of hard work as a glorification of God. The excitement of economic progress and the challenge of technology had an undeniable identification with thrift, industry, and self-discipline. So it was not accidental that Christianity was far from being a Sunday-only affair in the Jacksonian period. Both rural and urban faithful attended prayer meetings on week nights. Grace was said before meals in innumerable homes, and devotional services were held in family circles with parents and children devoutly kneeling.

A preoccupation with the expected return of Christ also experienced a boost in the mid-nineteenth century when William Miller, a farmer from upstate New York, claimed in 1842 that he had mathematically calculated the exact time of the second coming of Christ as March 21, 1843. According to Miller, the correct meaning of Daniel 8:14, which states that "the sanctuary will be cleansed after 2300 days," was that the earth would be destroyed by fire 2,300 years after the prophecy, thus mandating Christ's return in 1843. Miller also concluded that the earth would be 6,000 years old on that date.

Miller published his conclusions in the 1830s and began preaching at churches and camp meetings, rapidly building a following. It is estimated that by 1843, some 50,000 Americans believed Miller's predictions and an estimated million more expected "something" to happen. Miller and his followers gave away their worldly belongings in March of 1843, donned white robes and flocked to the hills and tops of buildings to wait for Jesus' return. March 21 passed without incident, causing Miller to recalculate several times; but Christ failed each time to return.

Miller died in 1848 as a discredited prophet in terms of the date of his prediction. His followers continued to adhere to his teaching that Christians must still "Remember the Sabbath and Keep it Holy" and, therefore, must worship on Saturday (instead of Sunday) and perform no work on that day. Miller's followers eventually became known as the Seventh Day Adventists who continue to honor the Sabbath as Miller instructed in the twenty-first century.

MORMONS

Perhaps no new religious group of the early nineteenth century has placed a greater stamp on America than the Mormons, founded by Joseph Smith of Palmyra, New York, in the 1820s. Smith claimed to have been visited by the Angel Moroni, who led him to dig on a particular day for some golden plates buried in the ground near his home. Written on the plates in an indecipherable language, which Smith described as "reformed Egyptian," were more than 500 pages of the Book of Mormon. Smith also uncovered two sacred stones, Urim and Thummim, with which he could interpret the plates.

Smith then went about the business of interpreting the plates and dictated the Book of Mormon to a scribe who wrote down what Smith interpreted from behind a curtain. Some witnesses were amazed that Smith could interpret the plates using the Sacred Stones when the plates themselves were under a sheet. At least eight other people testified, however, that they had personally seen the plates before Smith returned them to the Angel Moroni.

The plates described the one true church and a "lost tribe of Israel" that had been missing for centuries. The Book of Mormon essentially provided an explanation that had bewildered Christians everywhere for centuries as to how the Native Americans had come to be in the Western Hemisphere. The Native Americans were explained to be the lost tribe of Israel, and Jesus Christ had come to America after his Resurrection and preached to the Native Americans. The original sight of the Garden of Eden was identified as a place near Independence, Missouri. The Book of Mormon also predicted the appearance of a prophet in America who would establish a new, pure kingdom of Christ in the United States. The Book also predicted the coming of the Civil War, proof later to many that Smith was a true prophet of God.

Skeptics point out, however, that the book also mentions the presence of horses, steel, and wheat in the Western Hemisphere prior to the arrival of Columbus. Furthermore, in 1835 Smith purchased and translated Egyptian Papyruses that he claimed were written by Abraham. Twentieth century Egyptologists, however, contend that Abraham did not write Smith's papyruses; but they are copies of the Egyptian Book of the Dead.

Theologically speaking, Smith's Mormonism is a protestant Christian religion. The teachings of Smith's Mormonism include not only belief in the one true God of Christianity, but in Jesus Christ as the Son of God and savior of all humanity. Smith's Mormonism also taught that human life on earth is part of the human progress toward eventual status in heaven equivalent to that of God in the Old Testament. The logic, essentially, is that if humans are God's children, then when humans "grow up" in the afterlife, they will be "Gods" residing on a distant planet near the orbiting the star Kolob, the closest place to God that keeps time. While in heaven, human males will be sexually active with wife or wives in a paradise of jewels and gold. In Mormonism, marriage is eternal, and people will be reunited in the afterlife.

While on earth, Mormons avoided strong drink, including alcohol, coffee, and tea. Mormonism also taught that prosperity is a path to Godliness; and, thus, the Mormons stressed work. Mormonism is also hierarchical, and a "First President" and 12 Apostles head the Church. At first, Mormonism also taught that converts must give all their property to the Church; but Joseph Smith found that the wealthy rebelled against the practice, so he changed the requirement from "all property," to a tithe. This alteration is an early example of the doctrine of "continuous revelation," which allows doctrine to evolve with changing times. Famously, Mormonism also allowed polygamy. Joseph Smith himself had 28 wives; but the Mormon Church abandoned the practice in 1890 after it was struck down as unconstitutional by the United States Supreme Court.

Polygamy, of course, was controversial and caused the Mormons to be persecuted by the larger communities around them. Mormonism also requires evangelism, which aids in the growth of Mormonism but, also, alienates those who do not care to be evangelized. Thus, Smith and his followers were forced to migrate from Palmyra, New York, to Ohio, Missouri, and then Nauvoo, Illinois. Nevertheless, Nauvoo had a Mormon population of 15,000 by 1844, and Smith petitioned Congress for separate territorial status and even ran for president. The entire Mormon population at the time of Smith's untimely death at the hands of an angry mob in 1844 is estimated at 26,000.

The persecution of Mormons by the larger community was undoubtedly severe, thus leading to the multiple migrations. Smith's (and later Brigham Young's) Mormonism itself was not entirely pacific, and the Mormons at times lashed back at their persecutors. Mormonism contained the idea of "blood atonement," whereby Mormon believers can kill enemies of the Church. Furthermore, those who had fallen away from the Mormon Church could be justly killed by believers. Those that had fallen away and desired to return to the Church could regain their salvation by killing the enemies of the Church. In doing so, the throats of the victims were slit, and it was required that their blood be spilled on the ground. At Haun's Mill near Kirtland, Ohio, in 1838, 17 people were killed in this manner when they refused to migrate with the rest of the Mormon community. Even more horrific, in 1857 at Mountain

Brigham Young

Meadows, Utah, Mormons slaughtered 140 men, women, and children from Arkansas who were in the process of crossing Utah in a wagon train. Twenty children age seven and under were spared as "innocents," adopted by the Mormons, and later as adults lived to tell the truth of the massacre. If it were not for the coming of the Civil War, the United States government might have invaded Utah and arrested Brigham Young for his responsibility in the Mountain Meadows massacre; but the magnitude of the sectional crisis in the United States at the time forced the United States government to direct its energy elsewhere. More discussion of Brigham Young and the Mormon's migration to Utah will be presented in Chapter 11.

THE UNITARIAN INFLUENCE

For the Christians whose ardor and faith have just been depicted, God the Son and God the Holy Ghost were as integral in the deity as God the Father. But concurrently spreading in New England was the influence of Unitarians, who rejected the doctrine of the trinity, believing that God exists in only one person.

Unitarians accepted Christian revelation, but only so far as it accorded with what they conceived to be human reason. The Calvinistic belief in the doctrine of election was not for them because it implied an arbitrary God. Instead, Unitarians underscored the deity's benevolence. They declared that Jesus was divine in the sense that all people are divine. To a degree, they were reacting against both the creed and the formalism of Congregationalists and the fire-and-brimstone evangelism of the Great Awakenings, although one also finds links between the latter and Unitarian individualism. To Unitarians, the life of Jesus represented an example to be emulated by persons who already were innately good and spiritually free.

A spokesman for Unitarian thought and action was the Boston clergyman, William Ellery Channing. Implicit in his ideas was the prominence of the individual—independent, yet spiritually obliged to "transcend" individualistic self by intimate identification with the Deity. Though Channing had been reared in the creed of Calvinism, he came to deny the doctrine of original sin and to believe firmly in the freedom of the will. Many of the era's reformers and intellectuals were Unitarian in their beliefs.

ROMANTICISM REVISITED

It is not difficult to understand why Channing and other Unitarian thinkers appealed to young scholars and writers who had been impressed by the ideas of Romanticism because the belief in human possibility was very congruent with Romanticism. Romanticism had already had an important influence on the thinking of the young republic. Now, in 1824–1848, Romanticism's influence was, if anything, even more pervasive.

Romantic writers and artists had as their goal the "liberation" of the individual—the full realization of the human potential. To accomplish this, they felt that individuals should give free rein to imagination and emotion, experimenting with new ways and new ideas. The emphasis was on informality, the picturesque, the exotic, and the sensuous as ways of appreciating external nature and capturing the transient aspects of life. They shunned tradition, feeling that human intuition and poetic sensibility were best qualified to lead people to truth.

The growth of democratic government during the Jacksonian period also reflected this new emphasis on the value of the individual and faith in the ability of the common person. This individualism was not necessarily "nonconformist": Most Americans still took their cue for behavior from the majority. They did tend, however, to admire the rugged individualists among them, whether in life or in literature, such as the heroes of James Fenimore Cooper (*The Last of the Mohicans*), to be discussed shortly.

The ultimate liberated men were those who invaded the wilderness, drove the Native Americans out, and established settlements in the West. These men saw themselves as economically self-reliant and capable of almost any achievement and developed versatility, robustness, and resilience, along with the physical courage and (sometimes) moral obtuseness that was required of them.

The Romantics felt that society was a growing organism that could be changed and improved. Thus, Romanticism as well as Christianity nourished the reform movements of the period. Most American Romanticists, however, thought their country already had the political foundations it needed and so concerned themselves largely with social and humanitarian reforms.

THE GOLDEN AGE OF LITERATURE

EMERSON AND TRANSCENDENTALISM

The period from the triumph of Jacksonian democracy to the Civil War was one of the greatest eras in American literary history. It has been called "The Golden Day," "The New England Renaissance," and

"The Flowering of New England." We begin with Ralph Waldo Emerson, Margaret Fuller, and Henry David Thoreau, who were among the leading proponents of the Boston-based transcendentalist movement into which the two intellectual streams we have just observed, Unitarianism and Romanticism, flowed.

Transcendentalism has been defined philosophically as "recognition in man of the capacity of knowing truth intuitively, or attaining knowledge transcending the reach of the senses." Transcendentalists believed that the power of the solitary individual was limitless and that people should not conform to the materialistic world. Instead, people should look within themselves and within the natural world for guidance.

In his first little book *Nature*, published in 1836, Emerson asked penetrating questions:

> Foregoing generations beheld God and nature face to face; we, through their eyes. Why should not we also enjoy an original relation to the universe? Why should not we have a poetry and philosophy of insight and not of tradition, and a religion by revelation to us, and not the history of theirs?

Emerson pointed out that Jesus "spoke of miracles," for Jesus felt "man's life was a miracle" and man's "daily miracle shines, as the character ascends." The churches' interpretation of the word miracle, Emerson added, gave a false impression and was "not one with the blowing clover and the falling rain."

The allusion to clover and rain as miracles symbolized the transcendentalists' search for revelations of divinity in external nature as well as in the individual's own nature. Emerson viewed the different aspects of the universe as diverse manifestations of a central spirit, which he called the Over-Soul. Man and woman, according to Emerson, could be channels for the higher truths of the Over-Soul by developing their intuitive powers to

Statue of Ralph Waldo Emerson

the fullest. Emerson's doctrine of the Over-Soul also implied a belief in self-reliance, as expounded in his famous essay of that name. When he wrote about self-reliance, Emerson's meaning was that the human being could reach a direct, exalted relationship with the universal spirit.

Emerson's philosophy was essentially a variety of philosophical idealism, as distinct from materialism. Broadly speaking, an idealist is one who sees basic reality as spiritual; the materialist is one who sees it as physical or material. Emerson's idealism was concerned ultimately with the conduct of life. For this he felt that men and women have the capacity to draw upon a power greater than their own.

One of Emerson's chief allies in the transcendentalist project was Margaret Fuller, America's first great woman intellectual. A few years younger than Emerson, Fuller was unable to attend Harvard as so many men did, but she pursued a ferociously ambitious program of reading and was able to hold her own with any and all of the other transcendentalists. In the fall of 1836 a number of these Boston intellectuals began meeting informally in what evolved into the Transcendentalist Club. For a brief period they published a journal, the *Dial*, of which Fuller was the editor. A brilliant conversationalist, Fuller would visit the Emerson household in Concord, where she and her host would talk by the hour. After her untimely death in 1850, Emerson wrote a memoir about her.

HENRY DAVID THOREAU

Although Emerson published many volumes of poetry and essays, he was more widely known in his lifetime as the most popular lecturer of his day, while Fuller was known for her journalism, of which more will be said later in the chapter. In contrast, Henry David Thoreau's contacts with his contemporary Americans were minimal. Very few bought or read his *A Week on the Concord and Merrimack Rivers* (1849) or even his now-celebrated *Walden* (1854), both of which related his experience and thinking in the 1840s.

Today Thoreau is considered one of the major American writers of all time. Emerson comprehended the younger man's greatness as a stylist, testifying that "Thoreau illustrates with excellent images that which I convey in a sleepy generality." An erstwhile schoolteacher and local handyman, Thoreau spent the years 1845–1847 in a shack on the edge of Walden Pond near Concord. Here he dwelt among the birds and beasts, reading and writing with few distractions. "I went to the woods because I wished to live deliberately" he explained, "to front only the essential facts of life."

Any Romanticist, any fellow-transcendentalist, would have no trouble grasping the logic of what Thoreau said. "... I had not lived there a week before my feet wore a path from my door to the pondside. ... How worn and dusty, then, must be the highways of the world, how deep the ruts of tradition and conformity."

Henry David Thoreau

Independence and self-reliance dominated Thoreau's life. He actively helped the "underground railroad" to convey runaway slaves to the freedom of Canada. He spent a night in jail rather than pay a tiny tax to support a government then prosecuting what he considered an unjust war against Mexico.

Out of the latter experience came *Civil Disobedience*, a highly influential political essay that the modern author and critic Henry S. Canby referred to as "Gandhi's textbook in his campaign of passive resistance" against the British in twentieth-century India. Together Thoreau and Mahatma Gandhi later greatly influenced the nonviolent resistance of Martin Luther King, Jr. Thoreau declared it the duty of citizens to deny allegiance to a government they feel is wrong.

Such an attitude is essential to the health of a democracy. It is the opposite of that apathy which prevents citizens from taking a stand, allowing important contests to go by default. Thoreau was not antisocial. He merely took his duties as a citizen more seriously than most Americans.

THE BOSTON BRAHMINS

In his own day, Thoreau was not nearly so well known as Henry Wadsworth Longfellow, James Russell Lowell, or Oliver Wendell Holmes. Each of these was an admired poet (and Holmes, somewhat later, the author of well-regarded prose). Although Lowell and Longfellow attacked slavery in verse, all three were primarily literary aristocrats. Holmes applied the label "Brahmin caste of New England" to the cultivated, exclusive class he typified.

These "Brahmins" were inclined to view literature as something lofty and ennobling. Much of the time in their writing, they erected barriers against unpleasant or perplexing social and philosophic questions. In the 1830s and 1840s, the dreamy utopias of Emerson and the back-to-nature living of Thoreau were not for them—nor were the portrayals of evil that characterized the books of Nathaniel Hawthorne and Herman Melville. Benevolent toward others, the "Brahmins" were usually satisfied to savor the pleasant intellectual life of Boston and Harvard—where all three were professors. Although (or perhaps because) he had a sense of humor, Holmes considered Boston "the thinking center of the continent, and therefore of the planet."

NATHANIEL HAWTHORNE

The writer who most brilliantly opposed transcendentalist tendencies was Nathaniel Hawthorne of Salem, Massachusetts. He was the chief inheritor, in literature, of the old Puritan tradition, and his works—particularly his novel *The Scarlet Letter* (1850)—embodied Puritan ideas. His ancestors had been Puritan magistrates charged with persecuting Quakers and condemning "witches" at Salem court. While disapproving of their bigotry and cruelty, he recognized the ancestral tie: "Strong traits of their nature," he said, "have intertwined themselves with mine."

Hawthorne rejected both the optimism inherent in transcendentalism and the reform movements abetted by it. He held the Puritan belief that people are innately sinful, that evil is an ever-present reality (not an illusion to be brushed aside), and that self-reliant individualism alone cannot save a person from destruction. In Hawthorne, we see the persistence of the Puritan point of view into the Jacksonian Era.

Unlike Emerson, who denied that evil existed in an ultimate form, Hawthorne made evil central in his stories and novels. *The Scarlet Letter* deals with secret guilt, the effects of crime on man and woman, and the need for expiation through confession or love. In *The House of the Seven Gables* (1851), evil appears as a hereditary taint visiting the sins of the fathers on the children in a study of degeneration and decay. *The Blithedale Romance* (1852) is, in part, a satire on the secular community Brook Farm—the villain showing how a reformer's zealotry can mesh with unconscionable ambition and thus serve evil rather than good.

HERMAN MELVILLE

A writer close to Hawthorne both in his concern with the "deep mystery of sin" and in his revulsion against Emersonian currents of optimism was Herman Melville. Born in New York, reared there and in the Berkshires of Massachusetts, Melville as a youth shipped as a sailor on a merchantman plying the Atlantic and later on a whaler bound for the South Seas. On these voyages he saw first hand, a world of violence, crime, and misery.

Such early Melville books as *Typee* and *Omoo* were popular, but his increased pessimism caused the novelist to be neglected after the 1840s. He was "rediscovered" in the 1920s by post-World War I readers, to whose mood of disillusionment *Moby Dick* (1851) had a powerful appeal.

Although Melville, like Hawthorne, was a philosophical pessimist, he arrived at his pessimism along intellectual avenues differing from Hawthorne's in three ways. First, Hawthorne still cherished Calvinist values though critical of them and all others, whereas Melville rebelled against the religious conservatism he had known as a boy. Second, in Liverpool and in the South Seas Melville was shocked by the roughness and cruelty of "civilized" men—brutalities that neither Hawthorne nor Emerson experienced. Finally, just as he lacked Emerson's optimism, he lacked Hawthorne's resignation.

Said Hawthorne in reference to an 1856 meeting with Melville in England:

> Melville, as he always does, began to reason of providence and futurity, and of everything that lies beyond human ken, and informed me that he had "pretty much made up his mind to be annihilated"; but still he does not seem to rest in that anticipation; and, I think, will never rest until he gets hold of a definite belief. It is strange how he persists—and has persisted ever since I knew him, and probably long before—in wandering to-and-fro over these deserts, as dismal and monotonous as the sand hills amid which we were sitting. He can neither believe, nor be comfortable in his unbelief; and he is too honest and courageous not to try to do one or the other.

Modern literary critics give Melville high ratings and are fascinated by his imagery. Sometimes they remind us that we should not forget his love of the exotic, the sensually attractive, and the humorous, for Melville was a many-sided man. While the dilemma of the author of *Moby Dick* has been variously analyzed, it is probable that Hawthorne's interpretation was not wide of the mark.

JAMES FENIMORE COOPER

The disparity between the dream of a peaceful, democratic society in the virgin wilderness and the reality of frontier life was frequently reflected in the thought and literature of this period. The real Western frontier posed many problems of adjustment for its settlers. Land speculation, political corruption, and immorality were common in the poorly organized towns. In short, the real frontier bore little resemblance to the literary legend or to the popular tall tale.

The first major writer of fiction to exploit the literary potential of the frontier was James Fenimore Cooper, whose series of "Leatherstocking Tales" both romanticized the wilderness and conveyed the loss many Americans felt when they became aware of the crude fashion in which the frontier was being settled. For instance, Cooper convincingly expressed the tragedy of the Native American, pushed out of ancestral lands by the advancing white settler.

Although it is easy to lampoon his didacticism, stock characters, and strained and starchy dialogue, at his best Cooper was a captivating storyteller with a talent for both description and perceptive social criticism. "The Leatherstocking Tales" represents a Romantic view of the West, just as Sir Walter Scott's novels and ballads romanticized with charm and skill the people and places of a lost Europe. Cooper's West, however, was confined mainly to upper New York state before 1800. He himself never saw the prairie, never neared the Rocky Mountains—in fact, never even crossed the Mississippi River.

SOUTHERN ROMANTICISM

The South produced numerous authors before the Civil War, yet there were few direct literary connections with New England. Sectional interests influenced literature, just as they influenced politics. With many Southerners convinced that slavery must be maintained and allowed to spread, Southerners liked to idealize their plantations as happy feudal domains where blacks benefited from the most humane treatment. Southern writers praised Greek democracy where *inequality,* rather than *equality,* had prevailed. There and in the American South, they held, competent individuals directed and cared for the less competent—acting in the interest of all.

Because of the feudal emphasis, the dominant influence on Romantic Southern literature during these years was the British author Sir Walter Scott. Scott's fictional recreation of the Middle Ages, his knights in shining armor, his defenders of glamorous ladies in distress, and his heroes' exemplary characters fitted in with notions of Southern chivalry—as opposed to Northern commercialism and reformism.

A number of American writers attempted to romanticize the "feudal" South in works of fiction. One of the best of those novels was

John P. Kennedy's *Swallow Barn* (1832), which depicted rural Virginia in the 1820s. A resident of Baltimore, Kennedy strung together sketches of idealized plantation aristocracy with a minimal plot. In it the master of the estate of Swallow Barn is genial and generous, his relatives and friends are virtuous, their hospitality is bountiful, and the blacks are cheerful.

EDGAR ALLAN POE

Reared as a foster child in Virginia, Edgar Allan Poe nevertheless can be treated only partly as a Southerner. Although in his personal life he was—or wanted to be—a conservative Southerner, and although he supported the works of other Southern authors and praised the Southern defense of slavery, Poe's writings rarely reveal a Southern

Edgar Allan Poe

tone or setting. In his tales he was more influenced by the "Gothic" tradition in English fiction—the kind of fiction that used certain stock properties like old castles, decayed houses, dungeons, secret passages, ancient wrongs, and supernatural phenomena.

Poe was not concerned with portraying contemporary scenes or providing moral reflections on life. He believed that poetry, for example, should exist for its own sake, never as an instrument of instruction. It may be that no other American has maintained more consistently that literature exists primarily and perhaps solely to entertain; but Poe did not take this function lightly. In his own poetry and prose, he applied the theories of literary technique that he expounded in his critical writings. There was a great deal of originality in Poe's writing, particularly in his short stories and detective stories. Both his poetry and his prose were enormously admired abroad, especially in France.

JOURNALISM AND POPULAR CULTURE

WRITING FOR THE PEOPLE

Americans of the time read newspapers more avidly than even the most exciting fiction. New York City produced some of the best journalism in Horace Greeley's *Tribune* and poet-editor William Cullen Bryant's *Post*. James Gordon Bennett's New York *Herald*, a pioneer in the "penny press" field, presented national and world news alongside lurid accounts of murders and sex scandals. Nowhere else had there ever been so many newspapers as there were then in America. While quality varied from town to town, Americans knew more about what was going on than any other general population anywhere.

After stereotyping began in 1811 and electrotyping in 1841, the influence of technology on popular culture was evi-

Statue of *New York Tribune* editor Horace Greeley

dent. Printers used steam presses to mass-produce books which, cheaply bound and extensively distributed, sold for as little as 25 cents. Intellectuals read such magazines as the *North American Review* and the *Southern Literary Messenger*. Tillers of the soil preferred the *American Farmer*, the *American Agriculturist*, and the *Southern Cultivator*. In addition to agricultural articles, these offered fiction and verse to farm families.

Religious periodicals abounded—notably the *Biblical Repertory* (Presbyterian), the *Biblical Repository* (Congregationalist), the *Christian Review* (Baptist), the *Christian Examiner* (Unitarian), the *Methodist Magazine,* and the *United States Catholic Magazine*. Carrying theological arguments and sectarian messages, many of them also disseminated miscellaneous culture. "Of all the reading of the people," a commentator observed in 1840, "three fourths is purely religious." In 1848, 52 religious journals were published in New York City alone.

MAGAZINES AND BOOKS FOR WOMEN

Discerning innovators discovered that women could comprise one of the most dependable magazine markets. From 1830 on, a Philadelphia periodical called *Godey's Lady's Book* enjoyed an enviable circulation, helped along by the efforts of its gifted editor, Sarah Josepha Hale. By the 1850s, its subscription list reached 150,000. Eventually, its publisher amassed a million-dollar fortune. *Graham's Magazine*, which made its bow in 1841, instantly appealed to both women and men. Soon it had 40,000 subscribers and a $50,000 annual profit. Its contents? Short stories, essays, poetry, colored fashion plates, book reviews, and a department on fine arts. Bryant, Cooper, Lowell, and Longfellow contributed to *Graham's*. For a time Poe was literary editor, and some of his best work graced its pages. Combining the insipid and sentimental with better things, *Graham's* and *Godey's* provided exactly what their readers wanted.

Women writers were widely published during the period. Authorship lent opportunity to women when most other vocational doors were shut. Mrs. Ann Stephens, co-editor of the *Ladies' National Magazine,* sent florid but thrilling tales to the *Lady's Wreath* and similar media. Poems (often lachrymose by modern standards) and articles by Mrs. Lydia Sigourney won acceptance in countless journals. Among women authors with large followings were Catharine M. Sedgwick and Mrs. Anna Mowatt. Mrs. Caroline Lee Hentz and Mrs. E.D.E.N. Southworth, popular novelists of the 1850s, got their start in the previous decade. Margaret Fuller edited the *Dial* in Boston, as we have noted; and later, in New York on Greeley's *Tribune*, she gained more admirers of her astute criticism. Her volume, *Women in the Nineteenth Century*, drawn from her writings for the *Tribune*, projected advanced views on women's rights.

SPORTS, HUMOR, AND REALISM

One of the liveliest periodicals was New York's *Spirit of the Times*. Its editor featured sports and pastimes like horse racing, boxing, hunting, shooting, and fishing. He also had an eye for realism and amusing exaggeration in fiction. In the *Spirit* and in books, small farmers and reckless frontiersmen of the Old Southwest—from Georgia to Arkansas—became subjects of wildly humorous yarns by such frontier writers as Thomas B. Thorpe, William T. Thompson, Augustus B. Longstreet, J. J. Hooper, and George W. Harris. Authentically depicting the speech, customs, and scenery of their region, they produced comedy combined with realism.

Harris, who wrote for the *Spirit* in the 1840s, created his fictional character Sut Livingood a bit later. There is no better example of the breed of men inhabiting these humorists' stories. A lanky mountaineer and self-confessed "nat-ral-born durn'd fool," Sut loves liquor and women but hates Yankees and circuit-riding preachers, whom he describes as "durn'd, infurnel, hiperkritical, potbellied, scaley-hided, whiskey-wastin'." These storytellers delighted in the boast and brag of the "tall tale":

> I'm that same David Crockett, fresh from the backwoods, half-horse, half-alligator, a little touched with the snapping-turtle; can wade the Mississippi, leap the Ohio, ride upon a streak of lightning, and slip without a scratch down a honey locust; can whip my weight in wild-cats—and if any gentleman pleases, for a ten-dollar bill, he may throw in a panther. ...[1]

Here—chauvinism, boastfulness, and exaggeration—all reflected the influence of the West and Southwest on thinking and reading tastes. There are historians who believe that the "starting point of a truly American literature" can be located on the frontier, in just such tales, more logically than in the East.

[1]Vernon Louis Parrington, *Main Currents in American Thought,* II (New York: Harcourt Brace Jovanovich, Inc.,1927), p. 176.

ARTS, SCIENCES, AND POPULAR TASTE

THE "HIGHER CULTURE"

As in literature, so in other arts: Americans valued both the light and the serious. Classical music had numerous appreciators, particularly in urban centers with their orchestras and choral societies. No actor won more plaudits than Edwin Forrest, who played major Shakespearean parts like Brutus and King Lear. No lecturer was more respected than Emerson, who discoursed on intellectual topics annually from New England westward. Margaret Fuller's "conversations," in Boston, attracted audiences of women—eager participants—hungry for mental stimulation; and in 1826 in Millbury, Massachusetts, Josiah Holbrook organized a series of public lectures that were to form the basis of the National American Lyceum movement. This movement, which was dedicated to the spread of information about the arts, sciences, history, and public affairs, spread to other states and became an important force in adult education and social reform.

Despite the fact that serious research was beyond the reach of most teachers, the period witnessed advances along scientific lines. There was keen public interest in science, and young and older people crowded scientific exhibitions and marveled at scientific experiments. Benjamin Silliman, professor at Yale, published *Elements of Chemistry* in 1830 and wrote learnedly on subjects ranging from gold deposits to sugar planting. Other scientific pioneers were Elisha Mitchell, geologist and botanist at the University of North Carolina; Edmund Ruffin, Virginia soil chemist; and Matthew F. Maury of the United States Navy, his generation's expert in navigation and oceanography. George Ticknor at Harvard was the American trailblazer in the study and teaching of modern foreign languages. In the historical field, William H. Prescott was publishing his monumental works on Mexico and Peru, and another first-rate historian, Francis Parkman, was writing *The Oregon Trail* and *The Conspiracy of Pontiac*.

In some of the arts and sciences, America still leaned on Europe for much of its leadership. Thus John James Audubon, the ornithologist and painter whose *Birds of America* is a classic, was born in the West Indies and reared in France. Duncan Phyfe, famous for the furniture he produced in New York, came to America from Scotland. Louis Agassiz of Switzerland, who joined the Harvard faculty, did as much as anyone to arouse American interest in zoology and geology. Young Americans of promise went to Germany and France for

Soprano Jenny Lind, the "Swedish Nightingale"

graduate study. In philanthropy, too, the Old World pointed the way: an Englishman endowed Washington's Smithsonian Institution.

Among highly regarded performing artists appearing in the United States were many Europeans, including an Austrian ballet dancer, a Norwegian violinist, and countless British actors and actresses. The Swedish soprano Jenny Lind—the "Swedish Nightingale"—was one of the most beloved performers of her day. Presented by the famed impresario, P. T. Barnum, Lind packed concert halls in several American cities. Objects from a style of crib to a locomotive were named in her honor.

POPULAR MUSIC AND DRAMA

Americans by no means depended exclusively on Europe for all their culture. Much folk art and folk craft—the beautiful furniture of the Shakers, for example—was far from being purely derivative, although many songs Americans hummed—"Home, Sweet Home" is an illustration—were at least partly of European origin. Well-loved ballads, fiddle tunes, and folk songs fused the native and imported. The same was true of hymns, work songs, political chants, and comic airs. Some were totally native. All were intimately integrated into the lives, worship, and fun of average people.

On the stage, light plays and musicals competed with the classical—though even the plays of Shakespeare might well have been presented in so rollicking a fashion as to constitute popular entertainment. With low admission prices, the urban theater boomed. Rowdy comedies and farces played to rowdy audiences. The versatile James H. Hackett helped make Rip Van Winkle famous and ridiculed "high society" in *The Moderns, or A Trip to the Springs*. The lighter side of cultural life developed with zest in rural areas as well. Heroes were applauded and villains hissed and booed in smaller cities and towns—even in barns and log houses and on boats on Western waters.

Among indigenous American entertainments was the minstrel show with its interlocutor and end men, banjos, bones, and tambourines. The minstrel show featured white men wearing blackface make-up, and it was both a racist spectacle deriding black people and a vehicle for calling attention to aspects of African American folk culture. Audiences cheered minstrels like Ohio's Daniel Emmett, the singer and composer who subsequently gave "Dixie" to the South. Enchanting were the tunes of Stephen Collins Foster, the Pennsylvanian who immortalized Florida's "Swanee" River and evoked tears with the strains of "My Old Kentucky Home." Love of the spectacular as well as good music—in the case of Jenny Lind—led multitudes to line the pockets of Phineas T. Barnum, who amazed gaping compatriots with his museum of curios—from the woolly horse and bearded lady to the midget "General Tom Thumb."

SCULPTURE, ARCHITECTURE, PAINTING

American sculptors had a remarkable vogue. Among the most celebrated were Hiram Powers, whose "Greek Slave" Londoners greeted with admiration, and Thomas Crawford, whose "Armed Freedom" surmounts the Capitol in Washington, D.C. Pseudoclassical portrait busts were produced by the thousands. Average Americans took pride in this art form, although the nude "Greek Slave" did not please the prudish and Horatio Greenough's "George Washington"—partly draped in a Roman toga—drew its share of outraged criticism.

The Jefferson-Latrobe influence remained strong in Greek Revival architecture. But in the 1830s and 1840s young architects considered classical columns and porticos too formal and artificial. Devotees of Romantic theories, they stressed the organic in plan and construction. A multiplicity of styles, especially the Gothic, characterized the work of Alexander J. Davis and of Richard Upjohn, who designed Trinity Church in New York City. While most Americans did not employ architects, thousands of houses showed the influence of architectural handbooks.

Although, like Upjohn, the most successful portrait painter, Thomas Sully, had come to the United States from England, the canvases of the American-born artists John Neagle and Henry Inman also were popular. "Storytelling" or anecdotal painting—in which common human situations were depicted nostalgically or humorously—likewise was growing in public favor. Scenes of life on the farm or of raftsmen poling their flatboats upstream or of prairie schooners and Native Americans appeared in the work of George Caleb Bingham,

William Sidney Mount, and Alfred Jacob Miller. Romanticism and American pride in the land combined to inspire a group of painters known as the Hudson River School, who romantically portrayed the wilderness of forests, mountains, and streams.

SLAVERY AND DEMOCRACY

GARRISON AND ABOLITION

For all the progress and all the pride in the white American of these years—for all the artistry of the gifted, the technology of the inventive, and the fun and frolic and misery and strivings and achievements of the masses of people—the dark cloud of slavery deeply troubled first the few and then the many.

In the 1820s the ranks of abolitionists tended to be filled by Quakers, such as the Philadelphian, Benjamin Lundy. Then in Boston in 1831 a journeyman printer named William Lloyd Garrison founded *The Liberator*, a new kind of abolitionist paper, new because it carried an unprecedented tone of moral urgency. Garrison could see no good in the legal sanctions protecting slavery in half the country. Constitutionalism meant far less to him than securing freedom for his fellow human beings. It was no happenstance that Garrison's insistence on this reform occurred at the very time when other movers and shakers were spurring other reforms—both religious and secular.

According to Garrison's concept of Christianity, slavery was sinful. As *The Liberator's* editor, he was motivated primarily by this sinfulness. Fervent in his conviction, he attacked the Constitution as "a covenant with death and an agreement with hell" and called for an immediate end to slavery. It was hardly surprising that most "respectable" northerners would not subscribe to what was seen as extremism in a day when John Quincy Adams, himself against slavery but no Garrisonian, described the abolitionist faction as small and shallow.

Garrison was persistent, however. In 1843, he began the first of 22 terms as president of the American Anti-Slavery Society. The seed nourished by Garrison and fellow abolitionists eventually flowered in the emancipation of blacks from bondage. Long depicted in historical writing as a fanatic, Garrison is now regarded as one of the era's most influential reformers, primarily but not exclusively for his abolitionism. He also espoused women's rights and pacifism.

Yet, it must be stated that it would be the possibility of slavery's westward extension—rather than the existence of slavery in states where it was legal—to which millions of Northerners would strenuously object from the outbreak of the Mexican War forward. The approach to the slavery issue of Abraham Lincoln and other political leaders was anything but that of Garrison.

Second only to Garrison in national fame among abolitionists, perhaps, was Frederick Douglass, an African American who had escaped from slavery and become an agent of the Massachusetts Anti-Slavery Society. Of commanding appearance and a gifted orator, Douglass established an antislavery paper—the *North Star*—and was well received by both American and British audiences. Another well-known black abolitionist was the eloquent Charles L. Remond, born free, who for a time rivaled Douglass on abolitionist platforms. Black clergymen also had significant parts in the antislavery cause. Two, the Presbyterian Henry H. Garnet and the Congregationalist Samuel R. Ward, held pastorates in upstate New York but were known chiefly as abolition spokesmen. Finally, there were a number of clubs composed of black women abolitionists; and two women, Frances Watkins Harper and the former slave Sojourner Truth were touring anti-slavery lecturers.

THE LITERARY ANTECEDENTS TO CIVIL WAR

From 1833 on, the New England Quaker, John Greenleaf Whittier, contributed poems and prose to the abolitionists' campaign. Longfellow in 1842 published a few antislavery poems but never became a Garrison adherent. James Russell Lowell wrote for the *National Anti-Slavery Standard*. Other younger authors—Thoreau, Melville, and Walt Whitman—were repelled by slavery and said so. Then, while Holmes and Hawthorne continued to abstain from the agitation, Emerson swung around in the 1850s to laud the abolitionist crusader John Brown and to compare Brown's gallows—Brown was executed after being captured in the attempt to lead a slave revolt in 1859—to the cross of Jesus.

It was a powerful novel, however, that proved to be the most effective tool deployed by any of those who opposed slavery. Written by Harriet Beecher Stowe—daughter, wife, and sister of Calvinist ministers and a woman abundantly aware of her own New England conscience—*Uncle Tom's Cabin* (1852) provided a searing indictment of "the peculiar institution." Stowe contended that God inspired the book, which depicted the separation of families, maternal loss, and other evils inherent in slavery. Inspired or not, it turned out to be the greatest work of propaganda ever written by an American, selling hundreds of thousands of copies and imbuing the anti-slavery crusade with a moral fervor that captured Northern attention and sympathy in an unprecedented way. Truly, it changed the nature of the discourse Stowe's treatment of slavery caused many Americans to

Harriet Beecher Stowe

see, for the first time, blacks as human and face the inhumanity of slavery. Southern fiction produced by way of reply had no comparable punch, though it is noteworthy that the sectional conflict was fought with words before it was fought with bullets.

The ablest Southern arguments were in essay form and came mostly from politicians and educators. Many slaveholders agreed with John C. Calhoun and William Harper of South Carolina and Thomas R. Dew of Virginia that far from being harmful, slavery was a positive good. Other Southerners merely saw—or thought they saw—a practical necessity for retaining the slave labor system.

When *The Impending Crisis of the South,* a book attacking slavery on economic grounds, was published in 1857, its author, Hinton R. Helper of North Carolina, was bitterly assailed by Southerners. On the other hand, those who denounced Helper warmly praised the writings of a Virginian, George Fitzhugh, in the 1850s. In *Sociology for the South*, Fitzhugh said slavery was a social, political, and economic blessing—and avowed that people trying to eliminate it were blind to Southern realities.

ALEXIS DE TOCQUEVILLE'S AMERICA

Alexis de Tocqueville, the young French magistrate who spent nine months in the United States in 1831 and 1832, has been mentioned previously for his views on life in America. His noteworthy contribution to political science, sociology, and history was *Democracy in America* (1835). He concluded that American democracy was functioning successfully; that its success depended chiefly on separation of church and state and on the absence of centralization; that American political morality was important; and that American democracy was not for export to Europe until such time as Europeans elevated their standards of governmental morality.

Prints of Uncle Tom's Cabin

The Frenchman was particularly struck by what he saw as an American tendency toward the practical, an avoidance of traditions, and an optimistic hope that in the new social system people would be able to progress rapidly toward perfection. One of his principal theses was that the American system of government derived from a dominant principle—the will of the people—that had been felt all during the nation's history.

The French magistrate, who stayed long enough to look around thoroughly and to reflect on what he saw and heard, was by no means oblivious to problems involved in the questions of slavery and race. "The most formidable of all the ills which threaten the future existence of the Union," he wrote, "arises from the presence of a black population upon its territory; and in contemplating the cause of the present embarrassments or of the future dangers of the United States, the observer is invariably led to consider this as a primary fact."

Social mobility was a feature of American life that intrigued de Tocqueville. He believed that, with one exception, such mobility would prevent both class stratification and extreme social conflict resulting from it. This exception he found in black-white relationships. If and when Southern blacks "are raised to the level of freemen," he predicted, "they will soon revolt at being deprived of almost all their civil rights; and as they cannot become the equals of the whites, they will speedily show themselves as enemies." Northern whites, he observed, "Avoided the Negroes with increasing care in proportion as the legal barriers of separation are removed."

The French observer was not without other doubts concerning the American experiment. He saw a potential danger to freedom of the individual in the possibility that majorities would crush minorities or nibble away at minority rights. He also thought he discerned a trend toward mediocrity in popular leaders and in American culture—this in a country where Emerson, Fuller, Thoreau, Hawthorne, Melville, Stowe, and Lincoln all were living when de Tocqueville's book went to press. Still, while the French visitor guessed wrong at times, he was remarkably correct in the aggregate.

CHAPTER

10

THE GROWTH OF DEMOCRATIC GOVERNMENT, 1824–1844

THE ELECTION OF 1824

Four Political Factions
Adams Defeats Jackson

THE J. Q. ADAMS INTERLUDE

Adams in the White House
Democratic Republicans, National
  Republicans
Foreign Relations

JACKSON TRIUMPHANT

The Election of 1828
"King Mob"
Andrew Jackson: Man of the People
Reorganization of the Cabinet
Changing Problems, Changing
  Arguments
Webster's "Second Reply to Hayne"
Two Controversial Vetoes
The Election of 1832

"KING ANDREW"

Crisis Over Nullification
The United States Bank
Hard Money and Land

Jackson's Foreign Policy
The Supreme Court

**JACKSONIAN DEMOCRACY—
  A LOOK BACK**

The Influence of Economic Factors

Characteristics of Jacksonian
 Democracy
Evaluation of Jackson's Administration

DEMOCRATS AND WHIGS

The Election of 1836
The Panic of 1837

The Caroline Affair
Tippecanoe and Tyler Too
President Without a Party
The Webster-Ashburton Treaty
Return of the Democrats
Features of American Democratic
Growth

THE ELECTION OF 1824

FOUR POLITICAL FACTIONS

The sands of political allegiance never shifted more swiftly than in the last year and a half of James Monroe's administration, when the "Good Feelings" in the immediate aftermath of the War of 1812 degenerated into feuding so intense that the historian Sean Wilentz has recently labeled the period "The Era of Bad Feelings." Yet, there was still, for practical purposes, only one political party. Although the Federalist Party continued to exist for a while in enclaves like Delaware, most citizens called themselves Republicans, including the four leading candidates for the presidency in 1824.

Before 1824, the congressional caucus of the Republican majority had chosen the party's presidential candidates, but during Monroe's second administration the caucus—as a means of choosing Presidential candidates—met with increasing opposition. The public looked on the caucus as undemocratic and sought a reform in much the same spirit as the other efforts toward reforms discussed in Chapter 9. Moreover, since launching of the new nation, there had been an increasing groundswell of democratic organizing that had found its chief expression at the local and state levels—as Wilentz brilliantly demonstrates in *The Rise of American Democracy*—but which was poised to make itself felt at the national level in the mid-1820s.

There was also growing conviction that it was not in the country's best interest for a newly elected President to feel that he owed his office to Congress. This provides an excellent example of the evolution of the American party system, for criticism of the caucus eventually led to establishment of national party conventions in the 1830s.

Politicians, impressed by the strenuous objections against the caucus, moved to dissociate themselves from it. In a number of states either the legislature or state conventions nominated their own favorite sons, and a full three quarters of the states elected candidates by popular vote. The result was that when the Republican caucus was held in February 1824 only 66 of the 216 Republican congressmen even attended.

The caucus chose Secretary of the Treasury William H. Crawford, a Georgian, as their candidate. Most of Crawford's strength was in the Southeast, and his rivals and their many followers scorned his selection. New England supported John Quincy Adams of Massachusetts, son of John Adams and Secretary of State in Monroe's cabinet. Kentucky, Missouri, and Ohio looked to Speaker of the House Henry Clay of Kentucky. Meanwhile, Pennsylvania, most of the West, and some of the Southeast rallied behind "Old Hickory," General Andrew Jackson of Tennessee, the famous hero of New Orleans. Secretary of War John C. Calhoun of South Carolina also had supporters; but finding his support to be insufficient to win, he dropped out of the race early, seeking the vice-presidency instead.

ADAMS DEFEATS JACKSON

The real contest in the presidential election of 1824 was between Jackson and Adams. Jackson received approximately 153,000 popular votes to Adams' 108,000 and 99 electoral votes to Adams' 84; but Crawford and Clay, with 41 and 37 electoral votes respectively, split the total sufficiently that neither Jackson nor Adams received a majority of the electoral vote.

Constitutional procedure in such cases now called for the decision to be referred to the House of Representatives. Here each state had one vote, and the three candidates with the most electoral votes—Jackson, Adams, and Crawford—remained in the running.

House Speaker Clay, no longer a presidential candidate, held the balance of power in the House decision. Although he earlier had instigated an anti-Adams campaign in the West, Clay personally disliked Jackson more than Adams and feared him as a future Western rival. As a consequence, Clay made amends with his former adversary and decided to support Adams.

With Clay's support in the House, Adams was elected on the first ballot on February 9, 1825. The new President promptly appointed Clay his Secretary of State. Just as promptly, Jacksonians angrily charged that a "corrupt bargain" accounted for both Adams' election and Clay's appointment. There probably was an implicit—if not explicit—understanding between Adams and Clay that the latter would receive the Cabinet post in exchange for his support, but no evidence exists to demonstrate corruption. In fact, whether or not such a bargain is corrupting at all, or just good Democratic politics, remains a matter of debate. The appointment of Clay was, however, an enormous political problem for the Adams administration, because it saddled both men with tarnished reputations and ensured that the new administration would commence under a cloud. To Jackson support-

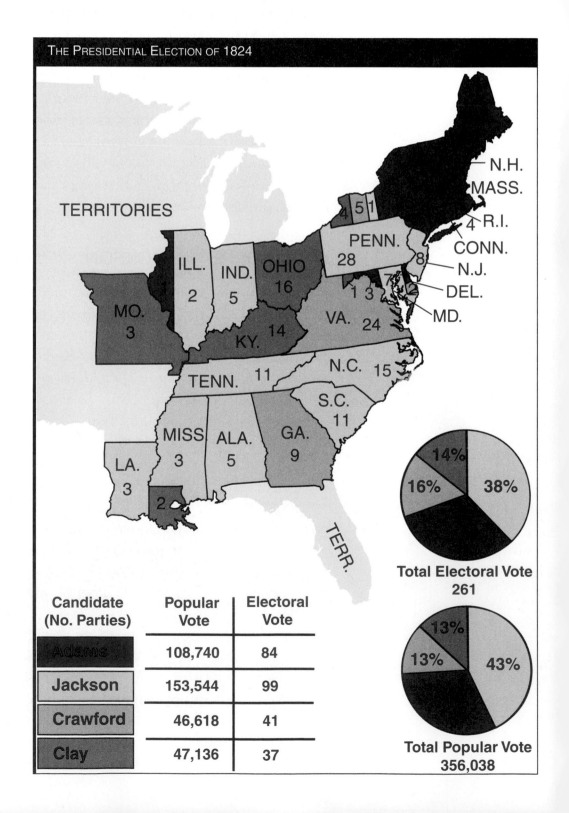

THE PRESIDENTIAL ELECTION OF 1824

Total Electoral Vote
261

Total Popular Vote
356,038

Candidate (No. Parties)	Popular Vote	Electoral Vote
Adams	108,740	84
Jackson	153,544	99
Crawford	46,618	41
Clay	47,136	37

ers, the idea that the man who won a plurality of both the popular vote and the electoral vote would not be President violated their sense of justice.

One of the often-unseen pivots of history is discernible in the election of 1824. Adams was almost exclusively a New England candidate until the New York General Assembly gave him 26 of New York's 36 electors. This resulted from tricky maneuvering by Adams' Albany managers, who were able to divert from Clay several of the electoral votes he had counted on. If Clay instead of Crawford had been the third candidate, it is possible that the popular Speaker of the House of Representatives would have appealed to his fellow representatives more than either Adams or Jackson.

THE J. Q. ADAMS INTERLUDE

ADAMS IN THE WHITE HOUSE

President Adams projected a bold domestic program. An intellectual like his father before him, in his first annual message Adams called for laws creating a national university (first proposed by Washington), a naval academy, and a national astronomical observatory. Adams likewise advocated a uniform national militia law, a uniform bankruptcy law, an orderly, federally financed system of internal improvements, and a Department of the Interior to manage America's vast public land holdings. Most of these ideas were highly imaginative; and had his program gone into effect, the second Adams today would be identified with legislation of those kinds.

Such accomplishments, however, simply were not forthcoming. From the outset Adams made little effort to push his policies once he had enunciated them. A principal cause of this failure was his view that the executive should abstain from what he considered undue interference in the legislative branch. As a

John Quincy Adams

consequence, numerous White House proposals, made year after year, were never introduced in Congress as legislative bills or resolutions. This is in spite of the fact that Adams was endowed with a sharp mind and a Puritan work ethic that had him awake and working at 4:00 a.m. daily. Adams wrote so much as President that he learned to write with both hands so as to alleviate writer's cramp.

Despite his work ethic and intellectual prowess, Adams had personal defects that prevented his being a natural leader. A man of determined character and possessed of a high degree of moral rectitude, Adams was aloof and unpleasant toward many associates, disliked public contact, and was incapable of appearing to good advantage when little knots of admirers gathered to greet him on his limited travels. Though a man with his diplomatic background should have overcome such traits, he could appear ungracious and petty in the most minor human relations.

Compounding such personal handicaps were continuing complexities as to what was constitutional and what was not. Politicians had conflicting ideas on (1) what the federal government's role in the economy should be and (2) how much authority the federal government should have over the states. While these problems were not peculiar to the period 1825–1829, the White House provided no strong directing force toward helping to solve them.

Disagreements among senators and representatives over the construction of the Constitution, coupled with their local interests, contributed to Congress' refusal to develop a systematic national public works program. This was one of Adams' greatest disappointments. Furthermore, Congressional appropriations followed no logical pattern, and legislative logrolling—the exchange of favors among lawmakers—left undone some of the most necessary projects.

Despite this slapdash approach, however, internal improvements during Adams' tenure were significant. Rivers were dredged and harbors made more serviceable with more federal appropriations voted for those purposes than in the previous 30 years. Lack of funds had halted work on the National Road in 1818, but new federal money permitted construction to resume in 1825. By mid-century this important highway stretched from Cumberland, Maryland, to Vandalia, Illinois.

DEMOCRATIC REPUBLICANS, NATIONAL REPUBLICANS

Off to an inauspicious start in the first half of his term, Adams was hopelessly beset after 1826 by a congressional coalition fighting him at every turn. The old Republican Party was no more. Increasingly,

Jackson people were known as Democratic Republicans, and Adams-Clay people as National Republicans. Jacksonians would not forget that a "deal" had made Adams President despite the electorate's clear preference for Jackson. Sectional hostilities were increasing, and states' rights adherents opposed Adams' bold plans to expand federal authority. Political idealists might praise Adams for being one of the least dominating of all our chief executives, but his effectiveness suffered for this very reason. His opponents played politics to the hilt, especially after they came to control Congress.

Sectionalism and partisanship were most flagrant in the area of tariff debates and tariff votes. One reason for the passage of the tariff of 1824, enacted while President Monroe was still in office, had been its inclusion of duties on raw wool and other farm products. These schedules were attractive to the West, but Eastern manufacturers of woolen textiles complained that their profits diminished because raw materials were so expensive. Yet in 1827 a bill containing a compromise that was supposedly acceptable to both Northeast and Northwest was defeated in the Senate by Vice-President Calhoun's tie-breaking vote.

Original Senate Chamber, restored in 1976

The next year a tariff crisis occurred that would lead to others. In drafting the tariff bill of that year, Jacksonians in Congress gave top priorities to the protectionist features desired by Middle Atlantic states, where Jackson hoped for strong support in the next presidential election. His congressional friends virtually ignored New England interests, assuming that Adams' fellow New Englanders could not avoid voting for a high tariff in any case., but the measure was offensive to a wide variety of individuals and sections, especially the Southeast.

Painted into a corner by the shrewd strategy, Adams signed the bill with loathing. Then, because of his signature, he—not the Jacksonians—bore most of the blame for it. Thereafter, his name was associated with what critics appropriately labeled the "Tariff of Abominations."

FOREIGN RELATIONS

Adams' background in diplomacy had led his supporters to believe he would leave a memorable record in foreign affairs, yet he achieved nothing as President on a par with his earlier success as Secretary of State. During his presidency, the United States failed to obtain from England the right of free navigation of the St. Lawrence River. Furthermore, American shippers had to resort to a roundabout trade when the ports of the British West Indies were closed in 1826, as tightly as they had ever been, to Yankee merchantmen. Adams retaliated by closing American ports to England, with the result that American trade with England diminished precipitously; and the American economy sagged as a result.

Other diplomatic problems also went unsolved during the Adams years. Old claims against France for damages arising out of the wars of the French Revolution were no nearer settlement in 1829 than in 1825. Additionally, though delegates were sent to the Congress of Panama in 1826, which had been called for the purpose of establishing cooperation among the republics of the Western Hemisphere, one died en route to Panama, and the other arrived too late, so the mission accomplished nothing.

In the entire field of foreign relations, Adams could point with pride only to an unprecedented number of minor treaties and to the renewal in 1827 of the Anglo-American agreement covering joint occupation of Oregon.

JACKSON TRIUMPHANT

THE ELECTION OF 1828

The election of 1828 has long been seen as a watershed in American political history, owing partially to the vastly increased voter turnout that year; but it also marked the beginning of a new era, because it was the first presidential election after two momentous deaths that occurred on July 4, 1826. On that day—exactly 50 years since the Declaration of Independence—both Thomas Jefferson and John Adams died. Washington having died in 1799, the country had now lost its first three presidents—its most important living links with the Revolution. Moreover, his awe-inspiring father would no longer be around to challenge—and sometimes torment—John Quincy Adams.

Even if Adams' personality had been more attractive, his attitude more gracious, and his leadership more compelling, he would have had trouble in any contest with the forces arrayed against him. As early as 1825, the general assembly of Tennessee placed Andrew Jackson on the track for the 1828 presidential race. Moreover, except for New England, enthusiasm for Jackson appeared everywhere. From New York to Illinois and from Pennsylvania to Louisiana, acclaim for Jackson reverberated. Furthermore, Jackson had impressive allies. Vice-President Calhoun, an outstanding South Carolinian who had been Monroe's Secretary of War, did little to conceal his antipathy toward Adams. Another important addition to the Jackson high command was Senator Martin Van Buren of New York. Formerly a Crawford lieutenant, the ingratiating Van Buren worked dexterously with Calhoun and others to weld a powerful combination of Southerners and Northerners opposing Adams and favoring Jackson. The combination was especially powerful in that it included both established men and those representing popular democratic movements.

In the 1828 election, backers of both Adams and Jackson indulged in disreputable tactics. Pro-Adams journalists made much of Jackson's reputation for military highhandedness. They dragged the name of Mrs. Jackson through the gutters of partisan filth by reminding voters that her divorce from another man had not been final in the 1790s when she became Jackson's wife. Furthermore, Jackson's detractors pointed out that there was no record of Jackson's actual marriage to Rachel and argued, therefore, that he was "living in sin." This

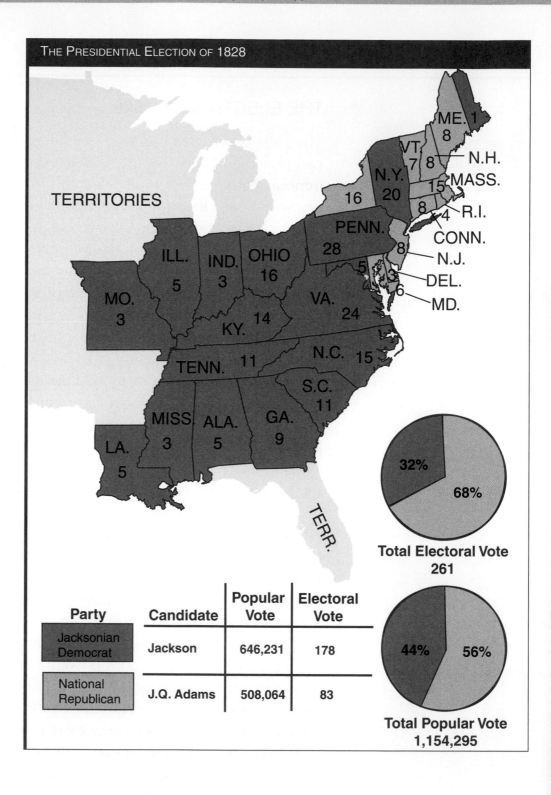

THE PRESIDENTIAL ELECTION OF 1828

TERRITORIES

ME. 1
8
VT 7 8 N.H.
N.Y. 15 MASS.
16 20 8 4 R.I.
PENN. CONN.
28 8 N.J.
5 DEL.
6 MD.

ILL. IND. OHIO
5 3 16
MO.
3
VA.
24
KY. 14
TENN. 11
N.C. 15
S.C. 11
MISS. ALA. GA.
3 5 9
LA.
5
TERR.

32%
68%

**Total Electoral Vote
261**

44% 56%

**Total Popular Vote
1,154,295**

Party	Candidate	Popular Vote	Electoral Vote
Jacksonian Democrat	Jackson	646,231	178
National Republican	J.Q. Adams	508,064	83

infuriated Jackson and Jackson "remarried" Rachel during the campaign so as to satisfy the critics. The underhanded publicity and criticism may have had something to do with Mrs. Jackson's death from a heart attack soon after the election. Pro-Jackson editors, however, were no innocent bystanders when the mud was slung; and Adams was pilloried as a billiards-playing aristocrat out of touch with the plain people. That Jackson himself was a wealthy plantation owner was beside the point.

Substantive issues were not entirely ignored. Since the country had not reached the period of national conventions and platforms, there was no formal enunciation of principles; but Jackson in some minds was linked with proposals for tariff reform, and Adams—fairly or unfairly—with the Tariff of Abominations. Critics of the Second Bank of the United States hoped that Jackson, as President, would oppose it. Some advocates of the federally funded construction of roads and canals and the dredging of rivers and harbors preferred Adams because he had spoken out in favor of federal appropriations for these purposes. Yet, there was no unanimity here; others believed that Jackson would support federal funding for internal improvements more heartily than Adams.

If serious citizens held serious opinions, a simple "Hurrah for Jackson!" was the rallying cry that appealed to most Americans. About three times as many people voted in 1828 as four years before, and the results were recorded with more care. Jackson, the Democratic-Republican candidate, scored a clear triumph with approximately 647,000 popular votes to 508,000 for Adams. In the Electoral College the margin was two to one, with 178 votes for Jackson and 83 for Adams. This growth in the size of the electorate reflected population growth, an increased turnout of eligible voters, *and* a growth in the size of the pool of those eligible to vote, so that the pool was now composed of all adult white males. That property qualifications had been more or less eliminated by this time in many states represented the fruit of decades of democratic struggle by urban mechanics and small farmers in many parts of the country.

"KING MOB"

Jackson's inauguration in March 1829 was accompanied by a demonstration unparalleled in American history. The thousands of people assembled in Washington behaved well outside the Capitol while Jackson read his inaugural address; but when the time came for the White House reception, "King Mob" took over. Men, women, and children crashed, trampled, and crushed their way in muddy boots and shoes into and through the mansion. Only when someone thought of placing refreshments on the White House lawn did the crowd move outdoors.

Jackson's political enemies were shocked by this public demonstration. They talked darkly of a reenactment of French Revolution excesses on American soil. Actually, the scene had been more a

The inauguration of President Andrew Jackson in 1829

matter of bad manners and an explosion of pent-up energy than anything else. The base of governmental support had broadened appreciably in the past few years, but no excesses other than social ones upset the evolutionary development of an increasingly democratic state. Nevertheless, when the multitude faded away shortly after inauguration day, the symbol of "King Mob" remained as a counterweight to "King Caucus" of old.

ANDREW JACKSON: MAN OF THE PEOPLE

Andrew Jackson resonated so well with the common people partially because of his humble roots. Though Jackson was a wealthy planter at the time of his election, he was born in a humble log cabin in North Carolina and made his reputation as the hero of the Battle of New Orleans and one of the country's greatest Native American fighters. Jackson also connected with the common people through his speech, which was laden with incorrect grammar like that of the common people. Jackson had little formal education, was a poor writer, and an atrocious speller. Like the common people that loved him, Jackson also chewed tobacco incessantly, spitting tobacco juice into spittoons while entertaining guests at the White House.

Jackson also had a deserved reputation as a real-life tough guy. In the words of one of Jackson's fellow law students, he was the "most roaring, rollicking, game-cocking, horse racing, card playing, mischievous fellow." His nickname was "Old Hickory" because hickory was such a hard wood. Jackson also had a very Southern sense of honor,

Major General Andrew Jackson, seventh president of the United States

which he said he got from his mother who told him to "never lie, cheat, steal, or sue anyone at law for insults. Handle insults to one's honor yourself." As a consequence, Jackson was twice wounded by gunshot defending his honor: once in the shoulder in a bar fight and once in the chest from a duel in 1806. The bullet from the duel lodged in Jackson's ribs (Jackson allowed his opponent to shoot first) and caused Jackson pain the rest of his life.

REORGANIZATION OF THE CABINET

The Democratic-Republican Party of 62-year-old President Jackson charted its administrative course in an atmosphere of confusion. Though Van Buren became Secretary of State, several cabinet members were more closely identified with Vice-President Calhoun than with either Jackson or Van Buren.

Almost at once there erupted one of those odd controversies that occasionally have influenced American political history, a controversy whose ramifications played themselves out over a course of two years. Secretary of War John H. Eaton, a Jackson appointee who had long been on intimate terms with the new President, had recently married a young widow whose comeliness was said to have attracted him before her first husband's death. The story goes that Mrs. Calhoun and the wives of Calhoun's cabinet friends took the lead in snubbing Mrs. Eaton. Jackson resented the social chill, associating it with the shameful treatment of his own late wife during the campaign.

Van Buren, who endeared himself to Jackson by siding with the Eatons (and who, being a widower, had no wife to consult about the matter), offered to resign from his cabinet post, knowing that a cabinet reorganization would enable Jackson to be rid of the problem. Eaton followed Van Buren's example, and in the spring of 1831 Jackson requested resignations from all the remaining cabinet members except one. Calhoun's supporters were excluded from the succeeding cabinet while Van Buren retained the confidence of Jackson, who promptly named him minister to Britain. Looked at in one way, the Eaton affair was a tempest in a teapot. On the other hand, it also demonstrates the increasing social power and moral authority of women, even when, as in this case, these phenomena were deployed in a snobbish cause. Eaton eventually resigned from the Cabinet as Washington women continued to snub his wife, Peggy. Happiness, however, did not come to the Eaton household with John's resignation; Peggy, age 59, subsequently left her husband for a 19-year-old dance instructor.

CHANGING PROBLEMS, CHANGING ARGUMENTS

Meanwhile, a more fundamental division between Jackson and Vice-President Calhoun developed over two other issues. First, the President was greatly disturbed by the discovery that, years before, Calhoun had recommended that Jackson be court-martialed for his conduct during the Seminole War of 1818. Second and more significant, Jackson hotly disapproved of Calhoun's contention that a state had the right to nullify a federal statute. It was concerning this "nullification" question that the smoldering antipathies of the two ranking officials of the country flared into the open.

The nullification stand of the Vice-President and his fellow South Carolinian, Senator Robert Y. Hayne, resulted from their state's opposition to the tariff tendencies of the United States—especially the Tariff of Abominations. They believed that while the industrial Northeast benefited, the agricultural South was damaged by the rising customs duties.

Economic conditions in the Southeast were steadily worsening. The extension of cotton planting to the rich bottomlands of Alabama, Mississippi, Louisiana, and then the Southwest expanded production of the staple; and cotton prices consequently dropped. Many planters in the Southeast, threatened with ruin by their inability to compete on relatively poor soil, pulled stakes and took their slaves to the Southwest for a fresh start. The consequent loss of population compounded the Southeast's financial difficulties. There were also political reverberations, since fewer people would mean smaller representation in Congress for South Carolina and similarly affected states.

Calhoun had lately joined Hayne and other South Carolina politicians in the conviction that most of their state's troubles could be traced to the tariff. In 1828, while running for reelection to the vice-presidency as a Jackson adherent, Calhoun had secretly written the "South Carolina Exposition." This document, published without his name, declared protective tariffs unconstitutional. It went on to assert the right of any state to "nullify" or prevent the enforcement within its boundaries of what it deemed to be an unconstitutional act of Congress. Calhoun's authorship of the "Exposition" was not generally known in 1830, but his new position was becoming clear in some minds, including Jackson's.

In 1830, the Vice-President carefully coached the less brilliant Hayne when the latter eloquently defended the extreme states' rights position in a dramatic Senate debate with Senator Daniel Webster of Massachusetts. As Massachusetts had become more industrialized and accordingly adopted a high tariff policy, Webster had abandoned his low-tariff convictions (he opposed the Tariff of 1824); and by 1830 he was a high-tariff advocate. Moreover, Webster identified Massachusetts' changed economic attitude with a political nationalism that contrasted with the growing sectionalism of South Carolina. In so doing, he sought to equate the North's economic interest with patriotic virtue.

The famous Senate debate of 1830 arose as the result of a resolution by Connecticut Senator Samuel A. Foot, which had as one aim a restriction of the sale of public land. The land question was a vital matter to congressmen from the West. Current land laws, in effect since the early 1820s, provided for (1) a minimum purchase of 80 acres, (2) a minimum price of $1.25 an acre, (3) no credit system, and (4) exceptions which recognized but did not wholly satisfy Western insistence on lower land prices and on the preemption principle by which genuine settlers would have the first chance to buy at the minimum price. Already in the air were proposals for liberalizing land policies. Eastern laborers joined Western farmers in favoring such liberalization, and Southerners saw an advantage in linking Western land desires to Southern low-tariff hopes. Thus the opposition to Foot's restrictive resolution was not limited to any single section.

Senator Thomas H. Benton of Missouri resoundingly assailed the Foot Resolution. Benton saw it as a scheme of New England manufacturers, fearful of losing factory operatives to the lure of the West, to make cheap land inaccessible and so keep their workers in the East. Hayne took the issue to Benton's supporters, but took a different approach. If Foot's proposition were put into effect, he said, future prices of Western land would be high. The income would then constitute "a fund for corruption," adding to the power of the federal government and endangering the independence of the states. Thereupon Webster launched his first reply to Hayne. Denying that the East was illiberal toward the West, the erstwhile sectionalist from Boston proclaimed his nationalism.

Hayne again spoke, reminding his listeners of New England's anti-Union attitude during the War of 1812. Where, he asked, were New England nationalists then? Had not residents of Webster's section, plotters of the Hartford Convention, favored the same constitutional arguments contained in the "South Carolina Exposition"? The Northeastern sectionalists of old, Hayne insisted, currently championed theories that they formerly had decried. Their sincerity, he implied, was open to grave doubts, and their past words and tactics hovered as reminders of appalling inconsistencies.

WEBSTER'S "SECOND REPLY TO HAYNE"

After Hayne spiritedly elaborated on the extreme states' rights point of view, Webster answered him in what is widely regarded as the greatest speech ever delivered in Congress. In New England, he said, what Hayne had discussed was consigned to a bygone time. New Englanders were thinking not of the past but of the present and the future. Vital now was the wellbeing of America as a whole. Nothing could be more preposterous than the idea that 24 states could interpret the Constitution as each of them saw fit. The Union should not be "dissevered, discordant, belligerent." The country should not be "rent with civil feuds, or drenched … in fraternal blood." It was delusion and folly to think of "Liberty first, and Union afterwards." Instead, "dear to every true American heart" was that blazing sentiment—"Liberty *and* Union, now and forever, one and inseparable!"

In bygone days, countless young Americans memorized the peroration of Webster's "Second Reply to Hayne," regarded at the time and subsequently in the nineteenth century as a particularly eloquent statement of democratic nationalism. Calhoun, the idea man for Hayne, had morphed from an ardent defender of a strong central government to a defender of states rights in order to protect his key constituency, the South Carolina planters, while Webster had gone in the other direction.

Calhoun and Jackson succeeded Hayne and Webster in the public spotlight during the spring of the same year, 1830, when a Jefferson birthday banquet was held in Washington's Indian Queen Hotel. Jackson offered fellow Democratic-Republicans a toast: "The Federal Union, it must be preserved!" Calhoun countered with a toast of his own: "The Union, next to our liberty, most dear!" The disparate sentiments were not lost upon the diners. The President had hurled down the gauntlet, and the Vice-President had picked it up. After that,

Daniel Webster

their relations became ever more strained; and before Jackson's first term ended, Calhoun had resigned the vice-presidency.

TWO CONTROVERSIAL VETOES

Jackson sternly opposed the Bank of the United States and objected to most proposals to use federal funds for internal improvements. The improvements question loomed large in 1830, when Congress passed a bill authorizing subscription of stock in a private company constructing a road between Maysville and Lexington, Kentucky. Jackson vetoed the proposition on the ground that the Maysville Road lay wholly in one state and therefore was not entitled to financial support from Washington.

Jackson's controversial veto seemed tyrannical to many, and enemies dubbed him "King Andrew." Henry Clay and other transportation-minded Americans charged the President with being an impediment in the march of progress. Clay, it should be noted, was the prime advocate of the so-called "American System," a plan that encompassed a national bank, high tariffs, and federal aid for internal improvements. The veto, however, was well received by Southern strict constructionists and by others resentful of what they deemed undue interference by the federal government in purely state affairs. Moreover, Jackson's selection of a Western road as a target of his disapproval pleased those in New York and Pennsylvania who had financed their own projects locally and saw no reason why people in other regions should get the kind of Washington help they themselves had failed to obtain.

Jackson was hostile to the Bank of the United States for at least four reasons. First, he held the Jeffersonian strict-construction view, maintaining that Congress was not empowered by the Constitution to incorporate a bank outside the District of Columbia (in spite of the fact that the Supreme Court had ruled the Bank constitutional in 1819 in *McColloch v. Maryland*). Jackson also doubted that the Bank would serve the nation's welfare and accused it of not having established a sound and uniform currency. His third objection was that the Bank played politics in election campaigns and influenced congressmen by lending them money or placing them on its payroll. Finally, Old Hickory had an ingrained suspicion of the note issues of all banks—with the Bank of the United States the most notorious offender because it was far and away the most powerful. Jackson erroneously argued that foreigners controlled the bank.

Moreover, it should be noted that there was a political payoff to the antibank stance: one of the key elements of the Jacksonian constituency, the urban workingmen, tended to see the Bank as an un-democratic monopoly, and these workers were organizing into parties in cities such as New York and Philadelphia. (We will deal more with workers in the following chapter.)

To be fair, under Nicholas Biddle's leadership the Bank of the United States had made important contributions to American economic stability. Regardless of what Jackson said, it did provide a sound currency; and its monetary standards and the financial power it wielded often exerted a salutary effect on the fluctuating currencies of state banks—many of which were dangerously weak. However, the charge of political activity and legislative influence was, for the most part, warranted. Jackson came to consider the Bank a monopoly; but though government deposits were exclusively entrusted to it, the Bank was not a monopolistic enterprise in the customary sense of the term.

The Bank's charter had four years to run in 1832; but Clay, now a United States senator, was in full accord with Bank President Biddle's desire to see the institution rechartered long in advance of the legal deadline. Clay pushed a Bank Bill through both houses of Congress. Then, chosen by the National Republicans as their standard bearer in opposition to Jackson, he strove to make the Bank the main issue in the campaign of 1832. Jackson lost no time in vetoing the rechartering act in July 1832. Thus he and Clay set the stage for a showdown on the issue.

THE ELECTION OF 1832

It can be argued that Clay was handicapped in his presidential race by the existence of an Anti-Masonic third party that considered the Masonic fraternity an aristocratic threat to democratic institutions and objected to both Jackson and Clay because they were Masons.

The Anti-Masons nominated William Wirt of Maryland, himself ironically also a Mason and for 12 years Attorney General under Monroe and Adams. They chose their candidate by a party convention, foreshadowing the method soon to be adopted by all the parties. The National Republicans' choice was Clay, while the Democratic-Republicans (now beginning to be called Democrats) of course were for Jackson, with Van Buren as his running mate. In most states the anti-Jackson following was concentrated behind either Clay or Wirt, with the other man staying out of the contest. Even with this tactical advantage, neither Clay nor Wirt had a very good chance to oust the popular Jackson. Furthermore, the Bank issue did not aid Clay as he had anticipated it would.

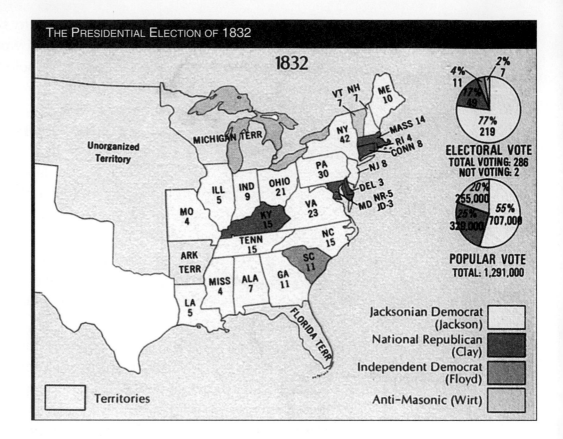

THE PRESIDENTIAL ELECTION OF 1832

1832

Unorganized Territory

MICHIGAN TERR

VT 7 NH 7 ME 10

NY 42

MASS 14
RI 4
CONN 8

PA 30

NJ 8

ILL 5 IND 9 OHIO 21

DEL 3
MD NR-5 JD-3

MO 4

VA 23

KY 15

TENN 15

NC 15

ARK TERR

SC 11

MISS 4 ALA 7 GA 11

LA 5

FLORIDA TERR

4% 11   2% 7
17% 49
77% 219

ELECTORAL VOTE
TOTAL VOTING: 286
NOT VOTING: 2

20% 255,000
25% 329,000
55% 707,000

POPULAR VOTE
TOTAL: 1,291,000

Jacksonian Democrat (Jackson)
National Republican (Clay)
Independent Democrat (Floyd)
Anti-Masonic (Wirt)

Territories

Not all historians agree on the exact size of the popular vote. It is clear, however, that Jackson won easily; his popular vote was approximately 687,500 against 530,000 for Clay and Wirt combined. Jackson was victorious in nearly the entire South and West, plus the "big" states of New York and Pennsylvania. In the Electoral College, Jackson scored 219 to Clay's 49 and Wirt's 7. South Carolina, still voting through its legislature, refused to back any of the regular candidates and cast 11 protest ballots for John Floyd of Virginia.

"KING ANDREW"

CRISIS OVER NULLIFICATION

No sooner was the 1832 election decided than South Carolina brought the nullification controversy to a head. The issue immediately in question was the Tariff of 1832, which lowered customs duties but not enough to satisfy critics in the Palmetto State. The newly elected state legislature, composed predominantly of "nullifiers," ordered a special state convention to deal with the problem. The convention met in Columbia in November and took three major steps: It declared the tariffs of 1828 and 1832 null and void within South Carolina, called on the state legislature to prohibit collection of duties in the state after February 1, 1833, and warned that South Carolina would secede if the federal government used force to collect duties.

Jackson responded to South Carolina's saber rattling by dispatching naval and military units to that state and issuing a stirring Nullification Proclamation, which declared in part:

> I consider, then, the power to annul a law of the United States, assumed by one State, incompatible with the existence of the Union, contradicted expressly by the letter of the Constitution, unauthorized by its spirit, inconsistent with every principle on which it was founded, and destructive of the great object for which it was formed.

Possible bloodshed was averted when Senator Clay of Kentucky sponsored a compromise tariff bill providing for a gradual reduction of duties year by year until 1842. Though the protectionist New England and Middle Atlantic states bitterly opposed such a tariff reduction, Congress passed the compromise bill and Jackson signed it on March 2, 1833. On the same day, a Force Bill—giving Jackson congressional authority to use arms to enforce collection of customs—became law.

The Compromise Tariff of 1833 was much more reasonable by South Carolina's standards than preceding tariffs had been. The Columbia convention met once again and withdrew its nullification ordinance, but as a face-saving gesture the convention nullified Jackson's Force Bill. The President regarded this last defiant act as of little practical significance. Both sides now considered the issue closed, and both claimed victory.

THE UNITED STATES BANK

Jackson, interpreting his success in the 1832 election as a mandate from the voters to continue action against the Bank of the United States, decided to remove federal deposits from the Bank gradually and deposit them in selected state banks. An order to this effect was issued on September 26, 1833; and when Secretary of the Treasury Duane refused to carry it out, Jackson replaced him with Roger B. Taney, until then Attorney General. By the end of the year 23 state banks—dubbed "pet banks" by anti-Jacksonians—had been selected as depositories.

Jackson's move against the Bank met with considerable political opposition, and his policy was attacked in Congress. In December

1833 Henry Clay introduced Senate resolutions to censure both the Treasury action and the President for having "assumed upon himself authority and power not conferred by the constitution and laws, but in derogation of both." By the spring of 1834 President Jackson's opponents even had a new name: the Whig party. This name played off the idea that Jackson was acting as if he were "King Andrew", because it was the Whig party in Britain that espoused the limiting of royal power.

When the Senate resolutions were adopted, Jackson formally protested that that body had charged him with an impeachable offense but denied him an opportunity to defend himself. The Senate, however, rejected Jackson's protest and, as a further measure of defiance, would not approve Taney's nomination as Secretary of the Treasury. Only after a three-year Senate battle did Jackson's supporters succeed in having the resolution of censure expunged from the Senate record. Nevertheless, in eliminating the Bank of the United States, Jackson had eliminated a security measure against a banking crisis and rendered the banking system more volatile.

HARD MONEY AND LAND

Jackson's Bank policy contributed to a series of severe nationwide economic reverses. Even though the administration withdrew federal funds from the United States Bank only gradually, using them to meet current expenses while depositing new revenue in "pet banks," the Bank's decline was sharp enough to touch off an economic recession in 1833–1834. Nicholas Biddle's actions aggravated the situation: To make up for the lost federal deposits and to force congressional reconsideration of the Bank's charter, Biddle took the unnecessarily harsh step of calling in outstanding loans, thus creating demands for credit from state banks which they could not meet. Only under strong pressure from businessmen and from the governor of Pennsylvania did Biddle at last reverse his policy.

The country pulled out of the economic doldrums and almost immediately headed into a dangerous inflationary spiral. States chartered hundreds of new private banks, each issuing its own banknotes and each setting its own interest rates, which were typically much higher than prior to Jackson's bank veto. These factors, along with an influx of silver from Mexican mines, caused prices to rise 50 percent between 1834 and 1837. State banks also used their newly acquired federal funds for speculative purposes. At the same time, the federal government greatly increased its sale of public land, inadvertently encouraging the most reckless speculators.

Although political leaders were divided in their reaction to the inflationary trend, Jackson agreed with Senator Benton's prediction that "the present bloat in the paper system" could foreshadow another depression. On July 11, 1836, Jackson chose to issue a Specie Circular, which provided that after August 15 all public lands purchased from the federal government were to be paid for only in gold or silver, with one exception: Until December 15 people actually settling on the land were permitted to use state bank notes to purchase parcels of land up to 320 acres. The impact of Jackson's action was to greatly diminish the value of the money supply since paper banknotes could not be used to purchase federal land.

Jackson's sudden policy reversal sharply curtailed western land sales and weakened public confidence in the state banks. It encouraged the hoarding of specie (hard money) and was a factor in bringing on the Panic of 1837.

The western land problem figured repeatedly in congressional debates from Jackson's day to Lincoln's and beyond. Benton and other Westerners favored the policy of "graduation," by which prices for the less desirable portions of the public domain would be reduced from $1.25 an acre to $1.00, 50 cents, or less, depending on the length of time they had been on sale. Westerners also wanted the

Assassination Attempt on Andrew Jackson, 1835

policy of preemption, that favored squatters, who lived on the land, rather than speculators, who bought the land for the purpose of re-sale at a profit.

Although Congress passed no graduation bill until 1854, a temporary Preemption Act in 1830 authorized settlers to buy up to 160 acres of public land at a minimum price of $1.25 an acre. The act was renewed regularly and remained in force until 1842.

Not to be confused with preemption was Henry Clay's advocacy of "distribution." In 1833, the Kentuckian drove through both the House and Senate a bill stipulating that most of the revenue derived from public-land sales be distributed among all the states, with a smaller fraction earmarked for states where the sales took place. That was a typical example of Clay's desire to appeal politically to two sections at once. Jackson, however, pocket-vetoed the bill, thwarting his adversary and identifying himself further with the actual settlers of the Northwest and Southwest. Jackson was the first President to use the pocket veto, whereby any bill passed by Congress during the last 10 days of a session does not pass without the President's signature. Since Clay's distribution bill was passed during the last 10 days of a Congressional session, Jackson did not have to formally veto the bill to kill it. He merely did not sign the bill and thus accomplished the same result.

JACKSON'S FOREIGN POLICY

Jackson's handling of foreign affairs was at times as headstrong and unconventional as one might expect of an old border captain. The only real diplomatic crisis of his two terms concerned claims against France for seizures of American ships during the Napoleonic wars. Adams and preceding Presidents had failed to collect, but at Jackson's urging France agreed to pay $5 million in a series of indemnity installments. The first $1 million was due in 1833. When the French made no payment then or the following year, but made payment to England, Jackson viewed it as an insult to American honor and favored war with France. Jackson was ready to take coercive action, uttering, "I know them French—They won't pay unless they are made to." In December 1834, Jackson requested Congressional support for an ultimatum to France in demand of payment. Jackson also urged Congress to authorize reprisals on French property unless the money was speedily sent. The French responded with a demand for a "satisfactory explanation" of Jackson's ultimatum, which they viewed as an insult to French honor. For a few months there appeared to be danger of war, but the British offered mediation of the dispute and persuaded the French to accept Jackson's address to Congress asking for an ultimatum as an "explanation." The French desired to avoid war and accepted the British solution. Payment of the debt began in 1836.

Jackson also faced the problem of whether to recognize the independence of Texas, established in 1836. (This is a topic to be discussed more fully, along with Native American removal, in the following chapter, that deals with the West). Because Texas was a potential slave state, Jackson trod carefully in order not to inflame the American people over the slavery issue and possibly jeopardize Van Buren's presidential hopes in the election of 1836. Jackson was fearful also of angering Mexico, which insisted that Texas was still a Mexican State in rebellion and that any American interference with Texas could mean war with Mexico, a situation that Jackson sought to avoid. Though there was no question about Jackson's personal sentiment—his sympathy for the Texan revolutionists was strong—he withheld recognition from the Texas republic until the very day he left office in 1837.

THE SUPREME COURT

Andrew Jackson's most enduring influence on the Supreme Court came indirectly through the justices whom he elevated to the bench. When he retired, five of the sitting judges were his appointees. The number included slavery advocate Roger B. Taney, who had succeeded John Marshall as Chief Justice on the latter's death in 1835.

Among the principal early decisions under Taney was *Briscoe v. The Bank of Kentucky* (1837), which reduced the application of constitutional limitations on state banking and currency matters. This decision held that it was not unconstitutional for a state that owned stock to issue bank notes. More famous is *Charles River Bridge v. Warren Bridge* (1837), which stressed community responsibilities of private property and modified the contract doctrines of Marshall. In *Bank of Augusta v. Earle* (1839), the Chief Justice denied that corporations had all legal rights of natural persons. He also held that while corporations could take part in interstate commerce, any state had the right to exclude another state's corporations.

In later cases there sometimes was a lack of agreement or consistency regarding federal power to regulate commerce on the one hand and the states' internal police power on the other. This is traceable in part to the Court's changing personnel after Jackson's presidency, and in part to the alterations in Taney's own ideas.

The Supreme Court chamber. Andrew Jackson influenced the Supreme Court through the justices he appointed; five of his appointees were still sitting judges when he retired.

For many years, it was the fashion to be hypercritical of Taney's Supreme Court record. Continuing on the tribunal until he died during the Civil War, he became very unpopular in the North because of his position in favor of states' rights and because of the infamous Dred Scott decision in 1857 (see Chapter 13). Actually, the judicial philosophies and influences of Marshall and Taney had many similarities. Taney and most of his associates believed that the growing power of corporations needed supervision by states in the public interest, but they were not unsympathetic toward property rights as such. Modern authorities on judicial history see no sharp break between most constitutional interpretations of the two jurists.

JACKSONIAN DEMOCRACY—A LOOK BACK

THE INFLUENCE OF ECONOMIC FACTORS

In Jackson's time, as now, political changes were often tied to economic changes and alliances formed and reformed over economic issues. What had been the Republican Party had, by 1836, split into two parties known as Democrats and Whigs, with opposing views on government and its proper role in the economy.

To find consistency in the political actions of Democrats and Whigs is difficult, chiefly because of shifts brought about by economic factors. Daniel Webster, for example, had begun his career as a champion of New England shipping interests and free trade. After the War of 1812, however, domestic manufacturing was growing, and Webster caught the spirit of industrial progress. He and other Whigs felt that the fledgling industries needed all the government protection they could get. Thus, by the late 1820s, Webster had become an aggressive advocate of protective tariffs that would foster American industry. Besides a protected market, he and his fellow Whigs felt that industry also needed a sound banking system, which would provide a stable currency and ample credit.

Henry Clay, too, had changed his political convictions with changing times. Reared in the Virginia of Jeffersonian agrarianism, he migrated to Kentucky and was awakened to new Western economic ambitions. A spokesman for Western Whigs, Clay believed in a nationalistic program—his American System. Through federally funded internal improvements, a liberal policy of public-land sales, a central bank, and tariffs, the aim of this system was to reduce American dependence on foreign trade and provide a home market for the exchange of the North's manufactured goods and the West's agricultural products.

The Whigs felt that government aid to business would promote the economic progress and wellbeing of all Americans. The Whig party, however, also contained prominent Southern planters, though their reliance on cotton exports and low-cost imports caused them to oppose the protective tariffs advocated by the Northern Whigs. Like the leaders in other sections, those in the South took anguished turns in their search for adjustment. John C. Calhoun of South Carolina began as a "War Hawk" nationalist during the days of Jefferson and Madison. Later, he became a defender of states' rights in defiance of federal "authoritarianism." Politically, he shifted from the Democrats to the Whigs and back to the Democrats.

Jackson was able to cope with these shifting factions. With a military hero reputation that aided him in politics, he was looked upon as a champion of the plain people and an enemy of "privilege" to any one class or section. Often arbitrary in method, Jackson was at times headstrong and uncompromising, such as in the case of the Bank Veto. He did, however, at times try to find a middle ground, favoring a "judicious" tariff and avoiding the annexation of Texas so as to prevent a heightening of sectional tensions. He approved or opposed federal funding for internal improvements on the merits of

John C. Calhoun

each individual case, and he and his Democratic followers were more aware than the Whigs of the potential dangers of "monopolies".

CHARACTERISTICS OF JACKSONIAN DEMOCRACY

The policies identified with Jacksonian democracy have been associated with five major trends. First, Jacksonian democracy represented a trend toward equality and expansion of democracy, with more men participating more fully in the political process. While Jackson drew support from persons in many walks of life, common people were most inclined to identify themselves with Jackson and his policies. Second, Jacksonian democracy marked a departure from the domination of bankers and merchants, even though some bankers and merchants were steadfast Jacksonians. Third, Jacksonians were expansionists, committed to making room for white settlers on what had been Native American lands. Fourth, as seen in the South Carolina controversy, Jacksonian democrats resolutely opposed weakening the Federal union. Fifth, Jackson's followers approved Jackson's exercise of federal authority over the American economy.

To understand Jackson's influence, it is essential to understand why Jackson was so popular and what caused him to retain his popularity. The War of 1812, as we have seen, involved no other military victory on a par with Jackson's brilliant one. Fervidly admired because of his achievement, he intrigued fellow-Americans who found in him no mere child of luck but, rather, a man of iron will and ingenious battlefield prowess. Also (and this was nearly as important), he seemed to symbolize the "outs" or non-establishment people in contrast with the "ins" of Washington. He had come up in the world on his own and was a leader of forcefulness and determination—the very sort of dynamic figure who makes enemies and yet attracts hosts of followers and friends. No understanding of Jacksonian democracy can be complete without awareness of the charismatic Jackson image.

EVALUATION OF JACKSON'S ADMINISTRATION

As President, the active and dominant Jackson continued both to arouse strong adverse criticism and to inspire praise bordering on idolatry. The Tennessean's enemies did not hesitate to call him every unpleasant name in the book. They depicted him as "King Andrew," a would-be tyrant with slight regard for the ways of free people and with a ruthless intent to impose his will on the country. On the other hand, Jackson's friends (and they were a majority) loved him personally and held his political talents in the highest esteem.

In the perspective of the years, Jackson's record shows marked differences from issue to issue. Although moderation is not traditionally considered a trait of Jackson's, he was essentially a moderate on the tariff, and his attitude toward land policy was generally temperate. Though he did not block all internal improvements financed with federal funds, he was apt to be conservative or reactionary (depending on one's point of view) on projects in that category.

Many scholars have argued that Jackson's greatest mistake was his hostility to the Bank, and that his Specie Circular reflected a miscalculation in timing if not in principle. On the other hand, Jackson's foreign policy was successful, and his nationalism was tellingly asserted in opposition to the nullifiers.

A slaveholder with the manners and tastes of a Southern planter, Jackson had, nonetheless, an acute awareness of public preferences and the public interest. He also had an instinct for reaching the "common" people and for identifying their desires with his own. A simple man with a fighting heart, Jackson lived in constant pain, owing to injuries he had received in the duels he had fought. The pain contributed to an irascibility of temper. That said, it could still be concluded that Jackson judged each issue on its merits—as he understood them—and contributed vigorous leadership to every cause he championed.

Historians' opinions of Jackson, like their judgments of Jefferson and other Presidents, have changed from generation to generation. The principal recent charges against Jackson are that his Native American policy, to be discussed in the next chapter, was too harsh. Yet, indisputably, Jackson brought major long-lasting changes to American politics. Jackson ushered in the era of mass partisan politics with more people involved in the political process than ever before and mass-based political parties emerging as the driving forces of politics. Jackson also strengthened the power of the executive in a number of ways, but among them was his use of the veto for something other than "unconstitutional" legislation and his use of the pocket veto. Prior to Jackson, the veto had been used only nine times in American history—all on legislation that the vetoing Presidents viewed as unconstitutional. Jackson, himself, used the veto 12 times, more than all previous Presidents combined, and used the veto on bills that he simply opposed but did not consider unconstitutional.

DEMOCRATS AND WHIGS

THE ELECTION OF 1836

As Jackson's second term neared its end, Vice-President Martin Van Buren was the Democratic presidential nominee and received the endorsement of Andrew Jackson. The Whig opposition, tried to throw the contest into the House of Representatives by sponsoring several candidates on a regional basis. Van Buren faced Daniel Webster in the Northeast, Ohio's William Henry Harrison in the Northwest,

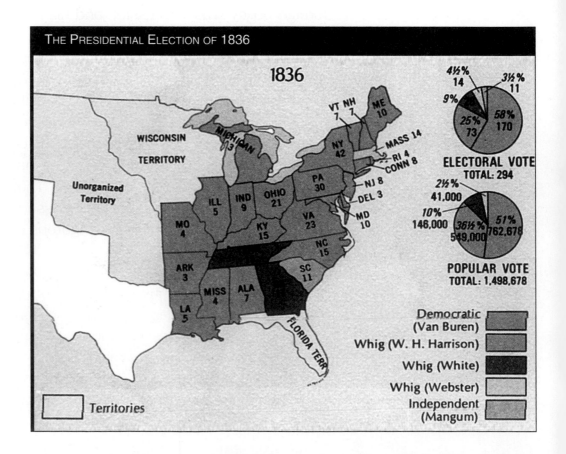

THE PRESIDENTIAL ELECTION OF 1836

and Tennessee's Hugh L. White in the South. These three Whigs won 14, 73, and 26 electoral votes respectively. South Carolina gave its 11 votes to the anti-Jacksonian Willie P. Mangum of North Carolina. Their combined total of 124 was well under Van Buren's figure of 170, and the Whig popular vote of 739,000 failed to match Van Buren's 765,000. So while the Whigs made gains, the 1836 regional scheme fell apart; and again the Democrats were victors.

THE PANIC OF 1837

The "Little Magician" or "Red Fox of Kinderhook," as Van Buren was nicknamed, proved to be an unlucky President. A New York lawyer of ability and a politician who up to now had proved himself adroit in difficult situations, Van Buren found himself confronted by an economic disaster beyond his control. In May 1837, only two months after his inauguration, a New York bank panic signaled the start of one of America's deep depressions. In part, the trouble stemmed from an English financial crisis during which many British creditors canceled their American investments. Jackson and Van Buren drew much of the blame because the panic began shortly after Jackson's Specie Circular caused a rapid decline in land sales, and some of Jackson's "pet banks" were among those that failed. Furthermore, while the Specie Circular checked speculation in western lands, it curtailed the activities of financiers who had been supplying funds to speculators.

The depression affected the lives and fortunes of people in every part of the country. Widespread unemployment developed in seaboard cities of the Northeast, spreading into interior communities and fanning out to the South and West. Bread lines and soup kitchens relieved the hunger of poor families, including thousands of recent immigrants. Farmers received low prices for their crops. Factories closed. Laborers walked the streets. Canal and railroad projects were halted. In 1839 the worst of the depression seemed to be over, but another decline occurred later that same year due to cotton overproduction and falling agricultural prices. Good times did not return to America as a whole until 1843.

In the meantime, Van Buren's fine display of statesmanship belied his reputation as a crafty politician. Beginning in 1837, he induced Congress to agree to a temporary issue of short-term Treasury notes. These amounted to $47 million in the next six years and enabled the government to meet its obligations. He also advocated an independent treasury, where federal funds could be safely retained without either running pet-bank style risks or resorting to another Bank of the United States.

Martin Van Buren

Most Whigs and some Democrats opposed the banking bill on the grounds that removal of federal funds from the state banks where they were deposited would restrict credit at a time when credit was sorely needed. The Independent Treasury Act finally was passed in 1840, but Van Buren's victory was short-lived. The next year, under the Tyler administration, the act was repealed, and for the next five years the Whig majority in Congress defeated Democratic efforts to reestablish this "subtreasury system."

THE CAROLINE AFFAIR

Another problem of the Van Buren regime concerned a spat along the Canadian border. In 1837 Canadian insurgents, dissatisfied with London's rule, fled to an island in the Niagara River, where American Anglophobes reinforced them with recruits and arms. The American steamer *Caroline* was employed in the supply service.

Canadian soldiers, crossing to the American side of the Niagara, set the *Caroline* afire and turned her adrift. Because of the high state of excitement, there was danger of mob invasions in either direction, and the slaying of an American citizen, Amos Durfee, on the night the vessel burned seriously complicated the situation. The Citizens of Buffalo placed Durfee's body on public display in the town square with a bullet hole in his forehead and blood still in his hair. New York newspapers called for war against England in the name of national honor and demanded an apology from Britain. No apology was forthcoming from Britain, however, because they argued that Durfee's death was an act of self-defense.

Three years later a Canadian deputy sheriff named Alexander McLeod was arrested in Lockport, New York, and indicted for murder and arson in connection with the *Caroline* affair after he had publicly boasted of killing Durfee in a Buffalo tavern. The British demanded the release of McLeod on the basis that if he had killed Durfee, it was a military action and he was acting under orders to defend a British territory (Canada) against insurgents. Furthermore, President Martin Van Buren had declared American neutrality in the Canadian rebellion; consequently, it was illegal under international law for the United States to aid Canadian rebels in the conflict—the United States would be violating its own neutrality. Although the Americans involved in aiding the Canadian rebels on the *Caroline* were doing so with private funds, the British pointed out that the United States had claimed—with Andrew Jackson's invasion of Florida in 1818—the right of one country to invade another if the country invaded does not sufficiently secure its own border. The British threatened war if McLeod were not released; on both sides of the border additional sums were appropriated for the strengthening of boundary defenses. Even after a New York court acquitted McLeod in 1841, the case seemed an unpromising preliminary to the Webster-Ashburton negotiations on border disputes that were to take place the next year.

TIPPECANOE AND TYLER TOO

During Van Buren's presidency, Webster and Clay continued to be prominent in the senatorial spotlight. Webster's oratorical ability was as outstanding as ever, and Clay distinguished himself as a parliamentary leader, thus helping to keep the Whig party in the spotlight.

Northern Whigs favored the creation of a new national bank and advocated a high tariff and federally financed internal improvements. If their anti-Jackson and anti-Van Buren confreres of the South did not agree about the tariff and the bank, the common bond linking all Whigs was the issue of "executive tyranny." Less domination by the President and more authority vested in Congress were aims that Southern and Northern Whigs shared. They also capitalized on the country's economic distress that had occurred under Van Buren's watch and were as one in their criticism of Van Buren as the 1840 election approached.

The Whigs played their cards cannily in the 1840 test of skill. In the first place, their standard-bearer was neither Clay nor Webster—able men who had many friends, but also many enemies—but William Henry Harrison of Ohio. Harrison had run well as a regional Whig candidate in 1836 and had won a measure of military glory in the dim past at the Native American Battle of Tippecanoe. Second, the Whigs turned to their own advantage a journalist's taunt that

The Battle of Tippecanoe

Harrison was unfit for the presidency. "Give him a barrel of hard cider, and settle a pension of two thousand a year on him," the newsman sneered," and (take) my word for it, he will sit the remainder of his days in his log cabin by the side of a 'sea coal' fire, and study moral philosophy."

Yes, the Whigs replied, their nominee was a man of the people who preferred a log cabin and hard cider to the frippery of red-whiskered Van Buren. In reality, Harrison dwelt in a mansion near Cincinnati and was an aristocratic Virginian by birth and rearing; but log cabins, barrels of cider, coonskin caps, and even live raccoons became Harrison symbols in the campaign.

For the vice-presidency the Whigs had chosen John Tyler of Virginia, a former states' rights Democrat who now was a spokesman for the minority Southern element within the Whig party. The Whigs' most typical campaign verse contained the best known of all jingles associated with elections:

What has caused the great commotion,

   motion, motion,

Our country through?

It is the ball a rolling on

For Tippecanoe and Tyler too—

   Tippecanoe and Tyler too,

And with them we'll beat

   little Van, Van, Van.

Van is a used up man.

As expected, the Whigs were victorious in 1840. Harrison's Electoral College showing was impressive (234 to Van Buren's 60), and his popular vote was 1,274,000 to 1,127,000 for the Democrat. Although the Whig margin was not vast in a number of critical states, it was large enough. North of the Mason-Dixon line Van Buren carried only New Hampshire and Illinois.

The 1840 election was not a "critical" or "realigning" one like those of 1800 and 1828. No permanent party changes stemmed from it; but the Tippecanoe campaign did have importance as it (1) showed

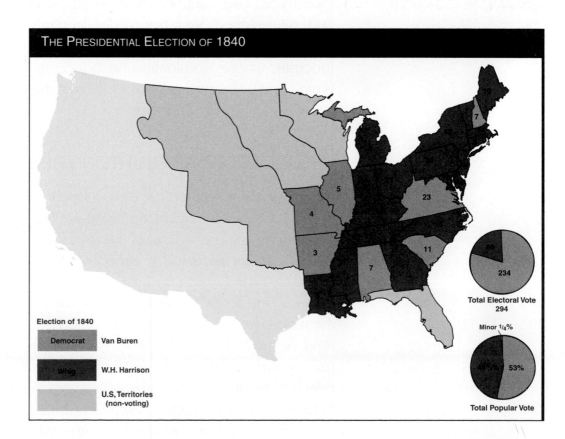

THE PRESIDENTIAL ELECTION OF 1840

Election of 1840

Democrat — Van Buren

Whig — W.H. Harrison

U.S. Territories (non-voting)

Total Electoral Vote 294

Minor 1/4%

Total Popular Vote

how adroitly Whigs could play the Democrats' game and (2) served as a model for presidential contests for more than a century.

PRESIDENT WITHOUT A PARTY

The sweet taste of triumph soon turned bitter in Whig mouths. Inaugurated in March 1841, the 68-year-old Harrison gave his inaugural address on a cold day in Washington with no hat and no coat. He died of pneumonia after a single month in office. Tyler, the first man to reach the presidency through the death of his predecessor, shared few of the ideas of the dominant Whig group in Congress. Twice he vetoed attempts to revive the Bank of the United States, and twice he vetoed Clay-sponsored tariffs. Thrice he defeated distribution to the states of proceeds from public-land sales. All members of Harrison's cabinet, which Tyler inherited, resigned after six months, with the exception of Secretary of State Webster, who stayed on only long enough to complete ongoing negotiations over the border with Canada.

John Tyler found himself in the unenviable position of a President without a party. He did agree with Northern Whigs that the Independent Treasury law should be repealed, and this was accomplished in 1841, but his vetoes of Clay's tariff measures made him a deserter in their eyes. The Tariff of 1842, which Congress reluctantly passed and Tyler signed, was but mildly protective. Tyler also approved a General Preemption Act and cooperated more and more with Democrats, whose nomination he hoped to obtain in 1844. Northern Whigs and border-staters like Clay rued the day when "Tyler too" had been tapped to run with "Tippecanoe."

THE WEBSTER-ASHBURTON TREATY

Before Webster entered the State Department, the *Caroline* affair was not the only border incident fanning the flames of international misunderstanding. There was also the undeclared Aroostook War, caused by conflicting claims to the Aroostook River region on the undefined Maine-New Brunswick boundary. England and the United States had disputed the actual boundaries since the Peace of Paris in 1783 when the map used by the negotiators turned out to be flawed. In 1827, the King of the Netherlands mediated the dispute and drew a compromise border in 1831 that the English accepted and the United States rejected. Eight years later, the government of New Brunswick granted land titles to its subjects in areas north of the border drawn in 1831, but still claimed by the United States When Canadian lumberjacks

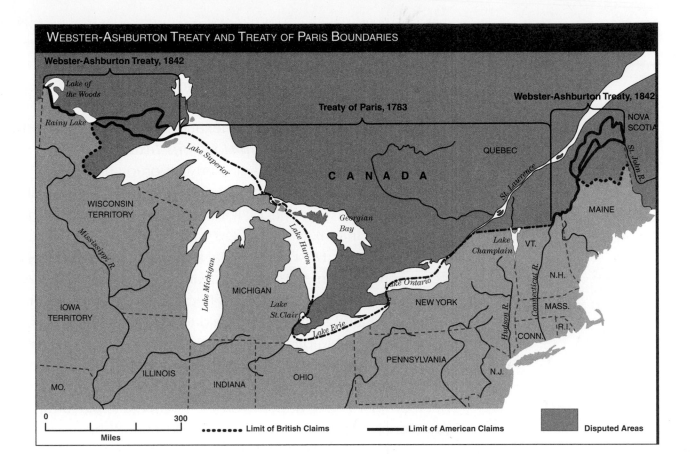

WEBSTER-ASHBURTON TREATY AND TREATY OF PARIS BOUNDARIES

Webster-Ashburton Treaty, 1842

Lake of the Woods

Rainy Lake

Lake Superior

Treaty of Paris, 1783

QUEBEC

Webster-Ashburton Treaty, 1842

NOVA SCOTIA

St. John R.

MAINE

WISCONSIN TERRITORY

Mississippi R.

Georgian Bay

Lake Huron

Lake Michigan

MICHIGAN

Lake St. Clair

Lake Erie

Lake Ontario

St. Lawrence

Lake Champlain

VT.

N.H.

NEW YORK

Hudson R.

Connecticut R.

MASS.

R.I.

CONN.

IOWA TERRITORY

MO.

ILLINOIS

INDIANA

OHIO

PENNSYLVANIA

N.J.

0   300
Miles

••••••••• Limit of British Claims   ▬▬▬ Limit of American Claims   ▨ Disputed Areas

moved into what Americans claimed was American territory in Maine, the Maine legislature authorized the Maine militia to expel the "Warriors of Waterloo." The Canadian lumberjacks clashed with the Maine militia and captured 50 American militiamen. General Winfield Scott and 10,000 Maine troops were committed in 1839 to the defense of the area subject to dispute. Instead of waging war with the Canadians, however, Scott arranged a truce that set the borders to be in the areas occupied by each side.

As the crisis eased, Secretary Webster met in a series of conferences with England's envoy, Lord Ashburton to settle all items in dispute. In their treaty of 1842, Webster accepted a border very similar to the one drawn by the King of the Netherlands in 1831 after the British produced an old Ben Franklin map with the line drawn much further south than the 1831 border. New Brunswick received 5,000 square miles of the 12,000 square miles in dispute, but the United States gained the area around Thunder Bay, Minnesota. The treaty was resented and Webster's popularity forever damaged in Maine, which felt itself shortchanged. Nevertheless, the Webster-Ashburton Treaty did help to achieve order and peace.

RETURN OF THE DEMOCRATS

Fresh issues exerted a vital impact on the election of 1844. Some had to do with the West, others with chattel slavery. Texans had won independence from Mexico in 1836, and now there was considerable sentiment for the annexation of the Republic of Texas by the United States. (See *"Sam Houston: Texas Hero and Jacksonian Democrat."*) Southerners particularly favored such a step, while expansion-minded Northerners hoped that Americans would wholly occupy Oregon instead of it being divided between the United States and Britain.

Henry Clay's 1844 presidential nomination by the Whigs came as no surprise. Former President Martin Van Buren, however, was shunted aside by the Democrats because he was thought to be anti-Texas; and little attention was paid to Tyler as a candidate since he was not a reliable party man. Instead, delegates to the Democratic national convention nominated James K. Polk, a former governor of Tennessee and Speaker of the House of Representatives, Polk seemed thoroughly at home on the Democratic platform, which euphoniously but none too accurately described the desired Western

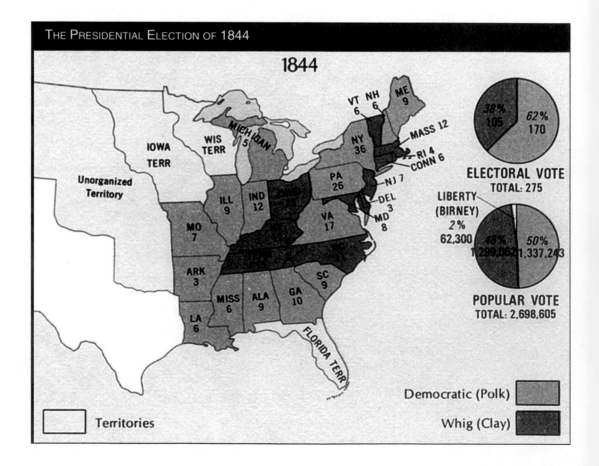

THE PRESIDENTIAL ELECTION OF 1844

1844

ELECTORAL VOTE
TOTAL: 275

38% 105 · 62% 170

LIBERTY (BIRNEY)
2%
62,300

48% 1,299,062 · 50% 1,337,243

POPULAR VOTE
TOTAL: 2,698,605

Democratic (Polk)
Whig (Clay)
Territories

policy as "the reannexa-
tion of Texas" and "the re-
occupation of Oregon."
Whigs made light of Polk's
qualifications. "Who *is*
James K. Polk?" they
asked. But Polk's cam-
paign strategy proved
more effective than that of
Clay, who tried to straddle
the Texas dilemma and
was impaled on the horns
of equivocation.

Into the close contest
came James G. Birney,
heading the first partisan
political expression of antislavery sentiment, the
Liberty Party. Birney si-
phoned off Clay votes in
New York and caused its

James K. Polk

electors to go to Polk, thus providing the difference for Polk. Polk received 170 electoral votes to Clay's 105. The popular outcome,
however, favored the Tennessean much more narrowly. Polk's
1,338,000 supporters outnumbered Clay's by only 38,000.

FEATURES OF AMERICAN DEMOCRATIC GROWTH

The years 1824–1828 were characterized by an increase in the number of elected officeholders, by a relative decrease in appointed officials at the state and local levels, and by some reflection of the popular
will by the Supreme Court. There was far greater participation in government than had been the case in prior eras. By the time the period
was well launched, all states except one chose presidential electors
by popular vote; and the popular vote itself steadily increased from
campaign to campaign, not only because the population was greater
but because such barriers as religious and property qualifications were
gradually lowered on a state-by-state basis. Jacksonians regarded
changes of these kinds as desirable reforms, whose democratizing
purposes and spirit bore resemblances to the era's social reforms.

The development of democratic government was not without its
growing pains. One of the most criticized aspects of the political
scene was the "spoils system," by which governmental posts were

PEOPLE THAT MADE A DIFFERENCE

Sam Houston: Texas Hero and Jacksonian Democrat

Sam Houston

Few Americans of 1828–1848 rival Sam Houston in epitomizing so many prominent characteristics of the Jacksonian period. First in war and then in politics, he was intimately identified with Andrew Jackson. Not even Jackson himself so vividly personified the dynamic thrust for Western expansion. Few fellow Americans became so involved, in and out of Congress, in the issue of federal-state authority. Significantly, Houston looms today as a consistent and colorful human link between the Unionism of President Jackson and the Unionism of Abraham Lincoln.

In a curious way, Houston also symbolized two major reform trends—temperance and religious conversion. He was a romantic personage who lived as close to nature as Thoreau, yet repeatedly combined his romanticism with an on-again-off-again practicality.

Born in Virginia in 1793, young Sam grew up in Tennessee and by choice spent three of his adolescent years living with the nearby Cherokee Indians. The Cherokees liked the teenager so much that they adopted him into their tribe. Returning to his white kinsmen, he volunteered at 19 for combat in the War of 1812. In 1814 his bravery at Horseshoe Bend, where General Jackson defeated the Creek Indians, won Houston great commendation. Severely wounded in this encounter, he managed to survive, although the battlefield injury he had received never healed.

Following the war, Houston studied law and served as district attorney in Nashville. A political protégé of Jackson, he won two elections to Congress and then the governorship of Tennessee. In 1829 Eliza Allen, an attractive girl half his age, became Houston's wife but abruptly left him after only two months of marriage. (Rumors spread as to the reason, which may have been related to his unhealed wound, but he and Eliza forever maintained absolute silence on the subject. Ultimately he divorced her on the ground of abandonment.) Immediately, in "moments of awful agony" [his words], he resigned as governor. He felt "overwhelmed by sudden calamities" and thought it "more respectful to the world" to retire. Boarding a riverboat and leaving all the familiar scenes of past political triumphs, he steamed away from white society.

Houston's destination? That part of what is now Oklahoma where his old Cherokee friends had gone, and where he was welcomed as one of them. Taking an Native American wife, Houston operated as a merchant and gave legal advice on the side. He also served his adopted Native American father and other Native American chiefs by twice representing Cherokee interests in Washington. There his old mentor, President Jackson, greeted him warmly. Sam was a rarity among whites—a Westerner who not only sympathized with Native Americans, but, also owing to the Jackson-Houston friendship, negotiated successfully on their behalf.

Houston drank heavily in the Cherokee country, as he had done previously and would also do later. He even acquired the nickname "Big Drunk." Still, it would be wrong to think of this as a "lost" period of his life. From the Cherokees' point of view, his achievements were impressive.

By 1833 Sam Houston was in Texas. Here he identified himself with the independence cause. In 1836, when war broke out between Texas and Mexico, he was chosen to lead troops assembled to oppose the Mexican army under Santa Anna. Houston's victory at San Jacinto that spring exemplified brilliant strategy and tactics. His trouncing of Santa Anna took only a few minutes but made the victor a hero in Texans' eyes and a natural choice for the new republic's presidency. Serving two nonconsecutive terms as president, Houston did much to strengthen and lend prestige to the Texas government.

Houston's Native American wife, who had not come to Texas, died a few years later, and in 1840 the hard-fighting, hard-drinking frontiersman wed Margaret Lea, a woman of deep religious conviction who set out to reform him and succeeded. This marriage was a happy one, blessed with eight children.

When the United States annexed Texas in 1845, Houston took his seat in the United States Senate and remained in that body 13 years. Here devotion to the Union distinguished him. He was one of only four senators who supported every provision of the Compromise of 1850. Though hailing from a slave state, he attacked the weaker 1854 Kansas-Nebraska Bill because it undid the Missouri Compromise of 1819, which had established a line dividing future free and slave states.

Later, as governor of Texas and in 1859–1861, he opposed Texas' secession from the Union—a stand totally unpopular with most of his constituents. Houston could have resorted to arms once more, leading Unionists against the Texas majority. Instead he relinquished the governorship at the age of 68 and retired to his Texas farm, where he died two years later. The year was 1863,

A mere résumé of his career fails to provide anything like an adequate impression of the impact of Houston's personality. Six feet two, with brown hair and penetrating gray eyes, he created the illusion of being bigger than he was. Extraordinarily popular when a young politician, and time and again as a Texas office seeker, he had military qualities like Jackson's and a gift for what really counted in battle. Possessing a natural dignity, he also could be charmingly informal. Spectators enjoyed spotting him in the senate—wearing a leopardskin vest and other quaint clothes—relaxed and whittling in the back row while colleagues strutted in the limelight. This casualness, together with his unswerving Unionism and his reputation for courage, made him a legend in his life.

Occasionally, Houston hurt his prospects with faulty decisions, like his identification with the anti-immigrant Know-Nothing movement of the 1850s. Another fault was his love of liquor. Converted to the Baptist faith and taking the anti-liquor pledge, Houston in his 50s and 60s not only reformed personally but spoke eloquently for the temperance cause far and wide on the lecture platform.

Houston's strong stand for the Union, in 1850 and thereafter, was signally reminiscent of Jackson's position earlier in the nullification crisis. While more attuned to Native Americans' needs than "Old Hickory" ever was, Houston fully shared Jackson's forthright expansionism and was the Southwest's outstanding statesman in the years after Jackson's death.

Governor of two states, congressman from two, and twice president of Texas, Houston might have made it to the White House if he had not been from the remote frontier and if, when young, he had flaunted fewer free-and-easy personal habits.

No other leader, active from the 1820s to the 1860s, was a more confirmed nationalist than the vibrant, exotic Sam Houston.

allotted as "spoils" of victory to members of the party triumphant at the polls. Under Monroe and Adams a small coterie of federal clerks and minor administrators had held offices on what amounted to a lifetime good-conduct basis. Jackson removed a number of these perennials because they had played the partisan game against him, because they were corrupt and inefficient, or because he wanted to make room for partisans of his own. In 1832 Senator William L. Marcy, a Jackson adherent, had remarked, "To the victor belong the spoils of the enemy"; and Jackson's enemies applied the phrase "spoils system" to Jackson's program of rewarding his political supporters with public office. Although the spoils system clearly leads to corruption and appointment of incompetent government officials, Jackson believed that most government jobs were so simple that they required little intellectual capacity and the damage was, therefore, mitigated.

Furthermore, during his entire presidency Jackson removed only a fifth of those holding office, but he did take a decisive step toward perpetuating an undesirable system. Jacksonians defended the policy as the quickest and surest path to reform; but for every Adams man like embezzler Tobias Watkins who was removed, Jackson's party contributed a scamp of its own—such as collector Samuel Swartwout of the port of New York, who embezzled more than a million dollars.

National party conventions, which came into being with the Anti-Masonic assembly held in 1831, were thoroughly established in the political structure by the end of Jackson's second term. Sometimes they have resulted in the choice of second-rate candidates for first-rate posts, but in the main the decisions of conventions have been sound, and they were and are more directly representative and democratic than "King Caucus" ever was. After momentarily striking a pose of aloofness from Jacksonian electioneering tactics, Whigs imitated their rivals by adopting slogans and symbols similar to Democratic ones. For over a century styles of campaigning were patterned, to an appreciable degree, on the 1840 ballyhoo techniques that promoted "Tippecanoe and Tyler Too!"

During Jackson's administration the personal advisers on whom the President relied came to be known as the "kitchen cabinet"—because they ostensibly conferred with Jackson more intimately than did members of his official cabinet. Later chief executives have followed Jackson's example by surrounding themselves with capable but unofficial counselors whose advice supplemented—or supplanted—that of department heads. It is doubtful that the "kitchen cabinet" would have originated as and when it did if Jackson had not owed his election in part to Calhounite Deep South support, which at least two cabinet members personified but on which he chose not to rely once his administration was underway.

It would be a mistake to minimize the role of the West in the period 1824–1844. Public lands, the tariff, internal improvements, the United States Bank, and almost all other issues were of interest to Westerners. The West had its own viewpoint or viewpoints of a predominantly sectional variety, yet it also exerted a nationalizing influence. The Southwest had much in common with the Northwest, and Jackson the Southwesterner—proved himself a foremost nationalist who was supported as consistently in the Northwest as in any other portion of the country. To the West we now turn.

WESTWARD EXPANSION AND ECONOMIC GROWTH, 1824–1848

THE BACKGROUND OF EXPANSION

Manifest Destiny
Native American Removal
The Pathfinders
The Santa Fe Trail
The Oregon Trail
Western Army Posts

CONQUERING THE WEST

A National Question
The Oregon Dispute
Settlement of Texas
War for Independence
The Republic of Texas
Annexation of Texas
War with Mexico
The Treaty of Guadalupe Hidalgo
Gadsden Purchase
Eruption of the Slavery Issue
Filling Out the West

THE ECONOMICS OF EXPANSION

The West and the Transportation
  Revolution
The Northeast and the Industrial
  Revolution
The Corporate Revolution
The Rise of Industrial Populations
The Rise of Labor
Growing Sectionalism

THE BACKGROUND OF EXPANSION

MANIFEST DESTINY

New York magazine editor John L. O'Sullivan proclaimed in 1845 that it was "the fulfillment of our manifest destiny to overspread the continent allotted by Providence for the free development of our yearly multiplying millions." O'Sullivan's exuberant words reflected the optimism of fervid nationalists that the American banner soon would wave over all of North America and beyond. For the exponents of Manifest Destiny, even the addition of Texas, New Mexico, California, and the Oregon country to the nation would not be enough: God had destined the United States to extend its sovereignty over Canada, Alaska, Mexico, Cuba, other West Indian islands, and Hawaii. Related to this outlook was the fact that millions of Americans firmly believed that God had singled out their country to play a special role in human history.

The dream of Manifest Destiny should be placed in the context of America's impressive achievements and realized dreams that had occurred since 1776: nearly anything seemed possible in the next half century. In 1803 the Louisiana Purchase had doubled the area of the American republic, and late that year Lewis and Clark had left on their historic expedition. When they returned two and a half years later, they brought back not only hard data about the flora and fauna of the upper Missouri and the Columbia watersheds, but also food for potent dreams about the West. By 1830 commerce with Europe was flourishing, and trade with Asia was burgeoning, with adventurers extracting fortunes from China. Wealthy speculators were willing to invest in almost any feasible enterprise. Americans thus had a sense of themselves as a risk-taking people. Moreover, in 1840 the Bostonian Richard Henry Dana published a vivid description of the California coast in *Two Years Before the Mast*, thereby feeding the imagination of his fellow Americans about that then remote region.

Dreams of Manifest Destiny were both an augury of future hemispheric expansion and a concomitant of the westward expansion actually taking place between 1824 and 1848. During this period, Native Americans were moved out of the way by the conquering whites, and the immense areas of the new Southwest and the Far West were added to the United States. It was a period that saw a rapid influx of European immigrants into the United States. Between 1830 and 1850 more than two million Europeans—most of them impoverished farmers or manual workers—crossed the Atlantic. Many

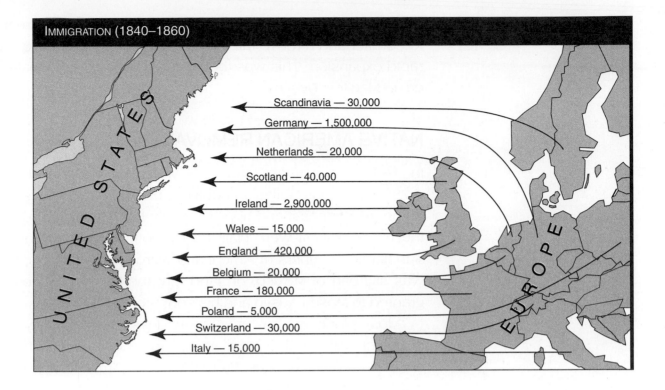

IMMIGRATION (1840–1860)

Scandinavia — 30,000
Germany — 1,500,000
Netherlands — 20,000
Scotland — 40,000
Ireland — 2,900,000
Wales — 15,000
England — 420,000
Belgium — 20,000
France — 180,000
Poland — 5,000
Switzerland — 30,000
Italy — 15,000

were of the new German and Irish wave of immigrants. Between 1830 and 1850 the population of the United States as a whole almost doubled, from about 12.9 million to over 23 million. Though immigration was significant, natural increase accounted for most of the growth, as these figures make clear.

Although much of the emphasis on the theme of expansion was frankly materialistic, and what would today be called racist, idealistic motives were present, too. Protestant and Catholic missionaries, active in Oregon and elsewhere, hoped for numerous Native American converts, though it should also be pointed out that most of them were quite culturally insensitive. Many Americans took pride in the contrast between freedoms flourishing in their own country and oppressions evident in foreign lands—often flattering their own country by exaggerating the contrasts. In fact, there was widespread concern that the intrigues of European imperialists would endanger the opportunities and liberties of ordinary Americans. Rumors spread that Britain and other powers were scheming to influence the internal and diplomatic policies of the Republic of Texas, to acquire Hawaii, and to control the Bays of San Francisco and San Diego as well as Puget Sound. (Some of the rumors had more substance than skeptics realized.) Would not encroachments of inimical courts and kings imperil the future of American democracy? Might they not also limit areas otherwise available for millions of oppressed Europeans, still hoping to come to American shores? Surely, it was God's and America's way to counter and remove the threat through a constructive program of rapid expansion. This was the sincere conviction of idealistic believers in Manifest Destiny.

NATIVE AMERICAN REMOVAL

In 1830 the nation's land and water area covered more than 1,780,000 square miles. In addition, more than 12,000 square miles in the far Northeast and approximately half a million square miles in the far Northwest were claimed by both Washington and London. Substantial numbers of Americans were living in Texas, which then was still part of Mexico, on land that the Mexican government had granted to Moses Austin and his son, Stephen F. Austin.

Most pioneers, however, were less concerned with Mexican Texas or with Anglo-American boundary differences than with the nearby Native Americans. From the Native Americans' points of view, it was utterly wrong for them to be forced out of their ancestral lands in order to make places for white settlers. Most whites had a very different attitude, considering Native Americans inferior and looking on them as in the way.

During this period, the pressure of frontiersmen and their families pushed tens of thousands of Native Americans west of the Mississippi River. In 90 treaties signed during Jackson's presidency—some less honorable than others—the Native Americans reluctantly accepted new western lands in lieu of their old homes.

North of the Ohio River there was relatively little trouble for the white Americans when what were left of the Shawnees, Wyandots, Delawares, and Miamis were moved to western reservations. Although the move was a difficult one, the Northern tribes were to suffer less than the tribes of the South.

The most dramatic example of resistance by Northern Native Americans in the 1830s was an exception to the rule. This involved a resolute Sauk, Black Hawk by name, who believed that a treaty ceding the Rock River region of southern Wisconsin and northwestern Illinois to the hated whites had been signed under conditions of trickery. Black Hawk reluctantly moved his people to the west bank of the Mississippi, but in 1832 he led them back to southern Wisconsin in search of fertile farm land. The ensuing Black Hawk War, won by the whites that summer, marked the end of organized Native American resistance in the Old Northwest. Westward migration of Sauk, Fox, Winnebago, and other tribes increased. Within six years both Wisconsin and Iowa became territories; within 16 years they became states, as settlers from the East populated the country of Native Americans again dispossessed.

Beginning in 1819, Congress began an assimilation policy under which they granted $10,000 annually to a number of missionary associations for the purpose of "civilizing" Native Americans by converting them to Christianity. The program included teaching the English language and English literacy to Native Americans as well as the teaching of traditional gender roles favored by whites. Not everyone agreed with the assimilation policy. Andrew Jackson stated to Congress in his 1833 address that the Native Americans had "neither the intelligence, the industry, the moral habits, nor the desire of improvement which are essential."

In the judgment of many whites, however, Southern Native Americans generally were making more progress toward "civilization" than those being prodded westward north of the Ohio. Sequoya, inventor of a set of characters for Cherokee syllables, enabled thousands of Cherokee adults and children to read and write. Because by white standards they were more advanced than other Native Americans, the Cherokees, Chickasaws, Choctaws, Creeks, and Seminoles are known in American history as the Five Civilized Tribes. Some of them, notably the Seminoles and the Creeks, did not always prove civilized if placidity is a criterion, but there is small wonder that enlightened leaders could not invariably remain placid in light of the whites' tricks and treachery.

The Indian Springs Treaty of 1825, involving Creek land in southern Georgia, was so unfair to the Native Americans that the United States Senate rejected it. Often treaties were said to be the result of corrupt deals in which Native American "leaders" sold out to the whites in return for handsome rewards. In any case, the treaties secured the land for the whites. The Treaty of Dancing Rabbit (1830) relinquished nearly eight million Choctaw acres in Alabama and Mississippi, and in the next decade other substantial cessions were made. Many Cherokees and other Native Americans were forced to move west. Not a few died along the way on what has been called the "Trail of Tears," suffering not only indignities but also agonies on the long trek from their homes into "Indian Territory" (present-day Oklahoma). Because Andrew Jackson was president during the period in which the legal basis for removal was enacted, it is he, more than any other political leader, who is held responsible for this dark page in American history. In Jackson's first annual message to Congress in 1829, Jackson declared that moving the Native Americans to territory west of the Mississippi River was the only way to "save" them from extinction. Jackson repeated this message in his next seven annual addresses to Congress. It was also under Jackson that Congress passed the Indian Removal Act of 1830 that appropriated $500,000 to relocate Native American tribes in the East on over 100 million acres to land west of the Mississippi—as Jackson had suggested the previous year.

Not all Southern tribes submitted passively to the whites' intrusions. Osceola, a Florida Seminole sub-chief, so resented the Treaty of Payne's Landing, which authorized removal of the Seminoles to west of the Mississippi, that he is said to have plunged his knife into the document when he was expected to sign it with his "X."

Resistance on the part of Micanopy, Alligator, Osceola, and other Native Americans—supported by some runaway slaves—culminated in the Second Seminole War. In 1835 the Seminoles ambushed and massacred 107 of the 110 officers and men of Major Francis L. Dade. Taking full advantage of Florida's maze of inland rivers and swamps to hide their women and children, they harassed United States troops and then rushed back to cover. Osceola was seized and imprisoned when, under a flag of truce, he came for an interview with an American general. He died in a military prison, but the war—the bloodiest and most expensive of all our conflicts with Native Americans—continued until 1842. Although there are Seminoles in Florida in our own time, most of the original tribesmen were forced to surrender or were tricked into capture by the whites. Usually they settled in Native American Territory.

Osceola

The Cherokee tribe of Georgia mounted a legal challenge to their removal. The Cherokee, perhaps more than any other tribe, had attempted to pacify whites through assimilation policies, adopted their own written constitution based on the American model, and adopted white ways in terms of clothing, housing, and cotton plantation agriculture—including the ownership of 1,000 slaves. In 1832 in *Worcester v. Georgia*, the United

States Supreme Court recognized the Cherokee nation as a sovereign entity with its own territory in which the laws of Georgia had no force. Andrew Jackson, understanding that it was the Executive Branch, not the Judiciary that had enforcement powers, simply ignored the ruling and pressed the Cherokees to move west.

In 1835, Jackson's side received a break when a small, unrepresentative group of Cherokees signed a treaty ceding all tribal land in exchange for $5 million and equal acreage west of Arkansas. Cherokee Chief John Ross petitioned the United States to ignore the unrepresentative treaty, but Georgia rapidly sold the Cherokee's land to whites. Most Cherokees refused to vacate their land until President Martin Van Buren sent federal troops to Georgia to force their evacuation. The 1200-mile journey of the Cherokees to Oklahoma became known as the "Trail of Tears" as a fourth of the Native Americans (approximately 4,000) on the journey died of exposure, disease, and other hardships on their way to Oklahoma.

Many Americans opposed the brutal treatment of Native Americans—such prominent Northern Whigs as John Quincy Adams and Daniel Webster, for example—but they were unable to prevail. One man whose bad conscience about Native Americans led him down the unusual path not of protest but of artistic rendering of Native Americans, was the artist George Catlin. Giving up his career as a Philadelphia lawyer, he made five trips into the Great Plains during the 1830s, so as to paint the Plains Indians—in the days before photography. Self-taught, Catlin was a man on a mission. When he completed his vast body of portraiture and scenes of daily life, he tried, unsuccessfully, to sell his paintings to Congress. In the end he had to travel to Europe to get the recognition he craved. Modern Americans are indebted to him—because he left an invaluable record—in some instances, such as the Mandans, of tribes that would subsequently be wiped out by the white people's pathogens. Over time, the paintings found their way into American museums, and today hundreds of them are in the collection of the Smithsonian Institution in Washington, D.C., among other repositories.

THE PATHFINDERS

By the 1830s, with the removal of the Native Americans, the trans-Appalachian West was a great complex of newly admitted states, and already people were moving beyond the Mississippi River. Missouri had been admitted as a state as early as 1821, and Arkansas followed in 1836. The wilderness beyond the Mississippi provided attractive commercial opportunities for aggressive American frontiersmen. The lucrative fur trade in the Northwest, for example, had early drawn rugged trappers and traders to that area.

The most successful of the early fur traders was German-born John Jacob Astor, who organized the American Fur Company in 1808 with the intention of establishing a monopoly of the fur trade throughout the West. Astor's acquisitiveness, ruthlessness, enormous capital, and efficient administration helped him take over Great Lakes and Mississippi Valley trading posts that originally had belonged to other companies. In the 1820s he pushed west and northwest, absorbing the Columbia Fur Company in the Oregon country and ruthlessly crushing rival trappers and traders.

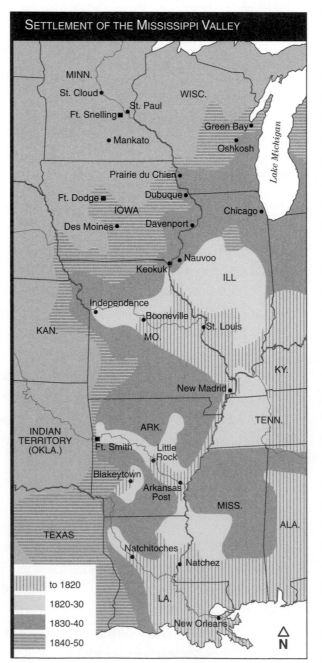

Astor's business methods met with severe criticism on the frontier. An army officer had this to say: "Take the American Fur Company in the aggregate, and they are the greatest scoundrels the world ever knew." Astor, undaunted by such criticism, continued to prosper. In 1834 he withdrew from the fur business to concentrate on New York City real estate.

William Henry Ashley of St. Louis was another who made a fortune from furs in the Northwest. Ashley's Rocky Mountain Fur Company originated the revolutionary "rendezvous" method of fur trading, by which company agents, instead of trading with the Native Americans, bought furs directly from white trappers at an annual "rendezvous" in the mountains. From 1822 to 1826, Ashley and the rugged trappers on his payroll pushed north and west, penetrating the country of hostile tribes and trapping beaver there.

When Ashley retired, he sold his Rocky Mountain Fur Company to Jedediah S. Smith, the "Knight in Buckskin" whose explorations greatly fostered American interest in the Far West. In the autumn of 1826 Smith led the first American overland expedition from Missouri to California. He carved an amazing career as "mountain man" and plainsman, accomplishing the daunting task of survival through self-reliance in the harsh elements of the Rocky Mountains, while using the methods and technology of Native Americans. Another fabulous character and "mountain man" was Jim Bridger, who may have been the first white man to see Salt Lake. Still another was Thomas Fitzpatrick, the noted guide and genuine friend of Native Americans.

Smith, Ashley, Bridger, Fitzpatrick, and the employees of the Astor interest—all were experts with the knife, the rifle, and the trap; but more important, they contributed significantly to frontier expansion and marked the paths for others. They had much to do with the development of communities like St. Louis and of states and future states in what is now the western part of the Middle West. Accounts of their exploits as men at one with nature while surviving the elements also turned Easterners' eyes and imaginations out to the Rockies and beyond.

Perhaps the most famous explorer among his contemporaries— so famous that he was known as the "Pathfinder" and won the Republican nomination for President in 1856—was John C. Frémont. Son of a French émigré schoolteacher, Frémont early in life formed a strong taste for meeting and mastering wilderness challenges. It was in 1838–1839, when employed on a survey of the broad plateau between the upper Mississippi and upper Missouri Rivers, that this army officer got his real start as a geological observer, mapmaker, and scientific reporter. In the 1840s he led several expeditions to the West—exploring the Oregon Trail, the Sierra Nevada, California, the Colorado River, and the Rio Grande. His well-written reports, avidly read in the East, stimulated further emigration to the West.

THE SANTA FE TRAIL

Santa Fe, in the Mexican territory of New Mexico, also provided attractive commercial opportunities for enterprising Americans. Though the volume of American trade in Santa Fe never was large, it was economically significant because American merchants were able to dispose of goods at handsome profit and because they brought away silver in an era when silver was at a premium.

William Becknell of Arrow Rock, Missouri, initiated the Santa Fe trade in 1821, when he sold his goods for 10 to 20 times what they would have brought on the banks of the Mississippi. Venturesome American merchants and farmers followed Becknell's example, carrying goods along the 800-mile Santa Fe Trail from Independence, Missouri, to the great bend of the Arkansas and into New Mexico, which was then a part of Mexico. Though the trip was arduous, confronting caravans with the dangers of rattlesnakes, heat, and storm, before 1843 Native Americans are reported to have slain only 11 whites —a figure that illustrates that the Santa Fe Trail was less dangerous than it sometimes has been depicted.

THE OREGON TRAIL

Mention of the Oregon Trail also conjures up visions of caravans moving west, but in this case the wagon trains carried not merely merchants but farmers and other permanent settlers. Back in Jefferson's time, Lewis and Clark had traversed part of what was to become the celebrated route to the Pacific Northwest. Other hardy spirits followed, adding discoveries of their own.

The Oregon idea was not difficult to sell to land-hungry Americans even though Oregon at that time was jointly occupied by the United States and Britain. The Hudson's Bay Company, an English concern, had long been established in the business of beaver pelts on the Columbia River. Church interest heightened when such American Protestant missionaries as Jason Lee, Samuel Parker, and Dr. Marcus Whitman and his wife Narcissa went out to Oregon to convert Native Americans. Thus national pride, missionary zeal, the lure of cheap land, and the favorable reputation of the region all played a part in enticing thousands to Oregon.

As in the case of the Santa Fe Trail, Missouri towns like Independence and St. Joseph were takeoff spots for the Oregon-bound. For a couple of days of travel, the two routes even coincided until one went south and the other bent north. Out across various rivers including the Platte, and beyond to Fort Laramie, the covered wagons and pack trains of those seeking homes in the Northwest wound their way in the 1840s. On to Fort Bridger and along the Snake River they proceeded to the Whitmans' mission. At last they saw the storied Columbia and reached Astoria on the Pacific Coast, or wherever they were going. The Oregon Trail stretched 2,000 miles—two and a half times the length of the Santa Fe journey.

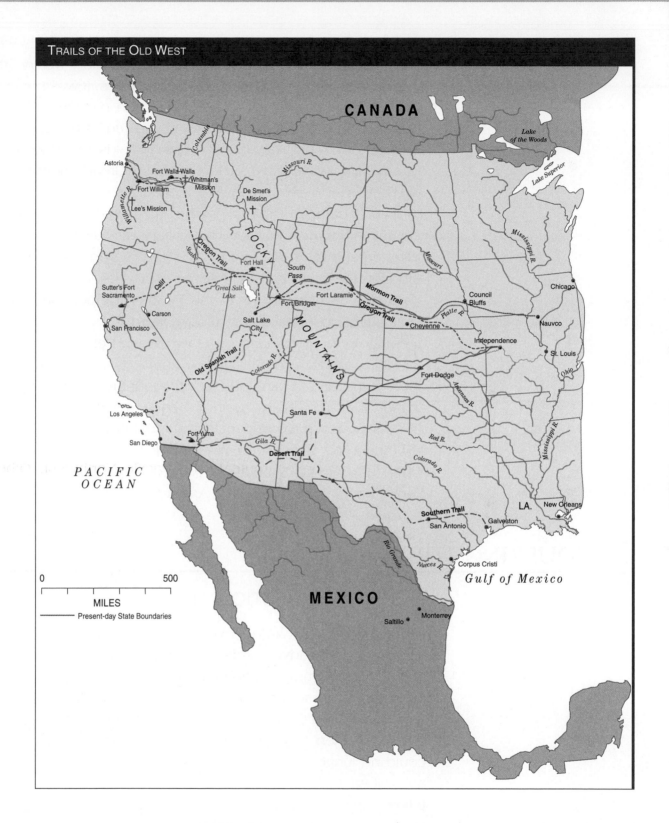

TRAILS OF THE OLD WEST

WESTERN ARMY POSTS

The exploits of the mountain trappers, the Santa Fe traders, and the Oregon pioneers should not tempt us to overlook the role of the professional soldiers. From the 1820s well into the 1840s, the United States army never was large, but its role in aiding the settlement of the West can hardly be exaggerated. Speculators and homesteaders were more likely to bring their families to areas when the military was nearby. Army posts in time became villages, towns, and cities. It was not unusual for a retired officer to become a respected civilian in a new community. Soldiers brought steamboats to Western rivers, constructed sawmills, and built their own forts. They farmed adjacent fields, introduced cattle, and disproved the widely credited legend that a "Great American Desert" existed between the Mississippi and the Rockies.

When it came to exploration, the army also played its part. In general, the information provided by military expeditions was better documented and more useful than the stories from the mountain men. Although these military expeditions were not so colorful as the exploits of a Jim Bridger or of the famous trapper, Native American fighter, and scout Kit Carson, they were nevertheless essential in opening up the previously unknown West. Perhaps most important was the expedition of Stephen S. Long (1819–1820) who surveyed parts of the Great Plains and Rocky Mountains. Long, however, described the Great Plains as the "Great American Desert," fit only for the Native Americans and the buffalo, but not for cultivation or white settlement. As a consequence, for decades many maps of North America would label the area between the Mississippi River and the Rocky Mountains as the "Great American Desert."

CONQUERING THE WEST

A NATIONAL QUESTION

As long as the westward movement was confined to a few explorers and commercial adventurers, Washington could act indecisively and put off any attempt to reach terms with London and Mexico City in connection with territorial disputes in the West. But as American settlers poured into the Far West and the Southwest, setting up communities and then local governments, the United States government could no longer hesitate. The dispute with Britain over the boundaries of the Oregon country had to be settled, and the aspirations of fellow Americans living in Texas had to be heeded. What had been social and economic developments in the West had by the 1840s risen to the level of national political questions.

THE OREGON DISPUTE

The "Oregon country" was a great deal larger than the present state of Oregon, including what are now the states of Idaho, Oregon, and

Washington as well as much of British Columbia. It was bounded roughly by the "Great Stony" Mountains on the east, the Pacific on the west, California on the south, and Alaska (then Russian) on the north. When informed men chatted about Oregon in the era after the War of 1812, they referred to a wondrously varied land with towering mountains and fertile valleys, swift-coursing rivers and magnificent forests. Details, however, eluded even the best informed of commentators; lack of surveys made it impossible to define its area precisely.

Early in the nineteenth century both Russia and Spain laid claim to sections of Oregon, but Spain bowed out of the picture in 1819, and Russia in the next decade acknowledged 54°40′ as Alaska's southern line. Britain and the United States were left in contention over the Oregon country between Russian Alaska and Spanish California.

The principal area in dispute was the territory between the Columbia River and the line of 49° latitude to the Pacific—the northwestern two thirds of the present state of Washington. Britain based its claims on the exploration, discovery, and occupation of the region by British subjects and the British fur trapping operations in the

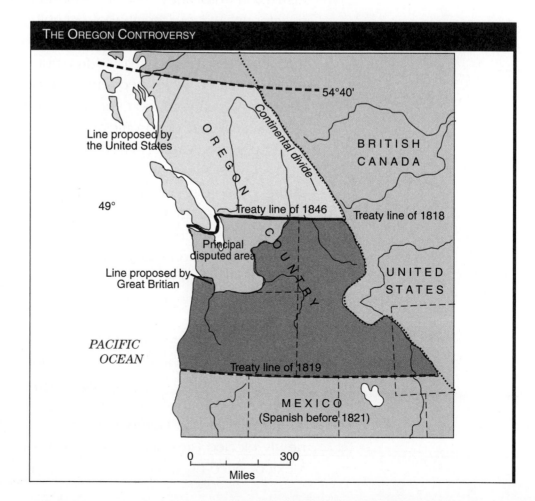

THE OREGON CONTROVERSY

Line proposed by the United States

54°40'

 O R E G O N

Continental divide

BRITISH CANADA

49°

Treaty line of 1846

Treaty line of 1818

C O U N T R Y

Principal disputed area

Line proposed by Great Britian

UNITED STATES

PACIFIC OCEAN

Treaty line of 1819

MEXICO
(Spanish before 1821)

0   300
Miles

Columbia River Valley. American claims also were based on exploration and occupation, including Captain Gray's original discovery of the Columbia River in 1792, the Lewis and Clark expedition of 1804–1806, and the presence of American missionaries and settlers in the area in the 1830s and 1840s.

During Anglo-American negotiations in 1818 the United States proposed the boundary line of 49° to the Pacific Ocean. Britain agreed except for the part north and west of the Columbia River; it was unwilling to relinquish its claims to the Columbia River, the "St. Lawrence of the West," and home to British beaver trapping operations. Unable to reach a satisfactory agreement, the two nations in 1818 settled upon a treaty of 10-year joint occupation of the area "on the northwest coast of America, westward of the Stony Mountains." In 1827 the treaty was renewed for an indefinite period, with the provision that either party could terminate it on a year's notice.

Neither in 1818 nor at any other time until 1845 did the United States or Britain provide for civil government in Oregon. No marshal, no sheriff, no jury, no judge was empowered to carry out legal procedures. No laws could be executed because none had been enacted, there being no enacting authority. As a consequence, men often took justice, or what they deemed was justice, into their own hands. A missionary, without the shadow of authority, might name a constable or a magistrate, and there were times when American traders and trappers tried alleged culprits for murder and other crimes. Maintenance of order, while frequently successful, was unofficial at best. Native Americans in the Oregon territory did not become subject to the slightest American official authority until 1843, when President Tyler appointed Oregon's first Native American agent.

That was the year when the first large body of American immigrants arduously entered the Willamette valley in Western Oregon. It was also then that a committee, composed of American pioneers and their French-Canadian neighbors, met in Champoeg and formed a provisional government. Once the government came into being, it was almost immediately effective. People of stamina and initiative determined to do in Oregon what Washington agencies had not done.

Soon the "Oregon fever" had hit the eastern United States, and British settlers in Oregon began to find themselves vastly outnumbered. This rapid influx of Americans prompted both Britain and the United States to try once again for a peaceful boundary settlement.

Soon after the Democratic victory in the election of 1844, the newly elected President Polk, faced with the possibility of war with Mexico, once again proposed to Great Britain the boundary line of

49°. When the British minister in Washington peremptorily rejected the American offer, the United States on April 26, 1846, gave the required one-year notice to terminate the joint-occupation treaty of 1818. Later that year the British government decided to settle for the 49° line because the British had over-trapped in the Columbia River valley, and their business in beaver pelts was no longer profitable. Britain submitted a draft treaty to this effect to the United States and Polk submitted the treaty to the Senate, which approved it on June 12 and formally ratified it a week later.

The Anglo-American settlement did not meet with unanimous approval in the United States: Northwestern exponents of Manifest Destiny and antislavery men charged that they had been betrayed by a South which, smugly complacent over the annexation of all of Texas, had been satisfied with less than all of Oregon. The Oregon Treaty, however, did have the important effect of preventing a possible third war between the United States and Great Britain at a time when the United States was involved in a war with Mexico over the question of Texas.

SETTLEMENT OF TEXAS

In the 1820s and 1830s a number of Americans—mostly Southerners—took Mexico's liberal colonization law that offered cheap land to settlers at face value and migrated to Texas. With the help of slaves and cotton gins they farmed the fertile soil and conducted business under the aegis of Stephen Austin and other *empresarios* who had contracted with the Mexican government to settle a certain number of families in Texas in return for large grants of land.

In three centuries the Spanish government had brought only 4,000 subjects to Texas. Now the population of the Austin communities alone expanded from 2,000 in 1828 to more than 5,500 three years later. By 1836 more than 25,000 white men, women, and children were scattered between the Sabine River and San Antonio de Bexar. Colonists from the United States far outnumbered those of Spanish ancestry.

Friction between Mexicans and Americans in Texas was probably inevitable. Mexicans, long accustomed to Spanish procedures, naturally were unprepared for the expectations of Anglo-style administrative and legislative procedures by the immigrants. Blunt and self-assertive Americans in Texas were certain that their way of life was freer, healthier, happier, and in all ways superior to that of the Mexicans. They looked upon themselves individually and collectively as proper agents to impose reform and progress on what they

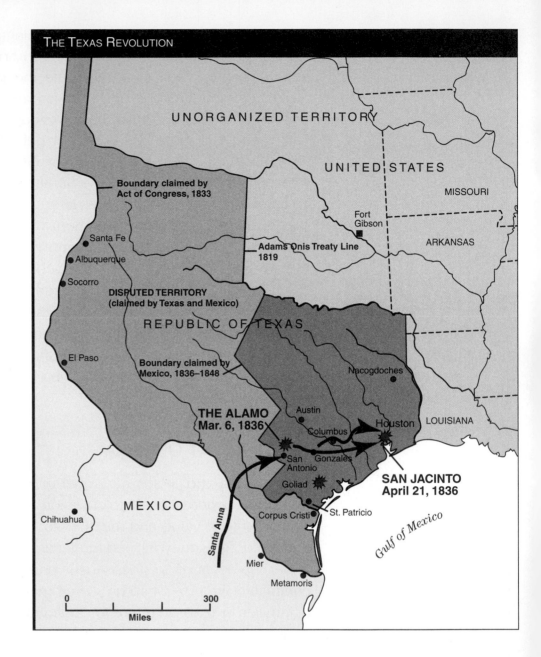

THE TEXAS REVOLUTION

UNORGANIZED TERRITORY

UNITED STATES

MISSOURI

Boundary claimed by Act of Congress, 1833

Santa Fe

Albuquerque

Socorro

Fort Gibson

Adams Onis Treaty Line 1819

ARKANSAS

DISPUTED TERRITORY (claimed by Texas and Mexico)

REPUBLIC OF TEXAS

El Paso

Boundary claimed by Mexico, 1836–1848

Nacogdoches

THE ALAMO Mar. 6, 1836

Austin

Columbus

Houston

LOUISIANA

Gonzales

San Antonio

SAN JACINTO April 21, 1836

Goliad

MEXICO

Corpus Cristi

St. Patricio

Chihuahua

Santa Anna

Gulf of Mexico

Mier

Metamoris

0   300

Miles

deemed to be a benighted society, handicapped for generations by superstition and sloth. The average newcomer failed to recognize the spirituality and gentility of Spanish culture and criticized the Mexican peasants for being illiterate and ignorant. Americans also overlooked the equally pertinent truth that both Mexican peasants and their grandee overlords were sensitive and proud.

Americans in Texas were distressed by gyrations in Mexican policy and the uncertainty of their own status. The Mexican government appeared indifferent to educational needs and law enforcement, and it did nothing to meet the Americans' request for the separation of Texas from the state of Coahuila, to which it had long been joined. This neglect—as well as the government's pressure to force the

Roman Catholic religion on the settlers, impose taxes, impose centralized rule from Mexico City, and to abolish slavery—contributed to a drift that widened the gulf between the native Mexicans and the immigrants from the north.

WAR FOR INDEPENDENCE

In Mexico City, meanwhile, a growing trend toward dictatorial rule reduced the likelihood of conciliation. The master spirit of despotism was Antonio Lopez de Santa Anna, who became president of Mexico in 1833. Santa Anna, "the Napoleon of the West," was ambitious, adept at intrigue, and an able field commander as long as fate favored him. As president he ruthlessly crushed every semblance of liberalism in Mexico's central government and then turned his attention to Texas, where Americans were vehemently protesting his abandonment of the 11-year-old "enlightened" Mexican federal constitution of 1824. The Texans' protests culminated in a proclamation of independence from Mexico on March 2, 1836.

Four days later Santa Anna and his Mexican troops swept into Texas and massacred every one of the 188 Americans at the Alamo mission in San Antonio. Davy Crockett, Jim Bowie, and William B. Travis were among the Americans who died defending the Alamo. That same month, at Goliad on the south bank of the San Antonio River, the severely wounded James Walker Fannin surrendered his tiny command to Mexican General José Urrea, with the understanding that the Texans would be accorded the humane treatment normally extended to prisoners of war. Instead, acting under Santa Anna's orders, Urrea mercilessly executed most of the 300 prisoners in cold blood, with Colonel Fannin the last to go. If the shots that killed them were not heard 'round the world in the tradition of Concord bridge, "Remember the Alamo!" and "Remember Goliad!" long served as rallying cries in Texas.

Mexican general Antonio Lopez de Santa Anna

During the war for Texan independence, as we have seen, the young republic's forces were in the capable hands of General Sam Houston, who had fought under Andrew Jackson in the War of 1812 and had later settled in Texas. Not quite two months after the Texans' stunning defeats at the Alamo and Goliad his troops surprised and defeated Santa Anna's forces at San Jacinto (near Houston) on April 21, 1836 and captured the Mexican dictator himself. Houston forced Santa Anna to sign the Treaty of Velasco, by which Mexico agreed to withdraw its forces from Texas and to recognize the Rio Grande as the southwestern boundary of the new Republic of Texas. Santa Anna also agreed to use his influence to induce Mexico to recognize Texas' independence.

THE REPUBLIC OF TEXAS

The Texans' proposal for annexation was initially rejected by the United States because of fear that a serious sectional controversy might develop over extending slavery into the area—as, indeed, it did. Thus the young republic, under the leadership of Presidents Sam Houston (who served two nonconsecutive terms) and Mirabeau B. Lamar, proceeded to develop its own foreign and domestic policies. One of its first problems was Mexico's refusal to recognize its independent status. Because Santa Anna had signed the Treaty of Velasco under duress, while a prisoner of war, and Mexico had never ratified the Treaty, the Mexicans denied its validity. Thus, though both Europe and the United States officially recognized Texas independence, Mexico withheld recognition and continued to consider Texas to be a Mexican state in rebellion.

Though the sizable volunteer army of the San Jacinto campaign was disbanded in 1837, Texas maintained armed troops against the danger of another military campaign by Mexico. The Texas Rangers, loosely organized until then, were developed to fight Native American raids and border incursions by Mexican cattle rustlers; and the Texas navy made its presence felt in the Gulf of Mexico. As late as 1843, Texan sailors fought against Mexican steam warships in the Gulf of Mexico.

Maintenance of the navy and defenses against marauding Native Americans and Banditos, as well as a Mexican army that twice invaded Texas and took over the town of San Antonio in 1842, demanded more money than Texas had. Texan troops also unsuccessfully invaded the Mexican towns of Mier and Santa Fe in 1842, with the result that some 500 Texans were either dead or imprisoned in Mexico after the failed expeditions. The republic's civil government also desperately needed financial support. Though bond issues were floated with varying degrees of success, the fiscal structure was never very solid in the period of the republic that was experiencing inflation, currency devaluation, and massive debt.

Nevertheless, Texas prospered in that its population grew rapidly due to immigration, and most of the immigrants continued to be Americans. Large in territory and rich in untapped resources, Texas was regarded with covetous eyes by those American politicians who viewed it as a promising field for expansion, exploitation, and the extension of slavery.

ANNEXATION OF TEXAS

Presidents Jackson and Van Buren had been concerned about the North's opposition to the annexation of Texas due to the numerical balance between slave states and free states. Jackson favored annexation and was more outspoken about it after he retired from the presidency. In fact, Jackson had recognized Texas' independence on his last day in office in 1837. Hamstrung by the Panic of 1837, Van Buren marked time; but neither of his successors, Tyler nor Polk, had qualms about working toward annexation. Although both were slaveholders, neither seems to have been thinking primarily about considerations of slavery when pushing for Texas' annexation (Polk's diary gives abundant evidence to this effect). Instead both couched their motives in terms of expansion: Would it be to the country's advantage to limit expansion of the federal domain? This was substantially the same question Jefferson had asked himself in 1803 with reference to the Louisiana Purchase. Like Jefferson, Tyler and Polk answered with a ringing "No!"

Antislavery elements in the North, however, viewed the situation differently. Most Northerners—excluding the tiny minority of abolitionists—agreed with their Southern brothers that the Constitution protected slavery where slavery then existed. Extension of slavery into the West, however, they strongly disapproved. Thus many citizens north of the Mason-Dixon line opposed the addition of Texas as a slave state.

Early in 1844 President Tyler, anticipating the presidential campaign of that year, sent a treaty for the annexation of Texas to the Senate. When the Senate rejected it by a vote of 35 to 16, Tyler recommended that Texas be annexed by joint resolution of both houses of Congress, since a joint resolution could be passed by a simple majority in both houses plus the President's signature, in contrast to the two-thirds Senate majority needed for treaty ratification. Congress

President John Tyler

adjourned before the measure could be brought to a vote, but when the second session convened on December 2, 1844, Tyler again urged a joint resolution to annex Texas.

Momentum gained for the measure in the fall of 1844 partially due to the election of James Polk, who campaigned for President on a Manifest Destiny platform that included the annexation of both Texas and Oregon. Many in Congress viewed Polk's election as a public mandate for expansion. Therefore, this time the resolution passed both House and Senate, and Tyler signed it on March 1, 1845. Under the terms of the resolution, Texas was offered statehood with the understanding that its territory might be subdivided into not more than four additional states. The Missouri Compromise line of 36°30' was extended westward to permit slavery in Texas.

Before the annexation resolution was passed, there had been hints and fears of British involvement in the fate of the Texas Republic. It was to England's, as well as to Mexico's, interest to see that Texas stayed out of the United States. A pending arrangement whereby Texas would ship cotton directly to Liverpool, for example, would mean the tightening of mutually advantageous Anglo-Texas economic ties.

The London government tried to induce Mexico to recognize Texas independence on the condition that the Lone Star republic would not become part of the United States. Mexico did assent to this proposal in May 1845, and Texans had a choice of being annexed to the United States or negotiating such a treaty with Mexico. The Mexican offer had come too late, however. Now that annexation to the United States was theirs for the taking, Texans, most of whom were recent immigrants from the United States, found this alternative the more desirable.

WAR WITH MEXICO

Already irate over Texas' independence, the Mexican government became exceedingly resentful when, in 1845, its erstwhile possession was formally annexed by the United States. Mexico had threatened to declare war on the United States if Texas was annexed. Now it withdrew its minister to the United States and severed official relations with the American government.

Mexico and the United States also disputed the official border between Texas and Mexico. The United States claimed that the border was the Rio Grande, based on the Treaty of Velasco signed by Santa Anna under duress and never ratified by Mexico. Mexico claimed that the border was the Nueces River (about 150 miles north of the Rio Grande) based on a border drawn by Spain in 1775 when Texas was part of New Spain prior to Mexican independence. In June 1845 President Polk ordered General Zachary Taylor and his troops into Texas to defend the territory. Taylor set up camp on the south bank of the Nueces River, about 150 miles from the Rio Grande. In November Polk dispatched John Slidell to Mexico on a special mission to discuss the outstanding issues between Mexico and the United States. Slidell was to propose that the United States assume the $2 million in claims of American citizens against the government of Mexico, in return for Mexico's recognition of the Rio Grande as the southwestern boundary of Texas. Polk also authorized Slidell to offer $5 million for New Mexico or $25 million for both New Mexico and California, (whose port of San Francisco seemed highly desirable to a people now committed to the China trade).

When the new Mexican government under President José I. Herrera refused to receive Slidell because public sentiment in Mexico was against the sale of territory to the United States, Slidell wrote to President Polk and argued, "Nothing is to be done with these people until they have been chastised. War is desirable and we can never get along with them until we have given them a good drubbing." Polk ordered Taylor to proceed to the Rio Grande, a movement of troops that was bound to be taken as provocative since Mexico claimed that the area was on Mexican soil. Polk also sent the United States navy to the coast of California so that the United States could easily take over the ports of California if Mexico attacked American troops in Texas.

On April 12, Mexico warned Taylor to withdraw to the Nueces River; but Taylor refused and instead instituted a blockade of the Port of Matamoros, an act of war under international law. On April 25,

The Battle of Molino del Rey (the king's mill), one of the bloodiest battles of the Mexican-American War

1846, Taylor's troops were attacked by Mexican troops, and 11 men were killed. Congress declared war on the Republic of Mexico after Polk declared to Congress on May 11, "blood has been shed on American soil" and "War exists" between the United States and Mexico. One young Congressman from Illinois opposed the war declaration on the grounds that the spot where blood was shed might not have been American soil. For demanding to know the "spot," on which American blood had been shed, Congressman Abraham Lincoln gained the nickname, "Spotty Lincoln."

President Polk aided the return of the exiled Santa Anna to power in Mexico, believing that Santa Anna would quickly negotiate peace in return. Instead, Santa Anna raised a 25,000-man army and moved north to meet Taylor's forces.

The battles of Palo Alto and Resaca de la Palma followed; the first was an inconclusive artillery duel, the second a smashing American victory. These opening engagements of May 1846 were followed by the major encounters of Monterrey the next September and Buena Vista in February 1847. General Zachary Taylor, bearing battlefield and theater responsibility in the Monterrey area, displayed great gallantry and was popular with his men; however, he did not make much progress in the direction of Mexico City, partly because Polk transferred most of the seasoned soldiers from Taylor's command to that of Major General Winfield Scott on the southeastern Mexican coast.

It was Scott, who landing at Vera Cruz in March 1847, made that Gulf port his supply base and advanced inland to the mountain pass of Cerro Gordo, where he routed Mexican General Santa Anna. Other battles took place in 1847, and all were American victories. Scott entered Mexico City in September, but it was blood-soaked Buena Vista, more than half a year earlier, which would make Taylor the next President. Before Scott entered Mexico City, Santa Anna offered, through the British Minister in Mexico City, to accept peace on the receipt of $10,000 up front and $1 million to be paid later after a treaty was ratified. Scott made the $10,000 payment through a secret service fund, but Santa Anna then announced that the Mexican legislature

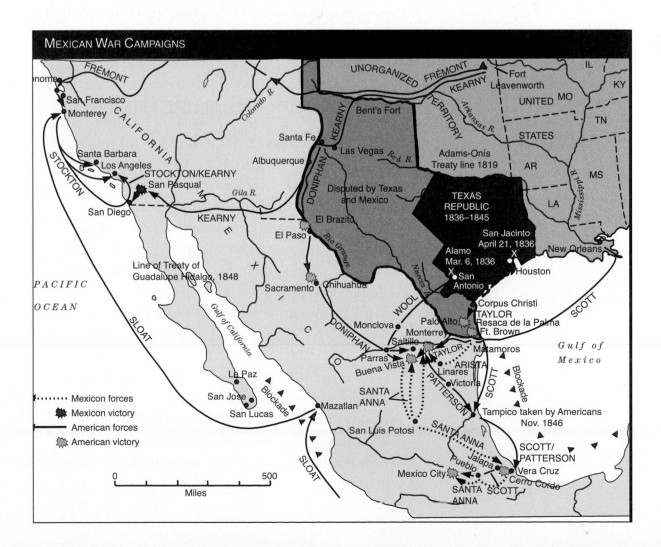

MEXICAN WAR CAMPAIGNS

opposed peace talks. On August 23, as Scott prepared for an assault on the capitol city, Santa Anna offered a cease-fire through the British embassy. Scott, however, distrusted Santa Anna due to the failed $10,000 bribe debacle and stormed the city anyway. Scott secured Mexico City on September 14, 1847, and Santa Anna resigned two days later.

Although the United States declared war on Mexico in May 1846, the news did not reach California for a number of weeks. Meanwhile, a group of California settlers, aided by explorer John C. Frémont and by American naval officers, had revolted against Mexican rule and proclaimed California an independent republic. They raised a flag on which a grizzly bear, a red star, and the legend "Republic of California" were juxtaposed. When news that the United States had declared war against Mexico was received, however, the significance of the Bear Flag Revolt was greatly diminished.

In the summer of 1846 Colonel Stephen W. Kearny and a detachment of about 1,700 troops took possession of Santa Fe in the name of the United States. Polk subsequently ordered Kearny to take charge of American operations in California. The American elements previously led by Commodore R. F. Stockton were brought together under Kearny, and by autumn of 1846 the conquest of California was complete.

THE TREATY OF GUADALUPE HIDALGO

In April 1847 President Polk, eager to end the fighting as quickly as possible, delegated Nicholas P. Trist, chief clerk of the State Department, as peace commissioner to Mexico. Trist's instructions were to negotiate a treaty recognizing the Rio Grande as the southwest boundary of Texas and ceding to the United States for $15 million the Mexican states of upper California and New Mexico. The United States also would assume the claims of United States citizens against Mexico up to $3.25 million.

Mexico's new government demanded a peace treaty that set the boundary at the Nueces River. Trist forwarded this demand to Polk, who was incensed over the demand; and Trist was peremptorily recalled by Polk. Trist, however, believing that the time for peace talks was immediate because the moderates in power in Mexico could fall at any time and a less amiable government could take their place, sent a 65-page letter to Polk explaining the situation. Trist refused to return to Washington and, with no official authority, signed on February 2, 1848, a treaty that incorporated all the provisions of his annulled instructions. Polk was furious at Trist's disobedience, declaring that Trist had acted "worse than any man in the public employ whom I have ever known," but he immediately sent the treaty to the Senate for ratification. Though two vocal minorities—those who had demanded the cession of all of Mexico and those who wanted none of the southwestern territory denounced the Treaty of Guadalupe Hidalgo—the Senate ratified it on March 10, 1848. The United States now found itself in possession of the mammoth region that includes the present states of California, Nevada, and Utah, most of Arizona and New Mexico, and parts of Colorado and Wyoming. It also found itself with a considerable number of Spanish-speaking residents, many who belonged to families that had lived there for generations. According to the treaty, they became United States citizens, and their property rights were entitled to respect.

The territory, however, had come at a great cost. The United States lost 13,000 men (11,550 from disease) from its army of 105,000, the highest death rate of any foreign war in United States history. The cost was even greater for Mexico, which lost 50,000 men and approximately half its territory. The war also created ill will toward the United States in Mexico that lasted for generations.

GADSDEN PURCHASE

Santa Anna returned to power in Mexico in the 1850s, and his government was desperate for money. Santa Anna knew that the United States coveted land in the Mexican Northwest for the construction of a railroad from Texas to California. Santa Anna, therefore, let President Franklin Pierce know that he would be willing to give up more borderland in the desert Mexican Northwest in exchange for a generous offer. To avoid political dissent in Mexico, however, Santa Anna required that the United States amass its army near the Mexican border and appear to threaten another military incursion. President Pierce, therefore, dutifully sent the United States military to the Rio Grande in a charade of force; and the United States Minister to Mexico, James Gadsden, secured 54,000 sq. miles of what is now southern Arizona and New Mexico for $10 million.

ERUPTION OF THE SLAVERY ISSUE

Northern reactions to the War with Mexico were even more intense than Northern reactions to Texas' annexation. No matter how moderate they had previously been, anti-extension Northerners began to heed the abolitionists' arguments that the South's "slave power" must be checked. According to this version of affairs, the South, having dominated the federal government since its establishment, now was afraid of population growth in the North. The proliferation of free states in the Northwest would destroy its political advantage. Hence the South sought to strengthen itself by spreading an evil, that enlightened folk deplored. The threat would affect the Southwest (as a result of the Mexican War), the West as a whole, and Northern states as well. The "slave power," the argument continued, would try to annex every Mexican mile and Central America and the West Indies in the bargain.

At the same time, many Southerners blamed the North as the aggressor. The pamphlets of abolitionists stirred up blacks, they asserted. Slave insurrections had resulted and would continue to result from the "senseless" agitation. As an example, Southerners pointed to the Nat Turner revolt of 1831, which Southerners blamed on Northern agitators. Most notably, David Walker, a freeborn black man living in Boston published his *Appeal to the Coloured Citizens of the World*, which was an open invitation to all slaves to rebel. Walker's work was found in the hands of Virginia slaves, the state where Nat Turner launched his bloody revolt. Coincidentally, William Lloyd Garrison of Boston published his first issue of *The Liberator*, an abolitionist publication, the same year as Nat Turner's revolt.

Nat Turner was a Virginia slave who in his twenties claimed to receive the Spirit of God, who appointed him as a Divine instrument against slavery. On August 22, 1831, Turner and six slave followers attacked their master and all of the white people on their plantation, beheading the slave master and his wife in front of their children with an axe. Turner and his followers visited 10 other plantations by noon and killed all of the white men, women, and children they encountered on each plantation. Fifty-seven white men, women and children were dead and Turner's following had grown to at least 50

William Lloyd Garrison

slaves. The next day, the whites raised a militia and killed all of Turner's followers. Turner successfully hid out for 10 weeks before being captured—after which he was tried, convicted, and executed. Twenty other slaves were also executed for aiding Turner in his revolt, the most deadly in American history.

Antislavery rhetoric had long been limited to a few Northern hotheads, but now they saw the zealotry as epidemic. Northerners had petitioned to do away with slavery in the District of Columbia and on federal property in the South, and the same "intolerance" had been manifested in opposition to annexing Texas. Furthermore, did not Northern states abysmally fail to live up to their constitutional commitments when they repeatedly refused to enforce the Fugitive Slave Law of 1793? So ran the Southern arguments.

As the world has often seen in situations where emotion interferes with reason, there were exaggerations on both sides rather than complete departures from truth. On the one hand, there simply was no "slave power" in the abolitionist sense of the term. There was no unanimity of Southern opinion as to policies. From Jefferson's day through Jackson's to Polk's, not all Southern officeholders in high places had been of one political mind. Contrary to what was charged, there was no widespread Southern *or* Northern conspiracy.

In the 1840s, the issues of slavery and antislavery, expansion and containment became intermeshed. If the Civil War had never taken place, we might not now be inclined to stress North-South antipathies respecting the West. But since the war did occur, it is evident that the relationship of the slavery question to the West involved problems loaded with political dynamite. In the North, the Mexican War sparked opposition from the young, one-term Congressman from Illinois, Abraham Lincoln, as well as from the New Englander, Henry David Thoreau—and countless others who were not destined to be so famous. The War of 1812 had triggered domestic opposition in the North on the basis of sectional self-interest. The Mexican War triggered opposition by principled opponents of slavery, and some of the arguments deployed by these opponents have inspired subsequent anti-war activists down to the twenty-first century.

FILLING OUT THE WEST

While settlement of Texas and the Oregon country was proceeding, other areas were luring pioneers westward in search of land or mineral wealth. Some who had started out on the Oregon Trail bound for the Northwest changed their destination to California. The path to California followed the Oregon Trail to the Continental Divide where, turning southwestward, it became the California Trail and led through the Sierra Nevada into California.

Before 1840, only fur traders penetrated to California, and whaling ships stopped there for supplies occasionally. In the early 1840s some farmers began to move into the Pacific Coast valleys; but when war with Mexico broke out in 1846, there were only about 700 Americans in California. The discovery of gold at Sutter's Mill near Sacramento in 1848 started the "gold rush," which brought the total population of the area to 90,000 by 1850, when California became a state. The gold seekers came by sea around Cape Horn or by sea after an overland crossing of Mexico or Central America or by various overland routes across the North American continent. The transcontinental journey was chosen by most immigrants, an estimated 40,000 using it in 1849 alone. The California gold rush brought people—a disproportionate share of them male in the first years—from all over the world and left an imprint on the region that is, arguably, felt to this day, in that California is one of the most ethnically diverse regions of the country. As New Mexico continues to be regionally distinct because it was the most populous region in the Mexican domain before being sold to the United States in 1848, as New Orleans and Louisiana still show many traces of the French and Creole cultures that preceded the Louisiana Purchase, so San Francisco and northern California are different today because "the world rushed in" in 1849. Two-thirds of the adult males in Oregon quickly immigrated to California in search of gold, and some 13,000 immigrants arrived in California from Mexico, South America, and Europe.

By the 1850s there were two frontiers in America, one moving westward beyond the Mississippi and the other moving eastward from California and Oregon into the Rocky Mountain

An 1849 handbill promoting the Gold Rush

area. The first settlement to fill the gap between them was made by the Mormons, who moved to Utah in 1847, (another region that continues to bear a strong imprint of its original settlement patterns). This religious group had been organized by Joseph Smith in New York State in 1830, after he announced finding golden tablets containing *The Book of Mormon* and convinced others of their religious truths. The Mormons had moved to Ohio in 1831 and to Illinois in 1839 to escape persecution. There, in 1844, Smith was murdered by a mob. That he had received revelations permitting polygamy had made him especially controversial. Then, once again to escape persecution and under the leadership of Brigham Young, the Mormons decided to move to a desert valley around the Great Salt Lake in 1846, where they hoped to find peace. The Mormons had chosen Utah because no one else wanted the barren territory, and they believed that they would be left alone. Thousands of Mormons migrated along the Mormon Trail some 1,300 miles from Iowa to Utah using handcarts. In one great exodus, 1,000 Mormons and their handcarts got stuck in the Rocky Mountain snow, and Brigham Young sent an entourage of Mormons with mules to save 800 of the stranded pilgrims. They had some misfortunes and near disasters in the first few years but eventually became prosperous due to ingenious canal irrigation of the Rocky Mountain snowmelt. Moreover, they continued to practice polygamy. Brigham Young installed himself as President of the Mormon Church and considered Utah to be an independent country. Along with having 23 wives, however, Young was prone to self-aggrandizement and claimed his own death and resurrection.

With the close of the Mexican War the Mormons lost the nominal Mexican jurisdiction under which they had been free to do as they pleased. Congress organized the Mormon lands into Utah Territory in 1850, naming Brigham Young as territorial governor. By 1860 there were 40,000 persons in Utah, but it was not admitted as a state until 1896 because the Mormon Church did not renounce the practice of polygamy until 1890. For a few years after 1849 the Mormons profited substantially from the sale of supplies to gold seekers on the way to California.

The treaty ending the war with Mexico filled out the present continental limits of the United States with the exception of a strip of land in what later became southern New Mexico and Arizona. It was purchased from Mexico in 1853 because it was thought to provide the best route for a railroad to California. With the Gadsden Purchase, the American "empire" was complete from Atlantic to Pacific.

THE ECONOMICS OF EXPANSION

THE WEST AND THE TRANSPORTATION REVOLUTION

From the beginning of human life on earth, people have lived in close association with rivers and streams. Waterways were the natural routes over which travelers moved both themselves and their goods, for rivers cut through wildernesses they could not penetrate in other ways. Therefore, when the settlers moving into the American frontier were forced to return to the most primitive conditions of living, rivers naturally became their first important means of inland transportation.

One of the great drawbacks to river transportation is that the river does not always go where the traffic needs to go. That became true in the United States as soon as the territory west of the Appalachian Mountains was opened for settlement. Rivers descended eastward from the Appalachian watersheds to the Atlantic or westward to meet the Ohio and Mississippi, but no waterway connected East and West. Thus the great enthusiasm for building national roads during the "Turnpike Era" from 1800 to 1830 was occasioned partly by the fact that roads were needed to connect the Ohio River system with the Atlantic coastal rivers.

Transportation of goods between West and East over these road and river routes, however, was prohibitively expensive except for light and very valuable merchandise. The best outlet for the bulky Western produce was not eastward, but southward on flatboats down the Ohio and Mississippi Rivers to New Orleans. Any attempt, however, to try to propel flatboats back up the river against the current was still impractical. Manufactured products needed by Western settlers—such as guns, ammunition, traps, axes, plows, tools, and even shoes and cloth—still had to come in overland from the East.

Because America's immediate economic problem was the need to move goods over great distances inexpensively, the new steam power developed in England in the eighteenth century was applied in America to water transportation even earlier than to industry. Beginning with John Fitch in 1786, a series of American inventors worked on the problem of driving a boat with steam, culminating with Robert Fulton's commercial success in powering his *Clermont* up the Hudson River in 1807. In the following decade steamboats were successfully tried on the Ohio and Mississippi Rivers. By 1829 there were 200 steamboats in operation on the Western rivers, and by 1842 the number had reached 450. A decade later there were

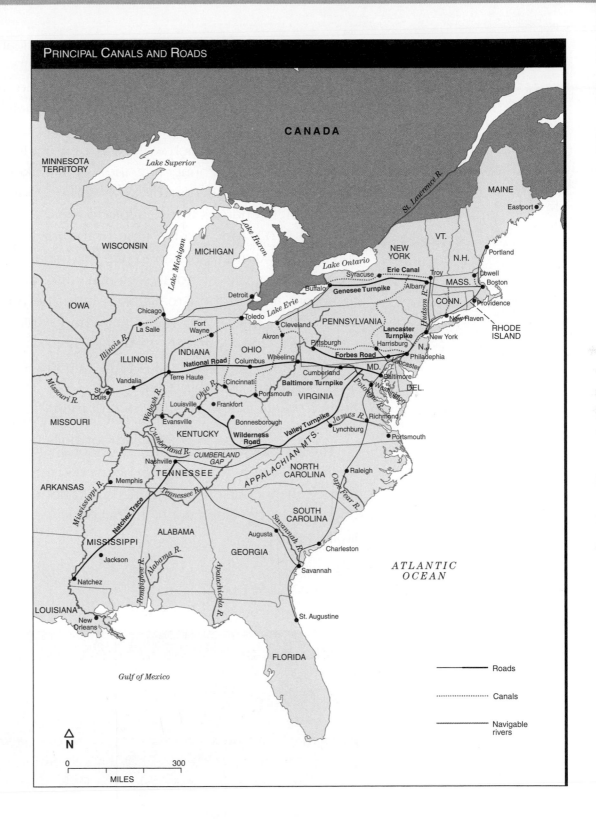

PRINCIPAL CANALS AND ROADS

considerably over 1,000. Partly because of the special needs of the West and partly because early steamboats were too fragile for ocean use (trans-Atlantic steamer service was not frequent until mid-century), more steamboats were in service on the Mississippi River system than anywhere else in the world. Pittsburgh, Cincinnati, and

Louisville began as river towns, and New Orleans became one of America's greatest ports.

Meanwhile, in an attempt to avoid the roundabout route through New Orleans, Northerners turned their attention to canal building, which had been so successful in England in the 1760s and 1770s. The first such waterway of great importance was New York's Erie Canal, connecting the Great Lakes with the Hudson River (and thus the port of New York). Upon its completion in 1825, freight charges from Buffalo to New York City were cut from $100 to $10 a ton, and the time of the trip was reduced from 20 days to six. Migrants began to use the canal to gain access to the West. Buffalo, Cleveland, Detroit, Chicago, and other cities began to sprout around the Great Lakes, and the area began to fill up with settlers just as the Ohio Valley had earlier. As a result of the canal trade, New York City grew rapidly in wealth and population, becoming the greatest port on the Atlantic seaboard. The nation was propelled into the "Canal Era" (1825–1840), with other sections from Illinois to Massachusetts trying to imitate the success of New York.

Rivers and canals had their shortcomings, however. During winter, frozen waterways could not be used in the North. Rivers followed inconvenient courses, and canals could not be built in rough or hilly country. The development of the railroads would overcome all these limitations.

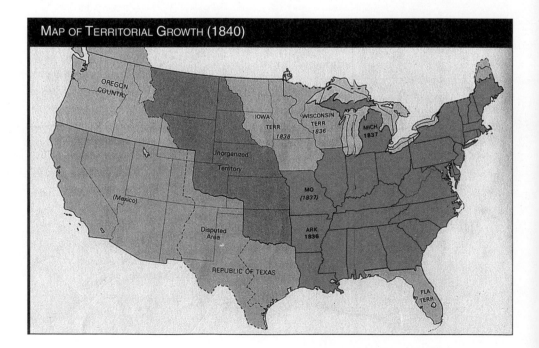

MAP OF TERRITORIAL GROWTH (1840)

Steam-powered rail locomotives had already won success in England when the Baltimore and Ohio Railroad started the first few miles of American rail service in 1830. Soon other short lines were built elsewhere, and by 1840, 2,808 miles of track had been laid. Ten years later the mileage had more than tripled, to 9,029 miles, and by 1860 it had tripled again, to 30,626 miles (as compared to industrial Britain's 10,410 miles). The railroads, which connected the Atlantic coast with Chicago and St. Louis by the 1850s, for the first time provided the West with exactly the kind of transportation it needed. Western products, no matter what their bulk, could now be moved regardless of weather or terrain directly to Eastern markets for overseas shipment. Manufactures from the East and abroad could come in freely. Traffic on the rivers and canals simultaneously declined. With the coming of the rails, the commercial and industrial Northeast and the agricultural Northwest were tied more closely together by common economic bonds.

THE NORTHEAST AND THE INDUSTRIAL REVOLUTION

Under the impact of continually expanding trade, each section of the country underwent a characteristic economic evolution of its own. New England, for example, the section that had achieved the lead in

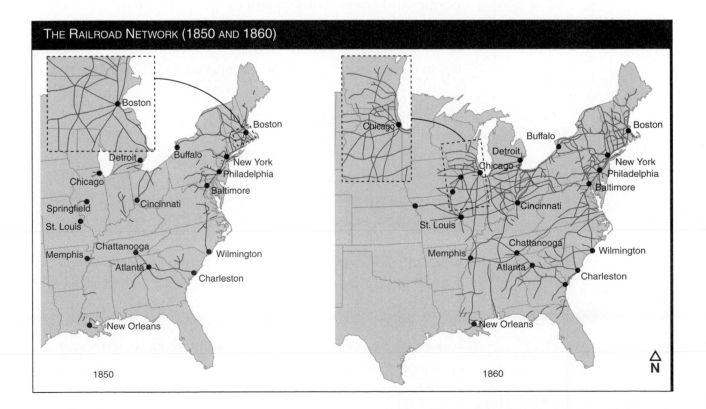

THE RAILROAD NETWORK (1850 AND 1860)

1850

1860

population in the colonial era, was the first to pass from agriculture to commerce and industry. The absence of good soil for agriculture and the abundance of good harbors adjacent to ample supplies of pine and hardwood had turned its people to shipbuilding, fishing, and overseas commerce in colonial days. It was no accident, too, that industrialism should have entered America through New England, for towns well located for commerce were also attractive for manufacturers. Mills and factories need to be near shipping points, markets, or sources of raw materials. The Northeast provided both shipping points, with its excellent harbors, and markets, with burgeoning population.

Other circumstances contributed to the growth of industrialism in the Northeast. In the early stages, streams were still a must for turning the water wheels that drove the machinery of mills and factories, and the Northeast was favorably endowed with waterpower. In Chapter 8 we saw how the Embargo and the War of 1812, in restricting overseas trade, had driven idle commercial capital into investment in domestic industry. The tremendous potentialities of trade with the West, facilitated first by the Erie Canal and then by the railroads, provided further incentive for the manufacture of industrial products. Finally, even after steam had replaced waterpower in industry, manufacturing continued for a time to be located where capital and labor were already concentrated—in the Northeast.

The rise of industrialism in the northern United States had economic and social consequences of such a revolutionary character that it has been called—as in England—the Industrial Revolution. It revolutionized the nature of business organization, of labor, of population distribution, and of the life and welfare of all Americans.

THE CORPORATE REVOLUTION

The arrival of industrialism meant the beginning of the growth of large factories and large railroad networks; and as the size of businesses increased, the old methods of organizing and financing business enterprises by means of individual ownership or partnership became inadequate. The costs of maintaining trading ships or small mills did not exceed the personal fortune of individuals; however, with the coming of railroads and large-scale manufactures, the enormous costs of buildings, equipment, and stock began to run into millions of dollars. This was far beyond the financial resources of even most of the wealthiest persons, and the risks were too great to be undertaken individually. As a consequence, entrepreneurs turned increasingly to the corporate form of enterprise.

The chief disadvantage of the partnership was its "unlimited liability" for business debts. If the firm failed, creditors could force the sale of the owners' personal property, as well as their business property, to satisfy claims. The partnership, therefore, usually comprised a very few individuals who knew and trusted one another and who were willing to take the risks together. Moreover, the partnership had no permanence. It dissolved and the company collapsed when any single member withdrew. The corporation, on the other hand, is a separate legal entity or "person," distinct from its owners. An owner may sell his stock in the corporation without the assent of the other owners, and the corporation continues.

The most important feature of the corporation is the concept of "limited liability." If the corporation fails, the owners are liable to lose only what they paid for stock in the corporation; and the creditors have no claim on the owners personal resources. Finally, by the issuance of stock, the corporation can draw on the contributions of literally thousands of investors and accumulate the large amounts of capital needed for large industry.

In spite of its advantages, the corporate form was not without its opponents in the Jacksonian period. Jackson, Jefferson before him, and even the father of free enterprise or laissez faire and English economist Adam Smith, had attacked corporations as according "exclusive privilege" and limiting "free competition." Abraham Lincoln later warned that the power of corporations could subvert American democracy, but what they were attacking, however, was the kind of incorporation that was known before the 1830s. Before then corporation charters had been granted only through special legislation and only for some specific enterprise that had to be run as a monopoly in order to be profitable. Thus turnpikes, canals, bridges, and banks—enterprises of a semi-public character—were often conducted under charters granting exclusive privileges. Part of Jackson's hostility toward the Bank of the United States can be traced to what he viewed as its monopolistic charter. Even less clearly beneficial to all the public was the construction of industrial establishments.

Many thought that the government should have no authority over the economy; but the wider markets in the West and the new technical processes made increased capital so necessary to industry that corporation charters were sought more and more in spite of possible public opposition. To make incorporation democratic and consonant with Jacksonian equal-rights principles, Whigs and like-minded Democrats urged "general incorporation laws" (as distinct from special legislative grants) which would make corporation charters available to all who could meet certain legal requirements. Beginning in the

1830s and continuing into the 1840s and 1850s, corporations began to proliferate under the new system of general laws.

The Whig Party, which generally favored business interests (as would later its successor, the Republican Party), had advocated free incorporation as a method of inaugurating a kind of "democratic" capitalism. That is, business would no longer be dependent upon rich men but could gather the combined resources of countless small investors. This multiplication of ownership, however, eventually resulted in a revolutionary change in the nature of business organization. As the number of stockholders or owners in a corporation rose into the thousands and as they were dispersed about the country, actual management or "control" of the company fell into the hands of individuals who were not dominant owners or perhaps not even stockholders at all.

Under the system of individual proprietorship or partnership, ownership and control had been in the hands of the same person. The corporate system began the process of divorcing ownership from control and of creating a vast class of investors dependent, insofar as their profits were concerned, on the actions of others—the corporate managers. The inherent danger was that the managers might not act in the interests of the owners. In former days when the owners managed their own businesses, owners who defrauded the company defrauded themselves. With the separation of ownership and control, the "insiders" or managers could systematically loot a company for their own profit. Said a contemporary observer concerning the stock market scandals of 1854:

> The spring trade of '54 opened gloomily. ... In June it was discovered that the Parker Vein Company had flooded the market with an immense and unauthorized issue of stock. The first of the next month New York was startled by the intelligence that Robert Schuyler, President of the New York and New Haven Railroad, had been selling some 20,000 illegal shares at par,—and was now a defaulter for two millions. Almost simultaneously it was ascertained that Alexander Kyle, Secretary of the Harlem Railroad Company, had made an issue of forged stock to the amount of $300,000. Other developments of breaches of trust came flocking from the inland cities.[1]

[1] James K. Medbury, *Men and Mysteries of Wall Street* (Boston: Fields, Osgood, 1870), p. 309.

Scandals, very fortunately, represented only one phase of America's part in the Industrial Revolution. Another phase, at least equally significant, was the entirely new evaluation of the forces that affected the location of industry.

THE RISE OF INDUSTRIAL POPULATIONS

Before the steam engine was developed, the almost complete reliance on water power resulted in scattering manufacturing among a large number of small or medium-sized towns, for the capacity of any given dam site was limited. The first American factory, Slater's Mill, was built in Pawtucket, Rhode Island, in the 1790s by British immigrant Samuel Slater, who designed his textile mill from memory based on those with which he was familiar in England. At the time, it was illegal to take a written blueprint of a textile mill out of England.

The first American factory, Slater's Mill, was built in Pawtucket, Rhode Island

By 1815, New England had over 150 textile mills producing thread and yarn from raw materials. All the mills worked on water-power from water wheels in New England streams. This pattern would change, however, when the triumph of steam made it feasible for manufacturing to concentrate in large cities with locations off of riverbanks.

Industrial employment brought new problems not imaginable in the previous handicraft period of individual workshops. In America, as in England, people did not know how to cope with the problems of health and safety in the new factories because never before had such problems existed. (Even in England, factory laws were not introduced until the 1840s.) Moreover, congested living quarters in the growing industrial cities of New England and the Middle Atlantic states often resulted in a deplorable lack not only of sanitation but also of the minimum requirements for decent human existence. Hours of work were usually long, wages low, and schools for the children of workers inadequate. Workers could afford little for housing. The idea of public transportation had not been developed, so employees had to live within walking distance of their place of employment. All these conditions worked together to produce a type of housing for industrial workers that would become slums of the worst sort.

Unlike the earlier hand industries, the new steam-driven machines did not require workers with great skill or physical strength. Increasingly, women and even children were hired to perform the simple but arduous and monotonous tasks of factory work. The best-known early textile mills were in Lowell, Massachusetts, where the workers were young, unmarried New England farmwomen. By 1830, eight textile mills in Lowell employed over 5,000 women, most between 16 and 25 years of age. The young women lived in company owned boarding houses with company housemothers and slept with 4-6 women in each bed. Company rules provided for curfews at 10:00 p.m. and prohibitions against alcohol, gambling, and unsupervised courtship. There were soon several other mills in Massachusetts and New Hampshire, so that by the 1830s there were some 40,000 women working in New England textile production. Scholars have tried to assess how much their work represented opportunity for them—for most this was their first chance to earn money—and how much it involved exploitation. What is certain is that the workday was long and arduous; the women worked in hot and humid conditions, and the power looms they tended along with all the spinning gears and whizzing belts created an extremely noisy atmosphere. Nonetheless, the Lowell women found the energy to publish a literary magazine, the *Lowell Offering;* and when employers tried to cut wages in the 1830s, the women twice went on strike. It has been suggested that the fact that they lived in dormitories together (so as to reassure their parents that they were being supervised) may actually have promoted solidarity among them. For most of them, after a stint in the mills, they married, having been able to put some money aside for household necessities out of their wages. Research has disclosed that they also sent money home to help educate their brothers or for other needs of their families of origin. Once Irish immigrants began to arrive in large numbers, in the 1840s, the newcomers supplanted the native-born women as textile workers.

Urban industrialism resulted not only from new production techniques and new Western markets but also from increased efficiency in agriculture: Improved farm methods and farm machinery permitted more people to be siphoned off into industrial production. In addition, a good many immigrants settled immediately in the cities. As a result, between 1820 and 1850 the cities grew much faster than the population as a whole. In 1820 only one person in fourteen lived in a city of 2500 or more. In 1850 nearly one person in six lived in such a city. This meant an increase of more than fivefold in the population of cities, while the whole population had increased just over twofold during those years.

The great majority of Americans were still rural, still untouched by conditions developing in the Northeast. Those that watched the cities fill with immigrants and develop slums, vice, and crimes were deeply disturbed. Many associated crowded cities and the factory grind with a Europe of decadence and oppression. The traditional Jeffersonian vision of America—the land of democratic simplicity— seemed to be threatened by new problems of industrial complexity.

THE RISE OF LABOR

Among the first to react to these unsatisfactory conditions were the workers themselves. Although workers were influential in contributing to trends toward better education, their moves in the direction of unionization were in the main separate and distinct from most other reforms of the period.

The oldest labor organizations in America date back to the late eighteenth century, when various skilled craftsmen banded together to obtain higher wages, shorter hours, and other benefits from their merchant-artisan employers. It was not until the late 1820s and the 1830s, however, that aggressive union activity began with the establishment of strong craft unions in Philadelphia, Boston, New York,

MAP OF DISTRIBUTION OF UNITED STATES POPULATION (1840)

DISTRIBUTION OF POPULATION
1840

★ Center of Population

Scale 224 Miles to Inch

Providence, and other cities. An attempt was even made in 1834 to form a National Trades Union; but though the group held conventions for several years, the effort failed to achieve an enduring result.

The most successful of the early unions were local groups that were primarily political in their objectives, working especially hard for various social reforms like free public schools. Aided by favorable public opinion, they were able to make substantial gains by legislative action. By the middle of the nineteenth century the idea of free public education, at least through the primary grades, was pretty generally accepted.

Nowhere was the political presence of workingmen more visible than in New York City. There they organized as the short-lived New York Workingmen's Party in 1829 and again made their presence felt as the radical, anti-bank wing of the Democratic Party, the Loco Focos (so-called after a type of match that they struck at meetings), in the 1830s. With so much democratic ferment taking place, there was also an audience for radical lectures and a radical press. Perhaps the most colorful of the lecturers was the Scottish-born Fanny Wright, a woman who defied the taboo against women speaking in public—and then defied it even more thoroughly by advocating a number of reforms for workers and, in addition, the reform of marriage laws in the direction of more freedom, even to the extent of "free love." Sean Wilentz suggests that her advent in January 1829 marked the beginning of worker insurgency in New York City.

Beginning in the late 1840s, a number of important states began to establish the 10-hour day as the legal maximum workday, but it was usually possible for workers to make a special contract with their employers to work longer. Economic necessity frequently drove them to do so, nullifying the effect of the statutory provision. Nevertheless, such laws represented a gain for labor since they helped to establish the idea of a 10-hour limit.

Finally, in the 1850s, unions less interested in political activity than in "bread-and-butter" issues (wages, hours, and working conditions) gathered momentum. During this period, the first permanent national unions of separate trades were set up, beginning with the National Typographical Union in 1852.

The appearance of solid and enduring national unions was a sign of the end of America's industrial adolescence. Many more decades were to pass before economic conditions would convince even a substantial minority of American workers or employers that unions were a good and permanent element in industrial relations. The individualistic tradition and conditioning of both workers and employers, and an excess of labor, prevented that result sooner. However, national unions were here to stay and their very existence testified to the arrival of a new period in American economic history.

GROWING SECTIONALISM

While the economic bonds were tightening between Northeast and Northwest, the South depended increasingly on exporting cotton and other plantation products to the European market. Although there were notable exceptions, basically Southerners were pulling away from their earlier common interests with other parts of the country. The South's growing identification with an international market economy was natural for the specialized producer of seven-eighths of the world's cotton fiber.

Certain financial obstacles, however, prevented the South from completely freeing itself from dependence on the North. A growing demand for slaves meant continually rising prices for them. To buy land and slaves for the expansion of cultivation required new increments of capital, which the planter class—a leisure-loving economic aristocracy—simply could not provide for itself. The new capital, therefore, had to be acquired in the financial markets of the North and Europe in competition with an expanding and increasingly productive mechanized industry.

Likewise the shipping and sale of cotton tended to be handled by mercantile agencies in the principal Northeastern seaports, because the highly specialized shipping requirements of the Southern economy could not be met efficiently except in conjunction with the more general trade of the major ports. Southern ports did not offer such possibilities of pooling cargo and warehouse space. Southerners complained that Northern merchants who obtained the profits of the cotton trade and kept the Southern planters dependent upon them for mercantile credit took business away from Southerners.

Nevertheless, the South continued to follow its policy of determined divergence from the economies of the other sections of the nation and continued to seek a free world market. Not all whites living in the South were in agreement on means and methods, but the most extreme elements felt that there was only one way in which their section could escape economic submission to the North and West. Only through secession from the Union, they were convinced, could the Southern states avoid being damaged by future economic policies that would destroy slavery and the plantation system. Ultimately the South would indeed choose the path of secession, a path that would lead not only to the end of the institutions they had sought to save but also to the most destructive event in our national history—the Civil War.

CHAPTER 12

THE NATION AT MID-CENTURY

A MODERNIZING UNITED STATES

Characteristics of Modernization
American Modernization
Education and Innovation
Technology and Agriculture

THE SOCIAL IMPACT

Ready-Made Clothing
The "Balloon-Frame" House
Plumbing, Lighting, and Heating
The Icebox
The Emergence of the Modern Family

MODERNIZATION AND REFORM

The Protestant Ethic and Reform
Temperance
Public Education
Higher Education
The "Media"
Women's Rights

The Broadening Antislavery Movement

PREJUDICES, POLITICS, AND POLARIZATION

The New Immigration

A MODERNIZING UNITED STATES

CHARACTERISTICS OF MODERNIZATION

Many scholars have used the concept of "modernization" to describe and analyze the rapid change experienced by Americans in the North in the middle decades of the nineteenth century. According to this thinking—which can provide a useful way of organizing information about such a transformative period—modernization is characterized by four factors, all of which, it must be said, were present in the mid-century North. The first is a heavy investment in "social overhead capital," or improved transportation and communication. This produces a transition from a localized subsistence economy to a regionally or nationally integrated market economy. The second factor is a rapid increase in the output per man-hour that results from technological innovation and the substitution of machines for human labor. The third factor is the evolution from decentralized handcraft manufacturing to centralized industry producing standardized, interchangeable parts. Last is the accelerated growth of the industrial sector as compared with other sectors of the economy.

Socially, modernization is marked by a growth in education, literacy, and mass communication and by a transition from a static, predominantly rural populace to an urbanizing population in which farms and villages become cultural as well as economic satellites of the urban/industrial market. Politically, modernization is accompanied by the rise of nationalism and centralized authority and by increased popular participation in government. Ideologically, an outlook that emphasizes change rather than tradition characterizes modernization. In sum, modernization is the transition from a rural, village-oriented system of traditional personal and family ties to a dynamic, urban, market-oriented system of impersonal relationships. Once again, this set of descriptions fits the North in mid-nineteenth century very well.

Modernization was both the cause and the effect of the growing differences between North and South. As a labor-intensive economic system, tying up large amounts of capital in the ownership of human beings, slavery inhibited technological innovation. Capital was diverted in the South from investment in factories to investment into human inventory, thus stunting technological advance. The South feared change, while the North welcomed it and came increasingly to see slavery and the South's conservatism as obstacles to the progress and greatness of America.

AMERICAN MODERNIZATION

In nearly every index of modernization, this period marked the transition of America—with the partial and significant exception of the South—from a pre-modern to a modern society. In the 1850s middle-aged Americans could look back upon unprecedented changes in their own lifetimes. Since 1815 the development of steamboats, canals, macadamized roads, and railroads had radically increased the speed and reduced the cost of inland transportation. In 1815 the average cost of shipping freight had been 40¢ per ton-mile by wagon and 6¢ by water; in 1855 it was less than 3¢ by rail and 1¢ by water. Goods sent from Cincinnati to New York in 1817 took more than 50 days to reach their destination; by the early 1850s they required only six days. The same trip for passengers was reduced from three weeks to less than two days.

A few simple statistics will illustrate the pace of change in other indices of modernization also. While all sectors of the economy grew rapidly from 1840 to 1880, the rate of growth in the manufacturing sector was more than twice that of agriculture. The percentage of the labor force engaged in manufacturing nearly doubled during the same period, and the proportion of the population living in urban areas increased more than two and one half times. As a measure of the increased efficiency and higher standard of living produced by a modernizing economy, the per capita commodity output increased 72 percent and *per capita* income doubled during the same years.

This growth was a mixed blessing. The industrial working class did not share equally in the rising prosperity, for the real wages of blue-collar workers rose less than the income of other groups. Furthermore, no one can measure the human consequences of the transition from a craft-oriented system of manufacturing, in which skilled journeymen and apprentices worked alongside master craftsmen in small shops, to a factory system in which unskilled or semiskilled workers performed repetitious tasks at a machine. The loss of skills and of pride in craftsmanship, the growing separation of a working "class" from its employers, and the sense of relative deprivation caused by unequal distribution of increasing national wealth lay behind much of the labor unrest of this period.

In contrast with Europe, however, wages in America were high because of a relative shortage of labor. Despite rapid population growth, the supply of workers was never sufficient to meet the demand. This labor shortage in turn continued to stimulate technological innovation. New machines and new methods of production had to compensate for labor scarcity. Eli Whitney's attempt in 1798 to manufacture interchangeable rifle parts was sparked by the lack of skilled labor to make rifles in the traditional way. Although making interchangeable parts by machine was not exclusively an American development, it became known as the "American System" of manufacturing. By the 1850s, according to a team of visiting British industrialists, the American System was used for the production of a wide variety of goods including "doors, furniture, and other woodwork; boots and shoes; ploughs and mowing machines; wood screws, files, and nails; biscuits; locks, clocks, small arms, nuts and bolts."

EDUCATION AND INNOVATION

A high level of literacy, openness to change, and that intangible quality known as "Yankee ingenuity" also contributed to American technological progress. Economists consider education an investment in "human capital" that is vital to economic growth. The United States (with the exception of the South) had a higher percentage of its population in school than any other country in 1850. Literacy in the North and especially in New England was nearly universal. It was no accident that most technological advances came out of New England, the most industrialized and modernized section of the country. As one observer wrote in 1829: "From the habits of early life and the diffusion of knowledge by free schools there exists generally among the mechanics of New England a vivacity in inquiring into the first principles of the science to which they are practically devoted. They thus frequently acquire a theoretical knowledge of the processes of the useful arts, which the English laborers may commonly be found to possess only after a long apprenticeship."

Although Prussia and France were far ahead of the United States in basic science and Britain had a clear lead in engineering and machine-tool capacity, American entrepreneurs and engineers, much like those of Asian countries today, had a knack for adapting foreign technology to their own needs and improving it through dozens of incremental changes. Thus, while the basic inventions of textile machinery were British, most of the important improvements in such machinery in the 1820s and 1830s were American. "Everything new is quickly introduced here," wrote a German visitor. "There is no clinging to old ways, the moment an American hears the word 'invention' he pricks up his ears."

Moreover, in some ways we can trace the dawning of today's "Information Revolution" to this period; because as transportation became faster and cheaper, then ideas and the people disseminating

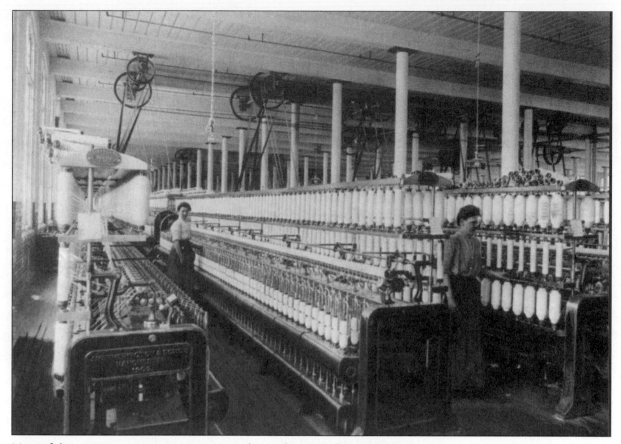

Most of the important improvements in textile machinery in the 1820s and 1830s were American.

them could circulate more widely. As an instance in point, once it became possible to travel from Cincinnati to New York in two days, then it also became possible for leading Northeastern intellectuals and reformers to appear on lecture platforms in a wide geographical area.

TECHNOLOGY AND AGRICULTURE

Although industrial and urban growth outpaced that of farm and village during this period, farming remained the principal occupation of Americans and the backbone of the economy. It provided most of the exports that earned foreign exchange and helped provide the capital to launch America's industrial growth. Yet in most elements of husbandry, American farmers were incomparably careless and wasteful. Crop rotation was only occasionally practiced, fallow lands were not plowed to preserve fertility, and millions of tons of manure were allowed to wash away unused each year. Not until after the Civil War did most American farmers begin to approach the careful scientific farming of Europe.

The reason for such wastefulness, of course, was the existence of seemingly limitless fertile virgin land. It was cheaper to exhaust the soil in one area and move westward than to nourish the fertility of Eastern land. The constant extension of the frontier was the main reason for the abundance of American agriculture, but after 1830 the mechanization of farming and especially of the harvesting process became an increasingly important cause of rising productivity. Insofar as the substitution of machines for human muscles is an index of modernization, Northern agriculture (there was little mechanization in the South with its supply of slave labor) was at the forefront of this process before the war.

For centuries there had been little improvement in farm implements. Plows were hardly better than those used by pre-Christian Egyptians: "In culture, harvesting and threshing of grains," writes one historian, "the colonists were not much advanced beyond Biblical times." Suspicion of "newfangled" ideas was stronger among farmers than among other groups, but the same problem that stimulated innovation in manufacturing—a shortage of labor—overcame this conservatism on the expanding frontier. The first improvements came with the development of an iron plow by Jethro Wood of New York in the 1810s and of a steel plow by John Deere of Illinois in the 1830s (further improved by John Oliver of Indiana in the 1850s). Drills for faster planting of seed also came into use during the early nineteenth century. These implements, which increased the acreage a farmer could plow and plant, actually made worse the chief bottleneck of farming-the harvest. A farmer could grow more grain than he and his family could reap.

In the 1830s, Cyrus McCormick of Virginia and Obed Hussey of Maine vastly improved the invention of the horse-drawn reapers—the most revolutionary development in nineteenth-century agriculture. Two workers and a horse could now harvest as much grain in a day as 20 workers with sickles. Of course, even this quantum leap in productivity would have meant little had not similar improvements in threshing come along at the same time. Here the principal invention was a combined threshing and fanning machine patented by John and Hiram Pitts of Maine in 1834. These inventions and the continued expansion of grain farming onto the prairies enabled wheat farmers to double their productivity per man-hour between 1835 and 1880 and to multiply the total wheat harvest sixfold. McCormick's reaper even made it possible for Northern farms to increase the production and export of wheat during the Civil War, despite the military enlistment of nearly a million farmers.

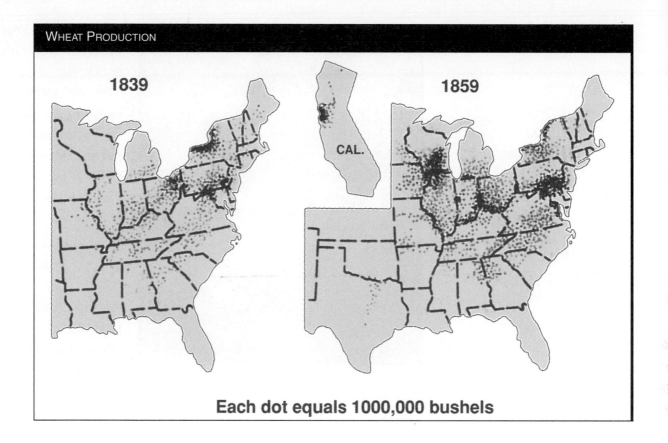

WHEAT PRODUCTION

1839

1859

CAL.

Each dot equals 1000,000 bushels

THE SOCIAL IMPACT

READY-MADE CLOTHING

Although crude sewing machines had been developed in France and America during the 1830s, Elias Howe of Massachusetts perfected the first patented machine with the crucial capacity to sew interlocking stitches in 1846. Howe exhibited his machine at the Quincy Hall Clothing Manufactory in Boston, where amazed visitors watched him sew 250 stitches in a minute—seven times the speed of a fast seamstress. In the next few years several other technicians made improvements in Howe's original machine. One of them, Isaac M. Singer of upstate New York, began to sell sewing machines, without paying Howe a royalty. Howe finally won the resulting patent suit in 1854. To avoid more patent battles several manufacturers merged in 1856 to form the "Great Sewing Machine Combination," the first monopoly in American industrial history. By the 1870s nearly a million sewing machines were manufactured each year, three-quarters of them by I. M. Singer Company, heir of the 1856 merger.

In 1856 several sewing machine manufacturers merged to form the "Great Sewing Machine Combination"—the first monopoly in American industrial history.

The Civil War was the catalyst for the ready-made clothing industry. The demand for millions of uniforms was a powerful spur to standardized production. When the Union government supplied manufacturers with a series of graduated measurements for soldiers, producers developed the concept of "sizing" and soon began to make clothes in regular sizes. By the end of the century, nine-tenths of the men's clothing in the United States was ready-made. Although a smaller percentage of women's clothes were commercially manufactured, the development of standardized dress patterns helped democratize female fashions as well.

Technological changes and the Civil War also profoundly affected the shoemaking industry. In the 1850s adaptation of the sewing machine to leather hastened the trend to standardized production; but the sewing of uppers to soles remained handwork until 1862, when Gordon McKay, a Massachusetts entrepreneur, patented an improved sewing machine that mechanized this process. This invention and later ones not only enabled manufacturers to fill government contracts for army boots, but also laid the groundwork for a mechanized, mass-production shoe industry after the war. By the century's end factory shoes, like ready-made clothing, dominated the market.

These developments illustrated both the positive and negative impacts of mechanization. On the one hand, they lowered the cost of clothes and shoes, improved their quality and fit for the lower and middle classes, and democratized a consumer product that in Europe continued to function as a symbol of class differences. The sewing machine also lightened the drudgery of housewives while providing new employment opportunities for women and children outside the home. On the other hand, sweatshops (shops or lofts where women and children worked long hours at sewing machines for piecework wages) became a byword for labor exploitation. Not until unionization in the twentieth century did garment workers begin to win decent wages and working conditions. The mechanization of boot and shoe production destroyed an ancient craft and caused strikes and strife as skilled workers were replaced by machines or demoted to the status of machine tenders.

THE "BALLOON-FRAME" HOUSE

Americans lived in a greater variety of houses a century ago than they do today. Ranging from the rickety wooden cabin of the slave or sharecropper and the log cabin or sod hut of the pioneer farmer to the substantial stone house of the Pennsylvania Dutch farmer and the Georgian or Neo-classical mansion of the rich, these structures had the virtues of variety and individuality. In an era of rapid growth, however, they also had disadvantages. Stone or brick construction was slow and required many skilled workmen. The same was true of substantial wooden houses, which for centuries had been built with thick timbers joined by mortise and tenon and fastened by wooden pegs. The skilled carpenters necessary for this kind of construction were in short supply in the mushrooming Midwestern cities of the period.

The lack of skilled workers inspired a new technique of inexpensive, speedy, standardized home construction—the "balloon-frame" house. This was the now-familiar combination of machine-sawed boards (two-by-fours, two-by-sixes, etc.) nailed together as wall plates, studs, floor joists, and roof rafters to form the skeleton of a frame house. Augustine Taylor, a Connecticut Yankee who moved to Chicago, the boomtown of that decade, probably invented the technique. A severe housing shortage was solved by these balloon-frame structures, so-called by skeptics who sneered that the first strong wind would blow them away. In fact they were remarkably strong, for the boards were nailed together in such a way that every strain went against the grain of the wood. Such houses could be built in a fraction of the time and at a fraction of the cost of a traditional house. So successful was the "Chicago construction" that it spread to all parts of the country. By the end of the nineteenth century at least half of all American homes were built in this fashion.

The balloon-frame house would not have been possible without a related revolution in the manufacture of nails. New England factories pioneered in the mechanization of the handcraft methods of nail making in the 1820s, cutting the price of nails by two-thirds and creating another mass-production industry.

PLUMBING, LIGHTING, AND HEATING

Changes inside homes also had a large impact on the way middle-class urban Americans lived. Bathing was a once-a-week occurrence at best when water had to be pumped by hand, heated in an open fireplace, carried to a tin tub, and drained by bailing after the bath. Before mid-century, wealthier homeowners and better hotels had installed tubs with running water heated by pipes passing through a boiler, but such contrivances were rare in modest urban homes and virtually nonexistent for the majority who lived in rural areas. The same was true of toilets, which first appeared in the 1830s but made little headway at a time when relatively few cities had municipal water systems (about 100 places had them by 1860) and even fewer had sewer systems. By the 1880s many middle-class urban homes had hot and cold running water and "modern" bathroom equipment, but the outdoor privy and the Saturday night hand-filled bathtub remained standard for rural Americans. Even as late as 1900 Baltimore had 90,000 outdoor privies.

Improvements in lighting, cooking, and heating spread more widely than improvements in plumbing. For light, most houses before 1860 used candles or lamps that burned one of several kinds of animal or vegetable oil. Whale oil was the cleanest and safest fuel, but it was expensive. Coal, oil, lard, and camphene (turpentine and alcohol) were cheaper, but the first two were dirty and the last dangerous. Gas derived from coal had been used for lighting as early as 1806. While most cities had piped-in gas supplies by the time of the Civil War, this form of lighting was confined mainly to streets, public places, and homes of a few wealthy. In 1859 after the discovery that petroleum could be used as a fuel and the first commercial oil well was drilled at Titusville, Pennsylvania, kerosene lamps became the ubiquitous source of home lighting, persisting long after Thomas A. Edison perfected the incandescent electric light bulb in 1879.

As late as 1840 in most homes, food was still cooked in an open fireplace. In 1834 Philo P. Stewart—a Connecticut-born abolitionist, missionary to the Native Americans, founder of Oberlin College, and inveterate tinkerer—patented a stove that with subsequent improvements became the standard wood- or coal-burning kitchen appliance for the second half of the nineteenth century.

Another Connecticut Yankee, Eliphalet Nott, president of Union College, patented several improvements of the basic Franklin heating stove and invented the first stove to burn anthracite coal. By the 1840s many homes were heated by such stoves, and European visitors were already complaining that Americans kept their houses too warm. Central heating with hot air first made its appearance in the 1830s. The "radiator" heated by steam or hot water piped from a basement boiler became common in the last three decades of the century.

THE ICEBOX

The use of ice to preserve food was mainly a nineteenth-century development. The icebox was entirely so. Nothing better illustrated Yankee ingenu-

Eliphalet Nott

ity and enterprise than the career of Frederic Tudor of Boston, the "Ice King." A passing remark at a party in 1805 gave him the idea of exploiting one of New England's few natural resources—the ice on its ponds. By 1825 Tudor and his Cambridge partner Nathaniel Wyeth had perfected an ice-cutting machine, which mechanized the "harvesting" process, and through trial and error had worked out the best methods for building and insulating ships to transport the ice as well as icehouses to store it. The old underground icehouses had suffered a seasonal loss from melting of at least 60 percent. Inside Tudor's heavy-timbered double walls with sawdust insulation the loss was only 8 percent.

In 1833, Tudor sent one of his ships with 180 tons of ice from Boston to Calcutta, crossing the equator twice in a voyage of four months and arriving with the cargo intact. Although the main export markets for ice were the American South and the West Indies, Tudor shipped his product all over the world. In the 1850s Boston exported up to 150,000 tons of ice per year.

Tudor's achievements helped make possible the "icebox" (an American word), which by 1860 was a common feature of American households. These large wooden boxes on legs, lined with tin and zinc and interlined with charcoal, improved the American diet and extended the season for fresh fruits and vegetables. Meat could be preserved longer without salting. Ice cream became a widely enjoyed pleasure instead of a rare luxury. Americans began to put ice in their drinks, to the consternation of European visitors. Even that abomination in British eyes, iced tea, made its appearance before the Civil War. After the war the development of refrigerated railroad cars further improved the quality and variety of fresh fruits and vegetables available in all parts of the country. It also permitted the meatpacking industry to become centralized in Chicago and to serve a national market with its products.

THE EMERGENCE OF THE MODERN FAMILY

Scholars have identified a new type of family that was coming into being in these years under the impact of such rapid economic change. In the traditional family men and women both worked at home, though their chores were probably gender-specific. Industrialization removed male work from the home, except in rural areas; and it also made a large number of children less economically valuable since their work was no longer required on a farm. Further, more women were gaining more education. For all of these reasons, the birth rate began to drop in the early nineteenth century, and the family began to be a more democratic institution. Scholars have called this new style "the modern family."

Modernization and Reform

THE PROTESTANT ETHIC AND REFORM

Economic growth and a rising standard of living depend not only on material factors but also on intangibles such as social values. The openness to change and the emphasis on education in Northern states have already been mentioned as important contributors to economic development. Equally important were attitudes toward work. There is universal agreement that nineteenth-century Americans (at least those in the North, and especially those in New England) were infused with the work ethic. "The national motto," wrote a British observer of the United States, "should be 'All work and no play.'" This produced some unlovely habits, such as the tendency of Americans to bolt their food in order to lose little time from labor, but it also reinforced a value system that was well adapted to a modernizing society.

This value system was more or less synonymous with what is generally called the Protestant Ethic, or sometimes the Puritan Ethic, since its roots lay in Puritan attitudes toward work as a glorification of God and idleness as an instrument of Satan. Emphasizing hard work, thrift, sobriety, reliability, self-discipline, self-reliance, and the postponement of immediate gratification for the sake of long-range goals, the Protestant Ethic reinforced precisely those values best suited to capitalist development. There was also a close relationship between the Protestant Ethic and many of the reform movements. These movements grew out of the evangelical enthusiasm of the Second Great Awakening (1800–s1830) and the radical idealism of transcendentalism. In addition to urging Christians to stop committing such social sins as fornication, drunkenness, violation of the Sabbath, and enslavement of other human beings, reformers sought to instill in the poor, the idle, the depraved, and the intemperate "the virtues of true Protestantism—industry, sobriety, thrift and piety"—to enable them to reform themselves.

The voluntary associations that carried on reform activities provided another link between reform and modernization. The social network of pre-modern societies is confined mainly to kin and village. An essential element of modernization is the transcendence of these localized and prescriptive ties by supralocal voluntary organizations formed for a specific purpose—trade unions, missionary societies, reform associations, pressure groups, and the like. This was precisely what happened in the United States. There were only a few such associations in the eighteenth century, but by 1832 their number and variety astonished the French visitor, Alexis de Tocqueville. "Americans of all ages, all conditions, and all dispositions constantly form associations," he wrote in *Democracy in America*, "associations to give entertainments, to found seminaries, to build inns, to construct churches, to diffuse books, to send missionaries to the antipodes ... to found hospitals, prisons, and schools .... Wherever at the head of some new undertaking you see the government in France, or a man of rank in England, in the United States you will be sure to find an association."

Four of the reform movements, all related to the modernization process (though it would be too limiting simply to see them in those terms), had a crucial impact on American society after 1848: the movements for temperance, improved education, women's rights, and abolition.

TEMPERANCE

In the early nineteenth century Americans consumed an extraordinary amount of liquor. The average annual intake of spirituous and distilled alcohol per person of drinking age in the 1820s, for example, was seven to 10 gallons—at least five times today's average. In addition, the average person consumed 30 gallons of some combination of hard cider, beer, and wine. The most common distilled liquor in

New England and seaport cities was rum. In the rest of the country it was usually whiskey. Beer and wine were drunk everywhere, but the most popular fermented drink in those days was hard cider (about 20 proof). No social occasion, whether a corn-husking bee or the installation of a clergyman, was complete without heavy drinking. Whiskey was a form of money on the frontier, and even church subscriptions were payable in liquid coin. Wretched transportation facilities before the 1820s meant that grain could be marketed over distances only in distilled form. Liquor was cheap, untaxed in most areas, and constituted a considerable portion of people's daily calorie intake. Many men greeted each day with a gill (four fluid ounces) of grog. John Adams regularly drank a pint of hard cider before breakfast. European visitors were astonished by the "universal practice of sipping a little at a time ... (every) half an hour to a couple of hours." Rum was included in the standard daily rations for members of the American army and navy, and colleges typically served ale by the pint to students with their meals.

The temperance movement arose partly as a reaction to excessive consumption. Beginning as a local religious and moral reform led by ministers, doctors, and women, the movement had expanded by the 1830s into a well-organized national crusade. In 1826, Connecticut minister Lyman Beecher founded the American Temperance Society, dedicated to the reduction of the consumption of alcohol because of its deleterious effects on society. Beecher argued that drunkenness led to crime, unemployment, poverty, and domestic violence. Following Beecher's example, temperance lecturers rode from town to town lecturing on the damaging effects of alcohol. At the height of its power in 1836, the American Temperance Union, a federation of 8,000 local and regional societies, claimed a membership of 1.5 million; but this Union fragmented as members divided over the question of temperance versus prohibition. At first the movement had been for *moderation* in drinking,

Lyman Beecher

urging the elimination only of distilled spirits while endorsing temperate consumption of beer, wine, or cider. By the 1830s, however, temperance advocates became more militant, taking on the character of Christian perfectionism and moral regeneration that characterized other reform crusades of the decade. Like the abolitionists, who demanded universal emancipation, prohibitionists began to call for the total abolition of *all* alcoholic beverages. The requirement that members pledge total abstinence caused a dramatic drop in the membership of the American Temperance Union by 1840.

Up to this time temperance had been primarily a middle-class Protestant movement. Its goal was to impose the values of the Protestant Ethic, especially sobriety, upon the whole society. It was here that temperance intersected with modernization. Work patterns in pre-modern society were task-oriented rather than time-oriented. Artisans typically worked in bursts of effort until a particular job was completed and then took several days off, perhaps to spend their wages in heavy drinking. This irregularity was unsuitable to mechanized factories in which successful operation of complex and dangerous machinery required punctuality, reliability, and sobriety. Work became time-oriented rather than task-oriented.

It was no coincidence that the temperance movement in both Britain and America coincided with the Industrial Revolution in those countries. As part of the effort to instill the values of reliability and self-discipline in the working classes, employers supported the temperance movement and often forbade their workers to drink on *or* off the job. Many employers began requiring their employees to take a temperance pledge where employees "volunteered" to cease alcohol consumption as a condition of their employment.

Many workers, especially Irish and German immigrants, did not take kindly to such discipline, but in 1840, Protestant workingmen began to organize the Washington Temperance Societies. The first such society was founded in Baltimore by six heavy-drinking workmen who had been converted by a temperance lecture. Proudly declaring themselves "reformed drunkards," they moved with missionary zeal to organize societies all over the Northern and Western states. Native-born workers pointed to their endorsement of temperance as evidence of their superior dependability as compared to immigrant laborers.

The Washingtonian movement rejuvenated the temperance crusade. It was this period that produced an outpouring of sentimental songs with such titles as "Father, Dear Father, Come Home with Me Now" and the play *Ten Nights in a Bar Room*, which did for temperance what *Uncle Tom's Cabin* did for the antislavery movement.

The alliance of middle-class prohibitionists and Washingtonians helped push prohibition laws through 15 state legislatures in the decade after Maine passed the first in 1846; but these laws had little impact on drinking habits. In a dress rehearsal for the national prohibition of the 1920s, they were widely evaded and most were eventually repealed. Whatever success the temperance cause enjoyed was the result of other factors, especially the evangelical revivals of the Second Great Awakening. In any case, the per capita consumption of alcohol appears to have declined sharply, perhaps as much as fivefold in the two decades before 1850. It never again approached the earlier level and rum and hard cider almost disappeared as American drinks.

PUBLIC EDUCATION

Traditional histories of education emphasize the great reforms inspired by Horace Mann, Secretary of the Massachusetts State Board of Education from 1837 to 1849. Before then, so the story goes, the New England common schools had fallen into decay, the few public schools elsewhere were "pauper" schools to which self-respecting parents would not send their children, teachers were semiliterate, and most children outside New England grew up with scarcely any formal schooling. Although this picture contains some truth, historians have recently uncovered evidence of a vigorous and growing educational system in the generation before 1837. It now appears that in New England and New York at least three-quarters of the school-age children were in school and that in 1830 the average adult in those states had completed eight or nine years of schooling (though the typical school term was only three or four months each year).

Elsewhere the picture was less bright although a mixture of public, private, and church schools provided some education for well over half the white population, except on the frontier and in parts of the South. If this had not been true, one would have difficulty explaining the 95-percent literacy rate for the Americans in the North.

In some respects, however, things were as bad as the reformers of the 1840s painted them. Formal teacher training was almost nonexistent. Educational standards varied widely. Schools were generally ungraded. With rare exceptions, no public school system worthy of the name existed in the Deep South and the white illiteracy rate in the slave states was above 20 percent. Black illiteracy was close to 90 percent. Pennsylvania, New Jersey, and the Western states had little in the way of public school systems before 1835.

What Horace Mann and his fellow New England reformers did was to rationalize and centralize the existing patchwork pattern of public schools, to professionalize the calling of teacher, and by force of example and crusading zeal to spread this system through most of the North by 1860. Mann founded the first "normal" school for training teachers at Lexington, Massachusetts, in 1839. During the next two decades such institutions were established in several states, and half a century later they evolved into teachers' colleges.

Massachusetts also pioneered in other reforms: a standardized graded curriculum, extension of public education to the secondary level, and the first compulsory attendance law (1852). Indeed, Mann did his work so well that some revisionist historians have criticized him for inaugurating a bureaucratic educational establishment that they regard as rigid and reactionary.

Revisionists have also condemned the school reformers for creating a system designed to impose Protestant middle-class values on all children in order to perpetuate the class structure through repression of ethnic minorities and the poor. It is true that the schools tried to teach the values of the Protestant Ethic. An essential task of

An early school room

education, wrote the Massachusetts Superintendent of Schools in 1857, was "by moral and religious instruction daily given" to "inculcate habits of regularity, punctuality, constancy and industry." *McGuffey's Readers* and the various readers and spellers of Noah Webster, which taught hundreds of millions of nineteenth-century children to read, reiterated these lessons. The reformers of the time, however, considered this progressive, not reactionary. The purpose of reform, after all, was not to keep the poor content in their humble station but to lift them out of poverty by equipping them with the skills and values they needed to function and hold their own in a modernizing, fluid, competitive, capitalist economy. "Nothing but Universal education can counterwork this tendency to the domination of capital and the servility of labor," wrote Horace Mann in 1848. Education "does better than to disarm the poor of their hostility toward the rich; it prevents being poor." If this was unrealistic, it nevertheless bespoke the faith that all classes of Americans have placed in education.

HIGHER EDUCATION

Ever since the founding of Harvard College in 1636, higher education had been associated primarily with the churches. In 1860, of the 207 colleges existing, churches had founded 180—most of them during the previous generation as population flowed westward and the Protestant denominations struggled to educate a ministry and a lay leadership that would preserve and expand the faith on the frontier.

Many of the 6,000 "academies" (with only 12,000 teachers) that provided nearly all the country's secondary education were also church-supported. In 1860 there were only 321 public high schools, nearly a third of them in Massachusetts.

After the Civil War, higher education became more secular and more broadly available. By 1890 twenty-five states outside the South had followed the lead of Massachusetts and passed compulsory school-attendance laws. By 1900 there were 6,000 public high schools. The need for technical and scientific training to keep pace with rapid advances in these fields led to the founding of several schools modeled on the earlier examples of Rensselaer Polytechnic Institute (1824) and Massachusetts Institute of Technology (1865). In 1862 the Morrill Act created the land-grant colleges by setting aside public lands to support universities that emphasized "agriculture and mechanical arts." Eventually, universities would develop, such as Texas A&M and Alabama A&M, that would encapsulate the spirit of the Moral Act in the very name of the University itself.

In the postwar decades the modern university outgrew the confines of the old Christian college. In 1869 Charles W. Eliot became the first non-clergyman president of Harvard and proceeded to liberalize the curriculum. Men that may not have Church affiliation dominated boards of Regents, and students were recruited and donations were solicited from persons of all faiths. In 1868 Andrew D. White launched another real university at Cornell, and in 1876 Daniel Coit Gilman started America's first true research university at Johns Hopkins.

THE "MEDIA"

Not all education took place in schools, of course. In addition to such institutions as the family, church, and voluntary associations, many channels existed for the dissemination of information and ideas. One of the most important was the public lecture. Abolitionists, temperance workers, and other reformers found lecturing to be the most effective means of spreading their message, with women having won the right to appear on the lecture stage by the 1850s. Debating societies, literary associations, and the like grew up in almost every crossroads village. In 1826 Josiah Holbrook, a Massachusetts educator and friend of Horace Mann, founded the American Lyceum of Science and the Arts. The Lyceum was the first national agency for adult education, bringing lecturers on almost every conceivable subject to cities and hamlets throughout the nation. In 1838, young Abraham Lincoln spoke at the Springfield, Illinois Lyceum on "The Perpetuation of Our Political Institutions." Lyceums and debating societies fostered independent thought and new ideas, in addition to providing lecture forums for well-known thinkers such as Ralph Waldo Emerson.

Overshadowing all other means of communication, however, was the popular press. America was a newspaper culture. Technological advances in printing brought explosive growth in newspaper circulation after 1830. The expansion of the railroad network enabled urban dailies to print weekly editions for rural areas. By 1860 the weekly edition of Horace Greeley's New York *Tribune* had the unprecedented circulation of 200,000 copies. Samuel F. B. Morse's invention of the telegraph in 1844 made possible the instantaneous transmission of news over long distances and led to the formation of the Associated Press in 1848. The number of newspapers, which had doubled between 1825 and 1840, doubled again by 1860, reaching a total of 3,300. Widespread literacy, the highly partisan nature of American journalism, and universal white manhood suffrage help explain the remarkable politicization of the population, an important factor in the emotion-charged controversies that led to civil war. Though women could not vote, the print culture gave them the opportunity to weigh in on issues related to the sectional conflict, *Uncle Tom's Cabin* being the outstanding (but not unique) example of this phenomenon.

Popular magazines such as *Godey's Lady's Book* (started 1830), *Harper's Monthly* (1850), and the *New York Ledger* (1851) also enjoyed an expanding readership. Prominent features in newspapers as well as magazines were sentimental poetry and moralistic fiction. Most novels were serialized in weeklies before appearing between hard covers, and they often focused on domestic situations revolving around such themes as marriage, home, family, religion, and death. Most of the authors were women, who poured forth serialized novels year after year, reaching a huge audience—also mostly women —through the mass-circulation magazines and inexpensive books. Susan Warner's *Wide, Wide World* (1850) and Maria Susanna Cummins' *The Lamplighter* (1854), for example, were two of the best-sellers. Marion Harland's first novel, *Alone* (1854), sold half a million copies. She wrote dozens more, the last one in 1919. Mary Jane Holmes produced a book a year from 1854 to 1907.

By all odds the leader of this school was Mrs. E. D. E. N. Southworth, who wrote her first novel, *Retribution* (200,000 copies), in 1849 after her husband had deserted her. She followed with 61 more in the next four decades. Serialization of her books lifted the *Ledger's* circulation to 400,000 by 1860. Not surprisingly, given her personal history, many of her novels—such as *The Deserted Wife* (1850)—were highly critical of the gender norms of her day. Indeed, many modern critics have discerned an underlying political strain in the domestic novels in general because so many of them featured women trying to establish their autonomy under difficult conditions—and using the moral authority of the home and the housewife to achieve this.

A particularly noteworthy work of fiction by a woman in these years was Harriet Wilson's *Our Nig* (1850), the first known novel by an African American woman. Wilson, who had herself been a servant, wrote a narrative that inverts many of the conventions of the domestic novel because it depicts the home, not as the site of female empowerment a la *The Wide, Wide World*, for example, but rather as the site of the oppression of a free black servant in a northern state.

WOMEN'S RIGHTS

The preeminence of women in popular literature was only one sign of the growing opportunities and achievements of women at mid-century, but there was, however, ambivalence in these achievements. Literary themes and popular culture reinforced the tenets of domesticity and the sexual double standard that tied women to home, marriage, and family—while men managed affairs in the outside world. At the same time, however, economic modernization was taking many women out of the home and putting them into the wage-earning labor force. The textile and garment industries were large-scale employ-

The inventions of the telegraph, typewriter, and telephone created new jobs for women.

ers of women (and children). The inventions of the telegraph (1844), typewriter (1874), and telephone (1876) created new white-collar jobs for women.

The expansion of public education and the professionalization of teaching opened a major career opportunity for women, though women were paid less than male teachers. By the 1850s the "schoolmarm" was a familiar figure, especially in the Northeast. In the decades after Oberlin opened its doors to women in 1837, several other colleges followed suit. Beginning with Vassar (1865) and Wellesley and Smith (1875), numerous women's colleges were founded after the Civil War. (Mount Holyoke, founded in 1837, did not become a full-fledged college until 1888.)

The spirit generated by antebellum reform movements spurred demands for an end to women's inferior legal and political status. Female abolitionists began to speak out against sexual as well as racial slavery. As we have seen, the first women's rights convention was organized by Elizabeth Cady Stanton and Lucretia Mott and held at Seneca Falls, New York, in 1848. The movement's first priority was abolition of laws that treated unmarried women as minors and forced married women to turn over all property to their husbands. By 1861, more than half the states had taken steps toward ending such legal inequalities.

After the war, feminist leaders decided to concentrate on winning the right to vote, believing that the ballot was the key to open other doors to sexual equality. (See "*Julia Ward Howe: Hymnist of Freedom.*") By 1890 women had won the right to vote in school-board elections in 17 states and territories. Wyoming territory granted women general suffrage in 1869 and, with its admission to statehood in 1890, became the first state to do so. Colorado followed in 1893, Utah and Idaho in 1896. Although no more states enfranchised women until 1910, the nineteenth century movement laid the groundwork for passage of the Nineteenth Amendment in 1920.

Elizabeth Cady Stanton and her daughter Harriet

THE BROADENING ANTISLAVERY MOVEMENT

In 1831 in Boston, William Lloyd Garrison began his publication, *The Liberator,* with the uncompromising goal of immediate and complete abolition of slavery. The next year, Garrison's supporters began the New England Anti-Slavery Society, and New York and Philadelphia followed with similar groups in 1833. In the late 1830s and 1840s the antislavery movement began to reach out to—and convince—more Northerners, with 1,300 local antislavery societies comprised of some 250,000 members by 1837. Similarly, abolitionist newspapers and anti-slavery lecturers began to permeate the northern states.

One of the key elements in this transition was the so-called "gag rule" in the House of Representatives and the battle against it by the one-term president and subsequent House member, John Quincy Adams. Antislavery advocates were circulating petitions attacking the "peculiar institution" as it existed in the District of Columbia itself and sending them to Northerners in Congress. In 1836 Southerners in the House succeeded in enacting the gag rule, whereby the petitions were tabled without being officially acknowledged. Adams's battle took eight years but he ultimately managed to get the rule overturned. During those eight years, many people began to see the antislavery effort as involving the defense of free speech as well as the opposition to slavery itself, and this broadened its appeal.

In 1839–1841 there was another important issue in which Adams—known as "Old Man Eloquent"—played a crucial role: the *Amistad* case. The *Amistad* was a Spanish slave ship carrying 53 slaves on which there had been a mutiny before it could reach its destination in Cuba. Slaves picked the lock on their hold with a nail and took over the ship. Understanding that they had sailed away from the morning sun on their way from Africa to Cuba, the slaves ordered the Spanish sailors to sail into the morning sun. The Spanish, therefore, sailed east by day but west and north by night and zigzagged their way up the North American coast. In August, 1839 some of the mutineers came ashore in Long Island, New York, the ship being just offshore. Over the next two years there was a sustained legal dispute, with Spanish owners trying to get the slaves back, slaves who were in American custody. Going against the Spanish cause was the fact that the Spaniards had been engaged in the slave trade in violation of a treaty of 1817 between their country and Britain, a treaty which had prohibited the importation of slaves into Spanish colonies. The crucial evidence in the case was that none of the slaves seemed to be able to speak Spanish, though the Spaniards claimed they were all born in Cuba, and none would answer to their Spanish names. If the slaves were born in Cuba, they were legally the property of their Spanish slave owners. If they were from Africa, then they were imported to the Western Hemisphere in violation of the 1817 Treaty and would be given their freedom. Adams successfully argued for the slaves' freedom before the United States Supreme Court. The Spanish then tried for compensation but to no avail.

With so much ferment going on, the anti-slavery movement entered politics in 1840 with the founding of the Liberty Party. The only previous antislavery organization had been the American Colonization Society, founded in 1817, by Southern planters who favored gradual individual emancipation and the return of the slaves to Africa. The Colonization Society failed to take hold, however, even though several thousand slaves were repatriated to Liberia in the 1820s, because of the enormous cost of repatriation and the fact that most American slaves in the 1820s were born in the United States and had no knowledge whatsoever of Africa.

In contrast some Liberty Party men insisted that the Constitution empowered the federal government to abolish slavery. Officially, however, the party stood only for the exclusion of slavery from new territories and states, for its abolition in the District of Columbia, and for prohibition of the interstate slave trade. In 1848 the Liberty Party was absorbed by the more broad-gauged Free Soil Party, which adopted a similar platform (omitting reference to the slave trade) but attracted many members who were more opposed to Southern political power than to slavery as such.

PEOPLE THAT MADE A DIFFERENCE

Julia Ward Howe: Hymnist of Freedom

by Holman Hamilton and Glenna Matthews

Julia Ward Howe

It would be easy-but utterly misleading-to depict Julia Ward Howe (1819-1910) solely in terms of literary success. She was very successful in that way, for she wrote "The Battle Hymn of the Republic," containing the most celebrated lyrics connected with the Civil War. In her long, fruitful life, she became the most famous American woman in the eyes of many of her contemporaries.

In both respects, her life was very different from those of the great majority of Africans brought to America. Yet her story represents the importance of the forced migration from Africa, not only because the numbers of people involved exceeded the migration of peoples from Western Europe in the colonial eighteenth century, but also because of the many talents brought to America by Africans. Unlike many other blacks, Phillis Wheatley was encouraged to develop her talents and was accepted into white society.

But there is a far greater significance in the Howe story-significance not alone in terms of her own times but also as people see her today. To grasp the importance of what she did, and all she represents, it is essential to understand the status of women in the first half of the nineteenth century. Most daughters of upper-class families, sheltered from infancy on, had no active part in improving the lot of the masses of humanity and were not supposed to. They took it for granted that they were not to plunge into causes, particularly those deemed unpopular or unfashionable. It was a rare wife and mother, of courageous conviction, that chose to dedicate herself to helping black people or to leading the fight to obtain the right to vote for the female half of the population. Such a wife and mother was Mrs. Howe.

Born in New York City, Julia Ward moved to Boston upon marrying Dr. Samuel Gridley Howe. Her choice of a husband indicated the qualities she valued, for Dr. Howe, a Massachusetts physician, devoted his career not to conventional practice but to aiding seriously handicapped children, adolescents, and adults. He gave "light" to the blind, "sound" to the deaf, and meaning to the retarded. Samuel's was a pioneering venture in medicine, psychology, and mercy. However admirable he was as physician and reformer, Dr. Howe was a domestic tyrant where his wife was concerned. Indeed, he believed that it was wrong for a married woman to engage in public life. Therefore, in becoming so well known, his wife's courage had to be deployed in defying her husband as well as on other fronts. Though the parents of six children, the Howes saw their marriage totter on the brink of divorce on more than one occasion.

Nonetheless, they also worked together in reform causes. In an era when most whites looked down on blacks and did little or nothing on their behalf, Julia gave her best efforts to opposing slavery with her sharpest weapon-her pen. Together, Samuel and Julia edited The Commonwealth, an antislavery paper. Julia had a major role in the enterprise, possessing both talent as a writer and persistence as a reformer.

Nor were writing and editing the only means the Howes used in their antislavery activities. Abolitionist men and women needed a headquarters where they could gather and exchange ideas and plan the next moves in their campaigns. Julia Ward Howe provided that headquarters in her own house, not simply as hostess but as a catalytic agent for freedom's cause. As she later said, she had "the honor of pleading for the slave when he was a slave."

Most authors become famous only when they address themselves to topics in which they have deep interest. Julia Ward Howe's literary growth perfectly illustrates this fact. In 1854, at 35, she published a first volume of poems. Three years later, a second book of poetry followed, as well as a play. But the latter was not a stunning triumph and the verses received little attention. The limelight, where she would soon shine was reserved for a period of national upheaval. Author, subject, mind, and emotion found their inspiration in the Civil War. The accomplishment was entirely logical because now religious conviction the Howes were Unitarian-and aggressive opposition to slavery blended with the cause of the Union, in which she also devoutly believed. Visiting the city of Washington, D.C., and the Union soldiers stationed nearby, she was inspired to write a series of stanzas to the familiar tune of "John Brown's Body."

Lyrics came to Julia one night when she could not sleep. She was scarcely able to read what she scrawled in the dim light, and then-at last drowsy-was asleep.

When she wakened, she reviewed the words of the "Battle Hymn":

Mine eyes have seen the glory of the
    coming of the Lord
He is trampling out the vintage where
    the grapes of wrath are stored;
He hath loosed the fateful lightning of
    His terrible swift sword;
    His truth is marching on.

Although its publication brought her only four dollars in cash, the poem had a sensational impact. So stirring were her lines that almost immediately they echoed and re-echoed throughout the North. Eventually they became integral in the nationwide musical and poetic tradition.

Julia did not rest on "Battle Hymn" laurels. With blacks freed and the Union saved, the vote for women was her next theme. This was another unpopular cause from many people's points of view, yet she adhered to it with all the enthusiasm she had earlier devoted to freeing the slaves. The Nineteenth Amendment, granting woman suffrage, would not be adopted until 1919, nine years after Julia Ward Howe's death at the age of 91, but younger women with whom she had been working carried to spectacular completion this second major reform.

By the time of her death, Julia Ward Howe was regarded as a spiritual leader as well as a literary figure.

Indeed, in her later years, she preached in Unitarian and Universalist pulpits although she had not been ordained. In 1908, just before her death, she became the first woman to be elected to the American Academy of Arts and Letters.

Genuine abolitionists watched these and subsequent developments leading to the founding of the Republican Party in 1854 (treated in Chapter 13) with mixed feelings. While they welcomed the growth of antislavery sentiment in the North, they were well aware that it was often based on dislike of both slavery *and* blacks. Moreover, Garrison and his adherents advocated non-resistance, rather than political parties as the means of ending slavery. Hence, abolitionists kept their societies alive and continued to work for the equal rights and education of Northern blacks.

Women played prominent roles in the abolition movement, forming women's auxiliaries and raising funds to support abolitionist lecturers. William Lloyd Garrison published a letter by Angelina Grimke in *The Liberator* that made her an overnight celebrity among abolitionists. Grimke and her sister Sarah quickly became in-demand lecturers on the abolitionist lecture circuit. The Grimke sisters, however, also wrote and spoke about women's rights, thus sewing discord among the abolitionists themselves—though some abolitionists, such as Garrison, favored women's rights as well. One famous African American woman who lectured both against slavery and for women's rights was Sojourner Truth. Truth gave her famous speech, "Ain't I a Woman" in Akron, Ohio in 1851, arguing for equal rights for both blacks and women. Truth dictated her memoirs of slavery to a friend, and Garrison published those memoirs as *The Narrative of Sojourner Truth: A Northern Slave,* in 1850.

By the 1850s there was a robust anti-slavery discourse, fed most importantly by the publication of *Uncle Tom's Cabin* in 1852, but also by the writings and lectures of many former slaves, Frederick Douglass being the best known. In 1845 Douglass published his *Narrative of the Life of Frederick Douglass.* He also began publishing an abolitionist newspaper, *The North*

Isabella van Wagenen, who called herself "Sojourner Truth"

Star. Another former slave who became well known in the antebellum United States was Sojourner Truth. Born a slave in New York in 1797, Isabella van Wagenen began to call herself "Sojourner Truth" after a religious conversion. She was a familiar presence on the lecture platform in the North, and in 1850 appeared the first version of her autobiography, as dictated to Olive Gilbert.

Finally, public opinion in the North began to be more favorable to the antislavery cause because of certain political developments such as the Compromise of 1850 and the Kansas-Nebraska Act, both of which will be more fully discussed in Chapter 13. For now what is important to point out is the fact that the Compromise of 1850 contained as one of its key elements, a new and tougher fugitive slave law. After its passage, as we will see in the next chapter, there were a number of notorious cases that kept the issue of slavery in the public eye.

PREJUDICES, POLITICS, AND POLARIZATION

THE NEW IMMIGRATION

In the first 40 years of the Republic immigrants did not come in large numbers. As late as the 1820s the number of immigrants averaged less than 13,000 per year, but rapid population growth, land shortages, and labor surpluses in Northern Europe, combined with cheap land, labor shortages, and higher wages in America, brought a quadrupling of this average in the 1830s. During the decade from 1845 through 1854, the number of immigrants averaged nearly 300,000 annually.

Although these newcomers provided much of the labor force necessary for rapid economic growth, many of them received a cold welcome in the United States. Actually, anti-immigrant sentiment (or nativism) was not directed primarily against immigrants as such, but against *Catholic* immigrants. Nearly 40 percent of the immigrants to America during these years were Irish Catholics, driven to emigrate by the potato famine after 1845. Another 12 or 13 percent were German Catholics.

Settling mainly in cities, the Irish were the most concentrated and visible of the immigrant groups. They were poor, clannish, fiercely loyal to their church, hostile toward abolitionists and toward free blacks (with whom they competed for jobs), and therefore favorable toward slavery and the Democratic Party. This aroused a nativist anti-Irish movement that strongly influenced the politics of several states in the 1840s and 1850s. The movement was fueled by traditional Protestant anti-Catholicism and by temperance reformers, abolitionists, proponents of public schools, and Protestant workingmen, who saw the Irish influx as a threat to their reforms, values, or status. In the 1840s there were numerous anti-Catholic riots and some pitched battles between Protestant and Catholic workingmen. In Philadelphia in 1844, a Catholic church was burned, 13 people were killed, and the state militia had to be called in to restore order.

In 1843, nativists in New York established the American Republican Party, which won 23 percent of the vote in New York City that year. The next year the Whigs made an alliance with the nativists, supporting their local candidates in return for American Republican support of Whig Presidential candidate Henry Clay. Though the nativist-laden Whigs were unsuccessful in the Presidential race, they won six Congressional races in New York City and Philadelphia and won the mayor's offices in New York and Boston.

Nativism reached its height in the Know-Nothing movement, in which the main goal was to exclude "foreigners" from political power by lengthening the naturalization period from five to as much as 21 years. In 1849 a secret nativist society called the Supreme Order of the Star-Spangled Banner was organized in New York City. When questioned about the Order, members would reply, "I know nothing." The Know-Nothings began to endorse political candidates, and by 1854 their strength had mushroomed to formidable proportions in several states, where under the name of the American party they elected legislators, governors, and congressmen. In the 1850s, the Know-Nothings dominated politics in Massachusetts and received a third of the vote in New York.

Then, within two or three years, the Know-Nothing movement subsided as quickly as it had risen. This was partly because of a falling off in immigration after 1854. More important, however, was the blazing intensity of the slavery issue. Northern nativists were absorbed into the new Republican Party, while those in the South (remnants of the Whig Party) retained the name American party and nominated Millard Fillmore for President in 1856.

The Know-Nothing legacy persisted in Northern politics, however; and during the next 40 years most Catholics voted Democratic, while evangelical Protestants usually voted Republican. Southern Whigs demanded that the Party support slavery while Northern Whigs demanded abolition. The result was the eventual dissolution of the Whigs, and the rise of the Republicans as the Northern Abolitionist Party. Local and state elections often turned on such issues as temperance, parochial schools, and the like.

The animosities expressed by the Know-Nothings flared up again in the American Protective Association (APA) of the 1880s and 1890s and in continuing patterns of prejudice against Catholics and immigrants.

The Know-Nothings were a party that had a brief, if significant, heyday. The other new party born in the heat of sectional conflict in these years, the Republican Party, is with us still. To that dramatic chapter in American history we now turn.

Millard Fillmore

THE SECTIONAL CRISIS, 1848–1861

THE ORIGIN OF SECTIONALISM

The Transcontinental Republic
The Southern Way of Life
Slavery
The Northern Way of Life

THE BASES OF SECTIONAL ANTAGONISM

Economic Causes
The Growth of the Slavery Issue
The Question of Extending Slavery
The Wilmot Proviso
The Doctrine of Popular Sovereignty

THE COMPROMISE OF 1850

Early Secessionist Sentiment
The Clay Compromise Proposals
The Douglas Strategy
The Fugitive Slave Act
Resistance Against the Fugitive
  Slave Law
The Election of 1852

KANSAS AND NEBRASKA

The Douglas Bill
"Appeal of the Independent Democrats"
The Election of 1854
"Bleeding Kansas"
"The Crime Against Kansas"

The Character of Franklin Pierce

ON THE EVE OF WAR

The Election of 1856
The Dred Scott Decision
The Lincoln-Douglas Debates
John Brown's Raid
The Election of 1860
The Democrats
The Republican Victory
Secession
The Failure of Compromise
Fort Sumter

"CAUSES OF THE CIVIL WAR"

THE ORIGIN OF SECTIONALISM

THE TRANSCONTINENTAL REPUBLIC

Between 1846 and 1848, with the settlement of the Oregon question and the Treaty of Guadalupe Hidalgo, the United States became in the full sense a two-ocean transcontinental republic. Except for Alaska, Hawaii, and a small segment of Arizona and New Mexico that would be acquired by the Gadsden Purchase in 1853, the country had reached its present territorial limits.

In one sense, the acquisition of the Southwest marked a fulfillment of American nationalism. No other nation on earth had grown so rapidly, and no people were prouder of their nation than the Americans, who boasted incessantly of the superiority of republican institutions. Yet, ironically, the climax of national growth also brought with it a crisis of national unity, for it precipitated a bitter rivalry between two dissimilar sections of the country—areas divided by the Mason-Dixon line and the Ohio River.

The problem of geographical rivalries was not a new one in the United States. In a country larger than all of Western Europe—with immense diversity of soil, terrain, and climate—conflicts had arisen more than once between the economic interests of one area and those of

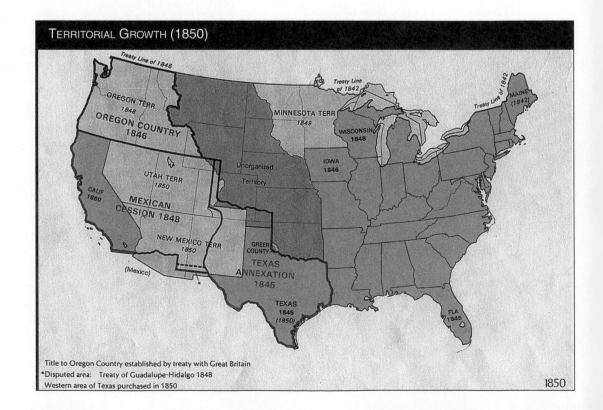

TERRITORIAL GROWTH (1850)

Treaty Line of 1846

OREGON TERR 1848

OREGON COUNTRY 1846

Treaty Line of 1842

Treaty Line of 1842

MAINE (1842)

MINNESOTA TERR 1849

WISCONSIN 1848

CALIF 1850

UTAH TERR 1850

MEXICAN CESSION 1848

Unorganized Territory

IOWA 1846

NEW MEXICO TERR 1850

(Mexico)

GREER COUNTY

TEXAS ANNEXATION 1845

TEXAS 1845 (1850)

FLA 1845

Title to Oregon Country established by treaty with Great Britain
*Disputed area: Treaty of Guadalupe-Hidalgo 1848
Western area of Texas purchased in 1850

1850

another. In fact, American history has been full of such conflicts, a division between East and West has often marked them. This was true, for instance, in the contest over the Bank of the United States at the time of Jackson and, later, in the battle between the advocates of the coinage of silver and the defenders of the gold standard in 1896. The theme of sectional rivalry has been so persistent that historians sometimes dispute whether the deepest antagonisms in American history have been between conflicting social classes or ethnic groups or religious denominations or between conflicting sections.

Thus, the sectional crisis between North and South, which approached its climax between 1848 and 1860, was in no sense unique; however, it did reach a unique pitch of intensity. Usually, competitive sectional forces have sought only to gain advantage over one another within a Union which both accept, but on this occasion the South became so alienated that it made a titanic effort to withdraw from the Union.

THE SOUTHERN WAY OF LIFE

Historians have never been able to agree on any one factor as the primary cause of this division, but they do agree in recognizing a cluster of contributing factors. As far back as the seventeenth century, North and South had developed along dissimilar lines. Virginia, Maryland, and the colonies to the South had based their economy on crops that were limited to latitudes of warm climate and a long growing season. Tobacco, the first of these to be introduced in the colonies, was followed by rice and indigo in Carolina and sugar in Louisiana, and, most importantly, by cotton throughout the lower South after the invention of the cotton gin in 1793. For the cultivation of these crops the plantation had evolved as the economic unit of production. Within the plantation system the labor supply had evolved to consist primarily of black slaves.

Actually, slave labor did not become dominant until the eighteenth century; but by the time of the American Revolution, slaves had come to outnumber free persons in many plantation districts. In 1850, 32 percent of the South's total population was held in slavery. In South Carolina and Mississippi a majority of the population consisted of slaves.

SLAVERY

Slavery presented a supreme paradox; for while slaves were human beings, they were also mere property. The complex relationships

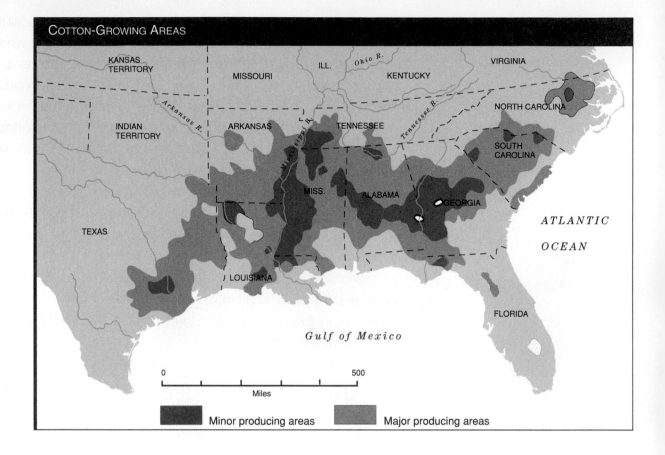

COTTON-GROWING AREAS

Minor producing areas   Major producing areas

between masters and slaves reflected this paradox. On the one hand, most white Christians recognized the slaves' humanity and believed that they had immortal souls to be saved. (Of course the idea of a better life after death could also be useful in diverting slave unrest into religious zeal.) The law viewed slaves as human beings to the extent of making them liable to punishment for serious crimes. Some masters permitted a wedding service for slave couples even though they could not legally be married. On plantations where blacks and whites mingled closely in everyday life, relations of intimacy and affection often developed. Even the proslavery stereotype of the "happy and carefree" slave, a reflection more of the whites' wishful thinking than of reality, was a backhanded way of admitting the slave's right to human happiness.

On the other hand, slaves were chattels—pieces of property. They could be bought, sold, mortgaged, bequeathed by will, or taken in payment for debt if their owners became bankrupt. They could not legally marry, or own property, or in most states, be taught to read or write. Owners might let them have a family, earn money, and even buy their freedom, but until they were free, money, spouse, and children could be taken away at any moment.

The evils of slavery can be looked at in several ways. Many abolitionists condemned slavery primarily for its physical harshness—the flogging and branding of slaves; the separation of mothers from children at the auction block, the brutal labor conditions, especially for slaves who had been "sold down the river" to work in the sugarcane fields; and the low standard of diet, clothing, and housing. Slaves experienced much cruelty and hardship no doubt; but, in some instances slaves may have been kindly treated.

The worst feature of slavery may well have been its social and cultural impact on both slave and master. The slave's powerlessness tended to create a sense of dependency and to discourage self-reliance. Stable family life was difficult in a situation where parents and children might be sold away from each other, white men could sexually exploit female slaves, and a slave father was legally helpless to protect his wife and children. The master's power over fellow human beings tended to create feelings of superiority and domination, including vis-à-vis his wife as well as his slaves. The racial theories that

A group of slaves on a South Carolina plantation

bolstered slavery bred in most white people a belief in black inferiority. Some blacks, also subscribed to this notion.

Of course this does not mean that all or even most slaves carried the psychological scars of dependence and inferiority. On many plantations the black driver, rather than the overseer, exercised authority in day-to-day operations. As a sort of labor leader as well as "boss," the driver could do much to win better working conditions for the slaves. Drivers, slave artisans, highly-skilled cooks, and other blacks with critical skills played important roles in Southern life and provided other slaves with role models of self-respect and limited power within a system from which few could hope to escape.

Moreover, despite repression the slaves sustained a vigorous black culture largely independent of surrounding white institutions. Natural leaders in the slave quarters often became eloquent preachers in the "invisible institution" of the black church, whose congregations worshipped apart from whites (sometimes secretly) in spite of laws against separate worship. Some of these preachers, especially Gabriel Prosser in 1800 and Nat Turner in 1831, plotted armed insurrections to strike for freedom. The slaves created the most original and moving music in antebellum America—the spirituals—that expressed their longing for freedom as well as their resignation to sorrow, and evolved after the Civil War into the blues and eventually jazz.

Recent research suggests that while slavery made stable family life difficult—and sometimes brutal—a majority of slaves nevertheless formed strong ties of kinship and family. Thus although slavery's impact on black people could be repressive, the countervailing force of a positive black culture provides an impressive example of survival in the face of adversity.

Furthermore, there were many mechanisms for resistance, some more successful than others. Some slaves—predominantly male—managed to run away. Others succeeded in being truant for a short while though they may have faced severe punishment upon their return. Scholars have suggested that slaves may have deliberately broken farm implements or worked at a relatively slow pace by way of proving to themselves their independence from the master's interests—or maybe even to punish the master. For women, as a recent book by Stephanie Camp suggests, the assertion of self may have taken the form of making themselves party clothes out of whatever materials they could cobble together so that they could then sneak away from the quarters at night for an unauthorized good time in their dress-up clothes. The slaves' freedom of movement was constantly at risk of being monitored by slave patrols, so the bondspeople had

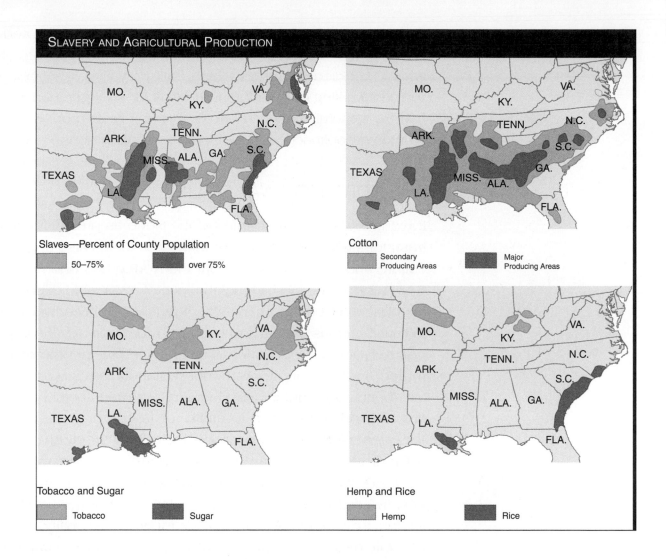

SLAVERY AND AGRICULTURAL PRODUCTION

Slaves—Percent of County Population
- 50–75%
- over 75%

Cotton
- Secondary Producing Areas
- Major Producing Areas

Tobacco and Sugar
- Tobacco
- Sugar

Hemp and Rice
- Hemp
- Rice

to be prudent in order to carve out time and space for either surreptitious religious services or for "frolics."

Slavery also put Southern whites on the defensive, ever fearful of slave insurrection and ever conscious that slavery was condemned throughout most of the Western world. As a result they isolated themselves more and more, imposing an "intellectual blockade" to keep out not only abolitionist ideas but also any social ideas implying freedom or change. To defend their system, they idealized their society as romantic and chivalric. At best, they realized their ideal in the attainment of a real aristocracy, but the tradition was maintained at a high cost.

By 1850 the Southern system, its rural life and its slave labor, had led to the development of a somewhat conservative temper, a marked stratification of social orders, and a paternalistic type of society. The power of all landowners to rule their own workers on their own plantations had prevented the growth of a strong public authority. As a result, violence was frequent, and qualities of personal courage and physical prowess were especially valued. For instance, the practice of dueling, which had died out in the North, still prevailed. The taboo against women working outside the home was far stronger than in the North; and, in general, gender norms were far more conservative. Even women schoolteachers in the South were often Northerners.

THE NORTHERN WAY OF LIFE

It would be a mistake to think of the North as presenting a total contrast, for the majority of people in the free states also engaged in agriculture and lived a rural life; but the Northern economy and culture were more diversified. In the absence of a valuable export crop such as tobacco or cotton, many New England Yankees had turned early to commerce as a means of securing money to buy the imports they needed. During the Napoleonic wars, when their commerce was disrupted and the supply of imported manufactures was cut off, they had begun a manufacturing industry. As manufacturing grew, cities grew with it.

Prosperity and rapid economic growth in the North fostered a belief in progress and innovation quite different from the more traditional (or static) attitudes of the South. Although the factory system brought with it a certain amount of exploitation of labor through low wages, the fact that all men were free made for greater mobility, greater equality, more democracy, and less sharply defined social stratification than in the South. The modernizing North grew to value the commercial virtues of thrift, enterprise, and hard work, in contrast to the more traditional and military virtues that held a priority in the South.

Such differences as these can easily be exaggerated, for a great deal of frontier Americanism prevailed in both the North and the South. Similarly, evangelical Protestantism was the dominant religion of both sections. The materialistic pursuit of wealth motivated cotton planters as well as Yankee industrialists. To a European, all Americans seemed bumptiously democratic; and in the South the Whig party, favored by most planter aristocrats, could not have competed against the Democratic Party at all unless it had adopted the democratic symbols of the log cabin, the coonskin hat, and the cider barrel.

THE BASES OF SECTIONAL ANTAGONISM

Regional dissimilarity, however, need not lead to conflict. In the United States today there are profound differences between the red states and the blue states, the rural and the urban regions, but no one is talking about secession, let alone war. The antagonism that drove North and South to war in the mid-nineteenth century, therefore, needs to be explained.

ECONOMIC CAUSES

In one sense the antagonism was economic, for the dissimilar economic interests of the North and the South caused them to favor opposite economic policies and therefore to clash politically. Essentially, the South with its cotton economy produced raw materials for a textile industry centered in Britain. Accordingly, the South sold on the world market; and, in return, it needed to buy its manufactured goods where they were cheapest, which was also in the world market, and to keep down taxes and governmental costs as much as possible.

For the more diversified Northern economy, the needs were different. Northern manufacturers and workers wanted tariffs to protect them from the competition of low-priced goods produced by cheaper labor abroad. Manufacturers and farmers alike needed improved transportation facilities ("internal improvements") in the form of roads, canals, and railroads to foster inter-regional exchanges of goods. As a result, Northern economic groups and their congressional representatives therefore, supported state and federal appropriations to build better roads and to assist canal and railroad construction.

Some of the upper South states like Kentucky and Maryland, with urban and manufacturing centers of their own, supported appropriations for these purposes but the cotton-growing South did not fit into this scheme. Most of the cotton and tobacco crop was shipped by river or by short, locally built railroads to river or coastal port cities for export abroad. Internal improvements meant only that the South would be paying part of the governmental costs of a program from which it did not benefit. Indeed, the new transportation routes diverted trade away from the South's own Mississippi River system, which drew trade southward toward New Orleans. In addition, the tariff meant that the South would be prevented from buying its manufactures from those who bought its raw materials and would be forced by law to pay a higher, tariff-supported price for its manufactures. As the Virginian, John Randolph of Roanoke, had angrily declared, "we shall only pay more for worse goods." Because of these economic factors, North and South tended to vote against each other on questions of tariff, internal improvements, and other extensions of the power of the central government. Their rivalry had reached a crisis at

John Randolph

the time of the Nullification Controversy in 1833, when South Carolina was ready to defy federal law (see Chapter 10). The crisis had only been averted when other Southern states had not committed to take up arms in supported of South Carolina. The South as a whole had resented federal economic policies but had never opposed them to the point of breaking up the Union, to which most Southerners felt strong patriotic loyalty.

THE GROWTH OF THE SLAVERY ISSUE

A deeper cause of division, however, was the institution of slavery. Until the 1770s slavery had scarcely been regarded as a moral question at all, except by the Quakers. In one form or another the institution had existed in other lands for thousands of years, and the slave trade had been essential to the colonization of the Western Hemisphere. As late as 1780 there was no division into slave states and free states; slaves were held in every state of the Union. They were less numerous in the North only because they were less profitable there. In the late eighteenth century (during the Age of Reason, or the Enlightenment), however, slavery came under attack from believers in natural law, human equality, and human rights. At the same time, emphasis in the churches shifted from a limited concern with the personal salvation of the individual to a fuller application of Christian teaching in relation to human society. Thus, the savage penal code of earlier times was modified, various social reforms were adopted, and slavery came under attack.

The states from Pennsylvania northward shared in this movement against slavery. By 1804 all of them had adopted laws for the gradual or immediate emancipation of their slaves, and Congress had prohibited the importation of any more slaves from Africa after 1808. For a time it appeared that the South might also participate in this movement. Southern Enlightenment leaders like Jefferson condemned slavery in the abstract, and antislavery societies were active in the South. Furthermore, slavery was restricted to the rice and tobacco economy, which was static and no longer very profitable. This meant that the Southern economy as a whole did not depend on slave labor.

Jefferson, however, never freed more than a handful of his own slaves since his exorbitant spending habits rendered him to a state of indebtedness virtually all of his life; slaves were his primary assets that not only could be sold at any time to pay debts, but also multiplied naturally. The Southern antislavery societies devoted their efforts mainly to encouraging the emigration of free blacks. The tenor of antislavery sentiment among Southerners, apart from the Quakers and the early Methodists, was one of anguished hand wringing over an inherited evil rather than vigorous action for its abolition.

The introduction of cotton and the cotton gin injected greater vitality into the slave system. In one generation, the cultivation of short-staple cotton spread across the lower South from middle Georgia to the banks of the Brazos in Texas. During every decade from 1800 to 1860 the value and the volume of the crop doubled. In this dynamic and expanding economy, the price of slaves rose and fell with the price of cotton. Slavery accompanied cotton as it expanded into the new areas. By 1820 both slavery and cotton were completely interwoven into the whole Southern system.

While this was happening, the humanitarian crusade against slavery in Great Britain (which abolished slavery in the West Indies in 1833), in France (which abolished it in 1848), and in the Northern states (where the abolitionists became increasingly militant in their denunciations) led the South to a defensive reaction. By 1830 Southern leaders were no longer saying, as some had said earlier, that slavery was an evil but too deeply rooted to be abolished at once. Instead, they were beginning to assert that slavery was a positive good. They defended it with claims that it had been sanctioned in the Bible and that the Negro was biologically inferior to the white. They argued that the exploitation of Negro workers by the slavery system was not so harsh as the exploitation of white workers by a wage system in which the worker received only a bare subsistence when he was working and no subsistence at all when he was not. They held that, since social divisions were inevitable, assigning leadership to one class and subordination to another was better than having an endless struggle between classes.

These clashing arguments polarized the two sections more and more with each decade after 1830. As the abolitionists became more militant in their crusade against the "sin" of slavery, the South became so defensive about criticism that it would not tolerate any expression of antislavery opinion.

In spite of this disagreement on the ethics of slavery, several factors prevented a legal or physical clash over the question. To begin with, slavery was widely regarded as a matter for the states locally rather than for the federal government nationally. (South Carolina's attempt at nullification was actually a challenge to the government's authority in this area, as well as in setting tariffs). At that time, people regarded the federal system more as a loose association of states and less as a consolidated nation, and they were willing to leave many important questions to state action. Further, it was generally understood that the Constitution, in its "three-fifths" and fugitive slave clauses (see Chapter 7), protected the South's right to practice slavery. It was on the basis of such provisions that the Southern states had agreed to join the Union.

Apart from the question of legal or constitutional obligation, many Americans took the position that the harmony of the Union was simply more important than the ethics of slavery—that the slave question must not be permitted to weaken the Union and that the abolitionists were wrong to keep up constant agitation on an issue that caused sectional antagonism. The abolitionists, who were in the minority, felt that the Union was not worth saving unless it was based upon freedom.

THE QUESTION OF EXTENDING SLAVERY

All this meant that as long as the institution of slavery was confined to the existing slave states, few Northerners were willing to act against it; and it was not an explosive question politically. When the question of extending slavery to new areas arose, however, the opposition was far more determined. As early as the Ordinance of 1787, the old Congress under the Articles of Confederation had agreed to exclude slavery from the region north of the Ohio River. Some people, motivated by sincere antislavery sentiments, were determined to "contain" slavery. Others cared nothing about the evils of slavery but wanted to reserve unsettled areas for white residents only. Furthermore, many people wanted to bring these new areas to the support of the North in the economic struggle between North and South. The South, conversely, was equally convinced that the growth of the country should not be all on the side of the North, reducing the South to a defenseless minority. This feeling made the South unwilling to concede even the areas where there was little prospect of extending slavery.

Because of these attitudes, the acquisition of any new area, the organization of any new territory, and the admission of any new state had always involved a possible flare-up over the slavery question. There had been such a crisis in 1819, when Missouri applied for admission to statehood as the first state (except Louisiana) to be formed out of the Louisiana Purchase. In the same way, the prospect of acquisition of territory from Mexico as a result of the Mexican War brought on a more protracted and more serious crisis beginning in 1846.

A few months after the beginning of the Mexican War, President Polk asked Congress to appropriate $2 million to be used in negotiating for land to be acquired from Mexico at the termination of the war. Many Northern Democrats were at this time angry with Polk, partly because he had vetoed a rivers and harbors bill important to mid-western economic development and partly because they felt he had violated the expansionist promises on which he was elected. His platform had called for the "reoccupation" of Oregon, the "reannexation" of Texas, and for "all of Oregon or none." In fact, a Polk campaign slogan had been "Fifty-four forty or fight," suggesting that Polk would prefer to go to war with England rather than settle for a Canada/Oregon border that did not include much of what is now British Columbia all the way to the southern tip of Alaska. This had put the question of expansion on a bisectional basis by promising Oregon, sure to be free territory, for the North and Texas, which already had slavery, for the South. After becoming President, however, Polk had compromised on Oregon by accepting the boundary at the forty-ninth parallel instead of at 54° 40´ and thus avoiding confrontation with England, while pushing expansion toward the southwest to the fullest extent by waging war with Mexico.

THE WILMOT PROVISO

This was the state of affairs when David Wilmot, a Democrat from Pennsylvania, introduced a resolution in the House of Representatives that slavery should be prohibited in any territory acquired from Mexico with the $2 million Polk requested. This free-soil resolution passed the House where the North was stronger, but failed to pass in the Senate where the South had equal strength. The disagreement of Senate and House marked a deadlock in Congress that lasted for four years, blocking the organization of governments for the new areas. The result was a steady increase in sectional tension.

In 1848, at the end of the Mexican War, the victorious United States acquired territory embracing the present states of Nevada,

California, and Utah, most of Arizona and New Mexico, and parts of Colorado and Wyoming. Mexico also relinquished all claims to Texas above the Rio Grande. In the same year gold was discovered in California, and by 1849 the Gold Rush was in full swing.

The need for organizing the new land was urgent, and the territorial question became the foremost issue in public life. At one extreme on this question stood Wilmot and the "free-soilers," both Whig and Democrat, who demanded the exclusion of slavery from the new areas by act of Congress. At the other extreme, most Southern Whigs and Democrats adopted the position of John C. Calhoun, who argued that the territories were owned in common by all the states (rather than by the federal government, which was only a joint agent for the states) and that all citizens had an equal right to take their property (including slaves) to the common territory. Therefore, in Calhoun's logic, Congress had no power under the Constitution to exclude slavery from any territory.

THE DOCTRINE OF POPULAR SOVEREIGNTY

Political leaders who wanted some kind of adjustment or middle ground were not satisfied with either Wilmot's or Calhoun's alternative—one of which conceded nothing to the South, the other nothing to the North. They sought a more "moderate" position, and some of them advocated an extension of the Missouri Compromise line of 36° 30′ to the Pacific. Most of them, however, were more attracted, however, by a proposal sponsored by Lewis Cass, senator from Michigan, for what was called "popular sovereignty" or "squatter sovereignty." Cass contended that the fairest and most democratic solution would be to let the people in the territories decide for themselves whether they would have slavery, just as the people in the states had already decided. Cass' proposal offered an attractive means for keeping the slavery question out of federal politics, but it contained one ambiguity that he adroitly refused to clarify. It did not specify *when* the people in the territories should make the decision. If they could make the decision as soon as the territory was organized, free soil could be attained by popular vote as easily as by congressional vote. According to Calhoun, popular exclusion at this stage would be just as wrong as congressional exclusion, for it would mean that Congress was giving to the territory a power that Congress did not have and, therefore, could not give. If, however, the voters in a territory could decide on slavery only when they applied for statehood, this would mean that the territories would have been left open to slavery quite as much as by Calhoun's position.

Far from reducing the amount of support for popular sovereignty, however, this ambiguity actually added to the attractiveness of the doctrine. Antislavery people argued that popular sovereignty would result in free territories while proslavery advocates contended that it guaranteed slavery a fair chance to establish itself during the period before statehood.

THE COMPROMISE OF 1850

While these various positions on the territorial extension of slavery were being developed, the impasse in Congress continued. For three entire sessions, covering most of the Polk administration, nothing could be voted for California or the Southwest. It was only after long delay that an act to organize the Oregon Territory without slavery was adopted.

In 1848, when the two national parties faced this question in a presidential election, both of them evaded it. The Democrats nominated Cass whose reputation was based on the idea of "popular sovereignty," on a platform that still did not say *when* the people of a territory could vote on slavery. The Whigs nominated a military hero, Zachary Taylor, who had never been in politics, without any platform whatever. Further muddying the waters was the development of the

Free Soil Party, which held its inaugural convention in Buffalo. The Free Soil Party nominated former President and Jacksonian Democrat Martin Van Buren for President and Charles Francis Adams of the Whig Party for Vice President on a platform of "Free soil, free speech, free labor, and free men." In the election campaign, the Free Soilers were successful in making slavery the main issue of the campaign, but they did not carry a single state. In the main contest between Taylor

Martin Van Buren and Charles Francis Adams

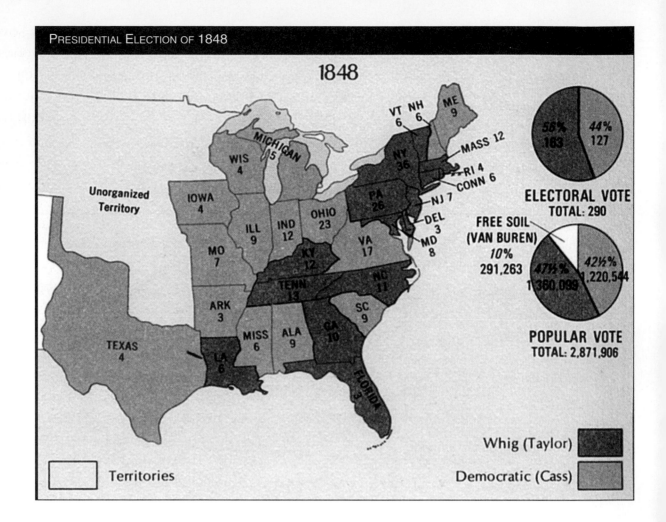

PRESIDENTIAL ELECTION OF 1848

1848

Unorganized Territory

MICHIGAN 5

WIS 4

IOWA 4

ILL 9 IND 12 OHIO 23

MO 7

ARK 3

TEXAS 4

LA 6

MISS 6 ALA 9 GA 10

TENN 13

KY 12

VA 17

NC 11

SC 9

FLORIDA 3

VT 6 NH 6 ME 9

NY 36

MASS 12

RI 4 CONN 6

PA 26

NJ 7

DEL 3

MD 8

ELECTORAL VOTE TOTAL: 290

56% 163 44% 127

FREE SOIL (VAN BUREN) 10% 291,263

47½% 1,360,099 42½% 1,220,544

POPULAR VOTE TOTAL: 2,871,906

Territories

Whig (Taylor)

Democratic (Cass)

and Cass, however, which turned out to be a contest between frank evasion and concealed evasion, Taylor, who owned over 100 slaves on plantations in Mississippi and Louisiana, was triumphant. Taylor was inaugurated as President in 1849.

EARLY SECESSIONIST SENTIMENT

Meanwhile, the House of Representatives had repeatedly voted in favor of Wilmot's principle of free soil by congressional action. The seeming imminence of a free-soil victory had, in turn, aroused bitter resentment in the South. For the first time many Southerners began to think of withdrawing from the Union if Congress voted to prevent them from taking their slaves into areas they had helped to win and to pay for. By 1848, Southerners in Congress were beginning to speak rather freely of disunion. After Taylor was elected, he sent envoys to California and New Mexico to persuade settlers in the newly acquired territories to draft constitutions and apply for admission to the Union as states, rather than as territories. The inhabitants of both territories were predominantly anti-slavery. In California, gold rushers did not want to have to compete with gangs of slave labor in gold prospecting. In New Mexico, the climate was simply too arid to grow cotton and slave labor was not necessary on the open range. Southerners realized that, although he was a Louisiana slaveholder that brought slaves with him to the White House that he kept hidden in the White House attic, Taylor was not going to block free-soil legislation; and they began to organize Southern resistance. Jefferson Davis of Mississippi argued, "We are about permanently to destroy the balance of power between the sections."

In October 1849 a state convention in Mississippi called for a convention of Southern state delegates to meet at Nashville, Tennessee, the following June to work out a united Southern position. Five Southern states officially elected delegates to such a convention, and representatives were unofficially chosen from four others.

Thus, when Taylor's first Congress met in December 1849, the need for organizing the area acquired from Mexico was urgent; and the relations between North and South were at a crisis. This crisis became more acute when Taylor announced his support for admitting California directly to statehood, without going through a territorial stage, and his intention to support the same plan for New Mexico in due course. Technically, this plan bypassed the question of congressional exclusion from the decision on slavery; but in substance, however, it would represent a free-soil victory, for the proposed states seemed fairly certain to be free states. At this prospect Southern protests were intensified. Though historians today disagree as to whether the country was close to disunion, certainly many prominent leaders at the time feared that it was.

A separate issue threatening disunion at the time was a border dispute between the United States and the new state of Texas. According to

Zachary Taylor

the 1836 Treaty of Velasco under which Texas had staked its claim to independence, the Texas southern and western border was the Rio Grande. Texans sent envoys to the upper Rio Grande Valley (present day Albuquerque) and Santa Fe to organize county governments, but the residents rebuffed them. At Santa Fe, the Texan envoys were ordered to "cease and desist at every peril" by United States Army General Kearney, who exercised political authority in Santa Fe in the aftermath of the War with Mexico. Nevertheless, Texans still claimed their rights to the territory, and Peter Hansborough Bell won the Texas Gubernatorial election of 1849 on a platform of retaining Santa Fe by force. Though Texas had fought for a decade to join the Union and had not been an American state for even four years, the Texans were threatening war with the United States over Santa Fe. Under Texas' Articles of Annexation, however, a provision stated that Congress would settle border disputes. Northerners opposed Texas possession of Santa Fe primarily because they viewed it as an extension of slave territory into New Mexico. The Santa Fe issue would, therefore, become connected to the entire sectional debate.

THE CLAY COMPROMISE PROPOSALS

Among those leaders fearing disunion was Senator Henry Clay of Kentucky. As a spokesman of the border states, one who was always anxious to promote sectional harmony and as one who had played a leading part in arranging the compromises of 1820 (Missouri) and 1833 (Nullification), Clay was a natural leader of compromise. Although a Whig, he was at odds with President Taylor. Accordingly, Clay came forward early in the congressional session of 1850, with an elaborate compromise designed to cover the slavery question in all its national aspects. Clay's plan called for: (1) admitting California as a free state; (2) organizing the rest of the Mexican cession into two territories, Utah and New Mexico, which were to decide for themselves whether slavery should be permitted or abolished; (3) awarding New Mexico part of the area on the upper Rio Grande claimed by Texas, including Santa Fe, but compensating Texas through federal payment of the $10 million Texas debt contracted before annexation; (4) abolishing the sale of slaves in the District of Columbia but guaranteeing slavery itself in the District; and (5) enacting an effective law to compel the return of fugitive slaves who had escaped into the free states.

Clay's proposal brought on a long, brilliant, and famous series of debates in Congress. Clay himself made an immensely eloquent appeal for his plan as a means of saving the Union, giving 70 speeches urging its passage. Calhoun, who did not support the compromise directly, helped it indirectly by coming into the Senate almost in a dying condition to warn solemnly of the danger to the Union and the determination of the South to maintain its rights. The most important speech of the session was made by Daniel Webster, who was Clay's only peer as an orator and who was generally regarded as an antislavery man. On the seventh of March, Webster announced his support of the compromise and made a powerful argument that slavery was naturally excluded from the west by climatic, physical, and agricultural conditions and that there was no need to bring on a crisis by adopting an antislavery law, such as the Wilmot Proviso, to accomplish what had already been settled by physical environment. "I would not re-enact a law of God," said Webster, impressively, "I would not reaffirm an ordinance of nature."

Despite great oratorical support, Clay's "omnibus bill," incorporating all his proposals in one measure, faced heavy opposition. President Taylor was waiting to veto it, and in July it was cut to pieces on the floor by a process of amendment in which Northern and Southern extremists voted together to prevent its passage.

Clay, Calhoun, Fillmore, and Webster in the Senate

Clay—old, worn out, and badly discouraged—went off to Newport for a rest.

THE DOUGLAS STRATEGY

Even before this vote was taken, however, the tide had turned. President Taylor died, and his successor, Millard Fillmore, favored the compromise and immediately began to exert presidential influence to support it.

Meanwhile, Stephen A. Douglas, a young and vigorous senator from Illinois, took over the management of the compromise forces in Congress. Douglas was not a great orator, but he was a supremely effective rough-and-tumble debater, a man of immense energy ("a steam engine in breeches" was the phrase) and a most sagacious political tactician. He perceived that there was not a clear majority in favor of the compromise and that it could not be passed in the form in which Clay had presented it; but he realized that if Clay's proposals were taken up one by one, they could be passed by a combination of those who favored the compromise as a whole and those who favored each particular measure. (For instance, a majority composed of compromise men and antislavery men could admit California, while the Fugitive Slave Act would be adopted by a combination of compromise men and proslavery men.) Douglas applied this strategy so effectively that within a few weeks Clay's entire program was enacted into law.

The adoption of the "Compromise of 1850" ended the crisis. It also broke the long deadlock and gave badly needed political organization to California and the Southwest. Because it brought a great sense of relief to those who had feared for the safety of the Union, it was hailed as a great and final settlement that defused the slavery issue once and for all as a source of discord in the Union. Free-Soiler Salmon Chase, however, drew the ominous conclusion that "the question of slavery in the territories has been avoided. It has not been settled." Unfortunately for the nation, Chase's conclusion would prove to be correct.

THE FUGITIVE SLAVE ACT

In fact, the Compromise of 1850 settled far less than it appeared to settle. For Utah and New Mexico the Compromise of 1850 admitted them to the Union as territories with "popular sovereignty" to determine the status of slavery in each territory. These provisions left open the explosive question Lewis Cass had so carefully avoided:

Could the citizens of the territory outlaw slavery in the territory? More important, while laying to rest the explosive issue of the Wilmot Proviso, it brought to life the even more explosive issue of the fugitive slave. The question of the slave in the territories was a legal and abstract question—a question of what was later called "an imaginary Negro in an impossible place"—but the question of the runaway slave was dramatic and real, involv-

Lewis Cass

ing a human creature in quest of freedom that was being hunted down by his fellow humans.

Finally, the compromise had never commanded a real majority and had been enacted only by finesse. The Southern states accepted it somewhat reluctantly, but Georgia spoke for the rest of them when its legislature voted resolutions that if the compromise were not fully enforced, Georgia would withdraw from the Union. In fact, while the Southern disunionists were agreeing not to demand secession at this time, the Southern unionists were almost forced to agree to the *principle* of secession in order to get the secessionists to agree not to exercise it at that time. Meanwhile, in the North the anti-slavery forces were pouring their denunciations upon the Fugitive Slave Act and upon Daniel Webster for supporting it. Perhaps never before in American politics had political invective been so bitter.

For a time, the fugitive slave question raised a terrific furor. To appreciate the uproar, one must understand that the law contained a number of very extreme features. The general idea was that when slaves successfully escaped their captors in the South and fled to territory in the North where black persons could be free, Northerners were obligated to help the Southerners apprehend the runaway slaves and return them to their masters. Additionally, the Fugitive Slave Act denied trial by jury in the case of alleged fugitives and provided for their cases to be decided by a special federal commissioner. Those accused of being fugitives could not testify in their own defense; hence, if anyone were captured in a case of mistaken identity, he or she would not be able to say so in court. Further, it paid the commissioner a fee that was higher in cases where the alleged fugitive was returned to slavery than in cases where the fugitive was set free. Though this arrangement was defended on the ground that there was much more paper work in one case than the other, it led to severe criticism. Still further, the law stipulated that any citizen could be called upon to participate in the enforcement process, which meant that those who opposed slavery must not only permit the capture of fugitives but might possibly be made to help in their capture. Those Northern citizens who failed to assist in the capture of a slave when they were able to do so could be subject to both fines and imprisonment. The very idea that Northerners would have to assist Southern slave masters in recovering their "property" was abhorrent to Northern abolitionists, but to be jailed or fined for failing to do so was a double indignity.

Apart from these features of the law itself, the act aroused criticism because in operation it applied not only to slaves who were then running away but also to any slaves who had ever run away. There were many fugitives who had lived quietly in the North for many years and who had been quite safe from arrest under the relatively ineffectual Fugitive Slave Law of 1793. Under the act of 1850, they found themselves in real danger. Some Southerners went north rounding up black people with little consideration of how long they had been free or, in some cases, if they in fact had ever been slaves. For example, in 1851 a black man who had lived in Indiana for 19 years was torn from his family and sent into slavery. Throughout the North, the law terrorized blacks, for those who were not fugitives had reason to fear being kidnapped quite as much as actual runaways had reason to fear being arrested. Consequently, a wave of migration to Canada set in, and several thousand blacks moved to Ontario. Northern abolitionists added fuel to the fire of sectional tensions over the Fugitive Slave Act by impeding the capture of fugitives even when there was no question that the person was a recent runaway.

The problems with the Fugitive Slave Act reflect the fact that the 1850 Compromise had never commanded a real majority and had been enacted only by finesse. The Southern states accepted it somewhat reluctantly; but Georgia spoke for the rest of them when its legislature voted resolutions that if the compromise were not fully enforced, Georgia would withdraw from the Union. In fact, while the Southern disunionists were agreeing not to demand secession at this time, the Southern unionists were almost forced to agree to the *principle* of secession in order to get the secessionists to agree not to exercise it at that time. Meanwhile, in the North the antislavery forces were pouring their denunciations upon the Fugitive Slave Act and upon Daniel Webster for supporting it. Perhaps never before in American politics had political invective been so bitter.

RESISTANCE AGAINST THE FUGITIVE SLAVE LAW

A series of fugitive slave episodes followed which kept the country at a high pitch of excitement. In Boston, leading citizens openly asserted their intention to violate the law. In October a "vigilance committee" headed by one of the foremost citizens of Boston, the Reverend Theodore Parker, smuggled two undoubted slaves out of the country. Four months later a crowd, mostly black, seized a prisoner, Shadrach, from the courtroom and spirited him away to Canada. Finally, in April 1851 the government succeeded in returning a slave from Boston, from which city it was boasted that no slave had ever been returned. This was accomplished only after mobs had surrounded the courthouse for several days. Only once again was a slave, Anthony Burns, returned from Boston. In his case a mob stormed the courthouse in an effort to rescue him, and a large military force was required in order to prevent his rescue.

In other cities, also, rescues and attempted rescues kept the pot boiling, and the fugitive slave question became for a time the foremost issue of the day. Yet the excitement and emotion that the issue generated have made it hard to get at the facts about whether the escape of slaves from the South was numerically significant. On the one hand, Northern antislavery advocates boasted of their resistance to the law and claimed that they were operating a vast "underground railroad" which had helped 80,000 slaves to escape their pursuers. On the other, spokesmen of the South, indignant at the open violation of the law, complained bitterly that 100,000 slaves had been abducted over a 40-year period. These were probably inflated figures. The Underground Railroad was probably more extensive

Anthony Burns

in legend than in reality and more important as a weapon of psychological warfare than as an escape route for slaves. It also appears that in many parts of the North the Fugitive Slave Act had public support and was well enforced.

There is no doubt, however, that the fugitive question dramatized the issue of slavery to a spectacular degree. The human being in quest of freedom, trying to escape from bloodthirsty pursuers, was an immensely moving figure. By changing the focus of the slavery question from the legal status of an imaginary chattel in a remote territory to the human plight of an individual human being in a nearby street, the Compromise of 1850 had, perhaps, created more tension than it relieved. In the final analysis, the Fugitive Slave Act was largely an unenforceable failure as evidenced by the fact that in the decade between the passage of the act and the Civil War, only 300 slaves were returned to their masters under the act. Given that a major fear of many northern whites was that blacks would leave the southern plantations and move north, one might have expected at least as many slaves to be returned to their masters during this period—even if the act had never been passed.

It is by no means an accident that *Uncle Tom's Cabin* (1851–1852), the classic literary protest against slavery, was published less than a year after the enactment of the fugitive law. In fact, Harriet Beecher Stowe's sister-in-law urged her to write something in response to the new law, and the novel was the result. The book's most dramatic scene was that of the fugitive slave woman, Eliza, crossing the ice-bound Ohio River with her son in her arms as a slave trader pursued her. This book, one of America's all-time best sellers, forced readers to see the humanity of the slaves and wrung sympathy and tears from countless people who had never previously been moved by the abolitionists.

THE ELECTION OF 1852

If the Fugitive Slave law dramatized the issue of slavery, the crisis preceding the Compromise of 1850 had dramatized the issue of Union. Many Northerners who thoroughly disapproved of slavery felt that the question of Union was more important and must have priority. Consequently, despite fugitive slave episodes, the compromise received strong support throughout much of the country; and though there had not been a clear majority in favor of adopting it, there was certainly a clear majority in favor of maintaining it.

The firmness of public support for the Compromise of 1850 showed up clearly in the election of 1852. As it approached, Millard

Fillmore, who had signed the compromise acts while serving out the term of Zachary Taylor, aspired to a term of his own. In the party convention, however, Northern Whigs blocked the effort of Southern Whigs to nominate Fillmore and forced the nomination instead of General Winfield Scott, who had captured Mexico City in the Mexican War. Scott was the Whigs' third military hero, and they hoped that, like Harrison and Taylor he would win the White House on his military record.

The adoption of a platform revealed a deep division among the Whigs. The majority secured the adoption of a plank accepting the Compromise of 1850, including the Fugitive Slave Act, as a final settlement; but there was strong opposition, consisting mostly of delegates who supported Scott. Scott, who was pompous and politically clumsy, tried to get out of this dilemma by saying merely, "I accept the nomination with the resolutions attached;" however, it was clear that he was not a thoroughgoing supporter of the Compromise.

The Democrats settled their differences between rival candidates by agreeing on a dark horse, Franklin Pierce of New Hampshire, who had served with gallantry in the Mexican War. Pierce later proved a weak man, with a serious alcohol addiction (later as President even being arrested in Washington for recklessly trampling a woman with his horse while intoxicated) and a depressed wife (Jane) who wrote letters to their dead son. However, he was an attractive candidate—handsome and pleasing in his manner—and the Democrats gave him united support on a platform that proclaimed the finality of the Compromise.

Franklin Pierce

The position of the two parties gave the voters a fairly clear choice on the question of compromise—Pierce and his Democratic Party were united on it; the Whigs were not. The voters exercised their option in a decisive way. Pierce carried all but four states—two in the North and two in the South.

The defeat smashed the Whig Party, which was

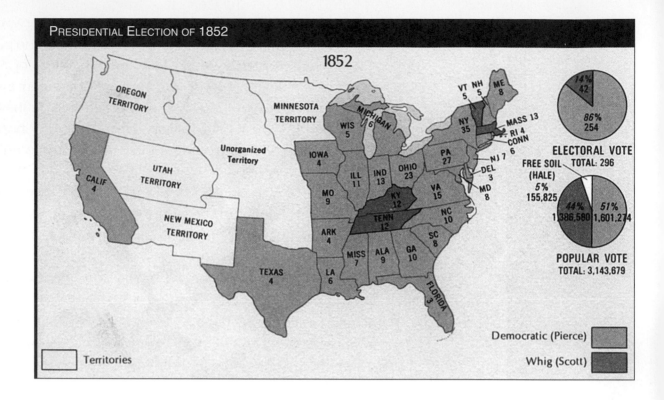

PRESIDENTIAL ELECTION OF 1852

1852

OREGON TERRITORY

MINNESOTA TERRITORY

MICHIGAN 6

WIS 5

VT 5 · NH 5 · ME 8

NY 35 · MASS 13 · RI 4 · CONN 6

IOWA 4

Unorganized Territory

PA 27 · NJ 7 · DEL 3 · MD 8

UTAH TERRITORY

ILL 11 · IND 13 · OHIO 23

CALIF 4

MO 9

KY 12 · VA 15

NEW MEXICO TERRITORY

TENN 12 · NC 10

ARK 4

SC 8

TEXAS 4

MISS 7 · ALA 9 · GA 10

LA 6

FLORIDA 3

ELECTORAL VOTE TOTAL: 296
14% 42
86% 254

FREE SOIL (HALE) 5% 155,825
44% 1,386,580
51% 1,601,274

POPULAR VOTE TOTAL: 3,143,679

Democratic (Pierce)
Whig (Scott)

Territories

already badly divided between the "Cotton Whigs" of the South and the "Conscience Whigs" of the North. Though many important figures—including Abraham Lincoln—remained in the Whig organization somewhat longer, it was never a national party after 1852. This meant that only one national party—the Democratic—was left, which in turn meant that there was now only one remaining political organization in which Northern and Southern leaders were still seeking to smooth out sectional disagreements for the sake of party victory.

KANSAS AND NEBRASKA

THE DOUGLAS BILL

Pierce's campaign had promised harmony for the Union and finality for the Compromise, but his administration brought just the opposite. His first Congress had barely met in December 1853, when the territorial question arose again in a new form. Stephen A. Douglas wanted to organize territorial government for the region west of Iowa and Missouri. This area lay within the Louisiana Purchase; and since it was north of 36° 30´, it had been closed to slavery by the Missouri

Compromise of 1820. Douglas, therefore, at first introduced a bill to organize free territories.

Southern senators, however, voted against his legislation and thus blocked it. They did this in part because they knew that Douglas wanted to promote a transcontinental railroad west from Chicago or some other Northern terminus to the Pacific. They were equally eager to run such a road west from New Orleans. There was simply no reason for them to give their votes to organize another free-soil territory for the purpose of facilitating a Northern railroad.

Douglas felt that he had to have their votes; thus, in January 1854 he was led to take the fatal step of agreeing to change his bill so that it would repeal the Missouri Compromise line and would leave the status of slavery in the Kansas-Nebraska region to be settled by popular sovereignty. Douglas made the plausible argument that what he advocated was nothing new and that the legislation of 1850 had already replaced the principle of geographical division with the principle of popular sovereignty.

"APPEAL OF THE INDEPENDENT DEMOCRATS"

In a widely disseminated tract entitled "Appeal of the Independent Democrats," antislavery advocates rejected Douglas' argument with furious indignation. They insisted that the act of 1850 applied only to the Mexican cession and was thus merely supplementary to the Missouri Compromise. The South, they asserted, was violating a sacred pledge; in 1820 it had promised to recognize freedom north of 36° 30′ in return for the admission of Missouri, and now it was defaulting on the agreement. To the Northerners, the territories had been free soil ever since the Missouri Compromise, and Douglas' proposal was, therefore, the "reintroduction" of slavery into the territories.

The Northern arguments were not entirely accurate. To mention but one point, a majority of Southern congressmen had voted against the act of 1820, but the act had stood for 34 years. Douglas was at least reckless, if not wrong, to tamper with it.

The furious blast of indignation that greeted his amended Kansas-Nebraska bill must have told him that he had made a major blunder; however, Douglas was bold, aggressive, and tenacious. After committing President Pierce to his bill, he staged an all-out parliamentary battle for enactment. His own resourcefulness in debate enabled him repeatedly to throw his attackers on the defensive, and he conducted a brilliant campaign by which he succeeded in forcing the bill through both houses of Congress.

THE ELECTION OF 1854

Douglas' success, however, came at a terrible price. He had correctly foreseen that the repeal of the Missouri Compromise would "raise the Hell of a storm;" but he had not foreseen, as he later said, that he would be able to travel to Chicago by the light of his own burning effigies. Six months after the act was adopted, the congressional elections of 1854 took place. All over the North "anti-Nebraska" parties sprang up to capitalize on free-soil anger at the Kansas-Nebraska Act. In Wisconsin and Michigan these parties took the name "Republican," and this name soon spread to other states. In the Northeast, however, the main beneficiary of the voter uprising in 1854 was not the newborn Republican Party but rather the anti-Catholic Know-Nothings, who shared the Republicans' hostility to the extension of slavery but were even more concerned about the apparent threat of

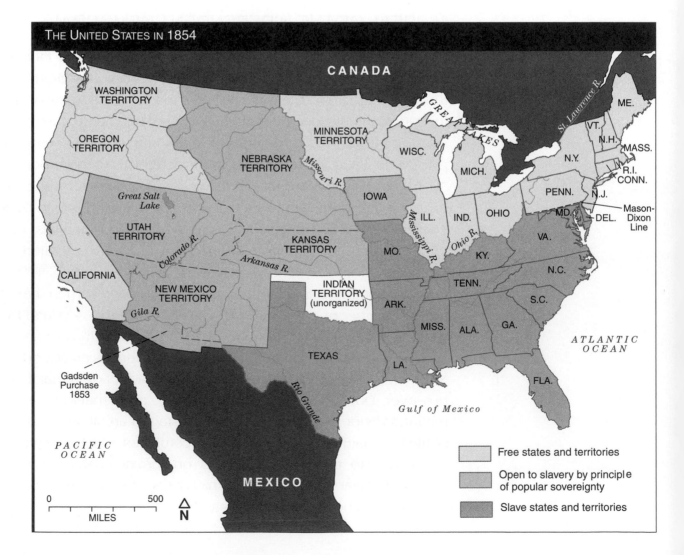

THE UNITED STATES IN 1854

CANADA

WASHINGTON TERRITORY
OREGON TERRITORY
MINNESOTA TERRITORY
NEBRASKA TERRITORY
Missouri R.
GREAT LAKES
WISC.
MICH.
ME.
VT.
N.H.
MASS.
N.Y.
R.I.
CONN.
Great Salt Lake
UTAH TERRITORY
Colorado R.
IOWA
Mississippi R.
ILL.
IND.
OHIO
PENN.
N.J.
MD.
DEL.
Mason-Dixon Line
St. Lawrence R.
CALIFORNIA
KANSAS TERRITORY
Arkansas R.
MO.
Ohio R.
KY.
VA.
N.C.
NEW MEXICO TERRITORY
INDIAN TERRITORY (unorganized)
ARK.
TENN.
S.C.
Gila R.
MISS.
ALA.
GA.
Gadsden Purchase 1853
TEXAS
LA.
FLA.
Rio Grande
Gulf of Mexico
ATLANTIC OCEAN
PACIFIC OCEAN
MEXICO
0   500
MILES
N

Free states and territories

Open to slavery by principle of popular sovereignty

Slave states and territories

Catholic immigrants. The Know-Nothings won enough votes to gain 40 seats in the House of Representatives.

Whatever the name of their opponents, the Democrats suffered a stunning setback in the Northern congressional elections. The number of Northern Democrats in the House fell from 91 to 25, and the Northern congressional Democrats functioned thereafter as the tail to the Southern Democratic dog. From 1854 forward, the Democratic Party would function as a Southern, sectional, proslavery party.

In the long run, however, the Republicans rather than the Know-Nothings proved to be the main beneficiaries of the 1854 electoral revolution, gaining 100 seats in the House of Representatives. Northern opposition to the expansion of slavery proved deeper and more intense than Protestant dislike of Catholic immigrants. By the end of 1855 the Republican Party had emerged as the successor to the Whigs as the country's second major party. Unlike the Whigs, however, the Republicans were entirely a sectional party with no strength at all in the slave states.

"BLEEDING KANSAS"

The worst thing about the new Kansas-Nebraska Act was that, even at the price of causing the bitterest kind of sectional hostility, it did not create a real basis for stability in the new territory. Instead it merely changed the terms of the contest, for Douglas and many Northern Democrats believed that popular sovereignty could make Kansas and Nebraska free territories just as well as congressional action could. Proslavery leaders, on the other hand, took the repeal of the Missouri Compromise to mean that slavery should prevail in at least one of the two new territories.

Both antislavery and proslavery groups prepared to rush supporters into Kansas to defend their respective positions there. In New England, antislavery advocates organized an Emigrant Aid Society to send free-soil settlers to Kansas. In 1854 and 1855, the Society sponsored 1,240 settlers. Though the society never officially purchased weapons for these settlers, the leaders of the society bought rifles with separate funds to arm the emigrants against the proslavery groups.

From Missouri, proslavery advocates, known as Border Ruffians, had a way of riding over into Kansas on Election Day to vote and intimidate the free-soilers before riding back to Missouri. Missouri Senator David Rice Atchison publicly encouraged the election fraud. Atchison proclaimed, "There are eleven hundred coming over from Platte County to vote, and if that ain't enough, we can

Senator William H. Seward

send 5,000 to kill every God-damned abolitionist in the territory." Atchison led a contingent of armed men from Missouri to vote and frighten away Free Soil voters. On the other side, Senator William H. Seward of New York retorted, "Come on then, Gentlemen of the Slave States ... since there is no escaping your challenge, I accept it in behalf of the cause of freedom. We will engage in competition for the virgin soil of Kansas, and God give the victory to the side which is stronger in numbers as it is in right."

In March 1855, an election was held in Kansas to elect a territorial legislature. Of the 2,905 eligible voters, somehow 6,307 votes were cast; and Kansas quickly assembled a proslavery legislature elected through fraud primarily by proslavery zealots from Missouri. The new proslavery legislature quickly passed a law outlawing the abolition of slavery, a position that was opposed by a strong majority of the people that actually lived in Kansas.

It would have taken a strong President to keep order in Kansas, and Pierce was not strong. He appointed a succession of able governors for the territory, but he would not vigorously support them when they needed his backing. Affairs, therefore, went from bad to worse. After the proslavery faction had stolen an election and Pierce had given recognition to the government thus elected, even replacing the Kansas Governor who had objected to the election fraud, the free-soil advocates formed another government of their own. Kansas then had two governments—a proslavery one at Pawnee, legal but not honest, and an antislavery one at Topeka, honest but not legal. The antislavery legislature not only banned slavery from the state, but also passed a measure banning all blacks from the state, slave or free.

It is a great mistake to think of frontier Kansas as inhabited entirely by people who went there as missionaries for slavery or for freedom. Many settlers were simply land-hungry pioneers like those who swarmed into all new territories. Such settlers were often quick to violence, and not all the shooting that took place in Kansas was because of slavery; however, the slavery issue did accentuate the violence and give a pattern to the lawlessness of the frontier.

With President Pierce denouncing the free-soil government for its illegality, the proslavery forces secured an indictment of the free-soilers by a grand jury that was, of course, of the proslavery men's own choosing. With this indictment a proslavery federal marshal led an armed mob, or "posse" as it called itself, and marched on the free-soil headquarters at Lawrence. There they shot cannon balls into the Free State Hotel, destroyed the printing press of the free soil newspaper, and burned or looted a good deal of property—both shops and private homes—while taking over the free soil government buildings.

Four days later in May 1856, John Brown (a free-soiler who carried his views to fanatical lengths) and six companions (four of them his sons) avenged the sacking of Lawrence and the killing of several free-soil settlers by leading a body of men to Pottawatomie Creek, where they took five unarmed proslavery settlers from their homes in the dead of night and murdered them. Brown argued that his action was just and stated, "It was better that a score of bad men should die than that one man who came here to make Kansas a free state should be driven out."

These events were part of an escalation of terror and violence in "Bleeding Kansas" that followed. Both Brown and proslavery groups roamed the countryside shooting and looting for their causes. Probably 200 people met violent deaths before a new territorial government used federal troops to restore order four months later. Brown was neither captured nor killed by the federal troops, but forced to flee Kansas and go into hiding in October 1856.

Though things in Kansas were surely bad enough, exaggerated reports of the violence in the nation's newspapers made them even worse, further heightening sectional tensions. For example, one editor of a proslavery newspaper claimed that abolitionists came to Kansas "for the express purpose of stealing, running off and hiding runaway negroes from Missouri, and taking to their own bed ... a stinking negro wench." Rumors circulated Missouri that 20,000 abolitionist migrants were coming to Kansas, a gross exaggeration that bore little relation with reality, but believed nonetheless. The reality was that most Kansas residents were migrants from Missouri who came to Kansas for land ownership. The vast majority was against slavery, but not for racial equality, and opposed the presence of free blacks in Kansas as well. In the words of one Kansas clergyman, "I kem to Kansas to live in a free state and I don't want niggers a— trampin' over my grave."

"THE CRIME AGAINST KANSAS"

Meanwhile, the intensity of sectional ill will was both illustrated and heightened by an occurrence in Washington. Charles Sumner, an antislavery senator from Massachusetts, delivered an oration entitled "The Crime Against Kansas" in which, in addition to castigating the slave power as bitterly as he could and denouncing what he termed as "murderous robbers" and "assassins," he spoke in extremely personal terms about elderly Senator Andrew P. Butler of South Carolina, accusing him of "cavorting with the harlot, slavery." He, also, alluded to "the loose expectoration" of the elderly Butler's speech. A nephew of Butler's in the House of Representatives, Preston Brooks, went to the Senate chamber when the Senate was not in session, found Sumner seated at his desk, and beat him severely with a cane. In the words of Brooks, "I gave him 40 first-rate stripes."

For several years after the assault, Sumner was incapacitated either by the blows that he received or, according to the best modern medical opinion, by his psychological reaction to the assault. The public significance of this affair, however, lay less in the attack itself than in the fact that a large part of the Northern press made a martyr of Sumner and pictured all Southerners as barbarians, while the South made a hero of Brooks and typed all Yankees as rabid fanatics.

THE CHARACTER OF FRANKLIN PIERCE

Preston Brooks

By this time the Pierce administration was ending as a disaster because of the weakness of the President and the extent to which he let himself be dominated by Southern influence. After failing to prevent repeal of the Missouri Compromise, Pierce might still have saved the peace of the country if he had stood firm for real popular sovereignty in Kansas. Instead, however, he had backed a proslavery regime that was palpably fraudulent, had allowed violence to go unrestrained, and had finally given his support to the idea of statehood with a proslavery government. At this point Stephen A. Douglas had broken with the administration and was fighting hard in Congress to defeat this proslavery government. Thus the political division now was less between free-soil and proslavery forces than between the honest application of popular sovereignty and the perversion of it.

Indeed, Pierce had backed the south at almost every point. He had negotiated the Gadsden Purchase (1853) with Mexico for what is now the southernmost part of Arizona and New Mexico because the land in question was strategic for the construction of a transcontinental railroad by the southern route from New Orleans. He had permitted three of his diplomatic emissaries in Europe to meet at Ostend, Belgium, in October 1854 to propose American annexation of Cuba by purchase or, if that failed, by "wresting it from Spain." Cuba had almost 400,000 slaves and would strengthen the power of slavery. This "Ostend Manifesto," however, aroused such worldwide indignation that the administration was forced to repudiate it.

Moreover, the administration did nothing effective to prevent expeditions by adventurers, called *filibusterers*, who invaded Latin countries from American shores. One such expedition from New Orleans against Cuba failed. Another, against Nicaragua, was temporarily successful, installing American William Walker as the leader of the country. These efforts to acquire new slave territory for the United States sparked Northern anger and brought new recruits into the Republican Party. As for Pierce, he would sink even deeper into alcoholism and die of what historians believe to be cirrhosis of the liver. Pierce once explained his alcohol addiction by stating, "After the Presidency, what is there to do but drink?"

ON THE EVE OF WAR

THE ELECTION OF 1856

At the end of Pierce's term even the Southern Democrats knew that he could not be reelected. The Democrats nominated James Buchanan of Pennsylvania, who, as minister to England, had been out of the country at the time of the Kansas-Nebraska Act (although as one of three authors of the Ostend Manifesto, he was particularly acceptable to the South). Buchanan had been Secretary of State under Polk and was a veteran of American politics—an old Public Functionary, as he called himself.

James Buchanan

Buchanan was also a bachelor, making him a bit out of the ordinary for American Presidents, and thus reliant on close friends as his confidants. Buchanan's closest confidant with whom he roomed for a number of years was Alabama Senator Rufus King. Andrew Jackson referred to Senator King as "Miss Nancy," a common term of the era for a man with effeminate mannerisms. Clearly, Buchanan relied on King; and the two had a close enough relationship that Congressman Aaron Brown of Tennessee referred to King as Buchanan's "better half and wife" in a letter he wrote to Mrs. James Polk. In 1844 when King was appointed Ambassador to France, Buchanan wrote a friend that he was now "solitary and alone," adding, "I have gone wooing to several gentlemen, but have not succeeded with any of them." Buchanan would have even less success in keeping the country from falling apart.

To run against him, a remnant of the Know-Nothings and Southern Whigs calling themselves the American Party nominated Millard Fillmore, but the principal opposition came from the new Republican Party. The Republicans passed over their most prominent leaders to nominate the dashing but politically inexperienced young explorer of the Rocky Mountains and the Far West, John C. Frémont.

In the election that followed, Buchanan carried all the slave states (except Maryland, which voted for Fillmore) and four free states, thus winning the election. The majority of the North, however, was now backing the Republican Party, that denounced slavery as a "relic of barbarism" and that had no organization whatever throughout half the Union.

It is questionable whether, by this time, anyone could have brought the disruptive forces of sectional antagonism under control. Certainly Buchanan could not do it. Southern Democrats dominated his cabinet as they had Pierce's. In February 1858, Buchanan forfeited his claim to impartial leadership by recommending admission of Kansas to state-

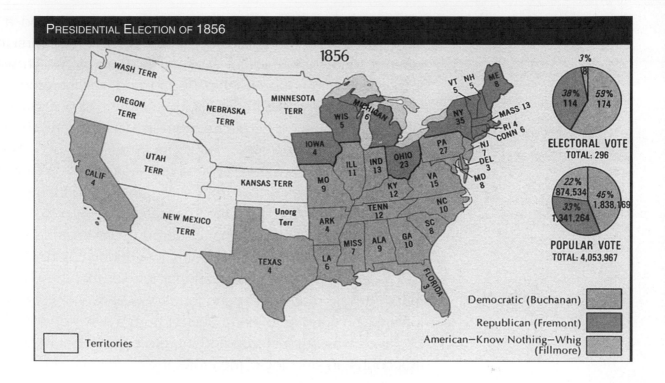

PRESIDENTIAL ELECTION OF 1856

hood under a proslavery constitution fraudulently adopted by a rump convention that met at Lecompton, Kansas. Free Soil forces, suspecting a sham, had boycotted the Lecompton constitutional convention, so conventioneers drafted a proslavery constitution without opposition and refused to allow Kansas voters to ratify the document.

Stephen Douglas and other Northern Democrats resisted the Lecompton constitution and rejected the bill to admit Kansas unless the Kansas voters ratified the Lecompton constitution. In January 1858, in spite of the fact that slavery advocates from Missouri again stuffed the ballot boxes, the voters of Kansas rejected the Lecompton constitution by a 2 to 1 margin. A second referendum was held at the insistent urging of the President, and this time fewer proslavery voters were able to cross the border. The Lecompton constitution was voted down by an even larger 6 to 1 margin. Stephen Douglas' role in opposing the Lecompton constitution lost for him the Southern support that he had won in 1854, and the Democratic Party became deeply divided. Douglas would defeat Abraham Lincoln in 1858 to retain his Illinois Senate seat, but it would be the last victory of his political career.

THE DRED SCOTT DECISION

Meanwhile, in 1857 the Supreme Court had handed down a decision that may have been intended to restore sectional peace but had exactly the opposite effect. This ruling concerned a Missouri slave, Dred Scott, who had been carried by his master first to the free state of Illinois and then into Wisconsin Territory, which was within the Louisiana Purchase north of 36° 30′ and was therefore, under the Missouri Compromise, free territory. After he had been taken back to Missouri, Scott sued for his freedom in Missouri; and the case was eventually carried up on appeal to the Supreme Court. The justices divided in various ways on several questions that were involved, but essentially the five justices from slave states held that Scott was still a slave, while the four from the free states divided two and two.

The principal opinion was rendered by 80 year-old slaveholding Chief Justice Roger B. Taney, stating that during colonial times blacks had "been regarded as beings so far inferior that they had no rights that the white man was bound to respect." Following Taney, the majority of the court held that a person born a slave or the descendant of slaves was not a citizen and therefore could not bring suit in federal courts. In strict logic, therefore, the court need not have ruled on the other questions Scott raised; but it went on to state that even if he could have sued, he still would not have been free, for the Missouri Compromise was unconstitutional because Congress had no power to exclude slavery from the territories.

In a literal sense the Dred Scott decision added nothing new to the debate about the extension of slavery, for it merely declared void a law which had already been repealed by the Kansas-Nebraska Act three years earlier. In another sense, however, it had a shattering effect in that it strengthened a conviction in the North that an evil "slave power," bent on spreading slavery throughout the land, was in control of the government and must be checked. It justified Southerners, on the other hand, in believing that the free soilers were trying to rob them of their legal rights.

It even struck a deadly blow at the one moderate position—that of popular sovereignty—which lay between the extremes of free-soil and proslavery contentions. If, as the Court ruled, Congress had no power to exclude slavery from a territory by its own act, certainly it could not give a power that it did not possess to the territorial legislatures; and without such power there could be no effective popular sovereignty. It made compromise by act of Congress almost impossible. Slavery, which had been illegal north of the Missouri Compromise line since 1820, was now legal everywhere unless state legislatures passed laws against it. Slaves could now be brought into northern territories such as Oregon or Minnesota.

As for African Americans, the decision was devastating. It convinced many free blacks that they had no future in a country that denied them citizenship. Further, it intensified the growing mood of Black Nationalism and spurred movements for emigration to Haiti or Africa.

THE LINCOLN-DOUGLAS DEBATES

The effect of the Dred Scott decision in polarizing sectional extremism showed up clearly in 1858, when Stephen A. Douglas ran for reelection to the Senate from Illinois and was challenged to a series of debates by his Republican opponent, Abraham Lincoln. Lincoln, a former Whig, was deeply opposed to slavery. He regarded it as morally wrong—"if slavery is not wrong then nothing is wrong"—and he insisted that the Dred Scott decision be reversed. Slavery must be kept out of the territories and placed "in the course of ultimate extinction."

Lincoln was by no means an abolitionist. He did not advocate racial equality, stating clearly in the debates, "I am not, nor ever have been, in favor of bringing about the social and political equality of the white and black races." Lincoln also opposed black suffrage, interracial marriage, black citizenship, the repeal of the fugitive slave act, and allowing blacks to serve on juries. Lincoln even predicted that slavery would last another hundred years, though he personally favored the repatriation of slaves to Africa.

Lincoln recognized, however, both the complexity of the slavery question and the fact that slavery was protected by constitutional guarantees which he proposed to respect—even to the enforcement of the fugitive slave law. Lincoln defined the dilemma the Dred Scott decision had created for Douglas and for all moderates. If slavery could not be legally excluded from the territories, how could the people of the territory, under popular sovereignty, exclude it? Concerning Southerners, Lincoln phrased the situation as, "They are merely what we would be in their situation."

Douglas replied at Freeport, Illinois (the

Abraham Lincoln

"Freeport doctrine"), that unless a territory adopted positive laws to protect slavery by local police regulations, slavery could not establish itself. Thus by merely refraining from legislation, lawmakers could keep a territory free. This answer was enough to gain reelection for Douglas, but it cost him what was left of his reputation as a national leader with strong bisectional support. At one time, Southerners had applauded him for repealing the slavery exclusion of the Missouri Compromise. Now they saw him as a man who was supporting the free-soilers in Kansas and who was advocating a theory that would deprive the South of rights guaranteed by a decision of the Supreme Court.

Though Lincoln lost the election for Senate, he came to the attention of people throughout the country with his careful exposition of the issues raised by the Dred Scott decision. He consolidated his growing reputation with a speech given at Cooper Union in New York City on February 27, 1860. No doubt aware of the opportunity provided by this forum, Lincoln conducted extensive research on the opinions of signers of the Constitution on the question of slavery in the territories and dazzled his audience with his logic and his erudition. The historian Harold Holzer calls it "the speech that made Abraham Lincoln president."

JOHN BROWN'S RAID

If the Dred Scott decision brought to a climax the Northern feeling that freedom was being dangerously threatened by a sinister conspiracy of the "slave power," John Brown's raid on Harpers Ferry created an even more intense feeling below the Mason-Dixon line that abolitionist fanaticism posed an immediate danger to the social order and even to human life in the South. After the "Pottawatomie massacre" in Kansas, Brown had dropped out of sight; but during the night of October 16, 1859, he suddenly descended with a band of 18 men (including five blacks) on the town of Harpers Ferry, Virginia, seized the federal arsenal there, and called upon the slaves to rise and claim their freedom.

Brown's plan was to arm the slaves that he expected to flock to his side for a massive revolt, after which a black republic would be established in the mountains of Virginia. Then he and his supporters would wage a war against the slaveholding South. Exactly how Brown expected droves of slaves to hear of his actions, get away from their plantations, and join his rebellion is a mystery known only to Brown. Instead, no slaves arrived to join the revolt, and within 36 hours Brown was captured by federal troops under the command of

John Brown being led to execution

Robert E. Lee. Ten of Brown's men were killed in the gun battle, and Brown was charged with treason, conspiracy, and murder. Later he was tried and hanged, but not before playing the role of the perfect martyr for Northern abolitionists. Brown proclaimed, "If it is deemed necessary that I should forfeit my life for the furtherance of the ends of justice ... I say let it be done."

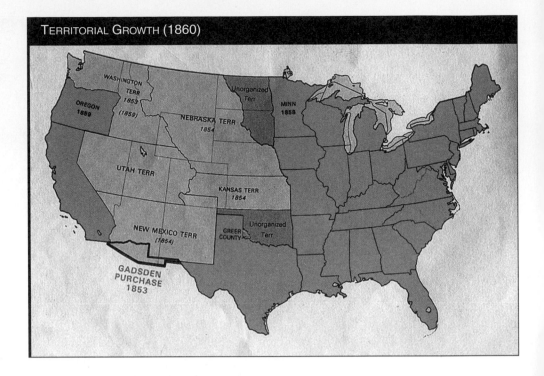

TERRITORIAL GROWTH (1860)

Brown's action had touched the South differently, however, and at its most sensitive nerve—its fear of the kind of slave insurrection that had caused immense slaughter at Santo Domingo at the beginning of the century and had periodically threatened to erupt in the South itself. Southern alarm and resentment would perhaps have been less great if the North had denounced Brown's act—as many Northerners, including Lincoln, did. The fact soon came out, however, that Brown had received financial backing from some of the most respected figures in Boston; and the day of his execution became one of public mourning in New England. Brown was called Saint John the Just, and Henry David Thoreau publicly spoke in support of Brown. Similarly, Ralph Waldo Emerson wrote an essay about Brown entitled, "Courage," in which Emerson argued that Brown would "make the gallows glorious like the cross."

THE ELECTION OF 1860

By this time, developments were rapidly moving toward a showdown. For more than a decade, sectional dissension had been destroying the institutions that held the American people together in national unity. In 1844 it had split the Methodist Church, and in 1845 the Baptist church had divided into separate Northern and Southern bodies. Between 1852 and 1856, sectionalism had split the Whig Party, and as matters now stood, the Democratic Party was the only remaining major national institution, outside of the government itself. In 1860, with another presidential election at hand, the Democratic organization, already strained by the tension between the Buchanan and the Douglas wings, also broke apart.

THE DEMOCRATS

Meeting at Charleston, the Democratic convention divided on the question of the platform. Douglas Democrats wanted a plank that promised, in general terms, to abide by the decisions of the Supreme Court but which avoided explicit expression of support for slavery in the territories. Southern Democrats, led by William L. Yancey, a famous orator from Alabama, wanted a categorical affirmation that slavery would be protected in the territories. When the Douglas forces secured the adoption of their plank, Yancey and most of the delegates from the cotton states walked out of the convention.

The accusation was later made that they did this as part of a deliberate plan or conspiracy to break up the Union by splitting the Democratic Party, letting the Republicans win, and thus creating a situation that would cause the South to secede. In fact, however, many of those who bolted were hoping to force Northern Democrats to come to terms or to throw the election to Congress, where there was a chance that the South might have won. For weeks, desperate efforts were made to reunite the Democrats, but in the end the Northern wing of the party nominated Douglas and the Southern wing nominated John C. Breckinridge of Kentucky, Vice-President under Buchanan.

Some of the conservative successors of the Whigs, now calling themselves Constitutional Unionists, nominated John Bell of Tennessee for President and Edward Everett for Vice-President on a platform that said nothing about the territorial question and called only for "the Constitution, the Union, and the enforcement of the laws."

THE REPUBLICAN VICTORY

The principal opposition to Douglas, it was understood, would come from the Republicans, whose convention was meeting at a new building called the Wigwam in Chicago. The leading candidate before the convention was William H. Seward, United States senator from New York, who had been the foremost Republican for some years. His talent for coining memorable phrases—"a higher law than the Constitution" and "the irrepressible conflict between freedom and slavery"—had won him a reputation for extremism, however.

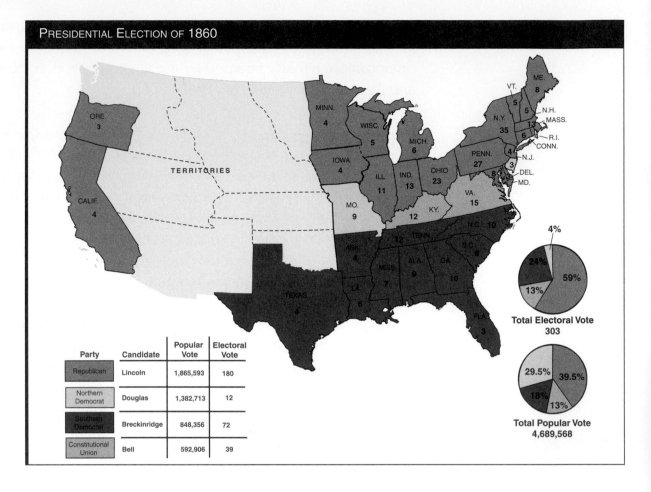

PRESIDENTIAL ELECTION OF 1860

Party	Candidate	Popular Vote	Electoral Vote
Republican	Lincoln	1,865,593	180
Northern Democrat	Douglas	1,382,713	12
Southern Democrat	Breckinridge	848,356	72
Constitutional Union	Bell	592,906	39

Total Electoral Vote 303

Total Popular Vote 4,689,568

The Republicans, seeing a good chance of victory after the Democratic split, decided to move in a conservative direction in order not to jeopardize their prospects. Accordingly, they nominated Abraham Lincoln, who had made his reputation in the debates with Douglas but who had never been militant on the slavery question. To balance this nomination they made Hannibal Hamlin, a former Democrat from Maine, their vice-presidential candidate.

To win, the Republicans needed only to hold what they had won in 1856 and to capture Pennsylvania and either Illinois or Indiana, which Buchanan had carried. As the election turned out, they won every free state except New Jersey (part of which went to Douglas), while Breckinridge won all the slave states except Virginia, Kentucky, and Tennessee (which went to Bell) and Missouri (which went to Douglas). Douglas ran a strong second in popular votes, but a poor fourth in electoral votes, while Lincoln was in the curious position of winning with only 40 percent of the popular vote. His victory resulted not from the division of his opponents, however, but from the fact that his strength was strategically distributed. His victories in many of the free states were narrow, and he received no votes at all in 10 Southern states. Thus the distribution of his popular votes had maximum effectiveness in winning electoral votes.

SECESSION

Lincoln's victory at last precipitated the sectional split which had been brewing for so long. As we can now see in the light of later events, Lincoln was moderate-minded and would have respected the legal rights of the South even though he deplored slavery. To the South, however, fearful of Northern aggression, his victory was a signal of imminent danger. Here was a man who had said that a house divided against itself could not stand and that the Union could not continue permanently half slave and half free. To the South he denied rights in the territories that the Supreme Court had said that the South possessed. He was supported by swarms of militant antislavery men, and his victory clearly represented the imposition of a President by one section upon the other, for 99 percent of his vote had come in the free states.

Southerners had controlled the United States government most of the time since its founding. Although, as we have already seen, there was some diversity in their political opinion, especially before 1845, their prominence had been a matter of pride in the South and—increasingly—a matter of concern in the North. From 1789 to 1861, 25 of the 36 Presidents Pro Tem of the Senate and 24 of the 36 Speakers of the House were Southerners. Twenty of the 35 Supreme Court justices were from the South. A Southerner was Chief Justice during all but 12 of these years, at all times the South had a majority on the Court. During 49 of these 72 years the President of the United States was a Southerner—and a slaveholder. In addition, during 12 additional years, including most of the crucial 1850s, the Presidents were Northern Democratic "doughfaces" who were sometimes more pro-Southern than Southerners themselves might have dared to be.

Thus when the news of Lincoln's election came in 1860, Charles Francis Adams, the son and grandson of the only truly Northern Presidents the United States had ever had and himself a founder of the Republican Party, wrote jubilantly: "The great revolution has taken place. ... The country has once and for all thrown off the domination of the slave-holders."

The slaveholders, too, regarded the 1860 election as a political revolution that foreshadowed a future dominated by the ideology and institutions of the North. To the Old South this would be disaster, and a counterrevolution of independence seemed the only answer.

Proponents of secession invoked the doctrine that each state had retained its sovereignty when it joined the federal Union.

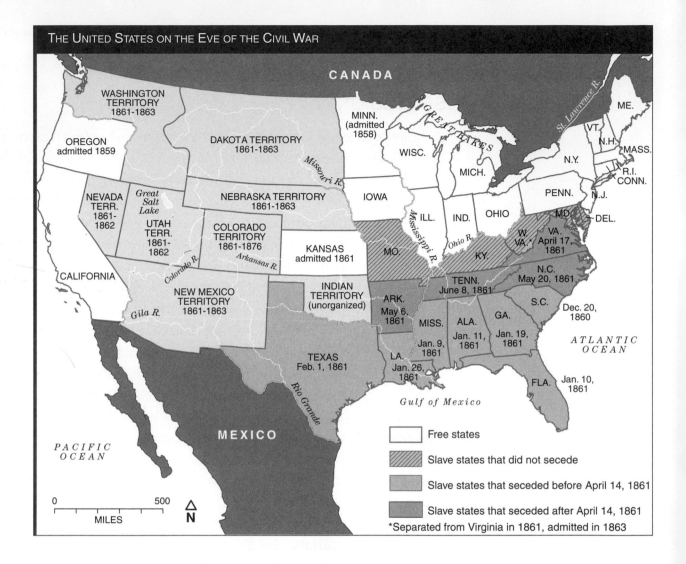

THE UNITED STATES ON THE EVE OF THE CIVIL WAR

Thus, in the exercise of this sovereignty, each state, acting through a special convention like the conventions that had ratified the Constitution, might secede from the Union. As soon as it learned of Lincoln's election, the South Carolina legislature called a convention to take the state out of the Union. Within six weeks the six other states of the lower South—Mississippi, Florida, Alabama, Georgia, Louisiana, and Texas—also called conventions. Delegates were elected by popular vote after short but intensive campaigns. Each convention voted by a substantial and in most cases an overwhelming majority to secede. By February 9, 1861, three months after Lincoln's election but almost a month before his inauguration, delegates from the seven seceded states had met in Montgomery, Alabama, to adopt a provisional Constitution for the Confederate States of America and to elect Jefferson Davis and Alexander Stephens as provisional President and Vice-President of the new republic.

THE FAILURE OF COMPROMISE

The actual arrival of disunion, which had been dreaded for so long, evoked strenuous efforts at compromise—especially by leaders in the border slave states, where loyalty to the Union was combined with sympathy for the South. From Kentucky, Senator John J. Crittenden, heir to the compromise tradition of Henry Clay, introduced proposals in Congress to revise and extend the Missouri Compromise line by constitutional amendment. Virginia took the lead in convening a Peace Convention, with delegates from 21 states, which met in Washington in February. Congress actually adopted a proposed amendment that would have guaranteed slavery in the states that wanted to keep it. This amendment was submitted to the states for ratification before the war came and made it obsolete.

President Buchanan professed himself powerless to prevent the secession. Buchanan denounced the action as illegal but, as a lame duck President, did not want to commit his successor to any course of action. In the meantime, the nation waited to see if the incoming President Lincoln would attempt to preserve the Union by force or peacefully allow the secession.

Unlike Buchanan, Lincoln was unwilling to make any concessions that would compromise the basic Republican principle of excluding slavery from the territories. The Crittenden Compromise would have permitted slavery in all territories south of 36° 30′ "now held, *or hereafter acquired*." In view of the South's appetite for the acquisition of new slave territory in the Caribbean and Central America, Republicans feared that adoption of such a compromise "would amount to a perpetual covenant of war against every people, tribe, and State owning a foot of land between here and Terra del Fuego" and turn the United States into "a great slavebreeding and slave-extending empire." Therefore, they defeated the Crittenden Compromise. In any case, it is

Senator John J. Crittenden

unlikely that adoption of this or any other compromise would have stemmed the tide of secession in the lower South where, by February 1861, the Confederacy was a *fait accompli*.

FORT SUMTER

Thus, when Lincoln was inaugurated on March 4, 1861, he was faced by a new Southern republic where seven states of the Union had been. This new Confederacy had seized federal post offices, customs houses, arsenals, and even federal forts, with the exception of Fort Sumter in Charleston harbor and Fort Pickens in Pensacola harbor. The federal forts in the South were by and large manned by Southerners and commanded by Southerners in the United States Army who turned over their forts to the Confederates without a shot. In Texas alone, 18 federal forts and all of their provisions were handed to the confederates without a fight. From North Carolina to the Rio Grande, these were the only two places where the Stars and Stripes still flew. There was great speculation at the time as to what position Lincoln would take, and there has been great dispute among historians since then as to what position he actually *did* take.

Certainly he made it absolutely clear that he denied the right of any state to secede and that he intended to preserve the Union, In his inaugural address, Lincoln denounced the secession as illegal; however, whether he intended to wage war in order to preserve it is not so clear. Lincoln also proclaimed that the North and South were not enemies, but friends. Furthermore, there were eight slave states (Virginia, North Carolina, Kentucky, Tennessee, Missouri, Arkansas, Maryland, and Delaware) still in the Union, and Lincoln was extremely eager to keep them loyal. As long as they remained in the Union, there was at least the possibility that they might help to bring the other slave states back. This split among the slave states represented a failure on the part of the secessionists to create a united South. Thus Lincoln had every reason to refrain from hasty action.

If he had been able to maintain the federal position at Fort Pickens and Fort Sumter, or even at one of them, he apparently would have been prepared to play a waiting game. Less than 24 hours after becoming President, however, he learned that Major Robert Anderson, commander at Fort Sumter, was running out of supplies and would soon have to surrender unless some were sent to him. Lincoln apparently gave serious consideration to the possibility of surrendering Sumter; and he might have done so if he had been able to reinforce Fort Pickens and make it the symbol of an unbroken Union. Attempts to reinforce Pickens, however, were delayed; and on April

6 Lincoln sent a message to the governor of South Carolina that supplies would be sent to Sumter. If the Southerners allowed the supplies in to the Union fort on Southern territory, no military reinforcement would be attempted.

Historians have disputed whether this was a promise not to start shooting if supplies were allowed or, rather, a threat to start shooting if they were not allowed. In any event, the Confederate government decided that the supplies could not be allowed. On April 12, 1861, after Major Anderson had rejected a formal demand for surrender, Confederate batteries opened a bombardment before dawn that forced Fort Sumter to surrender without casualties after 26 hours of furious shelling.

On April 15 Lincoln issued a call for the loyal states to furnish 75,000 militia to suppress the Southern "insurrection." All the free states responded with alacrity and enthusiasm. The four slave states of Virginia, North Carolina, Tennessee, and Arkansas responded by seceding and joining the Confederacy as they had promised they would. The other four slave states—Maryland, Delaware, Kentucky, and Missouri—remained uneasily in the Union, though many of their men went south to fight for the Confederacy. The bombardment of Fort Sumter marked the beginning of a war that lasted four years and, with the exception of the Napoleonic wars, was the greatest military conflict the world had seen up to that time.

"CAUSES OF THE CIVIL WAR"

Ever since 1861, writers have disputed what caused the Civil War and whether it was an "irrepressible conflict" in the sense of being inevitable. Southerners have argued that the war was fought not over slavery but, rather, over the question of states' rights. Several of the Confederate states, they point out, seceded only when the others had been attacked. Economic determinists have contended that the Northern public never would support the abolitionists on any direct question (which is certainly true), that Lincoln did not even venture to issue the Emancipation Proclamation until the war had been in progress for a year and five months (which is also true), and that the conflict was really between an industrial interest which wanted one kind of future for America and an agrarian interest which wanted another. Other historians, going a step beyond this, have pictured the North and the South as two "diverse civilizations," so dissimilar in their culture and their values that union between them was artificial and unnatural.

In the 1940s another group of writers, known as revisionists, emphasized the idea that Northerners and Southerners had formed distorted and false concepts of each other and that they went to war against these images rather than against the people they were really fighting. The war, they argued, grew out of emotions, not out of realities. Abraham Lincoln had no intention of leading a crusade against slavery in the South; but the Southerners perceived that he did, and that perception, unsupported by facts, became their reality.

Every one of these points of view has something to be said for it. The causes of the Civil War were certainly not simple, however; though each of the explanations points to something other than slavery, it is significant that the factor of slavery was involved in all of them. It is true that the South believed in the right of the states to secede whereas the North did not, but this belief would have remained an abstraction and never been acted upon if the Republican crusade against extending slavery had not impelled the South to use the secession weapon. Southerners were steadfast in their claim to states' rights, but it could be argued that the primary right that the Southern states claimed was the right to keep their slaves. At least to a degree then, the states' rights argument remained very much an argument about slavery. Evidence in support of this fact is present in the "Declaration of Causes" for secession in many Southern states, where slavery was mentioned prominently. For example, the declared "Causes" from the Secessionist Convention in Texas in 1861 included the following:

- The general government of the United States had administered the common territory so as to exclude Southern people from it (in other words, Congress had attempted to ban slavery in the Western territories).

- The Northern people had become inimical to the South and to their beneficent and patriarchical system of African slavery, preaching the debasing doctrine of the equality of all men, irrespective of race or color.

- The slaveholding states had become a minority, unable to defend themselves against northern aggression against slavery.

- The extremists of the North had elected as President and Vice-President two men whose chief claims to such high positions were the approval of the above wrongs, and these men were pledged to the final ruin of the slaveholding South.

Texans mentioned two more causes, blaming the United States government for the carnage in Kansas (which was, of course, also related to slavery) and for failing to defend Texans against raids from Native Americans and Mexican banditos. Taken together, the Texans' statements suggest that the states' rights argument may have been, at least partly, Southern propaganda to aid the South in their struggle to gain European (especially British) support for their cause, while the real cause was simply slavery. England was decidedly abolitionist and could not violate its own collective moral conscience to aid the South in a war to retain slavery. Aiding the South in its struggle for "states' rights," however, was much more palatable to the English sense of morality.

Slavery was clearly important as a moral issue, but also as an economic institution that divided two different and, in many ways, antagonistic societies. Both of these societies—the modernizing, free-labor, capitalist North and the conservative, agrarian, slave-labored South —were expansionist. Each believed that its social system must expand into the new territories in order to survive. Each saw the expansion of the other as a threat to its own future.

It is hard to imagine that without slavery the general dissimilarities between North and South, even their social and cultural separateness, would have been brought into such sharp focus as to precipitate a war. It is true that in the 1850s extremist leaders came to the fore and each section formed an emotional stereotype rather than a realistic picture of the other. (See "Hinton Rowan Helper: Antislavery Southerner."); but this is a process that typically occurs as antagonism deepens.

The point is that slavery furnished the emotional voltage that led to deep distrust and dislike in each section for the people of the other. In his second inaugural, Abraham Lincoln said, "All know that slavery was somehow the cause of the war." The operative word in his statement was "somehow," for the war was not in any simple sense a fight between crusaders for freedom all on one side and believers in slavery all on the other. Robert E. Lee, to name but one Southerner, did not believe in slavery at all, and many a Northern soldier who was willing to die, if need be, for the Union was deeply opposed to making slavery an issue of the war. But both antislavery

Robert E. Lee

PEOPLE THAT MADE A DIFFERENCE

Hinton Rowan Helper: Antislavery Southerner

Hinton Rowan Helper was the self-proclaimed spokesman for the non-slaveholding whites who constituted three-fourths of Southern white families. His book *The Impending Crisis* ranks with *Uncle Tom's Cabin* as one of the most important documents of the growing sectional conflict. It provoked a crisis in Congress and helped bring on the Civil War. In the end, however, Helper achieved little that he had hoped for and died of self-inflicted violence.

Hinton Rowan Helper was born December 27, 1829, in a section of North Carolina populated mainly by small farmers. After working as a youth on his father's farm and gaining a respectable education at a local academy, Helper went west in 1850 to seek his fortune in the newly opened goldfields of California. His unhappy failures there caused him to return east and publish in 1855 a derogatory book about California, The Land of Gold. The book's failure further disappointed him, and he poured some of the bitterness from this disappointment into the writing of his second and far more significant book, The Impending Crisis, published two years later.

Using selected statistics from the 1850 census, Helper portrayed a South stagnating in economic backwardness, while the free-labor North strode forward in seven-league boots. He contrasted the nearly universal literacy and comfortable living standard of Northern farmers and workers with the apparent ignorance and poverty of Southern "poor whites." The cause? "Slavery lies at the root of all the shame, poverty, ignorance, tyranny, and imbecility of the South," wrote Helper. Slavery monopolized the best land, degraded all labor to the level of bond labor, denied schools to workers, and impoverished all but the "lords of the lash" who "are not only absolute masters of the blacks [but] of all non-slaveholding whites, whose freedom is merely nominal, and whose unparalleled illiteracy and degradation is purposely and fiendishly perpetuated."

Although he demanded the total abolition of slavery, Helper wasted no sympathy on the slaves, whom he wanted shipped back to Africa. His book was aimed at the nonslaveholders that, like himself, disliked slavery because they disliked black people and resented their competition as laborers. Helper therefore assumed that the nonslaveholding whites would rally to the antislavery standard. He urged them to form state Republican parties in the South, use their votes to overthrow the slaveholders' rule, and free themselves from the curse of bondage.

Few nonslaveholding Southern whites read his message. No Southern printer had dared to publish the book, so Helper had had to move from his native North Carolina to the North to get it published in New York. The Impending Crisis was virtually banned in the South. Some states made it a criminal offense to possess or circulate copies of it.

Even if Southern whites had been able to read the book, however, it is unlikely that many of them would have accepted its arguments. Helper underestimated the strength of the ties that bound most whites, slaveholder and nonslaveholder alike, in a common culture. Although many residents of the South's upland and mountain regions were hostile to the plantation regime, most nonslaveholders elsewhere (who were the numerical majority of whites in the South) were loyal to the "Southern way of life," including slavery. Many were relatives of slaveholders. Others aspired to become slaveowners themselves. Even most whites, who had no connection with slavery or the planters supported the "peculiar institution" as the best means of controlling the black population and maintaining white supremacy.

The principle effect of The Impending Crisis in the South was to create a defensive-aggressive reaction to its popularity in the North. Republicans praised the book's economic indictment of slavery as a forceful expression of their own free-labor views. Leading Republicans raised money to print an inexpensive abridged edition and distributed it as a campaign document in the Congressional elections of 1858. This angered Southerners and contributed to one of the most serious sectional deadlocks in the history of Congress.

Republicans had a plurality, but not a majority, in the House of Representatives that convened in December 1859. Because their candidate for Speaker had endorsed Helper's book, the Democrats and ex-Whig conservatives refused to vote for him. The House remained deadlocked over the election of a Speaker for eight weeks until a compromise candidate finally won on the forty-fourth ballot. Tempers grew short, Northern and Southern congressmen hurled insults at each other, and nearly every member came to the House armed. Many observers actually expected a shootout on the floor of Congress. When war came, a little more than a year later, the clash over Helper's book was remembered as one of the many sectional irritants that had burst the bonds of Union.

During these years Helper lived in the North and tried with indifferent success to make a living as a lecturer. Described by a contemporary as a "tall, slim, peculiar-looking person, with short black hair, whiskers and a mustache, a very bronzed complexion, and a fierce military expression," Helper had become one of the most-hated men in the country as far as slaveholders were concerned. A North Carolina senator denounced him in a scathing congressional speech. Outraged and insulted, Helper rushed to the floor of the Senate and engaged the senator in a rough-and-tumble fistfight. Sympathetic Republicans paid his fine.

In 1861 President Lincoln appointed Helper United States Consul in Buenos Aires, where he served until 1866. While there he married an Argentine woman. After his return home his dislike for blacks turned into a pathological hatred. Sensitive of his heritage as a "poor white" and plagued by a sense of failure, he made blacks the scapegoats for the frustration and disappointments of his career. His 1867 book, Nojoque: A Question for a Continent, reaffirmed his earlier goal to "write the negro out of America" and expressed a desire "to write him out of existence." Another book of similar tenor, Negroes in Negroland, followed in 1868. Helper denounced the Republican Reconstruction program of equal rights for freed slaves. This time he received a much more sympathetic hearing in the South.

Much of the remainder of Helper's life was consumed in futile attempts to promote a trunk railroad from Canada to Argentina. During these years he made a scanty living as a lobbyist in Washington for claims against South American countries. In 1899 his wife left him. On March 8, 1909, living alone and in poverty in Washington, he took his own life.

Southerners and proslavery Northerners were caught in the web woven by the issue of slavery.

Could this issue have been settled without war? Was the crisis artificial? Was the territorial question a contest over "an imaginary Negro in an impossible place"? Was war really necessary in a situation where it seems doubtful that a majority of Southerners wanted to secede (only seven out of 15 slave states seceded before the firing on Fort Sumter) or that a majority of Northerners wanted to make an issue of slavery? (Lincoln had only 40 percent of the popular vote, and he promised security for slavery where it was already established.) Were the American people, both North and South, so much alike in their religion (overwhelmingly evangelical Protestant), their speech (American variants of English), their ethnic descent (mostly from British, Irish, and German stock), their democratic beliefs, their pioneer ways, their emphasis upon the values of self-reliance and hard work, their veneration for the Constitution, and even their bumptious Americanism—were they so much alike that a war between them could and should have been avoided? This in turn raises the question whether disagreements are any less bitter among parties who have much in common.

What was happening in America was that the center of gravity was gradually shifting from a loosely organized agricultural society to a modern industrial society with much greater concentration of power. As this happened, the United States was being transformed from a loose association of separately powerful states to a consolidated nation in which the states would be little more than political subdivisions. In America's startling growth the North had outstripped the South and the equilibrium that previously existed between them had been destroyed. The proposal of the victorious Republicans to confine slavery—and in this sense to exclude the South from further participation in the nation's growth—dramatized this shift in equilibrium. It seems most unlikely that the South would ever have accepted the political consequences of this basic change without a crisis, especially since Southern whites greatly feared the possibility that a preponderant North in control of the federal government might ultimately use its power to abolish slavery. Southerners well understood that if the entire frontier west of Missouri eventually came into the Union as free territory, slavery would exist only in the southeastern geographic quarter of the continent; and the free soil areas would eventually have the votes in Congress to eliminate slavery democratically.

The brooding presence of race permeated this issue. Slavery was more than an institution to exploit cheap labor. It was a means of controlling a large and potentially threatening black population and of maintaining white supremacy. Any hint of a threat to the "Southern way of life," which was based on the subordination of a race both scorned and feared, was bound to arouse deep and irrational phobias and to create a crisis. Whether this crisis had to take the form of armed conflict and whether this phase of armed force had to occur precisely when it did—or might have come a month, a year, or a decade sooner or later—would seem to be a matter for endless speculation.

CIVIL WAR, 1861–1865

THE BLUE AND THE GRAY

The "American" War
The Resources of North and South
Southern Strategy
Northern Strategy

THE WAR IN THE FIELD

The Virginia Front
The Battle of Bull Run (Manassas)
Second Battle of Bull Run
Antietam
Fredericksburg
Chancellorsville
Gettysburg
The War in the West
Confederate Invasion of New Mexico
Pea Ridge
Forts Henry and Donelson
Shiloh
Vicksburg
Chickamauga and Chattanooga
Grant Takes Command
Presidential Election and the Peace
  Movement
The Fall of Atlanta
Sherman's March
Destruction of Hood's Army of
  Tennessee
Sherman's March in the Carolinas
Appomattox

THE WAR BEHIND THE LINES

The Problems of the Confederacy
The Importance of Sea Power
Prisoners of War
Economic Failures of the South
Northern Industrialism and
  Republican Ascendancy
The Transcontinental Railroad
The National Banking System
Women and the War
The Road to Reunion
Emancipation
Emancipation Proclamation
Lincoln
Black Americans and the War

THE BLUE AND THE GRAY

THE "AMERICAN" WAR

The American Civil War lasted four years, from April 1861 to April 1865. It was fought over more than half of the United States with battles that took place in every slave state except Delaware, a slave state that did not secede: and Confederate forces made incursions into Pennsylvania, Ohio, West Virginia, Kansas, and (raiding from Canada) Vermont.

From a total of 14 million white males, 2.9 million were in uniform—2.1 million for the Union and 800,000 for the Confederacy. This was over 20 percent of all white males—a higher proportion than in any other American war. The highest participation rate of any state came from Texas, where a staggering 75 percent of men between the ages of 18 and 45 served in the Confederate army. The Union total included 180,000 black soldiers and perhaps 20,000 black sailors, nearly one tenth of the men in the Northern armed forces. Either as battle casualties or as victims of camp maladies, 618,000 men died in service (360,000 Union troops and 258,000 Confederates). More than one soldier in five lost his life—a far heavier ratio of losses than in any other war in our American history. For the Confederate soldiers it was one in three.

Partly because the cost was proportionately so heavy, and partly because the Civil War was distinctly an American war, this conflict has occupied a place in the American memory and the American imagination that other wars—those more recent, more destructive overall, and fought on a global scale—have never held. On both sides, men were fighting for what they deeply believed to be American values.

Southerners were convinced that their right to form a Confederacy was based on a principle of the Declaration of Independence—that governments derive their just powers from the consent of the governed. They were also fighting to defend their states from invasion. "All we ask is to be let alone," said Jefferson Davis in his first war message to the Confederate Congress. Early in the war some Union soldiers captured a Southern soldier, who from his tattered homespun butternut uniform was obviously not a member of the planter class. They asked him why he, a non-slaveholder, was fighting to uphold slavery. "I'm fighting because y'all are down here," was his reply.

The North was fighting to defend the flag and to prove that a democracy was not too weak to hold together. Secession was the

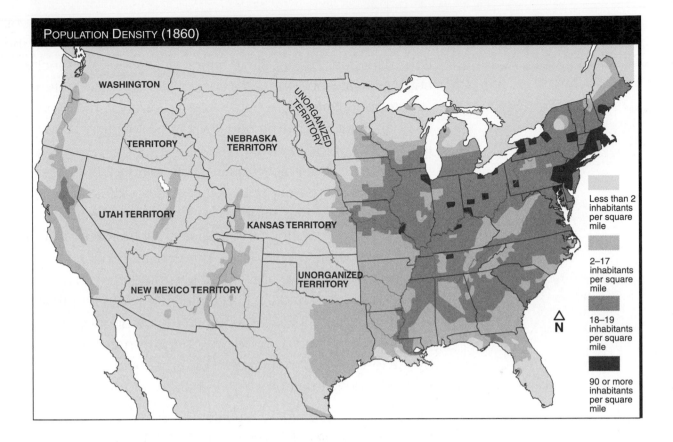

POPULATION DENSITY (1860)

WASHINGTON

TERRITORY

NEBRASKA TERRITORY

UNORGANIZED TERRITORY

UTAH TERRITORY

KANSAS TERRITORY

NEW MEXICO TERRITORY

UNORGANIZED TERRITORY

N

Less than 2 inhabitants per square mile

2–17 inhabitants per square mile

18–19 inhabitants per square mile

90 or more inhabitants per square mile

"essence of anarchy," said Lincoln. "The central idea pervading this struggle is the necessity of proving that popular government is not an absurdity. We must settle this question now, whether in a free government the minority have the right to break up the government whenever they choose." Abolition of slavery was not a motivation at all for most people in the North at the outset of the war. Instead, the abolition of slavery became a purpose in 1863 when Abraham Lincoln believed that the North needed a greater moral purpose as motivation. Until that time, preserving the Union was the primary Northern motive, but by the end of 1862 Lincoln found it insufficient to stir the masses. Thus, the greater moral purpose was added.

THE RESOURCES OF NORTH AND SOUTH

In later years, after the Confederacy had gone down to defeat, men said that the Lost Cause, as Southerners called it, had been lost from the beginning and that the South had been fighting against the census returns. In many respects this seems true, for the South was completely outnumbered in almost all the factors of manpower and economic strength that make up the sinews of modern war. The 11

Confederate states had a white population of 5,450,000, while the 19 free states had 18,950,000. These figures leave out both the population of the four border slave states of Missouri, Kentucky, Maryland, and Delaware and the slave population of the Confederate states. Greater population, of course, also translated into more soldiers. At its peak, the Union army had 690,000 soldiers in 1863 as compared to 270,000 for the Confederates.

The four border slave states were divided, but most of their people and resources supported the Union side. Slaves strengthened the Confederate war effort in an important way, however, for they constituted a majority of the South's labor force and, thereby, enabled most white men to leave home to fight in the army.

The Union was far ahead of the Confederacy in financial and economic strength. It had a bank capital more than four times as great as that of the South. It led the South in the number of manufacturing enterprises by six and a half to one, in the number of industrial workers by 12 to one, and in the value of its manufactures by 11 to one. In railroad mileage, it led by more than two to one, and the Union also had a serious naval advantage in that the South, essentially, possessed almost no warships at the beginning of the War. This deficiency would allow the Union to blockade the South, which was particularly damaging to the Southern economy that was dependent upon cotton exports for its revenue and upon foreign trade for its manufactured goods.

Against these ratios of strength must be placed the fact that the Union was undertaking a vastly more difficult military objective. It should be noted that virtually every advantage enjoyed by the Union during the Civil War was also enjoyed by England during the American Revolution; yet the British still lost. Much like the British during the American Revolution, the Union was seeking to occupy and subdue an area larger than all of western Europe. This meant that armies had to be sent hundreds of miles into hostile territory and be maintained in these distant operations. This necessity involved the gigantic tasks of transporting the immense volume of supplies required by an army in the field and defending long lines of supply and communication, the longest in American history, which would be worthless if they were cut even at a single point. In wars prior to the Civil War, armies had depended upon the use of great wagon trains to bring supplies. As the supply lines lengthened, the horses ate up in fodder a steadily increasing proportion of the amount they could haul, until there was scarcely any margin left between what the supply lines carried and what they consumed in carrying it.

During the Civil War, for the first time in the history of warfare, railroads played a major part in the supply services. If these more efficient carriers of goods had not changed the whole nature of war, it is questionable whether invading armies could ever have marched from the Ohio to the Gulf of Mexico. Ten years earlier the United States had not possessed the railroad network that supplied the Union armies between 1861 and 1865. Therefore, at an earlier time, the defensive position of the South would have been far stronger.

Even with railroads, superior munitions, and superior industrial facilities, the military tasks of the Union were most formidable. America was a profoundly civilian country. The peacetime army numbered only 16,000; and few people on either side had any conception of the vast problems involved in recruiting, mobilizing, equipping, training, and maintaining large armies. It was an amateur's war on both sides, and many of its features seem inconceivable today.

Most of the troops were recruited as volunteers rather than drafted. At the outset of the war, Lincoln called for 75,000 90-day volunteers, reflecting a bit of naivety in Lincoln's inability to foresee a protracted conflict. In defense of Lincoln, his own war experience had consisted of the Blackhawk War in 1832, where by his own admission, he survived "bloody encounters with mosquitoes and led raids on wild onion patches." Even the larger war against Mexico that Lincoln had experienced as a young Congressmen had been over in a little more than a year of actual fighting; and that war involved the invasion of a country further away and with more territory than the Confederacy.

Nevertheless, by July 1861, Lincoln's call for 75,000 90-day volunteers had raised 186,000, and the South had simultaneously raised 112,000 volunteers. The massive recruitment effort simply overwhelmed organizational and supply capacity on both sides.

Southerners quickly began building new factories to supply their soldiers with uniforms and arms, but the Southern manufacturing and transportation capacity would never be sufficient. Although by April 1864 Josiah Gorgas, the head of the Confederacy's Ordnance Bureau, boasted that the South was making enough guns and ammunition to meet the needs of its soldiers, at the outset there were no factories in the South that made guns, swords, shells, or powder; and the Confederate army would remain under-equipped throughout the war. Even when the production capacity of the South was sufficient, such as in food production, the products often did not make it to the troops in the field due to a lack of rail transportation.

Both the Union and the Confederacy sold war bonds, both raised taxes, and both issued paper currency to fund the war. Much like the

American Revolution, however, the increased taxation and borrowing were not enough to fund the war effort; and Americans on both sides essentially paid for the War through the depletion of their savings, caused by the rapid inflation that accompanied the paper currency issues. Prices in the North increased approximately 80 percent during the War; but in the South, where the costs of the war per capita were far greater, inflation reached 9,000 percent by the end of the War.

The Confederacy enacted conscription in April 1862 and the Union in March 1863, but the real purpose of these laws was to stimulate volunteering rather than to institute a genuine draft. Both the North and the South allowed drafted men to hire substitutes until the Confederacy abolished this privilege in December 1863. The Union government also exempted a drafted man upon payment of a $300 commutation fee, until this privilege was abolished in July 1864 due to popular discontent. In the North, the $300 commutation fee gave the common people reason to denounce the War as a "Rich man's war, poor man's fight." In the South, the idea that a central authority could force anyone, anywhere, to do anything against their will was a violation of the "states' rights" principles that the South was fighting for in the first place.

Union conscription was applied only in localities that failed to meet their quotas. Thus communities were impelled to pay "bounties" to encourage men to volunteer. This resulted in the practice of "bounty-jumping." A man would enlist, collect his bounty, desert, enlist again in some other locality, collect another bounty, and desert again.

Volunteers enlisted for specified periods, normally three years. The Confederacy's draft laws compelled them to reenlist even when their enlistment terms were up. On the Union side, by contrast, volunteers could not be compelled to reenlist, and in 1864 the North had to rely on bounties and patriotic persuasion to induce more than half of its three-year volunteers to reenlist.

Volunteer regiments at first elected their own officers, up to the rank of captain, and they frequently preferred officers who were not strict in matters of discipline. This was to handicap them in battle, however. Men without prior training as officers were placed in positions of command, and recruits were often thrown into combat with little basic training as soldiers. Even physical examinations for recruits were often a farce. It was, to a considerable extent, a do-it-yourself war because the machinery of the modern state was in its infancy, even in the North.

SOUTHERN STRATEGY

Southerners believed that they would win the war because of their "just cause," superior character, and—of course—because God was on their side. With foolhardy bravado, the Southerners believed that their rugged, country outdoorsmen with their frontier mentality would easily defeat the city boys from the North—whom they viewed as soft, flabby, and unprincipled. Southerners compared their position to that of the Colonists in 1776, who triumphed against insurmountable odds over the more powerful British.

Southerners also believed that the North would collapse without Southern cotton and that without the Southern market, Northern manufacturing would collapse in overproduction with no Southerners to purchase their goods. Southerners also believed that the Europeans, especially England, would be on their side because of the need for Southern cotton. The British imported 900 million pounds of cotton annually, three-fourths of which came from the American South. Twenty percent of Britain's workforce was involved in the textile industry; Britain would collapse without Southern cotton and would, therefore, ensure its supply with the world's largest navy. If England could be persuaded to join the Southern cause as a result of their need for cotton, then victory would be assured.

Confederate President Jefferson Davis termed the Southern strategy as an "offensive-defensive" strategy. Southerners recognized that a Union victory would require that they invade, defeat, and subjugate the South on its own soil (the challenge for the British in the American Revolution); but a Confederate victory only required the South to avoid annihilation until the North exhausted its resources and will to fight (the feat accomplished by the colonists in the American Revolution). This was the "defensive" part of the

Confederate President Jefferson Davis

Southern strategy. The "offensive" part of the strategy called for Southern offensives, preferably into Northern territory, that would produce shocking, "decisive victories," which would break the Northern will to fight and convince the Europeans to support the Southern cause as allies. In short, the Southerners sought a Civil War version of Saratoga, where a decisive victory by the Colonists brought France into the American Revolution as an ally, and a "Yorktown," where a decisive victory by the Colonists convinced the British that the fight was too costly and induced them to negotiate peace and accept the independence of their former possession.

To combat the Union navy, the Southerners armed their merchant ships, often draping them with bales of cotton to provide protection from Union guns. These "cotton clads" seized Union merchant ships and cargo—not only disrupting Union trade, but also confiscating goods for the South. The Confederates also constructed the beginnings of a navy, purchasing ships from England.

NORTHERN STRATEGY

President Lincoln's primary objective in the War was to preserve the Union, and his primary means was military subjugation of the South through a massive land invasion and naval blockade. In order to accomplish his goals, Lincoln needed to keep the war domestic and prevent European intervention on the behalf of the South. Direct European military intervention on the behalf of the South would tip the balance and secure Southern independence, so it had to be avoided at all costs. Massive economic aid from Europe to the South could perhaps tip the balance in the favor of the South, as well, so Secretary of State William Seward advised a blockade on all Southern ports. This Lincoln announced on April 19, 1861. In the beginning, the blockade was really merely a paper blockade since the United States had fewer than 100 ships to guard 185 Southern ports and 3,500 miles of coastline. Furthermore, only 42 of the Union's ships were considered seaworthy in 1861, and only eight were in United States waters at the time of the proclamation. The Union would build more ships, however, with the result that the blockade effectively crippled Southern international trade by the end of the war.

The blockade also presented a problem for the Union under international law because a "blockade" under international law was considered an act of war. Therefore, Lincoln's blockade inferred, under international law, that the South was an independent nation (a point disputed by the Union) and that the Civil War was a war between two independent nations, rather than an insurrection or a domestic dispute. The rules of international law were different for wars between belligerents (two independent, warring nations) than they were for insurrections or domestic disputes. As a belligerent in a war between nations, the South could obtain loans and purchase war materials in Europe. Furthermore, European nations would have the right to trade nonmilitary goods with both warring nations, the same rights that the United States had

Secretary of State William Seward

claimed and fought for in the War of 1812. When Lincoln declared the blockade, he essentially inferred that the South was an independent warring nation and that the Europeans would have those rights. England immediately declared neutrality, therefore inferring that they were asserting their rights as neutrals to trade nonmilitary goods in Southern ports. If Lincoln interrupted this trade, he risked war with England—which would doom Union prospects in the conflict with the South.

Lincoln's other option would have been to allow the Europeans unlimited trade with the South under the premise that the South was not independent and was still part of the United States. The advantage would be that the European powers would not be able to aid the South as an "independent country." If the South were not independent, as England's Lord Lyons explained to Secretary of State Seward, however, then a blockade would not be binding because blockades under international law applied only to two nations at war. Lincoln essentially attempted to skirt international law and do both—treat the war as a domestic dispute and deny European aid to the South—while imposing a blockade (thus inferring that the South was independent) and shutting off European trade with the South. The result would be legal disputes with England over the seizure of ships at sea that would be settled after the war and a continual risk of bringing England into the war on the side of the South over Union violations of international law.

Instead of a long, protracted war of attrition and annihilation that the Civil War eventually became, Lincoln and his generals envisioned a quick strike invasion into the South that would provide a stunning and decisive victory that would quickly quell the rebellion by proving to Southerners that their rebellion had no chance in the face of Northern superiority. Given that Richmond was only 100 miles from Washington, D.C., many Northern generals evidently believed that a quick strike on the Southern capital could produce the decisive Union victory necessary to cause the South to abandon the rebellion before it was even well started.

Instead, it was the Union strategy that was derailed before it even began. On April 19, the 6th Massachusetts Regiment that had been mobilized for an assault on Virginia arrived in Baltimore, Maryland, a city in a slave state that had not chosen to secede. Sentiments in Maryland were divided, and tensions were high. In Baltimore, the Massachusetts Regiment had to change railroad lines, forcing the soldiers to cross the city on foot. As they marched through the streets, a mob of some 10,000 Confederate sympathizers flying Confederate flags attacked them at first with rocks and then bullets. Under orders from their commander, the Union troops returned fire, and the city of Baltimore erupted into riotous violence. Twelve citizens of Baltimore and four Union soldiers were killed before military force could end the riot. Secessionists cut the telegraph wires and burned the railroad bridges connecting Baltimore to both North and South, cutting off the town from the Confederacy and, also, from the rest of the Union. The destruction of the rail bridges also cut off Washington (South of Baltimore) from the rest of the Union. To prevent the nation's capital from being surrounded by hostile enemy territory, Lincoln ordered that federal forces turn Maryland into an occupied state.

In order to prevent further bloodshed, Lincoln ordered that troops be routed around Baltimore. Lincoln then suspended habeas corpus and ordered the arrest of Confederate sympathizers with the result that Baltimore's mayor, police chief, a judge, and 19 Maryland state legislators were imprisoned without a trial. Chief Justice Roger Taney, who had penned the Dred Scott decision, challenged the President's action and issued a writ of habeas corpus for the release of a Southern sympathizer, John Merryman. In his opinion in ex parte Merryman, Taney ruled that if the public's safety was endangered, only Congress had the right to suspend the writ of habeas corpus. Lincoln, however, essentially ignored the ruling throughout the war and imprisoned, without charges or trials, whomever he saw fit.

Many Confederate sympathizers from Maryland fled the state to Virginia, formed a Confederate Maryland government in exile, and either joined up with the Confederate army or simply launched guerrilla raids back into Maryland. Unionists won the Maryland state elections and gained firm control of the Maryland legislature in the fall of 1861, but Maryland would remain a battleground for invading armies throughout the war.

The situation in Missouri essentially mirrored that in Maryland. St. Louis erupted into a full-scale riot and pitched battle between Unionist and Confederate militias on May 10–11, 1861; 36 people were killed. Union commander Nathaniel Lyon led his troops in a summer campaign that drove the Confederate militia, along with Missouri's governor and pro-Confederate legislators, into Arkansas where they formed a Missouri Confederate government in exile.

While in Arkansas, the Missouri Confederates recruited Arkansas comrades to help them invade back into Missouri in August. On August 10, the Union commander in Missouri, Nathaniel Lyon, was killed at Wilson's Creek in southwest Missouri. The Confederates then marched northward along the Missouri River and captured a Union garrison at Lexington, Missouri, 40 miles east of Kansas City, on September 20, 1861. This early victory was the South's high watermark in Missouri. The Union would officially control the state throughout the war, but Confederate "bushwhackers" and Unionist "Jayhawkers" would launch hit-and-run raids and ambushes against each other throughout the war. Notorious postwar outlaws Jesse and Frank James, and Cole and Jim Younger rode with the Confederate bushwhackers. Throughout the war, Missouri—perhaps more than any other state—suffered from a "civil war" within the Civil War.

Kentucky confederates, outnumbered approximately two to one in Kentucky, also fled to the Confederacy and formed a state government in exile; but Kentucky remained solidly in the Union. Union sentiments were also strong in the western mountain portion of Virginia west of the Shenandoah Valley where most of Virginia's delegates had voted against secession. In fact, part of the reason for placing the Southern capital in Richmond was to shore up Confederate support in the state. Western Virginia, however, was a mountainous agricultural area of small farms where family labor sufficed, and slaves were few in number. Western Virginia's economy was much more linked with Ohio and Pennsylvania than to the rest of Virginia or the South at large. Western Virginia's largest city, Wheeling, was 330 miles over rugged mountain terrain from Richmond, but only 60 miles from Pittsburgh. With the help of Union troops, which crossed the Ohio River and won several minor battles against Confederate forces in Western Virginia in the summer of 1861, the people of Western Virginia seceded from the confederacy and created the state of West Virginia, which was officially added to the Union in 1863.

The Civil War in the border states even spread into Native American territory as Confederate sympathizers manning the Union forts in the territory turned over the Union facilities to Confederates from Texas without a shot. Several Native American tribes were coaxed into signing Treaties of Alliance with the Confederacy, including the five "civilized tribes" (Cherokees, Creeks, Seminoles, Chickasaws, and Choctaws). Other Native American tribes sided with the Union, however, and aided by Union regiments from Kansas and Missouri eventually gained control of Native American Territory for the Union.

THE WAR IN THE FIELD

THE VIRGINIA FRONT

From the very outset of the war, attention was focused on the Virginia front. After fighting had begun at Fort Sumter and the states of the upper South had joined the Confederacy, the Confederate government moved its capital to Richmond, Virginia, about 100 miles south of Washington. With the two seats of government so close together, the war in the East became a struggle on the part of the Union to capture Richmond and on the part of the South to defend it.

Between Washington and Richmond a number of broad rivers—the Potomac, the Rappahannock, the York, the Chickahominy, and other tributaries—flow more or less parallel with one another from the Allegheny Mountains in the west to Chesapeake Bay in the east. This grid of rivers afforded a natural system of defense to the South and presented an obstacle course to the North. Southern armies on the defensive could lie in wait for their attackers on the south banks of these streams as they did at Bull Run, Fredericksburg, Chancellorsville, and the Wilderness. When the Southern army was driven back after going on the offensive, it could later cross back to safety, reorganize, and recoup—as it did after Antietam (Sharpsburg) and Gettysburg.

For four years the principal army of the North, the Army of the Potomac, struggled against the principal army of the South, the Army of Northern Virginia, over this terrain. Each side placed its foremost commander here. Robert E. Lee headed the Army of Northern Virginia after Joseph E. Johnston was wounded in 1862, and Ulysses S. Grant was brought east to take overall command of Union armies in

Attack on Fort Sumter

1864 after his great successes in the West. Public attention centered primarily upon these campaigns, and they have continued to receive more than their share of attention in history.

THE BATTLE OF BULL RUN (MANASSAS)

During the first half of the war, the Union met with a long succession of disappointments and defeats on the Virginia front. In July 1861, when both armies were still raw and unseasoned, the Union sent General Irvin McDowell south with the slogan "Forward to Richmond" and with expectations of an easy victory. This was done in spite of the fact that General Winfield Scott and his field commander, McDowell, both had misgivings about the ability of their green, poorly trained, 90-day volunteers to fight a real battle. In fact, Scott had argued for a cautious, long-term strategy known as the "Anaconda Plan," where the North would weaken the South gradually through blockades on land and sea until the Northern army was strong enough to move forward and crush the weakened south. The public, however, demanded bold, quick action—as did Scott's commander-in-chief, Abraham Lincoln. Thus, McDowell and his army marched into Virginia against the military judgment of its most experienced

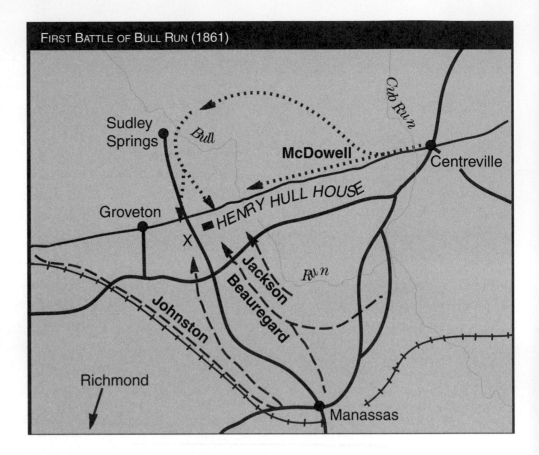

FIRST BATTLE OF BULL RUN (1861)

general. Twenty-five miles southwest of Washington, McDowell encountered the Confederate armies of Generals Pierre G. T. Beauregard, a West Point classmate of McDowell's known as the "Napoleon of the South," and Joseph E. Johnston with 25,000 strong, who had been deployed at Manassas Junction to defend a key rail junction at Manassas, Virginia. The Confederates named the ensuing battle from its location, whereas the Union named the battle after the creek that crossed the battlefield, Bull Run.

On July 21, the Union army forded Bull Run, a sluggish branch of the Potomac River, and engaged the Confederate troops on the Confederate left flank, at first driving them back. By early afternoon, the Union army appeared to be on the verge of breaking the Southern lines, but a Virginia brigade commanded by Thomas J. Jackson stood their ground. A South Carolina general, seeking to inspire his own troops, pointed to Jackson and his men—standing like a "stone wall" in repelling the Union troops. Afterwards, Thomas Jackson would be referred to in the South, affectionately, as "Stonewall Jackson." Jackson's stand, combined with the arrival of his 2,300 fresh Confederate reinforcements from the Shenandoah Valley (who hit the battlefield with a famed "rebel yell"), drove the green Union troops into a disorganized retreat. Union troops broke ranks and fled in a panic, trampling spectators who had stupidly arrived on the battlefield with parasols and picnic baskets to witness the romantic struggle of courage. Fleeing Union soldiers abandoned their weapons and stumbled past their abandoned supply wagons on their way back to Washington.

The inexperienced Southern troops lacked the organization and supply capacity necessary to press their advantage and, therefore, failed to pursue the fleeing Union army. Casualties on both sides were light by Civil War standards (2,800 for the Union and 2,000 Confederates), but the battle boosted Southern confidence while simultaneously proving to Lincoln and the Union that victory would not be swift and a broader strategy for winning the war would be necessary. In fact, for the South the victory may have engendered overconfidence, as some Southerners mistakenly believed that the war was won. Suddenly, the Union was more realistic and Congress

General Thomas "Stonewall" Jackson

General George B. McClellan

authorized the enlistment of up to a million three-year volunteers. Union men answered the call by the hundreds of thousands, and Lincoln and the Union settled in for a long, hard fight.

McDowell was replaced by 34 year-old George Brinton McClellan, who had campaigned successfully in West Virginia. McClellan was the child of wealthy parents in Philadelphia, educated in the best schools, and a graduate of West Point—where he finished second in his class and then served as an army engineer. A little man of supremely self-confident manner—he had gained the nickname, "The Young Napoleon." McClellan was much less the Napoleon than he appeared, however, because real resistance in West Virginia had been light; McClellan and the Union press overplayed the significance of his victories. Boldness in battle, which was the commodity Lincoln sought, would not prove to be McClellan's strongest suit.

McClellan possessed real ability as an organizer, and he had the good sense to realize that he must make his troops into an army before he took them campaigning. McClellan was a perfectionist, however; and he refused to mount an offensive until his army was trained to his own exacting requirements. Every commander has essentially two responsibilities: to win when engaged in military conflict and to keep as many of his own men alive as possible in the process. McClellan clearly believed that latter goal to be the more important of the two and sought every means by which he could avoid unnecessary loss of life and destruction of property. McClellan even stated that he expected to win by "maneuvering rather than fighting." McClellan was averse to risk and, of course, no military conflict can be waged completely absent of risk. The President prodded McClellan to speed up the process and become more aggressive, at one point stating, "If General McClellan does not want to use the army, I would like to borrow it." McClellan, however, was confident in his own abilities and had little respect for Lincoln, once referring to him as "the original gorilla." Consequently, there was no more major fighting on the Virginia front for almost a year.

When McClellan did at last move in April 1862, with an army of 130,000 strong, he persuaded President Lincoln to let him transport his troops by ship to Fort Monroe, a point on the Virginia coast within striking distance of Richmond. From this point he proposed to move up the peninsula between the York and the James Rivers (hence called the Peninsula Campaign) to capture the Confederate capital.

McClellan's plan was a brilliant solution to the difficult problem of supply, for he could now bring provisions for his army by ship without fear of Confederate raiders getting to his rear and cutting his lines. The plan had one important drawback, however, in that it left,

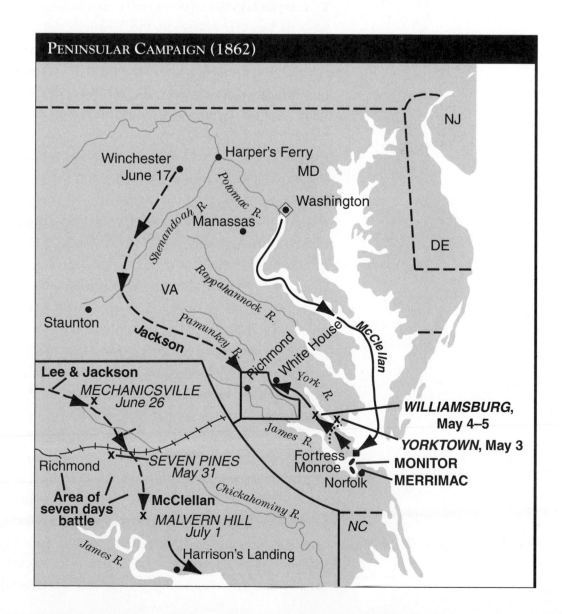

or appeared to leave, Washington exposed to the Confederates. Therefore, for the defense of the Capitol, President Lincoln insisted on withholding part (30,000) of the troops that McClellan wanted. So although McClellan launched his invasion from Fort Monroe toward Richmond, he failed to push his offensive with the vigor the North expected. McClellan also moved with methodical precision—so methodical, in fact, that it took him over 10 weeks to advance 65 miles. A small Confederate blocking force at Yorktown delayed McClellan for the entire month of April. McClellan insisted on bringing siege guns to the front to blast his way through an infantry that his immense army should have been able to crush on foot in a matter of days. Finally, McClellan and his men were within six miles of Richmond, close enough to hear the town's church bells.

While these developments were in progress, the Confederate commander, Joseph E. Johnston launched a counterattack on May 31–June 1, in what has become known as the Battle of Seven Pines. The battle was indecisive although the Confederates suffered 6,000 casualties and the Union 5,000. Johnston, however, was badly wounded in the shoulder in the assault and was replaced by Robert E. Lee.

Lee, a Virginia aristocrat, mild of speech and gentle of manner but gifted with a daring that was terrible to his adversaries, quickly perceived that he could play upon the Union's fear that Washington was too exposed. Accordingly, he sent his brilliant subordinate, Thomas I. ("Stonewall") Jackson, on a raid up the Shenandoah Valley, appearing to threaten Washington and causing the administration to hold there defensive troops that had previously been promised to McClellan. In the month between May 4 and June 9, 1862, Stonewall Jackson's Confederates, with only 17,000 men, marched over 350 miles in a month and defeated three separate Union armies in four engagements. Furthermore, the number of Union troops Jackson and his men defeated were more than twice the number than that of Jackson's Confederates.

When Jackson returned from his raid with phenomenal speed, Lee's reunited forces of 85,000 took the offensive against McClellan's 100,000 original forces south and east of Richmond in a series of engagements known as the Seven Days' Battles (June 25–July 1, 1862). McClellan fought hard and was not decisively defeated; but he lost his nerve, moved back to a base on the James River, and sent Washington a series of frantic messages that the government had deserted him. By the time McClellan had reached the water and the safety of Union naval support, the Union had suffered 16,000 casualties and the South 20,000. Though the South had suffered greater casualties, Lee had saved Richmond, forced the Union to retreat, and—at least temporarily—reversed the Union's momentum.

McClellan's retreat convinced Lincoln that the peninsula campaign would not work and that McClellan was not the right man to lead the Union Army. On July 11, Lincoln appointed General Henry W. Halleck, who had been the overall commander in the Western theater where the Union had experienced greater success, to be the new General-in-Chief.

SECOND BATTLE OF BULL RUN

Lincoln, who had never fully accepted the basic idea of operating by sea, through Halleck, withdrew McClellan's troops from the peninsula to northern Virginia where they would join a smaller force under the command of General John Pope, who had gained a reputation for aggressiveness in the West. The President hoped to launch another assault against Richmond via an overland route that he preferred. As McClellan departed from the peninsula by water, Lee quickly took advantage of the opportunity that was provided him by this separation of the two Union armies and moved north with his "Army of Northern Virginia" to engage Pope's troops before McClellan could reach him. Lee sent Stonewall Jackson to attack Pope from the rear, provoking Pope to launch a counter-attack against the Confederate contingency under Stonewall Jackson. Lee then hurled the main thrust of his army against Pope's flank before McClellan and the Army of the Potomac could arrive. An exasperated Lincoln removed Pope from command and reassigned him to fighting Native Americans in Minnesota. McClellan was restored to command and given a second chance.

ANTIETAM

When Lee decided to march north, cross the Potomac, and advance into Maryland, he believed that a decisive victory in Maryland could win the state for the Confederacy and influence the Union Congressional elections in November to an anti-war stance. A decisive victory in Maryland could, perhaps, bring recognition or intervention from England and thus win the war. However, Lee's movement into Maryland was fraught with difficulties from the start since Lee was greatly outnumbered (50,000 to 85,000), poorly supplied, and exhausted from the Richmond campaigns. Again Lee divided his forces, sending part of his army under Stonewall Jackson to capture Harper's Ferry, which lay amidst Lee's supply route from the Shenandoah Valley. Lee held the other part of his army on watch in the mountain passes west of Frederick, Maryland.

Union forces under McClellan had a stroke of good luck when they found a copy of Lee's battle plans at Fredrick, wrapped in three cigars and, evidently, dropped by a Southern officer. McClellan proclaimed, "Here is a paper ... with which if I cannot whip Bobbie Lee, I will be willing to go home." Even with a copy of Lee's secret orders in his hands so that he knew exactly what to expect, however, McClellan still did not move quickly or decisively. Twelve thousand of McClellan's men surrendered to Stonewall Jackson's Confederates at Harper's Ferry on September 15, 1862. McClellan's delay allowed Lee the time he needed to assume a position behind Antietam Creek near Sharpsburg on September 17. McClellan threw his 75,000 men at Lee's 40,000 Confederates even though McClellan, as was his nature, thought the Union was outnumbered. After a supremely hard-fought engagement at Antietam (Sharpsburg), Lee withdrew after the deadliest single-day battle of the war, bloodied, but not crushed, to the south bank of the Potomac. A total of 6,000 men were killed and 17,000 wounded in one day. McClellan's army almost broke through the Confederate lines on a road northeast of Sharpsburg (known after as Bloody Lane); but fearing counterattacks from reserves that Lee did not have, McClelland held back 20,000 of his troops in reserve. McClellan received reinforcements the next day and Lee did not; still McClellan did not renew his attack. The next night, the Confederates retreated back across the Potomac to Virginia.

Though the battle was a Union victory in that the Southern offensive was halted and Lee was forced to retreat, the victory was not complete because McClellan failed to press his advantage and allowed Lee's troops to return to Virginia to rebuild. Lincoln again replaced McClellan on November 7, this time with Ambrose E. Burnside. Britain and France, both of which had been considering intervention or recognition of the Confederacy, decided to withhold that recognition. Four days later on September 22, Lincoln issued his preliminary Emancipation Proclamation.

General Ambrose E. Burnside

FREDERICKSBURG

Ambrose E. Burnside was most certainly a more aggressive general than McClellan, but he proved to be a less than brilliant battlefield tactician. In December 1862 Burnside made an unimaginative frontal attack across the Rappahannock at Fredericksburg, Virginia, against prepared Confederate defenses. Fighting the Confederates on ground of their own choosing, Burnside launched his troops on an uphill charge where

General Joseph Hooker

he sustained terrible losses, more than twice the casualty rate of the Confederates, and was replaced by Joseph Hooker. After Lincoln heard the bad news from the battlefield, the President reportedly groaned, "If there is a worse place than hell, I am in it." Other than his failed frontal assault at Fredericksburg, Burnside is perhaps most noteworthy for his distinctive whiskers, from which the anagram "sideburns" became part of the English language.

Morale in the Union, both among the troops and among the public, reached a new low in the winter of 1862–1863, as did Lincoln's popularity. The army was suffering from high desertion rates, and the bleak outlook is what caused Lincoln to turn to "Fighting Joe" Hooker to lead the troops. Hooker was described as ill-tempered, vindictive, and deviously in favor of a military dictator for the United States. In his letter appointing Hooker to lead the army, Lincoln acknowledges that Hooker favors a dictatorship, while he did not; but the President was appointing Hooker to lead his army in spite of this fact. Lincoln did, however, believe Hooker to be a bold general in that he cautioned him against "rashness."

CHANCELLORSVILLE

Thus, Hooker seemed a man of boldness and decision and in command of 120,000 well-trained troops north of the Rappahannock River, opposite Fredericksburg. In May 1863, Hooker crossed the

Rappahannock north of Fredericksburg and moved his army toward the town and the Confederate army. After executing an excellent flanking march to maneuver Lee into battle on unfavorable terms, Hooker evidently lost his poise and drew his army back to what he thought was a defensive position in a desolate area of scrub trees known as the "Wilderness." Hooker allowed Jackson's corps to roll up the Union right flank in a surprise attack that rocked the Federals and eventually drove them back across the Rappahannock, in spite of the fact that the Confederates were outnumbered two to one. Although a great Confederate victory, the South paid a fearful price for Chancellorsville. Confederate casualties exceeded 12,000, and General Stonewall Jackson was accidentally wounded by his own troops and died a few days later.

GETTYSBURG

Hooker remained in command until Lee launched a second offensive against the North, this time into Pennsylvania. Lee understood that the South was losing a war of attrition, which favored the North; so he set his sights on scoring a decisive victory in the North that could break the morale of the Union and perhaps bring European intervention and recognition. When Lee escaped from Hooker on the northward march, Lincoln again changed commanders, turning this time to George Gordon Meade. By late June 1863, Lee's army had fanned out across southern Pennsylvania in a 50-mile arc from Harrisburg almost to Baltimore. Meade's army and Lee's army met at Gettysburg, though neither had planned it that way.

On July 1, Confederate troops in search of shoes in the town of Gettysburg clashed with a Union cavalry unit. Both sides sent out calls for reinforcement, and the two armies converged. On the first three days of July 1863, the South made its supreme effort, and the little town in Pennsylvania became the scene of the greatest battle ever fought in North America. Confederates broke the union lines on the afternoon of July 1, driving the Union to a defensive position on Cemetery Ridge south of town. General Richard Ewell, Stonewall Jackson's successor, judged the Union position too strong to defeat and chose not to attack further as darkness fell on July 1. The next morning, Lee and the Confederates occupied Seminary Ridge, facing Meade to the south on the high ground at Cemetery Ridge. General James Longstreet argued against a frontal assault. Instead he favored a maneuver to the south toward Washington, D.C., in an attempt to get the Union to attack the Confederates while they occupied a strong defensive position. Lee, however, reportedly pointed to the Union lines and said, "The enemy is there, and I am going to attack him there." On July 2, Lee threw his troops across a valley between the two against the Union positions in a series of bold attacks on the Union flanks. Having attacked the Union flank, Lee believed that the center of the Union lines might be weak; so on July 3, Lee ordered an assault on the Union center on Cemetery Ridge, where Meade's troops were dug-in with almost a mile of clear vision. After a two-hour

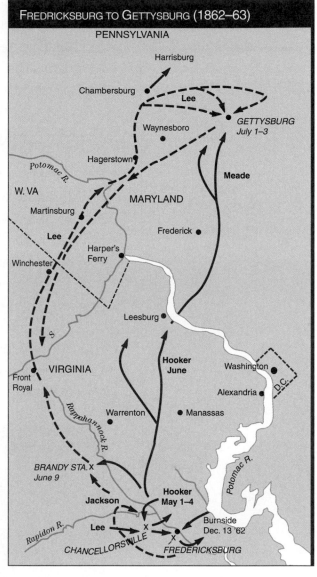

Confederate artillery bombardment, in an assault known as "Pickett's Charge," General George Pickett and 15,000 Confederates charged into Union cannon and rifle fire, but Meade's forces were too strong to be dislodged.

Pickett's assault was almost successful in that it actually broke the Union lines on the afternoon of July 3, but Union reinforcements drove the Confederates back before they could secure their positions. Approximately half of Pickett's men did not survive, and Lee lost over a third of his forces at Gettysburg. Lee realized his mistake and was heard to state, "It's all my fault." Nevertheless, Lee and his decimated army waited for more than a day to receive a counterattack that never came and then marched south. Meade did not pursue until too late, and 10 days after the battle Lee crossed back over the Potomac—unmolested. The Army of Northern Virginia had still never been driven from a battlefield, but its great offensive power was forever broken; and Lee would be able to mount no more Northern offensives. In this, the Battle of Gettysburg is generally considered the turning point in the Civil War. The Union had survived its greatest threat, and the South was reduced to fighting defensively in a losing war of attrition.

THE WAR IN THE WEST

While the War was raging in the East, the Union was also launching an offensive west of the Appalachians with the goal of dominating the Southern waterways and, thus, controlling Southern trade. Poor transportation, poor communications, and inadequate supplies hindered the Confederates in the West. For instance, many of the Confederate troops went into battle with out-of-date flintlock muskets against Union troops that had repeating rifles.

The whole region beyond the Alleghenies was far vaster and more fragmented geographically than the Virginia theater, and the Union campaigns in the West never had a single focus as they did in Virginia. Operations along the Mississippi were scarcely coordinated with operations in the central and eastern parts of Tennessee and Kentucky, and neither of these was synchronized with activities "west of the River" in Missouri, Arkansas, most of Louisiana, and Texas. Essentially, however, it was the objective of the Union to gain control of the Mississippi River and, thus, to cut off the western wing of the Confederacy. In this way Confederate armies would be deprived of reinforcements and supplies—especially of Texas cattle—a food source they vitally needed. A further division of the Confederacy would be undertaken

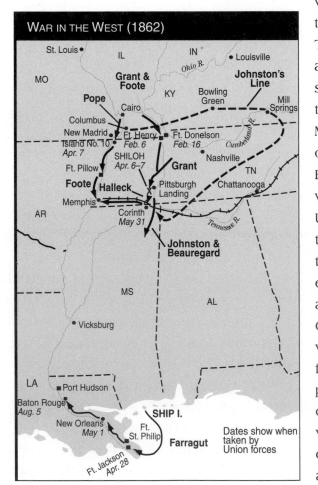

WAR IN THE WEST (1862)

by driving southeast through Kentucky and Tennessee, cutting vital Confederate rail connections at Chattanooga in eastern Tennessee and continuing, thence, into the heart of the Confederacy across Georgia to the sea. Such an operation would cut off the Gulf Coast region from the Atlantic seaboard and leave only Virginia, the Carolinas, and part of Georgia to support a hopeless cause.

It took three years and eight months for the Union to carry out these plans although they had begun sooner than the great campaigns in Virginia.

CONFEDERATE INVASION OF NEW MEXICO

Some Confederates had visions of a "manifest destiny" for the Confederacy that included expanding the Confederacy across the Mexican Cession of the southwestern United States. Some Southerners even envisioned a Confederate slave empire expanding throughout all of Latin America. In furtherance of these grandiose goals and with the specific objectives of securing the upper Rio Grande Valley (Albuquerque and Santa Fe) for the Confederacy and of establishing a Confederate Pacific port on the Gulf of California at the mouth of the Colorado River for the Confederacy (an area that through the twenty-first century remains under Mexican sovereignty), Confederate Colonel John R. Baylor on August 1, 1861, issued a proclamation establishing the "Confederate Territory of Arizona." This territory comprised of what is present-day New Mexico and Arizona, south of the 43 degrees north latitude. Baylor rode west with a Confederate force all the way to Tuscon, where he captured the federal garrison there from its unenthusiastic Union defenders. Baylor established a Confederate government in Tuscon, and he was made governor of the new Confederate territory.

In January 1862, three regiments of Confederate Texans under H. H. Sibley marched on the upper Rio Grande Valley and, in February 1862, defeated a New Mexico militia and a group of Union army regulars at Valverde, thus securing Albuquerque and Santa Fe for the Confederacy. The Confederate expansion was short-lived, however, as a Union regiment of Colorado miners, who had marched over the Rocky Mountains in winter, defeated the Confederate Texans at Glorieta Pass on March 26–28, forcing the Confederates to retreat all the way back to Texas. Of the 3,700 Confederates who had launched the New Mexico campaign, only 2,000 made it back to Texas due not only to battlefield losses but also insufficient food supplies and the harshness of the elements.

PEA RIDGE

Before the Union army could march on Tennessee, Union leaders believed they had to secure Missouri. Consequently, in March 1862, Union troops under General Samuel R. Curtis advanced across Missouri into northwestern Arkansas where they engaged and defeated 16,000 Confederates under General Earl Van Dorn at Pea Ridge. The Confederate army included three regiments of Native Americans from Native American Territory who had joined up with the Confederates hoping for greater autonomy than they enjoyed in the Union. Though Curtis' campaign swept the Confederate army out of Missouri, the state remained a hotbed of guerrilla activity and violence throughout the war.

FORTS HENRY AND DONELSON

In February 1862, Ulysses S. Grant, a man who had resigned from the army in 1854 as a failure and later been reinstated, captured two Confederate forts in western Tennessee, Henry and Donelson, which controlled the Tennessee and Cumberland Rivers. Unlike the streams of Virginia that cut across the paths of advancing armies, each of these rivers flowed in a "U"-shaped course from the southern Appalachians southward into northern Alabama (in the case of the Tennessee) or into central Tennessee (in the case of the Cumberland) and then reversed their courses almost due north to the Ohio River. Control of these river highways gave Grant easy entry deep into the South.

The Union's new "timberclad" gunboats, designed specifically for river warfare, took out Fort Henry without involvement by the Union infantry. At Fort Donelson, however, 27,000 Union forces under General Grant clashed with 17,000 Confederates. Grant famously demanded the "immediate and unconditional surrender" of 13,000 Confederate troops that, lacking options, surrendered on Grant's terms on February 16.

As a consequence of these victories, Union gunboats controlled the Tennessee River to Alabama and the Cumberland to Nashville. The Union army used the rivers to transport its troops, and on February 25, 1862, Nashville became the first Southern state capitol to surrender. Confederate army units withdrew from Kentucky and Tennessee to Corinth, Mississippi. From Corinth, the Confederate Western commander, Albert Sydney Johnston, planned to attack Grant's army at Pittsburg Landing just north of the Tennessee border from Mississippi.

The battle at Fort Donelson

Meanwhile, on April 26, 1862, a Union fleet under the command of David Farragut captured the port of New Orleans for the Union after running past forts south of the city. Besides securing and occupying New Orleans, Farragut proceeded to blockade the Gulf of Mexico and control traffic on the lower Mississippi. Farragut's exploits were so important to the Union that, in 1866, Congress created the rank of admiral specifically for Farragut.

SHILOH

On April 6, Johnston and 40,000 Confederates attacked 35,000 Union troops under General Grant near a church called Shiloh. The attack caught Grant and his men off-guard. Many of Grant's men were half-dressed, some were asleep, and others were brewing their morning coffee. Grant's army was pushed back, but the troops held their ground by the end of the first day. The Confederates lost Johnston, who bled to death from a shot to the leg. Grant received reinforcements overnight from a Union army of 25,000 under the command of

General Don Carlos Buell; and the Union counterattacked the next day, driving the Confederates back to Corinth, Mississippi.

A total of 13,000 Union and 10,000 Confederate troops were lost at Shiloh, more deaths than in all the battles of the American Revolution, the War of 1812, and the War with Mexico combined. A full day after the battle, 90 percent of the wounded were still lying on the battlefield in a heavy rain. Many of the wounded died of exposure, but some of them actually drowned in the downpour. The massive casualty rates and gruesome battlefield proved to citizens in both North and South that the war was not to be viewed as simply a romantic test of courage. Even Grant later stated that after Shiloh he "gave up all idea of saving the Union except by complete conquest." For Grant—personally—the high casualties, the fact that he was caught by surprise, and the fact that he allowed the battered Confederate army to escape, damaged his reputation and temporarily cost him his command.

After Shiloh, however, the Union victories continued in the West. By the end of May the Union armies under the general command of Henry W. Halleck expelled the Confederates from Corinth, the hub of several important railroads, while the Union gunboat fleet wiped out the Confederate fleet at Memphis on June 6. Moving North from New Orleans, Farragut captured Baton Rouge and Natchez before meeting up with Union gunboats from the North at Vicksburg. The Union fleet was unable to subdue the heavily fortified Confederate position at Vicksburg; however, the series of Northern victories after Shiloh had many in the North believing that the War was won in the West by the summer of 1862. Union victories in the spring of 1862 had brought over 50,000 square miles of Confederate territory under Union control.

The new Confederate Commander in the West, General Braxton Bragg, consolidated his troops in Chattanooga with plans to launch an offensive to retake Tennessee and Kentucky in the winter of 1862. A Union army under the command of Don Carlos Buell, and later William Rosecrans, whose goal was to capture Chattanooga, countered Bragg and the Confederates. The Confederates pushed north into Kentucky and had almost reached the Ohio River by September, but they were defeated at Perryville on October 8 and forced to retreat back to Tennessee. After several months of maneuvering, the two armies clashed again on December 31, 1862, at Murfeesboro (or Stones River); the Confederates were again forced to retreat and abandon their Tennessee offensive.

Problems for the Union in the Western theater persisted, however. Occupying and administering vast areas of territory in the South proved difficult and costly as soldiers for occupation had to be drawn from combat forces elsewhere. Furthermore, Union soldiers in the West were far from the Union infrastructure and at the end of long supply lines. The occupying Union soldiers, therefore, dangled in front of Confederate guerrillas as easy targets. During the last half of 1862, Southern cavalrymen under Nathan Bedford Forrest and John Hunt Morgan staged repeated guerrilla raids and sabotage—in which they burned bridges, blew up tunnels, destroyed railroad tracks, and stole Union supplies. The Southern guerrillas in the West very quickly reinforced the lessons learned by the British in the American Revolution: It is easier to defeat an inferior enemy in a frontal assault than to occupy and control a vast hostile country thousands of miles from home.

VICKSBURG

During the winter of 1862–1863, Grant began a campaign against the Confederate stronghold at Vicksburg where towering bluffs command the Mississippi. Deep in enemy country, Vicksburg was rendered almost impregnable by vast swamps, a succession of steep hills, and the river itself. After making a series of unsuccessful moves against this natural fortress, Grant at last hit on the bold and unorthodox plan of moving down the west side of the river, crossing below Vicksburg, abandoning his lines of communication, and living off the country during a final drive against the Confederate defenses. In furtherance of his plan, Grant first ran his ironclad river fleet down river past the Confederate guns overlooking the river from Vicksburg. Grant's troops then marched down the Mississippi's west bank to 40 miles south of Vicksburg where they were ferried across the river into Mississippi. Grant then deceptively marched his army east toward Jackson, Mississippi, instead of marching directly to Vicksburg. Grant's purpose was to scatter the Confederate forces that were concentrated at Vicksburg by making it appear that he was launching an assault on the Mississippi State Capitol. Grant also sought to destroy the Southern rails so that they would be hindered in attacking him from the rear when he turned his forces toward Vicksburg. During the first three weeks of May 1863, Grant fought and won five engagements with the Confederates in Mississippi and surrounded the 30,000 Confederate troops at Vicksburg, getting them stuck between the Union gunboats on the river and his army to their east. Grant launched assaults on the Confederate lines on May 19 and May 22, but he was repulsed. Grant then settled down to lay an old fashioned siege to the city with his army that now numbered over 70,000. After more than a month of siege warfare, the Confederates were running out of supplies. Finally, on July 4, 1863 the day on which Lee began his uncontested withdrawal, from Gettysburg John C. Pemberton, another Confederate general, surrendered an army of about 30,000 men—the largest that has ever been captured in North America—at Vicksburg. The man to whom he surrendered was Ulysses S. Grant, and the event marked the culmination of a series of campaigns in the West which had been much more decisive in their results than the eastern campaigns. After the battle an impressed Abraham Lincoln stated, "Grant is my man, and I am his the rest of the war." After over two years of searching, Lincoln had finally found his general. Five days later, the Confederate garrison at Port Hudson, 200 miles South of Vicksburg, also surrendered to the Union army, thus giving the Union control of the entire Mississippi.

CHICKAMAUGA AND CHATTANOOGA

For six months after the Battle of Murfeesboro (Stones River, December 31, 1862–January 3, 1863) William Rosecrans' Union Army of the Cumberland and Braxton Bragg's Confederate Army of Tennessee maneuvered against each other without major engagements. Finally, on June 24, 1863, Rosecrans launched an offensive designed to dislodge the Confederates from eastern Tennessee. Rosecrans' offensive forced the Confederates to retreat to Chattanooga. Rosecrans paused to take on supplies, connected with another Union army commanded by Ambrose Burnside, and drove the Confederates out of Knoxville on September 2, and Chattanooga on September 9. Thus, the Union army severed the South's only direct east-west railway, and with the capture of Chattanooga, the Union was in position to launch an invasion of Georgia.

On September 19, however, the Confederates counterattacked Rosecrans' army in the valley of Chickamauga Creek. Over the next two days of fierce fighting, the two armies suffered combined casualties of 36,000—the most of any battle at that point except for Gettysburg. On September 20, Confederates under James Longstreet broke the Union lines and forced a segment of the Union army to retreat to Chattanooga.

After the battle, Lincoln replaced Rosecrans—whom Lincoln described as "confused and stunned like a duck hit on the head"—with George H. Thomas, who gained the nickname "Rock of Chickamauga" for his firm stand against the Confederate assault. Lincoln then reinforced Thomas at Chattanooga with two Union armies from Virginia under "Fightin' Joe" Hooker and William Tecumseh Sherman. Lincoln also ordered General Grant to Chattanooga and appointed him to take overall command of the Union forces. By November 24, the tide had turned again in the Union's favor. On that day, Hooker's troops drove Confederates off Lookout Mountain, and the next day, Union forces broke the Confederate Lines at Missionary Ridge in Georgia, east of Chattanooga.

GRANT TAKES COMMAND

In March 1864, Lincoln brought Grant east to serve as general-in-chief and to take personal charge of the Army of the Potomac (Meade was not removed but was under Grant's command). By this time the Confederacy, outnumbered from the beginning, was fearfully handicapped by losses of men that could not be replaced as Union losses could. Grant, recognizing this handicap, settled upon a plan of operations that was far less brilliant than his operations in the West, but no less decisive. By steadily extending his flanks, he forced the Confederacy to extend also and to make its lines very thin. By continuing pressure, he gave his adversaries no rest.

The Confederates no longer had the manpower to launch invasions into the North in an effort to score the decisive victory that would cause the North to quit or the Europeans to intervene. The Southerners could still fight a guerrilla war of attrition on their own soil, however, as the Americans had done against the British in the American Revolution, and eventually exhaust the Union's will to sacrifice its children in the interest of saving the Union. In fact, by the summer of 1864, Lincoln's popularity may have been at an all time low. The Union Democrats nominated General George McClellan on a peace platform. There was a strong possibility that Lincoln and the Unionists would lose the election of 1864 and Lincoln's successor would end the war to satisfy the popular will. Thus, the Union would be lost, and secession successful.

In the spring of 1864, Grant placed himself in command in Virginia and General William Tecumseh Sherman in Georgia.

General Ulysses S. Grant

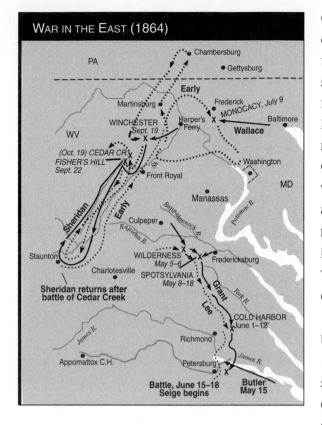

WAR IN THE EAST (1864)

Grant opted for an all-out offensive on all fronts so that the South could not shift troops to where the fighting was the hottest. Lee resisted with immense skill, attacking Grant in early May in the wilderness where Union artillery and superiority in numbers were greatly mitigated. In the Battle of the Tangled Wilderness, the Confederates inflicted 18,000 casualties on the Union, while suffering 12,000 themselves. Many soldiers were burned to death by fires started by exploding shells in the dry Virginia brush.

Grant, however, simply moved his army east toward Spotsylvania Court House, 10 miles closer to Richmond. Lee blocked the road junction between Grant's army and Richmond with the result that another 18,000 Union soldiers and 12,000 Confederates were killed, wounded, or captured in the 12 days between May 8 and May 19, 1864. Ahead of his time, Lee engaged in trench warfare tactics that would dominate World War I, some 50 years later.

Repulsed at Spotsylvania, Grant moved south in an effort to outflank Lee's forces, but Lee confronted him near the crossroads inn of Cold Harbor, 10 miles northeast of Richmond. Grant opted for an assault on Lee's entrenched forces at Cold Harbor on June 3, only to lose 7,000 men in less than an hour. Grant again tried to outflank Lee and moved his army to the James River at Petersburg, 20 miles south of Richmond. Lee again blocked Grant's troops, and in four days of fighting from June 15–18, 1864, Grant's forces suffered another 11,000 casualties.

Grant sacrificed men so freely in the Virginia campaign between May 5 and June 18, 1864 that his losses (65,000) almost equaled the total number of men in Lee's army and earned Grant the disparaging title, "Butcher Grant." During the same six weeks, the South, however, had suffered 37,000 casualties that they could ill-afford. Lee was winning the battles, but Grant was winning the war. Unable to break the

Confederate lines, as he had done at Vicksburg, Grant then settled down for a siege along the Petersburg-Richmond front. With Lee no longer mobile, it was only a question of time; but Lee held on for nine long months while Richmond remained the Confederate capital.

Meanwhile, Confederates also thwarted other Union efforts in Virginia. Union General Benjamin Butler attempted an attack up the James River against Richmond but was stopped by a rag-tag Confederate army under General Beauregard. A Union offensive in the Shenandoah Valley was stopped at Lynchburg by Stonewall Jackson's old troops under the command of Jubal Early. Early then led a daring raid across the Potomac almost to Washington, D.C., on July 11–12, before being driven back to Virginia.

PRESIDENTIAL ELECTION AND THE PEACE MOVEMENT

With Southerners reaching the outskirts of Washington, the high casualties, and Richmond still in Southern hands, the mood of the public in the North was decidedly anti-war and anti-Lincoln. If an election had been held in August 1864, many historians believe that Lincoln would have lost to an anti-war candidate and the fate of the United States might have been forever altered. Lincoln told a friend in August, "I am going to be beaten and, unless some great change takes place, badly beaten." Democrats called for Lincoln to drop the issue of emancipation and negotiate peace with the South with the understanding that slavery could continue if the South would return to the Union. Lincoln refused.

Union casualties during May through July 1864 had reached a staggering 110,000, double the casualty rate for any other three-month period of the war, and newspaper headlines boldly shouted to "STOP THE WAR!" Lincoln understood the public sentiments and even sent

1864 Abraham Lincoln presidential campaign poster

General George B. McClellan

New York Tribune editor Horace Greeley to attempt to negotiate peace with the Confederates at Niagara Falls—but with no success. In August, the Democratic Party nominated General George B. McClellan on a peace platform, and it appeared that the November election would be a referendum on Lincoln and the war and that Lincoln and his policy of continuation of the war would lose. Events in Georgia, however, would shift the mood of the public before the November election, sealing the preservation of the Union.

THE FALL OF ATLANTA

While Grant and Lee faced each other across the trenches at Petersburg, the Confederacy was being cut to pieces from the rear. Grant had first cut it at Vicksburg on the Mississippi, and the next cut was to take place from eastern Tennessee into Georgia. When Grant left for Virginia, William T. Sherman, a trusted subordinate, remained to face the Confederate forces under Joseph E. Johnston in the mountains of north Georgia.

By the end of June 1864, Sherman had advanced 80 miles, suffering 17,000 casualties to Johnston's 14,000. These losses were immense to be sure, but far less than the carnage conducted by Lee and Grant in Virginia. Johnston, a "retreating general" but a resourceful obstructionist, blocked and delayed Sherman at every step, all the way to Atlanta. At Peachtree Creek just outside Atlanta, Jefferson Davis removed Johnson because of his unwillingness to take the offensive; and John B. Hood was put in his place. Hood made the mistake of challenging Sherman in a series of direct attacks at Peachtree Creek, Atlanta, and Ezra Church. Hood was so badly defeated, suffering 15,000 casualties to 6,000 for Sherman, that he had to settle down into a purely defensive position by July 28.

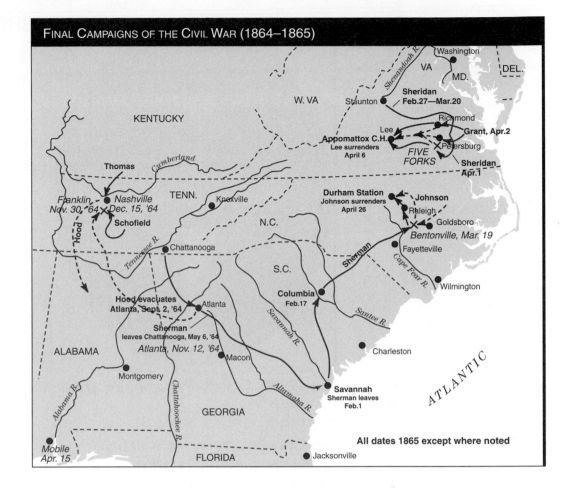

FINAL CAMPAIGNS OF THE CIVIL WAR (1864–1865)

After a month of stalemate, Sherman moved to attack the last rail link into Atlanta from the south at Jonesboro on August 31. On September 1, Sherman's men captured the railroad, and Confederate commander John Bell Hood abandoned Atlanta. Sherman moved his troops into the symbolic city on September 2. The news that Atlanta had fallen sent shockwaves throughout the South and waves of jubilation throughout the North. Southerners had believed that Lincoln would lose the election in November and his successor would quickly negotiate an end to the war that would result in Confederate independence with the retention of slavery. The fall of Atlanta, however, shifted the public sentiments in the North back to Lincoln and his policies of emancipation and military subjugation of the South. To most Northerners, the fall of Atlanta proved that the North had won. Similarly, the fall of Atlanta was a devastating blow to the morale of the South. Many Southerners now understood that they had lost; but they also understood that Abraham Lincoln, the man who had waged the irrepressible war against slavery and the South, would remain in the White House.

SHERMAN'S MARCH

General William Tecumseh Sherman

General William Tecumseh Sherman believed that taking Atlanta was not enough and that he must ensure that the Southerners understood what they had lost. Of all the Civil War generals, Grant and, especially, Sherman had the most "modern" conception of warfare. They were pioneers in the practice of total war. Sherman had become convinced that "We are not only fighting hostile armies, but a hostile people." Defeat of the Southern armies would not be enough to win this war. The railroads, farms, and factories that fed and supplied the armies must also be destroyed: the will of the civilian population that sustained the armies must be crushed. Sherman even killed the Southern livestock. "We cannot change the hearts of those people of the South," said Sherman in 1864, "but we can make war so terrible ... and make them so sick of war that generations would pass away before they would again appeal to it."

In order to ensure that the will of the people was crushed, Sherman believed that he must cut a path of destruction across the South so horrible that Southerners would never consider continuing the war or ever waging it again. He proposed to march his army from Atlanta to Savannah, destroying everything in his path.

After taking Atlanta on September 2, 1864, Sherman began his campaign of destruction by setting fire to the city and burning a third of the entire town, including much nonmilitary property. After assuring Lincoln and Grant that General George Thomas and his 60,000 men were sufficient to match Hood's Confederate army in Tennessee, Sherman and 60,000 Union troops marched out of Atlanta on November 16, beginning a march of destruction. Given that Hood's army abandoned Georgia for a campaign in Tennessee, Sherman was able to march unopposed across Georgia from Atlanta to the sea, cutting a path of charred destruction 60 miles wide for 280 miles. A Georgia woman's diary explained Sherman's impact:

There was hardly a fence left standing all the way from Sparta to Gordon. The fields were trampled down and the road was lined with carcasses of horses, hogs and cattle that the invaders, unable either to consume or to carry away with them, had wantonly shot down, to starve out the people. ... The dwellings that were standing all showed signs of pillage, and on every plantation we saw ... charred remains.

Sherman reached the port of Savannah on Christmas, 1864, while Grant was still outside Petersburg. The march of Sherman's army from Atlanta to the sea not only destroyed Confederate resources but also functioned as a form of psychological warfare. "It is a demonstration to the world," wrote Sherman, "that we have a power which Jefferson Davis cannot resist. This may not be war but rather statesmanship."

DESTRUCTION OF HOOD'S ARMY OF TENNESSEE

Hood's attempt to retake Tennessee rather than engage Sherman in Georgia turned out little better for the Southerners than Sherman's march. On November 30, 1864, the Confederates attacked the Union army at Franklin, 20 miles South of Nashville, but they were badly defeated. Hood then attempted to move on to Nashville where his army was almost wiped out by Union troops under General George Thomas. Of the 50,000 men under his command in July, only 15,000 remained after the defeat at Nashville. With no real army left to lead and a record only of defeat, Hood resigned in January 1865. The South's army in the West, for all practical purposes, was no more.

SHERMAN'S MARCH IN THE CAROLINAS

At the end of January 1865, Sherman's army of "total warriors" moved north from Savannah into South Carolina, destroying everything in their path as they had in Georgia. Sherman even left less standing in Columbia, South Carolina than he had in Atlanta. Sherman then continued his march all the way into North Carolina where he defeated a Confederate force under Joseph E. Johnston. Just as Sherman had intended, Southern morale was effectively destroyed everywhere he went. One South Carolina physician wrote, "All is gloom, despondency, and inactivity. ... Our army is demoralized and the people panic stricken. To fight longer seems to be madness."

APPOMATTOX

From this time, the South was completely fragmented and the Confederacy's cause was hopeless. Johnston, having returned to his command in the Southeast, held together a force that retreated across the Carolinas, with Sherman pursuing and wreaking havoc in South Carolina as he pursued. Lee, meanwhile, held against steadily increasing odds at Petersburg. By April 1865, however, the inevitable defeat could be put off no longer. Petersburg fell and Richmond was evacuated. As the Confederates fled Richmond, they set fire to all the military stores they could not carry, with the result that the fires spread out of control and destroyed more of Richmond than Sherman had destroyed of Atlanta or Columbia. Lee and his army headed west, hoping to join the remnants of Johnston's army in North Carolina; but the Union army under Philip Sheridan cut them off at Appamattox, 90 miles from Petersburg, on April 8. The next morning, Lee realized that his position against the superior Union army was hopeless. Lee stated, "There is nothing left for me to do, but to go and see General Grant, and I would rather die a thousand deaths."

Lee met Grant on April 9 at a farmhouse near Appomattox Court House, and in a moving scene surrendered the Army of Northern Vir-

Appomattox Court House

ginia to Grant, who accorded generous terms and told his troops not to cheer because, he said, "The rebels are our countrymen again." Southern leaders were not arrested, and Jefferson Davis was not to be "hanged from a sour apple tree" as Union newspapers had suggested. Instead, Southerners were to merely lay down their arms and go home. After Lee's surrender, General Johnston also surrendered at Greensboro, North Carolina, before the end of the month; and the Confederate government, which had fled south after the fall of Petersburg, simply evaporated.

THE WAR BEHIND THE LINES

THE PROBLEMS OF THE CONFEDERACY

Writers on the Civil War have piled up a vast literature—one of the largest bodies of literature on any historical subject—detailing the military aspects of the war: the battles and leaders, the campaigns and maneuvers, the strategy and tactics. This military record, however, does not fully explain the outcome of the war. For, in terms of strategy and tactics, the Confederate performance equaled that of the Union and, on the Virginia front, surpassed it until the last year of the war. The final result was registered on the battlefield, but the basic factors that caused Confederate defeat lay behind the lines. Essentially, the Confederacy failed to solve the problems of organizing its society and its economy for war. It faced these problems in a particularly difficult form; and when it proved unable to solve them, it went down to defeat.

One basic handicap of the Confederacy lay in the fact that while the North had a balanced agricultural and industrial economy that was invigorated by war, the Southern economy was based primarily on cotton production, which was dislocated and almost paralyzed by the war. In the North, war stimulated employment; and while wages failed to keep pace with inflation, civilian morale was generally high except among the underpaid urban poor. In the South, economic conditions deteriorated so badly that what may be called economic morale declined even while fighting morale remained good. During the spring of 1863 "bread riots" occurred in Richmond and several other Southern cities. Indeed, Drew Gilpin Faust has argued that because Southern women's interests were so little represented in the way the South publicly defined the war's meaning that the women lost heart and, in so doing, contributed substantially to the collapse of morale.

Essentially, the Confederacy, with its rural and agricultural society, needed two things. First, it needed access to the products of European—especially British—industry. Second, it needed to stimulate production of food, of horses, and of strategic supplies within the South. Ultimately, it was unable to meet most of those needs.

In order to be able to draw on British industry, the Confederacy needed to have buying power in the European market and to be able to ship goods freely to and fro across the Atlantic. Once war broke out, however, Lincoln proclaimed a blockade, which meant that federal naval vessels would try to seize the merchant vessels of any neutral country bringing goods to Confederate ports.

Southerners thought that the blockade would not work, partly because there were not enough Union ships to enforce it and even more because they believed in what has been called the "King Cotton delusion." They were firmly convinced that cotton was an absolute economic necessity to Britain, because textiles were the heart of British industry. Without cotton this industry would be prostrated. Britain's factories would stand idle, and its workers would be unemployed and would literally starve. When this started happening, the British government would decide to intervene to get cotton. The British navy, which still dominated the seas, would break the blockade.

Southerners were so confident of this idea that they were quite willing to see the British supply of cotton cut off for a while. In the first months of the blockade, while it was still largely ineffective, they deliberately kept their cotton at home instead of sending a part of it abroad to be held in British warehouses for later sale to give them funds for the purchase of supplies. The bumper crops of the previous two years had produced such a surplus, however, that British manufacturers were able to operate without interruption for nearly a year after the war broke out.

THE IMPORTANCE OF SEA POWER

For this and other reasons, the faith in cotton ultimately proved to be a fallacy. Britain got increased supplies of cotton from Egypt and India. Also, British antislavery sentiment generated a strong resistance to taking steps that would help the Confederacy. Britain was pleased to see America adopting a doctrine of international law concerning the right of blockade which she had always advocated and which was bound to be favorable to a nation with large naval power. Most importantly, British industry was not paralyzed because Northern wartime purchase stimulated it. Britain, as a neutral, enjoyed an economic boom from supplying war materials to the Union—a boom very similar to the booms the United States later enjoyed in 1914–1917 and 1939–1941 as a neutral supplying war materials to Britain.

Consequently, Britain and France, which was following Britain's lead, never did give diplomatic recognition to the Confederate government although they did recognize the existence of a state of war in which they would be neutral. This meant that they would treat Confederate naval vessels as warships and not as pirates.

The British recognition of belligerency was much resented in the United States; but, in fact, the real danger for the Union cause lay in the possibility of diplomatic recognition of the Confederacy, which would probably have resulted in efforts by the British to break the blockade. Such efforts would, in turn, have led to war with Britain; but this recognition, for which the Confederacy waited so anxiously, never came.

In November 1861 Confederate hopes were high when an eager Union naval officer, Charles Wilkes, stopped the British ship *Trent* on the high seas and took off two Confederate envoys to Britain, James Mason and John Slidell. Britain, at this point, actually prepared to fight. An emergency British Cabinet meeting demanded a formal apology to the British flag, reparations, and the release of Mason and Slidell. The British then put their navy on alert and sent 11,000 troops to Canada, departing England with a band playing "Dixie." President Lincoln, however, wisely admitted the error and set the envoys free, thus avoiding the possibility of war with England. Meanwhile, the blockade steadily grew tighter. One Confederate port after another was sealed off. Small Confederate vessels, built for speed and based in the Bahamas islands, continued to delight the South by running the blockade and bringing in cargoes of goods with high value in proportion to their bulk. Their volume was small, however; and they did not in any sense provide the flow of goods that the Confederacy so vitally needed.

In addition to depending on British naval might, the Confederacy made two important efforts to establish sea power of its own. To begin with, it fitted out the first large ironclad vessel ever to put to sea. A powerful steam frigate, the U.S.S. *Merrimac*, that the federals had scuttled in the Norfolk Navy Yard, was raised, renamed the *Virginia*, covered with armor plate, and sent out in March 1862—an iron giant against the wooden vessels of the Union navy. In its first day at sea it destroyed two large Union vessels with ease.

The entire Union navy appeared to be in acute danger, and there was panic in Northern coastal cities. The Union, however, had been preparing a metal-clad vessel of its own—a small craft that lay low in the water with a revolving gun turret. This *Monitor*, as it was called, challenged the *Virginia* on March 9, 1862. The battle ended in a draw, but with Monitor-type vessels the Union navy was again safe.

The Confederacy's second major endeavor at sea was to buy vessels and equipment in England. Unarmed ships built in England by private companies were then sent to the Azores Islands, outside of British Sovereignty, and outfitted with weaponry to produce fighting ships without violating Britain's neutrality. Such vessels could then raid merchant vessels flying the Union flag.

There were several of these raiders, the most famous of which was the *Alabama*. This great marauder, commanded by Admiral Raphael Semmes, roamed the seas for two years from Newfoundland to Singapore, capturing 62 merchant ships (most of which were burned, after careful attention to the safety of their crews and passengers). It also sank the U.S.S. *Hatteras* in a major naval battle. It was at last cornered and sunk off Cherbourg, France, by the U.S.S. *Kearsarge*, but its career had made the American flag so unsafe on the high seas that prohibitive insurance costs caused more than 700 American vessels to transfer to British registry. The American merchant marine never again attained the place in the world's carrying trade that it had held before the *Alabama* put to sea.

The U.S.S. *Kearsarge*

The Confederacy sought to have additional raiders built in British shipyards, and two immensely formidable vessels—the Laird rams—were actually constructed. There were vigorous protests from Charles Francis Adams, the American minister to England, however; and the British did not desire war with the Union, so the British government purchased the ships in September 1863 from the private British contractors at higher prices than those paid by the Confederates. After this the Confederate cause was lost at sea as well as on land, and the federal blockade tightened like a noose to strangle the Confederacy economically.

PRISONERS OF WAR

The issue of prisoners of war was one of the bitterest of the war, especially in the North, because the conditions in Southern prison camps were notoriously deplorable. After all, if Southern soldiers in the field had insufficient rations, what could one expect for Northern POWs in Southern prison camps? In 1862, the two sides had solved the problem by agreeing for the exchange of prisoners captured in battle, thus eliminating the need for large, long-term POW camps. This all changed, however, when the Union began enlisting former slaves into its army. The Confederate government announced that it would refuse to treat former slaves in Union uniforms as legitimate soldiers and would, instead, execute them when captured—along with the white Union officers for the crime of formenting slave insurrections.

In reality, the Southerners did not implement the official policy. Lincoln warned that he would retaliate against Confederate POWs held in the North if they did; however, Confederate troops did sometimes murder black Union soldiers and their white commanders on the battlefield when they tried to surrender. Other captured black soldiers were returned to slavery or put into forced labor for the Confederate Army. Because of these practices, Lincoln suspended the exchange of prisoners in 1863 until the Confederates agreed to treat white and black prisoners alike. The South, of course, refused—leading to the growth of large POW camps on both sides with squalid conditions for the POWs, especially in the South. Sixteen percent of all Union POWs held by the South died, while 12 percent of the Confederates held by the North also died.

The most notorious POW camp on either side was the Confederate's Andersonville Prison commanded by Henry Wirz, the only person executed by the Union after the war. Andersonville was a stockade with no cover that held 33,000 Union prisoners by the end of the war. Altogether, 13,000 Union soldiers died at Andersonville at a rate of 100 per day. The Southerners lacked the manpower to tend to all of the bodies with the result that an entire range of vermine invaded the prison. It is said that the ground essentially moved at Andersonville with all of the rats, roaches, flies, maggots, etc. that crawled amid the rotting flesh and human waste. The horrors of Andersonville would remain a symbol to the North of Southern barbarism for decades after the war.

It should be mentioned, however, that treatment of the civilian populations by the marauding armies was mild by war standards. Although much Southern property was destroyed—especially in Sherman's march—rape, murder, and the general terrorizing of civilians were less common. Although Northerners had sworn that they would execute Jefferson Davis, when he was finally captured in May 1865, he was imprisoned on charges of treason and murder, released in 1867, and never even brought to trial.

ECONOMIC FAILURES OF THE SOUTH

Meanwhile, on the home front, the Confederacy failed economically because it was caught between the need to stimulate production and the need to keep down prices and control inflation. The Southern government began with few financial assets other than land and slaves, neither of which could be readily transformed into negotiable currency. It faced a dilemma. It could either encourage production by buying goods in the open market at an uncontrolled price, in which case inflation would mushroom, or it could control inflation by a system of requisitioning goods for its armies at arbitrarily fixed prices, in which case production would be discouraged rather than stimulated. Help in reducing this problem would have required a program of heavy taxation, by which the government would take back the inflationary dollars that had been spent; but the Confederacy was afraid to use its taxing power. It raised less than 5 percent of its revenue from taxes—a smaller proportion than any other nation in a modern war. Its bond drives to raise funds by borrowing also fell short of hopes.

The South's main source of money was the printing press—the most inflationary method of all. Prices rose by 9,000 percent in the four years of war. Goods grew scarcer while money grew more plentiful. It was grimly said that at the beginning of the war people took their money to market in a purse and brought their goods home in a basket, but that by the end they took the money in a basket and brought their purchases home in a purse.

In short, the Confederacy died of economic starvation—an insufficiency of goods. Its government was too weak to cope with the nearly insoluble economic problems the war had caused. President Jefferson Davis was a bureaucrat who thought in legalistic rather than in dynamic terms. He was not an innovator but rather a conservative miscast as a revolutionist. The state governments also competed against the Confederate government for the control of manpower and supplies. They insisted upon their sovereign status so strenuously that it has been said that the Confederacy was born of states' rights and died of states' rights.

The best chance the Confederacy ever had—and it was perhaps a fairly good one—was to win a short war before the results of economic malnutrition set in. Once that failed, the cause was hopeless. A few Confederates, like Josiah Gorgas in the Ordinance Department, improvised brilliantly, and others did so desperately. In a country where a vitally necessary rail line could be laid only by tearing up the rails somewhere else and re-laying them, a long war against a dynamic adversary could have but one end.

NORTHERN INDUSTRIALISM AND REPUBLICAN ASCENDANCY

The problems and limitations of the Confederacy—problems of localism and decentralization, of an agricultural economy and of small-scale economic activities—were characteristic features of the kind of folk society the Confederacy was defending. While the South was making a last stand against the forces of the modern mechanized world, however, the war was rushing the North along the path toward industrial domination. Before the Southern states withdrew from the Union, they had blocked some of the governmental measures most conducive to the new industrial economy. Southern secession, however, left the new Republican Party in control. The Republicans combined a free-soil, antislavery ideology with the traditional Whig policy of using the government to stimulate economic growth. While this program was designed to promote the mutual interests of capital and free labor, Republican economic legislation in practice usually helped the former more than the latter.

Thus secession and the war enabled the Republicans to enact what one historian has called their "blueprint for modern America." In February 1861, while the empty seats of the departing Southern congressmen were still warm and even before President Lincoln took office, Congress adopted the Morrill Tariff that, though not very high, was higher than the existing tariff of 1857. This was the first of many tariff increases. There was not another perceptible reduction until 1913. Meanwhile Congress repeatedly strengthened the measures by which it gave American industrial producers more exclusive control in the American market, even if this forced American consumers to pay higher prices than they would have had to pay on the world market.

THE TRANSCONTINENTAL RAILROAD

In 1862 Congress broke the long deadlock the sectional conflict had created over the building of a railroad to the Pacific. For a decade, advocates of a southern route and supporters of a northern route had blocked each other. Now, with the Southerners absent, Congress created the Union Pacific Railroad Company, incorporated with a federal charter, to build westward from Omaha and to meet another road, the Central Pacific, a California corporation, building eastward from Sacramento. To encourage this enterprise, Congress placed very large resources at the disposal of the railroads. For each mile of track built it gave to the roads 10 square miles of land, running back

The completion of the transcontinental railroad

in alternate blocks from the tracks. In addition, it granted loans (not gifts) of between $16,000 and $48,000 a mile—according to the difficulty of the terrain where construction took place.

The value of the lands at that time was not great, and the munificence of this largesse has often been exaggerated; but the point is that the government was paying most of the costs of construction, whereas it might well have controlled or even owned the railroad. Instead, it placed these resources in the hands of private operators, who, if they succeeded, would become owners of the world's greatest railroad; if they lost, they would be losing the government's money rather than their own. It was "venture capitalism," as it is now called; but the government was doing most of the venturing and the private interests that constructed the road were getting most of the capital. Furthermore, the railroads committed fraud against the government by presenting fraudulent surveys that showed more mountainous terrain than actually existed (the government paid more per mile of track for mountainous terrain than for flatlands) and by needlessly zigzagging in their track construction so as to increase mileage that the government paid for.

In 1869, four years after the war ended, the Union Pacific and the Central Pacific met at Promontory Point in Utah, and a golden spike was driven to mark the event. Travelers to California no longer were obliged to go by wagon train or by a lengthy sea voyage. The United States was a long step closer to being a transcontinental, two-ocean republic in an operative sense as well as in a purely geographical one.

THE NATIONAL BANKING SYSTEM

One other major economic measure resulting from Republican ascendancy was the creation of a new and far more centralized system of banking and money. Ever since Andrew Jackson's overthrow of the Bank of the United States in 1832, the country had had a decentralized, loose-jointed financial system—one that today it is difficult even to imagine. The United States, of course, issued coins and also bills. For each bill in circulation, a corresponding value of precious metal was held in the Treasury and could be claimed by the holder of the bill. The government handled all its own transactions in such currency and was thus on a "hard money" basis.

Actually, however, this kind of money was not nearly sufficient to meet the economic needs of the country for a circulating medium. The principal circulating medium, therefore, had been provided by notes issued by banks operating under charters from the various states. State laws governing the incorporation of banks naturally varied, which meant that the financial soundness of the various banks also varied. This in turn meant that some of the notes circulated at face value, while others circulated at various degrees of discount from face value. So although the government was on a hard money basis, the economy of the country was not, and the federal government exercised no control whatever over the principal component in the monetary system of the country.

The Legal Tender Act of 1862 and the National Banking Act of 1863 changed all this. They grew out of the government's need to raise the immense sums required to fight the war. The Legal Tender Act authorized the issuance of Treasury notes—the famous greenbacks—that circulated as authorized money without a backing in metal held in the Treasury.

Primarily, however, the Treasury relied upon borrowing—that is, upon selling bonds. To borrow it had to make the bonds attractive as holdings for the banks. Accordingly, the National Banking Act provided that a bank which purchased government bonds to the amount of one third of its paid-in capital might issue federally guaranteed notes, known as national bank notes, in an amount equal to 90 percent of its bond holdings.

In 1865 a tax was laid on the notes issued under state authority by state-chartered banks. The tax had the effect of making these notes unprofitable and thus driving them out of circulation. As a result of government borrowing policy, therefore, the United States acquired a new, uniform, federally sanctioned circulating medium of national bank notes.

These notes became the principal form of money for the next 50 years, but they had a great defect—they made the amount of money dependent upon the volume of federal debt rather than upon the economic needs of the country. They were inflexible, and in 1913 Federal Reserve notes—a result of the establishment of the Federal Reserve System—largely replaced them. The principles that the United States should have a uniform currency in use throughout the nation, and that the federal government should be responsible for this currency, had come to stay.

WOMEN AND THE WAR

Although the Civil War brought suffering and loss to hundreds of thousands of American women, the war meant progress toward independence and equality for women as a group. It meant new opportunities for employment, broadened social and political interests, and demonstrations of competence in activities previously reserved for men. Some women went to war as nurses, spies, even as soldiers—most often masquerading as men; but the vast majority who served at home—including those who stayed in the home—did the most damage to the myth of the helpless female.

It is estimated that almost 400 women posed as men to join the Union and Confederate armies during the Civil War; and this may be an underestimate because there may be many more that were simply not discovered. So many smooth-faced and slightly built young boys joined both armies that many women could easily pass as young boys. Physical examinations on both sides were almost nonexistent; and women could merely cut their hair, bind their breasts close to their body, and show enthusiasm for the conflict. Sarah Emma Evelyn Edmonds, who joined the 2nd Michigan Volunteers as "Franklin Thompson," stated in her memoirs that her physical examination consisted only of a firm handshake. Although Edmonds' true identity was eventually discovered, she remained in service afterwards as a nurse and a spy. Many women managed to keep their true identities secret throughout the war. Albert D. J. Cashier, who served in an Illinois regiment in the Vicksburg campaign, was only discovered years later when "he" was hospitalized as a war veteran and doctors discovered that he was really Jennie Hodges. Others, such as Lyons Wakeman, who is buried at Chalmette National Cemetery in St. Bernard Parish, Louisiana, were only discovered in death. Wakeman, whose real identity was Sarah Rosetta Wakeman of Afton, New York, fought with General Nathaniel P. Banks in the Union's loss at Mansfield and also at Pleasant Hill before dying of dysentery.

Other women accompanied their husbands as camp followers. These women not only tended to their husbands' laundry and sewing, but also served as field nurses, kept weapons loaded, and carried water to cool both weapons and throats. One Rose Rooney, however, openly enlisted with the Crescent Blues Volunteers in the Confederate army at New Orleans in 1861. Her assigned duty was to serve as a cook and a laundress, but she eventually did much more than that. At the First Battle of Bull Run, she is credited with running through a field of heavy fire to tear down a rail fence so as to allow a battery of Confederate artillery to advance forward and help halt a Union charge. Rooney served in Lee's Army of Northern Virginia for virtually the entire war and remained in the ranks until Lee surrendered in 1865.

Aside from their roles on the battlefield, as in earlier wars—but in much greater numbers—women during the Civil War had to take their husbands' places as heads of households, running shops, managing farms and plantations, finding jobs to earn food for their families. In the South, many had to do housework—and field work—for the first time. Some had to face armed, hostile blacks as well as enemy soldiers. In Minnesota and elsewhere on the frontier, women had to survive Native American uprisings.

Job opportunities for women multiplied as men went off to fight or quit old occupations for better-paying ones. The war quickened the movement of women into school teaching, a profession once dominated by men. Many Northern women also went south to teach in schools for freed slaves. In both the Union and the Confederacy women also went to work for the government. By the end of the war thousands held government office jobs. Here, too, the change was permanent: Washington, D.C., would never again be without its corps of women workers. Many were employed, and some were killed, in government arsenals.

When the war began, women dominated the work force in the mills and factories of New England while in the South women industrial workers were a small minority—another situation that favored the Union war effort. As men joined the service, women took their places in industry and helped produce military equipment and supplies. The demand for what was considered women's work also expanded: Sewing women were hired by the thousands, and brutally exploited. In self-protection, the women organized, protested, and went out on strikes.

In addition to work for pay, there was a tremendous amount of unpaid activity by women in both South and North—though there was more in the North, because women in that region had a tradition of public activism lacking in the more conservative South. Women volunteered to nurse, and some of them, especially Clara Barton, became famous. They joined aid societies and organized activities to raise funds. They wrote and spoke for the causes they believed in and in a few cases, comprised part of the attendance at riots, in both the North and South. Overall, many women demonstrated talents of efficiency and leadership.

In the North women took the initiative to found an organization, the United States Sanitary Commission, which did valuable work in raising money and gathering materials for wounded soldiers. Their initial enthusiasm was somewhat alarming to the military authorities—the fear was of good-natured busybodies—hence men were officially in charge of the organization; but women supplied much of the energy. Over time, the women did so much good work that even the doubters came around. In an era when married women could not sign contracts (owing to the tenets of coverture), women raised hundreds of thousands of much-needed dollars for humanitarian relief.

The Civil War gave American women a chance to enter many new areas and prove themselves quite as capable as men. When the war ended, many lost their jobs to returning veterans. Some returned gratefully to domesticity, but there was no turning back the clock.

THE ROAD TO REUNION

Wars always bring results not intended by those who fight them. The Civil War accelerated the growth of mass production and economic centralization in the North while it destroyed much of the economic production in the South, convincing the rising generation of Southern leaders that future regional prosperity would depend upon industrialization. The war also caused an increase in federal power at the expense of the states, for no government could spend the funds, organize the forces, and wield the strength the federal government did, without increasing its power. The main purpose of the war, however, was to reunite a broken union of states, and there was a question whether the abolition of slavery was necessary to the objective of reunion. Some Republicans wanted to make emancipation one of the objects of the war, simply because they deplored slavery and did not believe that a Union which had slavery in it was worth saving. Others, who were relatively indifferent to the welfare of the blacks, believed that the slaveholding class, which they called the "slave power," was guilty of causing disunion. In order to make the Union safe, this power must be destroyed, and the way to destroy it was to abolish slavery. Still others, including many of the "War Democrats" and the Unionists in the border states, regarded the war as one against secession, having nothing to do with slavery.

EMANCIPATION

For his part, Abraham Lincoln had stated his belief long before he became President—the Union could not endure permanently as half-slave and half-free. He knew, however, that he could not free any slaves unless he won the war and that he could not win the war if he antagonized all the Unionists in the slave states of Delaware, Maryland, Kentucky (his own birthplace), and Missouri. As a result, he moved very slowly on the slavery question; and when two of his generals tried to move more quickly by emancipating slaves in the areas they had occupied, he countermanded their orders.

EMANCIPATION PROCLAMATION

Few people realize it today, but the war had raged for 17 months and was more than a third over before Lincoln moved to free the slaves in the Confederacy. In July 1862, Lincoln made up his mind to proclaim the freedom of slaves in the insurrectionary states, but he decided to wait for a victory before doing so. The Battle of Antietam (Sharpsburg) in September was not a great victory, but it sufficed. In that month Lincoln issued a proclamation that after January 1, 1863, all slaves in areas that were at that time in rebellion should be "forever free." This still did nothing about slaves in places like New Orleans, which was occupied by federal forces, or in the border slave states because those areas were not in rebellion. Therefore, the slaves in those areas were not free. The Emancipation Proclamation also did not free the slaves in areas under rebellion because those areas were obviously not under Union control and any proclamation by the President, whether concerning emancipation or otherwise, would be completely ignored. The emancipation proclamation also gave all the states of the Confederacy 100 days during which they could save slavery, provided the state came back into the Union. Clearly, the principle of the emancipation proclamation was not that

President Lincoln and the reading of the Emancipation Proclamation

one could not own slaves but, rather, that one could not own slaves and secede from the Union.

In December 1862, strongly believing in persuasion rather than force, Lincoln proposed a constitutional amendment for the gradual emancipation of slaves in the border states by the year 1900, with compensation to the owners; but this proposal was overtaken by events as the escalating impact of the war accelerated the destruction of slavery. On January 1, 1863, Lincoln issued the Emancipation Proclamation, which was to apply in all areas under Confederate control. Although it would require Northern victory to become a reality, this proclamation announced a new Union war aim—freedom for the slaves as well as restoration of the Union. Enthusiasm for the war in the North was already on the decline in late 1862; and Lincoln sought a moral cause for the war greater than merely the preservation of the Union, which by the end of 1862 was simply insufficient cause for far too many persons North of the Mason-Dixon line. Lincoln also surmised that the emancipation cause would help prevent English intervention on the side of the South. As the self-appointed world leader of the abolition movement, England could hardly join the war on the side of slavery if the Union had made abolition one of its goals.

The caution with which Lincoln had proceeded with emancipation reflects his own scruples about the Constitution and the prudence of his own temperament; but it, also, reflects the fierceness of the divisions within the North and the dangers that these divisions held for the administration. On one flank, the Democrats assailed Lincoln. A minority of War Democrats gave him vigorous support; but a majority of the Democrats, known as "Copperheads," constantly called for a negotiated peace and especially assailed any move against slavery, believing that any move against slavery would force the South to fight rather than negotiate. Democratic propagandists helped convince white workingmen that they were being used in a war to free blacks that would take their jobs away. It was this conviction that turned the "draft riots" in New York in July 1863, into mob assaults on blacks. More than 100 people, most of them white rioters shot down by police and troops, were killed in these assaults. The riots were so tumultuous that the draft was suspended in New York City for the remainder of the war.

On the other flank, pressure was coming from many sources, including from women and the black community. Susan B. Anthony and Elizabeth Cady Stanton organized their fellow suffragists into the Women's National Loyal League and gathered hundreds of thousands of signatures on an antislavery petition. Further, the more militant antislavery men in the Republican Party denounced Lincoln because he did not instantly take drastic action to end slavery. These "radical Republicans" hoped to dominate the administration by forcing all moderates on the slavery question out of the cabinet; and, in 1864, some of them sought to prevent Lincoln's nomination for a second term. Through unrivaled political dexterity and skill, Lincoln frustrated these attacks from both directions and maintained a broad base of support among abolitionists for the war.

As late as 1864, however, the House of Representatives defeated a constitutional amendment for the abolition of slavery. Congress did not finally vote the Thirteenth Amendment, abolishing slavery, for submission to the states until January 31, 1865. Maryland, Tennessee, and Missouri abolished slavery by state action at about this same time, but slavery was still legal in Kentucky and Delaware when the Civil War ended. The amendment was not ratified until eight months after Lincoln's death.

LINCOLN

Long after these events, people who had grown up with an oversimplified image of Lincoln as a Great Emancipator became disillusioned by this record, and in the ensuing century and a half, some critics have sought to tear down his reputation. Abraham Lincoln remains a figure of immense stature, however. Scholars and popular biographers continue to find nuances of his personality and achievements to explore.

Born in 1809 in a log cabin in Kentucky, Lincoln grew up on the frontier in Indiana and Illinois, doing rough work as a rail-splitter and a plowboy and receiving only a meager education. Lincoln's early life was filled with tragedy as his grandfather (the senior Abraham Lincoln) bequeathed none of his 5,544 acres to Abraham's father (Thomas Lincoln) and, instead, left it all in his will to Abraham's uncle Mordecai. Thomas Lincoln was then cheated out of the land he owned in Kentucky by land speculators who bribed crooked surveyors to allow them to stake claims to his land. The family moved to Indiana in 1816, where tragedy struck again as Abraham's mother, Nancy, died of "milk sickness" after drinking milk from cows that had eaten the poisonous white snakeroot plant. Thomas remarried Sarah Bush, with whom Abe had a good relationship; she, too, died in 1829.

Young Abraham spent two years on a flatboat on the Mississippi River and then managed a general store in New Salem, Illinois. When the store failed in 1834, Lincoln began his political career by becoming postmaster of New Salem. That same year, Lincoln ran and won a seat in the Illinois State Legislature at age 25, primarily because he needed the pay. After becoming a legislator, Lincoln realized he would benefit from studying law, so he studied law on his own and passed the bar. Later, he practiced law with a partner in Springfield and rode the circuit on horseback to follow the sessions of the court.

Lincoln's personal life of tragedy, however, continued. In 1835, Lincoln fell in love with a short, plump woman named Ann Rutledge, who tragically died of "brain fever." Lincoln, unfortunately, sunk into a fit of depression and would suffer from bouts of depression for much of the rest of his adult life. Later in 1844 Lincoln stated, "I am now the most miserable man living. If what I felt were equally distributed to the whole human race, there would not be one cheerful face on earth." Lincoln refused to carry a penknife out of fear that he might become self-destructive in a fit of depression, and on numerous occasions he cleared his house of all sharp objects so as to help eliminate any self-destructive temptations. Lincoln's law partner blamed his depression on chronic constipation; but it may have also been related to the medicine he took for his depression known as "blue mass," the ingredients of which included licorice, rose water, dead rose petals, honey, sugar, and mercury. Symptoms of mercury poisoning include insomnia, tremors, and rage attacks, all of which were suffered by Lincoln. Lincoln himself eventually made the connection and quit taking blue mass a few months into his Presidency because it made him "cross."

After the death of Rutledge, Lincoln had another failed relationship with a woman named Mary Owens, whom Lincoln described as "pleasingly stout, weighing between 150 and 180 pounds." Owens, however, ended the relationship, stating that Lincoln was "deficient in those little links which make up the chain of a woman's happiness." After the relationship failed, Lincoln wrote to Mr. O. H. Browning, "I can never be satisfied with anyone who would be blockhead enough to have me."

In 1837, Lincoln met Mary Todd, who at age 22 was "just short of being an old maid." Lincoln married Mary Todd, a Southern woman born of privilege, in 1842. Mary's sisters dropped her from their social circle because of her choosing a husband from such a low social status. Unfortunately, Mary was also known for her bad temper, suffered from headaches, was highly emotional, terrified of storms, dogs, robbers, and prone to panic. On one occasion, Mary chased Abe out of the House with a butcher knife. On another, she struck him on the nose with a piece of firewood. Her temperament was well known; and though she was the first President's wife to be known as "First

Abraham Lincoln

Lady," members of Lincoln's Cabinet frequently referred to her as "Hell-Cat."

While in the White House, Mary spent extravagantly, accepted gifts from office-seekers and those seeking favors, and ran up debts without Abe's knowledge. Mary sold furniture from the White House and manure from the White House stables to pay her debts. When that wasn't enough, she fired the White House Steward and kept the salary. She even presented Congress with fake vouchers for nonexistent purchases. At one point, the House Judiciary Committee investigated Mary for passing sensitive information to the South during the Civil War.

The Lincolns had four children. Willie and Eddie died of childhood diseases. Another son, Tad, evidently suffered from a hyperactive disorder and was wholly undisciplined. He was unable to dress himself at age nine and remained illiterate at the time of Lincoln's death.

To speak with the spirits of her deceased children, Mary held eight séances in the White House, one of which was attended by the President himself. Mary reportedly once told Abe that her deceased son Willie often came to visit her at night and often little Eddie (who died at age four) was with him! The deaths of her sons and a head injury Mary sustained as a result of a fall from a carriage may have led to her mental illness by the time of her husband's death. In 1875, the Lincolns' son Robert had Mary committed to a mental institution where she lived the rest of her life.

Lincoln was very much the frontiersman. Except for one term in Congress, 1847–1849, Lincoln rarely went east and was relatively unknown until the debates with Douglas gained him a reputation in 1858. In many ways, it is surprising that Lincoln became the one person most responsible for the end of slavery. In the 1840s, Lincoln opposed the Annexation of Texas, formerly a territory of Mexico, partially because he thought of the Mexicans as "greasers." Lincoln also viewed Native Americans as a "barbarous barrier to progress." He presided over the execution of 38 Native Americans by a military tribunal during the Civil War after the Native Americans had killed 350 whites because they had not paid the Native Americans for their land. This was the largest mass execution in American history. Concerning the slaves, Lincoln thought blacks to be inferior and opposed black suffrage, black equality, interracial marriage, blacks on juries, and the repeal of the Fugitive Slave Act. Lincoln also favored the repatriation of blacks to Africa as late as his debates with Stephen Douglas in 1858. In 1861, at a moment of crisis, this tall, gangling, plain-looking man, whose qualities of greatness were still unsuspected, became President.

Lincoln's relaxed and unpretentious manner masked remarkable powers of decision and qualities of leadership. Completely lacking in self-importance, he seemed humble to some observers; but he acted with the patience and forbearance of a man who was sure of what he was doing. He refused to let the abolitionists push him into an antislavery war that would antagonize Union men who did not care about slavery; and he refused to let the Union men separate him from the antislavery contingent by restricting war aims too narrowly.

He saw that the causes of Union and emancipation must support each other instead of oppose each other, or both would be defeated.

Patiently, he worked to fuse the idea of union with that of freedom and equality ("a new nation conceived in liberty and dedicated to the proposition that all men are created equal"). Thus, he reaffirmed for American nationalism the idealism of freedom and gave to the ideal of freedom the strength of an undivided union. Knowing that in a democracy a man must win political success in order to gain a chance for statesmanship, he moved patiently and indirectly to his goals. His opportunism offended many abolitionists; in the end, however, Lincoln struck slavery the fatal blow.

Once the Civil War started, Lincoln was very forceful in support of his goals. Lincoln closed newspapers that were too critical of his administration, arresting their editors and proprietors. He also allowed the arrest of preachers that preached sermons against the war. He allowed the arrest, trial, and conviction for treason by a military tribunal of former Ohio Congressman, Clement L. Vallandigham, who had spoken out strongly against the war. Lincoln then commuted Vallandigham's sentence from imprisonment to banishment to the Confederacy.

BLACK AMERICANS AND THE WAR

For black Americans, the Civil War years were a time of elation and rejoicing, frustration and despair. Black men and women alike worked hard for the Union cause. Black intellectuals wrote and lectured, both at home and abroad. Blacks organized their own aid and relief societies for the great numbers of freed slaves and went to them as teachers. Black women volunteered their services as nurses and hospital aids. Black men by the hundreds of thousands went to war for the Union as sailors in the navy and as servants, cooks, and laborers with the army. When they were finally allowed to do so, they also went as soldiers.

For a long time, however, blacks were not allowed to serve in the army. Not until the autumn of 1862 were blacks officially permitted to enlist, and it was another year before the bravery of black regiments in battle began to change the scornful attitude of whites, in and out of the service. Most instrumental in this shift was the heroic, if doomed, assault on Fort Wagner, South Carolina by a black regiment, the Fifty-fourth Massachusetts Infantry in July 1863. Overall, black servicemen established an admirable record, and 21 received the Congressional Medal of Honor. The officers in black regiments were mostly white men, however, and only a handful of black soldiers were promoted

The charge of the Fifty-Fourth Massachusetts Regiment on Fort Wagner

to the rank of lieutenant or captain. Not until June 1864, was the pay of black and white soldiers equalized.

Throughout the war, then, blacks continued to face injustice and discrimination, despite their major contribution to the Union cause. From the beginning, their most influential spokesman, Frederick Douglass, looked on Lincoln as much too conservative; and when the President delayed taking decisive steps toward freeing the slaves, Douglass was outspoken in his criticism.

Although Lincoln had his black supporters, including the beloved Harriet Tubman, he also gave offense by his continuing interest in some programs to move blacks out of the country to a colony in the tropics. In fact, there were some blacks that were so embittered that they welcomed the possibility of such separation. Martin R. Delany, who later joined with Douglass in working for black recruitment, favored the migration of American blacks to Haiti, a project that was tried unsuccessfully early in the war. After the rejection of black volunteers by the army, the subsequent mistreatment of black soldiers, and attacks on both black soldiers and black civilians in several Northern cities, there were blacks that agreed with white racists that

Influential African-American men involved in the reconstruction of the South

the Civil War was indeed a white man's war in a white man's country to which blacks owed no allegiance.

Nevertheless, there was progress. The Emancipation Proclamation was finally issued. The Thirteenth Amendment was adopted.

The great slave population, which—as Douglass had repeatedly pointed out—enabled the Confederacy to put so large a proportion of its whites into uniform, was finally freed. Many blacks, Union soldiers as well as former slaves, were also freed from the bonds of illiteracy through their own efforts and the efforts of dedicated teachers—both black and white.

After the war, blacks were recognized as full citizens by the federal government; and campaigns against discrimination in the law courts, the polling places, the schools, and public conveyances won victories in several states. In 1864 black representatives from 18 states formed the National Equal Rights League. The long, agonizingly slow march toward equality had begun.

EMANCIPATION AND RECONSTRUCTION, 1865–1877

LINCOLN'S PLAN OF RECONSTRUCTION

Johnson's Policy of Reconstruction

Congressional Radicals

Radical Reconstruction

The Fall of Radical Reconstruction

The Ku Klux Klan

Black Sharecroppers

Freedmen's Bureau

Johnson versus the Radicals

The Grant Administration

The Hayes-Tilden Election of 1876

LINCOLN'S PLAN OF RECONSTRUCTION

The process of readmission of Southern states to the Union had begun as early as 1862 when Union troops began reclaiming Southern territory. Lincoln appointed provisional governors for those parts of the Union controlled and occupied by federal troops. Although he had always opposed slavery on moral as well as political grounds, Lincoln was skeptical about the prospects for racial equality in the United States. The legacy of slavery and race prejudice, he believed, would prevent blacks from rising to the level of whites or prevent whites from allowing blacks to rise to their level. This was why Lincoln had supported the colonization abroad of freed slaves as a possible solution of the race problem.

By 1864, however, the President was convinced of the impracticality if not the injustice of this policy. The contribution of blacks to the Union war effort and the growing strength of Northern antislavery convictions also made him more hopeful about the chances for eventual black advancement and racial adjustment. On this question, though, Lincoln remained a moderate and a gradualist to the end of his life.

Lincoln and the Northern moderates also believed that victory in war could not really restore the Union. It could only prevent secession. The Union would be restored only if the Southern people again accepted the Union and gave their loyalty to it. To bring the South to that point, Lincoln wanted a conciliatory policy. In 1864 when Congress adopted a measure known as the Wade-Davis Bill that imposed stringent terms for the restoration of the former Confederates, including a requirement that Southerners could only establish state governments after the majority in a state had sworn a loyalty oath. Lincoln quickly disposed of the bill with the Pocket Veto (the President did not sign the bill during the last 10 days of a Congressional session, thus killing the bill through his inaction).

When people raised technical questions about the legal status of the Confederate states (Were they still states, or were they conquered territories? Had they committed "state suicide"?), Lincoln was impatient about such "pernicious abstractions." All that mattered was whether the states could be brought back into their proper relationship with the Union.

By 1864, the Union had regained enough control in Louisiana, Tennessee, and Arkansas to start a process of restoring these states to the Union, and Lincoln laid down generous terms on which this could be done. He would grant amnesty to former Confederates who took an oath of allegiance; and when as many as one tenth of the number who had been citizens in 1860 did so, he would permit them to form a new state government. When Southern government accepted the abolition of slavery and repudiated the principle of secession, Lincoln would receive it back into the Union. States did not have to recognize the rights of blacks or give a single black person the right to vote.

Louisiana was the first state reorganized on this basis; despite its denial of black suffrage, Lincoln accepted it, though he did ask the governor, "whether some of the colored people may not be let in, as for instance the very intelligent, and especially those who have fought gallantly in our ranks." In Virginia, Tennessee, and Arkansas, also, Lincoln recognized state governments that did not enfranchise the black Americans.

It was clear, however, that Republicans in Congress were suspicious of these states—more because of their leniency toward the former Confederates than because of their treatment of the blacks. Secondly, the Radical Republicans favored a reconstruction policy that would punish the South; and they, therefore, opposed Lincoln's plan because it was not punitive. Radical Republicans in Congress also disliked Lincoln's conciliatory "10 percent plan" because it allowed the President to establish reconstruction policy rather than Congress. It was also clear that Congress might deny the re-established states recognition by refusing to seat their newly elected senators and representatives.

In 1864, when the time came for a new presidential election, the Democrats nominated General McClellan to run against Lincoln. Some of the so-called Radical Republicans, who were dissatisfied with Lincoln's leniency, tried to block his renomination and put up the Secretary of the Treasury, Salmon P. Chase, in his stead. This effort failed, however, and Lincoln was renominated. In an effort to put the ticket on a broad, bipartisan basis, the party dropped the name Republican, called itself the Union party, and nominated for the vice-presidency a Southern Democrat who had stood firmly for the Union, Andrew Johnson of Tennessee.

In November 1864 Lincoln and Johnson were elected, carrying all but three Union states (New Jersey, Delaware, and Kentucky). In the following March, the new term began. Lincoln delivered his Second Inaugural Address, calling for "malice toward none and charity for all," in order "to bind up the nation's wounds." On April 9, Lee surrendered the Army of Northern Virginia. It was clear that the work of Reconstruction must now begin in earnest.

John Wilkes Booth

On April 14, however, as celebrations still continued in the North in the wake of the Confederate surrender, Lincoln attended a performance at Ford's Theater where an assassin, John Wilkes Booth, shot him. Booth broke into Lincoln's theater box and shot the President in the back of the head with a small pistol at point blank range. Then Booth jumped to the stage with a dagger in one hand, breaking an ankle in the process, and escaped through the back door of the theater. As he left the theater, Booth shouted the Virginia state motto, "Sic simper tyrannis" (thus always to tyrants). Lincoln died the next morning, without ever recovering consciousness; and Andrew Johnson, who was also stabbed in his bed by an attempted assassin while Lincoln was being shot across town, survived the attack and became President of the United States.

Unknown to Booth, a Southern sympathizer who evidently killed Lincoln in a spirit of Southern revenge, he had probably just killed the South's best friend. It does not appear that Lincoln favored any sort of punitive reconstruction, but he was in favor of allowing the South to manage their own affairs as much as would be possible. With Lincoln out of the way, the path was much more open for those in the North who favored a more punitive peace.

JOHNSON'S POLICY OF RECONSTRUCTION

Although a Southerner and the only Senator from a Southern state to remain loyal to the Union, Andrew Johnson was expected to be more severe in his Reconstruction policy than Lincoln. Johnson was the son of poor, illiterate parents in Raleigh, North Carolina, who could not afford to send their son to school. Instead, Johnson's mother apprenticed him to a tailor after his father died, and Johnson later worked as a tailor in Tennessee. The ambitious Johnson, who had been illiterate until his wife taught him to write, became not only a successful tailor but, also, accumulated a fortune in land and at one time even owned five slaves. He was a man of strong emotions; and as a Southerner with the roots of a common man, Johnson hated both aristocrats, whom he blamed for secession, and secessionists—in general. When his policy developed, it turned out that Johnson disliked abolitionists and radicals even more. In the end, Johnson proved even more lenient toward former Confederates than Lincoln had been. Johnson was a strong states' rights advocate, who as a Senator voted against everything that smacked of increased federal power. He even once voted against a bill to pave the streets of Washington, D.C.

Johnson was also a defender of slavery and accepted emancipation only grudgingly. Johnson's eventual opposition to slavery developed more out of his dislike for the planter class than out of any moral outrage against slavery or sympathy for blacks. Johnson believed blacks to be intellectually inferior and, naturally, more suited to manual labor.

On May 29, 1865, Johnson issued a broad amnesty to all who would take an oath of allegiance, including ex-Confederate government officials and military officers, although men with property valued at more than $20,000 (in other words, planters) were required to ask special pardon, which was freely given. In the six weeks after May 29 he appointed provisional governors in each of the remaining Southern states to reorganize governments for these states. Only men who had been voters in 1860 and who had taken the oath of allegiance could participate in these reorganizations. This meant, of course, that blacks were excluded. When the new governments disavowed secession, accepted the abolition of slavery, and repudiated the Confederate debt, Johnson would accept them. As to what policy should be followed toward the freedmen— that was to be determined by the states themselves.

Andrew Johnson

The Southern states moved swiftly under this easy formula. Before the end of the year, every state except Texas, which followed soon after, had set up a new government that met the President's terms. Two conspicuous features of these governments, however, were deeply disturbing to many Republicans.

First, these Southern states had adopted a series of laws known as "Black Codes," that denied to blacks many of the rights of citizenship—including the right to vote and to serve on juries. Blacks could not testify against whites, and laws were passed against interracial marriage. Of course, blacks were also denied the right to bear arms. Other laws were passed that excluded them from certain types of property ownership and certain occupations. In some cases, black employment was limited to agriculture and domestic servitude. Unemployed Negroes might be arrested as vagrants and bound out to labor in a new form of involuntary servitude. Black workers truant from jobs were forced to do public service until they returned to their former employer to whom they were contractually bound.

Secondly, the former Confederates were in complete control. Between them, the newly organized states elected to Congress no fewer than nine Confederate congressmen, seven Confederate state officials, four generals, four colonels, and Confederate Vice-President Alexander Stephens.

CONGRESSIONAL RADICALS

When Congress met at the end of 1865, it was confronted by presidential Reconstruction as a *fait accompli*. At this point, the Republicans were far from ready for the kind of all-out fight against Johnson that later developed, but they were not willing to accept the reorganized states. They were especially resentful because these states could now claim a larger representation in Congress with the free black population (only three fifths of the blacks had been counted when they were slaves), without actually allowing the blacks any voice in the government. It would be ironical indeed if the overthrow of slavery should increase the representation of the South in Congress and if the Rebels should come back into the Union stronger politically than when they left.

For some months, the Republicans in Congress moved slowly, unwilling to face a break with a President of their own party, and far from ready to make a vigorous stand for the rights of blacks. They would not seat the Southern congressmen-elect, however, and they set up a Joint Committee of the Senate and the House to assert their claim to a voice in the formulation of Reconstruction policy. They also passed a bill to extend the life and increase the activities of the Freedmen's Bureau—an agency created to aid blacks in their transition from slavery to freedom. The new duties Congress wanted to grant to the Freedmen's Bureau were to expand its responsibilities to include federal protection of blacks against white oppression in the South.

Johnson vetoed this measure as an unnecessary and unconstitutional use of the military during peacetime. In addition, he vetoed a Civil Rights bill that declared blacks to be United States citizens and denied Southern states the ability to withhold property rights on the basis of race. Tensions increased; and in April 1866, Congress re-passed the Civil Rights Act of 1866 over Johnson's veto, the first Congressional over-ride of a Presidential Veto in American history. The over-ride of the President's veto shifted the political upper hand to Congress, which would, henceforth, assume the lead in Reconstruction policy.

In June 1866, Congress voted a proposed Fourteenth Amendment, which clearly asserted the citizenship of blacks stating, "All persons born or naturalized in the United States are citizens," and thus effectively overturned the Dred Scott decision that held that blacks were not citizens and did not have standing to sue. It also asserted that they were entitled to the "privileges and immunities of citizens," to the "equal protection of the laws," and to protection against being deprived of "life, liberty, and property without due process of law." In effect, the Amendment was designed to overturn the Black Codes.

Lawyers have been kept busy for more than a century determining exactly what these terms meant, but one thing was clear. The amendment did not specify a right of black suffrage. It did, however, provide that states that disfranchised a part of their adult male population would have their representation in Congress proportionately reduced. It almost seemed that Congress was offering the Southerners a choice. They might disfranchise the blacks if they were willing to pay the price of reduced representation, or they might have increased representation if they were willing to pay the price of black suffrage. This might not help the blacks, but it was certain to help the Republicans. It would either reduce the strength of Southern white Democrats or give the Republicans black political allies in the South.

The Fourteenth Amendment also provisionally excluded from federal office any person who had held any important public office before the Civil War and had then gone over to the Confederacy. This sweeping move to disqualify almost the entire leadership of the South led the Southern states to make the serious mistake of following President Johnson's advice to reject the amendment. During the latter half of 1866 and the first months of 1867, 10 Southern states voted not to ratify the Fourteenth Amendment. By March 1867, Tennessee was the only Southern State that had ratified the Fourteenth Amendment.

RADICAL RECONSTRUCTION

Southern rejection of the Fourteenth Amendment precipitated the bitter fight that had been brewing for almost two years. Congressional elections of 1866, however, gave Radical Republicans a two thirds majority in Congress, thus solidifying their power to over-ride Presidential vetoes and take the lead in Reconstruction. Congress now moved to replace the Johnson governments in the South with new governments of its own creation. Between March and July 1867, it adopted a series of Reconstruction Acts that divided 10 Southern states into five military districts under five military governors. The governors were vested with "all powers necessary" to protect the civil rights of all persons, maintain order, and supervise the administration of justice. These governors were to hold elections for conventions to frame new state constitutions. In these elections adult males, including blacks, were to vote, but many whites, disqualified by their support of the Confederacy, were not to vote. The constitutions these conventions adopted must establish black suffrage, and the governments they established must ratify the Fourteenth Amendment. Then and only then might they be readmitted to the Union. Congress followed with a second Reconstruction Act that required military authorities in the South to register voters and supervise the election of the delegates to state constitutional conventions. Furthermore, new constitutions had to be ratified by a majority of voters. Thus, two years after the war was over, when the South supposed that the postwar adjustment had been completed, the process of Reconstruction actually began.

The period that followed has been the subject of more bitter feeling and more controversy than perhaps any other period in American history, and the intensity of the bitterness has made it hard to get at the realities. During 1867 the military governors conducted elections, and in late 1867 and early 1868, the new constitutional conventions met in the Southern states. They complied with the terms Congress had laid down, including enfranchisement of the black

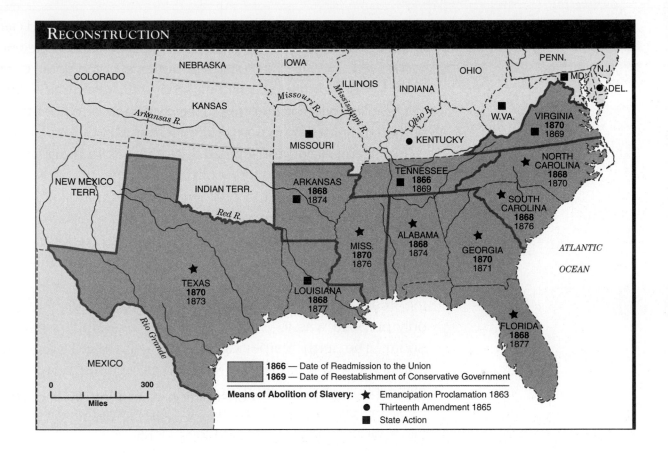

RECONSTRUCTION

1866 — Date of Readmission to the Union
1869 — Date of Reestablishment of Conservative Government

Means of Abolition of Slavery: ★ Emancipation Proclamation 1863
● Thirteenth Amendment 1865
■ State Action

men; however, many Southerners resisted. Military authorities in many places found that they could not get together a majority of voters at the polls, as Congress had required. In essence, the former Confederates protested their new constitutions, which they viewed as externally imposed, by staying home and not voting. In March 1868, Congress altered the rules to allow state constitutions to be ratified by the majority of those who voted in an election. Three months later, Arkansas fulfilled the requirements necessary for readmission to the Union. Within a year after the third Reconstruction Act (of July 1867), seven states had adopted new constitutions, organized new governments, ratified the Fourteenth Amendment, and been readmitted to the Union. In Virginia, Mississippi, Georgia, and Texas, however, the process was for one reason or another not completed until 1870. In July 1870, Georgia became the last Southern state to be readmitted to the Union.

All of these new governments, except the one in Virginia, began under Republican control, with more or less black representation in the legislatures. In one state after another, however, the Democrats, supporting a policy of white supremacy, soon gained the ascendancy. Military and "Radical" rule lasted for three years in North Carolina; four years in Tennessee (never under military government) and Georgia; six years in Texas; seven years in Alabama and Arkansas; eight years in Mississippi; and 10 years in Florida, Louisiana, and South Carolina.

Historians of the past and those of the present have interpreted, in completely different terms this experience of carpet bag rule—so named in reference to a popular nineteenth-century suitcase literally made from carpet and carried by many Northerners who moved south in search of economic opportunity. The earlier interpretation reflected the feelings of the Southern whites that resented this regime bitterly, seeing it as one of "military despotism" and "Negro rule." According to this version, later elaborated by a pro-Southern school of historians, the South was at the outset the victim of military occupation in which a brutal soldiery maintained bayonet rule. Then came the "carpetbaggers"—unscrupulous Northern adventurers whose only purpose was to enrich themselves by plundering the prostrate South. The term "carpetbagger" was also used disparagingly by Southerners in reference to Northerners who moved south and became involved in Southern politics.

In the view of Southerners, the carpetbaggers—in order to maintain their ascendancy—incited the blacks, who were essentially well disposed, to assert themselves in swaggering insolence. Thereupon, majorities made up of illiterate blacks swarmed into the legislatures where the carpetbaggers manipulated them. A carnival of riotous corruption and looting followed until at last the outraged whites, excluded from all voice in public affairs, could endure these conditions no longer and arose to drive the vandals away and to redeem their dishonored states.

This picture of Reconstruction has a very real importance, for it has undoubtedly influenced subsequent Southern attitudes; but it is an extreme distortion of the realities. Historical treatments since 1950 have presented quite a different version, stressing the brief nature of the military rule and the constructive measures of the "carpetbag" governments. As for bayonet rule, the number of troops in the "Army of Occupation" was absurdly small. In November 1869 there were 1,000 federal soldiers scattered over the state of Virginia and 716 over Mississippi with hardly more than a corporal's guard in any one place.

For certain, Southern politics during Reconstruction was fraught with factionalism and corruption, and some of the blame must be placed at the feet of the "carpetbaggers." For example, Illinois native Henry Clay Warmoth was elected Governor of Louisiana in 1868 with an annual salary of $8,000. Four years later, Warmoth had a net worth of over $1 million. A full 50 percent of the state budget in Louisiana during Warmoth's tenure went to state representatives and

FROM THE PLANTATION TO THE SENATE.

African Americans moved from the plantations to the state legislatures during the Reconstruction of the South.

their staff members for salaries and "mileage." This, however, was not the only incident of overpaid public officials. One year, South Carolina's legislature voted an additional $1,000 in salary for one member who had recently lost the same amount on a horse race. Inflated and corrupt government contracts were also rampant. For example, the state of Arkansas constructed a bridge one year at a cost of $500 and then repaired the bridge the next year at a cost of $9,000. To be sure, not all of the corruption was due to "carpetbaggers" in government, but for Southerners, the transplanted Northerners made easy

Mark Twain

targets. Among the American writers who familiarized the country with the looters and scoundrels was Mark Twain, whose fictional writings presented unscrupulous characters with which Southerners became all too familiar.

Among the carpetbaggers, though there were indeed looters and scoundrels, there were also idealists that did all they could to improve conditions in the South. Many Northern women came to teach the freed slaves. Many men came to develop needed industry, which even if it enriched the Northern carpetbagger in the process, was also good for the South as a whole. Many others worked with integrity and self-sacrifice to find a constructive solution for the problems of a society devastated by war and left with a huge population of former slaves to absorb and support. Many native Southerners, who joined with the "carpetbaggers" in their programs and who were denounced as "scalawags," were equally public-spirited and high-minded.

As for "Negro rule," the fact is that the blacks were in a majority only in the convention and the first three legislatures of South Carolina. Elsewhere they were a minority, even in Mississippi and Louisiana, where they constituted a majority of the population. In view of their illiteracy and their political inexperience, the blacks handled their new responsibilities well and they tended to choose educated men for public office. Thus many of the black legislators, congressmen, and state officials they chose were well qualified. They were, on the whole, moderate and self-restrained in their demands; and they gave major support to certain policies of long-range value, including notably the establishment of public school systems, which the South had not had in any broad sense before the Civil War.

As for the "carnival of corruption," the post-Civil War era was marked by corruption throughout the country. All the Southern states combined did not manage to steal as much money from the public treasury as did the Tweed Ring in New York City, led by William Marcy Tweed, commonly known as "Boss Tweed." New York was also famous for fraudulent elections, and the corruption in government spearheaded by Tweed would become a major issue in national politics in the 1870s. It was true, however, that the impoverished South could ill afford dishonesty in government. Nevertheless, much that was charged to "corruption" really stemmed from increased costs necessary to provide new social services such as public schools and to rebuild the Southern economy laid waste by war.

Finally, it should be noted that the Southern whites were never reduced to abject helplessness as is sometimes imagined. From the outset they were present in all of the Reconstruction conventions and legislatures—always vocal, frequently aggressive, and sometimes dominating the proceedings.

THE FALL OF RADICAL RECONSTRUCTION

For an average of six years, then, the regimes of Radical Republican Reconstruction continued. After that they gave way to the Democratic Redeemers—those who wanted to "redeem" the South to white rule—delaying until the twentieth century further progress toward equal rights for blacks.

When one considers that the South had just been badly defeated in war, that Radical Reconstruction was the policy of the dominant party in Washington, and that black and white Republicans constituted a majority of the voters in a half-dozen Southern states, it is difficult to understand why the Radical regimes were so promptly—almost easily—overthrown. Several contributing factors must be recognized.

First, the former slaves lacked experience in political participation and leadership. Largely illiterate and conditioned for many decades to defer to white people, they grasped the new opportunities with uncertain hands. Very often they seemed to wish, quite realistically, for security of land tenure and for education more than for political rights. At the same time, however, a number of articulate and able blacks, some of them former slaves, came to the fore and might have provided effective leadership for their race if Reconstruction had not been abandoned so soon.

Second, and more importantly, one must recognize the importance of the grim resistance offered by the Southern whites. With their deep belief in the superiority of their own race, these Southerners were convinced that civilization itself was at stake. They fought with proportionate desperation, not hesitating to resort to violence and terror.

THE KU KLUX KLAN

On Christmas Eve 1865, a half-whimsical secret society—known as the Ku Klux Klan (KKK)—was formed in Tennessee by six Confederate army veterans who were simply bored and restless after the war and sought something for their own amusement. The name "Ku Klux Klan" was derived from the Greek word "Kuklos," the root of the English word "circle." Since the six founding members were of Scotch-Irish ancestry, they added the word "Klan" and then added the made-up word "Klux" to add "mystery and baffle" as well as something "secret-sounding" and "nonsensically inscrutable." With nothing sinister in mind, Jon C. Lester reportedly said to his other listless five founding members, "Boys, let's start something to break the monotony and cheer up our mothers and girls. Let's start a club of some kind." The original purpose of the young men, evidently, was merely to play practical jokes and serenade women and had nothing to do with racism or terror.

In furtherance of their playful goals, however, the men donned white regalia and rode through the Tennessee countryside in search of adventure. Accidentally, the men discovered that their midnight marauding frightened the black refugees who were aimlessly wandering the Tennessee countryside in large numbers. This accident began to take on a more purposeful character, and the Klansmen began a campaign of scare tactics against the wandering black refugees. An unforeseen consequence was that blacks tended to avoid the roadways in the area where Klansmen were playing their games. Word of the KKK fun and games spread across the South. People in surrounding areas contacted the Klan wanting to know how they, too, could set up KKK Dens of their own for the express purpose of scaring vagrant blacks away from the roadways. Soon every Southern state had its organization of masked and robed riders, either as part of the Klan or under some other name. Klan tactics quickly escalated from jokes and scare tactics to naked violence, contrary to the original intensions of the Klan's founders. By use of threat, horsewhip, and even rope, gun, and fire, they spread fear not only among blacks but also, perhaps even more among the Republican leaders. By 1868, the Klan claimed to have 500,000 members, and their expressed purpose had grown from playful mischief to overt resistance to the Congressional Reconstruction Act of 1867.

Klan members were sworn to secrecy and had to swear that they were opposed to negro equality and in favor of a white man's government, including the "restoration of the civil rights to Southern White men." In its bylaws, the Klan stated a reverence for the "majesty and

Ku Klux Klan members burn a cross.

supremacy of the Divine Being" and recognized the supremacy of the United States Constitution. The Klan claimed that it was an institution of chivalry, humanity, mercy, and patriotism that existed to protect the weak, defend the Constitution, and execute all Constitutional laws.

In 1870, KKK violence had grown so steadily that it drew the attention of the Radical Republicans in Congress, who passed "An Act to Enforce the Provisions of the Fourteenth Amendment to the Constitution of the United States, and for Other Purposes"—more generally known as the First Ku Klux Klan Act. The Act imposed heavy penalties for violations of the Fourteenth and Fifteenth Amendments and gave the state governments the authority to take whatever action they deemed necessary against the Klan. In furtherance of the execution of the Act, Union troops and state militiamen arrested Klansmen and tried them for their crimes, sending many to prison. By the end of 1872, under this pressure from the federal and state governments, the KKK was no longer a force.

The dramatic quality of the Klan has given it a prominent place in the public's mental picture of Reconstruction. Though violence played a prominent role, the white South had other, less spectacular weapons that were no less powerful. Southern whites owned almost all of the land. Whites controlled virtually all employment, and they dominated the small supply of money and credit that was to be found in the South. They, also, dominated the legal system. In unspectacular ways they could make life very hard for individuals who did not comply with the system. These factors, perhaps more than the acts of night-riders and violent men, made the pressure against Radical rule almost irresistible.

Another important reason for the downfall of "Radical" Reconstruction was that it was not really very radical. It did not confiscate the land of plantation owners and distribute that land among the freed slaves, as radicals and abolitionists such as Thaddeus Stevens and Wendell Phillips had urged. It, also, did not reduce the former Confederate states to the status of territories for a probationary period as many Radicals also advocated. Furthermore, it did not permanently disfranchise the South's former ruling class, nor did it permanently disqualify more than a handful of ex-Confederate leaders from holding office. It did not enact Charles Sumner's bill to require universal public education in the South and to provide federal aid for schools there; hence, the former slaves were to remain largely uneducated. These would have been genuinely radical measures; but they went beyond what a majority of Northern voters were willing to support and perhaps they would have even risked the renewal of revolt in the South.

Indeed, even the limited radicalism of the Fourteenth Amendment and the Reconstruction Acts strained the convictions of most Northerners to the utmost. The North was not a racially equalitarian society. Black men did not have the right to vote in most Northern states at the time the Reconstruction Acts of 1867 enfranchised them in the South. The enactment of Negro suffrage in the South was accomplished by the Radical Republicans—not because of a widespread conviction that it was right in principle but because it seemed to be the only alternative to Confederate rule.

Later, Republicans found that many Northern voters cared little about black suffrage in the South. They also found that the white South would not consent to a real reunion on this basis and that the restoration of former Confederates to political power did not threaten Northern or national interests. As a result, the Republicans let the existing forces in the South find their own resolution, which was one of white supremacy.

Yet Reconstruction was far from a total failure. It established public schools in the South that gradually brought literacy to the children of freed slaves. By 1900, illiteracy among blacks had dropped from 90 percent after the Civil War to an estimated 48 percent by 1900. It brought abolitionists and missionaries from the North to found such colleges as Howard, Fisk, Morehouse, Talladega, and many others. These colleges trained future generations of black leaders who in turn led the black protest movements of the twentieth century. Furthermore, though Reconstruction did not confiscate and redistribute land, many freed slaves became landowners through their own hard work and savings. In 1865 scarcely any black farmers owned their farms, but by 1880, one fifth of them did.

BLACK SHARECROPPERS

A full 80 percent of black farmers were not landowners, even of small plots, but became sharecroppers, often working for the same landowner that had once owned them on the same plantation. Sharecropping was a wage-labor system where blacks worked the land for the white owners and paid the white owners a percentage of their harvest (normally 25 percent of the cotton crop and a third of other crops) for the privilege of working on the owner's land. Planters generally divided their plantations into small 25–30 acre plots and signed contracts with individual black sharecroppers to work each plot. Landowners supplied the sharecroppers with the necessary mules, seed, plows, and tools, while the sharecroppers were responsible for their own food and necessities. A system of credit developed where local merchants would advance goods to black sharecroppers with payment due at the time of harvest.

Sharecropping allowed blacks the beginnings of economic freedom and, also, the freedom to decide which

Sharecroppers, such as the man in this photo, worked the land for its white owners and paid the owners a percentage of the harvest.

family members would work the land, how long they would work each day, and how the labor would be divided. Blacks, typically, moved out of the slave cottages and into their own dwellings. On some plantations, however, blacks worked for wages in gangs, as they had under slavery, complete with white overseers and even whippings in some instances.

Still, change did come with emancipation in that a full third of the black women that had worked in the fields abandoned fieldwork either to tend to the home and child rearing or for paid domestic servitude. Indoor work, even if it consisted of cleaning and laundry, was much preferable to working in the field in the hot southern sun.

FREEDMEN'S BUREAU

Reconstruction also created the Freedmen's Bureau, which was perhaps charged with more responsibility than any federal agency in history. The Freedmen's Bureau was created for the purpose of aiding the former slaves in their transition to freedom. Though woefully undermanned and inadequately funded, the Freedmen's Bureau provided food, clothing, medical care, and shelter for former slaves. In the first two years after the War, the Freedmen's Bureau issued over $20 million to needy black Americans and treated 450,000 illnesses. The Bureau also constructed 40 hospitals across the South to help meet the medical needs of the former slave population.

After the Civil War, the Southern roadways were literally clogged with refugees as Southern plantation owners, who had no money with which to hire their labor, released thousands of free blacks. With nowhere to go, thousands of blacks wandered aimlessly across the South. These refugees, without shelter on the roadways, made easy targets for terrorizing by the night rides of the KKK. The Freedmen's Bureau helped transport the dislocated refugees to shelter, helped blacks find family members from whom they had become separated either before or after the War, and performed formal marriage ceremonies for many blacks that wanted legal sanction for the de facto marriages within which they had lived under slavery. In the first two years after the war, the Freedmen's Bureau helped resettled 30,000 displaced black Americans.

The Freedmen's Bureau also attempted to ensure fair trials for blacks in the South, to provide for black education, and to serve as an employment agency for the thousands of unemployed black refugees. In total, the Freedmen's Bureau constructed over 4,300 schools in the first two years following the Civil War.

Finally, Reconstruction also left as a permanent legacy the Fourteenth and Fifteenth Amendments, which formed the constitutional basis for the civil-rights movements of the post-World War II generation.

JOHNSON VERSUS THE RADICALS

The Republicans did not abandon their program all at once; rather, it faded out gradually although the Radicals remained militant while Johnson remained President. Johnson had used his administrative powers to evade or modify the enforcement of some Republican Reconstruction measures. This convinced most Republicans that his removal was necessary if their policy was to be carried out in the South; and in 1868, they tried to remove him by impeachment. The immediate pretext for impeachment was Johnson's dismissal of Secretary of War Stanton in February 1868.

A year earlier Congress had passed a series of acts designed to strengthen the legislative branch at the expense of the executive. Among these laws was the Tenure of Office Act, which forbade removals of public officials who had been confirmed by the Senate without first obtaining Senate approval. The Tenure of Office Act was subsequently found to be unconstitutional by the Supreme Court; but at the time that Johnson removed Stanton, who was reporting to the Radicals what went on in administration councils, there had been no judicial ruling. Therefore, the House of Representatives voted to impeach Johnson, which meant that the Senate must try him on the articles of impeachment.

The trial was conducted in a tense atmosphere and scarcely in a judicial way. Immense pressure was put on all Republican senators to vote for conviction. When a vote was finally taken on May 16, 1868,

A Congressional document showing the impeachment of President Andrew Johnson conviction failed by one vote of the two thirds required. Seven Republicans had stood out against the party. Johnson was permitted to serve out his term, and the balance between executive and legislative power in the American political system, which had almost been destroyed, was preserved. Johnson, however, would fail to win the Democratic Party's nomination for President at their national convention two months later.

The determination of Republicans to achieve congressional domination of the Reconstruction process also manifested itself in restrictions on the judiciary. When a Mississippi editor named McCardle appealed to the Supreme Court to rule on the constitutionality of one of the Reconstruction acts, under which he had been arrested by the military, Congress—in March 1868—passed an act changing the appellate jurisdiction of the Court so that it could not pass judgment on McCardle's case.

THE GRANT ADMINISTRATION

In 1868 the country faced another election, and the Republicans turned to General Grant as their nominee. He was elected over the Democratic candidate, Governor Horatio Seymour of New York, by a popular majority of only 310,000—a surprisingly close vote. Without the votes of the newly enfranchised blacks in the seven reconstructed Southern states, Grant might have had no edge in popular votes at all. The Radical Republicans were alarmed at their narrow margin of victory and, therefore, sought to find ways to add more black voters to the ranks. Although the Fourteenth Amendment theoretically forced black suffrage in the South, the issue of suffrage for blacks had been generally ignored in a number of Northern states. Between 1865 and 1869, a number of Northern states had held referendums on black suffrage; voters in Kansas, Ohio, Michigan, Missouri, Wisconsin, New York, and the District of Columbia all voted down black suffrage. The vote in the District of Columbia was an overwhelming 6,521 to 35 against black suffrage. Of the Northern states that held elections on the issue, only Iowa and Minnesota passed laws granting the franchise to blacks. To implant Negro suffrage permanently in the Constitution—for the North as well as the South—Congress in 1869 passed the Fifteenth Amendment, forbidding the states to deny any citizen his right to vote "on account of race, color, or previous condition of servitude." The Amendment was ratified in 1870; and it had almost immediate impact as black men, just five years removed from slavery, were elected to public office. Though blacks were still severely under-represented in the 1870s, 17 black men served in Congress, one served in the United States Senate, and one black man served as Chief Justice of the South Carolina Supreme Court. For a brief interlude, blacks even held a majority of the seats in the South Carolina legislature.

President Grant supported the measures of the Radicals and in some ways gave his backing to their policies. Like the good military man he was, he believed that where violence broke out, it should be put down uncompromisingly. Accordingly, he favored the adoption of Enforcement Acts for the use of federal troops to break up the activities of the Ku Klux Klan. When these laws were passed, he did not hesitate to invoke them; troops were sent in on a number of occasions.

Fundamentally, however, Grant was not a radical. He wanted to see tranquility restored, and this meant reuniting North and South on any basis both would be willing to accept. Accordingly, he urged a broader extension of amnesty to all former Confederates, and he grew to resent the frequent appeals of Republican governments in

President Ulysses S. Grant delivering his inaugural address at the U.S. Capitol on March 4, 1873.

the South for troops to uphold their authority. Though he realized that the tactics of the Redeemers were very bad—"bloodthirsty butchery" and "scarcely a credit to savages"—he became convinced that constant federal military intervention was worse in the long run.

During the eight years of Grant's presidency, Republican governments were overthrown in eight of the Southern states. As Grant's second term neared its end, only three states—Louisiana, Florida, and South Carolina—remained in the Republican ranks. The program of Radical Reconstruction still remained official policy in the Republican Party, but it had lost its steam. The country was concerned about other things.

In foreign affairs, Secretary of State Hamilton Fish was busy putting through an important settlement by which Great Britain and the United States adopted the principle of international arbitration. This was a means of settling American claims that had grown out of the raiding activities of the *Alabama* and other ships, which British shipyards had built for the Confederacy.

In financial circles there was a controversy over what to do about the greenback dollars issued during the war. Since greenbacks were not backed by gold, people had saved the more valuable gold dollars and spent the less valuable greenback dollars, thus driving gold out of circulation. The government was willing to give gold for greenbacks even though such a policy would tend to increase the value of the dollar. Debtor interests (such as farmers), who wanted a cheap dollar, fought hard against the policy of redemption; but the policy was adopted in 1875.

In politics, public confidence in the government was shaken by a series of disclosures concerning government corruption. In 1869, investors Jay Gould and Jim Fisk began purchasing gold futures for the purpose of driving up the price of gold, which skyrocketed from $4.00 per ounce to $25.00 per ounce. It was expected that at a certain point the United States Treasury Department would place U.S. gold reserves on the market in an effort to stabilize the gold market. Grant's brother-in-law in the Treasury Department struck a deal, unknown to Grant, with Gould to inform him in advance about when the Treasury Department would release its gold reserves so that Gould could sell before the prices dropped. Grant's brother-in-law dutifully sent Gould a telegraph the morning that the Treasury Department released its gold to the open market, but Gould was out of the office and did not get the message. Prices quickly fell back to the pre-panic price of $4.00 per ounce, and Gould's losses were $16 million.

In 1872 it was revealed that several congressmen had accepted gifts of stock in a construction company, the Crédit Mobilier, which was found to be diverting the funds of the Union Pacific Railroad—including the funds the government had granted to it—with the knowledge of the officers of the road. In 1875 Grant's private secretary was implicated in the operations of the "Whiskey Ring," which, by evading taxes, had systematically defrauded the government of millions of dollars. The following year, the Secretary of War was caught selling appointments to Native American posts. Meanwhile, in

Jay Gould

the New York City government, the Tweed Ring, headed by Tammany boss William Marcy Tweed, was exposed as guilty of graft and thefts that have seldom been equaled in size and have never been surpassed in effrontery.

The epidemic of corruption inspired a revolt by reform Republicans, who bolted the party in 1872, organized the Liberal Republican party, and nominated Horace Greeley, editor of the *New York Tribune*, for President. Although the Democrats also nominated Greeley and formed a coalition with the Liberal Republicans, Grant easily won reelection because most Northern voters were not yet prepared to trust the Democrats.

In the economic orbit, the country was trying to weather the financial depression that began with the panic of 1873. All in all, the problems posed by the South and the blacks seemed more and more distant, less and less important, to the people of the North.

THE HAYES-TILDEN ELECTION OF 1876

The election of 1876 brought to an end the program of Reconstruction, which probably would have ended soon in any case. In this election the Republicans, who were badly divided, turned to a Civil War veteran and governor of Ohio, Rutherford B. Hayes, as their nominee. Hayes was a conspicuously honest man, and so was his

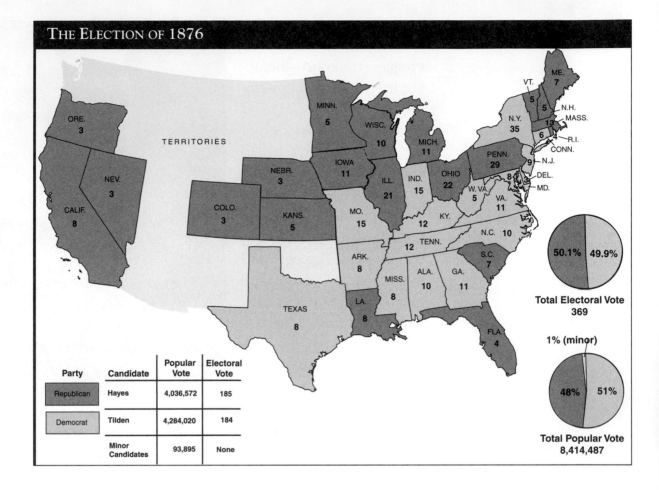

THE ELECTION OF 1876

Party	Candidate	Popular Vote	Electoral Vote
Republican	Hayes	4,036,572	185
Democrat	Tilden	4,284,020	184
	Minor Candidates	93,895	None

Total Electoral Vote 369
50.1% / 49.9%

1% (minor)
Total Popular Vote 8,414,487
48% / 51%

Democratic opponent, Samuel J. Tilden of New York, who owed his reputation to his part in breaking up the Tweed Ring.

When the votes were counted, Tilden had a popular majority (obtained partly by the suppression of black votes in some Southern states) and was within one vote of an electoral majority. However, there were three states—Florida, Louisiana, and South Carolina—in which the result was contested; and rival officials filed two sets of returns—though Tilden had clearly won the popular vote in all three states. To count the votes in such a case, the Constitution calls for a joint session of the Congress, but the House of Representatives, with a Democratic majority, was in a position to prevent an election by refusing to go into joint session with the Senate. Congress agreed to appoint an Electoral Commission to provide an impartial judgment, but the commission divided along party lines with eight Republicans and eight Democrats, voting eight to seven for Hayes. As late as two days before the inauguration it was doubtful whether the Democrats in the House would accept the decision.

Many Northern Democrats were prepared to fight to a finish against what they regarded as a stolen election, but the Southern Democrats had found that one civil war was enough. Moreover, various negotiations had been in progress behind the scenes. Important groups of Southern Democrats who had been left out when the government largesse of the Union Pacific-Central Pacific was distributed now hoped for a Texas and Pacific Railroad that would provide bountiful federal grants for Southern interests. They received assurances from friends of Governor Hayes that he would look with favor upon such programs of internal improvement. Moreover, they were assured that he would withdraw the last remaining federal troops from Louisiana and South Carolina, which meant that their Republican governments would collapse and the score of states would be: redeemed, 11—reconstructed, none.

With these understandings, Southern congressmen voted to let the count proceed so that Hayes would be elected. Later, when they were explaining their conduct to their constituents, they thought it best to say quite a great deal about how they had ransomed South Carolina and Louisiana and very little about their hopes for the Texas and Pacific Railroad and other such enterprises. Thus a legend grew up that there had been a "compromise" by which Reconstruction was ended.

What had really happened was that Southern Democrats and Northern Republicans had discovered that there were many features of economic policy on which they were in close harmony. The slaves were emancipated, the Union was restored, and bygones were bygones. The harmony of their views made reconciliation natural and Reconstruction unnecessary. There was still the question of the blacks, but only a few whites had ever supported black suffrage or racial equality for its own sake. It had been an expedient; and now that the expedient was no longer needed, it could be laid aside. Such was the spirit of reconciliation.

Thus, the country ended a period of intense friction and entered upon a long era of sectional harmony and rapid

Rutherford B. Hayes

economic growth. This was done, however, at the expense of leaving the question of racial relations still unattended to—even though slavery itself had, at immense cost, been removed.

THE DECLARATION OF INDEPENDENCE

When in the course of human events, it becomes necessary for one people to dissolve the political bands which have connected them with another, and to assume among the Powers of the earth, the separate and equal station to which the Laws of Nature and of Nature's God entitle them, a decent respect to the opinions of mankind requires that they should declare the causes which impel them to the separation.

We hold these truths to be self-evident, that all men are created equal, that they are endowed by their Creator with certain unalienable Rights, that among these are Life, Liberty and the pursuit of Happiness. That to secure these rights, Governments are instituted among Men, deriving their just Powers from the consent of the governed, That whenever any Form of Government becomes destructive of these ends, it is the Right of the People to alter or to abolish it, and to institute new Government, laying its foundation on such principles and organizing its Powers in such form, as to them shall seem most likely to effect their Safety and Happiness. Prudence, indeed, will dictate that Governments long established should not be changed for light and transient causes; and accordingly all experience hath shewn, that mankind are more disposed to suffer, while evils are sufferable, than to right themselves by abolishing the forms to which they are accustomed. But when a long train of abuses and usurpations, pursuing invariably the same object evinces a design to reduce them under absolute Despotism, it is their right, it is their duty, to throw off such Government, and to provide new Guards for their future security. Such has been the patient sufferance of these Colonies: and such is now the necessity which constrains them to alter their former Systems of Government. The history of the present King of Great Britain is a history of repeated injuries and usurpations, all having in direct object the Establishment of an absolute Tyranny over these States. To prove this, let Facts be submitted to a candid World:

He has refused his Assent to Laws, the most wholesome and necessary for the public good.

He has forbidden his Governors to pass Laws of immediate and pressing importance, unless suspended in their operation till his Assent should be obtained; and when so suspended, he has utterly neglected to attend to them.

He has refused to pass other Laws for the accommodation of large districts of people, unless those people would relinquish the right of Representation in the Legislature, a right inestimable to them and formidable to tyrants only.

He has called together legislative bodies at places unusual, uncomfortable, and distant from the depository of their Public Records, for the sole purpose of fatiguing them into compliance with his measures.

He has dissolved Representative Houses repeatedly, for opposing with manly firmness his invasions on the rights of the people.

He has refused for a long time, after such dissolutions, to cause others to be elected; whereby the Legislative Powers, incapable of the Annihilation, have returned to the People at large for their exercise; the State remaining in the mean time exposed to all the dangers of invasion from without, and the convulsions within.

He has endeavored to prevent the population of these States; for that purpose obstructing the Laws of Naturalization of Foreigners; refusing to pass others to encourage their migrations hither, and raising the conditions of new Appropriations of Lands.

He has obstructed the Administration of justice, by refusing his Assent to Laws for establishing Judiciary Powers.

He has made judges dependent on his Will alone, for the tenure of their offices, and the amount and payment of their salaries.

He has erected a multitude of New Offices, and sent hither swarms of Officers to harass our People, and eat out their substance.

He has kept among us, in times of peace, Standing Armies, without the consent of our legislature.

He has affected to render the Military independent of and superior to the Civil Power.

He has combined with others to subject us to a jurisdiction foreign to our constitution, and unacknowledged by our laws; giving his Assent to their acts of pretended legislation—

For quartering large bodies of armed troops among us;

For protecting them, by a mock Trial, from Punishment for any Murders which they should commit on the Inhabitants of these States;

For cutting off our Trade with all parts of the world;

For imposing Taxes on us without our Consent;

For depriving us in many cases, of the benefits of Trial by Jury;

For transporting us beyond Seas to be tried for pretended offences;

For abolishing the free System of English Laws in a neighboring Province, establishing therein an Arbitrary government, and enlarging its Boundaries so as to render it at once an example and fit instrument for introducing the same absolute rule into these Colonies;

For taking away our Charters, abolishing our most valuable Laws, and altering fundamentally the Forms of our Governments;

For suspending our own Legislatures, and declaring themselves invested with Power to legislate for us in all cases whatsoever.

He has abdicated Government here, by declaring us out of his Protection, and waging War against us.

He has plundered our seas, ravaged our Coasts, burnt our towns, and destroyed the lives of our people.

He is at this time transporting large armies of foreign mercenaries to compleat the works of death, desolation and tyranny, already begun with circumstances of Cruelty & perfidy, scarcely paralleled in the most barbarous ages, and totally unworthy the Head of a civilized nation.

He has constrained our fellow Citizens taken Captive on the high Seas to bear Arms against their Country, to become the executioners of their friends and Brethren, or to fall themselves by their Hands.

He has excited domestic insurrections amongst us, and has endeavoured to bring on the inhabitants of our frontiers, the merciless Indian Savages, whose known rule of warfare, is an undistinguished destruction of all ages, sexes and conditions.

In every stage of these Oppressions We have Petitioned for Redress in the most humble terms: Our repeated Petitions have been answered only by repeated injury. A Prince, whose character is thus marked by every act which may define a Tyrant, is unfit to be the ruler of a free People.

Nor have We been wanting in attentions to our British brethren. We have warned them from time to time of attempts by their legislature to extend an unwarrantable jurisdiction over us. We have reminded them of the circumstances of our emigration and settlement here. We have appealed to their native justice and magnanimity, and we have conjured them by the ties of our common kindred to disavow these usurpations, which, would inevitably interrupt our connections and correspondence. They too have been deaf to the voice of justice and of consanguinity. We must, therefore, acquiesce in the necessity, which denounces our Separation, and hold them, as we hold the rest of mankind, Enemies in War, in Peace, Friends.

We, therefore, the Representatives of the United States of America, in General Congress, Assembled, appealing to the Supreme judge of the world for the rectitude of our intentions, do, in the Name, and by Authority of the good People of these Colonies, solemnly publish and declare, That these United Colonies are, and of Right ought to be Free and Independent States; that they are Absolved from all Allegiance to the British Crown, and that all political connection between them and the State of Great Britain, is and ought to be totally dissolved; and that, as Free and Independent States, they have full Power to levy War, conclude Peace, contract Alliances, establish Commerce, and to do all other Acts and Things which independent States may of right do. And for the support of this Declaration, with a firm reliance on the Protection of Divine Providence, we mutually pledge to each other our Lives, our Fortunes and our sacred Honor.

THE CONSTITUTION OF THE UNITED STATES

We the people of the United States, in Order to form a more perfect Union, establish justice, insure domestic Tranquility, provide for the common defense, promote the general Welfare, and secure the Blessings of Liberty to ourselves and our Posterity, do ordain and establish this Constitution for the United States of America.

Article I

SECTION 1. All legislative Powers herein granted shall be vested in a Congress of the United States, which shall consist of a Senate and House of Representatives.

SECTION 2. 1. The House of Representatives shall be composed of Members chosen every second Year by the People of the several States, and the Electors in each State shall have the Qualifications requisite for Electors of the most numerous Branch of the State Legislature.

2. No person shall be a Representative who shall not have attained to the Age of twenty-five Years, and been seven Years a Citizen of the United States, and who shall not, when elected, be an Inhabitant of that State in which he shall be chosen.

3. Representatives and direct Taxes[1] shall be apportioned among the several States which may be included within this Union, according to their respective Numbers, which shall be determined by adding to the whole Number of free Persons, including those bound to Service for a Term of Years, and excluding Indians not taxed, three fifths of all other Persons.[2] The actual Enumeration shall be made within three Years after the first Meeting of the Congress of the United States, and within every subsequent Term of ten Years, in such Manner as they shall by Law direct. The Number of Representatives shall not exceed one for every thirty Thousand, but each State shall have at Least one Representative; and until such enumeration shall be made, the State of New Hampshire shall be entitled to chuse three, Massachusetts eight, Rhode Island and Providence Plantations one, Connecticut five, New York six, New Jersey four, Pennsylvania eight, Delaware one, Maryland six, Virginia ten, North Carolina five, South Carolina five, and Georgia three.

4. When vacancies happen in the Representation from any State, the Executive Authority thereof shall issue Writs of Election to fill such Vacancies.

5. The House of Representatives shall chuse their Speaker and other offi-

[1] See the Sixteenth Amendment.
[2] See the Fourteenth Amendment.

cers; and shall have the sole Power of Impeachment.

SECTION 3. 1. The Senate of the United States shall be composed of two Senators from each State, chosen by the Legislature thereof,[3] for six Years; and each Senator shall have one Vote.

2. Immediately after they shall be assembled in Consequence of the first Election, they shall be divided as equally as may be into three Classes. The Seats of the Senators of the first Class shall be vacated at the Expiration of the second Year, of the second Class at the Expiration of the fourth Year, and of the third Class at the Expiration of the sixth Year, so that one third may be chosen every second Year; and if Vacancies happen by Resignation, or otherwise, during the Recess of the Legislature of any State, the Executive thereof may make temporary Appointments until the next Meeting of the Legislature, which shall then fill such Vacancies.[4]

3. No Person shall be a Senator who shall not have attained to the Age of thirty Years, and been nine Years a Citizen of the United States, and who shall not, when elected, be an Inhabitant of that State for which he shall be chosen.

4. The Vice President of the United States shall be President of the Senate, but shall have no vote, unless they be equally divided.

5. The Senate shall chuse their other Officers, and also a President pro tempore, in the absence of the Vice President, or when he shall exercise the Office of President of the United States.

6. The Senate shall have the sole Power to try all Impeachments. When sitting for that purpose, they shall be on Oath or Affirmation. When the President of the United States is tried, the Chief justice shall preside: And no person shall be convicted without the Concurrence of two thirds of the Members present.

7. Judgment in Cases of impeachment shall not extend further than to removal from Office, and disqualification to hold and enjoy any Office of honor, Trust, or Profit under the United States: but the Party convicted shall nevertheless be liable and subject to Indictment, Trial, judgment and Punishment, according to Law.

SECTION 4. 1. The Times, Places and Manner of holding Elections for Senators and Representatives, shall be prescribed in each state by the Legislature thereof; but the Congress may at any time by Law make or alter such Regulations, except as to the Places of Chusing Senators.

2. The Congress shall assemble at least once in every Year, and such Meeting shall be on the first Monday in December, unless they shall by Law appoint a different Day.

SECTION 5. 1. Each House shall be the judge of the Elections, Returns and Qualifications of its own Members, and a Majority of each shall constitute a Quorum to do Business; but a smaller number may adjourn from day to day, and may be authorized to compel the Attendance of absent Members, in such

[3] See the Seventeenth Amendment.
[4] See the Seventeenth Amendment.

manner, and under such Penalties, as each House may provide.

2. Each House may determine the Rules of its Proceedings, punish its Members for disorderly Behavior, and, with the Concurrence of two thirds, expel a Member.

3. Each House shall keep a journal of its Proceedings, and from time to time publish the same, excepting such Parts as may in their judgment require Secrecy; and the Yeas and Nays of the Members of either House on any question shall, at the Desire of one fifth of those Present, be entered on the journal.

4. Neither House, during the Session of Congress, shall, without the Consent of the other, adjourn for more than three days, nor to any other Place than that in which the two Houses shall be sitting.

SECTION 6. 1. The Senators and Representatives shall receive a Compensation for their Services, to be ascertained by Law, and paid out of the Treasury of the United States. They shall in all Cases, except Treason, Felony, and Breach of the Peace, be privileged from arrest during their Attendance at the Session of their respective Houses, and in going to and returning from the same; and for any Speech or Debate in either House, they shall not be questioned in any other Place.

2. No Senator or Representative shall, during the Time for which he was elected, be appointed to any civil office under the Authority of the United States, which shall have been created, or the Emoluments whereof shall have been increased, during such time; and no Person holding any Office under the United States shall be a Member of either House during his continuance in Office.

SECTION 7. 1. All Bills for raising Revenue shall originate in the House of Representatives; but the Senate may propose or concur with Amendments as on other bills.

2. Every Bill which shall have passed the House of Representatives and the Senate, shall, before it become a Law, be presented to the President of the United States; If he approve he shall sign it, but if not he shall return it, with his Objections, to that House in which it shall have originated, who shall enter the Objections at large on their journal, and proceed to reconsider it. If after such Reconsideration two thirds of that House shall agree to pass the bill, it shall be sent, together with the objections, to the other House, by which it shall likewise be reconsidered, and if approved by two thirds of that House, it shall become a Law. But in all such Cases the Votes of both Houses shall be determined by Yeas and Nays, and the Names of the Persons voting for and against the Bill shall be entered on the journal of each House respectively. If any Bill shall not be returned by the President within ten Days (Sundays excepted) after it shall have been presented to him, the Same shall be a Law, in like Manner as if he had signed it, unless the Congress by their Adjournment prevent its Return, in which Case it shall not be a Law.

3. Every Order, Resolution, or Vote to which the Concurrence of the Senate and House of Representatives may be necessary (except on a question of

Adjournment) shall be presented to the President of the United States; and before the Same shall take Effect, shall be approved by him, or being disapproved by him, shall be repassed by two thirds of the Senate and House of Representatives, according to the Rules and Limitations prescribed in the Case of a Bill.

SECTION 8. The Congress shall have Power

1. To lay and collect Taxes, Duties, Imposts and Excises, to pay the Debts and provide for the common Defense and general Welfare of the United States; but all Duties, Imposts and Excises shall be uniform throughout the United States;

2. To borrow money on the credit of the United States;

3. To regulate Commerce with foreign Nations, and among the several States, and with the Indian Tribes;

4. To establish an uniform Rule of Naturalization, and uniform Laws on the subject of Bankruptcies throughout the United States;

5. To coin Money, regulate the Value thereof, and of foreign Coin, and fix the Standard of Weights and Measures;

6. To provide for the Punishment of counterfeiting the Securities and current Coin of the United States;

7. To establish Post offices and post Roads;

8. To promote the Progress of Science and useful Arts, by securing for limited Times to Authors and inventors the exclusive Right to their respective Writings and Discoveries;

9. To constitute Tribunals inferior to the Supreme Court;

10. To define and punish Piracies and Felonies committed on the high Seas, and Offences against the Law of Nations;

11. To declare War, grant Letters of Marque and Reprisal, and make Rules concerning Captures on Land and Water;

12. To raise and support Armies, but no Appropriation of Money to that Use shall be for a longer Term than two Years;

13. To provide and maintain a Navy;

14. To make Rules for the Government and Regulation of the land and naval forces;

15. To provide for calling forth the Militia to execute the Laws of the Union, suppress Insurrections and repel invasions;

16. To provide for organizing, arming, and disciplining the Militia, and for governing such Part of them as may be employed in the Service of the United States, reserving to the States respectively, the Appointment of the Officers, and the Authority of training the Militia according to the discipline prescribed by Congress;

17. To exercise exclusive Legislation in all Cases whatsoever, over such District (not exceeding ten Miles square) as may, by Cession of particular States, and the acceptance of Congress, become the Seat of Government of the United States, and to exercise like Authority over all Places purchased by the Consent of the Legislature of the State in which the Same shall be, for the Erection of Forts, Magazines, Arsenals, dock Yards, and other needful Buildings; And

18. To make all Laws which shall be necessary and proper for carrying into

Execution the foregoing Powers, and all other Powers vested by this Constitution in the government of the United States, or in any Department or Officer thereof.

SECTION 9. 1. The Migration or Importation of such Persons as any of the States now existing shall think proper to admit, shall not be prohibited by the Congress prior to the Year one thousand eight hundred and eight, but a tax or duty may be imposed on such Importation, not exceeding ten dollars for each Person.

2. The Privilege of the Writ of Habeas Corpus shall not be suspended, unless when in Cases of Rebellion or Invasion the public Safety may require it.

3. No Bill of Attainder or ex post facto Law shall be passed.

4. No capitation, or other direct, Tax shall be laid unless in Proportion to the Census or Enumeration herein before directed to be taken.[5]

5. No Tax or Duty shall be laid on Articles exported from any State.

6. No Preference shall be given by any Regulation of commerce or Revenue to the Ports of one State over those of another: nor shall Vessels bound to, or from, one state, be obliged to enter, clear, or pay Duties in another.

7. No Money shall be drawn from the Treasury, but in Consequence of Appropriations made by Law; and a regular Statement and Account of the Receipts and Expenditures of all public Money shall be published from time to time.

8. No Title of Nobility shall be granted by the United States: And no Person holding any Office of Profit or

Trust under them, shall, without the Consent of the Congress, accept of any present, Emolument, Office, or Title, of any kind whatever, from any King, Prince, or Foreign State.

SECTION 10. 1. No State shall enter into any Treaty, Alliance, or Confederation; grant Letters of Marque and Reprisal; coin Money; emit Bills of Credit; make any Thing but gold and silver Coin a Tender in Payment of Debts; pass any Bill of Attainder, ex post facto Law, or Law impairing the obligation of Contracts, or grant any Title of Nobility.

2. No State shall, without the Consent of the Congress, lay any Imposts or Duties on Imports or Exports, except what may be absolutely necessary for executing its inspection Laws: and the net Produce of all Duties and Imposts, laid by any State on Imports or Exports, shall be for the Use of the Treasury of the United States; and all such Laws shall be subject to the Revision and Control of the Congress.

3. No State shall, without the Consent of Congress, lay any duty of Tonnage, keep Troops, or Ships of War in time of peace, enter into any Agreement or Compact with another State, or with a foreign Power, or engage in War, unless actually invaded, or in such imminent Danger as will not admit of delay.

Article II

SECTION 1. 1. The executive Power shall be vested in a President of the United States of America. He shall hold his Office during the Term of four Years, and,

[5] See the Sixteenth Amendment.

together with the Vice President, chosen for the same Term, be elected, as follows:

2. Each State shall appoint, in such Manner as the Legislature thereof may direct, a Number of Electors, equal to the whole Number of Senators and Representatives to which the State may be entitled in the Congress; but no Senator or Representative, or Person holding an Office of Trust or Profit under the United States, shall be appointed an Elector.

The Electors shall meet in their respective States, and vote by Ballot for two persons, of whom one at least shall not be an Inhabitant of the same State with themselves. And they shall make a List of all the Persons voted for, and of the Number of Votes for each; which List they shall sign and certify, and transmit sealed to the Seat of the Government of the United States, directed to the President of the Senate. The President of the Senate shall, in the Presence of the Senate and House of Representatives, open all the Certificates, and the Votes shall then be counted. The Person having the greatest Number of Votes shall be the President, if such Number be a Majority of the whole Number of Electors appointed; and if there be more than one who have such Majority, and have an equal Number of Votes, then the House of Representatives shall immediately chuse by Ballot one of them for President; and if no Person have a Majority, then from the five highest on the List the said House shall in like Manner chuse the President. But in chusing the President, the votes shall be taken by States, the Representation from each State hav-

ing one Vote; a quorum for this Purpose shall consist of a Member or Members from two thirds of the States, and a Majority of all the States shall be necessary to a Choice. In every Case, after the Choice of the President, the Person having the greatest Number of Votes of the Electors shall be the Vice President. But if there should remain two or more who have equal votes, the Senate shall chuse from them by Ballot the Vice President.[6]

3. The Congress may determine the time of chusing the Electors, and the Day on which they shall give their Votes; which Day shall be the same throughout the United States.

4. No person except a natural born Citizen, or a Citizen of the United States, at the time of the Adoption of this Constitution, shall be eligible to the Office of President; neither shall any Person be eligible to that office who shall not have attained to the Age of thirty-five Years, and been fourteen Years a Resident within the United States.

5. In Case of the Removal of the President from Office, or of his Death, Resignation, or Inability to discharge the Powers and Duties of the said Office, the same shall devolve on the Vice President, and the Congress may by Law provide for the Case of Removal, Death, Resignation, or Inability, both of the President and Vice President, declaring what Officer shall then act as President, and such Officer shall act accordingly, until the Disability be removed, or a President shall be elected.

6. The President shall, at stated Times, receive for his Services a Compensation, which shall neither be in-

---

[6] Superseded by the Twelfth Amendment.

creased nor diminished during the Period for which he shall have been elected, and he shall not receive within that Period any other Emolument from the United States, or any of them.

7. Before he enter on the execution of his Office, he shall take the following Oath or Affirmation: "I do solemnly swear (or affirm) that I will faithfully execute the Office of President of the United States, and will, to the best of my Ability, preserve, protect, and defend the Constitution of the United States."

SECTION 2. 1. The President shall be Commander in Chief of the Army and Navy of the United States, and of the Militia of the several States, when called into the actual Service of the United States; he may require the Opinion, in writing, of the principal Officer in each of the executive Departments, upon any subject relating to the Duties of their respective Offices, and he shall have Power to Grant Reprieves and Pardons for Offences against the United States, except in Cases of Impeachment.

2. He shall have Power, by and with the Advice and Consent of the Senate, to make Treaties, provided two thirds of the Senators present concur; and he shall nominate, and by and with the Advice and Consent of the Senate, shall appoint Ambassadors, other public Ministers and Consuls, judges of the supreme Court, and all other Officers of the United States, whose Appointments are not herein otherwise provided for, and which shall be established by Law: but the Congress may by Law vest the Appointment of such inferior Officers, as they think proper, in the President alone, in the Courts of Law, or in the Heads of Departments.

3. The President shall have Power to fill up all Vacancies that may happen during the Recess of the Senate, by granting Commissions which shall expire at the End of their next Session.

SECTION 3. He shall from time to time give to the Congress Information of the State of the Union, and recommend to their Consideration such Measures as he shall judge necessary and expedient; he may, on extraordinary occasions, convene both Houses, or either of them, and in Case of Disagreement between them, with respect to the Time of Adjournment, he may adjourn them to such Time as he shall think proper; he shall receive Ambassadors and other public Ministers; he shall take Care that the Laws be faithfully executed, and shall Commission all the officers of the United States.

SECTION 4. The President, Vice President and all civil Officers of the United States, shall be removed from Office on Impeachment for, and Conviction of, Treason, Bribery, or other high Crimes and Misdemeanors.

Article III

SECTION 1. The judicial Power of the United States, shall be vested in one supreme Court, and in such inferior Courts as the Congress may from time to time ordain and establish. The judges, both of the supreme and inferior Courts, shall hold their Offices during good Behaviour, and shall, at stated Times, receive for their Services, a Compensation, which shall not be diminished during their Continuance in Office.

SECTION 2. 1. The judicial Power shall extend to all Cases, in Law and Equity, arising under this Constitution, the Laws of the United States, and treaties made, or which shall be made, under their Authority;—to all Cases affecting Ambassadors, other public ministers and consuls; to all cases of admiralty and maritime jurisdiction;—to Controversies to which the United States shall be a party;[7]—to Controversies between two or more States; between a State and citizens of another States;—between Citizens of different States;—between Citizens of the same State claiming Lands under Grants of different States, and between a State, or the Citizens thereof, and foreign States, Citizens or Subjects.

2. In all Cases affecting Ambassadors, other public Ministers and Consuls, and those in which a State shall be Party, the supreme Court shall have original Jurisdiction. In all the other Cases before mentioned, the supreme Court shall have appellate jurisdiction, both as to Law and Fact, with such Exceptions, and under such Regulations as the Congress shall make.

3. The trial of all Crimes, except in Cases of Impeachment, shall be by jury; and such Trial shall be held in the State where the said Crimes shall have been committed; but when not committed within any State, the trial shall be at such Place or Places as the Congress may by Law have directed.

SECTION 3. 1. Treason against the United States, shall consist only in levying War against them, or in adhering to their Enemies, giving them Aid and Comfort. No Person shall be convicted of Treason unless on the testimony of two Witnesses to the same overt Act, or on Confession in open Court.

2. The Congress shall have power to declare the Punishment of Treason, but no Attainder of Treason shall work Corruption of Blood, or Forfeiture except during the Life of the Person attainted.

Article IV

SECTION 1. Full Faith and Credit shall be given in each State to the public Acts, Records, and judicial Proceedings of every other State. And the Congress may by general Laws prescribe the Manner in which such Acts, Records and Proceedings shall be proved, and the Effect thereof.

SECTION 2. 1. The Citizens of each State shall be entitled to all Privileges and Immunities of Citizens in the several States.[8]

2. A Person charged in any State with Treason, Felony, or other Crime, who shall flee from justice, and be found in another State, shall on demand of the executive Authority of the State from which he fled, be delivered up, to be removed to the State having jurisdiction of the crime.

3. No Person held to Service or Labour in one State, under the Laws thereof, escaping into another, shall, in Consequence of any Law or Regulation

---

[7] See the Eleventh Amendment.

[8] See the Fourteenth Amendment, Section 1.

therein, be discharged from such Service or Labour, but shall be delivered up on Claim of the Party to whom such Service or Labour may be due.[9]

SECTION 3. 1. New States may be admitted by the Congress into this Union; but no new State shall be formed or erected within the Jurisdiction of any other State, nor any State be formed by the junction of two or more States, or parts of States, without the Consent of the Legislatures of the States concerned as well as of the Congress.

2. The Congress shall have Power to dispose of and make all needful Rules and Regulations respecting the Territory or other Property belonging to the United States; and nothing in this Constitution shall be so construed as to Prejudice any Claims of the United States, or of any particular State.

SECTION 4. The United States shall guarantee to every State in this Union a Republican Form of Government, and shall protect each of them against Invasion; and on Application of the Legislature, or of the Executive (when the Legislature cannot be convened) against domestic Violence.

Article V

The Congress, whenever two-thirds of both Houses shall deem it necessary, shall propose Amendments to this Constitution, or, on the Application of the Legislatures of two-thirds of the several States, shall call a Convention for proposing Amendments, which, in either Case, shall be valid to all Intents and Purposes, as part of this Constitution, when ratified by the Legislatures of three-fourths of the several States, or by Conventions in three-fourths thereof, as the one or the other Mode of Ratification may be proposed by the Congress; Provided that no Amendment which may be made prior to the Year One thousand eight hundred and eight shall in any Manner affect the first and fourth Clauses in the Ninth Section of the first Article; and that no State, without its Consent, shall be deprived of its equal Suffrage in the Senate.

Article VI

1. All Debts contracted and Engagements entered into, before the Adoption of this Constitution, shall be as valid against the United States under this Constitution, as under the Confederation.[10]

2. This Constitution, and the Laws of the United States which shall be made in Pursuance thereof; and all Treaties made, or which shall be made, under the Authority of the United States, shall be the supreme Law of the Land; and the judges in every State shall be bound thereby, any Thing in the Constitution or Laws of any State to the Contrary notwithstanding.

3. The Senators and Representatives before mentioned, and the Members of the several State Legislatures and all executive and judicial Officers, both of the United States and of the sev-

---

[9] See the Thirteenth Amendment

[10] See the Fourteenth Amendment, Sec. 4..

eral States, shall be bound by Oath or Affirmation, to support this Constitution; but no religious Test shall ever be required as a qualification to any Office or public Trust under the United States.

Article VII

The Ratification of the Conventions of nine States, shall be sufficient for the Establishment of this Constitution between the States so ratifying the same.

Done in Convention by the Unanimous Consent of the States present the Seventeenth Day of September in the Year of our Lord one thousand seven hundred and Eighty seven, and of the independence of the United States of America the Twelfth. In Witness whereof We have hereunto subscribed our Names.

(Names omitted)

* * *

Articles in addition to, and amendment of, the Constitution of the United States of America, proposed by Congress, and ratified by the legislatures of the several States, pursuant to the fifth article of the original Constitution.

Amendment I
(December 15, 1791)

Congress shall make no law respecting an establishment of religion, or prohibiting the free exercise thereof, or abridging the freedom of speech, or of the press; or the right of the people peaceably to assemble, and to peti-

tion the Government for a redress of grievances.

Amendment II
(December 15, 1791)

A well regulated Militia, being necessary to the security of a free State, the right of the people to keep and bear Arms shall not be infringed.

Amendment III
(December 15, 1791)

No Soldier shall, in time of peace, be quartered in any house, without the consent of the owner, nor in time of war, but in a manner to be prescribed by law.

Amendment IV
(December 15, 1791)

The right of the people to be secure in their persons, houses, papers, and effects, against unreasonable searches and seizures, shall not be violated, and no Warrants shall issue, but upon probable cause, supported by Oath or affirmation, and particularly describing the place to be searched, and the persons or things to be seized.

Amendment V
(December 15, 1791)

No person shall be held to answer for a capital or otherwise infamous crime, unless on a presentment or indictment of a Grand jury, except in cases arising in the land or naval forces, or in the Militia, when in actual service in time of War or public danger; nor shall any person be subject for the same offence to be twice put in jeopardy of life or limb; nor shall be compelled in any criminal case to be a witness against himself, nor be deprived of life, liberty, or property, without due process of law; nor shall private property be taken for public use, without just compensation.

Amendment VI
(December 15, 1791)

In all criminal prosecutions, the accused shall enjoy the right to a speedy and public trial, by an impartial jury of the State and district wherein the crime shall have been committed, which district shall have been previously ascertained by law, and to be informed of the nature and cause of the accusation; to be confronted with the witnesses against him; to have compulsory process for obtaining witnesses in his favor, and to have the Assistance of Counsel for his defense.

Amendment VII
(December 15, 1791)

In suits at common law, where the value in controversy shall exceed twenty dollars, the right of trial by jury shall be preserved, and no fact tried by a jury, shall be otherwise reexamined in any Court of the United States, than according to the rules of the common law.

Amendment VIII
(December 15, 1791)

Excessive bail shall not be required, nor excessive fines imposed, nor cruel and unusual punishments inflicted.

Amendment IX
(December 15, 1791)

The enumeration in the Constitution, of certain rights, shall not be construed to deny or disparage others retained by the people.

Amendment X
(December 15, 1791)

The powers not delegated to the United States by the Constitution, nor prohibited by it to the States, are reserved to the States respectively, or to the people.

Amendment XI
(January 8, 1798)

The judicial power of the United States shall not be construed to extend to any suit in law or equity, commenced or prosecuted against one of the United States by Citizens of another State, or by Citizens or Subjects of any Foreign State.

Amendment XII
(September 25, 1804)

The Electors shall meet in their respective States and vote by ballot for President and Vice-President, one of whom, at least, shall not be an inhabitant of the same State with themselves; they shall name in their ballots the person voted for as President, and in distinct ballots the person voted for as Vice-President, and they shall make distinct lists of all persons voted for as President, and of all persons voted for as Vice-President, and of the number of votes for each, which lists they shall sign and certify, and transmit sealed to the seat of the government of the United States, directed to the President of the Senate; The President of the Senate shall, in the presence of the Senate and House of Representatives, open all the certificates and the votes shall then be counted; The person having the greatest number of votes for President, shall be the President, if such number be a majority of the whole number of Electors appointed; and if no person have such majority, then from the persons having the highest numbers not exceeding three on the list of those voted for as President, the House of Representatives shall choose immediately, by ballot, the President. But in choosing the President, the votes shall be taken by states, the representation from each state having one vote; a quorum for this purpose shall consist of a member or members from two-thirds of the states, and a majority of all the states shall be necessary to a choice. And if the House of Representatives shall not choose a President whenever the right of choice shall devolve upon them, before the fourth day of March next following, then the Vice-President shall act as President, as in the case of the death or other constitutional disability of the President.

The person having the greatest number of votes as Vice President, shall be the Vice-President, if such number be a majority of the whole number of Electors appointed, and if no person have a majority, then from the two highest numbers on the list, the Senate shall choose the Vice-President; a quorum for the purpose shall consist of two-thirds of the whole number of Senators, and a majority of the whole number shall be necessary to a choice. But no person constitutionally ineligible to the office of President shall be eligible to that of Vice-President of the United States.

Amendment XIII
(December 18, 1865)

SECTION 1. Neither slavery nor involuntary servitude, except as a punishment for crime whereof the party shall have been duly convicted, shall exist within the United States, or any place subject to their jurisdiction.

SECTION 2. Congress shall have power to enforce this article by appropriate legislation.

Amendment XIV
(July 28, 1868)

SECTION 1. All persons born or naturalized in the United States, and subject to the jurisdiction thereof, are citizens of the United States and of the State wherein they reside. No State shall make or enforce any law which shall abridge the privileges or immunities of citizens of the United States; nor shall any State deprive any person of life, liberty, or property, without due process of law; nor deny to any person within its jurisdiction the equal protection of the laws.

SECTION 2. Representatives shall be apportioned among the several States according to their respective numbers, counting the whole number of persons in each State, excluding Indians not taxed. But when the right to vote at any election for the choice of electors for President and Vice-President of the United States, Representatives in Congress, the Executive and Judicial officers of a State, or the members of the Legislature thereof, is denied to any of the male inhabitants of such State, being twenty-one years of age, and citizens of the United States, or in any way abridged, except for participation in rebellion, or other crime, the basis of representation therein shall be reduced in the proportion which the number of such male citizens shall bear to the whole number of male citizens twenty-one years of age in such State.

SECTION 3. No person shall be a Senator or Representative in Congress, or elector of President and Vice-President, or hold any office, civil or military, under the United States, or under any State, who, having previously taken an oath, as a member of Congress, or as an officer of the United States, or as a member of any State legislature, or as an executive or judicial officer of any State, to support the Constitution of the United States, shall have engaged in insurrection or rebellion against the same, or given aid or comfort to the enemies

thereof. But Congress may by a vote of two-thirds of each House, remove such disability.

SECTION 4. The validity of the public debt of the United States, authorized by law, including debts incurred for payment of pensions and bounties for services in suppressing insurrection or rebellion, shall not be questioned. But neither the United States nor any State shall assume or pay any debt or obligation incurred in aid of insurrection or rebellion against the United States, or any claim for the loss or emancipation of any slave; but all such debts, obligations, and claims shall be held illegal and void.

SECTION 5. The Congress shall have the power to enforce, by appropriate legislation, the provisions of this article.

Amendment XV
(March 30, 1870)

SECTION 1. The right of citizens of the United States to vote shall not be denied or abridged by the United States or by any State on account of race, color, or previous condition of servitude

SECTION 2. The Congress shall have power to enforce this article by appropriate legislation.

Amendment XVI
(February 25, 1913)
The Congress shall have power to lay and collect taxes on incomes, from whatever source derived, without ap-

portionment among the several States, and without regard to any census or enumeration.

Amendment XVII
(May 31, 1913)

The Senate of the United States shall be composed of two Senators from each State, elected by the people thereof, for six years; and each Senator shall have one vote. The electors in each State shall have the qualifications requisite for electors of the most numerous branch of the State legislatures.

When vacancies happen in the representation of any State in the Senate, the executive authority of such State shall issue writs of election to fill such vacancies: Provided, That the legislature of any State may empower the executive thereof to make temporary appointments until the people fill the vacancies by election as the legislature may direct.

This amendment shall not be so construed as to affect the election or term of any Senator chosen before it becomes valid as part of the Constitution.

Amendment XVIII
(January 29, 1919)

Section 1. After one year from the ratification of this article the manufacture, sale, or transportation of intoxicating liquors within, the importation thereof into, or the exportation thereof from the United States and all territory subject to the jurisdiction thereof for beverage purposes is hereby prohibited.

Section 2. The Congress and the several States shall have concurrent power to enforce this article by appropriate legislation.

Section 3. This article shall be inoperative unless it shall have been ratified as an amendment to the Constitution by the legislatures of the several States, as provided in the Constitution, within seven years from the date of the submission hereof to the States by the Congress.

Amendment XIX
(August 26, 1920)

The right of citizens of the United States to vote shall not be denied or abridged by the United States or by any State on account of sex.

Congress shall have power to enforce this article by appropriate legislation.

Amendment XX
(January 23, 1933)

Section 1. The terms of the President and Vice-President shall end at noon on the 20th day of January, and the terms of Senators and Representatives at noon on the 3d day of January, of the years in which such terms would have ended if this article had not been ratified; and the terms of their successors shall then begin.

Section 2. The Congress shall assemble at least once in every year, and such meeting shall begin at noon on the 3rd day of January, unless they shall by law appoint a different day.

SECTION 3. If, at the time fixed for the beginning of the term of the President, the President elect shall have died, the Vice-President elect shall become President. If a President shall not have been chosen before the time fixed for the beginning of his term, or if the President elect shall have failed to qualify, then the Vice-President elect shall act as President until a President shall have qualified; and the Congress may by law provide for the case wherein neither a President elect nor a Vice-President elect shall have qualified, declaring who shall then act as President, or the manner in which one who is to act shall be selected, and such person shall act accordingly until a President or Vice-President shall have qualified.

SECTION 4. The Congress may by law provide for the case of the death of any of the persons from whom the House of Representatives may choose a President whenever the right of choice shall have devolved upon them, and for the case of the death of any of the persons from whom the Senate may choose a Vice-President whenever the right of choice shall have devolved upon them.

SECTION 5. Sections 1 and 2 shall take effect on the 15th day of October following the ratification of this article.

SECTION 6. This article shall be inoperative unless it shall have been ratified as an amendment to the Constitution by the legislatures of three-fourths of the several States within seven years from the date of its submission.

Amendment XXI
(December 5, 1933)

SECTION 1. The eighteenth article of amendment to the Constitution of the United States is hereby repealed.

SECTION 2. The transportation or importation into any State, Territory, or possession of the United States for delivery or use therein of intoxicating liquors, in violation of the laws thereof, is hereby prohibited.

SECTION 3. This article shall be inoperative unless it shall have been ratified as an amendment to the Constitution by conventions in the several States, as provided in the Constitution, within seven years from the date of the submission hereof to the States by the Congress.

Amendment XXII
(March 1, 1951)

SECTION 1. No person shall be elected to the office of the President more than twice, and no person who has held the office of President, or acted as President, for more than two years of a term to which some other person was elected President shall be elected to the office of the President more than once. But this Article shall not apply to any person holding the office of President when this Article was proposed by the Congress, and shall not prevent any person who may be holding the office of President or acting as President, during the term within which this Article becomes operative from holding the office of President or acting as President during the remainder of such term.

SECTION 2. This article shall be inoperative unless it shall have been ratified as an amendment to the Constitution by the legislatures of three-fourths of the several states within seven years from the date of its submission to the states by Congress.

Amendment XXIII
(March 29, 1961)

SECTION 1. The District constituting the seat of Government of the United States shall appoint in such manner as the Congress may direct:

A number of electors of President and Vice President equal to the whole number of Senators and Representatives in Congress to which the District would be entitled if it were a State, but in no event more than the least populous State; they shall be in addition to those appointed by the States, but they shall be considered, for the purposes of the election of President and Vice President, to be electors appointed by a State; and they shall meet in the District and perform such duties as provided by the twelfth article of amendment.

SECTION 2. The Congress shall have power to enforce this article by appropriate legislation.

Amendment XXIV
(January 23, 1964)

SECTION 1. The right of citizens of the United States to vote in any primary or other election for President or Vice President, for electors for President or Vice President, or for Senator or Representative in Congress, shall not be denied or abridged by the United States or any State by reason of failure to pay any poll tax or other tax.

SECTION 2. The Congress shall have the power to enforce this article by appropriate legislation.

Amendment XXV
(February 10, 1967)

SECTION 1. In case of the removal of the President from office or of his death or resignation, the Vice President shall become President.

SECTION 2. Whenever there is a vacancy in the office of the Vice President, the President shall nominate a Vice President who shall take office upon confirmation by a majority vote of both houses of Congress.

SECTION 3. Whenever the President transmits to the President pro tempore of the Senate and the Speaker of the House of Representatives his written declaration that he is unable to discharge the powers and duties of his office, and until he transmits to them a written declaration to the contrary, such powers and duties shall be discharged by the Vice President as Acting President.

SECTION 4. Whenever the Vice President and a majority of either the principal officers of the executive departments, or of such other body as Congress may by law provide, transmit to the President pro tempore of the Senate and the Speaker of the House of Representatives their written declaration that the President is unable to discharge the powers and duties of his office, the Vice President shall immediately assume the powers and duties of the office as Acting President.

Thereafter, when the President transmits to the President pro tempore of the Senate and the Speaker of the House of Representatives his written declaration that no inability exists, he shall resume the powers and duties of his office unless the Vice President and a majority of either the principal officers of the executive departments, or of such other body as Congress may by law provide, transmit within four days to the President pro tempore of the Senate and the Speaker of the House of Representatives their written declaration that the President is unable to discharge the powers and duties of his office. Thereupon Congress shall decide the issue, assembling within forty-eight hours for that purpose if not in session. If the Congress, within twenty-one days after receipt of the latter written declaration, or, if Congress is not in session, within twenty-one days after Congress is required to assemble, determines by two-thirds vote of both houses that the President is unable to discharge the powers and duties of his office, the Vice President shall continue to discharge the same as Acting President; otherwise, the President shall resume the powers and duties of his office.

Amendment XXVI
(June 30, 1971)

SECTION 1. The right of citizens of the United States, who are eighteen years of age or older, to vote shall not be denied or abridged by the United States or by any state on account of age.

SECTION 2. The Congress shall have power to enforce this article by appropriate legislation.

Amendent XXVII
(May 7, 1992)

No law varying the compensation for the services of the Senators and Representatives shall take effect, until an election of Representatives shall have intervened.

PRESIDENTIAL ELECTIONS

YEAR	NUMBER OF STATES	CANDIDATES	PARTY	POPULAR VOTE*	ELECTORAL VOTE**	PERCENTAGE OF POPULAR VOTE
1789	11	GEORGE WASHINGTON	No party designations		69	
		John Adams			34	
		Other Candidates			35	
1792	15	GEORGE WASHINGTON	No party designations		132	
		John Adams			77	
		George Clinton			50	
		Other Candidates			5	
1796	16	JOHN ADAMS	Federalist		71	
		Thomas Jefferson	Democratic-Republican		68	
		Thomas Pinckney	Federalist		59	
		Aaron Burr	Democratic-Republican		30	
		Other Candidates			48	
1800	16	THOMAS JEFFERSON	Democratic-Republican		73	
		Aaron Burr	Democratic-Republican		73	
		John Adams	Federalist		65	
		Charles C. Pinckney	Federalist		64	
		John Jay	Federalist			
1804	17	THOMAS JEFFERSON	Democratic-Republican		162	
		Charles C. Pinckney	Federalist		14	
1808	17	JAMES MADISON	Democratic-Republican		122	
		Charles C. Pinckney	Federalist		47	
		George Clinton	Democratic-Republican		6	
1812	18	JAMES MADISON	Democratic-Republican		128	
		DeWitt Clinton	Federalist		89	
1816	19	JAMES MONROE	Democratic-Republican		183	
		Rufus King	Federalist		34	
1820	24	JAMES MONROE	Democratic-Republican		231	
		John Quincy Adams	Independent Republican		1	
1824	24	JOHN QUINCY ADAMS		108,740	84	30.5
		Andrew Jackson		153,544	99	43.1
		William H. Crawford		46,618	41	13.1
		Henry Clay		47,136	37	13.2
1828	24	ANDREW JACKSON	Democrat	647,286	178	56.0
		John Quincy Adams	National Republican	508,064	83	44.0
1832	24	ANDREW JACKSON	Democrat	687,502	219	55.0
		Henry Clay	National Republican	530,189	49	42.4
		William Wirt	Anti-Masonic	33,108	7	2.6
		John Floyd	National Republican		11	
1836	26	MARTIN VAN BUREN	Democrat	765,483	170	50.9
		William H. Harrison	Whig		73	
		Hugh L. White	Whig	739,795	26	49.1
		Daniel Webster	Whig		14	
		W. P. Mangum	Whig		11	
1840	26	WILLIAM H. HARRISON	Whig	1,274,624	234	53.1
		Martin Van Buren	Democrat	1,127,781	60	46.9
1844	26	JAMES K. POLK	Democrat	1,338,464	170	49.6
		Henry Clay	Whig	1,300,097	105	48.1
		James G. Birney	Liberty	62,300		2.3
1848	30	ZACHARY TAYLOR	Whig	1,360,967	163	47.4
		Lewis Cass	Democrat	1,222,342	127	42.5
		Martin Van Buren	Free Soil	291,263		10.1
1852	31	FRANKLIN PIERCE	Democrat	1,601,117	254	50.9
		Winfield Scott	Whig	1,385,453	42	44.1
		John P. Hale	Free Soil	155,825		5.0

* Percentage of popular vote given for any election year may not total 100 percent because candidates receiving less than 1 percent of the popular vote have been omitted.

** Prior to the passage of the Twelfth Amendment in 1904, the electoral college voted for two presidential candidates; the runner-up became Vice President. Data from *Historical Statistics of the United States, Colonial Times to 1957* (1961), pp. 682–883, and *The World Almanac.*

PRESIDENTIAL ELECTIONS (continued)

YEAR	NUMBER OF STATES	CANDIDATES	PARTY	POPULAR VOTE*	ELECTORAL VOTE**	PERCENTAGE OF POPULAR VOTE
1856	31	JAMES BUCHANAN	Democrat	1,832,955	174	45.3
		John C. Frémont	Republican	1,339,932	114	33.1
		Millard Fillmore	American	871,731	8	21.6
1860	33	ABRAHAM LINCOLN	Republican	1,865,593	180	39.8
		Stephen A. Douglas	Democrat	1,382,713	12	29.5
		John C. Breckinridge	Democrat	848,356	72	18.1
		John Bell	Constitutional Union	592,906	39	12.6
1864	36	ABRAHAM LINCOLN	Republican	2,206,938	212	55.0
		George B. McClellan	Democrat	1,803,787	21	45.0
1868	37	ULYSSES S. GRANT	Republican	3,013,421	214	52.7
		Horatio Seymour	Democrat	2,706,829	80	47.3
1872	37	ULYSSES S. GRANT	Republican	3,596,745	286	55.6
		Horace Greeley	Democrat	2,843,446	*	43.9
1876	38	RUTHERFORD B. HAYES	Republican	4,036,572	185	48.0
		Samuel J. Tilden	Democrat	4,284,020	184	51.0
1880	38	JAMES A. GARFIELD	Republican	4,453,295	214	48.5
		Winfield S. Hancock	Democrat	4,414,082	155	48.1
		James B. Weaver	Greenback-Labor	308,578		3.4
1884	38	GROVER CLEVELAND	Democrat	4,879,507	219	48.5
		James G. Blaine	Republican	4,850,293	182	48.2
		Benjamin F. Butler	Greenback-Labor	175,370		1.8
		John P. St. John	Prohibition	150,369		1.5.
1888	38	BENJAMIN HARRISON	Republican	5,447,129	233	47.9
		Grover Cleveland	Democrat	5,537,857	168	48.6
		Clinton B. Fisk	Prohibition	249,506		2.2
		Anson J. Streeter	Union Labor	146,935		1.3
1892	44	GROVER CLEVELAND	Democrat	5,555,426	277	46.1
		Benjamin Harrison	Republican	5,182,690	145	43.0
		James B. Weaver	People's	1,029,846	22	8.5
		John Bidwell	Prohibition	264,133		2.2
1896	45	WILLIAM MCKINLEY	Republican	7,102,246	271	51.1
		William J. Bryan	Democrat	6,492,559	176	47.7
1900	45	WILLIAM MCKINLEY	Republican	7,218,491	292	51.7
		William J. Bryan	Democrat; Populist	6,356,734	155	45.5
		John C. Woolley	Prohibition	208,914		1.5
1904	45	THEODORE ROOSEVELT	Republican	7,628,461	336	57.4
		Alton B. Parker	Democrat	5,084,223	140	37.6
		Eugene V. Debs	Socialist	402,283		3.0
		Silas C. Swallow	Prohibition	258,536		1.9
1908	46	WILLIAM H. TAFT	Republican	7,675,320	321	51.6
		William J. Bryan	Democrat	6,412,294	162	43.1
		Eugene V. Debs	Socialist	420,793		2.8
		Eugene W. Chafin	Prohibition	253,840		1.7
1912	48	WOODROW WILSON	Democrat	6,296,547	435	41.9
		Theodore Roosevelt	Progressive	4,118,571	88	27.4
		William H. Taft	Republican	3,486,720	8	23.2
		Eugene V. Debs	Socialist	900,672		6.0
		Eugene W. Chafin	Prohibition	206,275		1.4
1916	48	WOODROW WILSON	Democrat	9,127,695	277	49.4
		Charles E. Hughes	Republican	8,533,507	254	46.2
		A. L. Benson	Socialist	585,113		3.2
		J. Frank Hanly	Prohibition	220,506		1.2
1920	48	WARREN G. HARDING	Republican	16,143,407	404	60.4
		James M. Cox	Democrat	9,130,328	127	34.2
		Eugene V. Debs	Socialist	919,799		3.4
		P. P. Christensen	Farmer-Labor	265,411		1.0

*Because of the death of Greeley, Democratic electors scattered their votes.

PRESENTIAL ELECTIONS (continued)

YEAR	NUMBER OF STATES	CANDIDATES	PARTY	POPULAR VOTE*	ELECTORAL VOTE**	PERCENTAGE OF POPULAR VOTE
1924	48	CALVIN COOLIDGE	Republican	15,718,211	382	54.0
		John W. Davis	Democrat	8,385,283	136	28.8
		Robert M. La Follette	Progressive	4,831,289	13	16.6
1928	48	HERBERT C. HOOVER	Republican	21,391,993	444	58.2
		Alfred E. Smith	Democrat	15,016,169	87	40.9
1932	48	FRANKLIN D. ROOSEVELT	Democrat	22,809,638	472	57.4
		Herbert C. Hoover	Republican	15,758,901	59	39.7
		Norman Thomas	Socialist	881,951		2.2
1936	48	FRANKLIN D. ROOSEVELT	Democrat	27,752,869	523	60.8
		Alfred M. Landon	Republican	16,674,665	8	36.5
		William Lemke	Union	882,479		1.9
1940	48	FRANKLIN D. ROOSEVELT	Democrat	27,307,819	449	54.8
		Wendell L. Wilkie	Republican	22,321,018	82	44.8
1944	48	FRANKLIN D. ROOSEVELT	Democrat	25,606,585	432	53.5
		Thomas E. Dewey	Republican	22,014,745	99	46.0
1948	48	HARRY S. TRUMAN	Democrat	24,105,812	303	49.5
		Thomas E. Dewey	Republican	21,970,065	189	45.1
		J. Strom Thurmond	States' Rights	1,169,063	39	2.4
		Henry A. Wallace	Progressive	1,157,172		2.4
1952	48	DWIGHT D. EISENHOWER	Republican	33,936,234	442	55.1
		Adlai E. Stevenson	Democrat	27,314,992	89	44.4
1956	48	DWIGHT D. EISENHOWER	Republican	35,590,472	457*	57.6
		Adlai E. Stevenson	Democrat	26,022,752	73	42.1
1960	50	JOHN F. KENNEDY	Democrat	34,227,096	303**	49.9
		Richard M. Nixon	Republican	34,108,546	219	49.6
1964	50	LYNDON B. JOHNSON	Democrat	42,676,220	486	61.3
		Barry M. Goldwater	Republican	26,860,314	52	38.5
1968	50	RICHARD M. NIXON	Republican	31,785,480	301	43.4
		Hubert H. Humphrey	Democrat	31,275,165	191	42.7
		George C. Wallace	American Independent	9,906,473	46	13.5
1972	50	RICHARD M. NIXON***	Republican	47,165,234	520	60.6
		George S. McGovern	Democrat	29,168,110	17	37.5
1976	50	JIMMY CARTER	Democrat	40,828,929	297	50.1
		Gerald R. Ford	Republican	39,148,940	240	47.9
		Eugene McCarthy	Independent	739,256		
1980	50	RONALD REAGAN	Republican	43,201,220	489	50.9
		Jimmy Carter	Democrat	34,913,332	49	41.2
		John B. Anderson	Independent	5,581,379		
1984	50	RONALD REAGAN	Republican	53,428,357	525	59.0
		Walter F. Mondale	Democrat	36,930,923	13	41.0
1988	50	GEORGE BUSH	Republican	48,901,046	426	53.4
		Michael Dukakis	Democrat	41,809,030	111	45.6
1992	50	WILLIAM J. CLINTON	Democrat	44,909,806	370	43.0
		George Bush	Republican	39,104,550	168	37.5
		H. Ross Perot	Independent	19,742,240		18.9
		Andre Marrau	Libertarian	291,631		0.3
1996	50	WILLIAM J. CLINTON	Democrat	47,402,357	379	49.2
		Robert Dole	Republican	39,198,755	159	40.7
		H. Ross Perot	Reform	8,085,402		8.4
		Ralph Nader	Green	685,128		0.7
		Harry Browne	Libertarian	485,798		0.5

*Walter B. Jones received 1 electoral vote.
**Harry F. Byrd received 15 electoral votes.
***Resigned August 9,1974; Vice President Gerald R. Ford became President.

PRESIDENTIAL ELECTIONS *(continued)*

YEAR	NUMBER OF STATES	CANDIDATES	PARTY	POPULAR VOTE*	ELECTORAL VOTE**	PERCENTAGE OF POPULAR VOTE
2000	50	GEORGE W. BUSH	Republican	50,459,624	271	47.9
		Albert Gore, Jr.	Democrat	51,003,238	266	48.4
		Ralph Nader	Green	2,882,985		2.7
		Patrick Buchanan	Reform	449,120		0.4
		Harry Browne	Libertarian	384,440		0.4
2004	50	GEORGE W. BUSH	Republican	62,040,610	286	58.9
		John F. Kerry	Democrat	59,028,111	251	56.1
		Ralph Nader	Independent/Reform	463,653		0.0
2008	50	BARACK OBAMA	Democrat	69,456,898	365	52.9
		John McCain	Republican	59,934,814	173	45.6
		Ralph Nader	Independent	738,771		0.6
		Bob Barr	Libertarian	523,686		0.4

COPYRIGHT ACKNOWLEDGMENTS; PHOTO CREDITS

Chapter 1, p, 1: Library of Congress

Chapter 1, p, 5: http://karenswhimsy.com/public-domain-images

Chapter 1, p, 6: http://karenswhimsy.com/public-domain-images

Chapter 1, p, 8: http://karenswhimsy.com/public-domain-images

Chapter 1, p, 9: http://karenswhimsy.com/public-domain-images

Chapter 1, p, 14: www.pdimages.com

Chapter 1, p, 15: http://karenswhimsy.com/public-domain-images

Chapter 1, p, 16: Library of Congress

Chapter 1, p, 19: Library of Congress

Chapter 1, p, 21: www.pdimages.com

Chapter 1, p, 25: Library of Congress

Chapter 1, p, 26: http://karenswhimsy.com/public-domain-images

Chapter 1, p, 28: www.pdimages.com

Chapter 2, p, 31: A/P World Wide

Chapter 2, p, 36: Library of Congress

Chapter 2, p, 38: http://teachpol.tcnj.edu/amer_pol_hist/

Chapter 2, p, 40: Library of Congress

Chapter 2, p, 43: www.pdclipart.org

Chapter 2, p, 46: A/P World Wide

Chapter 2, p, 49: http://teachpol.tcnj.edu/amer_pol_hist/

Chapter 2, p, 52: Library of Congress

Chapter 3, p, 65: Library of Congress

Chapter 3, p, 73: Library of Congress

Chapter 3, p, 82: Library of Congress

Chapter 3, p, 85: Library of Congress

Chapter 4, p, 89: A/P World Wide

Chapter 4, p, 93: Library of Congress

Chapter 4, p, 94: www.pdclipart.org

Chapter 4, p, 97: http://teachpol.tcnj.edu/amer_pol_hist/

Chapter 4, p, 104: Library of Congress

Chapter 4, p, 112: Library of Congress

Chapter 4, p, 120: Library of Congress

Chapter 4, p, 121: http://teachpol.tcnj.edu/amer_pol_hist/

Chapter 4, p, 123: A/P World Wide

A

Abolitionists, 368, 369, 473, 477, 479, 484, 485, 486, 493, 495, 499, 500, 512, 518, 519, 525, 526, 527, 535, 537, 609, 620, 621

Dred Scott decision, 489, 523, 524, 525, 526

Abraham, 351, 369

Adams, 226, 237, 239, 241, 243, 253, 254, 271, 272, 273, 276, 277, 278, 279, 280, 281

Adams, Abigail, 209, 239

Adams, Charles Francis, 503, 531

Adams, John Quincy322, 328, 330, 332, 368, 375, 377, 381, 423, 480

Democratic Republicans, 378–380

foreign relations, 380

in the White House, 377–378

interlude, 377–380

National Republicans, 378–380

foreign relations, 380

Adams, John, 149, 151, 157, 160, 179, 199, 214, 226, 237, 243, 253, 254, 271, 272, 273, 276, 277, 278, 279, 280, 286, 290, 375, 381, 472

Alien and Sedition Acts, 279–280

election of 1800, 280–281

trial of, 277–281

Treaty of 1800, 278–279

XYZ Affair, 277–278

Adams, Sam, 189

Adams, Samuel, 239, 241

Agassiz, Louis, 365

Age of Reason, 498

Alabama A&M, 476

Alabama, the, 584

Albany Conference, 85

Alcoholism, 341

Alcuin, 209

Alexis de Tocqueville, 370–372

Alien and Sedition Acts, 226, 279, 280

Allen, Ethan, 157, 196

Alligator, 422

Almanac, Poor Richard's, 98, 123

America

and the war French-English war, 299–305

Bank of the United States, 316–317

election of 1808, 302

in the aftermath of the War of 1812, 315–317

Native American rights, 318–319

neutrality, 299–300

protective tariff, 316

resistance to federal policy, 320–321

transportation routes, 317

War of 1812, 304–305

war hawks, 304

westward movement, 318–321

American arts, 365–368

architecture, 219, 367–368

"higher culture", 365–366

music and drama, 366–367

musicians and painters, 221

native literature, 210

painting, 367–368

poetry, 213

prose, 211

quest for, 210

reading, 212

sculpture, 367-368

theater, 216

American credo, 188

American Fur Company, 424

American Protective Association (APA), 487

American Revolution, 134, 149, 157, 163, 182, 186

American society,

shaping of, 201

marriage, morals, and family life, 204

women's rights, 208

Ames, Fisher, 199, 259

Ames, Nathaniel, 199

Amistad, the case, 480

Anasazi, 5, 6

Anderson, Major Robert, 534

Andersonville, 585, 586

Andrews, Charles M., 27

Andros, Edmond, 66

Anglicans, 117–119

Anglo-American negotiations, 430

Anthony, Susan B., 595

Anti-Masons, 391

Antietam, 543, 554, 561, 562, 594

Antifederalists, 225, 241, 249, 250, 272

Antislavery, 459, 473, 480–485, 499, 500, 503, 507, 508, 509, 510, 511, 515, 517, 518, 520, 531, 537, 538, 582, 587, 595, 596, 599

Apache, 110

Appamattox, 580

Arnold, Benedict, 157, 158, 173, 175, 176, 177

Aroostook War, 408

Articles of Confederation, 134, 184, 185, 186, 228, 229, 237, 240, 244, 251, 500

Artistic independence, 223–224

Arts and sciences, *see American Arts*

Asbury, Bishop Francis, 197, 348

Ashley, William Henry, 424

Associated Press, 477

Astor, John Jacob, 424

Atchison, Senator David Rice, 517

Atlanta, fall of, 543, 576, 577

Attorney General, 255

Audubon, John James, 365

Austin, Moses, 420

Austin, Stephen F., 420

Authoritarianism, 399

Aviles, Menendez de, 23

Aztecs, 4, 19, 20, 264

B

Bacon's Rebellion, 65, 79, 81

Bacon, Francis, 119

Bacon, Nathaniel, 79

Bailey, Hachaliah, 218

Baker, James Nelson, 211

Bank of Augusta v. Earle, 397

Bank of the United States, 258, 390,
      391, 393, 394, 408, 451, 491,
      589

Banks, General Nathaniel P., 591

Baptist, 348, 349, 363

Barker, James Nelson, 216

Barlow, Joel, 189, 196, 213

Barnum, P. T., 366

Battle of Austerlitz, 300

Battle of New Orleans, 384

Battle of Seven Pines, 560

Battle of the Tangled Wilderness,
      574

Battle of Tippecanoe, 304, 305, 320

Battle of Yorktown, 176–177

Baylor, Colonel John R., 567

Balloon-frame house, 459, 467

Beaumont, William, 337

Beauregard, Generals Pierre G. T.,
      556, 575

Beaver trapping, 430

Becknell, William, 426

Beecher, Lyman, 348, 349, 472

Beecher,, Catherine, 339

Bell, John, 529

Bell, Peter Hansborough, 506

Bennett, James Gordon, 362

Benton, Thomas H., 388

Berkeley, Governor, 79, 80

Berkeley, John Lord, 59

Berlin Decree, 300, 307

Bible, 104

Biddle, Nicholas, 391, 394

Bigotry, 358

Bill of Rights, 279, 280

Billings, William, 221

Bingham, George Caleb, 367

Black
      codes, 610, 611
      education, 622
      refugess, 618, 622
      suffrage, 525, 607, 611, 612, 620,
            624, 629

Black Hawk War, 420, 547

Blacksmith, 73

Bleeding Kansas, 489, 517,
      517–519

Blockade, 546, 550, 551, 569, 582,
      583, 585

Blue and Gray, 544–554
      Northern Strategy, 550–554
      Southern Strategy, 549–550
      The "American" War, 544–545

Blue Jacket, Chief, 264, 265

Blue-collar workers, 461

Bonaparte, Napoleon, 278, 279,
      288, 299

Book of Mormon, 350, 351, 445

Booth, John Wilkes, 608

Border Ruffians, 517

Boston Massacre, 149–150

Boston Tea party, 133, 151

Boucher, Jonathan, 127

Bounty-jumping, 548

Bowdoin, James, 239

Bowie, Jim, 433

Braddock, Edward, 86

Braddock, James, 86

Bradford, John, 267

Bradford, William, 41, 45, 57

Brahmins, 333, 357, 358

Brant, Chief Joseph, 264

Breckinridge, John C., 529

Brent, Margaret, 38

Bridger, Jim, 425, 428

Briscoe v. The Bank of Kentucky,
      397

Brittish
      Albany Conference, 85
      early border conflicts, 83
      Fort Duquesne, 1755, 86
      Great War, 84
      King George's War, 84
      New France, 81
      Proclamation of 1763, 87
      Quebec, capture of, 87
      Seven Years War, 87
      supremacy in North America, 81

Brock, Isaac, 308

Brooks, Preston, 520

Brown, Aaron, 522

Brown, Charles Brockden, 209, 212

Brown, John, 369, 489, 519, 526,
      527

Brown, William Hill, 211

Browning, O. H., 597

Buchanan, James, 521, 522, 533

Buell, General Don Carlos, 570

Bulfinch, Charles, 219

Bull Run
      battle of, 555–561
      second battle of, 561

Buren, Martin Van, 381, 402, 404,
      405, 410, 423, 503

Burns, Anthony, 511

Burnside, Ambrose E., 562, 563,
      572

Burr, Aaron, 210, 273, 276, 296, 297

Burritt, Elihu, 344

Burton, John, 50

Bushwhackers, 553

Butler, General Benjamin, 575

Butler, Senator Andrew P., 520

C

Cabot, John, 25

Cabrillo, Juan Rodriguez, 23

Calhoun, John C., 188, 304, 308, 321, 322, 328, 370, 375, 399, 400, 502, 507

Calvert, George, 37, 38

Calvinists, 195, 196, 348, 349, 353

Cambridge, 43, 50, 114

Camp, Stephanie, 494

Canal Era, 448

Cape Horn, 444

Cape of Good Hope, 12

Carnival of corruption, 616

Caroline affair, 374, 404, 408

Carolus Linnaeus, 129

Carpetbaggers, 614–616

Carr, Peter, 286

Carroll, Charles, 199

Carroll,, Father John, 195

Carson, Kit, 428

Cashier, Albert D. J., 591

Cass, Lewis, 502, 508, 509

Catholic Church, the, 21, 28, 29

Catholics, 348, 363, 485, 486, 487

Central Pacific Railroad, 588, 589

Chalmette National Cemetery, 591

Champlain, Samuel de, 81

Channing, William Ellery, 342, 353

Charbonneau, Toussaint, 294

Charles River Bridge v. Warren Bridge, 397

Charleston, 61

Chase, Salmon P., 193, 607

Chase, Samuel, 291

Chenaworth, Richard B., 334

Cherokee, 9, 10, 412, 421, 422, 423, 554

Cheves, Langdon, 304

Chickasaws, 554

Chief Blue Jacket, 264

Chief Joseph Brant, 264

Chief Little Turtle, 264, 265, 266

Chief Tecumseh, 304, 320, 321

Chinook Indians, 295

Choctaw Indians, 421, 554

Christianity, 16, 349, 351, 354, 368, 421

Civil War, 463, 464, 466, 468, 470, 476, 479, 482, 483, 494, 544, 546, 547, 550, 552, 553, 554, 566, 577, 578, 581, 590, 591, 593, 596, 599, 600, 602, 611, 616, 621, 622

African Americans and, 600–603

Antietam, 561–563

Appomattox, 580–581

Atlanta, the fall of 576–577

Battle of Bull Run (Manassas), 555–561

second battle, 561

behind the lines, 581–603

causes of, 535–541

Chancellorsville, 563–564

Chickamauga and Chattanooga, 572–573

compromise, failure of 533–534

Confederacy, the, 581–582

Democrats, 529

Dred Scott Decision, 523–525

economic failures of the South, 586–587

election of 1856, 521–523

election of 1860, 528–529

emancipation, 593–596

eve of, 521–535

Forts Henry and Donelson, 568–569

Fort Sumter, 534–535

Gettysburg, 564–566

Grant, 573–575

in the field, 554–581

Hood's Army of Tennessee, 579

John Brown's Raid, 526–528

Lincoln, 596–600

Lincoln-Douglas debates, 525–526

northern industrialism and Republican ascendancy, 587–588

Pea Ridge, 568

peace movement, 575–576

prisoners of, 585–586

sea power, 582–585

national banking system, 589–590

New Mexico, 567

reunion, 593

Republican victory, 529–531

secession, 531–532

Sherman's march in the Carolinas, 579

Transcontinental Railroad, 588–589

Vicksburg, 571–572

Virginia front, 554–555

war in the West, 566–567

women and, 590–593

Civil-rights movements, 623

Clair, Arthur St., 265

Clark, George Rogers, 175, 292

Clark, William, 292

Clay Compromise Proposals, 506–508

Clay, Henry, 188, 304, 306, 308, 317, 322, 328, 375, 390, 394, 396, 399, 410, 486, 506, 533

Claypoole, Anna, 223

Clinton, De Witt, 210, 309

Clinton, George, 241, 250, 273, 297, 298

Clinton, Henry, 158, 174, 175

Clothing, ready-made, 465–467

Coleridge, 191

Colleton, John, 61, 62

Colonial period

  Bacon's Rebellion, 79

  cultural development, 90

  economy, 69

  English Regulatory Acts, 75

  environment, 92

  influence of English society, 90

  Native American conflicts, 77

  New England, 69

  Pueblo Revolt, 81

  social structure, 90, 94

  women, 92

Colonies

  middle, 74

  northern, 55

  Roanoke, lost colony of 25

  southern, 73

Colonization,

  background to, 10

  Christopher Columbus, 12, 17

  Conquistadores, 19

  Encomiendas, 23

  European expansion, 10

  factors in, 25

  Spanish colonization, 23

Colt, Samuel, 337

Columbus, 2, 5, 7, 11, 12, 13, 14,
    15, 16, 17, 18, 19, 20, 25

Common Sense, 159

Communitarianism, 345–347

Compromise of 1850, 489, 503–514

Compromise Tariff of 1833, 393

Confederacy, the, 225, 228, 230,
    232, 239, 240, 241, 242, 244,
    543, 544, 545, 546, 547, 548,
    552, 553, 554, 561, 562, 566,
    567, 573, 576, 580, 581, 582,
    583, 584, 585, 586, 587, 592,
    594, 600, 603

  army, 544, 547, 553, 564, 568,
    570, 572, 575, 578, 585, 591

confederation period, 232–239

  crisis and rebellion, 238–239

  finances, 237–238

  relations with Europe,
    235–237states, 532

  sympathizers, 552, 553, 554

  trade, 237

  western policy, 234–235

Constitution, 225, 232, 233, 240,
    242, 244, 245, 248, 250, 251,
    252, 253, 255, 256, 257, 258,
    259, 271, 272, 275, 281

  convention, 244–248

  Federalism, 241–242

  Federalists and Antifederalists,
    249–251

  framing, 240–253

  philosophy of, 242–244

  ratification of, 251–253

Constitutional Convention, 189

Continental Congress, 166

Cooper, Bryant,, 363

Cooper, James Fenimore, 212, 333,
    354, 359, 360

Cooper, Peter, 335

Copley, John Singleton, 207, 221

Copperheads, 595

Cordoba, Pedro de, 18

Cornwallis, 176, 177

Coronado, Francisco Vasquez de,
    23

Corporate Revolution, 450–453

Cortes, Hernan, 19, 20

Cotton gin, 336

Count Volney, 202

Crawford, Thomas, 367

Crawford, William H., 321, 322, 375

Creeks, 421, 554

Crittenden Compromise, 533

Crittenden, John J., 533

Crockett, David, 364

Crusades, 11

Cruzatte, Peter, 295

Culture, colonial roots of, 130–131

Cuneo, Michele de, 17, 18

Curtis, General Samuel R., 568

Czar Alexander I, 313

D

Dade, Francis L., 422

Dallas, Alexander, 273

Dana, Richard Henry, 418

Daughters of Liberty, 208

Davenport, James, 125

Davis, Alexander J., 367

Davis, Jefferson, 505, 532, 544,
    549, 576, 579, 581, 586, 587

Decatur, Stephen, 286, 287, 310

Declaration of Causes, 536

Declaration of Independence, 100,
    121, 133, 154, 160, 162, 163,
    166, 178, 183, 184, 191, 195,
    228, 230, 250, 251, 286, 327,
    381, 544

Declaration of Sentiments, 339–340

Deere, John, 464

Delany, Martin R., 601

Democratic Growth, 411–415

Democratic Republicans, 373, 378,
    379

Democratic-Republican, 268, 273

Democrats and Whigs, 402–415

  Caroline Affair, 404–405

  election of 1836, 402–403

  panic of 1837, 403–404

  return of the Democrats, 410–411

  Tippecanoe and Tyler Too,
    405–408

  Webster-Ashburton Treaty,
    408–409

Department of Navy, 278

Depression, 395, 403

Dew, Thomas R., 370

Dickinson, John, 94, 95, 148, 228,
    246

Dimple, Billy, 216

Disciples, 348

Divorce, 205, 207

Dix, Dorothea Lynde, 339, 342

Dixie, 367

Doctrine of the broken voyage, 299

Dorn, General Earl Van, 568

Doughfaces, 531

Douglas Bill, 514–515

Douglas, Stephen A., 508, 514, 521, 523, 525

Douglass, Frederick, 340, 369, 484, 601

Drake, Francis, 26

Dred Scott decision, 398, 552

Dulaney, Daniel, 146, 164

Durfee, Amos, 404

Dwight, Timothy, 211, 213

E

Earliest Americans, 2

Early, Jubal, 575

East India Company, 26, 151, 152

Eaton, John H., 386

Economic aid, 550

Economic causes, 497–498

Economics of expansion, 446–458
  Growing Sectionalism, 457–458

Edison, Thomas A., 468

Edmonds, Sarah Emma Evelyn, 591

Education
  and innovation, 462–463
  higher, 476–477
  progress in, 347–348
  public, 474–476

Einstein, 119

Election
  1804, 283, 298
  1824, 374–377
  1828, 381–383
  1832, 391–392
  1836, 402–403

1852, 512–514

1854, 516–517

1856, 521–523

1860, 528–529

1876, 627–630

Electoral College, 247

Eliot, Charles W., 477

Emancipation, 593, 605, 606, 607, 608, 609, 610, 611, 612, 613, 614, 615, 616, 617, 618, 619, 620, 621, 622, 623, 624, 625, 626, 627, 628, 629, 630

Emancipation Proclamation, 535, 543, 562, 594, 595, 602

Embargo Act of 1807, 301

Emerson, Ralph Waldo, 355, 477, 528

English
  administration of the colonies, 66
  colonial politics, 67, 69
  local government, 68
  settlements, 32
    Carolinas, 62
    Georgia, 63
    Jerseys, the, 59
    Maryland, 37
    New York, 57
    Pennsylvania, 60
    Plymouth, 40
    Virginia, 32
  Hutchinson Heresy, 45
  indentured servitude, 34
  Penn's experiment, 59
  Puritans, 43, 44, 46, 51, 54, 56
  Quakers, 60
  Reorganization, 34

Enlightenment, 119–121, 187, 191, 192, 194, 195, 196, 198, 201, 219
  in America, 129–130

Enumeration Act, 76

Era of Good Feelings, 322

Erik the Red, 10

European Aid to the Americans, 174

Eustis, William, 306

Everett, Edward, 529

Ewell, General Richard, 564

Expansion.
  background of, 418–428
  Manifest Destiny, 418–420
  Native Americans, 420–423
  Oregon Trail, the 426

F

Fallen Timbers, Battle of, 263, 266

Fannin, James Walker, 433

Farragut, David, 569

Faust, Drew Gilpin, 581

Federal Reserve System, 590

Federalism, 225, 228, 241, 244, 250, 259, 277

Federalists, 225, 226, 241, 242, 249, 250, 251, 256, 272, 273, 276, 277, 279, 280, 281

Filibusterers, 521

Fillmore, Millard, 486, 487, 508, 512–513, 522

Finney, Charles Grandison, 349

First Seminole War, 328

Fish, Hamilton, 626

Fisk, Jim, 626

Fiske, John, 232

Fitch, John, 446

Fitzhugh, George, 370

Fitzpatrick, Thomas, 425

Five Nation Iroquois, 7

Floyd, Charles, 294

Foot, Samuel A., 388

Ford's Theater, 608

Foreign policy,
  evolution of, 327–332
  isolationism, 331–332
  problems, 327–330

Forrest, Edwin, 365

Forrest, Nathan Bedford, 571

Forts
  Bridger, 426
  Dearborn, 308
  Donelson, The battle at, 569
  Duquesne, 65, 86, 87
  Greenville, 265–266
  Laramie, 426
  McHenry, 311–312
  Michimilimackinac, 308
  Monroe, 559, 560
  Niagara, 308, 309
  Pickens, 534
  Recovery, 266
  Sumter, 489, 534, 535, 540
Fourier, Charles, 347
Fourteenth Amendment, 611, 612, 613, 619, 620, 624
Fox, Winnebago, 420
Franklin heating stove, 468
Franklin, Benjamin, 85, 97, 98, 123, 129, 131, 147, 160, 164, 174, 179, 191, 193, 196, 199, 204, 207, 209, 213, 215, 241, 249
Fredericksburg, 563
Free-soilers, 502, 517, 519, 526
Freedmen's Bureau, 605, 611, 622
Freemen, 68
Frémont, John C., 425, 440, 522
French and Indian War, 85, 138, 140, 143, 264
French Revolution, 226, 266, 267, 268, 271, 380
Freneau, Philip, 196, 216
Frontier evangelism, 196–198
Fugitive Slave Act, 489, 508, 509, 510, 511, 512, 513, 525
Fuller, Margaret, 355, 356, 363, 365
Fulton, Robert, 446

G

Gadsden Purchase, 445, 490, 521
Gadsden, James, 441

Gallatin, Albert, 273, 290, 315
Gallaudet, Thomas H., 344
Galloway, Joseph, 164
Gardoqui, Diego de, 236
Garnet, Henry H., 369
Garrison, William Lloyd, 368, 442, 480, 484
Gates, Horatio, 173, 175
Genet, Edmund, 268
Gerry, Elbridge, 243, 246, 248, 250, 278
Gettysburg, 543, 554, 564, 565, 564–566, 572
Ghent, the treaty of, 312, 313, 314, 315, 318, 327
Gilbert, Olive, 485
Gilman, Daniel Coit, 477
Girty, Simon, 262, 263
Goethe, 191
Gold rush, 444, 502
Gold standard, 491
Goodrich, Sara, 223
Goodyear, Charles, 336
Gorgas, Josiah, 547, 587
Gould, Jay, 626, 627
Government,
  launching of, 253–259
    Federalist finance, 256–258
    Whiskey Rebellion, 258–259
Graham, Sylvester, 341
Grant, General Ulysses S., 554, 568, 569, 570, 571, 572, 573, 574, 575, 576, 578, 579, 580, 581, 624–627
Grant Administration, 624–627
Great Awakening, 123–126
  second, 349
Great Compromise, 246
Great Sewing Machine Combination, 465
Greek democracy, 360
Greeley, Horace, 362, 477, 576
Greenough, Horatio, 367

Grenville, George, 143
Grimke, Angelina, 484
Grundy, Felix, 304

H

Hackett, James H., 366
Hale, Sarah Josepha, 363
Halleck, General Henry W., 561
Halleck, Henry W., 561, 570
Hamilton, 240–244, 249–251, 254–259, 262, 263, 269, 271, 272, 273, 275, 277, 278, 280, 281, 286, 296, 297
Hamiltonians, 276, 280
Hamlin, Hannibal, 530
Hancock, John, 148, 162, 239
Happiness, Peggy., 386
Harland, Marion, 478
Harmar, Josiah, 265
Harper, Frances Watkins, 369
Harper, William, 370
Harris, George W., 364
Harrison, William Henry, 304, 309, 318, 320, 402, 405
Harvard, 43, 54, 196, 476
Hawthorne, Nathaniel, 333, 358
Hayes, Rutherford B., 627, 629
Hayne, Senator Robert Y., 387
Helper, Hinton Rowan, 370, 537, 538–539
Hemmings, Sally, 285
Henry Clay Warmoth, 614
Henry the Navigator, 12, 13
Henry, Patrick, 145, 184, 189, 241, 250
Hentz, Mrs. Caroline Lee, 363
Herrera, President José I., 437
Hewitt, James, 221
"Higher Culture", 365–366
Hodges, Jennie, 591
Holbrook, Josiah, 365, 477
Holmes, Mary Jane, 478

Holmes, Oliver Wendell, 338, 357

Holzer, Harold, 526

Hood, John B., 576, 577

Hooker, General Joseph "Fighting
    Joe", 563, 564, 572, 573

Hooker, Thomas, 43, 44

Hooper, J. J., 364

Hopis, 110

Horace Greeley, 627

Horse-drawn reapers, 464

Houston, Sam, 410, 412, *412–413*,
    434

Howe, Dr. Samuel Gridley, 344, 482

Howe, Elias, 337, 465

Howe, Julia Ward, 479, 482, 483

Howe, William, 157, 169, 174

Hudson's Bay Company, 426

Hudson, Henry, 57

Hussey, Obed, 464

Hutchinson, Anne, 45, 49, 55, 92

Hutchinson, Governor, 227

Hutchinson, Thomas, 50, 145, 149,
    151, 152

I

Icebox, 459, 469

Icehouses, 202

Immigrants, 418, 419, 430, 431,
    433, 435, 436, 444, 455

Immigration, 485–487

Incandescent electric light bulb, 468

Indentured servants, 35, 55

Indentured servitude, 91, 92

Independent Democrats, the appeal
    of, 515

Indian Springs Treaty of 1825, 421

Indians. *See* Native Americans

Industrial Revolution, 188, 193, 449,
    450, 453, 473

    rise of populations, 453–455

    in the Northeast, 449–450

Industrialism, 450, 455

Inflation, 548, 581, 586

Information Revolution, 462

Ironclad river fleet, 571

Iroquois, 7, 8, 9

Irving, Washington, 211, 212

Isabella, 13

Isolationists, 275

J

Jackson, Andrew, 284, 312, 314,
    321, 328, 373, 375, 381–392,
    395, 397, 402, 405, 412, 421,
    423, 434, 522, 589

    crisis over nullification, 392–393

    democracy 398–402

    election of 1828, 381–383

    election of 1832, 391–392

    hard money and land, 394–396

    Jackson's foreign policy, 396–397

    King Andrew, 373, 390, 392–398,
        401

    reorganization of the Cabinet, 386

    Supreme Court, 397–398

    United States Bank, 393–394

    vetoes, 390–391

    Webster's "Second Reply to
        Hayne" , 389–390

Jackson, Thomas J., 556

James, Jesse and Frank, 553

Jamestown, 32, 33, 34, 35, 37, 77,
    80, 117, 118

Jay Treaty, 226, 265, 269–271, 277,
    280

Jay, John, 236, 241, 269, 271, 273

Jayhawkers, 553

Jefferson, Thomas, 188, 189, 196,
    198, 199, 201, 210, 219, 220,
    222, 235, 239, 240, 242, 254,
    255, 257, 258, 259, 264, 271,
    272, 273, 275, 276, 277, 279,
    280, 281, 283, 284, 286, 381,
    498, 499, 505, 532

    Barbary Corsairs, 286–287

election of 1804, 298–299

"Essex Junto", 296–298

in power, 284–299

Louisiana Purchase, 288–290

opening the West, 292–295

political patronage, 290–291

Revolution of 1800, 284

Thomas Jefferson, 284–286

versus Marshall, 291–292

Jeffersonians, 276, 279, 280

John Brown's Raid, 526–528

Johnson, Andrew, 605, 607–612,
    623, 624

Johnson, Samuel, 127, 128

Johnston, Albert Sydney, 568

Johnston, General, 581

Johnston, Joseph E., 554, 556, 560,
    576, 579

Joint-stock companies, 39

Jones, Inigo, 219

Jones, Willie, 273

Journalism, 362–364

    magazines and books for women,
        363–364

    sports, humor, and realism, 364

    writing for the people, 362–363

K

Kant, 191

Kearny, Colonel Stephen W., 440

Kearsarge, the U.S.S., 584

Kennedy, John P., 361

Kerber, Linda, 210

Key, Francis Scott, 312

King George, 159

King George's War, 65, 84

King James, 32, 34, 37, 39

King Louis XVI, 266

King Mob, 373, 383, 384

King Philip, 78, 79

King Philip's War, 78, 79

King, friends of, 226

King, Rufus, 250, 299, 322, 522

Know-Nothing movement, 486, 516, 517, 522

Knox, Henry, 241, 250, 255, 260, 265, 318

Kramer, Heinrich, 51

Ku Klux Klan (KKK), 618–622

L

L'Ouverture, Touissaint, 288

Labor

  exploitation, 467

  organizations, 455

  rise of, 455–457

Lafayette, 177, 178

Lamar, Mirabeau B., 434

Land Bridge to Alaska, 2

Latin Americans, 24

Latrobe, Benjamin, 220

Laurens, Henry, 179

Leclerc, Victor, 288

Lee, 554, 560, 561, 562, 564, 565, 566, 571, 574, 575, 576, 580, 581, 591

Lee, Henry, 228, 259

Lee, Jason, 426

Lee, Richard Henry, 159, 228

Lee, Robert E., 527, 537, 554, 560

Legal Tender Act of 1862, 590

Lester, Jon C., 618

Letters from a farmer in Pennsylvania, 148

Lewis, Meriwether, 292, 295

Lewis and Clark, 292, 293, 294, 295, 418, 426, 430

Lexington and Concord, 155–159

Liberator, 368

Library of Congress, 285

Lincoln, 202, 221, 369, 438, 443, 451, 477, 489, 514, 523, 525, 526, 528, 530–537, 539, 540, 543, 545, 547, 550–552, 555,

557–564, 572, 573, 575–578, 582, 583, 585, 587, 593–601, 605–609

Lincoln-Douglas Debates, 525–526

Lind, Jenny, 366, 367

Liquor, 471, 472

Literature, The Golden Age of, 354–362

Little Turtle, Chief, 264, 265, 266

Livingston, Robert, 288

Locke, John, 160, 191, 194, 198, 214

Long, Crawford, 337

Longfellow, Henry Wadsworth, 357

Longstreet, Augustus B., 364

Longstreet, General James, 564, 572

Lord Grenville, 142

Lord Sheffield, 237

Louisiana Purchase, 290, 292, 296, 325, 326, 327, 328, 330

Louisiana Territory, 289, 295

Lowell, James Russell, 357, 369

Loyalists, 133, 163, 164, 165, 166, 167, 169, 172, 176, 226, 227

Lundy, Benjamin, 368

Lutheran, 348

Lyon, Mary, 339

Lyon, Nathaniel, 553

M

Macadamized roads, 461

Macdonough, Captain Thomas, 311

Macon's Bill No. 2, 303

MacPherson, John, 142

Madison, 202, 204

Madison, Dolley, 204

Madison, James, 240, 241, 242, 244, 246, 273, 290, 302, 307, 317

Madison's War, 283, 304, 305, 314

Magellan, Ferdinand, 15, 16

Maleficarum, Malleus, 51

Mandan Indians, 293

Manifest Destiny, 288, 305, 417, 418, 420, 431, 436, 567

Mann, Horace, 344, 474, 475, 476, 477

Maoris, 264

Marbury v. Madison, 291

Marbury, William, 291

Marcy, William L., 414

Marquette, Jacques, 82

Marshall, John, 249, 266, 273, 278, 290, 291, 297

Martin, Luther, 250

Martyr, Peter, 17, 19

Maryland Toleration Act, 38

Mason, George, 146, 248, 250

Mason, James, 583

Mason-Dixon line, 407, 435, 490, 526, 595

Masons, 391

Massachusetts Institute of Technology, 476

Mather, Cotton, 191

Mather, Increase, 45

Maury, Matthew F., 365

Mayflower, 40, 41

McClellan, General George Brinton, 558, 559, 560, 561, 562, 563, 573, 576, 607

McCormick, Cyrus, 335, 464

McDowell, General Irvin, 555

McGuffey's parables, 344

McGuffey's readers, 476

McKay, Gordon, 466

McLeod, Alexander, 404

Mechanics, The Best in the World, 193

Missouri Compromise, 334

Monroe Doctrine, 284, 330, 330–331

Medbury, James K., 452

Melville, Herman, 333, 358, 359

Mental health, 342–343

Merricmac, the, 583

Merryman, John, 552

Mestizos, 24

Methodist, 348, 363, 499

Mexican War, 369, 437–440, 442, 443, 445

Miami, 264, 265

Micanopy, 422

Military governors, 612

Miller, Alfred Jacob, 368

Miller, Samuel, 221

Miller, William, 350

Minorities in the Colonies, 95

   Native Americans, 103

   non-English settlers, 109

   slavery, rise of, 98

   Stono Rebellion, 101

Miriam, Sarah, 223

Miss Nancy, 522

Mississippi River system, 497

Missouri Compromise, 188, 325–327, 502, 514–515, 516, 517, 520, 524, 526, 533

Missouri Confederate, 553

Mitchell, Elisha, 365

Mitchill, Dr. Samuel Latham, 193

Moby Dick, 359

Modern Family, 470

Modernization, 459, 460–464, 470, 471, 473, 479

   education and innovation, 462–463

   technology and agriculture, 463–464

Mohawks, 264

Molasses Act, 77

Molly Pitcher, 184, 209

Monitor, the, 584

Monopolies, 400

Monroe Doctrine, 188, 334

Monroe, James, 202, 240, 273, 288, 313, 317, 321, 322, 323, 328, 330, 331, 374

Montesquieu, 191

Montezuma, 19, 20

Montgomery, Richard, 158

Morgan, John Hunt, 571

Mormon Trail, 445

Mormons, 333, 345, 347, 348, 350, 351, 352, 353, 445

Morrill Tariff, 587

Morris, Gouverneur Rober, 164, 165, 167, 242

Morse, Samuel F. B., 336, 477

Mott, Lucretia, 339, 340, 479

Mound-Builders, 6

Mount, William Sidney, 368

Mountain men, 425

Murray, Judith Sargent, 209

N

Nairne, Thomas, 98

Napoleon, 188, 218, 288, 299, 300, 301, 303, 305, 311, 313, 315, 332

Napoleon of the South, 556

Napoleonic wars, 496, 535

Narragansett Indians, 55

National Banking Act, 590

National Banking System, 589–590

National Republicans, 378, 379, 391

Nationalism, American, 188

Nationalists, 242, 248, 250

Native Americans, 3–5, 7, 9, 10, 14, 17–19, 21, 24, 26, 33–35, 38, 41, 42, 55–57, 59, 60, 62, 69, 71, 78, 80, 81, 84–87, 89, 92, 93, 95, 103, 106–111, 139, 152, 172, 183, 185, 188, 198, 200, 201, 213, 254, 259, 260–266, 293–295, 304, 308, 318–321, 328, 351, 354, 367, 384, 397, 400, 401, 405, 412, 413, 418, 420–426, 428, 430, 434, 554, 561, 568, 592, 599

policy, 259–266

Navajos, 110

Naval blockade, 550

Navigation Act, 76

Navy, department of, 278

Negro rule, 614, 616

Neutrality, 283, 299, 300, 332

   French Revolution, 266–267

   Genet Affair, 267–268

   Jay's Treaty, 269–270

   perils of, 266–270

   relations with Britain, 268

Neville, John, 258

Newton, Sir Isaac, 119, 120, 191, 192, 194

Newtonian science, 192

Noll, Mark, 198

Non-Intercourse Act, 302, 303

Norse, 10, 11

Northwest Ordinance, 235, 264

Northwest Passage, 57

Norton, Mary Beth, 78

Nott, Eliphalet, 468, 469

Noyes, John Humphrey, 346

Nullification Proclamation, 393

Nullifiers, 392, 401

O

O'Sullivan, John L., 418

Old Hickory, 375, 385, 390, 413

Old Man Eloquent, 480

Oliver, John, 464

Opechancanough, 77, 78

Orders in Council, 300, 307, 314

Oregon

   country, 418, 424, 428, 429, 443

   fever, 430

   territory, 503

Oregon Trail, 417, 425, 426, 443

Osceola, 422

Ostend Manifesto, 521

Oswald, Richard, 179

Ottawa, 139

Our Old Home, 227

Owens, Mary, 597

Oxford, 114

P

Paine, Thomas, 121, 159, 170, 189, 196, 199, 209

Pakenham, General Edward, 312

Parker, Samuel, 426

Parker, Theodore, 511

Parkman, Francis, 365

Parris, Betty, 54

Party Politics, The Emergence of, 271–273

Pastorious, Francis Daniel, 96

Paterson, William, 244

Pathfinders, 423–425

Patriotism, 619

Payne, John Howard, 216

Pea Ridge, 543, 568

Peace of Paris, 179–181261

Peale, Angelica Kaufmann, 223

Peale, Charles Willson, 221

Peale, Sarah, 223

Peninsula Campaign, 559, 561

Penn, William, 59

Pequots, 78

Perry, Captain Oliver Hazard, 309

Philadelphia, the, 287

Phillips, Wendell, 620

Phyfe, Duncan, 365

Pickering, John, 291

Pickering, Timothy, 273, 296

Pickett, General George, 565

Pierce, Franklin, 441, 489, 513, 515, 519, 520

Pike's expedition, 295

Pike, Zebulon, 295

Pilgrims, 31, 40, 41, 42, 60

Pinckney Treaty, 236, 270

Pinckney, Charles Cotesworth, 242, 278, 281, 298–299, 302

Pinckney, Eliza, 100

Pinckney, Thomas, 273, 276

Pinkney, William, 199

Pioneers, 430

Ppirates, 286, 287

Pitt, William, 65, 86

Pitts, John and Hiram, 464

Plains Indians, 423

Plumbing, Lighting, and Heating, 468–469

Plymouth, 78, 112

Plymouth Rock, 40

Pocahontas, 31, 35, 36

Poe, Edgar Allan, 333, 361

Political asylum, 268

Political Parties
    early, 271–277
    Federalists and Republicans, 276–277
    election of 1796, 273–276

Polk, James K., 410, 411, 430, 437, 438, 440, 501, 503, 521, 522

Polygamy, 352

Pontiac, 139

Poor Richard's Almanac, 98, 123

Pope, General John, 561

Popular Sovereignty, 502–503

Port Hudson, 572

Porter, Peter B., 304

Pottawatomie massacre, 526

Powhatan, 35, 36

Powhatans, 77

Prescott, William H., 365

Presidios, 109

Prevost, Sir George, 311

Prince Henry the Navigator, 12, 13

Prohibitionists, 473, 474

Promontory Point, 589

Prophet, the, 304, 320

Prosser, Gabriel, 494

Provincials Act, 155

Ptolemy, 13

Public education, 620

Pueblo Indians, 81

Puritans, 31, 38, 42, 43, 44, 45, 46, 47, 48, 49, 50, 51, 53, 54, 55, 56, 57, 58, 60, 198
    free thought, 116
    in America, 112–114
    in England, 111–112
    theology, 114–116

Putnam, Thomas, 54

Q

Quakers, 31, 46, 47, 48, 49, 50, 51, 59, 60, 61, 97, 113, 118, *343*, 358, 368, 498, 499

Quasi-War, 278

Queen Anne's War, 83

Quetzalcoatl, 19

Quincy Hall Clothing Manufactory, 465

R

Radiator, 469

Railroads, 335, 336, 461, 497, 547, 570, 578, 588, 589

Randolph, Edmund, 244, 248, 249

Randolph, John, 497, 498

Read, George, 244

Reason, Age of, 190, 191, 194, 195, 219

Rebel yell, 556

Reconstruction, 605, 606, 607, 608, 609, 610, 611, 612, 613, 614, 615, 616, 617, 618, 619, 620, 621, 622, 623, 624, 625, 626, 627, 628, 629, 630
    congressional radicals, 610–612
    Freedmen's Bureau, 622–623
    Grant Administration, 624–627
    Johnson's Policy of, 608–610
    Lincoln's Plan of, 606–630
    Radical Reconstruction, 612–617
    sharecroppers, 621–622

Reform, modernization and, 470–485
  Broadening Antislavery Movement, 480–485
  higher education, 476–477
  media,, the 477–478
  Protestant ethic and reform, 470–471
  public education, 474–476
  temperance, 471–474
  women's rights, 478–480
Religion, 333, 348, 349, 351, 355
Religious Change, 195–196
Remond, Charles L., 369
Republic, 225, 226, 227, 229, 231, 233, 235, 237, 239, 241, 243, 245, 247, 249, 251, 253, 255, 257, 259, 261, 263, 265, 266, 267, 268, 269, 271, 273, 275, 277, 279, 281
Republic of Texas, 417, 419, 434
Requerimiento, 16, 17
Revolution of 1800, 283, 284
Revolution, American
  Articles of Confederation, 184
  background of, 134
  Boston Massacre, 149
  character of , 134
  constitutional confrontations, 138
  Constitutional issue, 137
  effects of, 182
  in retrospect, 178
  in the North, 169
  in the South, 175
  Liberty Incident, 148
  problems of defense and western lands, 139
  provocations and crises, 135
  ramifications of, 142
  Stamp Act, 143–144
  westward movement, 182
Revolutionary Finance, 166–167
Richardson, Ebeneezer, 149

Rip Van Winkle, 212, 366
River warfare, 568
Rolfe, John, 34, 35, 36
Roman Catholics, 29
Romanticism, 187, 190, 194, 195, 197, 333, 344, 353, 354, 355, 360, 368
Rooney, Rose, 591
Rosecrans, William, 570, 572
Ross, Chief John, 423
Ross, General Robert, 311
Rousseau, 191, 198, 210
Rowson, Susannah, 211
Ruffin, Edmund, 365
Rush, Benjamin, 209
Rutledge, Ann, 597

S

Saber rattling, 288
Sacajawea, 294
Saint John the Just, 528
Salem Village, 31, 53, 54
Salle, Robert de La, 82
Sam Adams, 147, 151, 155
Santa Anna, Antonio Lopez de, 413, 433, 434, 437, 438, 439, 440, 441
Santa Fe Trail, 417, 425, 426
Sauk, 420
Scarlet Letter, The 358
Schiller, 191
Science, the professionalization of, 192
Scientific advances in society
  impact of, 465–470
  plumbing, lighting, and heating, 468–469
  ready-made clothing, 465–467
  "balloon-frame" house, 467
  modern family, 470
  icebox, 469–470
Scott, Dred, 489, 523, 524, 525, 526

Scott, General Winfield, 439, 513, 555
Scott, Sir Walter, 212, 360
Scott, Winfield, 409
Sea Power, the importance of, 582–585
Secession, 531–532, 606, 607, 609
  convention in Texas, 536
  Douglas Strategy, 508
  election of 1852, 512–514
  Fugitive Slave Act, 508–512
  sentiment, 504–506
Secessionists, 609
Second Great Awakening, 349
Sectionalism, 379, 388
  and Slavery, 324–325, 491–496
  origin of, 490–496
  northern way of life, 496
  southern way of life, 491
  Transcontinental Republic, 490–491
Secularism, rise of, 122–123
Sedition Act, 292, 279
Seminole Indians, 328, 422, 554
Seminole War of 1818, 387
Sequoya, 421
Seven Years War, 133, 138, 142
Seward, Senator William H., 518, 529, 550, 551
Shakespeare, 216
Sharecroppers, 605, 621
Sharples, Ellen and Rolinda, 223
Shawnee, 262, 264, 265, 320
Shays' Rebellion, 239, 240
Shays, Daniel, 239, 240, 259
Shenandoah Valley, 553, 556, 560, 561, 575
Sheridan, Philip, 580
Sherman, General William Tecumseh, 543, 572, 573, 576–580, 586
Sherman's March, 578–579
Sherman, Roger, 246

Shiloh, 569–571

Sibley, H. H., 567

Sigourney, Mrs. Lydia, 363

Silliman, Benjamin, 365

Singer, Isaac M., 465

Sioux Indians, 294

Slater's Mill, 453

Slavery, 235, 248, 284, 323–327,
    333, 336, 339, 357, 360, 361,
    368, 369, 370, 372, 397, 410,
    417, 433–436, 441–443, 458,
    460, 479–486, 489, 491,
    493–495, 498–503, 505–510,
    512, 514–526, 529–531, 533,
    535–540, 544–575, 577, 585,
    593–596, 599, 600, 606, 607,
    609–611, 622, 624, 630

    abolition, 368–369

    and democracy, 368–372

    and the Revolution, 168–169

    rise of, 98–101

Sleepy Hollow, the legend of, 212

Slidell, John, 583

Smallpox, 56

Smith, Adam, 451

Smith, Jedediah S., 425

Smith, John, 32, 33, 34, 35, 78, 118

Smith, Joseph, 350, 351, 352, 445

Smith, Sydney, 212

Smith, William, 164

Smithsonian Institution, 366

Social Problem, 199

Sons of Liberty, 189

Soto, Hernando de, 23

Southerners, 544, 545, 547, 549,
    550, 552, 557, 567, 573, 575,
    577, 578, 579, 581, 582, 585,
    586, 588

Southworth, Mrs. E. D. E. N., 363,
    478

Souza, Matthias de, 38

Sovereignty, Doctrine of Popular,
    502–503

Spanish Succession, War of, 83

Spotswood, Alexander, 69, 70

Sprenger, James, 51

Squanto, 41, 42

Stability,
    search for, 228–232
    balancing federal and local author-
        ity, 228–230

Stamp Act, 133, 143, 144, 145, 147,
    148, 164

Stanton, Elizabeth Cady, 339, 479,
    595

Staple Act, 76

Star-Spangled Banner, 312

State Governments, 230–232

States' rights, 548, 587, 609

Steam-powered cylinder press, 212

Steamboats, 428, 446, 447, 461

Stephens, Alexander, 532

Stephens, Mrs. Ann, 363

Stewart, Philo P., 468

Stockton, Commodore R. F., 440

Stonewall Jackson, 556, 560, 561,
    562, 564, 575

Stono Rebellion, 101–103

Stowe, Harriet Beecher, 339, 369,
    370, 512

Strong, Caleb, 243

Stuart, Gilbert, 221, 222, 223

Stuart, Jane, 223

Suffrage, 232

Sumner, Charles, 520, 620

Supreme Court, 255–256

Sutter's Mill, 444

Sweatshops, 466

T

Tait, Judge Charles, 327

Taney, Justice Roger B., 393, 397,
    524, 552

Tar heels, 62

Tariff of Abominations, 380, 383,
    387

Tax policies, 280

Taylor, Augustine, 467

Taylor, General Zachary, 437, 438,
    503, 505, 513

Tea Act Crisis, 151–154

Technology
    and agriculture, 463–464
    and economic development,
        334–338

Tecumseh, Chief, 304, 320, 321

Telegraph, 477, 479

Telephone, 479

Tenskwatawa, 320

Texas A&M, 476

Texas
    annexation of, 435–436
    settlement of, 431–433

Textile mills, 454

Thirteenth Amendment, 596, 602

Thomas, General George H., 572,
    578, 579

Thompson, William T., 364

Thoreau, Henry David, 333, 355,
    356, 357, 443, 528

Thorpe, Thomas B., 364

Ticknor, George, 365

Tilden, Samuel J., 628

Tippecanoe, 374, 405, 407, 408,
    414

Tituba, 54

Tobacco, 34, 35, 36, 38, 62, 118,
    491, 496, 497, 499

Tocqueville, Alexis de, 333, 349,
    370–372, 471

Todd,, Mary, 597

Toleration, growth of, 121–122

Tom Thumb, 367

Townshend Act, 147

Townshend Duties, 147

Trail of Tears, 421, 423

Transcontinental railroad, 515, 521,
    543, 588–589

Transcontinental Republic, 490–491

Transportation revolution, in the west, 446–449

Travis, William B., 433

Treaty of 1800, 226, 278, 279

Treaty of Dancing Rabbit, 421

Treaty of Greenville, 266

Treaty of Guadalupe Hidalgo, 417, 440, 441

Treaty of Velasco, 434, 437, 506

Tribes, the five civilized, 421

Trist, Nicholas P., 440

Trumbull, John, 213, 221

Truth, Sojourner, 369, 484, 485

Tudor, Frederic, 469

Turner, Nat, 442

Turnpike Era, 446

Twain, Mark, 616

Tweed, William Marcy, 617, 627

Tyler, John, 406, 408, 436

Typewriter, 479

U

U.S.S. Merrimac, 583

Uncle Tom's Cabin, 369, 371, 473, 478, 484, 512, 538

Underground railroad, 511

Union gunboats, 568, 570, 571

Union Pacific Railroad, 588, 627

Unitarianism, 196

Unitarians, 353

United States Constitution, 245, 247

United States Navy, 278

Unrestricted Trade, 182

Upjohn, Richard, 367

Urim and Thummim, 350

Urrea, José, 433

U.S.S. Philadelphia, 287

V

Vaca, Cabeza de, 23

Vallandigham, Clement L., 600

Vegetarianism, 347

Venture capitalism, 589

Vespucci, Amerigo, 15, 16

Veto, 390, 394, 396, 399, 402

Vicksburg, 571–572

Virginia front, 543, 554, 555, 559, 581

Virginia Plan, 244, 245, 246

Voltaire, 191

W

Wakeman, Lyons, 591

Wakeman, Sarah Rosetta, 591

Walden Pond, 356

Walker, David, 442

Walker, William, 521

Walter Raleigh, 25

War Hawks, 283, 304, 399

War of 1812, the, 188, 216, 283, 304, 305, 307, 309, 314, 315, 321, 323, 374, 388, 399, 400, 412, 429, 434, 443, 450

War of 1812, 305–315

at sea, 309–310

Canada, 314–315

Hartford Convention, 312–313

on land, 305–312

results of, 314

Ward, Samuel R., 369

Warmoth, 614

Warner, Susan, 478

Warren, James, 250

Warren, Mercy Otis, 209, 250

Warriors of Waterloo, 409

Washington, George, 84, 188, 213, 225, 236, 239, 241, 242, 249, 253–256, 258–261, 265, 266, 267, 268, 269, 271, 272, 273, 275, 280

Watkins, Tobias, 414

Wayne, General "Mad Anthony", 263, 265, 266

Webster, Daniel, 322, 387, 389, 399, 402, 507, 509, 511

Webster, Noah, 189, 210, 347, 476

Webster-Ashburton Treaty, 374, 408, 409

Weems, Parson Mason Locke, 213, 214

Wesley, John, 195

West, Benjamin, 221, 222

West Point, 174, 175, 556, 558

West, the

conquering, 428–445

Gadsden Purchase, 441

Oregon, 428–431

slavery , 441–443

Texas, 431–436

Treaty of Guadalupe Hidalgo, 440–441

War with Mexico, 437–440

Western Army Posts, 427–428

Wharton, Edward, 47

Wheatley, Phillis, 103, 104, 105, 106, 123

Whigs, 374, 398, 399, 400, 402, 403, 404, 405, 406, 407, 408, 410, 411, 414

Whiskey, 472

Whiskey Rebellion, 225, 258, 259, 280

Whiskey Ring, 627

White supremacy., 620

White, Andrew D., 477

White, Hugh L., 403

White-collar jobs for women, 479

Whitman, Dr. Marcus, 426

Whitman, Walt, 369

Whittier, John Greenleaf, 369

Wilentz, Sean, 374, 457

Wilkinson, James, 297, 314

William and Mary, 66

William of Orange, 38

William Robinson, 125

Williams, Abigail, 54

Williams, Roger, 55

Willing, Thomas, 164

Wilmot Proviso, 489, 501–502, 507, 509

Wilmot, David, 501

Wilson, Harriet, 478

Wilson, James, 189, 242, 245, 246, 250

Winthrop, John, 42, 92, 93, 113

Winthrop, Margaret, 209

Wirt, William, 391

Wirz, Henry, 585

Witches, 31, 47, 51, 52, 53, 54, 78, 358

Wollstonecraft, Mary, 209

Women
in Colonial America, 92–94
legal status, 206–208
rights, 187, 208, 209, 210, 338-340, 459, 471, 478, 479, 484

Wood, Jethro, 464

Wood, Peter, 238

Wordsworth, 191

Wyeth, Nathaniel, 469

Y

Yancey, William L., 529

Yankee industrialists, 496

Yankee ingenuity, 462, 469

Yeardley, George, 37

Young, Brigham, 352, 353, 445

Younger, Cole and Jim, 553